The Holocaust

Laurence Rees is the author of the award-winning *Auschwitz: The Nazis and the 'Final Solution'* – the world's bestselling book on the history of the camp.

A former Head of BBC TV History programmes, he has written six books on the Nazis and the Second World War, as well as writing and producing the accompanying documentary TV series. His work includes the TV series and books *The Nazis: A Warning from History, Auschwitz: The Nazis and the 'Final Solution', World War II: Behind Closed Doors* and *The Dark Charisma of Adolf Hitler.*

Laurence Rees was educated at Solihull School and Oxford University and holds honorary doctorates from the University of Sheffield and the Open University. For several years he was a visiting senior fellow in the International History Department at the London School of Economics and Political Science, London University. His many awards include a British Book Award, a BAFTA, a George Foster Peabody award, a Broadcasting Press Guild award, a Grierson award, a Broadcast award, two International Documentary awards and two Emmys.

The Holocaust

A New History

LAURENCE REES

VIKING

an imprint of

PENGUIN BOOKS

VIKING

UK | USA | Canada | Ireland | Australia
India | New Zealand | South Africa

Viking is part of the Penguin Random House group of companies
whose addresses can be found at global.penguinrandomhouse.com.

First published 2017
001

Set in 12/14.75 pt Bembo Book MT Std
Typeset by Jouve (UK), Milton Keynes
Printed in Great Britain by Clays Ltd, St Ives plc

A CIP catalogue record for this book is available from the British Library

HARDBACK ISBN: 978–0–241–29700–1
TRADE PAPERBACK ISBN: 978–0–241–29818–3

www.greenpenguin.co.uk

To Camilla

Contents

List of Maps and Illustrations

Maps

Illustrations

SECTION ONE

1. Adolf Hitler and a group of Nazi supporters in the 1920s (*Ullsteinbild / TopFoto*)
2. Dietrich Eckart (*Ullsteinbild / TopFoto*)
3. A young Joseph Goebbels (*World History Archive / TopFoto*)
4. A Freikorps unit marches through Munich in 1919 (*Ullsteinbild / TopFoto*)
5. President Paul von Hindenburg and Adolf Hitler in 1933 (*akg-images*)
6. Otto Meissner and former Chancellor Franz von Papen (*Ullsteinbild / TopFoto*)
7. Concentration camp prisoners in the 1930s (*Ullsteinbild / TopFoto*)
8. Prisoners at Dachau before the war (*akg-images*)
9. Adolf Hitler in 1936 (*Ullsteinbild / TopFoto*)
10. Joseph Goebbels marries Magda Quandt in December 1931 (*Topham Picturepoint*)
11. Theodor Eicke (*Ullsteinbild / TopFoto*)
12. Hermann Göring and Heinrich Himmler (*Topham / AP*)
13. Adolf Eichmann (*Ullsteinbild / TopFoto*)
14. Heinrich Himmler and Reinhard Heydrich (*Ullsteinbild / TopFoto*)
15. Jews are made to scrub the streets in Austria in the wake of the Nazi occupation in 1938 (*World History Archive / TopFoto*)

(While every effort has been made to contact copyright holders, the publishers will be happy to correct any errors of omission or commission.)

Prologue

To the Nazis, Freda Wineman's crime was simple. She was Jewish. In May 1944, at the age of twenty, she was arrested in Saint-Etienne in France by collaborators belonging to the paramilitary Milice. Together with her parents and her three brothers she was taken first to the notorious holding camp at Drancy in the suburbs of Paris and thence to Auschwitz Birkenau in Nazi-occupied Poland.

In early June 1944, the train carrying Freda, her family and nearly a thousand other Jews from France passed under the red-brick guardhouse of Birkenau and down a railway line directly into the camp. As the doors of the freight wagon opened and they emerged into the light, Freda thought she had arrived in 'Hell. The smell! The smell was awful!'[1] But Freda was still unaware of the true purpose of Birkenau. The place was huge and teeming with prisoners. Perhaps the new arrivals would all be put to work?

As she and her family stood on the area by the side of the railway track known as the 'ramp', events took an unexpected turn. Prisoners from a special unit called the Sonderkommando, dressed in pyjama-like uniforms, shouted out to the new arrivals, 'Give the children to the older women.' As a consequence, Freda's mother was handed a baby by a young mother in her twenties.

The Jews were told to form two lines on the ramp – men in one and women and small children in another. Bewildered by what was happening, Freda joined the line for women together with her mother who was still holding the baby. When her mother reached the head of the queue, an SS doctor – Freda believes it was Dr Mengele – told her to go with the baby to the right. Freda followed her mother, but then, she recalls, 'Mengele called me back, and he said, "You go to the left." And I said, "No, I won't. I won't be separated from my mother." And he said, in a most natural way, "Your mother, she will be looking after the children, and you will go with the young ones [that is, the younger adults]." '

Freda 'couldn't understand why we were separated. I couldn't understand why they had to give the babies to older women. My mother was only forty-six years old. I couldn't understand what was happening, it was too quick. It was all happening so fast.'

As Freda's mother walked away with the baby, her father and three brothers reached the head of their queue. All of them were told to stay together. But as they stood on the ramp, Freda's eldest brother David saw their mother moving off in another direction and thought that their youngest sibling, thirteen-year-old Marcel, should go with her. He reasoned that 'it might be easier' for Marcel if his mother was able to look after him. So David told Marcel to accompany her and Marcel, listening to the words of his elder brother, ran off to join his mother. Unwittingly, David had helped send Marcel to his death.

They did not know it at the time, but they had just participated in a selection process in which SS doctors, in a matter of seconds, decided which person should be allowed to live temporarily and which person should die at once. The great majority of people on this transport were selected to be murdered immediately in the gas chambers of Birkenau – including Freda's mother, along with the baby that had been placed in her arms. The Nazis did not want children, the old or the sick to last more than a few hours in the camp.

Freda, her father and her three brothers had been selected to work. Though the Nazis intended all Jews to die eventually, this was at least a postponement of execution. So by sending Marcel towards their mother, David had ensured that he joined the group that had been chosen to die at once. Marcel, as a thirteen-year-old, was borderline for selection and so the SS must not have cared if he went with his mother to be murdered. As Freda says, David's actions 'would have been the right thing [to do] in different circumstances'. But, amid the inhumanity of Auschwitz, 'it was the wrong decision.'

On the ramp, the Sonderkommandos had told the young mothers to hand over their babies because the only chance they had of surviving the initial selection was to appear in front of the SS doctor without their children. Even if a mother was young and fit, the SS would rarely try and separate her from her child during the final selection process for fear of causing panic among the new arrivals. Members of the Sonderkommando had taken a look at Freda's mother as she waited by the train and decided that she was too old to survive selection. Since she was certain to die, and since the baby was also sure to perish, both had been placed together. That way the young mother had the possibility of living for longer than this one day.

How could such a situation ever come to exist on this earth? How could standards of common decency and morality have been inverted so unspeakably that the compassionate gesture of a brother directing a sibling to be with his mother helped cause his death, and the only chance a young mother had of surviving more than one day was for her baby to be taken from her and murdered?

More broadly, what were the reasons the Nazis decided to exterminate an entire group of people? Why did they take millions of men, women and children and gas them, shoot them, starve them, beat them to death – kill them by whatever means possible? What was the place of this genocide amid the catalogue of other horrors that the Nazis were responsible for?

For twenty-five years I have thought about these questions as I wrote and produced a number of television documentary series about the Nazis and the Second World War. In the course of my work I travelled to many different countries and met hundreds of eyewitnesses from the period – including those who suffered at the hands of the Nazis like Freda Wineman, those who watched events as bystanders, and those who committed crimes as perpetrators. Only a fraction of the testimony gathered for my films has ever been published before.

The Holocaust is the most infamous crime in the history of the world. We need to understand how this obscenity was possible. And this book, drawing not just on this fresh material but also on recent scholarship and documents of the time, is my attempt to do just that.

1. Origins of Hate

In September 1919 Adolf Hitler wrote a letter of immense historical importance. But at the time no one realized its significance. That's because the Adolf Hitler who composed the letter was a nobody. He was thirty years old, and yet he possessed no home, no career, no wife, no girlfriend, no intimate friend of any kind. All he had to look back on was a life filled with crushed dreams. He had wanted to become a famous artist but had been rejected by the artistic establishment; he had longed to play a part in a German victory over the Allies during the First World War, only to witness the humiliating defeat of German forces in November 1918. He was bitter, angry and looking for someone to blame.

In this letter, dated 16 September 1919, and addressed to a fellow soldier called Adolf Gemlich, Hitler stated unequivocally who was responsible not only for his personal predicament, but for the suffering of the whole German nation. 'There is living amongst us', wrote Hitler, 'a non-German, foreign race, unwilling and unable to sacrifice its characteristics . . . and which nonetheless possesses all the political rights that we ourselves have . . . Everything which makes men strive for higher things, whether religion, socialism or democracy, is for him only a means to an end, to the satisfaction of a lust for money and domination. His activities produce a racial tuberculosis among nations.'[1] The adversary Hitler had identified was 'the Jew'. And he added that the 'final aim' of any German government had to be 'the uncompromising removal of the Jews altogether'.

It is a remarkable document. Not just because it allows us an insight into the thinking in 1919 of the man who would later instigate the Holocaust, but also because it is the first irrefutable evidence of Hitler's own anti-Semitic beliefs. In his autobiography, *Mein Kampf*, which he wrote five years later, Hitler claimed that he had hated Jews even when he was a struggling artist in Vienna in the early years of the twentieth century. But some scholars have cast doubt on his simplistic version of his own past,[2] and questioned whether he really held these strong anti-Semitic views during his time in Vienna and his service as a soldier in the First World War.[3]

But that is not to say that Hitler's anti-Semitism entered into his head from nowhere in September 1919. In writing this letter he drew on currents of anti-Semitic thought that had swirled around Germany before, during and immediately after the First World War. So much so that not one of the ideas that he wrote about in his September 1919 letter was original. While he would later become the most infamous proponent of anti-Semitism, Hitler built on a vivid history of persecution.

Anti-Semitism, of course, was not new. Its origins can be traced back several thousand years. At the time of the emergence of Christianity, for instance, even though Jesus was born Jewish himself, passages in the Bible emphasize that 'the Jews' were antagonistic to him. The gospel of St John, in the King James version of the Bible, records that the Jews 'sought to kill'[4] Jesus. At one point they even pick up stones to throw at him.[5] As for Jesus, he tells the Jews that they are children of the 'devil'.[6]

Harmful ideas about the Jews were thus built into the most holy Christian text; and generations of priests branded the Jews a 'perfidious' people who had 'wanted to have Lord Jesus Christ killed'.[7] So it's not hard to understand why Jewish persecution was commonplace in a medieval Europe dominated by Christian culture. In many countries Jews were banned from owning land, from practising certain professions and from living wherever they chose. At various periods, in a number of cities across Europe, the Jews were forced to live in ghettos and wear a special mark of identification on their clothing – in Rome in the thirteenth century it was a yellow badge. One of the few jobs open to Jews was that of moneylender, since Christians were prohibited from practising 'usury'. And as Shakespeare's *Merchant of Venice* illustrates, the Jewish moneylender subsequently became a hated figure. In Germany, in 1543, Martin Luther wrote *On the Jews and Their Lies*. The Jews, said Luther, 'are nothing but thieves and robbers who daily eat no morsel and wear no thread of clothing which they have not stolen and pilfered from us by means of their accursed usury'. He called on the populace to 'eject them forever from this country . . . away with them!'[8]

The Enlightenment brought a change in fortune for the European

Jews. During this era of scientific and political advancement, many traditional beliefs were questioned. Did, for instance, the Jews 'deserve' the treatment they had suffered or were they merely the victims of prejudice? Christian Wilhelm von Dohm, a German historian, wrote in 1781 in favour of Jewish emancipation and pointed out that 'Everything the Jews are blamed for is caused by the political conditions under which they now live.'[9] In France, following the 'Declaration of the Rights of Man' in 1789, Jews were made 'free and equal' citizens under the law. During the nineteenth century, in Germany, many of the prohibitions that had been placed upon Jews were lifted, including those that restricted what professions Jews could enter.

But all these freedoms came at a cost. For at the same time as the German Jews experienced these new opportunities, the country was undergoing enormous change. No country in Europe altered as quickly as Germany during the second half of the nineteenth century. Coal production increased from 1.5 million tons in 1850 to 100 million tons in 1906.[10] The population grew from just over 40 million in 1871 to over 65 million by 1911. Germany also changed politically, with the unification of the country in 1871. In the wake of all this upheaval, many asked profound questions about the cultural and spiritual nature of this new nation. Not least, what did it mean to be 'German'?

Believers in the power of the *Volk* provided one answer. Although it is normally translated as 'people', the concept behind the *Volk* can't properly be conveyed in English by just one word. For the *völkisch* theorists it meant the almost mystical connection a group of people, all speaking the same language and possessing a shared cultural heritage, had with the soil of their native land. In reaction to the sudden growth of cities and the pollution emanating from newly built factories, they preached the glories of the German countryside and in particular the power of the forest. In *Land und Leute* (Land and People), one of the most famous paeans to the *Volk*, Professor Wilhelm Heinrich Riehl wrote: 'A people must die out if it can no longer understand the legacy of the forests from which it is strengthened and rejuvenated. We must preserve the forest, not just to keep the stove going in winter, but also to keep the pulse of the people warm and happy so that Germans can remain German.'[11] Writing in the middle of the nineteenth century, Riehl warned against the dangers posed not only by the growth of cities, but also by that symbol of modernity, the railway: 'in particular the farmer feels that he cannot remain the "traditional farmer" by the side of the new railway . . . everyone fears to become someone different, and those who want to rob us of our characteristic way of life appear to be more spectres from hell than good spirits.'[12]

The concept of the *Volk* would subsequently become of immense importance to Hitler and the Nazis. The Nazi Propaganda Minister, Joseph Goebbels, even commissioned an extraordinary film, released in 1936, entitled *Ewiger Wald* (Eternal Forest) which glorified the power and importance of the forest and the peasant farmer. 'Our ancestors were a forest people,' said the press release issued with the film, 'their God lived in holy groves, their religion grew from the forests. No people can live without the forest, and people who are guilty of deforesting will sink into oblivion . . .'[13] The final commentary line in the film reinforced this link between the *Volk* and the forest: 'The people, like the forest, will stand for ever!'[14]

Before the First World War the most popular youth movement in Germany was the Wandervogel, an organization that called for young men and women to journey into the countryside and recapture the connection between the German people and the soil. 'It was a spiritual movement,' says Fridolin von Spaun, who joined the Wandervogel as an adolescent. 'It was a reaction against the Emperor Wilhelm era, which was all about industry and commerce.'[15] Other young Germans joined groups like the German Gymnastics League and exercised in the open air. 'The German Gymnastics League was the first time I ever came across the swastika,' says Emil Klein, who was a member before the First World War. 'The four F's – *frisch* [fresh], *fromm* [pious], *fröhlich* [happy], *frei* [free] – formed a double swastika on the badge that you had, a bronze badge that you wore as an insignia.'[16] The swastika was adopted by a number of *völkisch* groups. They believed that this ancient symbol, used by various cultures in the past, represented a link with their early ancestors, in part because similar markings had been found on German archaeological relics.

All these new developments were a problem for German Jews, since they were excluded from the concept of the *Volk*. Most German Jews lived in cities and worked in jobs that were the antithesis of the *völkisch* ideal – the Jews were demonstrably not people who 'came from the forest'. In *Soll und Haben* (Debit and Credit), an enormously popular German novel published in 1855,[17] the central Jewish character, the businessman Veitel Itzig, is portrayed as a loathsome individual, obsessed with money and cheating honest but naive Germans. Itzig is a parasite, living a life that could not be further away from the noble ideal of the peasant who tills the soil.

While not every individual who subscribed to the idea of the *Volk* was necessarily an anti-Semite, the Jew nonetheless became a symbol for the *völkisch* movement as a whole of everything that was wrong with the new Germany. If you were a peasant farmer who found it hard to cope with the sudden growth of cities and the reality of the railway that now cut through your land – you could blame the Jew. If you were a shopkeeper who found that customers were deserting you for new department stores – you could blame the Jew. If you laboured in a workshop making hand-crafted products and now couldn't sell them because of the presence in the market of mass-produced factory goods – you could blame the Jew.

These arguments rested, of course, on prejudice. If German Jews were living in cities, if they were starting up department stores and factories, it was to a large extent because they had been excluded from working in *völkisch* 'approved' occupations for hundreds of years. In short, the Jews were now being blamed for not being attached to the soil after they had been forbidden from owning land. This developing antipathy towards German Jews was all the more remarkable because there were hardly any Jews living in Germany. Fewer than 1 per cent of Germans were Jewish. Many Germans never came into contact with Jews. But the absence of Jews is no bar to anti-Semitism.

The old Christian-based prejudices against German Jews did not disappear as the *völkisch* movement grew, but were reinforced. Paul Lagarde, one of the most committed *völkisch* anti-Semites, ranted in terms that Martin Luther would have recognized. 'We are anti-Semites,' he wrote in *Juden und Indogermanen* (Jews and Indo-Germans), published in 1887, 'because in 19th-century Germany the Jews living among us represent views, customs, and demands that go back to the times of the division into peoples shortly after the Flood . . . because in the midst of a Christian world the Jews are Asiatic heathens.' The Jews were, according to Lagarde, 'A people that has contributed nothing to history over thousands of years'.[18]

The false perception that the Jews were both an alien force and the secret powerbrokers in the new Germany led Heinrich Class, the leader of the Pan-German League, to write *Wenn ich der Kaiser wär'* (If I Were Kaiser). Class's book, published in 1912, two years before the outbreak of the First World War, linked the need to 'return to health in our national life' with the demand that 'Jewish influence' be 'completely expunged or screwed back to a bearable, innocuous level'.[19] Class proposed a variety of restrictive measures against the Jews. He called for newspapers that were owned by Jews or employed Jewish writers to 'make this fact known' and for Jews to be excluded from serving in the army or navy and banned from professions like teaching or the law.

In parallel to both *völkisch* and 'traditional' Christian-based anti-Semitism, another very different way of attacking the Jews was also growing. It was the idea behind Hitler's call in his letter of September 1919 for 'anti-Semitism based on reason'. 'Modern' anti-Semites, like Hitler, attempted to rely on pseudo-scientific reasons to justify their hatred of the Jews, arguing that the Jews should be despised not because of their religion, but because of their 'race'.

The notion that human beings could be distinguished from each other by race, and that some 'races' were superior to others, had received quasi-intellectual backing with the publication in 1855 of *Essai sur l'inégalité des races humaines* (Essay on the Inequality of the Human Races) by Arthur de Gobineau.[20] Trained as a diplomat, not a scientist, Gobineau conjured up a world in which there were three races, 'the black, the yellow, and the white'. Of these 'the negroid variety is the lowest, and stands at the foot of the ladder.' Yellow people were 'clearly superior to the black' but 'no civilized society could be created by them; they could not supply its nerve force, or set in motion the springs of beauty and action.' At the top of the racial hierarchy was the 'white race'. They have 'a remarkable, and even extreme, love of liberty'. Thus 'the lesson of history' was that 'all civilizations derive from the white race, that none can exist without its help, and that society is great and brilliant only so far as it preserves the blood of the noble group that created it . . .' Gobineau also believed that all European 'civilizations' – including that of the 'German races' – had been created, 'at least in part', by a group called the 'Aryans' who had migrated to Europe from India.

Houston Stewart Chamberlain, a writer born in England who later became a German citizen, introduced an anti-Semitic dimension to all of this in his *Die Grundlagen des XIX. Jahrhunderts* (Foundations of the Nineteenth Century), published in 1899. The book achieved a wide readership – and not just in Germany. In his effusive Introduction to the English edition, Lord Redesdale wrote that the book had been 'speedily declared to be one of the masterpieces of the century' and that the 'full fruit' of Chamberlain's 'learning and scholarship' had now 'ripened for the good of the world'.[21] Chamberlain argued that while the Aryans represented the ultimate ideal, the Jew embodied precisely the reverse. Even though some Jews might be hard to tell apart from Aryans at first sight, the reality was that all Jews were an 'alien Asiatic people' who had 'by the vilest means acquired immense wealth'.[22] However, since only the Jews and the Germanic race had managed to keep themselves 'pure', it followed that these two 'races' – the Aryan and the Jew – were engaged in a mighty struggle for supremacy.

Understandably, Chamberlain and Hitler had a great deal in common. When they met in 1923 Chamberlain said that as a result of the encounter 'the condition of his soul' had been transformed 'at one fell swoop'.[23] In return the Nazis adopted Chamberlain as one of their own. His seventieth birthday in September 1925 received huge coverage in the Nazi paper the *Völkischer Beobachter*, and *Foundations of the Nineteenth Century* became a revered text.

Many people – especially those whom Chamberlain and de Gobineau said were 'superior' – were attracted by this racial theory. The idea that it was possible to assess the worth of an individual just by their physical appearance proved to be a seductive one. In the popular German novel *Helmut Harringa* (1910) a judge cannot accept that Harringa could be guilty, simply because he looks so pure.[24] It's a lesson that Heinrich Himmler, Reichsführer SS, seems to have taken to heart. On a visit to an SS unit in 1938, a soldier 'caught' his eye because of his 'appearance'. Merely because of his looks the man was judged by Himmler to be a 'capable, good-blooded German'. After investigating the soldier's background, Himmler called for him to be promoted.[25]

There is one further element to add to this toxic mix of 'traditional' anti-Semitism, *völkisch* anti-Semitism and 'racial' anti-Semitism – the emergence of the eugenics movement. The word 'eugenics' (literally 'good race' from the Greek) was coined by the English scientist Francis

Galton. In 1869 in *Hereditary Genius* he argued that the key question that society had to address was simple – who was permitted to breed? He wrote that by 'careful selection' it would be possible 'to produce a highly gifted race of men by judicious marriages during several consecutive generations'. Society had to recognize that 'each generation has enormous power over the natural gifts of those that follow' and thus owed a duty 'to humanity to investigate the range of that power, and to exercise it in a way that, without being unwise towards ourselves, shall be most advantageous to future inhabitants of the earth'.[26]

Galton never advocated trying to stop certain people from breeding by force, but others did. In 1895, Alfred Ploetz, a German supporter of eugenics, or 'race hygiene' as he called it, raised the possibility of doctors deciding whether babies should live or die based on their racial worth. He also said that 'Advocates of racial hygiene will have little objection to war since they see in it one of the means whereby the nations carry on their struggle for existence.' He even suggested that during a battle 'inferior' people could be used as 'cannon fodder' and placed in positions of particular danger.[27]

Many of the pioneers in the eugenics movement were not anti-Semites – Ploetz, for instance, thought the Jews were 'racial Aryans' – but their teachings were of enormous use to those who were. The idea that 'racial hygiene' was central to the health of a nation, combined with Houston Chamberlain's notion that the Jews were a racial threat to 'Aryan' people, added a potentially catastrophic element to the anti-Semitic brew. Traditional anti-Semitism had been based on religion. If the Jews converted to Christianity then they had a chance of escaping persecution. But the idea that 'Jewishness' was something inherent in an individual – that it was present, as the Nazis came to believe, in the blood – meant that there was no escape. Your 'race', over which you had no control, was your destiny. You could be the kindest, most generous person imaginable, but if your 'race' was assessed as inferior or dangerous then you were at risk of persecution.

Hitler explicitly stated in his September 1919 letter that 'the Jews are definitely a race and not a religious community.' This was fundamental to his anti-Semitic belief. It meant, for him, that the question of what religion 'Jews' practised scarcely mattered, since 'there is hardly a single race whose members belong exclusively to one particular religion.'

However, despite a desperate search to identify a test for Jewish 'blood', the Nazis – not surprisingly – never managed to find a scientific way of telling whether or not an individual was a member of the Jewish 'race' or not. As a result, once the Nazis started to persecute and eventually exterminate Jews, they had to rely on a 'Jewishness' test that was religious. They assessed whether or not you were a Jew according to how many of your grandparents had practised the Jewish faith. Nonetheless, the Nazis still believed that the Jews were a 'race' not a 'religion'. The primacy of 'race' in human history was so central to Hitler's worldview that he would never let the small matter of science get in the way of his belief.

It is at this point that a warning needs to be stated. Given this evidence of German anti-Semitic belief predating the emergence of Hitler and the Nazis as a political force, it would be easy to suppose that there is a straight line from the pre-First World War hatred of the Jews to the Third Reich and the Holocaust, that the horror that was to come was somehow inevitable. But such a view would be mistaken, for two important reasons. First, despite the vehemence of their views, the German anti-Semitic parties were not successful in convincing the rest of the country to support them. One calculation is that in the Reichstag of 1893 there were only sixteen elected representatives from anti-Semitic groups, plus about twelve more in other parties who supported their views.[28] An overwhelming majority of German voters – 95 per cent – were not prepared to support overtly anti-Semitic parties at the ballot box.

Of course, what these statistics don't reveal is latent prejudice against the Jews. There would have been a good deal of that, given – as we have seen – that Christian-based anti-Semitism had existed for centuries in Germany. But then, at the time, many other countries in Europe exhibited elements of anti-Semitism. Indeed, the second reason that German anti-Semitism should not be overstated is that if you had lived at the start of the twentieth century and had been asked to predict which country would later pursue an exterminatory policy against the Jews, it's highly unlikely that you would have chosen Germany. Most probably you would have picked Russia. The amount of anti-Semitic violence Russian Jews suffered before the First World War was truly horrific. In a pogrom (the word itself is Russian) against the Jews of Kishinev in

April 1903, hundreds of houses and stores were destroyed and forty-nine Jews murdered. The Jews had been falsely, and ludicrously, accused of killing children in order to use their blood in the preparation of bread for Passover. Two years later in Odessa, in October 1905, around 1,600 Jewish homes were destroyed and several thousand Jews were killed or wounded.[29] These are just two examples of murderous attacks on Jews in Russia during this period – there were many more. Altogether about 2 million Jews fled from Russia between 1880 and the outbreak of the First World War – all seeking a better and safer life. Nothing like this happened in Germany during the same period. German Jews would have read about the murderous attacks taking place in Odessa and Kishinev and considered themselves lucky to live in a civilized country where such barbarities did not occur.

What is harder to assess precisely is Hitler's own attitude towards the Jews before the First World War. He lived in Vienna between 1908 and 1913 and admired the mayor, Karl Lueger – a committed anti-Semite - who once claimed that Jewish power over newspapers and capital amounted to 'the direst terrorism' and that he wanted to liberate Christian people from 'Jewish domination'.[30] He also believed that the Jews were the 'greatest enemy of the German people'.[31] But it is debatable whether Hitler ever voiced such views himself at the time. What is certain is that he was prepared to do business with Jewish dealers when selling his pictures in Vienna.[32] Perhaps, as one leading scholar suggests, he was just being 'pragmatic' during his encounters with Jews and had nonetheless absorbed Viennese anti-Semitism.[33] We simply don't know for sure.

There is no doubt, however, that Hitler wholeheartedly supported the German cause in the First World War and relished the opportunity to take part in the conflict. In August 1914 he petitioned to join a Bavarian regiment and so became a soldier in the German, not the Austrian, Army. Hitler was a committed pan-German, and even though he had been born an Austrian, he considered himself first and foremost a German. He was a brave soldier and won the Iron Cross first class. In the Second World War, he would wear that same Iron Cross on his jacket. What he didn't mention was that it had been a Jewish officer, Hugo Gutmann, who had recommended that he receive it.[34]

By 1916 the war was going badly for the Germans. There was

stalemate on the front line and shortage of food back at home. The idea of a swift victory – on which the plans of the German General Staff had been predicated – was now revealed as a fantasy. People looked for someone to blame for Germany's difficulties; and many began to blame the Jews. The Prussian War Minister claimed that his ministry 'continually' received complaints from the 'population at large' that 'large numbers of men of the Israelitic faith' were shirking their duty to serve on the front line.[35] As a result a census was conducted to determine how many Jews were actually taking part in the war. The results of that survey were never officially published. The suspicion was that after the German authorities had discovered that the data they had collected demonstrated that German Jews were bearing their fair share of the burden of war they concealed the results, rather than see Jews exonerated from the falseness of the charge.

The fact was that German Jews enlisted in the army in the same proportion as non-Jews. Nonetheless, the lie persisted that they had somehow dodged their duty to the Fatherland. In the 1920s, for instance, the newspaper *Der Schild* ran a scurrilous story claiming that 'a field hospital for Jews was established near the front lines, beautifully equipped with the latest medical gear and an all-Jewish staff. After waiting for eight weeks it treated its first patient who arrived shrieking with pain because a typewriter had fallen on his foot.'[36]

The Jews, not for the first time in history, became a scapegoat. Walther Rathenau, a leading Jewish industrialist and politician, wrote prophetically to a friend in 1916: 'The more Jews are killed [in action] in this war, the more obstinately their enemies will prove that they all sat behind the front in order to deal in war speculation. The hatred will grow twice and threefold.'[37]

The circumstances in which the First World War ended for Germany afforded anti-Semites more opportunities to blame the Jews. First, because in the wake of the armistice in November 1918 there was a socialist uprising. The *Ruhr-Echo* proclaimed that 'The red flag must wave victoriously over the whole of Germany. Germany must become a republic of Soviets and, in union with Russia, the springboard for the coming victory of the World revolution and World Socialism.'[38] In April 1919, revolutionaries proclaimed a 'Soviet Republic' in Bavaria. Communists, led by Eugen Leviné, tried to impose extreme socialist policies on Munich and took expensive apartments from their owners in order to house the poor. They also used violence to gain their ends – ten prisoners were murdered on 30 April. In May 1919, right-wing paramilitaries, the Freikorps, marched through Bavaria, entered Munich and defeated the Communists. They took bloody revenge on the revolutionaries and killed more than a thousand of them.

A number of the key Communist revolutionaries had been Jewish. As a result young men like Fridolin von Spaun, who joined a Freikorps immediately after the First World War, found it easy to justify their anti-Semitism by making a crude link between the Jews and Communism. 'The people sent to Bavaria to set up a [Soviet] councils' regime were almost all Jewish,' he says. 'Naturally we also knew from Russia that the Jews there were in a very influential position. So that in Germany the impression gradually took hold that Bolshevism and Judaism are the same, near enough.'[39]

The Jews were not just blamed for trying to instigate a Communist revolution in Germany. They were also blamed for the loss of the war; the destruction of the old political regime based on the Kaiser; agreeing to the terms of the hated Versailles peace treaty; and participating in the Weimar government which presided over the hyperinflation of the early 1920s.

Anti-Semites pointed to alleged Jewish involvement in all of these contentious issues. For example, they noted that the Jewish lawyer Hugo Preuss had drafted the Weimar constitution; that the Jewish politician Hugo Haase was chairman of the Independent Social Democratic Party in 1917; that another Jewish statesman, Otto Landsberg, had travelled to Versailles as Minister of Justice and listened to the demands of the Allies at the peace conference after the war; and that the Jewish industrialist Walther Rathenau hadn't just worked in the War Ministry during the conflict, but had later served as Foreign Minister in the Weimar government.

All the above facts were true. But they did not represent the whole truth. Not only was it absurd to hold Jewish statesmen solely responsible for collective decisions in which they had only played a part, but also any attempt to 'blame' these people as individuals collapsed under examination. For instance, while it was true that Hugo Preuss had been involved in drafting the Weimar constitution, the final version was not his and contained clauses that he had not written. Equally, while Otto Landsberg heard the Allied demands at Versailles, the anti-Semites never mentioned that he was so opposed to the treaty that he resigned. As for Hugo Haase and Walther Rathenau, they were both assassinated shortly after the war – Haase in 1919 and Rathenau in 1922 – and so could hardly be held responsible for any subsequent political deficiencies in the Weimar state.

But prejudice works only if some facts are ignored and others are exaggerated, and many Germans were in no mood to question their emotional response to the dire situation in which they now found themselves. Millions of them were short of food as a result of the Allied naval blockade of Germany – a blockade that was maintained until the summer of 1919 in order to pressurize the new government into signing peace terms. Germans also endured the effects of the 1918 flu pandemic, which caused immense suffering and a large number of deaths. Given all this – and the fear of imminent Communist revolution – many turned to anti-Semitism as a convenient way of explaining their misery. Theodor Eschenburg, for instance, was fourteen years old when the war ended, and remembers that his father suddenly 'developed a racial anti-Semitism, which he didn't have before. The world revolution, the world bankers, the world press – all full of Jews.'[40]

It was against this background of a lost war and enormous discontent that a new political force would emerge in the south of Germany – the National Socialist German Workers' Party. Or Nazis, for short.

2. Birth of the Nazis

(1919–1923)

The Nazi party was born out of a fundamental change in the German political environment. For German anti-Semites didn't just hold the Jews responsible for even more problems now than before the war – their hatred gained an entire new dimension.

In 1912 the leader of the Pan-Germans, Heinrich Class, had entitled his attack on the Jews 'If I Were Kaiser'. Class thus imagined that the changes he called for could be made within the established political system of which the Kaiser was the head. But it was inconceivable in 1919 that a leading anti-Semite would call a new attack on the Jews 'If I were President of the Weimar Republic'. That is because the government was no longer seen as the means by which a solution to the Jewish 'problem' could be sought – the government was seen as *part* of the Jewish 'problem'.

Amid all this discontent, anti-Semitic groups flourished. The most powerful was the Deutschvölkischer Schutz- und Trutzbund (German People's Protection and Defiance League), founded in February 1919. By 1922 the League had 150,000 members; and every one of them had signed up to a constitution calling for the 'removal' of the 'pernicious and destructive influence of Jewry'.[1]

Bavaria, in particular, was a breeding ground for a whole host of radical anti-Semitic groups. In Munich, for instance, the Thule Society demanded that each prospective member swear that 'no Jewish or coloured blood' flowed 'in his or his wife's veins'.[2] Once they had fulfilled these entrance requirements, members of the society were exposed to the rhetoric of the founder – Rudolf Freiherr von Sebottendorff. His views became positively apocalyptic at the time of the defeat of the German Army in November 1918. He proclaimed that now 'our mortal enemy rules: Judah. We don't know yet what will arise from this chaos. We can guess. The time of fight will come, of bitter hardships, a time of danger! We, who are in this fight, are all in danger, for the enemy hates us with the infinite hatred of the Jewish race. It is now an eye for an eye, a tooth for a tooth . . . Now, brothers and sisters, it is no longer the time for contemplative speeches and meetings and feasts! Now it is time to fight, and I want to and will fight! Fight until the swastika [the symbol of the Thule Society] ascends triumphantly . . . Now we need to talk about the German Reich, now we need to say that the Jew is our mortal enemy . . .'[3]

Another leading member of the Thule Society was an alcoholic playwright in his early fifties called Dietrich Eckart – a man who would have a very considerable influence on the thirty-year-old Adolf Hitler. Eckart was a convinced anti-Semite. He was most famous for his adaptation of Ibsen's *Peer Gynt*, which he altered so as to make the trolls into caricature Jews.[4] In another of his plays, *Familienvater*, Eckart told the story of a courageous journalist who tried to expose the corrupt power of the Jews in the media; the journalist wrote a play in order to warn the public about the danger of the Jews, but the Jews used their influence to make it fail. In a twist of events that would be comic were the underlying history not so bleak, when Eckart's play about an unsuccessful playwright whose play failed because of the Jews was itself unsuccessful, Eckart blamed – predictably – the Jews.[5] For Eckart, 'the Jewish question' was the 'issue that actually contains every other issue. Nothing on earth would remain obscure if one could only shed light on its mystery.'[6] Furthermore, he wrote, 'No people in the world' would let the Jew live if they understood him: if they 'suddenly saw through what he is and what he wants, screaming in horror they would strangle him the very next minute'.[7]

Eckart was a supporter of a small political group in Munich called the German Workers' Party, which was loosely associated with the Thule Society, and it was through this association that he and Hitler came to form a special bond. On 12 September 1919, a week before Hilter sent his letter outlining the reasons for his anti-Semitism, he attended a meeting of the party in a beer hall in Munich. The German Workers' Party was one of many small Bavarian political groups on the far right. All of them followed the same essential script: German soldiers had lost the war because they had been 'stabbed in the back' by Jewish profiteers working behind the lines, and the Jews were the instigators of both Communist revolution and the hated Weimar democracy. At the meeting Hitler was talent-spotted by the chairman of the party, a railway mechanic called Anton Drexler. Recognizing Hitler's ability to express himself in forceful terms, Drexler pressed him to join.

Over the next months, however, it was Dietrich Eckart who most influenced Hitler's development. Paradoxically, the qualities in Hitler that Eckart valued were the very ones that had previously made him appear rather 'peculiar'[8] to his comrades during the First World War. Hitler's intolerance, his social inadequacies, his inability to engage in normal conversation and his absolute certainty that he was right – these, to Eckart, were all now positive attributes. There was, Eckart no doubt believed, a great deal to be angry about in the wake of the German defeat, and Hitler was anger personified. That, combined with his extreme views about who was to blame for the current situation, was exactly what the confused masses in Munich needed to hear. Above all, Hitler's service in the war as an ordinary soldier who had won an Iron Cross for his bravery marked him out from the old leadership elite who had so demonstrably failed the nation. 'The rabble has to be scared shitless,' said Eckart. 'I can't use an officer; the people no longer have any respect for them. Best of all would be a worker who's got his mouth in the right place . . . He doesn't need to be intelligent; politics is the stupidest business in the world.'[9] All of which led Eckart to make this prophecy about Hitler: 'This is the coming man of Germany, one day the world will speak of him.'[10]

As for Hitler, his relationship with Eckart was one of the closest he ever had with another human being. He revered Eckart almost to the point of hero worship. He said that when he first met Eckart, 'I was intellectually a child still on the bottle. But what comforted me was that, even with him, it hadn't all sprouted of itself – that everything in his work was the result of a patient and intelligent effort.'[11] Hitler felt that Eckart 'shone in our eyes like the polar star'.[12]

This odd couple – the bald, prematurely aged alcoholic and the socially awkward ex-soldier – had many adventures together before Eckart's death in December 1923. Some alleged escapades attained an almost mythical status. Later accounts claimed, for example, that in March 1920 they flew in a light plane to Berlin in an attempt to make contact with right-wing revolutionaries who had just overthrown the government in the 'Kapp Putsch'. After a journey battling through the elements, during which Hitler vomited over the side of the plane, they landed in Berlin. Eckart now posed as a businessman and Hitler pretended to be his assistant. In order to make the impersonation more effective, Hitler put on a fake beard. They made their way to the Hotel Adlon, the headquarters of Wolfgang Kapp, the leader of the short-lived Putsch, only to be told by his press officer that he wasn't there. Eckart looked at the press officer and told Hitler they had to leave at once – because the press officer was clearly Jewish. Hitler subsequently said that he had realized that the Kapp Putsch would fail, because the 'press chief of Kapp's government . . . was a Jew'.[13]

Three weeks before this alleged abortive trip to Berlin, the German Workers' Party – now renamed the National Socialist German Workers' Party (colloquially, the Nazis) – had launched a twenty-five-point party programme at the Hofbräuhaus beer hall in Munich. Point four of the programme, which was composed largely by Hitler and Anton Drexler, read: 'Only members of the nation may be citizens of the State . . . Accordingly, no Jew may be a member of the nation.'[14] The penultimate point elaborated further on the anti-Semitic policy of the party by announcing that the Nazi party 'combats the Jewish-materialist spirit within and without us'.

Over the next few months and years, Hitler preached his anti-Semitic beliefs at countless rallies and meetings of the National Socialist German Workers' Party. He said that 'solving the Jewish question is the central question for National Socialists' and that the Nazis could 'solve' it only by using 'brute force'.[15] He also claimed that 'the Jew destroys and must destroy because he completely lacks the conception of an activity which builds up the life of the community'[16] and that 'no salvation is possible until the bearer of disunion, the Jew, has been rendered powerless to harm.'[17] Hitler even attacked the Jews for bringing democracy to Germany – 'Democracy is fundamentally not German: it is Jewish'[18] – and repeated the traditional anti-Semitic fantasy that 'the Jews are a people of robbers. He [the Jew] has never founded any civilization, though he has destroyed civilizations by the hundred. He possesses nothing of his own creation to which he can point.'[19]

Hitler emphasized to his audience that there could never be such a thing as a 'good' Jew. Individual actions and achievements counted for nothing. For Hitler 'it is beside the point whether the individual Jew is 'decent or not'. In himself he carries those characteristics which Nature has given him, and he cannot ever rid himself of those characteristics. And to us he is harmful.'[20] For Hitler, the decision to emancipate the Jews was 'the beginning of an attack of delirium' because 'equality' had been given to a 'people' that was 'clearly and definitely a race apart'.[21] The official policy of the National Socialist German Workers' Party was for the German Jews to be stripped of their citizenship, but in an article in March 1921 for the *Völkischer Beobachter* – a newspaper bought for the Nazis with the assistance of Dietrich Eckart – Hitler went further, and suggested that Germany could also be protected by imprisoning Jews. 'The Jewish undermining of our *Volk* must be prevented,' he wrote, 'if necessary through confining its instigators in concentration camps. Briefly, our *Volk* must be cleansed of all the poison at the top and the bottom.'[22]

Hitler's radical anti-Semitism was obvious, even at this early stage in the history of the Nazi party, but it did not necessarily follow that all of those who joined the party at this time did so because they also felt strongly about the Jews. Some, like Emil Klein, were motivated primarily by disillusionment about the lost war and fear of a Communist revolution. 'We were a young war generation,' he says. 'We saw our fathers being called up. We saw them garlanded with flowers at the stations as they set off for war in France. We saw the weeping mothers they left behind.'[23] Then, after his father returned, defeated, in 1919 'at the time of the Munich collapse, we suddenly saw the red flags. Because the Communists had entered and bombarded the whole city in their vans, distributing leaflets. And they advertised for their party and for the revolution with the slogan, "Workers of the world unite!" '

Emil Klein's route to anti-Semitism came via the alleged link between Communism and Judaism: 'I looked into it at the time and I discovered that the ones at the top [at the time of the Munich "Soviet republic"] were mainly literary Jews – well, a whole series of them. It did cause enormous offence in Bavaria that Jews were setting the tone. And that's where the expression came from: "Jew republic".' Once exposed to the rhetoric of the Nazi party, Klein extended the scope of his anti-Semitism, and came to believe that the Jews were not just behind Communism, but responsible for the ills of capitalism as well. He thought that 'the fight against Jewry' contained within the Nazi party programme was 'not against the Jews as such, but against international high finance, the financial power of Jewry . . . So, not against the Jews as individuals, but against capitalism, which stems from Jewry, from Wall Street that is. Wall Street was always being mentioned.'

Hitler did much more, however, than merely tell Nazi supporters that the Jews were to blame for Germany's problems. He didn't only preach a doctrine of hate – he also offered hope. He painted a vision of a new Germany in which class differences would disappear and all 'Aryan' Germans would bond themselves together in a national community. Emil Klein was attracted by the idea that the Nazi party 'wanted to eradicate class differences, with the working class here, the bourgeoisie here and the middle classes here. These were deeply ingrained concepts that split the nation into two parts, and that was an important point for me, one that I liked . . . that the nation has to be united.'[24]

Jutta Rüdiger, who would later become a senior figure in the Nazi organization Der Bund Deutscher Mädel, the League of German Girls, also wanted to see a united German community: 'The fact that the family comes first, then the clan, then the community, then the nation and then Europe, [this was] not a nebulous concept but an idea based on the roots of the family . . . The concept was a real classless society without any differences, whereas previous youth movements, and that is partly true of the boy scouts, too, had consisted mostly of grammar school boys, with the working-class children kept mostly to themselves. We had united the young workers and the young people still at school into one entity. There was no difference between them and nobody would ask "what does your father do?" '[25]

Rüdiger's support for the idea of the 'classless' Germany was encapsulated by one experience after the Nazis came to power. 'It was shortly before Christmas and everybody was collecting money, especially on the Day of National Solidarity as it was called then.* And leading members of the party were present as well as ministers and industrialists. They were on the street in the wind and the rain.' A rich foreigner approached one of the German industrialists and asked why he was standing out in the cold asking the public for small change when all he needed to do was to 'put a thousand marks in the tin'. The German industrialist turned to Jutta Rüdiger and said simply, 'They do not get the point at all.'

Bruno Hähnel, who joined the Nazi party in the early 1920s, also felt

---

* The BDM collected, along with others, for the Winterhilfswerk des Deutschen Volkes (the Winter Relief of the German People), the highlight of which was the Day of National Solidarity.

drawn to the idea of a 'national community' (in German, *Volksgemein-schaft*). 'It simply means that there had always been two distinct strata in German society,' he says, 'the bourgeoisie and the proletariat. And so in order to bridge the gap, a national community was to be established, in order to ensure that both the intellectuals and the workers would join forces. The national community was expressed in the [Nazi party's] catchphrase, which I think most of us used again and again: "The public's interest comes first." Hence also the expression that we weren't merely National Socialists, but national-*minded* Socialists.'[26]

As a senior German officer, secretly recorded in captivity by the British during the war, put it: 'Some things will remain for ever. They will last for hundreds of years. Not the roads [the Nazis built] – they are unimportant. But what will last is the way in which the state has been organized, particularly the inclusion of the workingman as part of the state. He [Hitler] has made a place for the workingman in the state and no one has ever done that before . . . This principle of everyone working for the common cause, the idea that the industrialist is really the trustee for the capital represented by German labour and for the other capital, all sounds so easy, but no one managed it before.'[27]

However, the Nazi supporters who approved of 'classlessness' were also, as a consequence, supporting a darker idea altogether. That is because Hitler taught that this new 'classless' life would be possible only when those of a different 'race' were excluded from the society of 'true' Germans. 'We said to ourselves', Hitler declared, 'there are no such things as classes: they cannot be. Class means caste and caste means race.'[28] The notion of a 'classless' Germany followed, as far as Hitler was concerned, from an acceptance that 'race' was the most vital quality of all. The Jews were thus the barrier to a Germany in which everyone was united in the Nazi ideal of a classless world. It was the Jews who were preventing Germans becoming happy and prosperous. If their 'power' was not somehow neutralized, there could be no progress, no way out of the morass. In a speech in September 1922, Hitler summed up what he saw as Germany's predicament: 'We in Germany have come to this: that sixty-million people sees its destiny to lie at the will of a few dozen Jewish bankers.'[29]

The Nazi party was not the only organization promoting both anti-Semitism and the ideals of the *völkisch* movement. Up to seventy other groups listed in the *German Völkisch Yearbook* of 1921 all believed that by stripping the Jews of German citizenship the *Volk* could flourish anew.[30] One of them, the small Deutschsozialistische Partei (German Socialist Party), based in Franconia in northern Bavaria, established a newspaper in 1920. An article in the first edition tried to convert socialists to the cause of the radical right by arguing that, while the parties on the left claimed to 'fight against all capital, even the Jewish big loan money', they were actually sponsored by the Jews: 'Do you really think that the Rothschilds, Mendelssohns, Bleichröders, Warburgs and Cohns will ever let you near their supply of money? Don't believe this swindle after all! As long as the blood brothers of the Mendelssohns, of the Bleichröders and Cohns are your captains and as long as your group leaders are mercenaries of the Jews, you don't pose a danger to the big-money people. As long as you do not become leaders yourselves, as long as the black shadow of aliens is behind you, you are seduced and fooled. The black alien is interested in his own benefit, not in you.'[31]

The author of the article was a thirty-six-year-old schoolteacher and veteran of the First World War who would subsequently play a leading role in inciting anti-Semitism in Germany. His name was Julius Streicher. Like Hitler, Streicher had won the Iron Cross during the war, but unlike Hitler he had been born a German, not an Austrian. He had grown up around Augsburg in south-west Bavaria. This area changed a great deal during his childhood as the population increased and several thousand Jews moved into the district. Streicher traced his own dislike of the Jews to an incident that he claimed occurred when he was five years old. His mother bought some fabric from a Jewish shop and it later turned out that the material wasn't of high quality. His mother burst into tears and said that this deception was typical of a Jew.[32]

In the autumn of 1921 Streicher joined the Deutsche Werkgemeinschaft (German Working Community), and his attacks on the Jews became more extreme and more personal. He claimed that Jews in Nuremberg snatched Christian children and murdered them in order to obtain blood to use in baking bread at Passover – the same 'Blood Libel' that had helped incite the pogrom in Kishinev in Russia nearly twenty years before. On 5 September 1922, at the district court in Schweinfurt, in a judgment against Streicher for 'an offence against religion', the assessor stated that Streicher had 'accused the Jews of still maintaining the custom of ritual murder. He [Streicher] referred to the east, where he previously fought in the World War as an officer, and explained that the people over there spoke quite bluntly about ritual murders by the Jews. He added that in Germany one hundred children would mysteriously disappear every year around the Easter period and he asked: "Where do these children get to?" '[33]

In another speech in 1922 Streicher said it should not be considered a crime if 'one day we stand up and chase the Jews to hell' and 'grab the bastards for their lies'.[34] He also alleged that the Jews had been 'proven' to 'wish for Germany's misfortune' and that if 'the [German] people had known the contents of the secret treaties of the war, they would have slain all the Jews'.[35]

While Streicher's rhetoric was popular among a select group, it was also inevitably the cause of conflict. At least one meeting had to be called off after he inflamed the audience so much that they started to fight among themselves. Even the leadership of the Deutsche Werkgemeinschaft criticized Streicher for his antics. It was obvious to everyone that he was an aggressive and potentially dangerous individual who was obsessed with hatred of the Jews and foreign 'races'. As a result, he was precisely the kind of man that Hitler wanted in the Nazi party. Reminiscing about this period nearly twenty years later, Hitler remarked that 'More than once' Dietrich Eckart had told him that Streicher was a 'lunatic'. But, said Hitler, Eckart 'always added that one could not hope for the triumph of National Socialism without giving one's support to men like Streicher'.[36]

Late in 1922, Streicher travelled to Munich and listened to Hitler speak for the first time. At his trial at Nuremberg after the war, he described the experience: 'First slowly, hardly audible, then faster and more powerfully, and finally with overpowering strength ... He revealed an enormous treasure trove of thought in a speech of more than three hours, clothed with the beauty of inspired language. Each person felt it: this man spoke from a godly calling, he spoke as a messenger from heaven at a time when hell threatened to swallow up everything. And everyone understood him, whether with the brain or the heart, whether man or woman. He had spoken for everyone, for the entire German people. Just before midnight his speech concluded with the inspiring call: "Workers, blue collar or white! To you is extended the hand of a German people's community of heart and action." '[37]

Streicher now believed that it was his destiny to serve Adolf Hitler. Indeed, he seems to have experienced an almost religious conversion. 'I saw this man shortly before midnight,' he said at Nuremberg, 'after he had spoken for three hours, drenched in perspiration, radiant. My neighbor said he thought he saw a halo around his head, and I experienced something which transcended the commonplace.'[38] Shortly afterwards, Streicher persuaded his own followers to join the Nazi party and accept Hitler's leadership. In 1923 he launched his anti-Semitic newspaper *Der Stürmer* and he continued to preside over this infamous hate sheet until the end of the Second World War.

Around this time Hitler attracted others into the party who would subsequently become leading figures in the Nazi movement. Ernst Röhm, Hermann Göring, Hans Frank, Rudolf Hess – all of these people and more decided to follow Hitler in the early 1920s. Some of them were young and impressionable, but men like Röhm and Göring were hard-bitten, cynical veterans of the war. Both had served as officers and had distinguished themselves as leaders of men in battle. Now, in the wake of the German defeat, they had countless political parties to choose from in order to pursue their goals, and yet they decided to subordinate themselves to a former soldier from the ranks called Adolf Hitler.

In part, this was because they witnessed the power of his rhetoric. They saw how he could attract new followers to the cause – just as he had with Julius Streicher. But just as important, they shared Hitler's beliefs. In terms of policy, Hitler had to convince them of nothing. What he offered them, in large part via his speech-making, was a combination of clarity of vision and the promise of a radical method of turning this vision into a reality.

As a necessary precondition of this, Hitler spoke with absolute certainty. He laid out the alleged reasons for the mess Germany was in, and then he told his audience the way these troubles should be fixed. There was no debate, no discussion. Hitler's belief that he was right was so intense that it dominated everything else. At a rally in Munich in 1923 Professor Karl Alexander von Müller watched him walk to the stage. He had previously met the Nazi leader once or twice in private houses, but the man before him now was a different Hitler. 'Gaunt, pale features contorted as if by inward rage,' wrote Professor Müller afterwards, 'cold flames darting from his protruding eyes, which seemed to be searching out foes to be conquered. Did the crowd give him this mysterious power? Did it emanate from him to them? "Fanatical, hysterical romanticism with a brutal core of willpower" I noted down. The declining middle class may be carrying this man, but he is not one of them. He assuredly comes from totally different depths of darkness.'[39]

Many in the *völkisch* movement had longed for an individual to come forward and offer them a way through the disorder that appeared all around. As Stefan George, the prophet of the movement, put it in 1907: 'The Man! The Deed! *Volk* and high counsel yearn for The Man! The Deed!'[40] Now Hitler appeared to fulfil this destiny. As Nazi supporter Bruno Hähnel says: 'it was our aim that a strong man should have the say, and we had such a strong man.'[41]

Hitler was soon the undisputed leader of the Nazis, and in a memorandum he wrote in January 1922 he outlined where previous leaders of the *völkisch* movement had gone wrong. They had been intelligent but 'fantastically naive' and had 'lacked the warm breath of the nation's youthful vigour'. What Hitler believed the movement needed was 'the impetuous force of headstrong fire-eaters'.[42] And he found just such men in Streicher, Röhm and Göring. They were exactly the people he needed for what he called 'a party of struggle and action'.

Hitler thus offered not only a racist and anti-Semitic vision of the world; not only an analysis of why Germany had lost the war and was now losing the peace; not just a promise of a 'classless' nation. He also offered a way forward that was exciting, dangerous and calculated to appeal to the young. 'The old parties train their youth in the gift of the gab,' he said in a speech in July 1922, 'we prefer to train them to use their bodily strength. For I tell you, the young man who does not find his way to the place where in the last resort the destiny of his people is most truly represented, only studies philosophy and in a time like this buries himself behind his books or sits at home by the fire, he is no German youth! I call upon you! Join our Storm Divisions!'[43]

During that same year, 1922, a twenty-one-year-old agricultural student at the University of Munich called Heinrich Himmler was trying to make sense of his own life. In the process, he absorbed many of the beliefs of the radical right. However, he was not moved by the crude, emotional anti-Semitism of men like Julius Streicher. Instead, Himmler preferred the pseudo-academic analysis contained within Houston

Stewart Chamberlain's work. He wrote of *Foundations of the Nineteenth Century* that it was 'objective' and not full of 'hate-filled' anti-Semitism.[44] The young Himmler believed that he could deal with individual Jews in a professional fashion, while still understanding that racially the Jews were a threat. In January 1922, for instance, he met a Jewish lawyer and described him in his diary as 'Extremely amiable and kind', but nonetheless 'He cannot hide his Jewishness' because it was in his 'blood'.[45] Himmler also approved of treating in a brutal way those Jews who were perceived by fanatical nationalists to have harmed Germany. When he heard the news that the German Jewish Foreign Minister Walther Rathenau had been shot in June 1922, he wrote, 'I'm glad . . . he was a villain.'[46]

Like many who hadn't seen combat in the First World War, Himmler wanted to show that he could be a brave fighter. After hearing a speech in Munich from a general who in 1919 had fought in the Baltic against the Bolsheviks, he wrote in his diary, 'Now I know more certainly than ever, if there is another campaign in the east, I will go along. The east is the most important thing for us. The west is simply dying. In the east, we need to fight and settle.'[47] They were unconsciously prophetic words, given that Himmler would subsequently orchestrate genocide 'in the east' during the Second World War.

The Himmler that emerges from his diaries is a repressed, prissy young man who thinks a great deal of himself, and has trouble in his relationships with women. He believed that he was one of those 'types of people' who were 'melancholic' and 'strict' and 'who are necessary in the people's community, but who in my opinion will still fall one day if they don't get married or engaged soon enough, because the human animalistic nature is too powerful within us'.[48] He also believed that 'the objective that every man should have' was 'to be an upright, straight, fair man, who is never shy or afraid and that is hard'.[49] Like that of many others, Himmler's career development was damaged by the economic problems of 1922. He had hoped to stay on and study politics at the University of Munich after finishing his agricultural exams, but instead, by the autumn of 1922, he was working for a fertilizer company. It was a change in fortune almost certainly caused by the hyperinflation that was now rampant and that made it hard for middle-class parents to fund their children's studies. Himmler had not yet met Adolf Hitler, but he

was already predisposed by his intellectual beliefs and his personal circumstances to find his message an attractive one.

Above all else in these early years, Hitler and his party saw themselves
as revolutionaries. They lived in a time of revolution – from the Communist uprisings in Berlin and Munich in 1919 to the right-wing Kapp
Putsch in 1920. And by 1922 Hitler was not only prepared to talk about
violence as the route to power, he was ready to lead into battle his own
group of paramilitaries – the Stormtroopers or Sturmabteilung. Originally members of the euphemistically known 'gymnastic and sports'
section of the party, the Stormtroopers protected party rallies and beat
up political opponents.

In October 1922 Hitler hired a train to take around 800 Nazi
Stormtroopers to Coburg in the north of Bavaria, an area with strong
left-wing support. His aim at Coburg was to provoke a confrontation;
and he succeeded, as his Stormtroopers fought the socialists in the streets
before finally declaring themselves victorious. As a consequence of
actions like this, the true nature of the Nazi party was clear for all to see.

Like all revolutionaries, Hitler was not concerned whether his ideas
succeeded at the ballot box. He did not have to worry whether or not
a majority of Germans supported Nazi policies – such as his desire to
strip the Jews of their citizenship – which was just as well for him,
because there was no evidence that most Germans supported this radical
idea. The Nazis, it should be remembered, were still a fringe party
opposed by substantial groups who despised their anti-Semitic and racist beliefs. Indeed, a study of voting patterns at national elections in the
early 1920s reveals that a majority of Germans voted for parties who did
not agree with anti-Semitic policies.[50] Nor should it be forgotten that
there were many Germans, like Josef Felder, later a Social Democratic
member of the Reichstag, who felt revulsion when they heard what
Hitler had to say. He remembers listening to one of Hitler's anti-Semitic
diatribes in the early 1920s and afterwards remarking to a friend that
'hopefully' Hitler 'would never come to power'.[51]

However, in 1922 it appeared to Hitler and his followers that the omens
for a successful revolution were good. The same month that Hitler led his
Stormtroopers into the streets of Coburg, a fellow revolutionary – Benito
Mussolini – saw his Blackshirted followers march on Rome and provoke a

change in government. By the end of October that year Mussolini was Prime Minister of Italy. Meanwhile, in Germany the economic crisis escalated when French and Belgian troops crossed into German territory at the start of 1923 and occupied the Rhineland. The occupation – the result of Germany defaulting on reparation payments – was, not surprisingly, hugely unpopular. It appeared that the Weimar government could not even protect German borders. In the wake of the crisis, membership of the Nazi party more than doubled and by November there were about 55,000 members. It was one of the first signs that this was a movement that thrived on calamity.

In Bavaria, Gustav von Kahr became State Commissioner – effectively a dictator. Hitler now hoped to force Kahr and the German troops based in Bavaria to support the Nazis and other right-wing paramilitaries in a march on Berlin. What had worked for Mussolini in Italy would now, Hitler supposed, work for the Nazis in Germany. Nazi Stormtroopers interrupted a meeting that Kahr was holding at the Bürgerbräukeller in Munich on the evening of 8 November and then marched through the city the following day. Taking part in what became known as the 'Beer-Hall Putsch' were many who would go on to play important roles in the Nazi party, including Himmler (who had still not met Hitler personally), Göring and Streicher – all of them dedicated revolutionaries. During the march through Munich the Nazis and their supporters were confronted by police at the corner of the Feldenherrnhalle and the Odeonsplatz in the centre of the city. Shots were fired and sixteen Nazis and four policemen were killed that day.

The whole episode was misconceived from the beginning. Despite promising to support the Putsch when Hitler threatened him at the Bürgerbräukeller, Kahr disavowed the Nazis as soon as he was out of their hands. Hitler had misread the potential willingness of the right-wing Bavarian authorities to support his revolution and had no contingency plan to put in place once the revolutionaries were on their own. But despite all this, he was able to transform this humiliating defeat into a propaganda triumph.

He was arrested and put on trial in February 1924. Knowing, as a result of Kahr's initial support at the Bürgerbräukeller, that the Bavarian authorities themselves were implicated in the Putsch, Hitler used the courtroom as a stage to shout his political beliefs to the world. He announced that he was the 'destroyer of Marxism' and that far from practising 'high treason' he had wanted only to create conditions in Germany that would 'make it possible for the iron grip of our enemies to be removed from us'.[52] Hitler did not regret his actions. Instead, he appeared proud of them.

Hitler was found guilty of high treason – no other verdict was possible given the evidence against him. But the court was lenient. The judge, Georg Neithardt, was one of many leading figures in the Bavarian establishment who was sympathetic to the aims of the Nazis. As a result, Hitler received the lightest sentence possible – five years in prison – with the expectation that he would be out on probation long before that sentence had been served.

What is significant about this episode in any attempt to understand the origins of the Nazi party as a revolutionary, anti-Semitic movement, is not so much the individual character of Hitler – though that is important – as the noxious mix of circumstances that made the situation in Bavaria possible. It is hard to see how the rise of such a motley group of violent people could have been tolerated in a civilized state without the turbulent conditions of the time.

Germans wrestled in the years immediately following the First World War with a whole host of difficulties that made their lives potentially hazardous. Hyperinflation wrecked their savings, the Weimar administration appeared impotent in the face of foreign intervention – the arrival of French and Belgian troops on German soil in the Rhineland was a particular humiliation – and Communist revolutionaries still threatened. Democracy appeared to have brought little but chaos. But paradoxically, since the Nazis were a party of violence, they claimed to offer a path to stability. As a result, a small minority of Germans – and only a small minority at this stage – supported them.

Finally, at a time of enormous suffering, Hitler offered reassurance. 'Listen,' the subtext of his speeches seemed to say, 'none of these problems are your fault.' Over the next months as he served his prison sentence, he would elaborate on just whose fault he believed all of Germany's troubles were – and why.

3. From Revolution to Ballot Box
(1924–1933)

Hitler served his sentence at Landsberg prison, just over 30 miles west of Munich. Landsberg was a *Festungshaft* or 'fortress' prison, which meant that the accommodation was comfortable and there were few restrictions on visitors. One Nazi supporter later remarked that he thought he had 'walked into a delicatessen' when he visited Hitler, since he found that admirers had provided the Nazi leader with an abundance of 'ham, sausage, cake, boxes of chocolates and much more'.[1]

In these convivial surroundings, among many of his comrades who had also taken part in the Putsch, Hitler composed a book – *Mein Kampf* (My Struggle). Though written in a crude and hyperbolic style, *Mein Kampf* nonetheless offers valuable insights into Hitler's worldview. The book was not a blueprint for the Holocaust – Hitler did not outline a plan to exterminate the Jews – but he did lay bare the nature of his own anti-Semitism. He explained, in greater detail than in any of his previous utterances, just why he hated the Jews. It was a hatred that reads today as the product of a mind so deeply mired in prejudice as to be almost unhinged.

The subject of the Jews dominated the book. Indeed, it is not going too far to say that 'the Jew' was the glue that held Hitler's entire worldview together. 'The Jew' was, in this sense, helpful to Hitler in an almost calculated way. For he believed the 'great leader' should direct 'the struggle' against just 'one enemy'.[2] This was partly, he argued, because 'the receptivity of the great masses is very limited, their intelligence is small, but their power of forgetting is enormous.'[3] However, the tactical usefulness that Hitler found in linking the Jews to every problem Germany faced should not blind us to the reality that he genuinely believed in the threat the Jews posed. 'Was there any form of filth or profligacy, particularly in cultural life, without at least one Jew involved in it?' he wrote in *Mein Kampf*. 'If you cut even cautiously into such an abscess, you found, like a maggot in a rotting body, often dazzled by the sudden light – a kike!'[4]

Hitler attempted to outline in *Mein Kampf* not just a coherent vision of the way the world worked, but also the manner in which his own life had developed since his youth. We have already noted how doubts have been cast on the extent to which he held anti-Semitic views during his time in Vienna, but in *Mein Kampf* he asserted unequivocally that he had formed his destructive views about the Jews as a result of his time in the Austrian capital. In Vienna, he claimed, he had come to hate the Jews for a myriad of reasons. The Jews were dirty – 'by their very exterior you could tell that these were no lovers of water';[5] they were cunning – 'I didn't know what to be more amazed at: the agility of their tongues or their virtuosity at lying';[6] they were involved in sexual slavery – 'The relation of the Jews to prostitution and, even more, to the white slave traffic, could be studied in Vienna as perhaps in no other city of Western Europe, with the possible exception of the southern French ports';[7] and they were behind the political ideology he most despised – 'The Jewish doctrine of Marxism rejects the aristocratic principle of Nature . . .'[8]

Hitler wrote that he had vociferous arguments with Jews in an attempt to convince them of the dangers of their 'Marxist doctrine'. But the trouble was that 'Whenever you tried to attack one of these apostles, your hand closed on a jelly-like slime which divided up and poured through your fingers, but in the next moment collected again.'[9] Hitler portrayed himself during his time in Vienna as a political agitator who 'talked my tongue sore and my throat hoarse' in argument with Jews. It was a claim that was scarcely believable, since no one ever came forward subsequently and said they were part of any such discussion. But it is not hard to understand why Hitler wanted to craft this image of his pre-war self. That is because what he created in *Mein Kampf* was a mythic fable – almost an ersatz religious tract. The stages of his awakening, as he described them, are clear and logical. In Vienna as a young man he became a fanatical Jew-hater because he saw the dangers inherent in their 'race'. During the First World War he learnt of the way in which Jews, luxuriating back in Germany, were sabotaging the brave soldiers in the front line. As soon as the war ended, he was finally enlightened to his mission – 'I, for my part, decided to go into politics.'[10]

The reality was very different. During his time in Vienna and serving in the German Army he remained a solitary figure on the edge of the group. He never demonstrated any interest in a career in politics or in arguing for hours with Jews. After all, he already knew the career he wanted to pursue – he longed to be an artist. Even in the immediate aftermath of the war, and contrary to his assertion in *Mein Kampf*, he showed no desire to go into politics. He didn't join a paramilitary Freikorps but remained in the army. Only in the summer of 1919 after he had been assigned to work for Captain Karl Mayr, head of the army's Information Department in Munich, does he appear to have manifested any interest in becoming a politician.

The trouble for Hitler was that his true autobiography did not make him look heroic. In reality he was just like most people, knocked about by events over which he had no control. If it had not been for the outbreak of the First World War he would most likely have remained a struggling artist who was prepared to sell his pictures to Jewish dealers. If the war had not ended as it did, he would almost certainly have never entered politics. But Hitler was astute enough to realize that no potential follower of his would value his genuine personal history. He had to maintain that he was born to greatness. He had to claim that he was the master of events; they were not the master of him.

This is significant in the context of the Holocaust, because it means that one cannot explain the crime by arguing that Hitler was somehow destined to commit it. While it is true that by the time he wrote *Mein Kampf* he had developed an immense hatred of Jews, the real trigger for that emotion seems to have been the manner of the German defeat in November 1918 combined with the political and economic situation in Bavaria in the immediate post-war years. These circumstances also explain why many people were suddenly entranced by his speeches. Before the war, when Hitler had ranted on to his acquaintances about his views on art, no one wanted to listen. Now, talking about politics, he connected with his followers because they shared the same essential emotions and prejudices.

However, Hitler did more than merely parrot back to his followers the views they already held. His anti-Semitism and racism were so extreme that they legitimized his supporters as they extended and hardened their own hatred. When he wrote a hyperbolic sentence in *Mein Kampf* like the Jew 'is and remains the typical parasite, a sponger who like a noxious bacillus keeps spreading as soon as a favourable medium invites him',[11] he acted to push the boundaries of his supporters' existing anti-Semitic views and radicalize the latent or 'moderate' anti-Semite. It would have been much harder to infect with anti-Semitism an adult who was not already contaminated by such prejudice. As Aldous Huxley wrote: 'The propagandist is a man who canalizes an already existing stream. In a land where there is no water, he digs in vain.'[12]

Hitler's most radical statement about the Jews in *Mein Kampf* is notorious. 'If at the beginning of the War and during the War,' he wrote, 'twelve or fifteen thousand of these Hebrew corrupters of the people had been held under poison gas, as happened to hundreds of thousands of our very best German workers in the field, the sacrifice of millions at the front would have not been in vain. On the contrary: twelve thousand scoundrels eliminated in time might have saved the lives of a million real Germans, valuable for the future.'[13]

It seems unequivocal. Hitler was arguing that Jews should have been gassed during the First World War. But it would be a mistake to conclude from this that he necessarily had a similar fate in mind for all Jews at some point in the future. While we cannot look into Hitler's mind and know his unspoken intentions, we can say with some certainty that he did not argue publicly for the extermination of the Jews at this time. In his statement about 'poison gas' he was speaking about a specific number of Jews whom he considered had sabotaged the war effort. There was no suggestion that he wanted to extend this fate to entire Jewish families and murder Jews en masse. The policy of the Nazi party remained one of persecuting the Jews and removing their German citizenship – and that was the assumption about their future on which the rest of Hitler's comments in *Mein Kampf* were based.

However, there was one direct causal link between the views he expressed about the Jews in *Mein Kampf* and what was to come. That's because, believing as he did that the Jews had sabotaged Germany's chance of winning the First World War from behind the front line, he was determined that they would never get the chance to do the same thing again. 'That race of criminals has on its conscience the two million dead of the [First] World War,' he said in private on 25 October 1941, two years into the Second World War, 'and now already hundreds of thousands more . . .'[14] The idea that there was a straightforward 'lesson' to be taken from the First World War and that this legitimized the Holocaust is something that we will encounter later.

Equally, even though it is hard to sustain the argument that Hitler at the time he wrote *Mein Kampf* intended to institute a policy to kill all the Jews if he ever came to power, that is not to say that somewhere in his mind, even at this stage, he would not have liked them just to disappear. If, as he wrote *Mein Kampf*, he had been able to push a button that made all the Jews of the world vanish – without any repercussions to him or the Nazi party – then surely he would have pressed it. That doesn't mean he already had a plan to kill the Jews, merely that his hatred of Jews was so intense as to be almost overwhelming.

When it came to the underlying justification for anti-Semitism, Hitler was careful to make a reference in *Mein Kampf* to the traditional Christian-based prejudice against the Jews. He said that he believed he was 'acting in accordance with the will of the Almighty Creator: by defending myself against the Jew, I am fighting for the work of the Lord.'[15] Two years before, in a speech he gave in Munich, he had been even more explicit in his reference to Christianity. 'My feeling as a Christian points me to my Lord and Saviour as a fighter,' he said in April 1922. 'It points me to the man who, once in loneliness, surrounded by a few followers, recognized these Jews for what they were and who – God's truth! – was greatest not as a sufferer but as a fighter.'[16]

The fact that Jesus was born Jewish was obviously awkward for the Nazis, but the widespread adoption of Houston Chamberlain's argument that Jesus might have been not of Jewish but of Aryan descent overcame this difficulty. In his *Myth of the Twentieth Century* the Nazi theorist Alfred Rosenberg developed Chamberlain's idea and proposed 'Positive Christianity' – the establishment of a Christian church free of 'Jewish' influence, with Jesus descended from a Nordic ancestor.

However, Hitler's own position on Christianity was more complex than it first appeared. While in 1922 he explicitly said that he was a 'Christian', the motive behind this statement was almost certainly cynical, since he was well aware that he risked alienating many of his own followers if he said he was a non-believer. As he remarked: 'I need Bavarian Catholics as well as Prussian Protestants to build up a great political movement. The rest comes later.'[17]

Revealingly, two years later as he wrote *Mein Kampf*, Hitler did not say he was a Christian. Instead he made the ambiguous statement that he was acting in accordance with the 'Almighty Creator' and fighting for the 'work of the Lord'. The Christians who read this would have assumed that 'the Lord' in question was Jesus, but Hitler's words could also mean that he believed in a non-Christian creator God who left human beings to work out their own problems on earth, and that there was no afterlife except the life of the nation. His subsequent statements about Christianity make this interpretation persuasive. For instance, he later criticized the 'meekness and flabbiness' of Christianity.[18] In 1941 Goebbels wrote that Hitler 'hates Christianity, because it has crippled all that is noble in humanity'.[19] There is no evidence that Hitler genuinely believed in Jesus' divinity or resurrection or any of the other key tenets of the Christian faith. Instead, he was careful to point out that 'for the space of many millenniums, a uniform concept of God did not exist.'[20]

The whole thrust of the argument in *Mein Kampf*, apart from this mention of the 'Almighty Creator', was anti-religious. For Hitler, the issue that determined the nature of the world was not religion but race. The reason the Jews were dangerous was because of who they were in themselves. In *Mein Kampf* he wrote that the 'whole existence' of the Jews 'is based on one single great lie, to wit, that they are a religious community while actually they are a race – and what a race!'[21]

The 'sole' reason that cultures decline, he argued, was the interbreeding of different races and the 'resultant drop in the racial level'. Adopting Houston Chamberlain's argument, Hitler maintained that because the Jews jealously guarded their own blood, since 'The Jew almost never marries a Christian woman,'[22] they were particularly dangerous. The central struggle of existence was therefore the fight between the two most racially pure peoples – the Aryans and the Jews. None of this, it is worth stating, was true. In fact the German Jews were one of the most assimilated Jewish groups in Europe.

Two further ideas that Hitler outlined in *Mein Kampf* were important for what was to come. The first was the attraction he felt towards the idea, developed by the 'racial hygiene' theorists, of preserving the quality of the 'race' through controlling who was allowed to produce children. 'The demand', he wrote, 'that defective people be prevented from propagating equally defective offspring is a demand of the clearest reason and if systematically executed represents the most humane act of mankind.'[23] The second was Hitler's belief that more land must be obtained for the German people if the nation was to flourish. He explicitly said where this extra 'living space' (*Lebensraum*) was to be found. 'If we speak of soil in Europe today,' he wrote, 'we can primarily have in mind only Russia and her vassal border states.'[24] Moreover, the area of the Soviet Union coveted by Hitler – such as the fertile land of the Soviet republics of Belarus and Ukraine – also contained a large number of Jews. A confrontation with both the Soviet Union and the Jews was therefore inevitable if Hitler ever pursued his stated intention.

Mein Kampf was an immensely significant piece of work. It laid bare unequivocally the central pillars of Hitler's thinking. Everything was here: the enormity of the threat posed by the Jews; the centrality of the issue of race; the importance of policing who was allowed to breed; the need for Germany to gain territory in the east. The content was so explicit that it was as if Hitler was hiding his radical ideas in plain sight. As his first biographer Konrad Heiden wrote, it did indeed turn out that 'there was no more effective method of concealment than the broadest publicity.'[25]

What *Mein Kampf* did not contain was any mention of the planning or implementation of the Beer-Hall Putsch. Yet this was the event that had spread Hitler's name across Germany and was the one subject guaranteed to interest his readers. There was a simple reason, however, why Hitler would have wanted to avoid raking up once again the events of Munich in November 1923. As he sat in his well-appointed cell in Landsberg in 1924, he could not be sure when he would be granted release on probation; and once he was released, he needed the cooperation of the Bavarian authorities in order to re-form the Nazi party and practise politics once again. Why risk antagonizing powerful figures in Munich by naming – and potentially shaming – those figures in the administration who had been involved in the initial stages of the Putsch? Far better to let it all lie quiet. It thus followed that Hitler must have calculated that the views he expressed in *Mein Kampf* would not upset the Bavarian authorities and so stand in the way of re-establishing his political career.

By the autumn of 1924 Hitler hoped that he would soon be permitted to leave prison. But officials working for the Bavarian state prosecutor were against the idea. They reminded the court that Hitler had incited a revolution and had never expressed remorse for his actions. Furthermore, he had been sentenced to five years' incarceration and had served less than a year.[26] However, a number of influential figures supported his early release. The governor of Landsberg prison, Otto Leybold, for instance, wrote an effusive report in which he claimed that Hitler had 'undoubtedly become more mature and calm' during his imprisonment, and that he was 'a man of many-sided intelligences, particularly political intelligence, and possesses extraordinary will power and directness in his thinking'. Leybold's report also revealed that he was not only aware that Hitler had been writing *Mein Kampf* while behind bars, but knew of the contents: 'He is entirely taken up with the writing of his book, which is due to appear in the next few weeks. It consists of his autobiography together with his thoughts about the bourgeoisie, Jewry and Marxism, the German revolution and Bolshevism, and the National Socialist movement with the events leading up to November 8th 1923.'[27]

In a further report, written in December 1924, Leybold was even more emphatic, writing that Hitler was 'especially deserving of parole'.[28] The Bavarian Minister of Justice, Franz Gürtner, agreed with this judgement and Hitler was released on 21 December 1924. Hitler did not forget Gürtner's generosity. After the Nazis came to power, Gürtner served Hitler as Reich Minister of Justice.

Hitler emerged from Landsberg having made two crucial decisions. One was about the future tactics he would employ to overthrow the Weimar state. He resolved now to seek power through democratic means, remarking, 'If outvoting them takes longer than outshooting them, at least the results will be guaranteed by their own constitution.'[29] The second was about the Jews. In the summer of 1924, while working on *Mein Kampf*, he said this to a comrade: 'It is quite true that I have changed my view on the way of fighting the Jews. I have realized that I have been far too mild up to now. While working on my book, I have come to the realization that in the future, the harshest means of struggle need to be adopted in order to win through. I am convinced that this is a vital issue not only for our people, but for all peoples. For the Jews are the pestilence of the world.'[30]

Hitler found on his emergence from prison that the political climate in Germany had changed, and not to his advantage. The Allies had agreed via the Dawes Plan to restructure the debts the Germans owed and to end the occupation of the Rhineland. The Americans had arranged to loan the Germans money, which then helped them to pay the reparations owed to the Allies. As a consequence, the United States became a more prominent player in the European economy than before, and any subsequent financial problems that the Americans faced would impact strongly on Europe – as would be discovered five years later at the time of the Wall Street Crash. But at the end of 1924 it appeared that the worst might be behind Germany. The currency was stabilized and Gustav Stresemann as Foreign Minister was negotiating with the Western Allies to try and normalize relationships – a process that would result in the signing of the Locarno Treaties in 1925. At the Reichstag elections in December 1924 there was a massive fall in support for extremist parties. The Communists alone saw their share of the vote drop by 17 per cent.

The two volumes of *Mein Kampf* were thus launched in the mid-1920s into an indifferent world. The book did not sell well. Only 15,000 copies of the second volume had been bought by 1929. In part that was because of the lack of quality in the writing – Mussolini famously remarked that the book was so boring he had been unable to finish it[31] – but it was also because by the time of its publication interest in Hitler had cooled.

However, the prejudice against the Jews that had been vociferously fostered in the immediate post-war years could not so easily be extinguished. Arnon Tamir, a Jewish German who went to school in Stuttgart during the 1920s, recalls that his teachers 'never missed an opportunity to make disparaging remarks about the Weimar Republic. And the Republic was to a large extent identified with Jews.' He remembers that, 'even as a small boy, I had already experienced what anti-Semitism was. First of all I had it drummed into me, by my parents, how a Jewish child had to behave, in order not to be conspicuous.' When he was a young boy, his Jewish origin was 'betrayed' to the rest of his playmates by a friend. 'As a child I found it especially painful when my so-called best friend joined the others and then they roared out in chorus: "Jewish pig, cowardly Jewish pig!" or some other zoological expression. I learnt very quickly that I was different and seen differently, and then when I came home crying, my father said to me: "Don't put up with it when they pester you, hit back!" The consequence was that I came home every couple of days bloody from fighting, with torn clothes, but I had begun to defend myself. Now I had the misfortune to be the only Jew in a rather reactionary grammar school. There were teachers who were perhaps not expressly anti-Semitic, and one, a former major general with scars on his face, said: "Yes, in my regiment there were decent and brave Jews." But it sounded as if what he meant to say was that in other regiments, or among the Jews he didn't know, there were actually cowardly and ignoble people. That seeped in so, in some subterranean way, it was fed to us, drop by drop. And such remarks, and other remarks, they made me seem, to my classmates, a person set apart.'[32]

As Arnon Tamir struggled to reconcile his life as both a German and a Jew, around 320 miles to the north-east, in Berlin, Eugene Leviné wrestled with many of the same emotions. He shared a similar name to that of his father, and it was a name in Germany that was infamous – or famous – depending on your point of view. Eugen Leviné the elder had been one of the Jewish leaders of the Communist Revolution in Munich in 1919, and had been shot by a firing squad just after the Freikorps regained control of the city. For his son, this was a heavy history to carry: 'I was made to understand that he had been very brave the way he met his death – in fact, he had called out "Long live the world revolution!" As a little boy I didn't understand the whole thing, I just knew that this is what you have to say when they shoot you – and I used to practise saying, "Es lebe die Weltrevolution!" [Long live the world revolution]. And I also wondered, increasingly, would I be brave enough if they put me against the wall to be shot? When I was a little boy I used to practise going up to a wall, turning round and imagining I was going to be shot, because I realized it would be most important not to be frightened and to die bravely. And, somehow, I came to the conclusion as a boy that it would be all right on the day, and that I would be able to make it. Right throughout my young years I believed that an honourable person would die sooner or later – either on the barricades or put up against the wall.'[33]

Eugene's mother told him stories of her own childhood in Russia. How her family had sat huddled in their house at night with the lights out, as gangs of anti-Semites marched by, looking for Jews to attack. 'But Communism was to end all that,' says Eugene; 'under Communism the

Jews were simply one national minority and officially there was no anti-Semitism.'

During his own childhood in Germany in the 1920s, Eugene experienced some problems as a result of his Jewish background. On occasion bullies picked on him in school, but since he was keen on boxing he was able to fight back. Overall, he says, 'I had a very happy boyhood in Germany. I like German. I like German art, I like German poetry, I like German songs. I liked many of my comrades . . . I mean anti-Semitism was there, but if you'd said to most Germans, "Look, you're going to have a government that's going to kill six million Jews," they would have said, "No, no, no, no. This is a civilized country."'

'I'm not suggesting', he adds, 'that all the Germans were rushing around to be kind to Jews, but there was a lot of individual sympathy.' A number of the people he encountered made a distinction between their hatred of the supposed 'Jewish international conspiracy' and the individual Jews they met in everyday life: 'To an extent, some people realized that when you hate "the Jews" it isn't because you hate individual Jews, you just believe "the Jews" are bad – they've crucified Jesus Christ, they've lost the war, and they've done all sorts of things which are bad. But individual Jews can be OK. At one of the schools I was in, there was a Nazi and he said, "You really should be one of us," and I said, "Look, I can't, I'm a Jew." He would [then] say – and many Jews had that said to them – "We don't mean you. Decent chaps like you will be perfectly all right in the New Germany." After all I'd proved that I must be a decent Jew because I'd joined the fencing club so I can't be all that bad.'

Eugene Leviné even recalls that some Nazi Stormtroopers had Jewish girlfriends – a claim that might seem outlandish were it not for the fact that in the 1920s Joseph Goebbels, who would later become close to Hitler and offer enthusiastic support for the Holocaust, also had a girlfriend with Jewish ancestry. Goebbels, active in the Nazi party from 1924, dated a schoolteacher called Else who had a Jewish mother. He claimed that he had loved Else, and said she was 'good and beautiful'. But he was also anxious about her background, writing in his diary that the 'Jewish spirit in part of Else's nature has often tormented and depressed me'.[34] The fundamental problem, as far as he was concerned, was that she was a 'half-breed'.[35]

What is extraordinary about Goebbels' relationship with Else is that he was emotionally attached to her at precisely the moment that his own anti-Semitism was hardening. Shortly after the failure of the Beer-Hall Putsch, Goebbels wrote that 'the Jews are the poison that is killing the body of Europe' and that one wants to 'punch' the Jews 'in the face'.[36] In April 1924 he was one of the founder members of a group that supported the Nazis in his hometown in the Rhineland. Their first meeting was dominated by a discussion about the 'anti-Semitic idea'. Afterwards, Goebbels wrote that 'I am on the *völkisch* side: I hate the Jew with my instincts and my reason. I detest and dislike him from the depth of my soul.'[37] Yet a few weeks later he wrote of Else that she was 'a dear, good child. A bit boring. But a loyal, hard-working little servant. One can rely on her, and she'll do you every possible favour.'[38]

The fact that Goebbels could hold two contradictory ideas in his head – he hated 'the Jews' and yet he loved a woman of Jewish ancestry – is a powerful reminder of the reality that Eugene Leviné encountered: that it was possible for some Nazis to despise Jews in the abstract and yet care for an individual Jew in the flesh. As Bruno Hähnel, who was a Stormtrooper in the 1920s, says, 'I had relatives who were Jews and we would meet at family gatherings. I had a very warm relationship with two cousins who were Jewish.'[39] Yet none of that prevented Bruno Hähnel – or seemingly Joseph Goebbels – from becoming a committed Nazi.

Goebbels' journey to Nazism is also instructive because it demonstrates the key role the political and economic situation played in creating support for the far right. There is no evidence that Goebbels was a committed anti-Semite before the end of the First World War. He was twenty-one years old when the war ended and had been unable to serve in the army because of a disabled leg, an affliction which caused him to walk with a pronounced limp. Prevented from becoming a soldier, he had pursued an academic career. The supervisor of his thesis was a Jew – Professor Max von Waldberg. But this doesn't appear to have bothered Goebbels. The turning point in his life came in 1923 when the French entered the Rhineland. He had been born in the small town of Rheydt in the west of the Rhineland, and in 1923 was living at home with his parents. He was out of work, suffering like millions of others through a time of hyperinflation and political chaos, and now a despised enemy had just occupied his homeland; like many others he sought someone to blame for what was happening, and found an easy target in the Jews.

Once Goebbels started reading Hitler's speeches, he concluded that the Nazi leader could be the saviour that Germany needed. In March 1924 he wrote that he found Hitler 'liberating' because of his 'completely upright and honest personality. That's rarely found in our world of party interests . . .'[40] Three days later he added, 'Hitler is an enthusiastic idealist. A man who brings new faith to the German people. I'm reading his speech, inspired and carried to the stars. The path runs from the brain to the heart . . . The Jewish question cannot be solved, unless one is hard and rigorous and relentless.'[41]

Significantly, Goebbels was captivated by Hitler long before he met him face to face. The words of Hitler's speeches on paper were enough to convince him of his worth, for though emotional feelings played a part in Goebbels' journey to Nazism, so did rationality. He had looked around in order to find who was responsible for Germany's problems, decided it was the Jews, and then discovered in Hitler someone who first reinforced and then extended his hatred.

Goebbels also remained sane enough to recognize, when he attended a gathering in Weimar of the far right in August 1924, that some of his fellow Nazi supporters were – to put it mildly – rather odd. One encounter with Julius Streicher was enough for him to decide that he was a 'fanatic with pinched lips' and 'a bit pathological'.[42] But Goebbels remained true to the cause, and four months later when Hitler was released from Landsberg he wrote, 'Adolf Hitler is free! Now we can break away from the backward-looking *völkisch* people and be true National Socialists again. Heil, Adolf Hitler! Now we have faith again in the victorious power of the idea.'[43]

It was not until July 1925, when Goebbels attended another gathering in Weimar, that he finally encountered Adolf Hitler for the first time. The experience of seeing him in person was almost overwhelming. 'Weimar was literally a resurrection,' he wrote in his diary. 'A day I will never forget. I am still in a dream . . . What a voice. What gestures, what passion. Just as I wanted him to be.'[44] Goebbels, the man who would later write, 'the world war is here, the destruction of the Jews must be the inevitable consequence,'[45] was utterly entranced.

• • •

Goebbels may have been immensely positive about Hitler, but as we have seen the vast majority of Germans were not. In the middle 1920s Germany appeared to grow more prosperous, and the Nazi party seemed an irrelevance, an eccentric group on the fringes of political life. But it would be a mistake to pass over this period of the Nazi party's development. That's because the way Hitler structured the decision-making process within the party elite during these years offers an insight into how his leadership would come to function during the years of extermination.

Crucially, by the time Goebbels heard Hitler speak in the summer of 1925 the Nazis were not a normal political party, but a 'movement', led by a single individual who relied for his legitimacy primarily on the charismatic effect he had on his followers. 'Now I know that the man who leads is a born leader,' wrote Goebbels in his diary in July 1925. 'I'm ready to sacrifice everything for this man. In times of greatest need, history gives the people the greatest men.'[46] This notion that members of the Nazi party should subordinate themselves to their 'Führer' (leader) because he was somehow destined to lead them was thus central to the concept of the party long before the Nazis came to power.

However, this was not an organization in which Hitler dictated all detailed policy. Indeed, as long as he was confident that his subordinates unquestioningly accepted the principle of his leadership, he could be remarkably non-dictatorial for long periods. Goebbels, for instance, held very different views in 1925 about the Soviet Union to those of Hitler. In an article in the *Völkischer Beobachter* in November 1925, Goebbels wrote that it would be wrong to see Bolshevism as essentially the work of Jews. Instead Bolshevism should be understood as a potential route to a better society in Russia. Such views were anathema to Hitler, but the Nazi leader was still friendly to Goebbels when they both subsequently attended a meeting.[47]

By the start of 1926, Goebbels was part of a group within the party that was pressing for other changes. Led by Gregor Strasser, a leading Nazi from Bavaria now working in north Germany, this faction campaigned for the party to become more 'socialist'. This crossed a line for Hitler – it appeared that Strasser and Goebbels were challenging his authority, which was something he would never permit. At a conference in Bamberg in February 1926 he dealt with the threat not by debating with the dissenters but by giving a two-hour speech in which he repudiated their ideas. He reiterated that 'Bolshevism is a Jewish plot' and that the 'natural allies' of Germany did not include Russia but were, instead, Italy and Britain.

Goebbels was devastated. 'One of the biggest disappointments of my life,' he wrote in his diary. 'I don't completely believe in Hitler any more. That's the terrible thing: I've lost my inner conviction . . . I despair!'[48] But Hitler, recognizing the value of Goebbels to the Nazi cause, moved swiftly to soothe his ego. He invited him to Munich, allowed him the use of his car and driver, spent time with him personally and praised him. Hitler also spoke in general terms about his own vision for Germany in a collection of feel-good terms that rekindled Goebbels' enthusiasm. 'I love him [Hitler],' he subsequently wrote in his diary. 'He has thought it all through . . . I bow to the greater – the political mastermind!'[49]

Hitler had managed to manoeuvre Goebbels – a person he clearly valued – away from policies that he disagreed with and back to a position of unquestioning support. Moreover, he had achieved this without a personal confrontation. Hitler never berated Goebbels directly. He didn't attempt to best him in debate. He manipulated Goebbels by first giving a speech critical of his beliefs and then repairing the damage with a charm offensive. It is not the conventional image that many people have of Hitler as a leader. Taking their impression primarily from the antagonistic tone of his speeches captured on old black and white newsreels, they believe that he must have been an angry, rude and aggressive boss. But he was capable, as this incident demonstrates, of subtle man-management. Not only that, his dealings with Goebbels illustrated how Hitler's priority was always to ensure that his own ultimate authority was not challenged by his subordinates. He was much less concerned with the details of policy. By focusing on a broad 'vision' of the Germany he wanted to create, he could leave his followers to work out the specifics of how this vision could be crafted in practice, and then correct them later if he disagreed strongly with the methodology they had devised.

There was another important part of Hitler's leadership technique that Goebbels also encountered around this time. Hitler rarely defined an individual's exact responsibilities within the party, and so conflict between ambitious Nazis was inevitable. For example, after Goebbels had been appointed head of Nazi propaganda he found that other people still exercised control over aspects of radio, film and the training of speakers. He had to scheme and fight to gather as many of these strands to himself as he could. All this created immense dynamism within the party, especially since Hitler rarely intervened in disputes about areas of responsibility between his subordinates. As we shall see, this style of leadership would have considerable impact on the way the Holocaust developed.

In 1928, Hitler wrote a new volume of his thoughts. This time he focused almost exclusively on foreign affairs. The so-called *Second Book* was never published in his lifetime, but it nonetheless offers an insight into his developing political beliefs. What it tells us, in essence, is how Hitler used 'race' as a guide to foreign policy.

Hitler asked why it was that America so thrived as a nation, while Russia remained relatively backward; and he saw the answer in the question of race. He argued that because the 'best blood' from Europe had emigrated to America, it was not surprising that the country had prospered. On the other hand, since 'Jewish-Bolshevist' Russia was filled with people of lesser racial value it could never rise high as a nation.

Yet again, Hitler placed the Jews centre stage. 'The ultimate goal of the Jewish struggle for survival is the enslavement of productively active peoples,'[50] he wrote. 'His ultimate aim is the denationalization and chaotic bastardization of the other peoples, the lowering of the racial level of the highest, and domination over this racial mush . . . The Jewish international struggle will therefore always end in bloody Bolshevization . . .'[51]

In his *Second Book* Hitler said once again that Germany needed more land in order to prosper, and that this new territory would have to be gained by force: 'One does not obtain freedom through begging or cheating, or through labor and industriousness either, but exclusively through fighting – fighting one's own battles.'[52]

By the time he wrote his *Second Book*, Hitler had established himself as the dominant figure on the *völkisch* right. He had achieved this not just by producing works that demonstrated his 'visionary' credentials, and by exercising the kind of shrewd leadership that won over Joseph Goebbels, but by accepting into the Nazi party people he did not always wholeheartedly agree with. In 1927, for instance, Count Reventlow joined the Nazis. Reventlow had helped form the German Völkisch Freedom Party in 1924, but had now decided to 'subordinate' himself 'without further ado to Herr Adolf Hitler'. Why had Reventlow taken this action? Because, he said, Hitler 'has proven that he can lead; he has created his party on the basis of his views, his will, and his unified national socialist ideas, and leads it. He and the party are one, and represent the unity that is the essential prerequisite for success.'[53] Reventlow called on members of his old party to join the Nazis, claiming that 'the only possibility for making any advance is through the National Socialist German Workers' Party – the only!'

Reventlow believed strongly in the socialist ideas favoured by Gregor Strasser that Hitler had dismissed at the Bamberg conference in 1926. But despite this, Hitler welcomed him into the Nazis. He knew that he needed to tolerate a wide variety of opinion if he was to gather all of the various *völkisch* parties under the Nazi banner and stand a chance of winning power.

One policy Reventlow and Hitler could agree on was anti-Semitism. In March 1928, Reventlow said he wanted a law introduced that 'would prohibit all further Jewish immigration, expel all Jews who had entered Germany since 1914, and place those remaining under Alien Law, whilst reserving the right to expel them subsequently, and exclude them from all the rights associated with German citizenship'.[54]

That proposal came to nothing. But the fact that Reventlow felt he could voice such ideas demonstrated the confidence of Nazi anti-Semites. Despite the apparent prosperity and modernity of the Weimar state, anti-Semitism remained entrenched in certain areas of German life. Anti-Semitism was particularly rife, for example, among student and youth groups. So much so that many young Jews had to form their own hiking clubs in order to enjoy the countryside. Eugene Leviné was one of those who rambled in the German countryside during this period with an all-Jewish youth association. He recalls a surprising encounter with an anti-Semite when he and his friends were travelling back home from a hiking trip. 'Don't forget there were parts of Germany who'd never seen a Jew,' he says, 'so it was easy enough to hate the Jews. I remember in my hiking days being in a railway compartment going home to Berlin, with my rucksack and my brown shirt.' Sharing the compartment with Eugene and his friends was a farmer, who started: 'swearing about the Jews, and so we said, "Well look, we are all Jews." And he roared with laughter, and he said, "You must think that we country people are daft. You are obviously nice clean-living, sporting German boys. You're not going to tell me you're Jews." And he meant it. Because we weren't dirty, we didn't wear side locks, we didn't have a caftan, we didn't have a beard. We looked like any other German boys to his eye. I mean, there might be a longer nose or darker eyes, but lots of Germans have long noses and dark eyes. The comical thing is the racial idea of "the German" – most of the Nazis didn't look like that [an idealized "Aryan"], for God's sake!'[55]

Hitler claimed anti-Semitism was more present than ever within Germany. At the annual general meeting of the Nazi party in September 1928, he said that 'anti-Semitism grows as an idea. What was hardly there ten years ago is there today: the Jewish question has been brought to people's notice, it will not disappear any more and we shall make sure that it becomes an international world question; we shall not let it rest until the question has been solved. We think we shall live to see that day.'[56]

Nonetheless, despite Hitler's boast, there is no evidence that the majority of Germans supported the Nazis and their virulent anti-Semitism. Quite the contrary. As he spoke those words, Hitler knew that four months before, at the German general election in May 1928, the Nazis had polled just 2.6 per cent of the vote. It was a disastrous result for them. Yet within five years Hitler would be Chancellor of Germany, at the head of the largest political party in the country. What made this transformation possible was not Hitler's bogus claim of widespread concern within Germany about 'the Jewish question' but a factor that was wholly out of his control – an economic catastrophe.

The Weimar economy, reliant on American loans, was devastated by the Wall Street Crash in October 1929. In just one year – between September 1929 and September 1930 – German unemployment more than doubled from 1.3 million to 3 million. Democratic government effectively ended in Germany in March 1930 when the grand coalition that included the German People's Party and the Social Democrats broke down. The new government, under Chancellor Heinrich Brüning, had to rely on Article 48 of the constitution which allowed government by Presidential decree.

In the elections of September 1930 the Nazis gained over 6 million votes and became the second-largest political party in the Reichstag. It was an astonishing result. Millions of Germans, who had previously rejected Hitler and the Nazis, suddenly turned to them in these desperate times. But despite in 1928 trumpeting the alleged growth of anti-Semitism in Germany, Hitler understood the reality – these new supporters had not come to him primarily because of any anti-Semitic beliefs. So he downplayed his obsession with the Jews. A study of his speeches between 1930 and 1933 demonstrates that he now placed much less emphasis on the role of the Jews than previously. He even said, in October 1930, that 'we have nothing against decent Jews; however, as soon as they conspire with Bolshevism we look on them as an enemy.'[57]

Instead of ranting about the Jews, Hitler focused more on the need for the regeneration of Germany through the creation of a National Socialist state. He called for a rejection of the punitive measures imposed on Germany by the Allies after the end of the First World War, and warned of the dangers of 'Bolshevism'. 'Today,' he said to an audience of industrialists in Düsseldorf in January 1932, 'we are at the turning point in German destiny.' That was because Germany risked falling into 'Bolshevist chaos'.[58] Nowhere in his lengthy speech did he refer to the Jews.

But it does not follow from this that his audiences were hoodwinked into thinking that the Nazis had suddenly rejected anti-Semitism. Nazi propaganda had stated over and over again that the Jews were responsible for 'Bolshevism', for the hated Treaty of Versailles and for the corruption of capitalism that had brought about the economic slump. So when Hitler mentioned any of these concepts in his speeches, many of his audience would have understood that the Jews were ultimately to be held accountable.

When Jutta Rüdiger, then a twenty-one-year-old student, heard Hitler speak in 1932 she certainly understood that behind the word 'Bolshevism' lay the Jews. 'Jews were associated with Communism, definitely,' she says. 'There was a vicious joke making the rounds . . . that it was just as well that there was one goy – a slightly derogatory term for a non-Jew – among the Communists in Russia, because at least he could sign the death warrants on a Saturday [the Jewish holy day]. That is a bit vicious, but there was a strong connection between Communism and the Jews, definitely.'[59]

While Jutta Rüdiger says that she was chiefly attracted to Hitler and the Nazis in the early 1930s because she thought they offered a way out of the economic depression and a chance for Germans to be united in a common goal, she also believes that their anti-Jewish agenda was not a barrier to their success: 'There was actually a general feeling among people, which had already been present in Imperial times and which may have been present in other nations at some time, too, that the Jews were perceived as an alien element.'[60]

Johannes Zahn, in 1932 a banker in his mid-twenties, agrees with this assessment: 'The general opinion was that the Jews had gone too far in Germany.'[61] By 'too far' he meant that German Jews were present in disproportionate numbers in professions like the law, medicine and journalism. (It was hardly surprising that Jews had chosen jobs like these, since they had been banned from many other avenues for so long.) According to Johannes Zahn, 'one day it was just too much, the general feeling was that the idea that the Jews should be driven back was not opposed; but that they should be killed in the end, nobody, or very few people, in Germany would have approved . . .'[62]

However, the prime reason for the rise of the Nazi party remained Germany's dire economic situation. For large numbers of people, in this time of economic catastrophe, what mattered was to find a job and support a family in an atmosphere of political uncertainty. There were 6 million unemployed by the start of 1933, and the Communists were gaining support at the same time as the Nazis. It was as if the country was splitting to the extremes – Communists on one side and Nazis on the other. 'Six million unemployed means, with three people in one family, six times three equals eighteen million without food,' says Johannes Zahn. 'And when a man was unemployed at that time, then there was only one thing left: either he became a Communist or he became an SA man [Nazi Stormtrooper]. And so business thought that it was better for these people to become SA men, because there was discipline and order; and at the beginning – you really have to say this today – at the beginning you couldn't tell whether National Socialism was something good with a few bad side-effects or something evil with a few good side-effects, you couldn't tell.'[63]

Such statements are largely self-serving. That is because while it is true that Hitler did not emphasize his hatred of the Jews during the

Nazis' rise to prominence between 1930 and 1933, many of his followers were not so restrained. Not only did Julius Streicher continue to publish anti-Semitic filth in *Der Stürmer*, he made these remarks in a speech in 1932: 'We National Socialists believe that Adolf Hitler is an emissary for a new Germany. We believe that he has been sent by God to liberate the German people from the blood-sucker almighty Jewry.'[64]

Joseph Goebbels also continued to voice his anti-Semitic beliefs during this period. Ever since his appointment as Gauleiter (Nazi leader) of Berlin at the end of 1926 he had made the Jews of the capital his special target – in particular Dr Bernhard Weiss, the deputy police commissioner. Goebbels persistently referred to him as 'Isidor' Weiss in his propaganda magazine *Der Angriff* (The Attack), 'Isidor' being an archetypal Jewish first name in contrast to Dr Weiss's given name of Bernhard. 'Isidor' Weiss was caricatured in a variety of ways in *Der Angriff*: as a hooked-nosed, untrustworthy Jew and even as a donkey. After Weiss complained, and a court confirmed that the donkey caricature was indeed supposed to represent him, Goebbels reprinted the cartoon with a caption announcing that judges had agreed that Dr Weiss looked like a donkey.[65] Goebbels also supported action against Jews on the streets. At the Jewish New Year, in September 1931, Stormtroopers moved in force on to the main shopping street of the Kurfürstendamm in Berlin and harassed anyone they thought was Jewish. By now Goebbels had banished his half-Jewish girlfriend Else from his life and was seeing the blonde-haired, blue-eyed Magda Quandt. They married in December 1931.

During the early 1930s, Nazi propaganda also targeted economic interests that many believed were owned by Jews. For instance, a Nazi election pamphlet in northern Germany read: 'A new blow aimed at your ruin is being prepared and carried out in Hanover! The present system enables the gigantic concern WOOLWORTH (America), supported by finance capital, to build a new vampire business in the centre of the city in the Georgstrasse to expose you to complete ruin.'[66]

Many people would immediately understand this reference to 'Woolworth' as an attack on the Jews. That's because the Nazis had said for years that large department stores were predominantly Jewish owned and a threat to the traditional shopkeeper. These stores – symbols of modernity – were considered 'vampire' businesses by the Nazis because they supposedly sucked the lifeblood out of the traditional high street. The Nazis were so angered by the presence of department stores that one of the twenty-five points in the original Nazi programme had explicitly referred to them. Point sixteen called for department stores to be leased 'at a cheap rate to small traders'.

Once the Nazis came to power department stores were a particular target. The district president of Hanover reported that in December 1934 'riots against Jewish businesses reoccurred ... On the Sunday before Christmas, canisters of tear gas were thrown one after the other into Jewish stores and into the store F. W. Woolworth. Because of serious symptoms of poisoning, ten shop assistants of the Woolworth Company had to be taken to a hospital by ambulances.'[67] In fact, the founder of Woolworths was of Methodist, not Jewish, ancestry.

Goebbels approved of this policy of guilt by association. When ordinary Germans heard the words 'department stores' many thought 'Jewish ownership', when they listened to a speech about the dangers of Marxism they thought 'Marx was a Jew' and so on. Goebbels believed that propaganda was at its most powerful when an audience could be manipulated into thinking that they had reached their own conclusions about a subject.[68]

But even though support for Nazis was growing during this period, a majority of Germans still opposed them. In particular, many socialists found their anti-Semitism despicable. Communist supporters like Alois Pfaller felt that since non-Jewish and Jewish Germans 'spoke the same language' and 'went to the same school' then 'why should you hate them?' He and his friends understood that 'someone can't do anything about his birth, that was clear – nobody is responsible for his birth.'[69] For Pfaller what was important was not 'race' but creating a more equal Germany by restraining the power of the 'bosses'.

There were also prophetic warnings in the German press about what was likely to happen if the Nazis ever came to power. For instance, the Jewish journalist Lion Feuchtwanger wrote in the newspaper *Welt am Abend* in January 1931: 'National Socialism strives to depose reason and install in its place emotion and drive – to be precise, barbarity ... What the intellectuals and artists have therefore to expect once the Third Reich is definitely established is clear: extermination.'[70]

Most Germans, however, desired radical change. While the Nazis themselves never gained a majority of the popular vote, a majority of Germans did support parties that openly said they intended to remove democracy. In the general election of July 1932 the Nazis received 37 per cent of the vote and the Communists 14 per cent – so a total of 51 per cent between them. It was an extremely significant result, since it meant that most voters wanted to destroy the system of democratic government that existed at the time. Germans felt that they had been let down not just by individual politicians or parties, but by the entire mechanism of governance.

The aversion of Germans to democracy during the early 1930s excited comment at the time. 'Speaking for the victory of National Socialism, above all, is the fact that in this country democracy has never been won in bloody battle,' wrote the novelist Heinrich Mann in December 1931. 'In one historical moment, after the defeat in the war, it appeared as a possible way out, compared to the disaster of the monarchy and the threat of bolshevism – only a way out, not a goal, much less a passionate experience.'[71]

'The Germans have no democratic tradition,' claims Arnon Tamir. 'Never have had. There has been, in Germany, until today no democracy which the citizens themselves fought for.' Growing up as a Jew in Germany during the 1920s and 1930s, he also reached the conclusion that Hitler flourished only because of the crisis within the German state: 'The Nazis emerged in circumstances during the 1920s, after the world war had been lost, when the German people were oppressed and humiliated and staggering from one economic crisis and from one political crisis to another. So this actually was very propitious. Someone must be to blame for it. And the entire anti-Semitism of the Nazis is actually encapsulated in the words: The Jew is guilty, for everything, always.'[72]

While Hitler may have toned down his rhetoric on Jews during their period of electoral growth, Nazi policy remained clear – and it wasn't far from Arnon Tamir's paraphrase: 'The Jew is guilty.' As Gregor Strasser, a senior member of the Nazi party, said in October 1931, once in power the Nazis would make certain that 'the rule of Jews in Germany would come to an end.' This would be achieved by 'the exclusion of Jews from all areas in which they are in a position to obstruct the German economy'.[73] The 37 per cent of the electorate who supported the Nazis in July 1932 were therefore voting for a party that openly intended, if elected, to persecute German Jews. The Nazis did not pretend otherwise.

Many in the German political elite had common ground with the Nazis. They also wanted to restore order to Germany by eliminating democracy and crushing the threat from the Communist Party. In 1932 President von Hindenburg, the eighty-five-year-old former commander of German troops in the First World War, was prepared to remove democracy and support the establishment of a government of the right. The trouble, as far as Hindenburg was concerned, was that though the Nazis were by now the most powerful force on the right in German political life, Hitler was not acceptable as Chancellor. When the two of them met in August 1932, Hindenburg told Hitler that he 'could not justify before God, before his conscience or before the Fatherland, the transfer of the whole authority of government to a single party, especially to a party that was biased against people who had different views from their own'.[74] He reiterated this opinion when he met Hitler again in November 1932, saying that he feared that 'a Presidential Cabinet headed by you would inevitably develop into a party dictatorship with all its consequences, resulting in a worsening of the antagonisms within the German people . . .' Hindenburg added that he could not reconcile such a situation 'with his oath and his conscience'.[75]

Hindenburg's objections to Hitler as a potential Chancellor were partly based on class. He referred to Hitler as a 'bohemian corporal'.[76] But he also indicated that he did not support every Nazi policy – in particular he questioned the party's overt anti-Semitism. In August 1932 he wrote to the Central Union of German Citizens of the Jewish Faith condemning attacks against Jews. The Nazi deputies in the Reichstag had even ridiculed Hindenburg as the 'Jewish candidate' during his re-election campaign for the Presidency earlier that year.[77]

However, a number of those close to Hindenburg did hold anti-Semitic views. Franz von Papen, Chancellor of Germany for much of 1932, revealed in an interview with the London *Evening Standard* the following year that the large number of Jews in medicine and the law in Germany would be 'unthinkable' in Britain, and that it was necessary to combat the influence of the 'international Jews' who held high positions within the German civil service.[78]

The problem that Hindenburg faced was that neither of the

Chancellors he appointed during 1932 – Franz von Papen and Kurt von Schleicher – had mass support, and he feared that the disconnect between the governing class and the ordinary German voter might grow still wider in the future. It could even lead to civil war as the Communists and Nazi Stormtroopers fought on the streets.

Hitler positioned himself both as respectful of Hindenburg and as the young patriot determined to unite Germany. In a speech in Detmold on 4 January 1933, he said, 'What has brought the National Socialist movement into being is the desire for a true community of the German people . . . Fate has set us the great task of removing the disunity of the German people . . .' What was necessary, argued Hitler, was 'uncompromisingly [to] eliminate everything' that was pulling the country apart. He named 'Marxists' as one threat to the unity of the *Volk*, and though there was no specific mention of the Jews, once again many would have heard the reference to 'Marxists' as code for Jews.[79]

Franz von Papen finally managed to reconcile Hindenburg to Hitler. Papen had been forced to give up the Chancellorship to Kurt von Schleicher in December 1932 because his administration lacked popular support. Schleicher, a born intriguer, had attempted – and failed – to gain a broader base for his own government. Now Papen took revenge and proposed re-entering government as Vice-Chancellor with Hitler as Chancellor. Hindenburg agreed. Their theory was that Hitler as Chancellor would be 'tamed' as Papen and a number of other non-Nazis would be appointed to the cabinet.

On 30 January 1933, thirteen years after he had announced his party's programme at the Hofbräuhaus in Munich, and less than five years after the Nazis had gained just 2.6 per cent of the popular vote in the general election, Adolf Hitler became Chancellor of Germany. Now, at last, he could attempt to put his long-cherished beliefs into practice.

4. Consolidating Power

(1933–1934)

Millions of Germans saw Hitler's appointment as a positive development. They agreed with Goebbels' judgement that Germany was at 'a turning point in her history'.[1] Manfred von Schröder, a student, says, 'the young people were enthusiastic and optimistic, and believed in Hitler, and thought it was a wonderful task to overcome the consequences of the First World War, and especially the Treaty of Versailles. So we were all in high mood . . . So there was a feeling of national liberation, a new start.'[2]

'Naturally we were excited,' confirms Gabriele Winckler, a young secretary. 'We thought now everything will be different, and everything will be better.' She remembers that 'all the young people . . . were all beaming, because they were all happy.'[3] Günter Lohse, nineteen years old in 1933, believes that 'it was Hitler's personality which you trusted – that he would not only keep his promises, but also realize them. There was already a myth about him.'[4]

Torchlight celebration parades were held in many cities, and Luise Solmitz watched the one in Hamburg on 6 February 1933. Her description of what was happening in front of her was made against the background of a family history that was out of the ordinary – though she was a staunch nationalist and not Jewish, her husband had converted from Judaism to Christianity. 'It turned 10 o'clock by the time the first torches came,' she wrote in her diary, 'and then they followed each other, like waves in the sea, about 20,000 Brownshirts, their faces glowing with enthusiasm in the torchlight.' She recalled that Nazi Stormtroopers called out 'Death to the Jews', shouted 'The Republic is shit,' and sang of 'the Jewish blood which would squirt from their knives'. Alongside that last remark, Luise Solmitz subsequently wrote, 'who took that seriously then?'[5]

For many German Jews the impact of Hitler's Chancellorship was immediate. Eugene Leviné, a student at a mixed-religion school, remembers that a non-Jewish boy who had previously been friendly came up to him and asked, 'Well, Leviné, have you got your ticket to Palestine?' Eugene was shocked: 'But, you see, anti-Semitism's always there beneath the surface. And I knocked him down. But the interesting thing is he didn't get up and start a fight. I made him realize how angry I was and he felt guilty, and he just slunk away. So you see people's feeling depends very much on circumstances, and what you can do at any one time varies.'[6]

Arnon Tamir, in Stuttgart, faced a similar confrontation: 'The stupidest boy in the class, who was already coming to school in his Stormtrooper uniform, offered me a piece of cardboard, with writing on it: "Ticket to Palestine, out and no return, ever." And I got ready to lay into him, but the senior boys of the class intervened. One was the son of a general and another the son of an officer – they were the "noble" anti-Semites in the class. They intervened and said: "That's not an issue . . . it's nothing to do with him. He's nothing to do with the Bolshevik Jews, with the capitalist Jews, he's nothing to do with it." And then I was, for the first time, invited to their homes as a demonstration that there were also decent, honourable opponents. Of course I didn't accept that. In response to this honour, of being invited, I declined.'[7]

In Hamburg, the Jewish schoolgirl Lucille Eichengreen and her sister also experienced sudden discrimination: 'Hitler came to power in January 1933. The children that lived in the same building . . . no longer spoke to us. They threw stones at us, they called us names, and that was maybe three months after Hitler came to power. And we couldn't understand what we had done to deserve this. So the question always was why? And when we asked at home the answer pretty much was, "Oh it's a passing phase, it won't matter, it will normalize." What that actually meant we did not know. But we couldn't understand the change . . . The first thing they [her parents] told us was on the way home, in the bus or in the street car don't draw attention to yourself, stand in the back, don't talk loudly and don't laugh, just sort of disappear. And we couldn't understand, it didn't make sense to us. And questions were not answered . . . It made us afraid because when we walked to school it was a forty-five-minute walk. And we were shouted [at], other children were spitting at us. The adults were looking away. Although we had no markings we felt marked.'[8]

What these experiences demonstrated was how easy it was for many Germans who had never previously expressed anti-Semitic views to fall into the behaviour now expected of them by the regime. For some, these beliefs had always been latent; others just decided to follow the path of least resistance – especially since the mighty German state now had a Chancellor who was known to be a dedicated anti-Semite.

However, even though he had been appointed Chancellor, Hitler was not yet the undisputed dictator of Germany. His actions were constrained by a number of powerful forces – all of which he sought to control. To begin with, he knew he needed the support of the military. So it was no accident that one of his first decisions – just four days after his appointment as Chancellor – was to meet with leading figures in the armed forces. On 3 February he told them that he was committed to a massive programme of rearmament, and that they need have no fear that he would attempt to merge the regular army with the Nazi Stormtroopers. This message, unsurprisingly, was a welcome one to the professional soldiers. 'An army was to be built which was capable of really defending Germany,' says Johann-Adolf Graf von Kielmansegg, then a young army officer. 'Here was a revolutionary action.' What was also reassuring, and 'played a big role for the soldiers', was that President von Hindenburg 'had given his blessing to Hitler's behaviour. That was the important thing for us. You know, for the army, Hindenburg was not Hitler.'[9]

On 10 February 1933 Hitler delivered a lengthy speech at the Sportpalast in Berlin that was broadcast nationwide on radio. He was careful to be vague about the details of any specific policies that his government might implement, remarking that when his opponents said, 'Show us the details of your programme,' his response could only be, 'after your fine state of affairs, after your dabbling, after your subversion, the German *Volk* must be rebuilt from top to bottom, just as you destroyed it from top to bottom! That is our programme!' He did reiterate, however, that nothing would distract him 'from stamping out Marxism'.[10]

Hitler was proceeding with care. He had called an election for 5 March in an attempt to legitimize his new regime and to pass an Enabling Act that would allow him to govern both without parliament and without each piece of legislation needing the approval of President von Hindenburg. So he had to make a number of compromises. In order to ensure the support of the Centre Party, for instance, he promised that he would never enter an alliance with any party that wanted to destroy Christianity.[11]

On 27 February 1933, there was a surprising development. A Dutch Communist called Marinus van der Lubbe set fire to the German parliament, the Reichstag. Initially, as Goebbels recorded in his diary, Hitler was 'in a rage' as he saw the flames. 'Now is the time to act!' wrote Goeb-bels. A few hours later they had discovered the perpetrator – a man who encapsulated the dangers of Marxism. 'Just what we needed,' said Goebbels, 'a Dutch Communist.'[12] The convenient timing of the attack, one week before the election, together with the equally convenient political affiliation of the perpetrator, has led to a raft of conspiracy theories alleging some kind of Nazi involvement in the burning of the Reichstag. But the participation of the Nazis in the crime has never been proved conclusively.

What is certain is that this act of arson was of immense benefit to Hitler. The next day Hindenburg signed legislation that curtailed basic human rights in Germany, such as the right to assembly and the right to free speech, and a new impetus was given to the rounding up of German Communists. Hermann Göring, as Prussian Minister of the Interior, had already recruited large numbers of Nazi Stormtroopers as Auxil-iary Police in order to target the Nazis' former political opponents.

As for the German Jews, while there were sporadic attacks against individuals over the next weeks and months as the Stormtroopers celebrated their victory, they were not detained en masse, and most often the assaults were humiliating and distressing rather than murder-ous. In Nuremberg, for instance, Rudi Bamber's father was one of a number of Jews taken by the Stormtroopers to a sports stadium where they were made to cut the grass with their teeth. Rudi Bamber learnt about the attack only because the children of others who had suffered the same treatment told him that his father had been targeted as well. 'My father couldn't talk about it or wouldn't talk about it,' he says, 'he just came back very grey and ashen faced and that was that . . . I didn't think there was a coherent plan of anti-Semitism, it was simply every now and then an opportunity arose and some action would be taken against the Jews just to show them where they stood in relation to the Germans as such, to humiliate them, really. There were sort of vague instructions given which people could interpret in any way which they wanted to, and they knew they had carte blanche and they did whatever they felt like – if some people were anti-Semitic or anti-Jewish or had strong feelings or wanted to show-off to their colleagues.'[13]

But while Rudi Bamber's assessment of the actions of the Stormtroop-ers in Nuremberg during those early months of 1933 may well be correct – there was certainly little coherence in the way the Nazis chose to persecute individual Jews – there was shortly to be a nationwide action against the Jews that was very much a deliberate act of state-sanctioned terror. It occurred after the Nazis had won nearly 44 per cent of the vote in the 5 March election. Starting on 7 March in the Rhineland and then moving across Germany in the next few days, Stormtroopers and other Nazi supporters demonstrated outside Jewish shops, harassed Jewish shopkeepers and often forced the shops to close for the day.

On 24 March the Enabling Act Hitler had wanted was finally passed. This 'law to remedy the distress of the people and the Reich' gave Hitler sweeping powers to rule without the Reichstag, and was the legal basis for what became the Nazi dictatorship. Just four days later, on 28 March, Hitler instigated a call for a countrywide boycott of Jewish shops and businesses. The form of this appeal to 'National Socialists' and 'Party Comrades' is significant for a number of reasons. First, now that his new powers had been agreed, Hitler felt comfortable coupling the word 'Marxist' with 'Jewish' once again. The 'German *Volk*', he said, had put a 'lightning end to the Marxist-Jewish nightmare'. Second, the Nazis claimed that Jews who had fled from Germany were 'unfolding an unscrupulous, treasonous campaign of agitation' from abroad. And third, he argued that 'the parties responsible for these lies and slander are the Jews in our midst,' since the German Jews had the 'power to call the liars in the rest of the world into line'.[14] It was the same belief in a conspiracy of Jews across national boundaries that Hitler had talked about in the early 1920s, but which in recent years he had refrained from openly proselytizing. Hitler clearly wanted to demonstrate to the international community that foreign criticism of the Nazi regime, particularly of the Nazis' anti-Semitic policy, would not be tolerated. The German Jews were thus used as 'hostages' to try and stop foreign Jews denigrating the Nazis. It is the earliest example of what was to become a common Nazi response to criticism from abroad – the worse the attacks on Germany were in the foreign press, the more the Jews in Germany would be at risk. Finally, Hitler did not sign the document himself. It bore only the signature 'National Socialist German Workers' Party Leadership'. But we can be certain that Hitler was involved, not just because the content so mirrors his own previously expressed views, but because the *Völkischer Beobachter* reported that, at the first cabinet meeting to be held since the passing of the Enabling Act, Hitler had remarked that the measures to combat 'Jewish atrocity propaganda abroad' had been made necessary because otherwise 'the *Volk* itself' would have acted against the Jews, and that this would have 'perhaps assumed undesirable forms'.[15]

This pattern, of capitalizing on the desire of Nazi supporters to initiate anti-Semitic actions, sanctioning the attacks and then ensuring that his own name was never explicitly used on any formal order to attack the Jews, is – like the use of Jews as 'hostages' – one that we will see repeated a number of times in this history. Hitler later said that he wanted his generals to be like bull terriers on chains, and they should want 'war, war, war' and 'I should have to put brakes on the whole thing.'[16] That method of leadership – whereby those below called for action in areas of policy for which Hitler had already expressed support in principle – applied just as much to his Stormtroopers in the context of the attack on the Jews as to his generals with the approach of war. There were many advantages to Hitler in operating in this way – not least that he could preserve a certain distance from any policy that later proved unpopular or damaging, if necessary blaming what happened on 'hotheads' who could not be restrained. But Hitler was always ultimately in control. If he wanted something stopped, it stopped at once.

After he had learnt of protests held abroad by foreign Jews, Hitler almost certainly did believe that there was some kind of international Jewish conspiracy at work. Most famously, on 27 March 1933 a mass protest rally was held at Madison Square Garden in New York, with more than 50,000 protesters attending inside and outside the hall. Three days before, on 24 March, the front page of the *Daily Express* in Britain had read 'Judea Declares War on Germany – Jews of All the World Unite in Action'.

Two groups of German Jews – the Organization of German Zionists and the Centralverein (the Central Association of German Citizens of Jewish Faith) – sent delegations at Göring's request to London at the end of March to try and prevent the imposition of trade restrictions against Germany.[17] While their actions were understandable, in the warped world that Hitler inhabited they proved that there was a link between Jews that extended beyond nations. Jewish groups outside Germany were also well aware of the similar paradox they faced. If they said nothing, it looked as if they were abandoning the German Jews; if they spoke out, they fuelled Hitler's fantasy of the existence of an 'international conspiracy' of Jews. It was an impossible situation for them, and one that prevented a unified international response to Nazi anti-Semitic actions during the early years of Hitler's rule.

The Centralverein issued a press release on 24 March that illustrated the delicate line that this most influential of Jewish groups in Germany sought to tread. On the one hand, they dismissed as 'pure fiction' reports that were allegedly in the foreign press claiming that the bodies of Jews had been found dumped outside a Jewish cemetery in Berlin, and that there had been a round-up of Jewish girls. On the other hand, they did admit that 'some' Jews had been the subject of 'acts of political revenge and violence'. The situation for Jews in Germany was bad, they seemed to be saying, but not as bad as some people abroad were claiming.[18]

On the eve of the planned Jewish boycott Goebbels, authorized by Hitler, announced that the action would now take place only for one day – Saturday 1 April – but it would be reimposed if foreign attacks on the regime did not stop. Once again the Nazi regime sought to demonstrate that the welfare of German Jews depended on the behaviour of other countries towards Germany. Hitler and Goebbels were attempting to build a mental construct within which their assault on the German Jews could be seen as an act of self-defence against attacks by foreign Jews.

In Stuttgart, fifteen-year-old Arnon Tamir awaited the imposition of the boycott with trepidation. He had already heard 'stories of friends who had been beaten up. And I also had a friend, an older friend, who just happened to be home at the time. He told me that SA men [Stormtroopers] from outside the village came into the village to beat up and thrash all the Jews so badly that they were unable to sit down for weeks. One heard things like that. It was their [the Nazis'] particular technique not to have SA men from the same village attack the Jews but to bring in people from outside.'[19]

On 1 April, Arnon felt 'a deep chasm opened up inside' him: 'The SA marched and positioned themselves in front of all the Jewish shops. They daubed paint all over the shop windows and then one or two or three SA men stood outside each shop. The public was gathering around or passed by and it was said "Germans do not buy in Jewish shops," "the Jews are our misery" and so on. We were standing there and looked on, and it did happen that one or two Germans did enter the shop anyway and were not to be stopped, they went in demonstratively, that was still in '33 . . . And that's when the penny dropped, that if you could treat Jews like that, then all the stories suddenly came together, the stories about arrests . . . about beatings and manslaughter . . . I felt as if I was falling into a deep hole. That's when I intuitively realized for the first time that the existing law did not apply to Jews. Meaning that you could do with Jews whatever you liked, that nobody stood up for them, that a Jew was an outlaw. That's when I realized for the first time what it meant that anybody can do to you whatever they like, even beat you to death. That was deeply terrifying for me. I was a young lad, not even sixteen years of age. That's when it clicked, that's when I began to distance myself from the Germans. Basically, my parents did not really believe that something like this was possible. There were also German neighbours who said: "This is just a horrific episode, it will pass, they don't mean you, they mean the others, the big Jews, the moneyed Jews, the international Jews." '[20]

From the Nazis' point of view, the boycott was a mixed success. While it allowed the Stormtroopers to vent their splenetic hatred in an organized way, it also revealed the lack of broad public support for anti-Semitic actions of this brutish kind. Arnon Tamir's experience – that a number of Germans braved the Stormtroopers outside the shops and went inside as normal – was a common one. Few Germans appeared to relish the idea of Nazi thugs targeting defenceless shopkeepers – even if they were Jewish – and such a visible, state-sanctioned boycott was never repeated.

Having harassed the Jews in a physical way, the Nazis turned to the law. On 7 April 1933 Hitler's government passed their first pieces of anti-Semitic legislation. The Law for the Restoration of the Professional Civil Service called for officials who were not of 'Aryan descent' to be removed, and a similar law ordered 'non-Aryan' lawyers to cease practising. But, at the request of President von Hindenburg, a number of exemptions were made, chiefly for those who had fought in the First World War or whose close relatives had been killed in the conflict. This dulled the effect of the legislation and large numbers – including more than half the Jewish lawyers – were able to continue to practise. At the end of April a third law was announced, which limited the number of Jewish students in state schools and universities.

Tension continued between the wishes of fervent Nazi supporters for widespread anti-Semitic actions and the desire of Hitler and the Nazi leadership to minimize disruption to the economy. Jewish doctors, for example, had been excluded from the restrictive legislation in April 1933, but some local Nazi groups targeted them regardless. It was obvious that a number of Hitler's followers – no doubt influenced by their Führer's previous hate-filled rhetoric about the Jews – wanted swifter change.

Many Jewish businessmen suffered immensely. Arnon Tamir's father, for instance, owned a small cigarette factory in Stuttgart, and shortly after the April boycott the cigarette dealers in the city told him that they couldn't sell his cigarettes any more. This wasn't an 'official' action – the government would have known nothing about it – but that made little difference to Arnon Tamir's father who lost his business and was plunged into a deep depression.

However, there were other German Jews who found that their daily routine was relatively unaffected by the arrival of the Nazis. The quality of their life depended to a large extent on the attitude of the non-German Jews they lived among. Rudi Bamber in Nuremberg, for instance, felt that 'outside school hours' he was perfectly safe walking around the city. But in the months after Hitler came to power he did notice that the teaching changed at the mixed religious school he attended: 'A biology teacher began to teach German biology and the racist approach – the Jews were a different race to the Germans and lots of racist theories were held forth.' On one occasion he discovered that an anti-Semitic cartoon, torn from *Der Stürmer*, had been left on his desk: 'Everybody was looking and watching to see what my reaction would be to this, and I can't remember exactly what I did but it was quite clear to me that I'd have to be careful what I did – or didn't do – in order not to give too much gratification to the people. I think I probably lifted the lid up and shoved it inside the desk and left it there. But the teachers were keen to maintain control in the class so the pupils were aware that they couldn't go too far.'[21]

Just as there were Germans who expressed open anti-Semitism, so there were others who did what they could to help the Jews. Eugene Leviné discovered that good Samaritans could sometimes be found in unexpected places. Shortly after Hitler came to power Eugene was warned by a non-Jewish family friend that the flat he was living in was being watched. Eugene was particularly vulnerable, both as the son of one of the most prominent Communist revolutionaries and as a member of the Berlin Young Communists. But what surprised him was that the family friend who came to tell him he was in danger was a member of the Nazi party. Eugene has always been grateful to him, not least because 'he took quite a risk to do that.'[22] Subsequently, he discovered that other Jewish refugees had 'similar stories to tell'.

Around 37,000 German Jews left Germany in 1933 – 7 per cent of the country's 520,000 Jews.[23] Many of the German Jews who left went to neighbouring countries like France or the Netherlands; it was notoriously problematic to arrange a visa for the United States. Jews who wanted to emigrate also had to contend with stringent laws restricting the amount of wealth that they could take out of Germany – most left with virtually nothing. The Central Committee of German Jews for Relief and Reconstruction warned against a mass exodus: 'It will not help anybody to go abroad aimlessly . . . but only increase the numbers there who are without work and means.'[24]

There were also a whole series of emotional reasons why flight remained an unattractive option. 'My mother's parents were living with us,' says Rudi Bamber, 'and while it might have been possible for my parents perhaps to find something abroad, they couldn't take the old people, that would be impossible . . . my mother didn't feel that she wanted to abandon them to their fate. I was perhaps [also] influenced by my parents' optimism – the optimism of various people – that it's not going to get worse.'[25]

Today, we know how much worse life was going to get for the Jews who remained in Germany, which is why it is so important to remember that at the time it didn't even seem certain that Hitler would survive in office for more than a few months. After all, the last three Chancellors had struggled to control events and had been replaced – why wouldn't Hitler just be another in that long list? 'Many people thought, "Ah well! He can't cope with unemployment,"' says Eugene Leviné. ' "He can't do anything. He'll be finished. He'll make a lot of promises – he'll be finished . . ." That's why so many Jews stayed on, despite the pleading of their relatives and children to leave. Because who wants to become a refugee and live on next to nothing, when you've still got your comfortable flat?'[26]

The Jewish experience in Germany thus varied considerably during this period, to a large extent depending on geography. The majority of German Jews lived in big cities, particularly Berlin and Frankfurt – in

Frankfurt nearly 5 per cent of the overall population was Jewish.[27] In these large metropolises, German Jews were less subject to arbitrary attack than those who lived in the countryside. Away from the cities, signs reading 'Jews are not welcome here' sprouted in a number of villages and towns, particularly in the area of northern Bavaria known as Franconia. Julius Streicher was Gauleiter of Franconia, and this was a district where anti-Semitic sentiment ran high. Indeed, it was no accident that during these early years of Nazi rule the most infamous example of an attack against the Jews occurred here in Franconia – in the small town of Gunzenhausen, 30 miles south-west of Nuremberg.

On the evening of 25 March 1934, Kurt Bär, a twenty-two-year-old Stormtrooper, went with a number of his comrades to a pub in Gunzenhausen that was run by a Jewish landlord. It was Palm Sunday, a date of considerable religious significance to Christians, and the Stormtroopers had heard a rumour that an 'Aryan' might be drinking in the pub – something they considered outrageous. Once the Stormtroopers were in the pub, Bär claimed that Julius Strauss, the son of the landlord, spat on him – though Julius Strauss denied this ever happened. Bär proceeded to beat up not just Julius but his father and the rest of the Strauss family.

A crowd gathered in front of the pub and Bär stopped hitting the Strauss family long enough to give an impromptu speech. He asked how it was possible 'even in these days' that 'a Christian drinks his beer at a Jew's place, since the Jews are our mortal enemies and have nailed our Lord to the cross. Furthermore, the Jews are to blame for the two million dead of the world war and the 400 dead and 10,000 severely injured of the [Nazi] movement. Plus, how many Jews have already raped German girls and how many bastards run around in Germany now? Nowadays, if a Jew still dares to spit at an SA man it is as if he spits on Adolf Hitler and the whole movement.'[28] One witness said that 'around 200' people listened to Bär's speech and 'they all agreed' with it.[29]

The beating of Julius Strauss now resumed, with the crowd egging on the Stormtroopers, shouting 'Hit him! Hit him!'[30] Afterwards the whole Strauss family was taken to the local jail. According to an official report of the incident, once in the jail Mrs Strauss protested that she had done nothing wrong, and 'Kurt Bär struck her across the face and said, "You Jewish hussy, keep your trap shut." Mrs Strauss tried to hide behind the prison administrator and grabbed hold of his arm. This gave

Bär an excuse to strike her another blow, saying, "you Jewish hussy, you must not touch a Christian." '31

Several hundred – some reports say more than a thousand – citizens of Gunzenhausen now roamed the streets, yelling 'The Jews have to go!' Jewish property was attacked, around thirty Jews were arrested and two Jews died. One committed suicide when a mob threatened him. The other, Jacob Rosenfelder – who was found hanging in a shed – had almost certainly been murdered.

Although a large number of people had participated in the riot, only a handful of Stormtroopers were ever put on trial. In June 1934 the district court at Ansbach also decided that – despite evidence to the contrary – both the Jews who died had committed suicide. So the defendants only had to face charges of breach of the peace and causing minor injuries. Five of the defendants were discharged, seventeen received sentences of between three and seven months in jail, and Bär was told he would go to prison for ten months. None of those found guilty were taken into custody straight away, and on 21 August 1934 every sentence – apart from Bär's – was quashed on appeal.

During the investigation into the crime, the deputy of the 'Supreme SA leader of the government of Central Franconia' tried to shift the blame for the whole incident on to the Jews themselves. He wrote that despite the 'National Socialist Revolution no stop has been put to the dirty game of the Jews'. Furthermore, 'the Jews in this district nowadays are just as arrogant, brazen, barefaced and brash as they were before the revolution. A large number of inhabitants of the town of Gunzenhausen as well as the district of Gunzenhausen have been legitimately annoyed by this for some time.'32

The authorities in Berlin were concerned that local Nazis had taken the law into their own hands. 'I strongly request', wrote the Reich Minister of the Interior to the authorities in Bavaria, 'that measures be taken so that these riots don't repeat themselves, and that the police intervene to stop the singing of the song "And when Jewish blood splatters from the knife, everything will be fine again! SA comrades, hang the Jews, put the fat cats against the wall!" The Jewish question is to be handled by the government of the Reich, not by the SA of Gunzenhausen.'33

That wasn't the end of the incident. On 15 July 1934 Kurt Bär together with two of his comrades returned to the pub in Gunzenhausen where the riot had started. According to the subsequent indictment against him, 'Kurt Bär entered the room shouting, "Hands up",' and immediately fired two shots at Simon Strauss [the landlord] who sat directly in front of him and who was hit in the head by both shots.' Julius Strauss, the landlord's son, tried to escape, but Bär shot him as well. Bär was taken to the local jail where he shouted out through a window to a crowd that had gathered in the street 'I have shot two Jews. Be contented, I defended the honour of my SA comrades!'[34]

Simon Strauss died of gunshot wounds but his son survived, so Bär faced one charge of murder and one of attempted murder. In October 1934 he was sentenced to ten years in prison, but he was released just four years later. Julius Streicher had called for Bär to be treated leniently, saying, according to one eyewitness, 'It is wrong, naturally, that this Jew was killed, but I am naturally glad about every Jew that is being killed.'[35]

The events in Gunzenhausen were at the extreme end of the spectrum of anti-Semitic action against Jews during the first two years of Hitler's Chancellorship. Nothing like this happened again in Bavaria until the attacks of Kristallnacht in 1938. But it remains instructive. It reveals, first of all, how spontaneous the attacks against the Jews could be. There is no evidence that this level of violence was pre-planned. If Kurt Bär had not lost his temper in a pub then it is hard to see how the attacks would have happened. But while Bär's actions were the catalyst, the pogrom was only possible as a result of underlying tensions. The reason so many of the local population rose up in support of Bär was because they themselves were predisposed to hate Jews. It is also worth noting that Bär in his speech outside the pub focused on traditional Christian-based anti-Semitism. This part of Franconia was staunchly Protestant, and the content of Bär's verbal attack on the Jews would have been familiar to Martin Luther.

The disagreement between the local Nazis, who felt they could take whatever action they liked against the Jews, and the central government, with their response that 'The Jewish question is to be handled by the government of the Reich, not by the SA of Gunzenhausen,' is also revealing. As is the fact that Bär instinctively felt that Hitler would have supported his actions, when he said that spitting on an SA uniform was akin to spitting on Adolf Hitler. Finally, this unpleasant story also demonstrates the extent to which the German courts had already been tainted by the advent of the Nazi state. While it was the case that some of the Stormtroopers were initially put on trial and found guilty, the legal system subsequently failed the victims of the crime by releasing the Stormtroopers on appeal. Such a pattern would soon become commonplace, as the rule of law was corrupted by the Nazis.

In May 1934, two months after the Palm Sunday attack in Gunzenhausen, Julius Streicher demonstrated once again where he stood on the question of the Jews by publishing the notorious 'Jewish murder plot' edition of *Der Stürmer*. A cartoon on the front page showed two grotesquely caricatured Jewish men, one of them holding a bloodstained knife, collecting the blood of children. The text underneath said that the Jews practised 'superstitious magic' and sought to collect Christian blood in order to mix it into unleavened bread. Other illustrations showed Jews sucking the blood of a prostrate child through straws, and a reproduction of a stone relief on an Oberwesel church which featured an alleged thirteenth-century ritual murder of a sixteen-year-old boy – a youth later canonized as St Werner of Oberwesel. Another article claimed that the history of the Jews was 'an unbroken chain of mass murders and blood baths'.

This special edition of *Der Stürmer* also emphasized the link between the Jews and Communism, alleging that after the 1917 Russian revolution '35 million' people had been 'shot, murdered, tortured and starved', and that today in 'Jewish Bolshevik Russia' mass murders still continued, with the murderers 'mostly Jewish'. Over 100,000 copies of this 'Jewish murder plot' edition were sold, while other copies were pinned on display boards in the streets.

There was widespread protest about the lurid content of *Der Stürmer*'s special edition – not just from abroad, but from Christians within Germany. So much so that Hitler eventually ordered it banned. Significantly, he said that he had banned this edition not because of the lies it propagated about the Jews, but because it could also be construed as an attack on 'Christ's holy communion'.[36] It is revealing that despite recognizing the political necessity of distancing himself from the extreme content of this edition of *Der Stürmer*, Hitler still couldn't bring himself to criticize the paper for attacking the Jews.

While there was no official policy of physically segregating German Jews from the rest of the population, immense pressure could nonetheless be placed on Jews, particularly in the countryside, to move away from areas in which they were no longer wanted. The *Fränkische Tageszeitung*, for instance, reported on 26 May 1934 that 'on Thursday at 5 p.m. the swastika flag was hoisted on the property of the last Jew to leave Hersbruck [in Franconia]. The Hersbruck district is now definitely purged of Jews. With pride and satisfaction the population takes cognizance of this fact.'[37] The paper went on to say that it was to be hoped that other areas 'will soon follow suit and that the day is not now far off when the whole of Franconia will be rid of Jews, just as one day that day must dawn when throughout the whole of Germany there will no longer be one single Jew'.

Equally, though there was as yet no law prohibiting Jews from marrying or having sexual relationships outside marriage with non-Jews, there were a number of instances of local Nazi groups humiliating couples that were in a mixed relationship. The Jewish lawyer Kurt Rosenberg wrote in his diary in August 1933 how in Cuxhaven, in Lower Saxony, 'an Aryan girl and a non-Aryan man are led through the city wearing signs around their necks, "I am a pig because I took up with a Jew," etc. In other locales the names of Aryan girls who have been seen in the company of Jews are published. And elsewhere Jews are prohibited from entering streets and town squares.'[38]

However, amid all of these instances of state sanctioned and locally inspired persecution, it is also important to notice what was not happening. The German Jews were not being sent en masse to concentration camps. The first makeshift camps were created to hold the Nazis' political opponents, not the Jews. In Prussia, thousands of Stormtroopers hired by Hermann Göring as Auxiliary Police arrested their former political adversaries and took them to improvised jails in disused factories and warehouses, even to basements in the houses of the Stormtroopers themselves. Those captured were often beaten and humiliated in an orgy of celebratory revenge. In March 1933 Wilhelm Murr, the Nazi state president of Württemberg, said memorably: 'We don't say: an eye for an eye, a tooth for a tooth. No, if someone knocks out one of our eyes, we will chop off his head, and if someone knocks out one of our teeth, we will smash in his jaw.'[39]

In March 1933 Heinrich Himmler became acting police chief in Bavaria. By now he was also head of a specialized protection unit called the Schutzstaffel, or SS, originally formed as a group of bodyguards to protect Nazi speakers at public meetings. Himmler was in the process of turning the organization into an elite group of Nazi believers, albeit one still within the overall structure of the Stormtroopers under SA leader Ernst Röhm. Many members of the SS had been sworn in as Auxiliary Police and in this capacity staffed the first concentration camps in Bavaria.

Himmler justified the mass arrest of the Nazis' political opponents in a speech in March 1933 with an early example of the kind of paternalistic double-speak for which he would later become infamous: 'I have made quite extensive use of protective custody . . . I felt compelled to do this because in many parts of the city there has been so much agitation that it has been impossible for me to guarantee the safety of those particular individuals who have provoked it.'[40]

Himmler thus claimed that those who had been thrown into concentration camps had been sent there for their own good, as their 'safety' could not be assured on the streets because the rest of the population might turn on them. It was similar to the reasoning Hitler would attempt to use later that same month for the Jewish boycott – the Nazi state had to act or else the *Volk* would take matters into their own hands.[41] According to Himmler, 'protective custody' worked in two ways: the population were 'protected' from those the Nazis arrested, and those who were arrested were 'protected' from the rest of the population. This was the logic behind the otherwise bizarre statement which prisoners were required to sign on their release from concentration camps: 'I am aware that I may at any time apply for a further period of protective custody if I consider my physical well being to be in jeopardy.'[42]

Protective custody did not replace the existing system of justice in Germany but operated in parallel to it, as Hermann Göring explained at his trial in Nuremberg in 1946: 'You must differentiate between the two categories; those who had committed some act of treason against the new state or those who might be proved to have committed such an act, were naturally turned over to the courts. The others, however, of whom one might expect such acts, but who had not yet committed them, were taken into protective custody, and these were the people who were taken to concentration camps.'[43] It was an idea that went against all rules of natural justice. But it was consistent with the principles that Hitler had expressed in *Mein Kampf*. People should be judged for who they *were*, just as much as for what they *did*. It was all part of the same worldview that said that a Jew could never become a Christian by being baptized, because inherently that individual remained a Jew.

There was another consequence of this thinking. Prisoners in concentration camps did not serve a specific sentence – how could they when they had not necessarily committed any offence? Therefore no prisoner knew the date when they would be released. Maybe they would be released tomorrow – or maybe they would never be released. As one concentration camp commandant later said, 'the uncertainty of the duration of their confinement was something with which they could never come to terms. It was this that wore them down and broke the strongest wills.'[44]

Nor were these camps intended to be similar to normal prisons where the punishment was the incarceration itself. That was because, according to Nazi theory, the prisoners' detention was not supposed to be an act of retribution but an opportunity for them to change. 'We had to rescue these people,' said Göring, 'to bring them back to the German national community. We had to re-educate them.'[45]

The first concentration camp in Bavaria opened on 22 March 1933 in a town just 10 miles from the centre of Munich. The name of this place would become infamous – Dachau. Himmler had personally inspected the site, on the outskirts of the town in a disused factory, and decided that this would be the location for the camp. The nature of the institution was clear from the outset. 'Now we've got the power,' said Johann-Erasmus von Malsen-Ponickau, an SS commander, to the new SS guards at Dachau. 'If these swine had taken over, they'd have made sure our heads rolled in the dust. So we know no sentimentality. Any man in our ranks who can't stand the sight of blood doesn't belong here, he should get out.'[46] They were words that demonstrated the hypocrisy of Göring's claim that the role of the camps was to 'rescue' misguided Germans, or Himmler's assertion that the SS sought to ensure the 'safety' of those they imprisoned.

On Christmas Eve 1934, Josef Felder, the SPD (Social Democratic Party) politician, discovered personally what form this lack of 'sentimentality' could take. He had bravely voted against the Enabling Act in March the previous year, and – as one of the Nazis' political opponents – was a prime candidate for 'protective custody'. He was arrested and taken to Dachau where he was thrown into one of the cells in a building known as the 'bunker': 'They took away the bag of straw which was lying there . . . on the wooden boards [of the bed]. They took it out and said, "You won't be needing that, because you'll only be leaving this bunker as a corpse!" '47 Left alone in the dark cell, he could hear the guards becoming 'raucous' as they indulged in a drunken Christmas celebration. Around midnight one of the guards came back, opened the iron flap in the cell door and held out a plate with white sausages and pretzels on it in front of Josef Felder's face. 'That would make a nice meal before your execution,' he said. 'But you're not even worth this, you bastard! We know a lot about you! We'll take care of you!' The guard slammed the flap shut and left. Later that night he returned, holding a rope, and demonstrated to Josef the 'best way' to hang himself. Josef replied that he had a family, and if they wanted him to die they would have to kill him themselves. 'Yes,' said the guard, 'we'll do that! But we've got [plenty of] time!'

The psychological torture continued. After several days in the bunker Josef was told, 'You're getting out tomorrow,' but the words were a sick joke. 'They kept saying,' he recalls, ' "You're getting out tomorrow." They were just messing around with me.' For three days out of four he had only water to drink and a piece of bread to eat. Every fourth day he would be given tea and, if he was lucky, one hot meal. As he lay in a dark insanitary cell, deprived of proper sustenance, his mind tormented by anxiety, it was scarcely surprising that Josef found that his health started to break. A lung disease that he had first contracted several years before reappeared and then intensified. As a consequence, the guards locked him in a segregation area of the bunker along with ten other prisoners, all suffering from lung disease. 'The Nazis were very afraid of pulmonary tuberculosis,' he says, 'which was a serious disease in those days.'

Josef Felder recovered from his lung condition and was released after just over a year in Dachau. Most prisoners in the camp served a similar length of time, though some were freed after just a few months and others were never released. It depended on the whim of the Nazis. All the prisoners who were eventually freed were required to declare that they would never reveal what they had experienced inside the camp. If they did, they would be sent back.

As for the relationship between the German Jews and the first concentration camps, it was not a straightforward one. In his speech in March 1933, Himmler went out of his way to stress that Jews would not be targeted simply for being Jews: 'I must emphasize one point in particular:

for us a citizen of the Jewish faith is just as much a citizen as someone who is not of the Jewish faith and his life and property are subject to the same protection. We make no distinction in this respect.'[48] It was an odd statement for Himmler to make, especially when his own party's programme denied that the Jews were 'true' Germans. He probably made these disingenuous remarks as much for a foreign audience – in order to counter the alleged 'atrocity propaganda' – as for a domestic one. In any case, his Stormtroopers did not follow his instruction. A proportion of the Communist and socialist politicians sent to the camps were Jewish, and these Jews were often singled out for harsher treatment than was imposed on the other prisoners. Max Abraham, for example, wrote *Juda verrecke. Ein Rabbiner im Konzentrationslager* (Death to Juda: A Rabbi in a Concentration Camp) after he managed to leave Germany. In the book, published in 1934, Abraham recorded his own treatment at the hands of the Nazis, just months after Hitler came to power.

Abraham was arrested in June 1933 for allegedly assaulting a Stormtrooper, but since he was a member of the Social Democratic Party and had been active in the small Jewish community in his hometown of Rathenow it is likely that the Nazis were already looking to pick him up. The Nazis also bore a personal grudge against him because a Stormtrooper had been sentenced to five months in jail back in 1930 for attacking him.

After his arrest, Abraham was first hit with truncheons by the guards, and then a special sadistic element was added – he and three other Jews were forced to beat each other up as the Stormtroopers watched. 'We four Jews had to take turns maltreating each other with the truncheon,' said Abraham. 'When we wouldn't hit hard enough, the Stormtroopers threatened us with an even worse torture.'[49]

Abraham was taken to a small camp at Papenburg, 35 miles west of Oldenburg in the north of Germany. The Jewish New Year was approaching, and the guards had been planning their own way of marking this Jewish festival. On the first day of the holiday, the SS guards forced Abraham and several other Jews into a manure pit. 'SS Scharführer [Sergeant] Everling roared at me,' wrote Abraham, ' "There, Rabbi, you can hold your service here!" Everything in me rebelled against literally having our faith sullied. I kept silent.' Despite the SS man insisting he do as he was ordered, Abraham continued to resist, saying, 'I do not hold services in a manure pit!' As a consequence, he was dragged out of the pit and 'truncheons and [rifle] butts rained down' on him. When he passed out he was taken back to his bunk and 'lay there without consciousness' for two hours. In the afternoon, after he had recovered, Abraham was returned to the manure pit and ordered by Scharführer Everling to give a speech on Judaism to the other Jews and to the SS who were supervising them. 'The Jewish religion is, like other religions, based on the Ten Commandments,' said Abraham, 'and the most beautiful biblical sentence: "Thou shalt love thy neighbour as thyself!"' At this point Everling interrupted, saying, 'Knock it off, you pig, we will teach you our understanding of the grace of charity!' Abraham was now 'maltreated so horribly' that he 'developed a high fever and lapsed into convulsions. My body was made sore by beating; I could neither sit nor lie. I spent a horrible night like this in a cloudy and dreadful delirium. The next morning, I was in an alarming state and they brought me to the ward. Here I was among non-Jewish comrades, Social Democrats and Communists, who devotedly looked after me. I will never forget their comradely help.'[50]

Max Abraham was released after four months' incarceration, and managed to leave Germany for Czechoslovakia in 1934. Eventually he settled in Britain where he died in 1977.[51] His *Juda verrecke. Ein Rabbiner im Konzentrationslager* reminds us that Stormtroopers and SS treated Jews in sadistic ways in concentration camps long before the creation of the extermination centres of the Holocaust.

The Nazis did not hide the concentration camps. Their existence was well known and newspapers across the world carried stories about them. On 1 January 1934, for instance, the *Manchester Guardian* accurately described the reality of life in the so-called bunker in Dachau: 'The cells are of concrete, they have one barred window each (which can be darkened), they are damp, and without heating arrangements.' The article also revealed the nature of the beatings that the guards administered: 'This consists of flogging with an ox-hide thong that has a strip of steel, three or four millimetres wide, running along its whole length (these are made by the prisoners). The blows – the number varies from twenty-five to seventy-five according to the sentence – are counted out by an SS man. Two other SS men hold the prisoner down, one by the hands and the other by the head, round which a sack is wrapped so that the prisoner's cries are stifled . . . Some prisoners have also been beaten with lengths of rubber hosepipe. Some have been burnt with cigarette ends and some have been put to what Americans call the "water torture".[52]

Hans Beimler, a German Communist, published another early eye-witness account of the camp in 1933. He entitled his book *Im Mörderlager Dachau* (In the Murder Camp Dachau).[53] But while Beimler was justified in calling Dachau a 'murder' camp, given that a small number of prisoners were killed there during this period, these concentration camps should not be confused with the later extermination camps – like Treblinka – whose only function was to kill. Appalling as the regime was at Dachau before the war, the majority of those who were sent to the camp at this time survived the experience.

When Beimler was arrested on 11 April 1933 the Stormtroopers could scarcely contain their glee at capturing such a prominent Communist. In prison he was savagely beaten with rubber truncheons. After fourteen days he was transferred to Dachau where he was hit about the head and thrown into a cell in the bunker. Just as with Josef Felder, one of the guards visited Beimler in his cell, gave him a rope and demonstrated the best way he could use it to hang himself. Soon afterwards Beimler heard screams as other prisoners were tortured, before his own cell door swung open and half a dozen guards entered. They beat him so badly that he could scarcely touch anything for days without feeling pain, and it was impossible for him to sleep.

Astonishingly, Beimler was able to escape from Dachau. He detached the wooden board over a small, high window in his cell, squeezed through the opening and, possibly with the collaboration of at least one guard, traversed the barbed-wire fence that surrounded the camp. An extensive manhunt was launched in an attempt to catch him, but he was able to cross the German border to freedom. He died in 1936 at the age of forty-one, fighting in the International Brigades in the Spanish civil war.

The consequence of works like *Im Mörderlager Dachau* and *Juda verrecke. Ein Rabbiner im Konzentrationslager*, together with articles in the *Manchester Guardian* and other newspapers, was that the brutal nature of the Nazi regime was known to the world from the beginning. However, in parallel to these truthful accounts, misinformation was also published, especially in Germany, which sanitized life in the concentration camps. For example, the local paper for Dachau, the *Amper-Bote*, claimed in September 1933 that the prisoners spent their spare time 'contentedly' playing sport or games and had been observed 'cheerfully working'.[54] Many other German citizens took a similarly benign view of the camps. Erna Krantz, a Munich schoolgirl in the 1930s, says: 'You just knew of the existence of Dachau, but it was just a prison camp, wasn't it? We knew that there were Communists there, and criminals.'[55] Karl Boehm-Tettelbach, a young air force officer at the time, believed that 'In Dachau he [Hitler] collected all the professional criminals . . . and they had to work there . . . in addition, he got all the gigolos, especially the homosexuals, away from the streets. And they were there in Dachau in that working camp, and the people didn't object too much at this.'[56]

This idea that the inmates of camps like Dachau somehow deserved to be there – even though they had faced no criminal trial – was not uncommon. Walter Fernau, for instance, was a teenager when he first 'heard the words concentration camp' in 1935. He remembers that 'a son of a friend of my father's was flirting with a married woman in a café, and then her husband came in and he was an SS Hauptsturmführer. He took him to task. This son of my father's friend, he was idle and just lived off his father's fortune; his goal in life was just to mess around with women and hang around bars. He hit out and gave the SS man, who grabbed him, such a hook that he flew over two tables and slid down the wall. Then he took his girlfriend – that was the man's wife – and went out. Of course, the police arrested him shortly afterwards. My father told my mother this story over lunch. We children, my sister and I, were listening. And then he said: "Imagine, Adelbert's son, the big one, they've arrested him, he beat up an SS man and now he's being sent to a concentration camp." And then my mother said: "What's that then?" And my father said: "He'll finally learn the meaning of work there!" And so as a child of fifteen or sixteen I thought, "Oh, that wastrel who has done nothing all his life and just picks up strange women and drives around in fast cars, it'll do him good to learn how to work for a change." '[57]

Others were more realistic about the political situation. Manfred von Schröder, the suave son of a banker who joined the Nazi party in 1933, believed that the concentration camps were the understandable by-product of a 'revolution'. 'Have you seen in history', he says, 'any revolution without nasty aspects on one side or the other?'[58] The Austrian-born Nazi Reinhard Spitzy echoes this view: 'In all revolutions – and we thought we have a revolution, a Nationalist Socialist revolution – blood is running.'[59]

At first sight it might seem strange that so many people welcomed this revolution, even with these 'nasty aspects'. But it is less surprising if we remember that Germany had just experienced an existential crisis. The whole fabric of the country appeared to be coming apart as a result of the economic crash. Everyone knew what had happened in Russia in 1917 and there was a real fear of just such a revolution breaking out in Germany. As a result, enormous numbers of violence-hating Germans thought that the best way of gaining peace and security was to support Hitler and his Stormtroopers. They believed that a Nazi revolution was preferable to a Communist one, and that as a result of the actions of the Stormtroopers law and order would return once again. Many Germans also felt comfortable because the groups that the Nazis targeted seemed to be clearly defined, not just the Jews but Communists and socialists as well. So if you were not Jewish, or Communist or socialist, if you didn't cross the new regime in any other way, if instead you were a good, solid German who wanted a new start, then you were almost certainly not only safe from persecution but it was perfectly possible that you approved of what the Nazis were doing.

Given that Hitler's rhetoric had focused so much on fight, struggle and the crushing of enemies, it is also not surprising that controlling the guards who worked in the camps was a challenge for the regime. Himmler's solution was not only to staff the camps he oversaw with members of his SS, but to replace the commandant of his showpiece camp, Dachau, just three months after it opened. The first commandant, Hilmar Wäckerle, had represented the old way of thinking. He was a veteran of the First World War and of service with the paramilitary Freikorps. He was the archetypal 'old fighter' who had been attracted by the revolutionary nature of the Nazi party and now that Hitler had gained power had been promoted beyond his abilities.

Wäckerle's chief problem, as far as Himmler was concerned, was that he was attracting too much of the wrong kind of attention to Dachau. Emblematic of his leadership of the camp was the death of four Jewish prisoners on 12 April 1933. They had been taken outside the camp to nearby woods and shot 'while attempting to escape' – a euphemism for murder. It is still a mystery why these particular prisoners were selected and killed, though one officer, Police Lieutenant Schuler, later said that he thought Wäckerle had been frightened of a 'communist revolt' in the camp.[60] The

Bavarian prosecutor's office subsequently took an interest in the affair and the resulting inquiry was not helpful for Himmler, since the circumstances surrounding the death of the prisoners were at odds with his desire to portray Dachau as a disciplined institution with an emphasis on reform.

It was in the midst of this controversy, on 9 May, that Hans Beimler escaped from the camp. Not only did there appear to be a policy of extra-judicial murder in operation at Dachau, but the guards now seemed to be incompetent as well. By the end of the next month Wäckerle was gone. The new commandant, Theodor Eicke, would make his mark on Dachau, and indeed on the whole concentration camp system, in a way that Wäckerle never did.

The choice of Eicke to take over as commandant of Dachau revealed a great deal about the personal qualities Himmler thought important for a leading figure in the SS. Eicke was not an easy person to manage, and could scarcely have been more different in character from Himmler. Eicke was argumentative, passionate and dangerous, while Himmler was punctilious, organized and calm – some thought he looked like a village schoolteacher. In 1932 Eicke had been arrested for planning a bombing campaign in support of the Nazis. Sentenced to prison, he fled Germany while on bail and returned only after Hitler's appointment as Chancellor. Believing that Josef Bürckel, Nazi Gauleiter of the Palatinate, had double-crossed him at the time of his arrest, Eicke wanted revenge. He organized an armed raid and captured Gauleiter Bürckel. Eicke's victory didn't last long, however, as Bürckel had powerful friends and Eicke's actions appeared almost unbalanced. Eicke was arrested and sent to a psychiatric hospital, though the doctors said he was sane. It was Himmler who rescued him from this morass.

What Himmler now counted on, as well as the ability he saw in Eicke, was that Eicke would show immense personal loyalty to him. Without Himmler's intervention his career at the age of forty was not just on a downward trajectory but in a vertical dive. Himmler offered him a second chance. He gave a similar opportunity to others, most notably Reinhard Heydrich, who would later have a close personal involvement with the extermination of the Jews. Himmler saved Heydrich in 1931, after he had been thrown out of the navy.

Under Eicke the guards at Dachau changed from the original band of street fighters to a professional corps within the newly formed SS Death's

Head Division. Eicke introduced a whole series of new regulations, not in order to eliminate the violence directed against inmates, but to clarify when it could be used. For instance, Eicke's regulations stated that any prisoner could be executed 'who attacks a guard or SS man, refuses to obey an order, refuses to obey an instruction in the workplace, incites or calls upon others to do so for reasons of rebellion, leaves a marching column or workplace or incites others to do so, or shouts, cries out, agitates or makes a speech while marching or during working hours'.[61]

Eicke emphasized that he wanted his men to be tough and uncompromising, especially in the presence of prisoners. 'Anyone who shows even the slightest vestige of sympathy towards them', he said, 'will immediately vanish from our ranks. I need only hard, totally committed SS men. There is no place amongst us for soft people.'[62] By such comments, Eicke not only articulated the qualities he demanded of the men under his command, he also sought to build an awareness that to be a member of the SS at Dachau was not just to be a jailer, but to be an elite soldier, fighting against ruthless enemies of the state. Eicke wanted the SS at Dachau to be a brotherhood, to be men who looked out for each other and fought in a noble, common cause. Eicke preached that the job of the officer was not just to lead the men under his command, but to care for them. As a consequence, Eicke's men came, in the words of one of his soldiers, to 'adore' him.[63] 'The name "Papa Eicke" was coined even then,' said Max von Dall-Armi, one of the SS men at Dachau. 'He [Eicke] hates his enemies behind the barbed wire . . . He speaks of their destruction and annihilation. He instils this hatred into the SS through speeches and conversations. Eicke is a fanatical SS officer and ardent National Socialist for whom there is no compromise . . . "SS men must hate . . . the heart in their breasts must be turned to stone." '[64]

Eicke also employed a number of carefully chosen inmates – known as Kapos – in a supervisory role at the camp. The idea of employing selected prisoners to oversee other inmates was not new – prisoners had been appointed 'trusties' in ordinary jails and even concentration camps before – but Eicke embraced the idea as if it was his own. There were many advantages for the SS in such a system. Not only could the supervision of prisoners now extend to times when SS guards were not present, but the potential arbitrariness of the treatment meted out by the Kapos to their fellow inmates added a note of uncertainty and tension that would intimidate the prisoners still further. As for the Kapos, their lives in the camp were altered in a double-edged way by their promotion to the status of overseers. While they could exercise power over those in their charge, they still remained vulnerable. As Himmler said, speaking during the war, 'His [the Kapo's] job is to see that the work gets done . . . thus he has to push his men. As soon as we are no longer satisfied with him, he is no longer a Kapo and returns to the other inmates. He knows that they will beat him to death his first night back.'[65]

There was also one longer-term benefit for the SS in embracing the system of Kapos. Over time, the existence of Kapos allowed the SS more distance from the prisoners. It meant that instead of physically attacking inmates themselves, they could instruct the Kapos to do the beating for them. The guards could thus choose not to become covered in the sweat and blood of the prisoners as they were lashed. There were, of course, SS who remained directly involved in the physical abuse of prisoners, but the Kapo system allowed an alternative way of structuring supervision and punishment. It was a system that was to find its apotheosis at Auschwitz, where prisoners were at risk of the most appalling abuse – even murder – from the Kapos who were in charge of their individual barracks or work details.

Many of those who were later to obtain high positions within the concentration camp system trained under Eicke at Dachau – most notably Rudolf Höss, who became the first commandant of Auschwitz in 1940. He started work as an ordinary SS soldier at Dachau in 1934 and in many ways was the exemplar of the new hard man that Eicke sought to cultivate. He described how Eicke tried to convince his SS men that they were dealing with 'dangerous enemies of the state' and so had to treat the prisoners harshly as a consequence.[66] But it would be wrong to take Höss's words, written in the memoirs he composed after the war, entirely at face value. While no doubt Eicke's methods did have an effect on him, they are not the whole reason why Höss could later oversee the largest site of mass murder in the history of the world. Like many of those who joined the SS and came to Dachau, he had a past that predisposed him to embrace the values that Eicke sought to impart.

Höss was thirty-three years old when he joined the SS, and he carried with him a bloody personal history. Born in 1900, he fought in the First World War – having joined up when he was under-age. He won several decorations for bravery, including the Iron Cross first class, and at the age of seventeen became the youngest NCO in the army. In the wake of Germany's defeat he joined a paramilitary Freikorps and fought to suppress a left-wing uprising in the Ruhr in 1920. In November 1922 he became a member of the Nazi party and the following year participated in the murder of a fellow member of the Freikorps who was thought to be a traitor. He was caught shortly afterwards and sentenced to ten years in prison. Released as part of an amnesty in 1928 he joined the Artamans, a *völkisch* group that preached the importance of remaining close to the soil. Here, working as a farmer, Höss met his future wife Hedwig. He also came to the attention of Heinrich Himmler, who supported the ideals of the Artaman movement.

Thus, long before Höss came within the orbit of Theodor Eicke, he had not only made a number of life choices that demonstrated his commitment to the values espoused by Hitler and the Nazi party, but he had also participated in acts of extreme violence and experienced five years of imprisonment. If anyone was primed to develop 'hatred and antipathy' for the inmates of Dachau, it was Rudolf Höss. That is not to say, however, that Höss's memoirs are entirely unreliable. His description of his feelings at first witnessing the flogging of prisoners in Dachau certainly rings true. He wrote how two prisoners were bound to the 'whipping block' in the camp and received twenty-five lashes each, because they had been convicted of stealing cigarettes. Höss recounts how 'the first prisoner, a small impenitent malingerer, was made to lie across the block. Two soldiers held his head and hands and two block leaders carried out the punishment, delivering alternate strokes. The prisoner uttered no sound. The other prisoner, a professional politician of strong physique, behaved quite otherwise. He cried out at the very first stroke and tried to break free. He went on screaming to the end, although the commandant yelled at him to keep quiet. I was stationed in the front rank and was thus compelled to watch the whole procedure. I say compelled, because if I had been in the rear of the company I would not have looked. When the man began to scream I went hot and cold all over. In fact the whole thing, even the beating of the first prisoner, made me shudder. Later on, at the beginning of the war, I attended my first execution, but it did not affect me nearly so much as witnessing that first corporal punishment.'[67]

While Eicke attempted to mould the SS guards at Dachau into a professional yet heartless force, a parallel structure of concentration camps operated in the north of Germany. Hermann Göring as Minister President of Prussia oversaw this system – or rather tried to, since he had difficulty restraining the Stormtroopers and SS in his domain. In Prussia there was no Eicke to prevent the brutality of the guards turning to anarchy.

There were particular problems at the complex of camps in Emsland in north-west Germany. The SS were not cooperating with the Stormtroopers and both groups were causing unrest in the local area. In the nearby town of Papenburg the SS and the SA brawled in the open,[68] and the SS were accused of invading 'the area like a swarm of locusts. They were in hock to the small businesses, in the pubs they smashed the furniture, the girls were impregnated, and everywhere they went they met with animosity. Petitions for the withdrawal of the SS were addressed to the ministry from among the population.'[69] In the camp itself there were disagreements among the guards over the appropriate amount of sadism that should be directed towards the inmates. 'The prisoners had to jump off their beds in the middle of the night,' wrote one political prisoner in the camp,[70] 'and were not allowed to get dressed. They had to line up naked' and 'were beaten without pity . . . It was abominable – so abominable that it was even too much for some of the SS. A group of the SS men involved in this "punitive action" became openly mutinous. They threatened their comrades with their guns, saying: "Enough already! Stop it, or we will shoot you down!" '[71]

By November 1933, the situation was so bad that Hitler ordered the existing guards to be discharged from duty.[72] They were not happy at the news. They 'bellowed outside the camp, "We shit on the fat-cat republic!" '[73] Shortly afterwards they decided to take an even more radical step – and said that they would mutiny. 'The SS [guards] announced, "We won't let the police replace us, even if we have to wade through blood up to our knees." '[74]

According to another account, by Walter Langhoff, an inmate in the camp, the SS got 'carried away by an enormous warlike mood'. Langhoff recalled: 'The guards at the gate were strengthened, machine-gun emplacements were set up around the camp, and commandant Fleitmann issued the order: "Everybody who approaches the camp in a police uniform and ignores the request to stop will be shot at." In the camp, the SS men took us [prisoners] aside: "You know, when they arrive, we will give you weapons, and we will put down the attack together! And after that we will found the 'Freikorps Fleitmann' and then we will struggle along until we are in Austria and there we will start the revolution!" '[75]

The idea that the SS guards ever offered to arm the prisoners and start a 'revolution' seems bizarre. But a clue to their behaviour lies in the reference to the 'Freikorps Fleitmann'. Individual paramilitary Freikorps groups, formed in the aftermath of the First World War, often took their names from their leader and it was to this commander – known as their 'Führer' – that each man pledged absolute loyalty, rather than to any abstract constitution or higher official. Here, in a throwback to those anarchic, revolutionary days, the SS were saying that they wanted to follow their own leader – Fleitmann – rather than trust anyone else.

It is also possible that the SS guards were never entirely serious in their threat to mutiny. Alcohol certainly played a part in their behaviour. The night before the police were due to arrive to replace them, the SS got drunk and caused mayhem within the camp: they 'shat in the lockers, mixed salt into the sugar, smashed the windows in the troop barracks and the canteen and all kinds of other things'.[76] The following morning, 6 November 1933, no doubt hung-over after the enormous quantity of alcohol they had consumed the previous night, the SS trudged out through the gates without putting up a fight and left the camp to a detachment of police.

While the violent excesses in Emsland had been perpetrated by those on the ground, it was the lack of leadership at the top that had been a necessary precondition of the lawless way the camps had operated. Now, just as Himmler had made Dachau into a place of orderly – rather than chaotic – cruelty, he would be given the authority to reform the concentration camps in Göring's Prussian realm. Himmler also became responsible for all of the German police, although he remained as yet nominally subordinate to Göring within Prussia.

The big leap forward for Himmler came with the 'Night of the Long Knives' – the murder of Stormtrooper leader Ernst Röhm and others thought antagonistic to the regime. By June 1934 Röhm was a problem for Hitler that he wanted to solve. Hitler was anxious to avoid potential conflict between Röhm's Stormtroopers and the German Army, and the ailing President von Hindenburg and Vice-Chancellor von Papen were also concerned about the lawless behaviour of Röhm's Storm-troopers. Papen warned, in a speech on 17 June 1934, that 'no nation that would survive before history can afford a permanent uprising from below . . . Germany cannot be allowed to become a train hurtling into the blue with no one knowing where it will stop.'[77]

On 30 June 1934, Röhm was arrested at the spa resort of Bad Wiessee and taken to Stadelheim prison in Munich. The next day he was visited in his cell by two SS officers – one of them, chosen for this historic mission, was Theodor Eicke. In an action reminiscent of the old Dachau conceit where pressure was placed on selected prisoners to commit suicide, they gave Röhm a pistol loaded with one bullet and told him to kill himself. When he refused, Eicke and his SS colleague Michel Lippert murdered him by firing three shots into his body. They travelled back to Dachau where more than twenty other people were shot as part of the purge. Afterwards, the SS at Dachau held a celebration and allegedly drank more than a thousand litres of beer.[78] Eicke supposedly later said that 'I am proud that I shot this faggot swine [the homosexual Röhm] with my own hands.'[79]

Members of the SS – and most especially their leader, Heinrich Himmler – had proven their loyalty to Hitler during the Röhm affair. Hitler had wanted Röhm to disappear and Himmler – without a second thought – had made it happen. The motto of the SS was *Meine Ehre heisst Treue* (My honour is called loyalty) and Himmler had lived up to that promise. It was the first manifestation of an important truth within the Third Reich. Whenever Hitler wanted a ruthless task undertaken by people who could be guaranteed to carry out the action without question, he turned to the SS.

The benefits to Himmler and the SS of their involvement in the Night of the Long Knives were immediate. On 20 July 1934 the SS were given the status of an equivalent organization to the SA – previously Himmler's direct boss had been Röhm, now it was Hitler. Eicke was subsequently appointed inspector of the concentration camps and brought his organizational zeal to the entire network of protective-custody camps. Himmler and his band of followers were now at the centre of the security apparatus of the Nazi state.

As for Hitler, his hold over Germany was about to be consolidated still further.

5. The Nuremberg Laws
(1934–1935)

On 2 August 1934 the ailing President von Hindenburg finally died and Hitler became German head of state as well as Chancellor. It was an appointment that encapsulated the enormous change that had taken place in the eighteen months since Hitler had first been appointed Chancellor at the head of a cabinet which contained a number of people who were supposed to restrain him. Now, all talk of 'taming' Hitler was in the distant past. He was the undisputed ruler of Germany.

Shortly after Hitler became head of state, every member of the armed forces and civil service swore an oath of allegiance to him personally. Many of those in the army, like the young officer Johann-Adolf Graf von Kielmansegg, were pleased that Hitler had destroyed the power of the Stormtroopers and committed himself to rebuilding the German Army. Moreover, Kielmansegg and his comrades did not find it strange that they had been asked to swear an oath to Hitler. 'Prussian-German history is full of personal oaths of loyalty,' he says. 'Indeed we almost preferred that to swearing loyalty to a piece of paper. Before we had been sworn in on the Weimar constitution, which nobody knew.'[1]

In the months before this consolidation of power, Hitler had demonstrated that he did not want to increase the role of the concentration camps within the Nazi state. Quite the reverse. He sought to show the world that the initial phase of the revolution in which 'scores were settled' was now over. In the spring of 1934 he had ordered the release of several thousand prisoners in an action that Himmler later privately called 'one of the worst political mistakes the National Socialist State could have made'.[2] By the summer of 1935 fewer than 4,000 people were imprisoned within the concentration camp system – while more than twenty-five times as many were held in conventional prisons.

As for the German Jews, Nazi policy remained one of restricting their rights within Germany while simultaneously encouraging them to leave the country. But it wasn't easy for Jews to emigrate. As we have seen, Jews who decided to leave faced two enormous obstacles. The first was the Nazis' desire to steal their money before they went, and the second was the problem of finding a country that would take them. One attempted solution to this impasse was agreed just seven months after Hitler came to power in the shape of the Haavara Agreement, signed on 25 August 1933. The idea was that German Jews would use their money to purchase German equipment – mostly farm related – which would then be exported to Palestine. The Jews would then leave Germany – with virtually no money in their possession – and once they arrived in Palestine they would be reimbursed for the cost of the German equipment, which would by then have been sold to companies in Palestine. German companies benefited because not only did they manage to sell equipment for export but foreign currency would have to be used to purchase spare parts for the machinery. And, obviously, the German Jews who emigrated to Palestine benefited because they were able to take some of their wealth with them.

The background to the scheme was the perceived threat of a Jewish-organized world boycott of German goods. In June 1933 the German consul to Jerusalem, Heinrich Wolff, stressed to his colleagues back in Germany the propaganda value of cooperating with Jewish groups to facilitate the agreement. He even said that Sam Cohen, one of the architects of the deal, would use his influence with the Hebrew newspaper *Doar Hayom* to show Germany in a positive light.[3]

Not surprisingly, the Haavara Agreement was controversial. The president of the American Jewish Congress, Stephen Wise, condemned the deal. He thought the agreement damaged the prospect of an international boycott of German goods and amounted to conniving with Hitler.[4] Nonetheless, the advantages of the agreement were so beneficial to German Jews that the arrangement continued until the outbreak of war. While tens of thousands of German Jews were able to make use of this scheme and emigrate to Palestine, the significance of the Haavara Agreement in this history is much greater than just the number of Jews who were able to use it to protect their assets. What it illustrated was the ability of the Nazi authorities and Jewish agencies to work together. Indeed, it was this very notion of collaboration that so enraged many American Zionists at the time.

But what the Haavara Agreement most certainly did not demonstrate was that Hitler was somehow a 'Zionist' himself and in favour of the

creation of a Jewish state in Palestine. He made his position on this matter clear in *Mein Kampf*: 'It doesn't even enter their [that is, Jews'] heads
to build up a Jewish state in Palestine for the purpose of living there; all
they want is a central organization for their international world swindle, endowed with its sovereign right and removed from the intervention
of other states: a haven for convicted scoundrels and a university for
budding crooks.'[5] Thus, while an expedient mechanism to expel Jews
from the country quickly – like the Haavara Agreement – was acceptable for Hitler, a Jewish-controlled state was perceived as a phenomenally
dangerous development. He never wanted the Jews to be in a position to
control their own destiny.

Hitler continued, however, to be sensitive to foreign criticism of
Jewish persecution. Although there is no evidence that his personal
hatred of the Jews had lessened, he was concerned about spontaneous
attacks on Jews by ordinary Nazis. As the letter sent by the Reich Interior Ministry about the Palm Sunday pogrom in Gunzenhausen had
stated, 'The Jewish question is to be handled by the government of the
Reich,' not by local hotheads.[6] The problem Hitler faced was that many
of his supporters still felt that the measures taken so far to exclude the
Jews from the mainstream of German life had not been strong enough.
Local groups, for instance, fought to ban Jews from swimming pools
and ice rinks – even from whole towns. Rudi Bamber remembers that
by 1935 'one had to be more and more careful because many of the towns
and villages had notices, "Jews not wanted", so it was difficult to find
where one could go and be accepted as a Jew.'[7]

Even before the adoption of formal laws preventing sexual relationships
between Jews and non-Jews, the Nazi propaganda claiming that Jews were
'defiling' German maidens was having an effect on young Jewish men like
Arnon Tamir: 'Speaking for myself, I can only say that at the time – I was
just a young lad – the mere idea of becoming friendly, or more, with a German girl was poisoned right from the start by these horrible cartoons and
headlines which claimed that the Jews were contaminating German girls.
It was simply impossible for me . . . to approach a girl like any young person. We were afraid to give them the slightest justification for such claims. I
don't even want to talk about what happened to German men or women
and Jewish men and women who were friendly with or married to each
other. It must have been terrible for them.'[8]

In April 1935 the Deputy Führer, Rudolf Hess, wrote to party members warning them not to 'vent their feelings by acts of terror against individual Jews'. Such actions only made it harder for Hitler to 'rebuke at any time allegations of atrocities and boycotts made by Jews abroad'.[9] But the spontaneous attacks did not stop, and four months later Hjalmar Schacht, the Economics Minister, and the man charged by Hitler with generating enough money to finance a massive armaments programme, complained that illegal anti-Semitic actions were damaging the economy.[10] Schacht did not protest about the harassment and persecution of Jews on moral grounds, he simply wanted the illegality to stop. By implication, if the Nazi state could pass laws that codified and limited the scope of the persecution and in the process ended arbitrary actions against the Jews, that would represent a helpful step forward.

Legislation was finally introduced to outlaw sexual relationships between Jews and non-Jews in September 1935, when a new law for the Protection of German Blood and German Honour was passed at the time of the Nuremberg rally. Wilhelm Frick, the Minister of the Interior, had said at the end of July that legislation outlawing marriages between Jews and non-Jews was in preparation, but the speed with which this new legislation was finally adopted was extraordinary. The first hint that it was coming was in a speech given by Gerhard Wagner, Reich Doctors' Leader, on 12 September. The following day Hitler said that he wanted the law passed in Nuremberg. The only difficulty was that there was currently no law to pass. So a team of civil servants, including Bernhard Lösener, a specialist in Jewish matters at the Interior Ministry, flew from Berlin to Nuremberg to draft the proposed legislation. On the 14th Hitler decided that he wanted to add another law to the mix – stripping Jews of German citizenship – so this too was created.

On the evening of 15 September, at a specially convened session of the Reichstag held at the Cultural Association in Nuremberg, Hitler announced that he had been compelled to bring in this new anti-Semitic legislation because 'loud complaints of provocative actions by individual members of this race are coming in from all sides'. So it was necessary 'to prevent this behavior from leading to quite determined defensive action on the part of the outraged population'. Hitler argued that his proposed legislation was an attempt to permit 'tolerable relations' between the Germans and the Jewish population. But he warned that if the 'international Jewish agitation' continued, he would conduct a 'new evaluation' of the situation.[11]

It was a classic Hitlerian performance – a mix of threat and falsehood. Just as he had at the time of the April 1933 boycott, he framed his actions as necessary to ensure that the outrage felt by the general population at the actions of the Jews did not turn violent. He also implied that the treatment that the German Jews received was determined in part by the conduct of the international Jewish community. The unspoken assumption underlying the speech was that if other countries let Hitler pursue the policies he wished, the German Jews would be spared even worse persecution.

After Hitler had spoken, Hermann Göring as Reichstag President gave a speech in which he slavishly supported his Führer. He focused in large part on what, at first sight, might appear to be the least significant part of the legislation that Hitler proposed that day – the Reich 'flag' act. This law, which called for the adoption of the swastika flag as the symbol of Germany, seemed relatively innocuous when compared with the overtly anti-Semitic nature of the other two pieces of legislation, but the origins of the flag act are revealing. Up until this point Germany had two legal flags – the swastika and the black, white and red flag of the German Empire. Hitler when he came to power had been careful not to offend traditionalists like President von Hindenburg and insist that the old flag of the Empire be dropped completely. So – bizarrely – German merchant ships had flown two national flags. This was the background to an incident in New York in July 1935 when protesters boarded the German liner the SS *Bremen* and threw the swastika flag into the water. Because the swastika flag was not the sole legal symbol of Germany, it had been possible for the Americans to argue that Germany as a country had not been insulted. The Nazi government was particularly enraged when Louis Brodsky, a Jewish American magistrate, did not treat the case as seriously as they wished. Hans Frank, president of the Reich Academy of Law, said that Brodsky was part of a Jewish 'menace' and that it was 'most deplorable and also a most dangerous precedent when a Jew in so highly cultured a nation as the United States is permitted to debase the robe of judge to the extent of venting [the] undying hatred of his race . . .'.[12]

This new act changed the status of the swastika flag, and now – as Göring put it – 'he who offends this flag insults the nation.'[13] Göring professed to 'feel sorry' for the Americans in the context of the *Bremen* incident, because they had been forced to witness the actions of a 'brazen Jew'. But from now on the swastika flag symbolized that Germany would remain true to Nazism 'for all eternity'. Tellingly, he added that it was 'self-evident' that 'no Jew may be allowed to hoist this sacred insignia.' Shortly after Göring's speech all three elements of what became known to the world as the Nuremberg Laws were passed – the Reich Flag Law, the Law for the Protection of German Blood and German Honour, and the Reich Citizenship Law which revoked the citizenship of German Jews.

Hitler never revealed publicly why he chose to move so suddenly in September 1935 to pass this anti-Semitic legislation, though the idea that Jews should not be considered German citizens nor be able to have sexual relations with non-Jews was certainly not new. But one suggested reason for this precise timing is persuasive: that Hitler had actually planned to make a broad statement about his foreign-policy demands at Nuremberg, but had been dissuaded at the last minute from doing so by Konstantin von Neurath, the Foreign Minister. Since Hitler had already called for a special sitting of members of the Reichstag and now had nothing but the Flag Law to put before them, he suddenly decided to push forward with the anti-Semitic legislation instead, motivated chiefly by a desire to bridge the gap in expectations between the activists in the party who were persecuting the Jews on the streets and the officials in government like Schacht who wanted greater clarity in the regime's position on the Jews.[14] In addition, it might also have been that Hitler thought the anti-Semitic legislation fitted well with the sentiments behind the Flag Law. He would surely have felt humiliated by the spectacle of the swastika flag floating in the water of New York harbour – a city the Nazis always associated with the Jews – torn from the SS *Bremen*, the pride of the German merchant fleet. There was certainly a pattern in Hitler's behaviour, as we shall see later in the 1930s and again during the war, of lashing out against the German Jews in a reaction against foreign actions that angered him.[15]

In practical terms the new laws to a large extent only reflected the reality that already existed in much of Germany, since even before the legislation local Nazis had put pressure on non-Jews to separate themselves from Jews, whether in personal or business life. But nonetheless, the Nuremberg Laws marked a watershed in the attitude of the Nazi state towards German Jews. Now the law of the Reich – not just Nazi party hotheads – called for the ruthless separation of the Jews from the rest of the community. It was not only that the Jews were legally no longer 'true' Germans, the new legislation also invaded the private sphere of every German citizen. The German state had proclaimed that it had the right to decide with whom you could have sexual intercourse. The Gestapo – the secret police – could now examine what went on in private in each house. Everyone was vulnerable to denunciation by a mean-spirited neighbour. Who was that stranger of the opposite sex who visited you last night? Didn't they look 'Jewish'? More than that, the state could demand to know exactly what sexual acts you took part in behind closed doors, since they applied an extraordinarily wide definition of 'sexual intercourse'. The Reich Supreme Court declared the following year that 'the concept of sexual intercourse' did 'not include every indecent act, but is not confined to actual intercourse, i.e. apart from intercourse itself, [it includes] all sexual activities with a member of the opposite sex which are intended in place of actual intercourse to satisfy the sexual urges of at least one of the partners'.[16]

Then there was the continuing problem, for the Nazis, of working out who was a Jew and who was not – information that was vital in order to enforce the new legislation. But despite the opening sentence of the Law for the Protection of German Blood and German Honour declaring that 'purity of German blood' was 'essential' for the 'continued existence of the German people', the Nazis could not tell by examining 'blood' just who was a Jew and who was not, and there was no other definition of 'Jewishness' anywhere in the Nuremberg legislation. As a consequence the laws as passed on 15 September 1935 were unenforceable. Only in the middle of November 1935 were regulations finally announced which defined who was a 'Jew'. This document talked about 'Jewish blood' and 'racially full Jews', but it had to resort to a religious definition to describe who was Jewish and who was not. It stated: 'A Jew is anyone who is descended from at least three grandparents who are racially full Jews.' But then it said that a 'grandparent shall be considered as full blooded if he or she belonged to the Jewish religious

community'.[17] So the Nazis determined your 'race' by the religious affiliation of your grandparents.

The question of what to do about those Germans who had mixed
ancestry occupied a great deal of the drafters' time. Some Germans who
were ardent nationalists – and appeared to be living an 'Aryan' life – had
two Jewish grandparents. Yet other people with two Jewish grandparents were, to Nazi eyes, obviously Jews. The solution the Nazi officials
devised was complex. It relied, once again, on examining the religious
affiliation of the individuals concerned. So if you had two grandparents
who were Jewish – by the definition of the decree – but you yourself had
not married a Jew and were living a non-Jewish religious life, then you
were not Jewish. However, if you had two Jewish grandparents and had
married a Jew, or were worshipping as a Jew, then you were Jewish.

It was a mess. What the decree exposed was the utter fallacy of a blood
or racial definition of Jewishness. For if the Nazis were serious in their
racial beliefs, how could one person who had two Jewish grandparents be
considered not Jewish, whereas another who had two Jewish grandparents be considered Jewish? Their background ought to mean that the
amount of 'Jewish blood' flowing within their veins was exactly the same.

Nonetheless, Hitler proclaimed the Nuremberg Laws a success and
called for the nation not to 'stray from the straight and narrow path of
the law'.[18] He clearly saw these anti-Semitic measures not only as an
ideological statement of the values of the Third Reich, but also as a
means of restraining the wilder elements in the party who sought to
pursue their own attacks. The day after the laws were passed, he
reminded the party faithful that they should 'continue to refrain' from
taking 'independent action' against Jews.[19]

Emil Klein, who joined the Nazi Party in the early 1920s, saw nothing unusual in these discriminatory measures. 'There wasn't only
apartheid in Germany alone,' he says, 'one heard about apartheid in
America. It was nothing special that happened in Germany. It was actually only a part of what was taking place – here and there – the whole
world over.'[20] And while he is right – and it is important to remember –
that racial discrimination was not confined to Germany at the time,
these comments are also disingenuous. For something 'special' was
happening in Germany, since the vehemence with which the Nazis
embraced racial theory was astounding.

There were also, paradoxically, many German Jews who saw the Nuremberg Laws in an almost positive light. Yes, they were obviously discriminatory, but the new laws appeared to outline the limits of persecution. 'These were the rules,'[21] and German Jews should live within the rules. It was as if the new anti-Semitic legislation offered Jews protection from arbitrary persecution by local thugs.

Many ordinary Germans did not overly concern themselves with the measures taken against the Jews. What mattered more to them was the massive reduction in unemployment that had occurred since Hitler came to power – from 6 million unemployed in 1933 to fewer than 2 million by 1936. Even though the Nazis massaged the figures – for instance women were no longer included in the data – it was an undoubted success. 'It was in 1934 that you saw that something might be changing,' says Erna Krantz, then growing up in Bavaria. It was 'a glimmer of hope for everyone. Not just for the unemployed, but for, well, for everybody, because we all know that we were downtrodden, and in 1933 Germany had collapsed. We can't hide the facts, can we? And that's how it was, lots of things got better. The salaries for civil servants and white-collar workers got better. Everything was improving a little, I can't remember exactly, I only know about that time from our personal situation as a household. You saw the unemployed disappearing from the streets. That was already a big plus. Of course you did notice that there was a certain line behind it, the youth were being drawn into sport, drawn into community service above all, which was something very significant. They started the construction of the motorways, and all that provided work and took people off the streets. Yes, it definitely was a positive time, otherwise why in the end did the masses follow this man? Why?'[22]

This economic success was obtained primarily by borrowing on a large scale, most notably for a massive expansion in military spending. Between 1933 and 1935 expenditure on the German military increased from less than 1 per cent of German national income to nearly 10 per cent – a bigger and quicker increase than ever seen before in peacetime in a capitalist state.[23]

Hitler's primary focus during this period was not on the 'Jewish question', but on building up Germany's armed forces. Almost everything else was subordinate to this aim. As for his foreign policy, he wanted to deal with foreign nations one by one, rather than through the League of Nations. To this end – and to pursue his policy of rearmament – he withdrew Germany from the League soon after he came to power in 1933. Two years later, in June 1935, Hitler's ambassador to the United Kingdom, Joachim von Ribbentrop, signed the Anglo-German Naval Agreement in London, which laid down the permissible size of the German fleet as a proportion of the British navy. The agreement broke the Versailles treaty, but there were no adverse consequences for Germany. Hitler said the day the Anglo-German Naval Agreement was signed was the happiest of his life.[24]

None of this should have come as a surprise to anyone who had read *Mein Kampf*. Hitler considered Great Britain a possible ally, and he wanted strong armed forces so that he could gain new territory for Germany in the east. He had said all this back in the 1920s. However, he had also said how much he hated the Jews and that he saw them as a deadly threat. It would still be some years before he would act decisively on this issue – but that time was coming ever closer.

6. Education and Empire-Building
(1935–1938)

In pursuit of what he called the '*völkische* state',[1] Hitler sought to change
the consciousness of the entire German nation. 'The *völkische* state', he
wrote in *Mein Kampf*, 'must perform the most gigantic educational task.
And some day this will seem to be a greater deed than the most victorious wars.'[2] A crucial part of this 'educational task' was awakening
'Aryan' Germans to the danger of the Jews. But while Hitler could leg-
islate for persecution of the Jews via new laws, he could not so easily
change the mentality of the nation. And in September 1935, the same
month as the announcement of the Nuremberg Laws, it was clear that
he was some way from achieving his self-appointed 'gigantic educational task'.

That September one supporter of the Social Democratic Party in
Saxony wrote: 'the majority of the population, however, ignore the
defamation of the Jews; they even openly choose to shop in Jewish
department stores and adopt a rather unfriendly attitude to the
Stormtrooper on duty there . . .'[3] The situation had not changed nearly
two years later, when the Gestapo in Bavaria reported that Jewish cattle
dealers still controlled most of the market and large numbers of peasants
remained content to do business with them.[4]

Hitler had always known that the 're-education' of the nation
would take time, and that it was vital, in particular, to target the young
so that they would be prepared for the exacting tasks ahead. 'In our
eyes,' he said to an audience of 54,000 Hitler Youth at Nuremberg in
September 1935, 'the German youth of the future must be slender and
supple, swift as greyhounds, tough as leather, and hard as Krupp steel.
We must cultivate a new man in order to prevent the ruin of our *Volk*
by the degeneration manifested in our age.'[5]

Many of the young were receptive to Nazi propaganda because life
seemed to be getting better – both for them and for their parents. 'When
Hitler got to power, suddenly we had work,' says Wilhelm Roes,
who grew up in Germany during the 1930s. 'The bad mood at home

[changed], it was always a bad mood at home when I was a child, because my mother at eleven o'clock didn't know what to put on the table at twelve. In '34 my father got work. I think he earned 380 marks. Our situation greatly improved. And he said that's what the Führer did. Well, what was I supposed to feel? You didn't really have to brainwash me at all. I'd taken it up at my mother's knee.'[6]

Teachers within the Nazi education system spent a great deal of time telling their 'Aryan' pupils that they were superior to the Jews, so that the overall context in which anti-Semitism was taught was one of positivity. Maria Mauth, for instance, remembers her teachers in north Germany in the 1930s telling her that 'only Germans were valuable human beings – there was a little booklet called *German Inventors, German Poets, German Musicians* – nothing else existed. And we devoured it. We were absolutely convinced that we were the greatest.'[7] Erna Krantz, a schoolgirl in Munich at the same time, thought that 'A lot was done in the educational field, the young had many opportunities . . . everything was being organized. We weren't living in affluence like today, but there was order and discipline. And we also had very many role models. That was encouraged. Good writers, they were being emphasized, philosophers too were emphasized . . . Well, I have to say it was somewhat contagious, you used to say that if you tell a young person every day, "You are something special," then in the end they will believe you. Well, I mean they tried to breed the so-called German race. Again and again they were saying, we want this, and that, we want healthy people, we want strong, working people, fit people. Above all the Germanness came through, which had been drilled, strengthened, in those years, the Germanness.'[8]

Although it was relatively easy to tell children that they were better than others, it was harder to get across the message that Jews were dangerous, especially if the pupils knew Jews who were benevolent. Wilhelm Roes, for example, had trouble relating the anti-Semitism that he was taught to the real world around him. In the town where he lived there were Jewish shops, and he remembers how the Jewish owners donated 'clothes for orphans'. As a result he 'didn't like those caricatures in *Der Stürmer*. I couldn't understand them.'[9]

One way teachers countered this disconnect between the Jews of Nazi propaganda and the flesh-and-blood Jews that pupils encountered was to emphasize the alleged deceitful nature of the Jews.[10] The most infamous example of this was the children's book *Der Giftpilz* (The Poisonous Mushroom), published by Julius Streicher's own publishing company in Nuremberg in 1938.[11] The title story in the collection tells how a child learns from his mother that just as it can be hard to distinguish good mushrooms in the forest from poisonous mushrooms, so it can be difficult to spot the evil nature of Jews, especially when they try to 'disguise' themselves. The advantages for the propagandist of this story are obvious. Jews are seen to be at their most treacherous when they are charming and helpful – just as, by implication, the poisonous mushroom in the forest appears to be the most attractive, but in reality is the most dangerous.

The Jews were thus presented as the antithesis of 'Germanness'. True Germans had no need to hide their genuine nature, while the Jews felt compelled to conceal their duplicitousness. While the 'Aryan' pupils were 'something special', the Jews were something poisonous. In a pamphlet entitled *The Jewish Question in Education*, written in 1937 by Fritz Fink and publicized in *Der Stürmer*, teachers were told that they must 'plant the knowledge of the Jew deep in the hearts of our youth from their childhood' as it was vital that the young learnt about 'the true depravity and danger of the Jew'. For Fink, a school inspector, the 'racial and Jewish question' was the 'central' issue of Nazism. The most powerful way to get the message across that contact with Jews was to be avoided, he argued, was via the teaching of 'science'. For just as a 'herd of wild horses' is never led by a 'wild boar', so 'each kind sticks with its own, and seeks a leader of the same species.' Children should learn that animals naturally know what is best for them. It is only human beings who subvert nature by breeding with different races. 'Only inferior members of various races mix with each other,' wrote Fink, 'the bad mixes with the bad. It is thus clear that the bastard always gets the worst of it, that is, he unites only the bad characteristics of the races he comes from. A teacher who presents his students with such ideas will have an easy time in explaining the meaning of the Nuremberg Laws to the youth. The children will see in the Nuremberg Laws nothing other than a return to the natural, to the divine, order.'[12]

Hitler understood that it was easier for Nazi propagandists to influence impressionable children than less pliable grown-ups. For adults it could prove harder – but not impossible – to reconcile their theoretical understanding of the Nazi case against the Jews with their personal encounters with Jewish Germans. Karl Boehm-Tettelbach, for instance, as a young Luftwaffe officer, had good reason to be grateful to a German Jew in 1935. Boehm-Tettelbach crash-landed his plane in a field and was rescued by a German Jew. Wanting to say thank-you, he took his rescuer to dinner and was surprised when the man 'suddenly said he is a Jew' and asked 'if I was afraid of being with Jews'. Boehm-Tettelbach told the man that he wasn't – after all, this man had saved his life. 'That's the first time I realized that something could happen with the Jews,' says Boehm-Tettelbach. But this incident didn't make him alter his desire to support the regime. 'In Berlin especially,' he says, 'they [the Nazis] claimed that the lawyers were mostly Jews, so when they said they had too many lawyers, one understood that. To be anti-Semitic doesn't mean that you kill the people. You might not get socially close together, you might not like them very much, but that doesn't mean that you kill the people . . .'[13] While feeling 'sorry' for the German Jews in the wake of the Nuremberg Laws, Boehm-Tettelbach admits that 'it didn't worry me much.'

In his relaxed attitude to the persecution of the German Jews during the 1930s, Boehm-Tettelbach captures the mood of many non-Jewish Germans. They were open to the suggestion that 'something should be done' about the alleged power and influence of the Jews, and if they subsequently felt uneasy about any excesses in anti-Semitic actions, they just looked the other way. As for the Jews they knew and liked, they were treated as a class apart.

Leading Nazis emphasized not just what they claimed were the practical aspects of the 'Jewish problem' – like the number of Jewish lawyers in Berlin – but also the underlying issue of race. To them, issues like the disproportionate number of Jews in the legal profession were the symptom of this 'problem' but race was always the cause. 'We shall gather together the best blood,' said Walther Darré, the Agriculture Minister. 'Just as we are now breeding our Hanover horse from the few remaining pure-blooded male and female stock, so we shall see the same type of breeding over the next generation of the pure type of Nordic German.'[14]

Statements like these didn't just allow the Nazis to promote their virulent anti-Semitism. They also helped link their racial anti-Semitism with their eugenic beliefs – or, in Nazi terminology, 'racial hygiene'.

The connection between 'racial hygiene' and the persecution of the Jews was not immediately apparent at the start of the Third Reich, but the two ideas were always intertwined for the Nazis. For just as they thought it was essential that Jewish blood was not allowed to mix with 'Aryan' blood so it was also vital that those 'Aryans' who were the weakest were not allowed to breed at all. Just as, to use Walther Darré's analogy, a Nazi believer would not mate a Hanover horse with an inferior breed of horse, he would not mate a healthy Hanover horse with a sick one.

So important to Hitler was this belief that only healthy 'Aryan' Germans should be allowed to reproduce that at the 1929 Nuremberg party conference he had warned: 'Through our modern sentimental humanitarianism, we make an effort to maintain the weak at the expense of the healthy . . . Criminals are allowed to reproduce, degenerates are laboriously coddled in an artificial way. Thus we slowly grow the weak and kill the strong.'[15] He even went as far as to say: 'If Germany gained a million children a year and eliminated 700,000–800,000 of the weakest, then the final result would probably be an increase in strength. The most dangerous thing is for us to cut ourselves off from the natural process of selection . . .' The idea that Hitler was suggesting in 1929 – just four years before he became Chancellor – the possibility of murdering seven or eight out of every ten new babies born in Germany is hugely revealing. For Hitler, the creation of the *völkische* state meant, in principle, killing enormous numbers of 'weak' Germans.

Given his belief that Germany should be genetically remodelled, it was scarcely surprising that less than six months after he came to power Hitler signed the Law for the Prevention of Genetically Diseased Offspring. This legislation called for Genetic Health Courts to order the compulsory sterilization of any individual who had one of a number of named disorders. Some of these disorders were not 'genetic' at all, and allowed Germans deemed socially undesirable, such as alcoholics, to be sterilized.

The Nazis were not the first to pass legislation on forced sterilization – many states in America had already done so – but they did push the idea forward with greater zeal than anyone else. Paul Eggert, from the Rhineland, for instance, was forcibly sterilized as a child under this legislation. He did not have a 'genetic' illness, but was simply an objectionable citizen as far as the Nazis were concerned. He came from a deprived background and his father was an alcoholic. As a child he begged from local farmers, and if he didn't return home with food then his father beat him. Eventually, as he puts it, 'the [local] people had enough of it.'[16] So he was taken away from his parents and put in a special children's home near Dortmund where he was told that he needed to have a hernia operation. It wasn't until after the war that he learnt that he had not had an operation for a hernia, but had been sterilized.

From Hitler's perspective, the sterilization law was only a beginning. While the new legislation meant that future generations would be spared the 'burden', as he saw it, of caring for some of the state's most needy citizens, it did not deal with the immediate situation. Hitler's own aspirations were encapsulated in the film *Opfer der Vergangenheit* (Victims of the Past), released in 1937. This documentary, shown in every cinema in Germany, argued for the killing of the mentally disabled. There were two reasons, the film's commentary said, why this action was necessary. First, because it offended the 'Creator's law of natural selection and order' to keep these people alive, and second, because 'the money it takes to care for these people could be put to better use helping strong and healthy children.'[17]

Some German doctors approved of this murderous idea. In 1935 the psychiatrist Dr Karl Knab wrote that German 'asylums' contained not just 'idiots on the lowest level' but 'spiritual ruins'. Moreover, this 'patient material . . . as mere cost-occasioning ballast, should be eradicated by being killed in a painless fashion'. This was 'justifiable', said Dr Knab, for financial reasons in the context of 'a nation fighting for its very existence'.[18]

Gerhard Wagner, Reich Doctors' Leader, spoke in support of *Opfer der Vergangenheit* at the film's premiere. He, more than anyone, knew his Führer's own views on this subject, since in 1935 Hitler had told him that during a future war they should plan on murdering the seriously mentally ill.[19] It is significant that Hitler believed that a forthcoming war would allow him to pursue such a radical course of action – not least because it would be under cover of this war that he would also preside over the mass extermination of the Jews.

Meanwhile, compulsory sterilization was carried out in Germany on an enormous scale – between 300,000 and 400,000 people suffered as a result.[20] This led to a seismic shift in the role of the medical profession.

No longer was the sole interest of doctors the health of their patients. If doctors decided they wished to sterilize a patient under the criteria set by the new legislation, they were legally obliged to ignore their patient's objections. Gerhard Wagner saw no conflict of interest here, because he believed the prime consideration for doctors should be the wellbeing of the nation.[21] As a consequence, the Nazis claimed that doctors had a greater responsibility than previously – no longer ministering merely to the needs of the individual, but now to the entire *Volkskörper*, the body of the people, all in pursuit of the goal of the *'völkische* state'.[22]

What the *'völkische* state' represented was a country in which the state now had the legal right to question every life choice that you made. Nazis could inquire into your detailed family background to determine whom you could and could not marry in order to assess whether or not you had the 'right' to reproduce. If you became pregnant and the baby you carried was deemed racially useful, you were forbidden from having an abortion. No longer could you choose not to work; that would make you 'work shy' and liable to 'protective custody'. You could not even choose your friends, for if your neighbours disapproved of the company you kept you could be denounced as 'asocial' – someone who was not a reliable member of the racial community.

Yet, despite all of these restrictions, the majority of Germans still supported Hitler. In the 1934 referendum on the merging of the posts of President and Chancellor, for example, 88 per cent of the electorate wanted Hitler to become head of state after Hindenburg's death. At the elections in 1936, which also contained a referendum question asking if voters approved of Hitler's action in ordering the military reoccupation of Germany's Rhineland, support for the Nazis was more than 98 per cent. These elections, we should remember, were held in a non-democratic state with none of the safeguards present in truly free elections, and the data cannot be used to imply a precise statistical level of support for the regime – but nonetheless the results remain enlightening. It is easy to see why the leading scholar on Hitler concludes from all the available evidence that the 1936 result represented 'an overhelming show of acclamation for Hitler'.[23] Many Germans in the 1930s would no doubt have agreed with Erna Krantz, who, looking back after the war, said, 'It was, I thought, a better time [than today]. To say this is of course taking a risk. But I'll say it anyway.'[24]

For a young woman like Erna Krantz in the 1930s it was not just a question of the positives of life under the Nazis outweighing the negatives. To a large extent the negatives of the regime as we see it – the concentration camps, the isolation of minority groups targeted by the Nazis and so on – were perceived as part of the positive. The concentration camps were thought necessary to remove the undesirables from the streets; the new racial-based teaching was welcomed as it told the young they were special; and as for the exclusion of the Jews, well, as the banker Johannes Zahn says, there was a perception among a section of the population that they had 'gone too far'[25] in Germany. So as long as you conformed to the Nazi ideal – and millions of Germans did just that – it was possible to enjoy yourself in Hitler's Third Reich during the 1930s. Many of those who did would later say that they had no idea that the persecution of the Jews, encapsulated in the Nuremberg Laws and other restrictive legislation, would lead to the Holocaust. And while in one sense that is true – there is no evidence at this point that Hitler had a blueprint for what was to come – it is also misleading. Because a fundamental reason that millions of Germans could enjoy life in Hitler's Germany was that they enthusiastically supported the racial theories that were at the core of Nazi thought. They embraced the idea that they were better than others. As a consequence, it was possible to treat as lesser human beings those they were told weren't like them. The argument was not about others being inferior – that was accepted by large numbers of people – the argument was about how these 'lesser' people should be treated.

As for the Jews, the Nuremberg Laws confirmed that they were to be excluded from the new Germany. Increasingly, Jews confined themselves to their own communities. There, life was tolerable for many of them. Günther Ruschin, a teenager living in the heart of the Jewish community in Berlin, remembers that he had a 'good home' and 'we had no difficulties . . . We went to [a Jewish] school, we came home.' His father, who had fought in the German Army during the First World War, was a cantor at the local synagogue and 'told everybody, I'm a German Jew, nothing will happen to me'.[26]

Günther's father, along with many other German Jews, remained convinced that it would be best for them all to remain at home, safe – as he saw it – within the Jewish community in Berlin. And, broadly speaking, the evidence around them from the summer of 1935 to the summer of 1937 seemed to support that view. Though there were still isolated actions against Jews, and regulations further excluding the Jews continued to be issued – for example, from October 1936 civil servants were banned from visiting Jewish doctors – there was no systematic mass violence against the German Jews. But what many took to be a sign of the regime settling down was merely a pause before the implementation of more radical measures.

One reason for the relative inaction of the regime in relation to the Jews during this period was Hitler's desire to ensure the success of the 1936 Berlin Olympics. In the United States there had been calls – supported by public figures like Mayor La Guardia of New York – for America to boycott the games. But the president of the American Olympic Committee, Avery Brundage, convinced the American Athletic Union to send a team to Berlin. With the participation not just of the Americans, but forty-eight other countries, the Berlin games were a coup for the Third Reich. Not only did Germany win the most medals, but the event was a propaganda triumph for the Nazis, as they succeeded in subverting the Olympic ideal and turning it into a vehicle for the aggrandizement of their racist state. The Nazi message was encapsulated in the opening images of Leni Riefenstahl's film of the games, *Olympia*, in which the Olympic torch is carried into the Berlin Olympic stadium by a blond-haired athlete, the epitome of the 'Aryan' ideal, and welcomed by Nazi salutes.

Even more extraordinary, from the perspective of today, is the assessment of Hitler made by the former British Prime Minister, David Lloyd George, after he had visited the Berghof, Hitler's Alpine retreat near Berchtesgaden, in September 1936. Writing in the *Daily Express*, Lloyd George said that Hitler was 'a born leader of men. A magnetic dynamic personality with a single-minded purpose, a resolute will, and a dauntless heart.'[27] He had observed that Hitler was worshipped as a 'national hero who has saved his country from utter despondence and degradation'. In Germany, Lloyd George had detected 'a passion for unity' and now 'Catholic and Protestant, Prussian and Bavarian, employer and workman, rich and poor, have been consolidated into one people.' He wrote that 'There was a revivalist atmosphere. It has had an extraordinary effect in unifying the nation.' As a result 'the people are more cheerful.'

What, one might ask, about the German Jews? Lloyd George knew that they were subject to persecution within Germany – he even made a passing reference to it in his article.[28] So how could he say that 'the people are more cheerful' – unless, perhaps, he did not consider German Jews truly 'German'? The very possibility of this might appear surprising, given that Lloyd George had supported the Balfour Declaration of November 1917 in which the British government had said that they viewed 'with favour the establishment in Palestine of a national home for the Jewish people'. However, the exact motives of the politicians behind the Declaration have long been the subject of controversy. Indeed, one historian has concluded that 'the men who sired it [the Balfour Declaration] were Christian and Zionist and, in many cases, anti-Semitic. They believed the Jews controlled the world.'[29]

In Britain, Lloyd George was not alone in lauding Hitler despite the Nazi persecution of the Jews. While it is certainly the case that neo-Nazi beliefs never became widespread in the country – Oswald Mosley's British Union of Fascists did not come close to achieving an electoral breakthrough in the 1930s – there was still a good deal of casual anti-Semitism. For instance, Johannes Zahn, the German banker, remembers hearing anti-Semitic remarks from British financiers on a trip to London.[30] As for Eugene Leviné, he believes that he encountered more anti-Semitism in Britain in the 1930s than he had experienced in Germany in the 1920s. 'I feel that in the social way the English are more anti-Semitic [than the Germans]. As people so often very kindly say, "After all, we don't gas Jews." No . . . but they certainly don't let them join their golf club. And, if you say to people with whom you're quite friendly, why won't they let so and so into a golf club? [they answer] "Well you see, dear, if you let one of them in, they'll bring all their friends." '[31] Sentiments against admitting Jews from abroad could also be detected in newspapers – a *Sunday Express* editorial in 1938, for example, announced that 'just now there is a big influx of foreign Jews into Britain. They are over-running our country.'[32]

The prejudice that the Jews were a group apart – as described by Eugene Leviné – was behind much of the anti-Semitic rhetoric. As for Lloyd George, he appears to have subscribed to the view that the Jews were immensely powerful and operated across national boundaries – a view also held in an extreme way by Adolf Hitler.[33] Such common ground may have helped Lloyd George form his eulogistic assessment of the German leader – we can't know for sure. What is certain is that while in the afterglow of the 1936 Berlin Olympics, Hitler had been able to charm Lloyd George and reassure him about Germany's development, the following year he would present an altogether different face to the world.

Nineteen-thirty-seven was in many ways a turning point. With the Olympics behind him, Hitler's rhetoric returned to the fevered levels it had last reached in the early 1920s in the beer halls of Bavaria. In a speech at the Nuremberg rally on 13 September 1937, he claimed that Bolshevism was 'the greatest menace with which the culture and civilization of the human race have been threatened since the collapse of the nations in Antiquity'.[34] Crucially, he raised once again the link that he believed existed between the Jews and the Bosheviks. The 'increasing upheaval' that the world faced, he said, was caused by the 'rulers of Jewish Bolshevism in Moscow'. In case anyone had missed this linkage, he added, 'when I quite intentionally present this problem as Jewish, then you, my party comrades, know that this is not an unverified assumption, but a fact proven by irrefutable evidence.' Hitler proceeded to give his audience a history lesson – albeit a distorted and twisted one – starting with his views on 'Russia'. (Hitler persisted in referring to 'Russia' even though Russia was just one of a number of republics within the Soviet Union.) He claimed that the Jews had managed to 'penetrate' the ruling elite in 'Russia' and had succeeded in 'exterminating' the previous leadership. The Jews were a 'foreign race' who had seized 'utter control' of Russian civilization and now wanted to use Russia as a 'bridgehead' to conquer other peoples.

Hitler conjured up an almost depraved fantasy, in which 'insane masses' supported by 'asocials' would go wild and take the indigenous people to the 'scaffolds to bleed to death'. And behind all this mayhem were the Jews. That was because Jews found it necessary to 'undertake the extermination' of the elite within any country that they sought to control. Hitler reminded his audience that in Germany 'we have all experienced the same thing' – by which he meant the Spartacist uprising in Berlin, orchestrated by Communists and socialists in 1919, and the Bavarian Soviet Republic later that same year.

Hitler said that Germany had 'a serious interest in preventing this

Bolshevist plague from spreading even further in Europe'. He recalled that although Germany had fought against other European nations in the past, these wars had always been between 'civilized' nations. But Bolshevism was something different. The rulers in Moscow were an 'uncivilized, Jewish-Bolshevik, international league of criminals'. The Nazis deserved praise for having prevented Jewish 'scum' from dictating their demands to German workers. Moreover, Germans today were 'even better' soldiers than before, and stood ready to confront anyone who sought to bring the Bolshevik 'menace' into Germany.

It was the situation in Spain, claimed Hitler, where a civil war raged, that had motivated his bellicose speech, especially since Stalin had supplied weapons and a small number of combatants to the republicans in their struggle against the nationalists. But once again Hitler was being disingenuous, for he had held these views since the early 1920s but for a whole variety of reasons had not thought it expedient to voice them so aggressively in public for years. It was all a question of tactics, as he explained to a meeting of party leaders in April 1937, six months before his bloodthirsty Nuremberg speech. In this private forum, he said that he understood why there were those who wanted stronger measures to be taken against the Jews, such as 'marking' Jewish businesses with a special insignia, but activists needed to recognize that his 'main concern' was 'always to avoid taking a step that I might later have to retrace and not to take a step which could damage us in any way. You must understand that I always go as far as I dare – but no further. It is vital to have a sixth sense which tells you broadly: "What can I still do, what can I not do?" ' Thus, while they all agreed about the danger the Jews posed, he always had to bear in mind what was possible at any given moment.[35] It's a speech that offers a vital insight into Hitler's mentality – he admitted that he would like to be more radical in his persecution of the Jews, but saw that it was politically necessary to advance slowly towards his ultimate goal. Goebbels in his diary entry of 30 November 1937 reveals just what that goal was: 'Talked about the Jewish question [with Hitler] for a long time . . . The Jews must be ejected from Germany, from the whole of Europe. This will take a while, but it will happen and it must happen. The Führer is completely committed to this.'[36]

In parallel to this tactical approach to the 'Jewish question', Hitler was also careful about how he spoke of his other deeply held conviction – his wish to create a German empire in the western regions of the Soviet Union. He never voiced this desire in public during the 1930s. But in private, the year before his 1937 speech at Nuremberg, he had made clear his intention to confront the 'danger' of Bolshevism. In a memorandum he wrote in August 1936, at the time he appointed Hermann Göring head of the economic programme known as the 'Four Year Plan', Hitler reiterated that – on the military front – it was the destiny of Germany to deal with Bolshevism. Since Germany was overpopulated, it was necessary to gain more land, thus 'the final solution [to this problem] lies in extending our living space.'[37] The use of the words 'final solution' in this context is worth noting – since the plan to exterminate the Jews would also come to be known by the same two words. Here they are meant to distinguish the transitional phase, during which the Germans would build up their military strength, from the 'final solution' phase, when the actual military conflict would commence.

At a cabinet meeting on 4 September 1936, Göring read out Hitler's memo and stated that the logic of it was clear – 'the showdown with Russia is inevitable.'[38] Two months later, in November 1936, Goebbels confirmed that he too was aware that the time was rapidly approaching when Germany would have to confront the Soviet Union. After lunch with Hitler, he had a 'thorough talk alone with the Führer' and concluded that 'Rearmament continues. We're investing fabulous sums. In 1941 we'll have completed it. The confrontation with Bolshevism is coming . . . Dominance in Europe for us is virtually certain.'[39]

In his fiery speech at Nuremberg ten months later, in September 1937, Hitler made an attempt to close the gap between what he was saying in private and what he was saying in public, though he never went as far as to say that Germany would invade the Soviet Union. Instead, he told the world that it was necessary for Germany both to rearm and to be prepared to fight against the Bolshevik menace should the 'Russians' attack. And since, according to Hitler, behind the Bolsheviks stood the Jews, a military conflict with the Russians would also mean an armed conflict with the Jewish 'menace'. Even at this early stage, it was obvious that any war between Germany and the Soviet Union would be no ordinary fight, but a struggle between different ideologies, and – as Hitler saw it – different 'races'.

Those in the German government who did not enthusiastically

embrace this vision were soon discarded. Hjalmar Schacht, the Reich Minister of Economics, who had done so much to make rearmament possible by his creative reorganization of the German economy, was fired in November 1937. He was simply not radical enough. Schacht remained as President of the Reichsbank until he was sacked from that post too in January 1939. He was finally removed from the meaningless post of Minister without Portfolio at the start of 1943. The following year, after the 20 July attempt on Hitler's life, he was sent to a concentration camp.

Schacht's fall from power was characteristic of the fate of a number of those in the traditional right-wing elite who had supported Hitler in the early 1930s. Schacht's trajectory may have been extreme – not many of them gained such a high position in the Nazi state, and few fell so low as to see the inside of a concentration camp – but the journey from initial euphoria at the creation of the Third Reich to disillusionment at the subsequent aggressive policies of the regime was not uncommon. On 5 November 1937, a few weeks before Schacht lost his job as Economics Minister, Hitler briefed several more members of the old-school German elite on his radical thinking; and when subsequently they failed to manifest fervent approval of his ideas, their careers suffered the same fate as Schacht's. Present at the meeting in the Reich Chancellery that day were the commanders-in-chief of the army (Generaloberst Werner von Fritsch), the navy (Generaladmiral Erich Raeder) and the air force (Reichsminister of Aviation Hermann Göring), together with the War Minister (Generalfeldmarschall Werner von Blomberg) and the Foreign Minister (Konstantin von Neurath). The infamous Hossbach Memorandum – notes of this meeting taken by Colonel Hossbach, Hitler's military adjutant – reveals that Hitler openly expressed his desire to gain more territory for Germany in the next few years, and to risk war in order to achieve this end. He didn't mention at the meeting his most grandiose ambition, the invasion of the Soviet Union, most probably because he wanted to focus on shorter-term goals like the seizing of Austria and Czechoslovakia.

Hitler's statement at the meeting that 'the aim of German policy was to make secure and to preserve the racial community and to enlarge it. It was therefore a question of space . . .' was consistent with the worldview he had expressed as far back as *Mein Kampf* in 1924.[40] Hitler said that

Germany should push forward as quickly as possible with an aggressive foreign policy, because the lead that had been established in rearmament would not last much longer. He also revealed that he had finally grasped how unlikely it would be that Germany could form a partnership with Great Britain. This was unsurprising, given that Ribbentrop, sent as German ambassador to London in the summer of 1936, had failed to deliver the hoped-for alliance. Hitler now said that Great Britain would more likely be an adversary in the coming conflict.

Göring, as usual, supported Hitler in the discussion that followed, but the others were sceptical. In particular they feared, presciently, that Germany might be trapped in a war on two fronts between the Soviet Union and the Western Allies. These reasoned arguments were not what Hitler wanted to hear from his underlings, and all of those who voiced doubts at the meeting were to leave office within the next few months. Blomberg resigned on 27 January 1938 after making an unsuitable marriage to a young woman who had once posed for pornographic photos; Fritsch was forced out on 4 February after he was falsely accused of a homosexual liaison; and Neurath was moved from the Foreign Office on the same day and 'promoted' to the post of President of a new Cabinet Council, a consultative committee that never met.

All the replacements for these key positions within the Nazi state were either more compliant than their predecessors or more bellicose – or both. Ribbentrop, the former ambassador to Great Britain, became Foreign Minister, the obliging Walther von Brauchitsch took over from Fritsch as head of the army, and Hitler replaced Blomberg himself, abolishing the title of Minister of War. There is no evidence that Hitler planned to make every one of these changes in the wake of the Hossbach meeting, but he did seize on various opportunities, such as Blomberg's inopportune marriage, when they were presented to him. As a result of these moves his ability to push forward with a more radical foreign policy was considerably strengthened.

The first manifestation of that more aggressive approach came little more than four months after the Hossbach meeting, as tensions grew between Hitler and the government in the land of his birth – Austria. This confrontation would, in turn, lead to a seismic change in Nazi anti-Semitic policy.

• • •

The recent history of the Austrian Jews was similar in many ways to that of the neighbouring German Jews, prior to Hitler's Chancellorship. The status of Viennese Jews in the first half of the nineteenth century was illustrated by the building of the ornate Stadttempel in the centre of the city in the 1820s. On the one hand the interior, with ionic columns and domed ceiling, boasted of the wealth and success of the Viennese Jewish community, and on the other the understated entrance – largely concealed from the street – demonstrated their oppression, since the Jews were forbidden from building an open place of worship by the Edict of Tolerance issued by Emperor Joseph II in 1782.

In 1867 Austrian Jews finally received equal rights under the law, and a golden age of Jewish culture began in Vienna. This was the time of the composer Gustav Mahler, of the author Arthur Schnitzler and the psychiatrist Sigmund Freud – all of them born Jewish. But not every Austrian was pleased by the Jews' newfound freedom. Two politicians in particular voiced virulent anti-Semitism. One was Georg von Schönerer, a parliamentarian obsessed with three ideas: the desire for closer union with Germany, a rejection of Catholicism and a hatred of Jews. His anti-Semitism was based more on racial than religious grounds. 'Religion's only a disguise,' went one of his sayings, 'in the blood the foulness lies.'[41] The second was Karl Lueger, the populist mayor of Vienna. He criticized, in terms that would sound familiar to the Nazis, the over-representation of Jews in certain professions and the way Jews allegedly corrupted the body politic. 'Whenever a state has allowed the Jews to become powerful,' he said, 'the state has soon collapsed, while in those states where they understood enough to isolate the Jews, the monarchical principle was saved . . .'[42] Lueger was quick to capitalize on Viennese fears about the influx of Jews from eastern Europe, in particular those fleeing from Russia. There were calls for the Austrian border to be closed to prevent Jews entering the country, and a fear that the Jews brought with them both disease and the seeds of political revolution. Lueger told the Jews of Vienna, in a speech in November 1905, 'not to admit the [Jewish] Social Democrat revolutionaries. I warn the Jews, most expressly: for the same thing could perhaps happen [here] as in Russia. We in Vienna are anti-Semites, but are certainly not inclined to murder and violence. But if the Jews should threaten our fatherland, then we will show no mercy.'[43]

While a great deal of this Austrian anti-Semitic rhetoric would have been recognizable to anti-Semites in Germany, there was one major difference between the two countries when it came to the 'Jewish question' – the proportion of the population that was Jewish. In Germany fewer than 1 per cent of Germans were Jews, while in Vienna in 1890 around 12 per cent of the population was Jewish – about 100,000 out of 820,000. By the time the Nazis entered Austria in March 1938 there were more than 180,000 Jews in Vienna alone, perhaps as many as 200,000 – while in the whole of Germany there were now fewer than twice that number. Thus for the Nazis the Jewish 'problem' in Austria was proportionately even bigger than it was in Germany.

At the end of the First World War the victorious powers had decided to split the Austro-Hungarian Empire, and Austria became a separate country. The new government in Vienna wanted Austria to become part of the German Republic, but by the Treaty of Saint-Germain in 1919 the victors forbade a union between the two. The Austrians would not forget that this request had been denied – a decision seemingly at odds with President Woodrow Wilson's promise of national 'self-determination'.

But there was no escaping geographical reality, and during the 1920s and 1930s Germany played a part in the affairs of Austria. In the 1920s Austria – like Germany – suffered economic difficulties, though not on the same scale as its larger neighbour. In 1934 amid an atmosphere of political crisis, Austrian Nazis assassinated the Austrian Chancellor, Engelbert Dollfuss. Kurt Schuschnigg, who succeeded Dollfuss, struggled to establish an independent Austria in the presence of a Germany now led by a Chancellor who had been born an Austrian but considered himself a German – just as he believed every 'Aryan' Austrian was a German as well.

Hitler put political pressure on Austria and on Schuschnigg, but he was wary of taking direct military action in order to force a union – or 'Anschluss'. His greatest anxiety was that such an adventure would antagonize Mussolini, since Italy had guaranteed Austria's independence. Hitler hoped that some kind of union might still occur without violence, and this seemed possible after the signing in 1936 of an Austro-German agreement. Though under the terms of the agreement Hitler had recognized Austria's 'sovereignty', in return Schuschnigg had said he would include one Nazi supporter in his cabinet.

In the early weeks of 1938, the German ambassador to Vienna – the ex-Chancellor Franz von Papen – suggested to Schuschnigg that he should visit Berchtesgaden for a meeting with Hitler in order to correct any 'misunderstandings' between the two countries. The resulting conference, held on 12 February that year, is one of the most instructive examples of how Hitler unsettled his opponents. In the first discussion between Hitler and Schuschnigg, in his study on the first floor of the Berghof, Hitler threw a whole series of accusations at the Austrian leader: that Austria should have withdrawn from the League of Nations; that Austria had historically sabotaged any attempt at union with Germany; that Austria was now trying to fortify the border with the Reich, and so on. He coupled these charges with the threat that he was determined to 'make an end of all this' and warned that, 'Perhaps you will wake up one morning in Vienna to find us there – just like a spring storm. And then you'll see something.' Furthermore, said Hitler, after a successful invasion, the country would be occupied by Nazi Stormtroopers and the Austrian Legion, a paramilitary group formed by Austrian Nazis, and 'nobody can stop their just revenge – not even I.'[44]

Like many of Hitler's political opponents, Schuschnigg was something of an intellectual – a graduate in law who after the war became a professor of political science. For people like this, Hitler was an almost impossible adversary. He would pile false charge after false charge in such quick succession that they could not be answered. Schuschnigg was one of the first foreign statesmen to be thrown off balance by this tactic – and he would not be the last. He did not seem to understand that Hitler did not respond to intellectual argument. The German leader was not a 'normal' statesman. He did not want to come to a mutually agreeable compromise and it did not matter to him that his 'facts' were wrong.

Hitler used a similar rhetorical tactic in his attack on the Jews. His sweeping claim, for example, that various 'foreign Jews' were plotting to unsettle Nazi Germany was much the same as his blanket accusation to Schuschnigg that 'the whole history of Austria is just one uninterrupted act of high treason'. Equally, his intimidating statement that 'not even' he could stop the 'just revenge' of fanatical elements within the Third Reich if they entered Austria was akin to his statement, at the time of the 1933 Nazi boycott of Jewish shops and businesses, that there was a danger of the people taking the law into their own hands and attacking the Jews themselves. In both cases Hitler presented himself as a moderating force, holding back even more radical groups. It was an obvious but effective threat. If you did not accept what Hitler offered now, worse would follow.

Kurt Schuschnigg was certainly disconcerted by his meeting with Hitler at the Berghof. Dr Otto Pirkham, an Austrian diplomat who accompanied him that day, remembers that 'at luncheon, Schuschnigg was completely silent . . . very depressed, and his silence was due to the fact that what he had learned at the meeting with Hitler would not have been very agreeable.'[45] Schuschnigg left Berchtesgaden that evening having been bullied into signing a document that made a number of concessions to Hitler, including an agreement to appoint the Austrian Nazi supporter Arthur Seyss-Inquart as Minister of the Interior. On 20 February, Hitler gave a lengthy speech to the Reichstag, in the course of which he praised Schuschnigg for his 'great understanding and warm-hearted willingness . . . to find a way forward in the interests of both countries as much as in the interest of the German *Volk* – that entire German *Volk*, the sons of which we all are . . .'.[46] Four days later in Munich, at a celebration of the anniversary of the forming of the Nazi party, Hitler linked together both the Austrian and Jewish questions, when he spoke out against the 'filthy lies' in the foreign press about Germany's real intentions towards Austria. He singled out the British *News Chronicle*, which he said had claimed that German troops were massed on the border. These 'brazen accusations', he declared, according to a report in the *Völkischer Beobachter*, served to demonstrate 'how the Jewish international poisoners manufacture and spread lies'. Furthermore, 'we can learn a lesson from this. We shall vigorously combat the Jewish rabble-rousers in Germany. We know that they are agents of an International, and we shall treat them all accordingly.'[47]

Schuschnigg now attempted to outmanoeuvre Hitler by calling for a plebiscite in Austria on the question of unification with Germany. In response Hitler, with Göring urging him on, put more pressure on the Austrians by mobilizing troops in Bavaria. Schuschnigg resigned and Seyss-Inquart was appointed Chancellor of Austria. He 'invited' German troops into Austria and they crossed the border on the morning of 12 March. Austrian troops offered no resistance to the Germans

1. Adolf Hitler (seated, second from the right) and a group of Nazi supporters in the 1920s. Hitler was already conscious of his image, and projects his attempt at a 'great man' stare to camera.

2. Hitler's mentor in the early 1920s, the alcoholic playwright Dietrich Eckart. Hitler said of him: he 'shone in our eyes like the Polar Star'.

3. A young Joseph Goebbels as a rabble-rousing street orator, before the Nazis came to power.

4. A Freikorps unit marches through Munich in 1919. Despite their somewhat comic Bavarian costumes, these men were tough paramilitaries.

5. President Paul von Hindenburg (left) and Adolf Hitler immediately after Hitler's appointment as Chancellor in 1933. Their contrasting expressions at the news are revealing.

6. The ultimate Establishment figures – Otto Meissner, an official close to President von Hindenburg (left) and former Chancellor Franz von Papen. Papen's manoeuvring helped bring Hitler to power.

7. Concentration camp prisoners in the 1930s. 'We had to rescue these people,' said Herman Göring, 'to bring them back to the national community. We had to re-educate them.' This 're-education' consisted of subjecting these prisoners to one of the most brutal prison regimes ever devised.

8. Prisoners at Dachau before the war. Many of these inmates were sent to the camp because they were political opponents of the regime.

9. Adolf Hitler in 1936, the year the former British Prime Minister David Lloyd George described him as 'a born leader of men. A magnetic dynamic personality with a single-minded purpose, a resolute will, and a dauntless heart.'

10. Joseph Goebbels marries the blonde-haired Magda Quandt in December 1931. Hitler is to the right of Goebbels, wearing a hat.

11. Theodor Eicke, commandant of Dachau from the summer of 1933. Eicke wanted the SS under his command to be 'hard'. 'There is no place amongst us,' he said, 'for soft people.'

12. Hermann Göring (left) and Heinrich Himmler. Two men who could not have been more different in temperament or character – but who were both committed Nazis.

13. Adolf Eichmann, the SD officer who would help organize the Nazis' 'Final Solution' – in particular the killing of the Hungarian Jews.

14. Heinrich Himmler (left) and Reinhard Heydrich (right) in Vienna in 1938 just after the Nazis gained control of Austria. Security forces under their command would shortly start arresting those Austrians considered 'asocial', 'criminal' or simply 'disagreeable'.

15. Jews are made to scrub the streets in Austria in the wake of the Nazi occupation in 1938. 'You were completely outlawed,' says Walter Kammerling, a Jewish resident of Vienna. 'There was no protection from anywhere.'

16. Smashed shop windows in the aftermath of Kristallnacht – the Nazi attack on Jewish homes, businesses and places of worship in November 1938.

17. A synagogue burns as a result of Kristallnacht. More than ninety Jews died as a consequence of the attacks on 9/10 November 1938, and around 30,000 Jews were subsequently sent to concentration camps.

18. The main camp at Auschwitz, a place originally designed to strike terror into the hearts of Poles in the surrounding area, with the first mass transport of prisoners arriving in June 1940. The words 'Arbeit Macht Frei' (Work makes you free), made infamous by their use here, had previously been emblazoned on a gate at Dachau in the 1930s.

as they moved through the country and millions of ordinary Austrians welcomed the Wehrmacht, garlanding them with flowers. Many Austrians thought the arrival of the Nazis offered hope of a new, stronger Austria no longer beset by economic problems. For example, Susi Seitz, an Austrian teenager, says that she and her family saw Hitler as their 'saviour' because 'we really had to belong to Germany.'[48] They had wanted Austria to be joined to Germany after the First World War, and now at last it seemed that this 'dream' would be fulfilled.

Emil Klein, an 'old fighter' in the Nazi party, who had taken part in the Beer-Hall Putsch back in 1923, could scarcely believe what was happening now, fifteen years later: 'When I heard that the annexation march was under way – I was Senior Regional Commander of the Hitler Youth – I was so enthused, because I had some Austrian connections from my early years, and without permission from my superiors and without asking, I took my car and drove to Austria, following the troops through Passau. What I experienced there I will not experience a second time in my life. This enthusiasm! Neither I, nor the soldiers, I imagine, have ever received as many kisses as we did from the girls who rushed to us. Austria was stood on its head.'[49]

Hitler crossed the border into Austria on the afternoon of 12 March, just a few hours after his soldiers had made the same journey. His crossing point was symbolic – across the River Inn at his birthplace of Braunau am Inn. He drove in triumph, past cheering crowds, all the way to the city of Linz where he had gone to school. Reinhard Spitzy, an Austrian Nazi who had joined the German Foreign Office, was in the sixth car in the procession, driving behind Hitler. For Spitzy, this was a profoundly emotional moment: 'All my dreams of reuniting Austria with Germany – don't forget Austria was ruling Germany during 600 years and the German crown is in Vienna in the Hofburg. And so for me, after the defeat of the year 1918, for us it was a dream . . . I must tell you the enthusiasm was, I won't say a hundred per cent but let us say eighty-five per cent, it was overwhelming . . . I saw even police and nuns with swastika flags. We all thought it is a new peaceful big Reich, because for the Austrians – I'm Austrian myself – war is something we don't like. We lost so many wars against Prussia, against England and France, and so on, we are fed up with the wars . . . Anschluss was one of

the successes of Hitler without war, like the occupation of the Rhineland, and what he did is perfectly in order.'[50]

At the time, claims Spitzy, he thought he knew exactly what Hitler's
ambitions were: 'Hitler, from the very beginning, wanted to unite all
German-speaking countries, except Switzerland or Luxembourg, in the
old Holy Roman Empire of German nations. He wanted to restore the
injustice of the Thirty Years War, of the peace of Münster and Osna-
brück, he wanted to make Germany as big as it was in the Middle Ages.'

This idea that Hitler's ultimate aim was to reunite German-speakers,
rather than pursue a war of conquest in the east, was a common
misconception – and one Hitler encouraged in his public pronounce-
ments. Spitzy, who served in the German embassy in London in the
1930s, discovered first hand that plenty of members of the British ruling
elite saw little problem in a Europe where all German-speakers lived
together: 'as long as he [Hitler] did that, he got an understanding from
a great part of the British Establishment. They all had understanding.
They told me.'

In Austria, while the state had not imposed similar anti-Semitic
measures to those in Germany, there was still considerable 'traditional'
prejudice of the kind that Kurt Lueger, the former mayor of Vienna,
would have recognized. Walter Frentz, for instance, travelled to Vienna
in 1928 and claimed that he experienced the attitude of some Viennese
to Jews when he was travelling on a tram. 'Suddenly the tram made an
emergency stop in the street,' says Frentz, who would later become Hitler's cameraman. 'And there was a man on the track who hadn't seen the
tram coming. And, after breaking, the tram driver said something that
shocked me and left a deep impression. "Oh dear, it's a Jew. If I had
known, I would have continued driving!" And all the other Viennese
said: "Yes, that's what you should have done, the Jewish pig!" And they
didn't even know the man.'[51] Susi Seitz, who cheered as Hitler entered
Linz in March 1938, was another Austrian who had issues with the
Jews, though she expresses her feelings rather more diplomatically:
'I must say that the Jews were not very much liked in Austria . . . We
never had the feeling that they were the same as us, they were different,
completely different.'[52]

From the moment the Germans entered Austria the Jews were at risk.
'We heard the noises from the streets,' says Walter Kammerling, a

fifteen-year-old Austrian Jew living in Vienna, 'the whole Viennese population, that is obviously the non-Jewish population, in jubilation and enjoyment. And then the first problem starts, the Jewish shops were smashed.' In the immediate aftermath of the German invasion, 'you already had people molesting you . . . You were completely outlawed. There was no protection from anywhere. Anybody could come up to you and do what they want and that's it . . .'[53]

Infamously, Nazi thugs made Jews scrub the streets clean in a display of public humiliation. Walter Kammerling remembers watching a well-dressed woman hold up her little girl so that she could see a Stormtrooper kick an old Jew as he scrubbed. 'They all laughed,' he says, 'and she laughed as well – it was a wonderful entertainment [for them], and that shook me.'[54]

William Shirer, an American correspondent, witnessed the abuse in Vienna. 'All sorts of reports of Nazi sadism and from the Austrians it surprises me,' he wrote in his diary. 'Jewish men and women made to clean latrines. Hundreds of them . . . just picked at random off the streets to clean the toilets of the Nazi boys.'[55]

This initial upsurge of anti-Semitic action had been mostly spontaneous – a disorganized series of acts of local persecution similar, but on a larger scale, to those launched by Stormtroopers immediately after Hitler became Chancellor. But soon the Nazi leadership discouraged this impulsive brutality and instead the persecution became institutionalized. Heinrich Himmler, Reichsführer SS, entered Austria shortly after the first German troops and established his headquarters at the Hotel Metropol in Vienna. Reinhard Heydrich, his close associate and head of the SD – the Sicherheitsdienst, the counter-intelligence operation of the SS – was also soon in the city. On the night of 13–14 March – just thirty-six hours after the German Army had placed their boots on Austrian soil – the Gestapo began to seize works of art from Jewish homes. The priceless art collection of the Rothschilds, for instance, was distributed between Hitler, Göring and the museum in Linz. Less than a week after the occupation of Austria, the Nazis closed down the offices of Jewish organizations and put their leaders behind bars. By the end of March, Jews had been sacked from jobs in professions like the theatre and academia, and banned from serving in the Austrian Army. Jewish property and businesses were also targeted, as the Nazis seized Jewish apartments and took over department stores and factories. This process of 'Aryanization' was shortly to be repeated within Germany.

The first train left Austria for Dachau concentration camp on 1 April 1938. By the end of the year nearly 8,000 people had been sent there from Austria.[56] To begin with most were the Nazis' political opponents, many of Jewish descent. But in May the Nazis began targeting Jews they called 'asocial', 'criminal' or simply 'disagreeable'.[57] The terror reached such an extreme that a Jewish Austrian was at risk of arrest for simply eating in a restaurant or sitting in a public park at the same time as the authorities launched a search for Jews. Overall, during 1938, more than 75 per cent of the prisoners sent to Dachau by the Nazis were Jewish. On the trains to Dachau, the Austrians were often beaten and otherwise abused. One estimate – made by the SS themselves – was that about 70 per cent of those on one transport they investigated had been attacked.[58]

Some Austrian Jews tried to reason with their tormentors. Dr David Schapira, a Viennese Jew who was both a lawyer and a shop owner, was blind as a result of injuries he had suffered during the war. After his legal practice had collapsed and his shop had been taken away from him, he went with his wife to visit Nazi officials in Vienna and hand in a petition, hoping that if they saw his war decorations they would show him mercy. But he was told, 'Jewish scoundrel, you can shove that Habsburg stuff [his medals] up your ass. Shove off, and don't come back, or I'll throw you down the stairs – maybe then you'll be able to see again.'[59]

Suicides were rife among the Jews of Vienna, as many chose death rather than life under Nazi rule. William Shirer wrote how a friend of his saw 'a Jewish-looking fellow' standing at a bar. 'After a while he took an old-fashioned razor from his pocket and slashed his throat.'[60] Goebbels noted cynically in his diary on 23 March 1938: 'In the past, the Germans committed suicide. Now it is the other way round.'[61]

Adolf Eichmann, a thirty-two-year-old lieutenant in the SD, played an important role in the horror in Austria. He was familiar with the country and had gone to school in Linz – just as Hitler had. Afterwards, for six years he had worked in Austria for the Vacuum Oil Company. He joined both the Nazi party and SS in 1932 and the following year, having lost his job, returned to Germany, his country of birth.

Eichmann, by now specializing in 'Jewish affairs' in the SD, had been preparing for the Anschluss for some time, gathering intelligence on those Austrians the Nazis considered a threat. He recalled that 'for weeks in advance every able-bodied man they could find was put to work in three shifts: writing file cards for an enormous circular card file, several yards in diameter, which a man sitting on a piano stool could operate and find any card he wanted thanks to a series of punch holes.'[62] Eichmann thus arrived in Vienna in March 1938 with a list of people, including prominent Jewish figures, to be arrested. But the Nazi authorities discovered that locking up the leaders of the Jewish community led to problems. Since the Nazis were trying to force Jews to emigrate – having robbed them of their wealth – there was nobody, on the Jewish side, left in a leadership position to coordinate the expulsions. So Eichmann gained permission from his superiors to release some leading Jews so that they could help organize the exodus. In one case, Eichmann met Josef Löwenherz, a Jewish lawyer, for a discussion about how Jewish organizations could help the Nazis, and then sent Löwenherz back to his cell to work on the plans.[63]

Soon a radical solution emerged – a system Eichmann termed a 'conveyor belt'.[64] Jews seeking emigration would be summoned to one building and then passed between Nazi officials until their expulsion was finalized. In August 1938 this Central Office for Jewish Emigration started work, based in the Rothschild Palace. Altogether 80,000 Austrian Jews left the country between March 1938 and the end of the year.[65] By the time the war started in September 1939 the total had risen to nearly 130,000. The Jews were forced to pay for their own departure, with wealthy Jews funding poorer ones through Jewish organizations.

The invasion of Austria and the subsequent union of the country with Germany was an undoubted success for Hitler's regime. In particular, the way in which the Jews in Austria had been so quickly targeted, persecuted and expelled, demonstrated a way forward for the Nazis. As a consequence, the Jews within Germany were at greater risk than ever before.

7. Radicalization
(1938–1939)

Hitler's self-confidence rose to a new level in the wake of the Nazi conquest of Austria. In his speeches in the aftermath of the Anschluss he said that he personally had 'rendered the greatest service to the German *Volk*' and that 'the period of my leadership of Germany is a historic one of German greatness.'[1]

Hitler even claimed that his existence was part of a supernatural plan, boasting that 'Whoever believes in God must admit: when the fate of a people is altered within three days, then this is divine judgement . . .'[2] and that since God had now decreed that Germany and Austria should be united then, 'What the Lord has joined together, let no man divide.'[3]

But for all this talk of 'God' there is no evidence that Hitler was a practising Christian – as we have already seen in the context of *Mein Kampf*.[4] Indeed, he thought Christianity 'an invention of sick brains'.[5] The purpose of life, as he saw it, was for human beings to live and die for the 'preservation of the species'.[6] His personal task was to lead the German *Volk* towards a new world of prosperity and racial purity. In this endeavour he was helped by a mystical force he called 'providence'. Memorably, in a speech he gave in 1936 he said that 'neither threats nor warnings will divert me. I walk the way providence has assigned to me, with the instinctive sureness of a sleepwalker.'[7]

However, by spring 1938, Hitler felt that time was running out for him to fulfil the destiny that 'providence' had allotted to him. In a speech he gave in Vienna on 9 April, shortly before his forty-ninth birthday, he railed against the fact that he had 'used up'[8] his 'best years' in the struggle to gain power. All of this – his fear that time was running out for him to achieve the greatness he sought, his overconfidence in his own genius as a result of the success in Austria and his anxiety that other countries were now investing massively in their armed forces – created a combustible mix.

The Nazis now began to pursue more radical policies within Germany itself. In an operation that began on 21 April 1938 the Gestapo moved against 'work-shy' Germans. Those unemployed who had declined two separate offers of work were taken to Buchenwald concentration camp. The Criminal Police instigated a similar move against 'asocials' in June 1938. A significant feature of this operation was that any German Jew who had a previous criminal conviction was arrested as well.[9] It didn't matter if the Jews arrested were fit for work or not, it was enough simply to be a Jew with a criminal conviction and to have previously served one month or more in jail.[10] This was one of the first examples of how, in the enforcement of nationwide actions, Jews were treated more harshly than others.

As a result of these raids, more than 2,000 Jews were imprisoned in conditions that were appalling even by Nazi standards. In Buchenwald many slept in the open. For some of the SS guards the arrival of the Jews offered an opportunity for them to vent both their anger and their sadism. Once admitted to the camp, the Jews were given the hardest jobs and more than ninety died during the summer. Release for these Jews was often possible only if they could convince the SS that they would emigrate immediately.

Life was also getting worse for the rest of the German Jews. A whole host of anti-Semitic regulations during 1938 further restricted their freedom. Jewish doctors could no longer treat 'Aryan' patients, and Jews were banned from a whole raft of jobs, including that of travelling salesman. Concerted efforts were also made by the Nazis to identify and isolate Jews by insisting in a decree of 17 August 1938 that, if they did not already have a first name that was 'specified' as Jewish, they had to take the additional name of 'Israel' for men or 'Sara' for women.[11]

At the same time as the implementation of these official measures of persecution the Nazis turned on Jews in the streets, particularly in Berlin where Goebbels was keen to ratchet up the level of anti-Semitic action. Goebbels noted in his diary in June 1938: 'Spoke in front of three hundred police officers in Berlin. Really got them going. Against all sentimentality. Legality is not the motto, but harassment. The Jews must get out of Berlin. The police will help.'[12] As a consequence, Jews were targeted on the streets of Berlin in ways that had not been seen since the early days of Nazi rule.

A few weeks before his June speech, Goebbels had asked Count Helldorff, the chief of the Berlin police, to put together proposals for harsher anti-Semitic regulations. On 11 June, the day after he gave his speech, he received Helldorf's memorandum. Though not immediately implemented, it contained many of the ideas for increased persecution that the Nazis would later adopt during the war – such as forcing the Jews to live in separate areas of the city and labelling them with a special mark on their clothing.

In parallel with these actions against the Jews, 'asocials' and the 'work-shy', the Nazis also increasingly targeted other distinct groups. The first were the *Zigeuner* – or 'Gypsies'. Today these are pejorative words (arguably the German *Zigeuner* more so than the English 'Gypsy'). But at the time the predominantly dark-skinned people who had – many hundreds of years before – travelled to Europe from India and now lived an itinerant lifestyle were commonly known as Gypsies. All the legislation drawn up to persecute them, and all those in the camps in which they were later tormented, referred to them by this name. However, the generally accepted term across many countries for those who used to be called Gypsies is now 'Sinti and Roma', because the majority came originally from groups known by those names.[13]

As with the Jews, the history of the persecution of the Sinti and Roma predates the arrival of the Nazis by many years. At the end of the sixteenth century the Sinti and Roma were accused of aiding and abetting the Turks in order to destabilize the Holy Roman Empire, and during the seventeenth and eighteenth centuries many German states passed legislation that attacked them. Some laws, like the edict from the ruler of Hesse-Darmstadt in 1734, denied Sinti and Roma the right to enter specific territory and others, like an order passed in Mainz in 1714, even called for Sinti and Roma to be executed.[14] Sinti and Roma were denigrated because of their lifestyle – they were accused of living 'like dogs'[15] – and their physical appearance, categorized as 'black, dirty [and] barbarous'.[16]

Just like the Jews, the Sinti and Roma were perceived as shiftless 'wanderers' with no permanent home. But it was never clear to what extent they were condemned for qualities that they could not change, like their ancestry, or social attributes that they could alter, like the decision of many Sinti and Roma to travel the countryside rather than settle in one place. Cesare Lombroso, the Italian writer, was one of those who believed that the perceived negative qualities of Sinti and Roma were inherent. In 1902 he wrote that they had a tendency to criminal behaviour because they were born 'villains'.[17] Nonetheless, most of the anti-Gypsy legislation that individual German states passed in the early twentieth century was designed to moderate behaviour rather than to mount a full racial attack. In July 1926 the Bavarian parliament passed a Law for the Combating of Gypsies, Travellers and the Work-Shy,[18] which stated, among other restrictions, that no one could travel from place to place with a caravan without permission from the police.

Many of those who grew up in what the Nazis classed as Gypsy families during the 1930s felt that the problems they faced were caused not just by the new regime but also by centuries of prejudice. 'The general public has always been contemptuous of the Sinti and the Roma,' says Franz Rosenbach, who experienced life under Nazi rule in Austria. 'They have always been mistreated, they were not recognized, they have always been regarded as second- or even third-class citizens. On the whole, we actually had very little contact with the majority of the population, firstly because they didn't want to have anything to do with us, and secondly because our parents had told us not to approach them because they did not want us. The prejudice was based on the idea that the Sinti were people who stole children and did whatever else. But I have to say that this was simply not true.'[19]

Hermann Höllenreiner, from a Sinti family in Munich, remembers how those who were perceived as Gypsies suffered in the 1930s. 'My mother did send me to school,' he says, 'but I had a teacher who disliked me – I had to stand in the corner or go out and I got beatings from him . . . that's why I stopped going to school. He also mistreated other Sinti.' The prejudice against Sinti and Roma in the school was widespread. 'In the second grade as soon as they heard that we were Gypsies the [rest of the] children weren't allowed to talk to us any more – maybe because of their parents, I don't know.' Hermann believes that most Germans took the view that 'if a dog shits somewhere they say: "Gypsy!" [that is, a Gypsy did it] – yeah, that's the proverb of the Germans.'[20]

Hitler, however, did not appear to be much concerned about the Sinti and Roma – they are not even mentioned in *Mein Kampf*. Only gradually did measures directed explicitly at the Sinti and Roma population come to be implemented by the Nazis. One reason for this lack of urgency was almost certainly that many Sinti and Roma were already often caught up in moves against 'beggars' or 'antisocials'. Only as an afterthought were they included within the Nuremberg Laws. Wilhelm

Frick, the Interior Minister, stated in a decree of 26 November 1935 that the Nuremberg Law prohibiting Jews from marrying 'pure' Germans also extended to a ban on Gypsies marrying them.[21] Frick subsequently clarified this restriction on 3 January 1936 by saying that if an individual Gypsy had a 'quarter or less of alien blood' then he or she could marry an 'Aryan' German.

By this legislation the Nazis created another immense definitional problem for themselves. It was all very well to talk theoretically of percentages of 'Gypsy blood', but in practice there was no way of implementing such an idea – for the simple reason that it was impossible to work out how much 'Gypsy blood' any individual possessed. We have seen how, since they couldn't find a racial way of distinguishing between Jews and non-Jews, the Nazis fell back on a religious-based definition of 'Jewishness'. But such a method could not be used in the case of the Sinti and Roma, since those that practised a religion were overwhelmingly Christian.

In the wake of this extension of the Nuremberg Laws, the Nazis urgently needed to find a way of determining the percentage of 'Gypsyness' in an individual, just as they had previously needed to assess the percentage of 'Jewishness'. To this end a new research organization was created early in 1936 within the Reich Health Office under the leadership of Dr Robert Ritter. He and his team now set out to create a vast card index containing information on every potential Sinti and Roma in Germany – eventually around 30,000 people would be detailed. Ritter and his colleagues decided who was and who was not a Gypsy by inspecting birth and family records, and by investigating the lifestyle of each individual.

Ritter's conclusions about the nature of Gypsy life informed the first pronouncement from Himmler on the subject, a circular entitled Combating the Gypsy Plague, issued on 8 December 1938. The document stated that the 'Gypsy problem' should be treated as a question of 'race' and called for both 'settled and non-settled Gypsies' to be registered with the police. The life of Gypsies needed to be 'regulated', said Himmler, not least in order to prevent 'further intermingling of blood'.[22]

One of the many curious aspects of Himmler's circular was the statement that 'experience shows that part-Gypsies play the greatest role in Gypsy criminality'. This strange assertion was based on Dr Ritter's belief that the small minority of 'racially pure' Gypsies who carried on the traditional wandering life, travelling from village to village in horse-drawn caravans, were less dangerous than Gypsies who had decided to settle in one place and marry into the 'Aryan' German population. Though there was no reliable empirical evidence to support this proposition, Ritter maintained that the distinction was important. The theory was that some 'pure Gypsies' might be considered as a type of 'Aryan', since they had originated in the Indian sub-continent. But because large numbers of Gypsies had intermarried with non-Gypsies, they had 'polluted their blood' and so were especially dangerous. This convoluted logic led to the bizarre situation – implied in the circular on Combating the Gypsy Plague – that 'pure-blood' Gypsies were less of a problem to the Nazi state than 'mixed-blood' Gypsies. This state of affairs was precisely the reverse of the one in which the Jews found themselves, where the more Jewish an individual was perceived to be the more he or she was at risk. In practice, once the war began and the persecution of the Sinti and Roma escalated, the distinction between 'pure' and 'non-pure' Gypsies was to have little practical effect, but it nonetheless remains a valuable insight into the mentality of the perpetrators.

The year 1938 was significant not only for the promulgation of the circular on Combating the Gypsy Plague, but also because the regime increased the level of threat against the Sinti and Roma in other ways. Many German Sinti and Roma were picked up during an attack on the 'work-shy' in June 1938 and transported to concentration camps – one manpower report at Sachsenhausen camp, for example, registered the arrival of 248 Gypsies.[23] Austrian Sinti and Roma were also targeted and taken to the new concentration camp at Mauthausen near Linz, where they were forced to work in terrible conditions. Adolf Gussak, an Austrian classed as a Gypsy by the Nazis, recalled that 'In the quarry we had to carry heavy stones. With them on our backs we had to climb the 180 steps up [towards the camp]. The SS beat us. As a result there often was some pushing: everybody wanted to escape the blows. If anyone fell down he was finished off by a bullet in the back of his neck.'[24]

There appears to have been little concern among the general population about the persecution of the Sinti and Roma. In fact, one police report from Austria in January 1939 said that the local population wanted even more to be done to combat the 'Gypsy plague' because this 'race does nothing but steal from and swindle the Germans.'[25]

Members of the second group the Nazis targeted with increased severity in the late 1930s were unique among all of those persecuted in the Third Reich. That is because they suffered not because of an accident of birth, like the Jews or Sinti and Roma, but because of a spiritual choice. They were Jehovah's Witnesses – persecuted for their religious faith. While, as we have already seen, the Nazis had an ambivalent attitude to most Christian sects, they found the Jehovah's Witnesses utterly unacceptable: Jehovah's Witnesses refused to give the Nazi salute, to let their children join the Hitler Youth, to vote in elections and to join the German Army.

Immediately after Hitler came to power Jehovah's Witnesses sought to clarify where they stood on a number of issues by publishing a 'Declaration of Facts'. The Witnesses denied that they received any Jewish financial support and alleged that 'the commercial Jews of the British-American empire' had 'built up and carried on Big Business as a means of exploiting and oppressing the peoples of many nations'.[26]

Else Abt, a Jehovah's Witness who was arrested during the war and suffered in Auschwitz, recalls her own attitude towards Jews prior to her imprisonment. 'I never bought anything from a Jewish shop,' she says, 'because they always [charged] higher prices, and then they'd give a discount and the stupid people thought that they were only paying half price. That was true, I saw it in Danzig. They would put the prices up and they know that people like to pay a lower price – they'd calculate prices in a certain way, that's my opinion, but I don't have anything against Jews . . . For me personally I can say that I never loved the Jews and I wouldn't buy anything in a Jewish shop.'[27]

However, the attempt by Jehovah's Witnesses to show that they could coexist with the Nazi regime was fruitless. As Hitler and the Nazis saw it, the Jehovah's Witnesses simply refused to conform to the norms expected in the new Germany. In particular, their pacifism was seen as appalling. In December 1933, Heydrich said that all Jehovah's Witnesses who attempted to spread their beliefs were 'unbelievable fanatics'[28] and should be arrested. Theodor Eicke, commandant of Dachau in 1933, summed up his view of religion in general with the words: 'Prayer books are things for women and for those who wear panties.'[29]

The Witnesses were particularly vulnerable after an order issued in May

1937 declared that they could be sent to concentration camps on mere suspicion of wrongdoing. Once inside the camps, Jehovah's Witnesses were often singled out for terrible mistreatment. At the post-war trial of guards at Sachsenhausen, one builder working at the camp testified that 'During the autumn of 1938 I was working as a mason on construction when Block-führer Sorge and Blockführer Bugdalle came on the job site and ordered a group of prisoners to dig a hole to the depth of a man, and they put in a Witness whose name was Bachuba and buried him up to his neck. Sorge and Bugdalle laughingly made sport of him. Then, when there was nothing left but his head above ground they urinated on his head. They left him for another hour in the grave. When he was dug up and pulled out on the ground he was still alive but he couldn't stand on his legs.'[30]

Rudolf Höss, who would later become commandant of Auschwitz, was posted to Sachsenhausen concentration camp as adjutant in 1938, and presided over the brutal way in which the Jehovah's Witnesses were treated. He subsequently wrote that he had 'met many religious fanatics in my time' but the Witnesses in Sachsenhausen 'surpassed anything that I had previously seen'.[31] He remembered two in particular who 'almost ran to the place of execution. They wished on no account to be bound, for they desired to be able to raise their hands to Jehovah. Transformed by ecstasy, they stood in front of the wooden wall of the rifle range, seemingly no longer of this world. Thus do I imagine that the first Christian martyrs must have appeared, as they waited in the circus for the wild beasts to tear them in pieces.'[32]

According to Höss, his bosses Himmler and Eicke were fascinated by the zealous commitment the Witnesses showed to their religion: 'On many occasions Himmler, as well as Eicke, used the fanatical faith of the Jehovah's Witnesses as an example. SS men must have the same fanatical and unshakeable faith in the National Socialist ideal and in Adolf Hitler that the Witnesses had in Jehovah. Only when all SS men believed as fanatically in their own philosophy would Adolf Hitler's State be permanently secure.'[33]

Other prisoners observed that the Jehovah's Witnesses seemed able to manage the suffering they endured in the camps better than many others. Bruno Bettelheim, the art historian and later psychologist, was imprisoned first in Dachau and then in Buchenwald just before the outbreak of the Second World War, and while he felt that the Jehovah's

Witnesses would – according to psychiatric theory – 'be considered extremely neurotic and even delirious and therefore vulnerable to psychiatric disintegration in time of crisis', that was not what he saw in the camps. 'Not only did they display exceptional moral behavior,' he wrote after the war, 'they seemed protected against the influence of the camp environment that rapidly destroyed persons that our psychiatrist friends, and even I, would have judged well integrated.'[34] That was certainly the case with Else Abt in Auschwitz. 'I wasn't scared,' she said, 'because I thought my creator would help me. We believed that God would be able to help us in every difficult situation.'[35]

The increasingly radical way in which the Nazis sought to deal with those they perceived as enemies within the Reich also affected another group of people – homosexuals. Heinrich Himmler made clear his attitude towards homosexuals in a speech he gave to SS leaders in 1937. He claimed that a homosexual was both a 'coward' and a 'liar'. 'Unfortunately it's not as easy for us as it was for our ancestors,' he said, because then the homosexual 'was drowned in a swamp . . . This was not a punishment, but simply the erasure of an abnormal life. It had to be eliminated, just like we root up stinging nettles, throw them on a pile and burn them. It wasn't out of revenge, just that the person concerned simply had to go.'

One practical reason to tackle homosexuality now, Himmler argued, was that 'the sexual balance' of Germany had been 'deranged' because the 2 million homosexuals in Germany – added to the 2 million German war dead – meant there was a 'lack of four million sexually capable men' in Germany. 'Among homosexuals,' said Himmler, 'there are those who take the view: what I am doing is nobody else's business, it is my private matter. However, all things in the sexual field are not the private matter of every individual, but signify the life and death of the nation.'[36]

The Nazis, as we have seen, often tried to claim a link between anything that they could not tolerate and the Jews. This was even the case with homosexuality. In 1930, before the Nazis came to power, Alfred Rosenberg wrote an article in the *Völkischer Beobachter* in which he promised that the Nazis would punish by 'banishment or hanging' the 'malicious drive of the Jews to prevent the divine idea of Creation, through physical relations with animals, siblings and same-sex persons'.[37]

Thus, claimed Rosenberg absurdly, the Jews encouraged not just homosexuality, but incest and bestiality as well.

Hitler's own attitude to homosexuality, at least in the beginning, was not so straightforward. While he talked of the importance of the traditional family and of the duty of couples to propagate, he tolerated the homosexuality of Ernst Röhm, the leader of the Stormtroopers. It was also common gossip among the leadership of the Stormtroopers that another senior figure in the organization, Obergruppenführer (Lieutenant General) Heines, was so open about his sexual preference that he was nicknamed 'Fräulein Schmidt'.[38]

Hitler initially dismissed concerns about Röhm's homosexuality when they were brought to his attention. That all changed, however, when Hitler turned on Röhm in June 1934 in a desire to suppress the power of the Stormtroopers. It was now politically expedient for him to condemn homosexuality. After Röhm had been arrested at the holiday resort of Bad Wiessee in June 1934 – and in the bedroom opposite, Obergruppenführer Heines was discovered in bed with a young Stormtrooper – Hitler railed against the moral corruption of the SA.[39]

Homosexual acts between men had been illegal during the Weimar period, though the authorities had often turned a blind eye to the gay clubs in Berlin. But the Nazis now rejected any form of tolerance and in 1935 introduced tougher restrictions in Paragraph 175 of the German Criminal Code, attacking what they called 'lewd and lascivious acts' between men. Previously, the courts had interpreted the law as outlawing sodomy – something which proved difficult to enforce unless two men were actually caught in the act. But the new definition of 'lewd and lascivious acts' allowed the courts to punish almost any form of physical contact between men. As for female homosexuality, while there was no law specifically outlawing sex between women, there was scope for the regime to target lesbians as 'asocials'.

Those convicted under Paragraph 175 were sent either to conventional prisons or to concentration camps where they risked being tortured in order to reveal the names of other homosexuals. They could even be castrated. The law stated that homosexuals had to consent to such a drastic operation, but once in the camps they could be subjected to unrelenting pressure to make them agree.[40] Altogether around 10,000 homosexuals were sent to concentration camps during the Third

Reich; no one knows exactly how many of these died, but one estimate suggests that it was as many as 60 per cent.[41]

It's also significant, in the context of this expansion of Nazi terror, that the late 1930s saw the opening of the first concentration camp specifically for women at Lichtenburg in Saxony, with the first prisoners entering the camp in December 1937. Up to this point women had been imprisoned within the traditional prison system, or at a much smaller camp at Moringen administered by the Prussian state. Only a minority of prisoners within the concentration camp system were women, less than 12 per cent prior to the outbreak of the war.[42] But the number of women targeted by the Nazi security forces increased as they looked further afield for potential enemies, a development also illustrated by the opening of the notorious female concentration camp at Ravensbrück, north of Berlin, in the spring of 1939. This – the largest of the camps for women – absorbed all of the female prisoners from Lichtenburg and then expanded still further.

It would be wrong, however, to suggest that Hitler was preoccupied during this period with the expansion of domestic terror. The increasing persecution occurred against the background of another issue that occupied his attention to a much greater extent – the drive towards war.

On 30 May 1938 Hitler signed an order declaring, 'It is my unalterable decision to shatter Czechoslovakia by a military operation in the foreseeable future.'[43] The excuse for this brazen statement was the alleged suffering of the German-speaking minority who lived in the border region of Czechoslovakia known as the Sudetenland. But in reality there was more at stake. On 8 July that year, in an address to industrialists, Hermann Göring revealed that Germany now risked war with 'France and England, Russia [and] America'. Moreover, this was 'the greatest hour of destiny ever since there has been a German history'.[44]

With tensions so high, it is not surprising that the Nazis increased their attacks on those they perceived as their enemies inside the Reich. But political considerations of tactics – and especially timing – still existed. On 21 June 1938, at a meeting attended by both police and party representatives, a decision was made not to adopt the heavily restrictive proposals on Berlin Jews put forward, after Goebbels' initiative, by the Berlin chief of police, Count Helldorff. This was a particularly sensitive time in the relationship between the Nazis and the international community, because the Nazis wanted other countries to accept hundreds of thousands of German and Austrian Jews. And this very question was about to be debated at Evian-les-Bains, a spa town on the banks of Lake Geneva in France.

This meeting of the Intergovernmental Committee for Political Refugees had first been proposed by President Roosevelt back in March 1938 in the wake of the Anschluss, but had taken four months to organize. By now the situation was even worse for the Jews than it had been at the time Roosevelt suggested the conference. For as the delegates to the Evian conference settled into their rooms at the luxurious Hôtel Royal, they knew that the attack on the Austrian Jews had resulted not in the nations of the world opening their borders, but in many cases on ever greater controls on immigration.

In the wake of the Anschluss the Dutch had refused to accept Austrian passports as legitimate documents. Luxembourg and Belgium had increased security at their frontiers, while the Foreign Office in London had expressed the view that Britain was 'an old country' both 'highly industrialized' and 'densely populated' and thus, by implication, an unsuitable destination for large numbers of immigrants.[45] One MP in parliament warned in a debate on 22 March 1938 of the 'difficulty' that the British would face in the event of the arrival of large numbers of Jews, because the police would have to ensure that 'our own people are protected against those who might quite easily slip in – drug traffickers, white slave traffickers, people with criminal records'.[46] The Home Secretary, Sir Samuel Hoare, said in a cabinet committee in July that 'there was a good deal of feeling growing up in this country . . . against the admission of Jews' to British colonies.[47] As for the Swiss, they had imposed draconian visa restrictions in order to prevent large numbers of Jews entering the country. They had even refused to host the intergovernmental conference on Swiss soil. The original suggestion had been to hold the conference in Geneva, but after the Swiss had refused to cooperate, the venue was moved to Evian, further along Lake Geneva. Nor did the United States agree to relax immigration rules in response to the Austrian crisis. Indeed, when the Americans called for the Evian conference they had explicitly said that no country which attended would be required to take more immigrants than it was already doing.

Roosevelt's own attitude to the conference was ambiguous. While the gathering was his idea, he chose to send as head of the American delegation not a member of his government but a close friend, Myron C. Taylor, former head of US Steel. Nor was this even officially a conference about helping the 'Jews' – the proposal for the conference euphemistically mentioned 'political refugees' only.

The most likely, albeit uncharitable, explanation of all this is that although Roosevelt was concerned about the fate of the Jews in the Reich he did not necessarily expect the Evian conference to result in much practical assistance to them. This interpretation is confirmed by the content of a confidential memo written before the conference by George Strausser Messersmith, Assistant Secretary of State. He said that not many countries were 'approaching the problem with enthusiasm', and he feared that delegates would merely 'render lip service' to the idea of helping the 'refugees'.[48]

This is particularly relevant because Messersmith, more than most in the Roosevelt administration, knew the true nature of the Nazi regime. In a letter he wrote in June 1933 from the US embassy in Berlin to William Phillips in the State Department, he said that he believed the German government wanted 'to make Germany the most capable instrument of war that there has ever existed' and that 'a psychology is being developed that the whole world is against Germany.' Furthermore, 'with few exceptions, the men who are running this government are of a mentality that you and I cannot understand. Some of them are psychopathic cases and would ordinarily be receiving treatment somewhere.'[49]

While Roosevelt was thus well aware of the nature of the Nazi regime, he was always careful never to move too far ahead of American public opinion. He once confided to his speechwriter Samuel Rosenman: 'It's a terrible thing to look over your shoulder when you are trying to lead and find no one there.'[50] Roosevelt knew from opinion polls that a majority of Americans were against admitting large numbers of refugees into the country[51] and he was not about to go directly against the wishes of American voters – especially when he faced re-election as President in 1940.

However, even if Roosevelt had called the Evian conference only to publicize the fate of the Jews, he was still more sympathetic to the problem than a number of other statesmen in the free world. Take the views of Mackenzie King, Prime Minister of Canada, for example. On 29 March 1938 he wrote in his diary: 'A very difficult question has presented itself in Roosevelt's appeal to different countries to unite with the United States in admitting refugees from Austria, Germany etc. That means, in a word, admitting numbers of Jews. My own feeling is that nothing is to be gained by creating an internal problem in an effort to meet an international one.' King recognized that Canada might be seen as a refuge for Jews because of 'our great open spaces and small population', but still, 'We must nevertheless seek to keep this part of the Continent free from unrest and from too great an intermixture of foreign strains of blood . . . I fear we would have riots if we agreed to a policy that admitted numbers of Jews.'[52]

King knew Germany well – he had been a student in Berlin at the turn of the century. When he met Hitler on 29 June 1937, he told him that he had personally witnessed 'the constructive work of his regime'. Furthermore, he 'hoped that that work might continue. That nothing would be permitted to destroy that work. That it was bound to be followed in other countries to the great advantage of mankind.' King formed the opinion that Hitler 'is really one who truly loves his fellow men, and his country, and would make any sacrifice for their good. That he feels himself to be a deliverer of his people from tyranny.' In particular, King was 'impressed' by Hitler's eyes: 'There was a liquid quality about them which indicate keen perception and profound sympathy.'[53] What King did not raise in his meeting with Hitler, according to his diary, was the persecution of the Jews. Nor did he mention the concentration camps, nor the suppression of human rights, nor the elimination of democracy.

The following day King met with Neurath, the German Foreign Minister. Neurath told King that he 'would have loathed living in Berlin with the Jews'. Neurath went on to claim that the Jews had been gaining control of German business and finance and so it had been necessary to curb their power.[54] King does not appear to have made any protest about these anti-Semitic remarks. Instead, he and Neurath moved on to attend a luncheon party together which 'was one of the pleasantest I have ever enjoyed'.

Despite this background, the Evian conference still remained 'the only hope', as far as the World Jewish Congress was concerned, for 'hundreds of thousands of Jews who are today barbarously persecuted and evicted from positions which they had held for centuries'. A memorandum addressed to the delegates of the conference by Rabbi Stephen Wise, president of the World Jewish Congress, not only called for the international community to offer refuge for 'at least' 200,000 to 300,000 German and Austrian Jews over the coming years, but also touched on two further issues that were even more contentious. The first was the request that the conference should 'do everything in its power' to convince the German government to allow Jews to leave the Reich with some of their wealth intact. The second was that the conference should accept that 'The Jewish refugee problem cannot be discussed without taking into account the immense possibilities of Palestine as an outlet for Jewish immigration. The majority of the Jewish people has recognized a long time ago that nothing short of creating a Jewish State can restore the normal structure of the dispersed Jewish community.'[55]

There was never any possibility of the delegates at Evian supporting the demands of the World Jewish Congress. The British, in particular, were not about to announce a radical change to the status quo in Palestine where Arabs currently outnumbered Jews. Indeed, the British were not prepared to discuss anything about Palestine at Evian. There were even concerns within the Foreign Office that any attempt to make it easier for 'refugees' to leave Germany might result in other eastern European countries trying to use the same mechanism to expel their 'refugees' as well (everyone knew, of course, that 'refugee' was code for 'Jew'). It was therefore possible, by this logic, for officials at the Foreign Office to argue that any attempt to help the German and Austrian Jews could 'make the refugee problem even worse than it is at present'.[56]

Such fears were not entirely groundless. Poland, Hungary and Romania all enacted anti-Semitic legislation during the 1930s. In Poland there were around 3 million Jews – five times as many as in Germany and Austria combined – and by the start of the Evian conference they lived under a variety of restrictive measures. In August 1936, for example, all Polish shops were required to display the name of the owner on their signs. As a consequence it was obvious which shops belonged to Jews. The following year Jews were forbidden from entering the medical profession, and restrictions were placed on their ability to practise law. In March 1938 a new citizenship law was announced, which would take effect on 30 October that year, revoking the citizenship of Poles who had lived abroad for five years and had not kept 'contact' with Poland. This would have a devastating effect on Polish Jews living elsewhere.[57]

The Polish government was also contemplating removing Jews from Poland altogether. In early 1937 the Poles opened discussions with the French about the possibility of sending large numbers of Polish Jews to the island of Madagascar off the south-east coast of Africa. The idea that Madagascar, then a French colony, could become a Jewish settlement had previously been proposed by the anti-Semitic writer Paul de Lagarde in the nineteenth century. Now the Polish government were taking the notion seriously. In May 1937 a joint Polish–French task force under the direction of the Polish official Mieczysław Lepecki travelled to Madagascar in order to evaluate the idea. But after several months on the island, Lepecki and his team concluded that at most 60,000 Jews could be accommodated there – a small fraction of the 3 million Polish Jews.[58] So this fantastical idea was scrapped – only, as we shall see, for it to be resurrected by the Nazis three years later.

The Polish Madagascar initiative acted as a powerful reminder to the delegates at Evian that anti-Semitic initiatives were not just the preserve of the government of the Third Reich. The desire of other European countries in the 1930s to persecute and even remove their Jews has largely been forgotten in the public consciousness today – dwarfed by the scale and ferocity of the subsequent Nazi Holocaust.

The Evian conference began on 6 July 1938. The tone was set by the opening speech of Myron Taylor, head of the American delegation, who acknowledged the extent of the problem but refused, on behalf of America, to increase the number of refugees allowed into the USA from the existing 27,000 a year. Then, one after another, the remaining delegates followed the same script; they all deplored the current situation but couldn't promise to do much to help. The reasons given were many and various – high existing unemployment, the risk of creating racial unrest, the need for agricultural workers not 'clerical' types and so on.

Only the Dominican Republic offered to take large numbers of German and Austrian 'refugees', but that proposal was most likely a publicity stunt by the dictator Rafael Trujillo. His international reputation was in tatters because he had presided over the massacre of up to 20,000 Haitians the year before. Ultimately only a handful of Jews were admitted to the Dominican Republic and Trujillo's grand promises came to nothing.

Golda Meir, later Prime Minister of Israel, witnessed personally the combination of hot air and hypocrisy that characterized the Evian conference. She wrote that she felt a 'mixture of sorrow, rage, frustration and horror' and wanted to 'scream' at the delegates that these 'numbers' were 'human beings, people who may spend the rest of their lives in concentration camps, or wandering around the world like lepers, if you don't let them in'.[59]

At the final session of the Evian conference on 15 July 1938, Myron Taylor announced that the many speeches and discussions had achieved something concrete – the creation of a new committee: the Intergovernmental Committee for Political Refugees from Germany. It was a pitiful response to one of the most terrible human crises of modern times.

However, it must also be acknowledged that the delegates at Evian faced a tough dilemma. Even if their governments had allowed genuine discussion about the possibility of increasing the number of refugees that each country would accept, there remained, as we have seen, the concern that some countries in eastern Europe might then demand that their Jews be offered exit visas via the same process. And since the rest of the world was not prepared to accept several hundred thousand German and Austrian Jews, what hope was there of accommodating several million more? Equally, if the delegates at the conference had suggested that only the refugees from Germany and Austria should be offered safe haven, because of the intensity of the persecution they suffered, might that not have encouraged other eastern European nations to increase their own anti-Semitic actions, on the basis that the world community accepted Jews only after they had been appallingly mistreated?

Against that background, it is hard to see how anything of substance could have been accomplished at Evian without allowing discussion of the status of Palestine. Not only did the World Jewish Congress believe that 'a Jewish State' could solve the problem, but the Polish government also supported the idea of allowing large numbers of Jews into Palestine.[60] In that respect the British authorities must take responsibility for not allowing 'the immense possibilities of Palestine as an outlet for Jewish immigration' to be discussed. But by the time of the Evian conference the British must have believed they had enough problems controlling Palestine without adding more potential conflict to the existing mix. An Arab revolt had broken out in 1937, triggered by the report of a

British Royal Commission that had recommended partitioning the country between Jews and Arabs. In May 1939, after the revolt had finally been suppressed, the British rejected the idea of partitioning Palestine and announced that there would be no Jewish state in Palestine after all. Strict limits were placed on Jewish immigration to Palestine in order, many suspected, to ensure that Arabs remained in a majority. It was devastating news for the thousands of Jews who desperately wanted to find a way out of the Third Reich. To supporters of Zionism, who remembered the fine words of the 1917 Balfour Declaration, it was nothing less than a betrayal. Winston Churchill, a supporter of Zionism, called the decision a 'lamentable act of default'.[61] Moreover, it was obvious that the British government had acted in this way in an attempt to mollify the Arabs. Strategic British interests – like the Suez Canal – lay in Arab territory, and geopolitically the Jews had little to bargain with by comparison. As the British Prime Minister, Neville Chamberlain, stated at a meeting of a cabinet committee on Palestine on 20 April 1939, it was of 'immense importance' that Britain should 'have the Muslim world with us'. Consequently, 'If we must offend one side, let us offend the Jews rather than the Arabs.'[62] Once again political pragmatism triumphed over compassionate humanitarianism.

There were even some officials who, in rejecting Jewish requests, revealed their own anti-Semitic beliefs. Charles Frederick Blair, director of Canada's Immigration Branch, stated in a memo in October 1938 that even though the Jews faced potential 'extinction'[63] in Europe, they should still not be allowed in large numbers into Canada. In an earlier letter, written after the Evian conference, he said that it 'might be a very good thing' for Jews to ask themselves the question 'why they are so unpopular almost everywhere'.[64]

The delegates at the Evian conference could not even come together to condemn the Nazi persecution of the Jews. Arguably, some feared making the situation in the Reich worse for the Jews if they spoke out. William Shirer wrote that the British, French and Americans seemed 'anxious not to do anything to offend Hitler'. It was an 'absurd situation', thought Shirer, because they 'want to appease the man who is responsible for their problem'.[65]

The Nazi regime's view of the outcome of the Evian conference could not have been more blunt: the headline of the *Völkischer Beobachter* on

13 July was 'No One Wants to Have Them', with the strapline 'Fruitless debates at the Jew-conference in Evian'.[66] Hitler, in a speech at Nuremberg in September 1938, ridiculed the 'hypocritical' actions of the 'democratic empires'. Germany, he said, was criticized for acting with 'unimaginable cruelty' against the Jews, but then the same democratic countries who voiced this attack refused to accommodate the Jews, saying 'there is regretfully no space' for them.

Hitler couched his argument against continuing to accept the presence of the Jews – 'these parasites' as he called them – in terms of population density. He claimed that Germany had more than 140 people per square kilometre whereas the 'democratic world empires' had only a 'few people' per square kilometre.[67]

Hitler spoke these words at the same time as he planned on taking military action to gain Germany more space: first in Czechoslovakia and subsequently, as he had outlined thirteen years before in *Mein Kampf*, in the western regions of the Soviet Union. The two obsessions of his political life – his racial hatred of the Jews and his desire for Germany to gain more land – were, as we have seen, intertwined. There would be no point, as far as Hitler was concerned, in gaining the extra space that Germany needed if that space contained large numbers of Jews, which, in the case of Poland and the western parts of the Soviet Union, it most certainly did. The potential for a catastrophic fate to befall millions of Jews thus lay once again in the subtext of this September 1938 speech, a year before the war began.

That same month, September 1938, Hitler met with Józef Lipski, the Polish ambassador to Berlin. In a revealing conversation – on both sides – they talked about the 'Jewish question' in the aftermath of the Evian conference and the failure of the Polish attempt to pursue a Madagascar 'solution'. Lipski recorded in his notes that Hitler 'has in mind an idea of settling the Jewish problem by way of emigration to the colonies in accordance with an understanding with Poland, Hungary, and possibly Romania'. After hearing these words, Lipski said to Hitler that 'if he finds such a solution we will erect to him a beautiful monument in Warsaw.'[68]

Around the same time Hitler was talking with the Polish ambassador about sending the Jews to the 'colonies', the British were trying to reach a diplomatic agreement with him about the fate of Czechoslovakia. Part of the problem was that the British government appeared to believe

Hitler's claim that he did not want war and that his chief concern was genuinely with the German-speaking minority in Czechoslovakia. In an attempt to solve the dispute, the British Prime Minister, Neville Chamberlain, agreed at a conference in Munich at the end of September 1938 that German troops could occupy the Sudetenland, the predominantly German-speaking region of Czechoslovakia. The Czechs, infamously, had no say in the matter. By thus appeasing Hitler, the British hoped to prevent war.

The trouble was that Chamberlain failed to understand that Hitler was not at heart a conventional statesman who, like all sensible political leaders, would be loath to risk military conflict. Ernst von Weizsäcker, a German diplomat, tried to explain the reality of the situation to the British ambassador to Berlin, Sir Nevile Henderson: 'I have said to Henderson once again that this is not a game of chess but a rising sea. One cannot make the same kind of assumptions as in normal times and with normal people.'[69] Weizsäcker's metaphor of the 'rising sea' is not just striking but accurate – at least as far as the German Jews were concerned, for they were about to be engulfed.

Any wide-ranging war in the near future threatened to upset existing Nazi plans for the Jews, since it would begin before the majority of the Jews had been pushed out of the Reich. This was, for Hitler and the staunch anti-Semites in the Nazi party, a dangerous problem, since they believed that the Jews had acted as traitors behind the lines in the First World War and that they would be liable to act in the same way in the event of another conflict. One practical method of dealing with the situation was proposed by the head of the Jewish Department of the SD, Herbert Hagen. In September 1938 he wrote a memo entitled 'Activity of the Department in the Event of Mobilization' which proposed arresting all foreign Jews once the German Army had been mobilized for war, as well as imprisoning all other Jews in 'special camps' where they would be forced to work on armaments production. Hagen also suggested that some Jews might be subjected to 'special treatment'. It is unclear in the context of his memo exactly what he meant by this. He could have intended the phrase simply to mean that the circumstances of some Jews would need to be looked at more closely, but it is also possible that he imagined that the Security Services might perhaps find it necessary to kill some of the group, since 'special treatment' would subsequently become one of the accepted euphemisms for extermination.[70]

As for Hitler, his belief in a world Jewish conspiracy had not been damaged by the failure of the international community to offer help to the Jews at the Evian conference. In a speech in Saarbrücken on 9 October 1938 he said, 'we know that the international Jewish fiend looms threateningly behind the scenes . . . and it does so today just as it did yesterday.'[71] He now decided that if foreign countries would not voluntarily take Jews living in the Reich, the Nazis would dump some of them on their doorstep. On 28 October, the Nazis gathered together around 17,000 Polish Jews who lived in Germany, took them to the border with Poland and tried to push them on to Polish land.

The timing of this brutal action was influenced by the law the Poles had passed earlier that year, which from 30 October threatened to deny citizenship to Poles living abroad. By trying to shove the Polish Jews back across the border to Poland two days before the deadline, the Nazis sought to circumvent the new rule. The plight of these Jews – wanted neither by the Germans nor by the Poles – was horrific. As Josef Broniatowski, who had been taken from Plauen, west of Dresden, to the Polish border, recalled, 'Thousands of Jews ended up on the meadow and marched soaked up to their waists across the fields [after crossing a water-filled ditch]. As we were getting close to a Polish village, some Polish soldiers came and chased us back to the German border, all the while hitting people and shooting,' and during the night 'many old people and little children died.' Eventually they were driven to another border crossing where they were finally admitted into Poland. 'The suffering was terrible, in the village to which they chased us the miners, who are Catholics, started crying when they saw all this suffering and misery.'[72]

Sendel and Riva Grynszpan were two more Jews among the thousands who were taken to the Polish border. Sendel had owned a small tailor's shop in Hanover and had suffered much economic hardship as a result of Nazi anti-Semitic legislation. He recalled that at the end of October 1938 the Gestapo arrived and 'took us in police trucks, [and] in prisoners' lorries, about 20 men in each truck, and they took us to the railway station. The streets were black with people shouting: "Juden raus! Aus nach Palästina!" ("Out with the Jews! Off to Palestine!").'[73]

Their son, Herschel, had moved to France in 1936 at the age of fifteen in order to escape Nazi persecution, but he remained devoted to his mother and father. In Paris he struggled to survive as he was at constant risk of deportation. When he heard what had happened to his parents he decided take revenge on the Nazis, and on Monday 7 November 1938 he shot Ernst vom Rath, a diplomat at the German embassy in Paris. Vom Rath died two days later on 9 November, coincidentally one of the most sacred dates in the Nazi calendar – the anniversary of the failed Beer-Hall Putsch in Munich.

Goebbels, like all the leading Nazis, was in Munich for the commemoration. He relished the pretext that the assassination of vom Rath gave for a new attack on the German Jews. 'In the afternoon [of 9 November] the death of the German diplomat vom Rath is reported,' he wrote in his diary. 'Well, now it's done.' Goebbels met Hitler a few hours later at the party reception in the old Town Hall in Munich. 'I present the matter to the Führer. He decides: let the demonstrations [against the Jews] continue. Withdraw the police. The Jews are to experience the rage of the people. That's right. I immediately issue appropriate instructions to police and party. Then I briefly speak to the party leadership to that effect. Rapturous applause. Everyone dashed to the telephones. Now the people will act.'[74]

Goebbels' diary entry was disingenuous. It wasn't so much that the Jews would 'experience the rage of the people' as that they would experience the rage of Nazi Stormtroopers. Throughout the night of 9 November, and the early hours of 10 November, Jewish shops and homes were smashed, synagogues were burnt, and Jews beaten up, arrested or even murdered. There are no accurate figures for how many Jews died that night – it was certainly more than ninety. Around 30,000 Jews were arrested and taken to concentration camps.

Eighteen-year-old Rudi Bamber in Nuremberg learnt of the attacks only when the front door of his house was smashed open. It was the first of two visits from Stormtroopers that night. The first group confined themselves to wrecking the house, the second attacked the residents. One of the elderly women who lived with them in the house was dragged out and beaten up. The Stormtroopers then turned their attentions on Rudi and started hitting him. Eventually he was taken outside and put under guard. Then – for reasons he never understood – the Stormtroopers left him and moved on. He went back into the house and found that 'it was all so chaotic . . . the second lot [of Stormtroopers] had smashed pipes and the water was running through the floors and I was concerned in trying to find the main stop valve to stop the water from running further, and fighting one's way through – it was a bit like sort of after an air raid I suppose in a way, you know, stuff lying everywhere and furniture broken, glass, china, everywhere.'[75]

Upstairs he found his father – dying. The Stormtroopers had murdered him. 'I was absolutely in shock. I couldn't understand how this situation had arisen, from what we had before, the sort of usual average, normal life – "normal" in inverted commas. For this to happen seemed to be absolutely unacceptable and unbelievable . . . I really couldn't envisage that such a thing should have or could have happened. I'd heard of concentration camps before, of course; they were going already in Dachau and Buchenwald, but that was something different. [This was] violence of a totally unnecessary and uncalled for [kind]. I didn't know the people, they didn't know me. They had no grudge against me [personally] – they were just people who had come to do whatever they thought they should do . . . The whole thing is senseless and pointless.'

What particularly struck Rudi Bamber, as he tried to come to terms with the murder of his father, were the contradictions that lay within the Germany he now inhabited. The assault in the early hours of 10 November had been arbitrary and unpredictable – yet it had been carried out by Stormtroopers under the protection of the state. The next morning the police sealed off the building as if it was an official crime scene. They also wanted to prevent looting, which was still held to be against the law. After a few days Rudi went to the office of the Gestapo and asked if his family could now remove the seals and move back into the house. 'It seems strange to me,' he says. 'I had no fear in going to the Gestapo. Somehow there seemed to be some legitimacy somewhere in this system . . . it was a period which is incomprehensible to me now.'

One of the reasons Rudi Bamber found it hard to deal with what had happened was that 'I couldn't give expression to my anger,' because 'if one could really give vent to one's feelings it might be worse for us . . . I had no way of coping with this in a sort of sensible or rational way. The background of the Nazi propaganda, Nazi domination, had I think subdued me and other Jews as well, to accept many things, and I think this came out when people were deported and taken to the camps. Looking back at it now I find it almost unbelievable how I dealt – or rather didn't deal – with anything which had happened and had no particular reaction to it, which obviously any right-thinking person would have had. But I think it was the power of the system which held me down in a way and stopped me from dealing with it in an appropriate way.'

Across Germany the attacks on synagogues and the desecration of Jewish Holy Scriptures marked a new low even for the Nazis. In Berlin, Günther Ruschin witnessed the aftermath of the destruction of the synagogue in which his father was cantor: 'I went there and I saw the holiest things we have. They were dirty with excrement and it was awful. It was the first time I saw my father cry.'[76]

For Rudi Bamber, the lack of support from other Germans compounded the suffering. He remembers that his family received no comfort from the non-Jewish population. Most just walked past their wrecked family home, but 'one or two' even threw stones at the building. Similarly, Heinz Nassau reported from Essen that as the Jewish youth centre was burning in the city, a nurse asked a fireman whether the Jewish administrator and his family were still inside. She was told: 'They can perish quietly! After all they did away with vom Rath. Make sure you leave this area or we'll smash you up too.'[77]

The reaction across the rest of Germany was more varied. One police report recorded that 'the populace has divided views' with the majority of people believing that 'all this destruction was uncalled for.'[78] Another Jewish eyewitness report from Bavaria said that 'The mood amongst the Christian population of Munich is thoroughly against the operation. I was shown the liveliest sympathy and compassion from all sides . . . A completely unknown Aryan lady from the best social class came to my wife with the comment, "Madam, I am ashamed to be a German." Another unknown lady sent a bottle of wine.'[79]

This differing response to the atrocity that became known as 'Kristallnacht' – Night of Broken Glass – was also illustrated by the contrasting reactions of Uwe Storjohann's parents in Hamburg. Even though Uwe's father was an 'anti-Semite' he was 'really angry' about Kristallnacht because the 'holy temples' of the Jews had been 'desecrated'. But his mother was not so concerned. She was pleased when, in the aftermath of the attack, their Jewish neighbours left and two days later 'a transport van came and one of Hamburg's high-up SA leaders' moved into their flat. Uwe remembers that his mother 'thought it was great that the SA leader, who was very jovial and pretended to be close to the people, was now there'.[80]

For the thousands of Jews sent to concentration camps after Kristallnacht the experience was predictably traumatic. One Jewish man recorded how he witnessed the commandant of Sachsenhausen take off his gloves and repeatedly punch a prisoner, calling him a 'dirty Jewish pig'. He was also forced to watch as a prisoner who had tried to escape was punished: 'The man in question was strapped to a Bock [whipping block] and beaten with a heavy bull whip by two SA men, who had volunteered specially for this . . . The victim had to loudly count every blow up to 25 himself until he fell silent because he lost consciousness, but even then the animals did not stop their mistreatment. The Stubenälteste [room elder] reported that if the victim recovered even slightly, the second twenty five would be administered.'[81]

The newspaper of the SS, *Das Schwarze Korps* (The Black Corps), had been agitating in increasingly radical terms against the Jews for months prior to Kristallnacht. But in the wake of the attacks even more hatred burst through. 'Because it is necessary,' declared an article that appeared on 24 November, 'because we no longer hear the world's clamour, and because no power on earth can stop us, we will bring the Jewish question to its total solution. The programme is clear. It is: Total expulsion, complete separation!'[82]

Another article, published on 17 November, stated: 'Woe betide the Jews, if even one of them or one of their accomplices, hired and filled with hatred by them, ever lifts up their murderous hand against one German! Not one will be held responsible for a dead or wounded German, but they all will. This is what those should know, who haven't known after our first moderate warning . . . There is only one right, our right, our self-defence, and we alone are to decide the time and mode of its application.'[83] A subsequent edition of *Das Schwarze Korps* made the threat explicit: 'The day a murder weapon that is Jewish or bought by Jews rises against one of the leading men of Germany, there will be no more Jews in Germany! We hope we have made ourselves clear!'[84]

The SS newspaper made two more statements around this time that are important to our understanding of the mentality of these hard-line believers. The first was that though the SS accepted that anti-Semitism was not new – indeed, it had 'been vital within all healthy peoples and races for many thousand years' – they believed the Nazis were the only ones to have drawn from it the necessary 'effective and practical, albeit unsentimental conclusions'.[85] Second, the SS asserted that the Nazis had been forced to take action against the Jews because of the failure of the international community to help out, and so they saw their critics in the democratic nations as hypocrites: 'Neither Mr. Roosevelt nor an English archbishop, nor any other prominent Democrat would put his daughter into the bed of a sleazy east European Jew; but when it comes to Germany, they know at once no Jewish question, but only the "persecution of the innocent for the sake of their faith", as if we had ever been interested in what a Jew believes or does not believe.'[86] Thus, even before the war began, the SS claimed they could take violent action against the Jews for two reasons: first, all 'healthy' people in the world accepted that it was right to be anti-Semitic, but only the Nazis were tough enough to take the necessary action against the Jews, and, second, it wasn't the SS's fault if they had to attack the Jews, because other countries had decided not to offer the Jews safe refuge.

At the same time as these views were being voiced in *Das Schwarze Korps*, the SS in concentration camps were beating, whipping and otherwise tormenting thousands of Jews in the wake of Kristallnacht. What all this tells us, of course, is that the SS were prepared for radical action against the Jews nearly a year before the Second World War started.

The overall international response to Kristallnacht was, understandably, one of condemnation. But in most countries, just as at Evian, compassionate words did not lead to compassionate action. Roosevelt did allow 12,000 Austrian and German Jews already in the United States on short-term visas to extend their stay, but a proposal in Congress to allow 20,000 additional Jewish children into America was rejected. Roosevelt did not speak up in support of the bill and the proposal died.

Only in Britain was there a substantial increase in the number of refugees admitted. In a gradual process that had begun in the wake of the Anschluss and continued after Kristallnacht, restrictions were eased so that 50,000 Jews from Germany and German-controlled territory could enter Britain before the outbreak of war.[87] Around 9,000 children travelled to the country on what became known as 'Kindertransports'. Rudi Bamber and his younger sister were two of those who managed to get visas to come to Britain just before the war began. Rudi remembers that there had to be 'a lot of planning' put into his emigration. 'Every bit of clothing – everything which I took – had to be listed and approved by the authorities.' Before his exit was finally authorized, Rudi also had to appear before a tribunal: 'There were Nazi officials and army officers, Gestapo and police sitting round . . . It was absurd because the general who was in charge of this sort of said "Oh yes, you're in agriculture. You're going to go to the colonies presumably to farm there." I said "Oh yes." I would have said yes to anything . . . Nobody mentioned the word "Jew" at the time.'[88]

After Kristallnacht there was no pretending that Hitler was a normal politician in charge of a country that wanted peaceful relations with the rest of the world. Lord Halifax, the British Foreign Secretary, told a meeting of the Foreign Policy Committee that 'crazy persons' had managed to 'secure control' of Germany. He believed that 'the immediate objective [of the British government] should be the correction of the false impression that we were decadent, spineless and could with impunity be kicked about'.[89]

As for Hitler, there is no record of him saying anything in public or in private about Kristallnacht after the event, although at the time Goebbels in his diary had made it clear that the German leader approved of the action against the Jews. Almost certainly Hitler did not want to be associated with the violence. He prized his prestige as head of state, and did not want foreign leaders to hold him personally responsible. His silence also left him the option of blaming extremists within the party for the violence if there was discontent within Germany about the attacks. Manfred von Schröder, then a young German diplomat, remembers that many believed that Kristallnacht was the work of 'radical Nazis and SA people' and that the crime had not been 'agreed by Hitler'.[90] Given how Hitler acted over Kristallnacht, it should not come as a surprise to learn that he would subsequently adopt the same tactic during the war and never speak explicitly in public about how the security forces of the Third Reich were murdering Jews.

On 12 November 1938, Hermann Göring chaired a conference at the Aviation Ministry in Berlin to discuss the aftermath of Kristallnacht. It is one of the only high-level Nazi gatherings on Jewish policy for which a stenographic record of much of the meeting survives, and the contents are revealing.[91] In the first place the meeting laid bare the extent to which the Nazi hierarchy had not thought through the consequences of their own actions. The problem they had created for themselves with Kristallnacht was straightforward – not only were the Jews able to claim for the damage they had suffered to their property from German insurance companies, many of which were owned by non-Jews, but a considerable quantity of the glass that had been destroyed could be replaced only by buying it from abroad and thus wasting large amounts of money on the foreign exchange market. Göring said that it was 'insane, to clean out and burn a Jewish warehouse then have a German insurance company make good the loss'. He would much rather that '200 Jews' had been killed rather than property of such value destroyed.

The participants at the conference also discussed further restrictive measures against the Jews. Reinhard Heydrich suggested that Jews should be forced to wear 'a certain insignia' on their clothes. One consequence of this, he said, would be that it would stop foreign Jews 'who don't look different from ours' from 'being molested'. This, in turn, would prevent other governments from complaining about the mistreatment of their own citizens in Germany. Göring pointed out that this action, combined with the further seizure of Jewish businesses and greater restrictions on the ability of Jews to move about freely, would lead to 'the creation of ghettos on a very large scale, in all the cities'. But Heydrich was against this: 'We could not control a ghetto where the Jews congregate amidst the whole Jewish people. It would remain the permanent hideout for criminals and also for epidemics and the like. We don't want to let the Jew live in the same house with the German population; but today the German population, [in] their blocks or houses, force the Jew to behave himself. The control of the Jew through the watchful eye of the whole population is better than having him by the thousands in a district where I cannot properly establish a control over his daily life through uniformed agents.' This exchange is significant in the light of what was to come, since both measures – the marking of Jews with an 'insignia' and the creation of ghettos – would be implemented in parts of the occupied east little more than a year later.

The transcript of the meeting also demonstrates the outlandish nature of the debate between these leading Nazi figures. What emerges is a world in which any idea, no matter how radical or eccentric, could be floated and discussed. Goebbels suggested that 'this is our chance to dissolve the synagogues' and to replace them with other buildings or 'parking lots'. They also discussed forcing Jews to travel in special compartments on trains, but Goebbels said that wouldn't work because 'suppose there would be two Jews in the train and the other compartments would be over-crowded. These two Jews would then have a compartment all to themselves.' Göring countered by saying, 'I'd give the Jews one coach or one compartment. And should a case like you mention arise and the train be overcrowded, believe me, we won't need a law. We'll kick him out and he'll have to sit all alone in the toilet all the way!'

Goebbels proposed that they should consider forbidding Jews to enter the German forests, because the 'behaviour of the Jews is so inciting and provocative' with 'whole herds of them' running about the Grunewald, a forest outside Berlin. Göring latched on to Goebbels' idea and gave it a bizarre twist of his own, suggesting that while the Jews should be banned from most of the forest, an area could be reserved just for them. This section could be stocked with animals that 'look' like Jews – Göring suggested the elk, because it 'has such a crooked nose'.

Göring's remark about the elk captures the attitude of those attend-ing the 12 November meeting. No ethical restriction held them back. A plan to send the Jews to the moon could have been proposed were it not for the practical difficulties of making it happen. These Nazi leaders knew that Hitler liked to hear radical ideas, and as a consequence they felt exhilarated, and able to dream as fantastically as they liked.

By the time the meeting ended Göring and his colleagues had dis-cussed a whole range of new measures against the Jews, including plans to seize – or 'Aryanize' – Jewish businesses, establish a similar emigra-tion operation in Germany to the one Eichmann had created in Austria, and – in an act of pure double-speak – make the Jews pay a massive fine as a penalty for causing Kristallnacht, because vom Rath had been mur-dered by a Jew. Finally, Göring summed up the situation for the Jews who still lived under German rule: 'If, in the near future, the German Reich should come into conflict with foreign powers, it goes without saying that we in Germany should first of all let it come to a showdown with the Jews.'[92]

As for Hitler, his rhetoric was now almost apocalyptic. In his speech before the Reichstag on 30 January 1939, the sixth anniversary of the seizure of power, he made explicit threats against the Jews. In an address that lasted more than two and a half hours, he asserted that Germany wanted only to live in peace with other countries, but 'international Jewry' sought to 'gratify its thirst for vengeance'. Furthermore, 'At this moment, the Jews are still propagating their campaign of hatred in certain states under the cover of press, film, radio, theater, and literature, which are all in their hands.' Infamously, Hitler also said that if 'international' Jewish financiers within Europe and abroad should succeed 'in plunging mankind into yet another world war, then the result will not be a Bolshevization of the earth and the victory of Jewry, but the annihilation of the Jewish race in Europe'.[93]

What exactly did Hitler mean by this? A serious threat against the Jews, certainly. But did he explicitly mean that he intended to kill the Jews in the event of a world war? That is debatable, especially since there is no evidence that he had a detailed plan of destruction in mind for the Jews as he uttered these words. An alternative, more persuasive interpretation is that by 'annihilation' Hitler meant 'elimination', and thus one possible 'solution' to the Nazis' Jewish 'problem' remained the destruction of the Jews in Europe by forcibly removing them from the continent. Support for this view is offered by Hitler's statements earlier in his speech, when he denounced 'the entire democratic world' for their 'non-intervention' and failure to accept Jewish emigrants. These countries were 'filled with tears of pity at the plight of the poor, tortured Jewish people, while remaining hardhearted'. It was in this context that Hitler promised that Germany would 'banish this people' – that is, the Jews.

A further insight into Hitler's intentions is offered by his comments at a meeting with István Csáky, the Hungarian Foreign Minister, on 16 January 1938 – two weeks before his 'prophecy' speech. Csáky was no friend of the Jews and served in a government that had already implemented anti-Semitic legislation. Hitler told Csáky that he was 'certain' that 'the Jews would have to disappear from Germany to the last one'.[94] He also said that the 'Jewish problem' existed 'not just in Germany' and that he would support any other state that sought to confront it. The context of his use of the word 'disappear' in this meeting suggests that Hitler meant 'expulsion' rather than 'extermination'.

Additional backing for this reading of events is offered by Hitler's remarks on 21 January 1938. During a discussion with the Czechoslovakian Foreign Minister, František Chvalkovský, Hitler said that the Jews would be 'destroyed in Germany' in vengeance for '9 November 1918' and that one 'possibility' was for the countries that were 'interested' to select 'any location in the world' and 'put the Jews there'. The other 'Anglo-Saxon countries that are dripping with humanity' could then be told, 'Here they are; they either starve to death or you can put into practice your many speeches [and, by implication, look after them].'[95]

However, while on balance it is unlikely that Hitler's prophecy demonstrated that he already had a definite plan to murder the Jews in the light of any forthcoming 'world war', the importance of the linkage in his mind between the fate of the Jews and any future conflict should not be underestimated. If Germany was involved in a war, the Jews would suffer appallingly – that was the assurance he gave on 30 January 1939. What form that suffering would take – forced expulsion or something even worse – was yet to be decided.

At the same time, Hitler was ratcheting up the pressure on his European neighbours still further. The Slovaks, who had gained greater autonomy within Czechoslovakia in the wake of the Munich agreement, were pressured into declaring full independence from the Czech state. Göring, at a meeting with Slovak representatives, expressed himself with typical bluntness. 'Do you want to make yourselves independent?' he said. '[Or should] I let the Hungarians have you?'[96] In March 1939 the Slovaks did as they were asked and split from the Czechs. Under the Presidency of Jozef Tiso, a Catholic priest, the new regime in Slovakia implemented a series of anti-Semitic measures. The following month, for instance, they passed Decree 63/39 banning Jews from many professions in an attempt to ensure that Jews were 'excluded' from 'national life'.[97] 'Our lives turned upside down,' says Linda Breder, an orthodox Slovak Jew then fourteen years old. Linda was 'kicked out of school' and her father lost his job. She was particularly shocked because previously 'Jews and Christians had lived side by side.'[98] Otto Pressburger, a Slovak Jew who was seventeen in 1939, confirms that 'There used to be no difference between us, between Jewish and Christian youth.' But after the Slovak state had been established, 'I was sent back home from school and told I cannot go to school any more. We could not go anywhere and had to stay at home . . . Before we used to go dancing with girls – not only Jewish girls – something like a disco today. Then the signs were put up: "No Jews and Dogs Allowed".'[99]

Once Slovakia, the eastern part of the former Czechoslovakia, had split from the rest of the country, Hitler ordered German troops to march into the remaining Czech lands. The occupation was completed in a matter of hours, and on 16 March 1939, Hitler travelled to Prague and announced the creation of the German Protectorate of Bohemia and Moravia. Over 110,000 more Jews now came under German control, and they too were soon subjected to a whole series of anti-Semitic measures, including the 'Aryanization' of Jewish businesses.

Hitler's aggressive intentions were now obvious to the world. The occupation of the Czech lands could not be defended as part of a Nazi plan merely to regain German-speaking territory lost at the end of the First World War. As the permanent under-secretary to the Foreign Office, Sir Alexander Cadogan, wrote in his diary on 20 March 1939: 'I'm afraid we have reached the crossroads. I always said that, as long as Hitler could pretend he was incorporating Germans in the Reich, we could pretend that he had a case. If he proceeded to gobble up other nationalities, that would be the time to call "Halt!" '[100]

The British now offered guarantees against any future Nazi aggression to Poland, Greece and Romania. Roosevelt, recognizing the seriousness of what had just happened to Czechoslovakia, decided to write Hitler a letter. On 15 April 1939 he held a press conference at the White House and announced that he had asked Hitler to commit to solving problems by peaceful means. He had sought 'assurance' from him that German armed forces would not 'attack or invade the territory or possessions' of more than thirty different countries, from Finland to Yugoslavia, from the Netherlands to Portugal and from Sweden to Iran.[101]

Roosevelt's letter was a propaganda gift for Hitler. After all, what right did the President of the United States have to ask the leader of Germany for a public assurance that he did not intend to use German forces to invade Spain or Switzerland? Hitler replied to Roosevelt's letter in a tour de force of bitter sarcasm during a speech to the Reichstag on 28 April. He pointed out that America had played a part in imposing the hated 'Diktat of Versailles' on the German people after the First World War and so was ill qualified now to talk of raising a 'voice of strength and friendship for mankind' – especially since the Americans had refused to support the League of Nations. But most embarrassingly for Roosevelt, Hitler pointed out that a number of the countries named on his list, such as Syria, were 'presently not in the possession of their liberty since their territories are occupied by the military forces of the democratic states which have robbed them of all their rights'. Moreover, Hitler said, Ireland did not see Germany as a threat but 'England'; and it appeared 'to have slipped Mr. Roosevelt's mind that Palestine is not being occupied by German troops but by English ones'.[102]

This marks the moment when Hitler burnt any diplomatic bridges that had been left standing between Germany and America. He mentioned a number of times in the speech how America had intervened on the Allied side in the First World War, and his concern, though unspoken, was obvious – the Americans might do just the same thing in any future conflict in Europe. Since Hitler believed that the Jews held profound influence in America, it is not surprising that December 1941, the month that America did finally enter the war, is a key moment – as we shall see – in the evolution of the Holocaust.

Not that the knowledge that America might become an adversary in a future war deterred Hitler from pursuing the conflict. He knew that if the war in Europe began without delay then the German Army would have an opportunity to gain sufficient territory and win the war before America decided to take part. It was all a matter of timing. As he said to his generals in August 1939, 'all these favourable circumstances will no longer prevail in two or three years' time . . . A long period of peace would not do us any good.'[103] It was now necessary to 'close your hearts to pity' and to 'act brutally'. These were the sentiments of the authentic Hitler.

Hitler was about to take Germany to war, but it was not the war he had once planned. Years ago he had wanted Britain as an ally, not an adversary. More recently he had hoped Poland would cooperate with Nazi aggression and join the Germans in a war against the Soviet Union. Yet the Poles now opposed him as well. So in order to restrict the number of nations that Germany would have to confront in the short term, he dispatched Ribbentrop to Moscow to agree a non-aggression pact with Stalin, his greatest ideological enemy. But while one of Hitler's desires – war against the Soviet Union – would have to wait, the other – a radical reckoning with the Jews – could begin at once.

8. The Start of Racial War

(1939–1940)

German troops invaded Poland on Friday 1 September 1939 and initiated a rule of terror that would see Poland become the epicentre of the Holocaust. The Germans would build all of their most infamous extermination camps on Polish soil, and Poland would suffer a greater proportionate loss of population than any other single country in the war. Up to 6 million people living in Poland – at least half of them Jews – lost their lives. The vast majority of these people did not die in battle, but as a result of a deliberate policy of starvation, deportation and murder.

The Germans defeated the Polish Army in less than six weeks. In part this success was gained because of superior armaments and tactics, but the Germans also received assistance from an unlikely source – their ideological enemy. On 17 September, just over two weeks after the Germans had entered Poland from the west, the Red Army invaded Poland from the east. As a result Polish forces were crushed between two powerful adversaries. The Poles never stood a chance.

In Moscow, the Germans and the Soviets agreed in comradely fashion to put ideological differences aside and discuss the detailed division of Poland. Ribbentrop and Vyacheslav Molotov, the Soviet Foreign Minister, toasted each other at an extravagant banquet in the Andreevsky Hall of the Kremlin on 27 September. 'Hurrah to Germany, her Führer and her Foreign Minister!' said Molotov as he raised his glass.[1] This 'friendship' had begun with the signing of the Nazi–Soviet pact in August 1939 – a deal which had included a secret protocol about the allocation between them of 'spheres of influence' in eastern Europe. But it was only tactical as far as Hitler was concerned – just twenty-two months later Germany would invade the Soviet Union.

As the Wehrmacht crossed into Poland, Reinhard Heydrich arranged with the German Army High Command for more than 2,000 'Einsatzgruppen' – 'operational groups' or special task forces – to enter the country immediately behind the army in order to combat 'elements hostile' to Germany. Heydrich, who in September was appointed head of the Reich Main Security Office, ordered that 'the higher echelons of the Polish population need to be rendered as good as harmless.' The result was that around 16,000 Poles were murdered in the first weeks of the invasion – a mix of members of the intelligentsia, priests, Jews and anyone else considered 'hostile'.

The atrocities committed by the invading forces were many and various. Erich Ehlers, a member of Einsatzgruppe II, recorded in his diary in September how 'Polish cutthroats' were summarily executed. He wrote that 'one of them still ate a piece of bread, even after the pit had been dug and the guns were already pointed at him'.[2] Helmuth Bischoff, commander of an Einsatzkommando, reported that shortly after his arrival in Bydgoszcz he had decided to place '14 Jewish and Polish male hostages' in 'front of the hotel entrance' so that 'the Polish passers-by were well aware that with every shot fired that night in our street, one of them would be killed. Because even this did not discourage the Polish snipers, the fate of the hostages was sealed.'[3] One ordinary German soldier, a member of a transport regiment, remembers witnessing the SS Regiment 'Germania' conducting a mass execution of Jews near Kraków as the regimental band played.[4]

In early November 1939 the Nazis called academics at the Jagiellonian University in Kraków to a meeting in one of the lecture rooms. Once they arrived they were beaten with rifle butts before being transported to concentration camps. 'I had a very Catholic upbringing,' says Mieczysław Brożek, an assistant professor at the university, 'and it did not enter my head that something evil [like this] could happen . . . It was beyond our life experience.' Once in Dachau he was so appalled by the suffering that he felt a 'complete annihilation of values. After the experiences I had in the camp there are no values. I had a vision of the worthlessness of everything. The senselessness of everything. This tormented me desperately, to the brink of suicide.'[5]

As for the mass of Polish civilians, they soon discovered that the Nazis wished them to become a nation of slaves. They were classed as Slavs by the Nazis and were therefore deemed to be an inferior race. 'There were no schools [any more],' says Michael Preisler, who was twenty years old in September 1939 and lived in the west of Poland. 'The churches were closed too. Polish people couldn't ride buses together with Germans. They even said, "not allowed for Poles and dogs". We were actually treated just like animals. We were treated as something different than humans."[6]

Some members of the German Army were appalled by the atrocities their fellow countrymen were committing in Poland. Major Helmuth Stieff, for example, wrote to his family and said 'we don't feel like victors here, more like guilty criminals . . . This annihilation of whole families with women and children can only be the work of subhumans who no longer deserve to be called "Germans". I am ashamed to be a German.'[7] Famously, General Johannes Blaskowitz wrote a critical report about the activities of the German security forces in Poland that reached Hitler. Hitler was furious, saying that 'you do not lead a war with Salvation Army methods' and that 'he had never trusted General Blaskowitz'.[8]

Blaskowitz was an exception. Most senior officers did not complain to their superiors about the atrocities that were committed in Poland. Field Marshal von Brauchitsch, the head of the army, set the tone when he wrote on 1 November that the 'Jew is the fiercest enemy of the German *Volk*'. A few months later he reminded his troops that the 'ethnic-political measures ordered by the Führer for the security of German living space in Poland . . . inevitably must lead to what would otherwise be regarded as unusual, harsh measures against the Polish population in the occupied territory'.[9]

In many cases officers and men of the German Army assisted the Einsatzgruppen in their work – for example, by suggesting groups to be targeted.[10] The army also shot hostages as a reprisal for attacks, and this in turn empowered German soldiers to kill innocent Polish civilians.[11] Nearly 400 Poles were murdered for this reason in Bydgoszcz in early September.

All this brutality did not mean, however, that the invasion of Poland marks the beginning of the Holocaust as we know it. Though several thousand Jews were murdered in the early months of the occupation, Hitler and the Nazi leadership were also targeting the 'leadership class' within Poland at the same time, and the overarching policy as regards the Jews remained the same as before – persecution and expulsion. But while the outbreak of war appeared to have closed one possible avenue for removing the Jews – the large-scale emigration of the Jews to countries not under German control – it had simultaneously opened another – the possibility of expelling Jews to the furthest reaches of the new Nazi empire. In late September Heydrich said Hitler had approved the idea of deporting the Jews to the east, and as an initial measure Polish Jews were to be concentrated in cities in order to make them easier to control.[12]

Hitler announced in October 1939 that German-occupied Poland would be divided into two. One part would be incorporated into the Reich and 'Germanized' and a section in the south-east of the country, bordering Soviet-occupied Poland, would remain 'Polish', albeit under German occupation. This area, containing around 11 million people and including the cities of Warsaw, Lublin and Kraków, was to be called the General Government of the Occupied Polish Areas – subsequently shortened to the General Government. The potential for this area to become, in Nazi slang, a 'dustbin' for the Reich, was obvious from the beginning. The rulers of the territory to be Germanized, notably Albert Forster of Danzig/West Prussia, and Arthur Greiser of the Warthegau – the area centred around Poznań – were both keen to 'cleanse' their areas and hoped to send the unwanted Poles and Jews to the General Government. Hitler remarked himself, at the end of September, that territory in the east of Poland between the River Bug – the border with Soviet-occupied Poland – and the River Vistula, should accommodate 'the whole of Jewry', while slightly to the west, but still within the General Government, a 'form of Polish state' should be created.

The Jews already living in the General Government rapidly learnt that they were at the very bottom of the new racial order. In the town of Izbica, Toivi Blatt, a twelve-year-old Jewish schoolboy, discovered that it was not only the Germans who were dangerous – non-Jewish Poles could be almost as threatening: 'I [had] thought that now we have the same enemy – the same Nazis who are hurting Poland, they're hurting Catholics, they're hurting Jews – that we will get together.'[13] Instead, he could see that some Poles had realized 'the Jews are second class and you could do with them whatever you wanted.' Many of the Jewish merchants who traded around Izbica 'were beaten up' and had their 'money taken away' because Polish villagers understood that the Jews were now without protection from the state. Catholic Poles even turned on each other. Within two weeks of the Germans seizing control of Izbica, Toivi saw a Polish collaborator 'beating another Pole because he didn't obey some German order'.

The first concerted effort to expel Jews into the General Government began in October 1939, little more than a month after the war had started. The head of the Gestapo, Heinrich Müller, ordered Adolf Eichmann – the SD officer who had organized the deportation of many Austrian Jews in the wake of the Anschluss – to plan the expulsion of around 80,000 Jews from Katowice, a city in a part of Poland that was to be Germanized. Almost immediately the planned deportations were broadened to include Jews from within the Reich, and Eichmann started developing plans to expel Jews from Vienna. In a note he sent to the Nazi Gauleiter of Silesia he mentioned that, after the initial transports, he had to send a 'progress' report to his superiors, and then 'in all probability' this would be given to 'the Führer' who would then decide how many more Jews should be sent east.[14]

The precise destination for these Jews was the town of Nisko on the San river, around 50 miles south of Lublin in the far east of Nazi-occupied Poland. At the end of October nearly 5,000 Jews from Vienna and cities in western Poland were sent to this new Jewish 'reservation'. When they left the trains, a few of the Jews were told to help in the construction of a camp, but the majority were simply dumped in the countryside without food or shelter. The quasi-genocidal nature of this scheme was obvious from the beginning. As Hans Frank, ruler of the General Government, put it: 'What a pleasure, finally to be able to tackle the Jewish race physically. The more that die, the better.'[15]

Just a few days later these transports were halted on Himmler's orders[16] and the Nisko initiative was dropped. This was almost certainly a pragmatic, rather than an ideological, decision. Himmler now had other problems, or 'challenges' as he would have seen them, that impacted on the further transportation of Jews from Germany and Austria into eastern Poland. On 7 October 1939 he had been confirmed as Reich Commissioner for the Strengthening of German Nationality. This almost mystical-sounding title concealed a brutal reality. For Himmler was now in charge of deporting large numbers of Poles from the areas of Poland annexed by Germany into the General Government in order to free up homes for hundreds of thousands of ethnic Germans. Many of these *Volksdeutsche* were arriving as part of a deal the Nazis had negotiated with Stalin to allow them to leave territory now controlled by the Soviet Union – such as the Baltic States – and come 'back to the Reich' or 'Heim ins Reich' as the slogan went. Transporting all these people to the new Reich and then finding homes and jobs for them – all in the midst of a war – was a logistical task of formidable difficulty. But the Nazi leadership believed the racial component of the task was so central that there was never any question of delaying this influx of new German 'blood'.

The suffering of the Poles who were thrown out of their homes to make space for these new arrivals was – predictably – immense. Michael Preisler remembers how, a few weeks after Himmler had been appointed to his new job, there was a sudden 'knock at the door' at two o'clock in the morning and a gang of Nazis rushed into the family home. 'They went all over the rooms, where my sisters were dressing, and they were standing over them, watching them. We got dressed and we couldn't even take anything, they say you cannot take anything, no food, nothing, no extra clothes, nothing. And that's it – they were pushing, you know like Germans. Everything had to be done right away. Then we were marching on the street to a hall where there were other people. And then finally when they collected more families, they took us to the railway station.'[17]

Another Pole, Anna Jeziorkowska, was deported with her family from Posen (the name the Germans gave to Poznań). She remembers that when the Germans 'burst' into their flat, 'there was great chaos, crying, wailing. The Germans pushed us, they hit father on the face, and we got so frightened that we started crying. My younger brother, he was very delicate, started vomiting.'[18]

Thousands of Poles like Michael Preisler and Anna Jeziorkowska were taken on trains and dumped in the General Government. Michael Preisler and his family were housed in the west of the General Government, first in a 'big hall' and then the whole family was crammed into one room in a house. Anna Jeziorkowska and her family were abandoned in the small town of Golice and huddled together in the open in the town square until an old man took pity on them and offered them space to sleep on his floor.

The Germans conducted the deportations not only with great brutality but also in an atmosphere of administrative chaos. In January 1940, the

Higher SS and Police Leader in the General Government, Friedrich-Wilhelm Krüger, estimated that 110,000 Poles had been sent to the General Government – 30,000 of them without proper agreement.[19] As Goebbels put it, writing in his diary the same month: 'Himmler is presently shifting populations. Not always successfully.'[20]

Shortly after Goebbels had written those words, Hans Frank, ruler of the General Government, decided that these mass deportations had to stop. Frank acted not out of compassion at the fate of those who had been transported into the General Government, but because of the turmoil that had resulted. As one of Frank's senior officials puts it: 'How can you organize anything, when you don't know [beforehand] that a train will arrive at X or Y or some place? There was nothing to organize . . . I didn't know where the transports would arrive. The district leadership didn't know this either . . .'[21] At a meeting with Göring and Himmler on 12 February, Frank asked for the timetable for the deportations to be reassessed. An uneasy agreement was reached by which future deportations were not supposed to be sent into the General Government without Frank's prior consent.

As for the new ethnic German settlers, many of them did not find life as rosy as they had hoped. They had been promised that they were going 'home to the Reich' so it was a surprise to discover that while they were – according to the Nazis – arriving in the 'Reich', it wasn't the 'Reich' they had necessarily been expecting. Irma Eigi, a seventeen-year-old ethnic German from Estonia, remembers how unhappy she and her family were to discover that they had to begin their new lives not in Germany but in Poland. 'We hadn't reckoned on that at all,' she says. 'When we were told we were going to the Warthegau, well, it was quite a shock, I can tell you.'[22]

A sense of disappointment about this whole enterprise was not confined to the arriving *Volksdeutsche* – some of the Germans who lived in the part of Poland that had been taken from Germany at the end of the First World War were just as displeased with the new arrivals. 'Quite a few times we welcomed trains carrying resettlers [from Volhynia, an area that bordered Poland to the east],' says Charles Bleeker Kohlsaat, from an ethnic German family. 'They spoke poor German, they had a terrible accent which nobody could understand and we almost took them for Poles. I remember particularly clearly one family with a boy – the boy might have been, perhaps ten years old, perhaps he was only nine . . . And when this boy arrived with his German parents – "German" in inverted commas – he was wearing a Polish boy scouts' cap, [and] he had used an indelible pencil to draw a swastika on the cap, this square cap . . . Basically we were appalled by the quality of these resettlers, because they were shabbily dressed, they arrived with unsightly bundles. Later, as refugees, we also carried such bundles, but we were not to know that at the time . . . So we said to ourselves, good heavens, what is the point of pushing out these old-established Polish families – farming families – and moving in these semi-Polish resettlers instead? And they gave the impression of being rather under-developed . . . besides, they were dressed in exactly the same fashion as the Polish farmers. They wore the high fur hat, they wore the long fur made out of unsheared sheepskin, they wore high boots and they rolled their cigarettes like the Poles did. And among themselves they spoke Polish. Well, we said: "One lot out, one lot in, what is the difference?" To us they were not genuine Germans, they were third-class Germans, if that.'[23]

Despite the meeting in February, and further protests by Hans Frank, the deportations into the General Government never entirely stopped. Between May 1940 and January 1941 around 90,000 Poles and 2,500 Jews were deported from the Warthegau into the General Government to create space for the arrival of the ethnic Germans.[24] Himmler made his own attitude clear in a memo he wrote in May 1940, when he said the population of the General Government should eventually consist of an 'inferior remnant'.[25]

Amid this administrative infighting, the Nazis began to place greater emphasis on a short-term solution to their Jewish 'problem' – ghettos. Since it was obviously not possible to transport at once all of the Polish Jews to the General Government, and given that it was a central tenet of Nazi ideological belief that the Jews were dangerous, both as supposed carriers of disease and as spiritual corruptors, it is not surprising that the idea of containing them within designated areas of Polish cities became widespread – nothwithstanding the concerns about ghetto 'security' that Heydrich had raised at the time of the November 1938 conference held in the wake of Kristallnacht.[26]

The first large ghetto to be constructed was in the city of Łódź – renamed Litzmannstadt by the Germans – in the Warthegau. This was an enormous task for the Nazis, since one in three of the 700,000 population of Łódź was Jewish. In a secret order of 10 December 1939, the German governor of the city, Friedrich Uebelhoer, wrote: 'Of course, the creation of the ghetto is only a transitional arrangement . . . the ultimate objective must be to completely burn out this plague spot.'[27] The first public order, calling for Jews to live within a designated area within the city, was published in early February 1940, and the ghetto was secured on 1 May. After this date any Jew found outside the wire fence of the ghetto without permission was liable to be shot.

Prior to the creation of the ghetto, the Jews of Łódź had already suffered at the hands of the Nazis. Soldiers of Einsatzkommando 2 entered the city in the first days of the invasion and with the assistance of ethnic Germans instigated riots, tormented Jews they found on the streets and carried off others to work in forced-labour gangs. In his diary entry for 12 September 1939, one Łódź Jew, Dawid Sierakowiak, wrote that 'the local Germans freely indulge their whims.' Jews were 'beaten and robbed', others were 'sadistically abused. Some Jews were ordered to stop working, to remove their clothes and stand facing the wall, at which point they were told they'd be shot. Shots were fired in their direction, and though nobody was killed this was repeated a few times.'[28]

Shortly after they seized control of the city in September 1939, the Nazis banned the Jews from working in the textile industry – a major source of Jewish employment – and all Jewish businesses were handed over to Germans. Jews were told not to ride on buses or possess radios or visit the synagogue or own a car, and from 12 November Jews were ordered to wear a Star of David marking on their clothing.

The Łódź ghetto, however, was to be a step change for the worse in the suffering of the Jewish population. Conditions within the ghetto were unsanitary and overcrowded. By the time the ghetto was sealed 70,000 Jews had left Łódź – many had either been deported or had fled to other parts of Poland – but 164,000 Jews still remained, all of whom were now crammed into an area of 1.5 square miles.

Max Epstein, a fifteen-year-old schoolboy, was one of the Łódź Jews imprisoned within the ghetto. Before the war he had lived a comfortable life – his father was a prosperous businessman who owned a lumberyard in the city. Now, Max, his father and his mother were confined to one room in an old house within the ghetto. As soon as Max's father arrived in the ghetto he made a fateful decision. 'My father was already in his middle fifties,' says Max Epstein, 'and his philosophy was, I don't want to live. He didn't dare to commit suicide, because you just don't. But he said: "That's the end of it. I really don't want this. I've lived my life and I don't want to live." So he closed the shutters, it was always dark in our room . . . He didn't shave, he just sat there with our shutters closed. He didn't want to see the world outside.' But Max, supported by his mother, tried to make the best of life in this new world. 'When you are young,' he says, 'you don't think of death. I'm not suggesting that we were not aware of the gravity of the situation . . . But you still think of the ridiculously mundane things.'[29]

Estera Frenkiel, another Jewish teenager trapped in the ghetto, felt 'just as though a bomb had gone off over our heads . . . We were used to anti-Semitism. Anti-Semitism was also rife amongst the Poles . . . Polish anti-Semitism was perhaps more financial. But German anti-Semitism was: "Why do you exist? You shouldn't be! You ought to disappear!" '[30]

Part of the Nazis' plan was to make the ghetto as self-governing as possible. They imposed a 'Jewish Council' or 'Council of Elders' to oversee the ghetto and established a Jewish police force to keep discipline. The German authorities told the chairman of the Council of Elders, 'You must particularly ensure order in economic life, food provisions, use of manpower, public health, and public welfare. You are authorized to take all necessary measures and issue all necessary instructions to attain this goal, and to enforce them by means of the Jewish police force that is under your command.'[31]

The Nazis had sought to establish Jewish committees across Poland in the wake of their invasion and now transferred the idea to the ghettos. Their creation helped the Nazis in a number of important ways. Chiefly, the Jewish leadership groups distanced the German occupiers from contact with most of the other Jews. This meant, in turn, that the perceived risk of 'infection' from the Jewish population was reduced. In January 1940, four months before the ghetto had been sealed, the police-president of Łódź had warned about the 'danger' of 'typhoid fever' and 'dysentery'[32] spreading from the Jewish-occupied districts of the city. The Nazis had precipitated this situation, of course, by previously depriving the Jews of adequate food and healthcare. An additional consequence of this distancing effect was that German soldiers did not have to see the suffering within the ghetto – there was little danger of them witnessing sights that might potentially cause them emotional disquiet. Another benefit for the Nazis in devolving administrative responsibility to the Jews was the consequent conflict within the ghetto. The Jewish councils eventually were forced by the Germans to choose some of those who would be deported from the ghetto – thus deciding who among their fellow Jews would be sent to an even worse fate. The members of the Jewish councils could also decide to give themselves a less onerous existence, which in turn made many other Jews angry. And a ghetto divided against itself suited the Germans perfectly.

In Łódź, the chairman of the Council of Elders was a sixty-three-year-old Jew called Mordechai Chaim Rumkowski. A former director of a Łódź orphanage, he was a domineering character with little formal education. In his role as chairman of the ghetto he would become one of the most controversial Jewish figures of the Holocaust.

Rumkowski knew from the beginning that he was a servant of the Germans, and that they would punish him severely if he did not do as he was asked. On 11 November 1939, every single member of the original Łódź Jewish Council – apart from Rumkowski and two others – had been arrested and sent to Radogoszcz prison. More than twenty of them were subsequently killed. Their only crime had been not to function as effectively as the Germans had wished. Members of the new Jewish Council, formed shortly afterwards and still under Rumkowski's chairmanship, were thus well aware that their position of relative privilege could potentially lead to their torture and death.

Within the ghetto, Rumkowski's power was immense. 'Toward his fellow Jews,' wrote Yehuda Leib Gerst, a survivor of the ghetto, 'he was an incomparable tyrant who behaved just like a Führer and cast deathly terror on anyone who dared to oppose his lowly ways.'[33] When Rumkowski subsequently visited the Warsaw ghetto, the Jewish leader, Adam Czerniaków, thought him 'replete with self-praise' and 'conceited'. Rumkowski was also 'dangerous', wrote Czerniaków, because 'he keeps telling the authorities that all is well in his preserve.' Czerniaków came to the conclusion, having read the newspaper published by Jews in the Łódź ghetto, that Rumkowski's 'main concern' appeared to be 'that "his people" should not bother him in the streets by handing him propositions and petitions'.[34]

The initial Nazi plan, after the Łódź ghetto had been sealed, was to make the Jews pay for their own food. As a consequence, Jews were forced to part with whatever they owned at a fraction of its real value. One ethnic German who profited on the black market from these one-sided exchanges later confessed that 'I saw it from the point of view of a businessman. They [the inhabitants of the ghetto] couldn't nibble on a ring, but if they could get a piece of bread for it, then they could survive for a day or two. If I got something in my hand for 100 marks and it was worth 5000 marks, then I'd be stupid not to buy it.'[35]

Jacob Zylberstein and his family had no money to buy food from the Germans at the inflated prices they demanded. So he realized that, if he didn't find a way of smuggling in food and bypassing the Germans, they would all die. He knew that their lives depended on his ability to make contact with a Pole outside the ghetto. This was a task that was immensely difficult since Jews worked almost exclusively within the confines of the ghetto. But Jacob had one advantage – his house backed on to the ghetto fence. Because of this proximity, in the early days of the ghetto he was able to come to an arrangement with a Pole on the other side of the wire. The Pole gave Jacob a loaf of bread; Jacob kept half for his family to eat, sold the other half within the ghetto and then passed on to the Pole the money he had earned. 'He helped us for two months,' says Jacob. But then the Pole was caught and killed by the Germans. 'Still,' remembers Jacob, 'two months was a very long time.'

Jacob could not believe that the Germans could be so cruel: 'You can't comprehend it as a human being, that such a thing can happen to you. How could a normal human being understand it? Hundreds died – weeks after the ghetto was closed . . . I remember that the hunger was so colossal that my mother went to pick weeds, and she cooked the weeds. You [even] got hold of potato peels – it's more than a luxury, it was the best food ever.'[36]

The outbreak of war did not just bring increased suffering to Jews and Poles. Other categories of people who had been targeted in the past by the Nazis were also at much greater risk – most notably the mentally and physically disabled. The way in which they were now treated would, in turn, have an impact on the development of the Holocaust.

As we have seen, Hitler despised the disabled. But, while the Nazis had introduced compulsory sterilization, they had so far refrained from authorizing the killing of the disabled – a policy known euphemistically as 'euthanasia'. That all changed just before the war began, when Philipp Bouhler, head of the Führer's Chancellery, brought to Hitler's attention a letter written by the father of a severely disabled child. The father, a believer in 'euthanasia', asked Hitler for permission for his child, who was a few months old, to be killed.

Hitler authorized his own doctor, Karl Brandt, to investigate the case and, if he found that the father's description of his son's condition was accurate, to arrange the child's murder. Brandt did as he was asked and subsequently organized the killing. Recent research has shown that the murder was carried out towards the end of July 1939.[37] That is several months later than had previously been thought, and offers further evidence that Hitler believed the forthcoming war would provide useful cover for drastic action against the disabled. He was fulfilling the prophecy he had made to Gerhard Wagner, Leader of the Reich Doctors, back in 1935, that he would 'radically solve' the 'problem' of the mentally ill in the event of a future conflict.[38]

The death of this one child led Hitler to authorize Bouhler and Brandt to murder other children who were similarly disabled – not just babies but older children as well. A whole administrative structure was subsequently constructed to oversee the process. In August 1939 the Interior Ministry issued confidential guidelines that called on midwives to report any newborn children who were suffering from conditions such as deformity or paralysis. These reports were then sent to three separate doctors who marked each document with a plus or a minus. If a majority wrote down a minus, the child was sent to a special clinic. Here the children who had been selected to die were killed, often by an overdose of morphine or another sedative. In the official record their deaths were recorded as the result of another plausible disease like measles.

The whole operation was conducted in great secrecy. The general public was never supposed to find out what was happening to children inside these special units. But within the walls of the hospital, it was difficult to hide the evidence of the crime. During the war, Paul Eggert – assessed as a 'delinquent' – was sent to Aplerbeck, one of the children's hospitals that also served as a killing centre. He remembers how every few weeks a nurse would come into the dining room during supper and select children. Next morning they were taken to the doctor's consulting room – supposedly they were to be immunized against diphtheria or scarlet fever. But Paul noticed that these children 'never came back' from their visit to the consulting room. He remembers that on occasion the selected children would hold on to the older boys in an attempt not to be taken away, but 'the doctor or the nurse would say, "Come now", or something [like that].' Long after the war Paul recalled 'the screams' and the terrified backward 'glances' from the children as they were led away to be killed. It was 'hopeless', he says, 'it was terrible.'[39]

Hitler didn't just want to kill disabled children, he also wanted to murder disabled adults. In June or July 1939 – the exact date isn't known – he asked Dr Leonardo Conti, the state secretary for health, to widen the 'euthanasia' scheme. Philipp Bouhler, of the Chancellery of the Führer, wasn't happy about Conti's planned role, as his department was already involved with the children's euthanasia operation. An expert in internal Nazi politics, Bouhler quickly managed to manoeuvre Conti out of the way and control both schemes.[40]

What this bureaucratic manoeuvring demonstrated was the flexibility of the administrative structure of the Nazi state – especially when it came to secret tasks like the killing of the disabled. German doctors were already murdering children in special units without any law to permit their action having been passed, and without the knowledge of the vast majority of Germans – including those in the government departments that would have expected to oversee such a policy had it been approved by the state in any formal way.

Job titles meant nothing to Hitler, as long as you could fulfil the task he wanted. The department that was running this large murder operation was called the Chancellery of the Führer and had previously had nothing to do with medical issues. Bouhler, the head of the Chancellery, was a thirty-nine-year-old party bureaucrat who, up to now, had worked on party-related business. His deputy, Viktor Brack, had once been Himmler's chauffeur. Neither Brack nor Bouhler possessed any medical qualifications.[41] But in the Nazi state, all this was irrelevant. What mattered was that these were ideologically committed, ambitious men keen to progress their careers and serve their Führer. If Hitler wanted mentally and physically disabled patients to be killed, then they would make it happen.

On 9 October 1939 Viktor Brack chaired a meeting attended by medical professionals sympathetic to the idea of killing the adult disabled. Here they discussed the mechanics of how the system should work. They decided that first a list of all the institutions where 'mental patients, epileptics, and the feebleminded' were currently treated should be compiled.[42] Staff at the named institutions would then be told to fill in forms outlining the nature of each patient's disability. Medical professionals would examine these forms, and decide who should live and who should die. One factor these doctors used in reaching their verdict was the extent to which the patients could still perform useful work. The selection was thus made on economic as well as medical grounds.[43]

The question of how exactly to kill the adult disabled was also discussed at the 9 October meeting. The Nazis were aware that there would probably be too many people to murder – an estimated 70,000 – just by medication, injection or starvation. So Brack consulted Arthur Nebe, head of the Criminal Police, about the best method of killing the disabled in large numbers. Nebe in turn suggested that Brack talk to Dr Albert Widmann, who ran the chemical department of the Criminal Technical Institute. Like a number of those who came to be involved in these secret schemes, Widmann was young and relatively inexperienced. He was just twenty-seven years old when he was asked to help devise methods to kill the disabled, and had received his doctorate in chemical engineering only the year before. At his trial after the war, Widmann said that he had been told by Nebe that 'animals in human form' were to be killed under the new scheme. At a subsequent meeting, Widmann said that in his expert opinion 'carbon monoxide gas' would be the best killing agent. He suggested that the gas could be 'discharged into the wards at night and thus "euthanize" the mental patients'.[44]

In an attempt to ensure the secrecy of this enormous murder operation, the euthanasia action was known only as 'T4' after the address of the headquarters of the scheme, Tiergartenstrasse 4 in Berlin. A number of those involved even adopted pseudonyms. Brack himself used the alias 'Jennerwein', the name of an infamous nineteenth-century poacher. But there still came a point, late in 1939, when those involved thought some kind of official authorization for their actions was necessary. So Hitler was approached, most likely by Bouhler, and asked to confirm in writing that he had ordered the project. The result was a short note, signed by Hitler, which said that Bouhler and Dr Brandt had been given the 'responsibility' of authorizing doctors to grant 'a mercy death' to those suffering from 'incurable' illnesses. Significantly, Hitler back-dated the note to '1 September 1939', the day of the invasion of Poland. He thus emphasized once again the connection between his decision to kill the disabled and the outbreak of war. This link between the war and the creation of an apparatus for the mass murder of the disabled was important not just for Hitler. As many of those involved in the killings were told, why should the disabled and unproductive be allowed to live at a time when the healthy were dying on the battlefield?[45]

Hitler's intense loathing of the disabled – particularly the mentally disabled – was on show that autumn during a meeting attended by Hans Lammers, head of the Reich Chancellery and Hitler's closest legal adviser. At the Nuremberg trials after the war, Lammers testified: 'On this occasion, the Führer discussed, in my presence for the first time, the problem of euthanasia. He explained that he thought it fit to remove "life unworthy of life" – that is the lives of the seriously mentally ill – through medical intervention causing death. He mentioned, if I recall correctly, by way of example, serious mental illnesses in which mentally ill people could only sleep on sand or sawdust because they would soil themselves constantly – cases in which these sick people would eat their own excrement as food. And he explained how it was the right thing to end this "life unworthy of life". He also explained how through this, there could be savings in the cost of hospitals, doctors and nursing staff.'[46]

On 4 January 1940, Dr Widmann conducted a gassing experiment in Brandenburg an der Havel at a prison converted into a euthanasia unit. The gassings took place in a tiled room with fake water pipes along the ceiling. The patients to be murdered were told to undress outside the room because they had to take a shower. Once the patients were locked inside the pretend shower room, Widmann personally turned on the valve to release the gas from bottles of carbon monoxide. The gas flowed through pipes into the room and the twenty or so patients were murdered. After they had died the room was ventilated and the bodies taken away to be burnt.

Dr Widmann's original idea of gassing the patients as they slept in their dormitories had been considered impractical, but this fake-shower method proved to be an effective method of committing mass murder. From the Nazi perspective it solved a number of practical problems. First, the patients who were to be killed were calm almost until the last moments of their lives. There was no need for them to be anxious about something as prosaic as taking a shower. Large numbers of patients could also be killed simultaneously, and fewer staff needed to be involved than in any previous killing method. Finally, the use of fake showers meant that the killers were distanced from the act of killing. Instead of having to look into the eyes of patients as they injected or shot them, all the killers needed to do now was to turn on a valve. The murderers were not just emotionally separated from the moment of killing, but physically separated as well.

Dr Karl Brandt, who personally witnessed the gassing at Brandenburg, did not mention any of these advantages for the Nazis when talking about the decision to gas patients at his trial after the war. Instead, he claimed that he had talked to Hitler about the choice between killing by injection and by gas and Hitler had asked, 'Which is the most humane way?'[47] For Brandt the answer was 'clear' – gassing. A number of other Nazis who were aware of this method of murder later claimed that they thought the same. They fantasized that the killers were being kinder to their victims by sparing them the torment of anticipating their own deaths, and that by deceiving them until the moment that gas came from the pipes above them, they were demonstrating an element of humanity. But the idea that death in a gas chamber was necessarily less horrific than death by any other method was a lie, as subsequent testimony from those involved in the gassing at the extermination camps makes clear.[48]

Dr Brandt also maintained that the 'experiment' of killing the disabled by gas was 'just one example of [what happens] when major advances in medical history are being made. There are cases of an operation being looked on at first with contempt, but then later on one learned it and carried it out.'[49] And so, believing that he was part of a 'major advance in medical history' and with a 'good conscience', Brandt pushed forward with the adult euthanasia scheme.

No doctor was compelled to participate in this project. Those who objected could excuse themselves – for instance, by saying they were too 'weak' for the task – but the majority of those who were asked went along with the scheme with various degrees of enthusiasm. Some made the argument that by killing the most severely disabled they released more funding for other patients. Others subscribed to the official belief that the role of the doctor in the Nazi state was to look after the well-being as much of society as of the individual patient – especially at a time when the country was at war. Whatever excuse the doctors gave themselves, they knew that without their participation this murderous scheme could not function. Medical professionals were central to the whole process – from initially selecting the patients to die, to reassuring the patients as they prepared to enter the gas chamber, to turning on the gas valve, to certifying that the patients were dead, and to inventing fake causes of death to write on the official documentation that was sent to the relatives of the deceased.

The Nazis created six euthanasia centres, five in Germany – Brandenburg, Grafeneck, Bernburg, Hadamar and Sonnenstein – and one in Austria at Hartheim, close to Linz. Typical was the one at Sonnenstein, on a hill in the suburbs outside the town of Pirna, not far from Dresden. Built originally as a fortress, the building was turned into a mental hospital in the nineteenth century. In 1940 work began on converting several rooms in the basement into a killing facility. One small room was made into a gas chamber and disguised as a shower room, with an airtight door linking it to a mortuary. Selected patients were taken in buses from other mental institutions in the area and on arrival at Sonnenstein told to enter the basement to take a shower, as part of the admissions procedure into the new hospital. Once the patients were in the fake shower room the gas valve was turned on and they were murdered. After they had been gassed and pronounced dead, their bodies were taken into the mortuary and any gold fillings or gold teeth in their mouths were removed. The bodies were then moved next door into a room that contained two cremation furnaces made by the Berlin firm of Heinrich Kori GmbH. The corpses were placed on a steel frame – normally two at a time – and pushed inside the furnace. Finally, their ashes were thrown out at the back of the building on to a hillside. During the operation of the Sonnenstein killing centre, from June 1940 to August 1941, an estimated 14,751 people were murdered in this way.[50]

The similarities between the process of killing at the euthanasia centres in the Reich in 1940 and the death camps in Nazi-occupied Poland in 1942

were many and varied, as we shall see. Not only were the techniques of killing much the same, but so were a number of the personnel. Present at
the first experimental killing at Brandenburg euthanasia centre in January 1940 were two men who in different ways would help shape the
Holocaust. The first was a medical professional, Dr Irmfried Eberl, who
was the director of the Brandenburg killing centre. He was a twenty-
nine-year-old Austrian, born in Bregenz and educated at Innsbruck
University. Eberl's life was devoted to the Nazi cause, from the trivial –
he sported a Hitler moustache and wore his hair slicked back – to the
criminal – he was intimately involved in the murders conducted in
Brandenburg. Eberl 'always considered' it 'his responsibility'[51] to turn on
the gas valve, according to the testimony of his deputy, Aquilin Ullrich.
Another member of the staff at Brandenburg, who was a keen gar-
dener, said that Dr Eberl had told him that just as 'all weeds needed to
be destroyed' so 'people not worthy to live ought to disappear.'[52] A different T4 official said that Dr Eberl was so enthusiastic about his task
that he 'wanted to gas all the world and his brother'.[53]

Dr Eberl believed, like Dr Brandt, that through his work he was fur-
thering medical science. The brains of children killed at Brandenburg
were sent to Professor Julius Hallervorden, head of the Neuropathology
Department of the Kaiser Wilhelm Institute for Brain Research in Berlin. Eberl's notebook records that Professor Hallervorden even visited
Brandenburg and took part in autopsies conducted at the killing
centre.[54] Hallervorden subsequently said at the Nuremberg trials that 'those
brains offered wonderful material' and 'it really wasn't my concern
where they came from . . .'[55]

Eberl's career was clearly on an upward trajectory within the Nazi
state. It is hard to imagine any other circumstances in which a junior
doctor like Eberl could have contributed so much to the researches
of a famous neurologist like Professor Hallervorden. Dr Eberl, just
like Dr Widmann, discovered that killing could be a way to swift
advancement.

The second person who witnessed the gassing experiment that January, and who would later participate in the Holocaust, could not have
been more different from Dr Eberl in age, education and life experience.
Christian Wirth was fifty-five years old when he was appointed administrative director of the euthanasia centre in Brandenburg. As a young

man he had trained as a carpenter before becoming a policeman. He won an Iron Cross in the First World War and after Germany's defeat joined the Nazi party while still pursuing his career in the police force. Immensely tough and practical, Wirth was a fearsome figure. His behaviour was so infamous that he came to be known as the 'wild Christian'. Once involved with T4, he had no qualms about participating in the killing process directly – he once personally shot four women patients who had been sent to a euthanasia centre and were thought to have typhus. He told those who worked for him that the 'mentally ill' were a 'burden on the state' and so had to be eliminated. One of those under Wirth's command described him simply as 'a beast'.[56] Franz Stangl, another policeman who joined the adult euthanasia programme and who would later go on to command a death camp, described Wirth as 'a gross and florid man. My heart sank when I met him.' Wirth spoke with 'awful verbal cruelty': 'He spoke of "doing away with useless mouths" and said that "sentimental slobber" about such people "made him puke".'[57] Wirth and Eberl, who worked together at Brandenburg killing centre in early 1940, would meet again two years later in the occupied east in even more appalling circumstances.

The disabled were murdered not just in Germany and Austria but in Nazi-occupied Poland as well. In the autumn of 1939 members of the Eimann Special Guard, an SS unit from Danzig, together with the Einsatzgruppen, shot thousands of mental patients in the territory of the newly Germanized area of Danzig/West Prussia. Those targeted were not just unfit for work – every Polish or Jewish patient was killed regardless of the severity of their illness.[58]

By early 1940 a new method of killing the disabled was in operation in Poland. A unit under the command of Herbert Lange, a thirty-year-old SS officer, used a mobile killing machine – a van with the words 'Kaiser's Coffee Company' written on the side. Once selected patients had been locked inside the van, bottled carbon monoxide was pumped in from outside. Lange's van travelled up and down the roads of Poland and the borderland with Germany murdering several thousand disabled.[59] The gas van had an obvious advantage for the Nazis over a fixed gas installation since it could travel to the location where the patients were hospitalized. There were, however, equally obvious disadvantages with this new killing method. There was a risk, for example, of the van becoming notorious – since no one who climbed into the back ever reappeared alive. But as long as the van was not overused in one particular area then secrecy could be preserved.

Within Germany, to begin with, disabled Jews were selected in much the same way as other patients – the doctors focused on clinical criteria as well as whether the patient could do useful work. But that changed in April 1940 when Herbert Linden, a doctor involved in 'race hygiene' and one of the functionaries supporting the T4 campaign, asked local authorities to reveal the names of all their Jewish mental patients. Every one of these patients was then selected to be killed.[60]

The outbreak of war also had dire consequences for Jews within the concentration camps that had been established on German territory before the conflict. While there is no evidence of an order from above calling on the Jews in the concentration camps to be murdered en masse, the SS within the camps knew that the febrile atmosphere of the war meant they could act against the Jews more or less as they wished. The arrival of a number of Polish Jews within the system only exacerbated the desire of the SS to torment the Jewish inmates. At Sachsenhausen outside Berlin the SS let their sadistic imagination run wild – thirsty Jewish prisoners were made to swallow their own urine, and those who were hungry had to beat each other up for food.[61] At Buchenwald near Weimar, more than twenty Jews were taken out of the camp and shot in November 1939, in revenge for an attempt on Hitler's life that had taken place in Munich the day before.[62]

The war also led to greater abuse of non-Jewish inmates in the concentration camps. In January 1940, for instance, Rudolf Höss, then an SS officer at Sachsenhausen, ordered 800 prisoners to stand for hours in the freezing cold and wind on the roll-call square. The senior prisoner – the camp elder – begged Höss to have mercy, but to no avail. The prisoners had to stand and suffer. Altogether in 1940 around 14,000 prisoners died within the concentration camp system. In 1938, the year of greatest fatalities before the war, 1,300 had lost their lives. The war thus brought more than a tenfold increase in the death rate.[63]

The war also led to an expansion in the overall concentration camp system, as the Nazis opened new camps in occupied territory. On 2 September 1939, the day after the Germans had invaded Poland, a concentration camp was established at the town of Sztutowo (Stutthof to the Germans) near Danzig. But it wasn't until the spring of 1940 that preparations were made to open on Polish soil what would become the most infamous camp within the whole Nazi system – Auschwitz.

When Rudolf Höss, transferred from Sachsenhausen as the newly appointed commandant of the camp, arrived at Auschwitz in April 1940, he had no idea that the facility he was to create and run would become the site of the largest mass murder in the history of the world. That's because he had been ordered to build not an extermination camp, but a more extreme version of Dachau – the 'model' camp run by Theodor Eicke in which Höss had originally trained. The town of Auschwitz, Oświęcim in Polish, was in Upper Silesia, a part of Poland that the Nazis wanted to Germanize, and the purpose of Höss's new camp was to strike terror into the local Polish population.

This camp, the original Auschwitz, was established next to the Sola river close to Auschwitz town, and was based around a collection of red-brick former Polish Army barracks. From the beginning the death rate at Auschwitz was much higher than in pre-war Dachau – more than half of the 20,000 Poles first sent to the camp were dead by the start of 1942.

Jerzy Bielecki, a Polish political prisoner, was on the first transport into the camp in June 1940. He remembers how the SS guards beat the prisoners all the way from the railway station to the gate of the camp: 'There was a young boy standing next to me, maybe he was sixteen – fifteen even – and he was crying, tears were falling. And his head was cracked and blood was dripping on his face . . . We were afraid, we didn't know where we were. It seemed to me that we found ourselves in hell. You cannot describe it any other way. And it turned out that this was hell.'[64] Bielecki, who had been sent to Auschwitz because the Germans believed that he was a member of the Polish resistance, was put to work along with the other prisoners, building the camp.

Jerzy Bielecki also recalls the brutality of the Kapos – German criminals sent to Auschwitz from Sachsenhausen – who supervised their work: 'I got used to seeing death, beatings and maltreatment,' he says. After 'three or four months I got used to that sight'. When he was part of a construction 'commando' he witnessed a Kapo, who was angry at the work of one of the prisoners, take a spade and 'cut his neck so that blood spouted and the spade was immersed to halfway in his neck. I'll never forget this . . . I see it in my dreams.'[65]

Only a small percentage of those sent to Auschwitz in 1940 were Jewish, but just as in camps within the pre-war borders of the Reich, Jews who were imprisoned in Auschwitz were liable to suffer appallingly. Kazimierz Ablin, who was also on the first transport into Auschwitz in June 1940, remembers that the Germans 'fished out' any Jews from among the prisoners, along with 'priests and monks' who 'were treated almost as badly as the Jews'.[66]

Wilhelm Brasse, who arrived in Auschwitz in August 1940, recalls that the Germans selected Jews and Catholic priests and told them to 'chant religious songs and hymns'. They would 'beat the priests and then the Jews, and would yell at them that they were lazy because they didn't chant loud enough. The impression this made on me was just terrifying. I've never imagined anything like this [could happen].'[67]

From the day the camp opened a variety of techniques were used to torment the prisoners. Punishments were not just cruel – a common one was to tie a prisoner's hands behind his back and then suspend him by his wrists from a pole – but often arbitrary. Every inmate knew that they were at permanent risk of a beating, or worse, and there was little they could do to prevent it. To exacerbate all of this suffering, the Germans insisted that life be conducted at speed. The sight of all the prisoners scurrying around the camp reminded August Kowalczyk, who was sent to Auschwitz at the end of 1940, of 'an anthill that someone had kicked. The anthill opens and then you see the ants running in all directions.'[68]

In May 1940, just days after Höss had arrived at Auschwitz, Himmler outlined his vision for the whole occupied east. This memo, which Himmler intended to submit to Hitler, was entitled – rather modestly given the sweeping nature of the proposals – 'Some Thoughts on the Treatment of the Alien Population in the East'.[69] A large section of the memo dealt with Himmler's plans to conduct a search among the Polish population in order to find children that were 'racially first class' and who 'came up to our requirements'. These children would then be transported to Germany and raised as German citizens. Himmler believed this policy would not just allow the Nazis access to more German 'blood' but deprive the Poles of the potential for a leadership class. As for the rest of the Polish children, they would receive the most basic education – taught only to count 'up to 500' and to write their own names. 'I consider it unnecessary to teach reading,' said Himmler. More important, he maintained, was that Polish children should learn that it was 'God's commandment to be obedient to the Germans and to be honest, hard working and well behaved'. When they grew up, these children would become part of a 'leaderless labouring class' that the Germans could use in 'road building, quarries' and 'construction'.

Himmler also said in his memo that the idea of 'physically exterminating a people' was 'fundamentally unGerman and impossible' – a view that he would change once the Holocaust began. But even though he would not, for the moment, countenance mass murder, his proposal for the Jews was still radical. 'I hope', he said, 'to see the term "Jew" completely eliminated through the possibility of a large-scale emigration of all Jews to Africa or to some colony.' He obviously had in mind something like the Madagascar plan which, as we have seen, the Poles themselves had been seriously considering just before the war. It was a striking departure from the policy expressed by Heydrich in the autumn of 1939, which was one of deporting the Jews to the eastern part of the new German Empire.

The reason Himmler felt able to float the idea of sending the Jews to Africa was because of what was happening elsewhere. By 15 May 1940, the date of the document, the German Army was five days into a major offensive against France and the Low Countries. While it was not yet certain if the Wehrmacht would achieve victory, the assumption underlying Himmler's vision of relocating the Jews to Africa was that once the Germans had triumphed and had occupied France, Belgium, Denmark, the Netherlands and Luxembourg, then Britain would make peace. This, in turn, would allow the Germans to use merchant ships, mostly captured from their opponents, to transport the Jews south, either to Madagascar – which the Germans would now lay claim to as former French-controlled territory – or to some other African country.

At first sight, especially given what happened later, it sounds like a fantasy. But the trail of documents the Nazis left through the summer of 1940 demonstrates that this potential 'solution' to the 'Jewish problem' was taken seriously. Just over a week after the defeat of France, on

3 July, Franz Rademacher, head of Jewish Affairs in the German Foreign Office, wrote a memo in which he said, 'France must make the island of Madagascar available for the solution of the Jewish question.'[70] Nine days later, Hans Frank remarked that there would be 'no more transports of Jews into the General Government'.[71] This was because the plan now was to send 'the whole pack of Jews' to an 'African or American colony' and that 'Madagascar is being considered, to be ceded by France for this purpose.'

Though the Nazis' Madagascar idea was not an immediate plan for the extermination of the Jews, it would have led to the deaths of millions. That's because the Polish commission that had investigated the possibility of mass emigration to Madagascar before the war had concluded that only 60,000 Jews could survive on the island, yet Eichmann's office sent a memo to Rademacher on 15 August saying that 'four million' Jews would be settled there.[72] Nor, under the Nazi plan, were the Jews to be allowed any form of self-government on Madagascar. The island would be 'under the control of the Reichsführer SS' and a 'police governor'.[73] Two further indications that the Nazi plans were quasi-genocidal was the fact that Philipp Bouhler – one of the originators of the adult euthanasia scheme – was mentioned as a possible 'Governor' of Madagascar, and that by late summer 1940 Rademacher had revised up his estimate of the number of Jews to be sent to the island still further – from 4 million to 6.5 million.[74]

The reason this scheme could even be discussed during the summer of 1940 was because of the Germans' swift victory in western Europe. In just six weeks in late spring 1940 the Wehrmacht had accomplished more than the German Army had achieved during the whole of the First World War. Popular myth tells us that this victory was inevitable, that the German armed forces were destined to win because their forces were more armoured, more motorized, more modern in every way than their opponents. But this is simply not the case. The reality was that the Western Allies possessed more tanks – and better ones – than the Germans. Victory in the west was not a foregone conclusion for Hitler's forces.

The background to this immense German success is significant in the context of the development of the Holocaust because of the change in perception of Hitler that occurred as a result of the victory. Towards the end of 1939 senior figures in the German Army had considered removing Hitler from power. Not because they were outraged by the appalling atrocities the Germans were committing in occupied Poland, but because they believed that Hitler was leading Germany to disaster by planning to invade western Europe. General Franz Halder, Chief of Staff of the German Army, wrote in his diary on 3 November 1939, 'None of the Higher Hq [Headquarters] thinks that the offensive ordered by OKW [the Supreme Command of the Wehrmacht, which worked directly for Hitler] has any prospect of success.'[75] One senior officer expressed his view more succinctly, saying the invasion plan was simply 'mad'.[76]

In November 1939, that judgement was almost certainly correct. For if the plans to invade the west as they existed at that time had been implemented, the Germans would most probably have suffered a catastrophic defeat. Only a change in strategy, caused in part by the Allies gaining intelligence about the Germans' original intentions, created the necessary precondition for success. The new idea was an enormous gamble – a swift attack through the seemingly impassable Ardennes forest towards the French city of Sedan, coupled with a diversionary thrust further north into Belgium. Hitler bet his entire future, and the fate of Germany, on the assumption that the Allies would not spot the movement of German armour through the Ardennes until it was too late to prevent the panzers of the Wehrmacht crossing the River Meuse at Sedan and dashing over the plains of central France to the Channel. It is scarcely possible to exaggerate either the radical nature of this plan or the element of risk involved. But, as we all know, it worked – chiefly because of the incompetence of the Allied military leadership who, as Hitler had gambled, did not understand the significance of the German advance towards Sedan until too late.

Hitler was now fêted by his military commanders. General Wilhelm Keitel, head of the OKW, the Supreme Command of the Wehrmacht – promoted to field marshal after the victory over France – announced that Hitler was 'the greatest military leader of all time'.[77] Most of the German population was just as ecstatic; the mass crowds that greeted Hitler on his return to Berlin from the western front on 6 July 1940 were almost hysterical as they demonstrated their gratitude for their Führer's apparent genius.

As a result of all this adulation, Hitler would have been reconfirmed in his own assessment of himself as one of the most important individuals that had ever existed. As he had told his generals in August 1939, 'essentially all depends on me, on my existence . . .'[78] He had also reiterated, in a speech to his military leaders three months later, on 23 November, that he saw the conflict in which they were now all embroiled in equally epic terms. The choice was either 'victory or defeat'; it was therefore necessary to 'annihilate' the enemy or risk annihilation oneself. This 'racial struggle' was inevitable, according to Hitler, because 'the increasing population [of Germany] needs larger *Lebensraum*.'[79]

The message that victory in the west sent out to the millions of Germans who were predisposed to support the Nazi movement was clear. It was no longer necessary to worry about the future. They could throw away their individual doubts and anxieties, because their Führer had shown that he was always right. Hitler had not 'hypnotized' these people. It was not that they agreed with him because their own better judgement had somehow been usurped. They chose to trust him because recent events had demonstrated that this appeared to be the most sensible thing to do. But that mindset was immensely dangerous. It meant that later on, when the Jews started vanishing from the streets, they could attempt to dismiss any anxieties they might have by hiding once again behind the familiar rubric – the Führer knows best. Hitler had shown in the past that he knew best, so he would know best in the future as well. If he ordered that the Jews should suffer more than ever before, then it was the right thing for Germany and the policy should be supported.

After the German victory on mainland Europe, Hitler expected Britain to make peace. In his Reichstag speech on 19 July 1940 he appealed to the British to see 'reason'. He said: 'I am still sad today that, in spite of all my efforts' no 'friendship' had been established with 'England'.[80] Churchill, who had become Prime Minister two months before, was against any such accommodation, as was the government he led. And once it was clear that the British would carry on fighting, Hitler faced a dilemma. He could direct his armed forces to invade Britain, or he could turn his attention east and confront the enemy he had identified in *Mein Kampf* in 1924 – the Soviet Union. For Hitler, this was an easy choice. He had never wanted war with Britain, and the German Navy lacked the warships capable of protecting a cross-Channel invasion fleet. At a meeting on 31 July 1940 he raised with his military commanders the possibility of invading the Soviet Union – even before Britain had been defeated. He justified this course of action by using somewhat twisted logic. He argued that one of the reasons the British had carried on fighting was because they hoped that eventually the Soviet Union would come to their aid, saying that 'Russia is the factor on which Britain is relying the most.[81] So destroying the Soviet Union's chances of entering the war on the British side, Hitler implied, would make Churchill sue for peace. It was a bizarre argument, not least because the British war effort depended on aid from America, not the Soviet Union. Nonetheless, no one spoke up against the idea.

Hitler didn't completely reject the idea of invading Britain. Plans were still put in place to launch an aerial bombardment, and despite the gloomy prospects for a cross-Channel attack outlined by Grand Admiral Raeder at the 31 July 1940 meeting, half-hearted preparations were made for Operation Sealion – the invasion of the British mainland. But Hitler was never committed to this option, and his hopes for another military triumph rested on the plans that were developed during the rest of 1940 for a massive strike against the Soviet Union the following year.

Hitler had said, as far back as 1924, that Germany needed to gain land in the east – and the war necessary to win this new territory was getting nearer.

9. Persecution in the West

(1940–1941)

While plans were drawn up to invade the Soviet Union, the Nazis had to resolve a pressing question that had arisen as a consequence of their victory in the west. Now that the Germans had many more Jews under their control, how should they treat them?

The way in which they answered that question, between May 1940 and the invasion of the Soviet Union in June 1941, tells us a great deal about the flexibility of their anti-Semitic policy during this first phase of the war. It also shows, once again, that no decision had been taken at this stage to implement mass murder. For the Nazis still clung to the belief that, in the long term, the way to 'solve' their 'Jewish question' was by expulsion.

On 10 May 1940 the German Army invaded Luxembourg, the Netherlands and Belgium. In Luxembourg, by far the smallest of the three countries, there were around 3,500 Jews out of a population of 300,000.[1] A *Volksdeutsche* movement within the country called for Luxembourg to 'come home' to the Reich, and Gauleiter Gustav Simon[2] instigated an extensive programme of 'Germanization', with the Nuremberg Laws put into effect as early as September 1940. Jews were pressured to travel across the border into France, and the Nazis set various deadlines in the autumn of 1940 by which they wanted all Jews to have left the country. Some Jews were just taken to the border and simply abandoned.[3]

In neighbouring Belgium the situation was different. Just before the Nazis invaded there were about 65,000 Jews in the country, out of a total population of 8.3 million. Most of these Jews did not hold Belgian citizenship but had fled from Nazi Germany or other eastern European countries. Unlike in Luxembourg, the Germans made no attempt to force the Jews to leave the country, but starting in October 1940 they imposed anti-Semitic legislation. New laws decreed who was a Jew and who was not, and the Nazis demanded that Jews be expelled from various professions. However, the absence of any concerted violence on the streets, together with the fact that the Nazis permitted the Jews to continue to work in the diamond industry in Antwerp, led some Jews to return to Belgium in the summer and autumn of 1940 from neighbouring countries. Nazi policy started to change in November 1940, when Göring demanded that Jewish enterprises be 'Aryanized', although the process did not gain full momentum until well into the following year.

There were isolated acts of protest in Belgium against the German persecution of the Jews. In October 1940, for instance, Belgian government officials initially refused to obey a German request to apply anti-Semitic measures, though they did subsequently implement the legislation once the Germans forced it on them. Academics at the Free University of Brussels also protested when the Germans demanded that Jewish academics be deprived of their jobs – but their remonstrations were ignored.

The King of the Belgians, Leopold III, decided to stay on in the country, and was placed under house arrest by the Germans. In the power vacuum that resulted, the government-in-exile based in London played an influential role. Headed by the pre-war Prime Minister of Belgium Hubert Pierlot, the government-in-exile stated in January 1941 that all stolen goods and property would be returned to the true owners once the Germans had been defeated, and that those Belgians who sought to profit by stealing property from others would be held to account. Though this statement did not specifically mention the anti-Semitic measures that the Germans had imposed on Belgium, the effect of the declaration was to warn of eventual retribution for those who stole from Jews. That was certainly how the words were understood by the American Jewish Congress, and Rabbi Stephen Wise wrote to Prime Minister Pierlot in London to thank him for his support.[4]

In occupied Belgium there were also those who welcomed both the racism and the anti-Semitism of the Nazis. The Rexists, for instance, a far-right Belgian political party under the leadership of Léon Degrelle, came to embrace Nazi ideology. Jacques Leroy, a committed Rexist, confirms that he was also a dedicated 'racist'. 'The difference', he says, 'between the people whom you call *Übermenschen* [a superior race] and the ones whom you call *Untermenschen* [an inferior race] is that the *Übermenschen* are the white race . . . In those days we were proud to belong to the white race.'[5] As for his attitude towards the Jews, Jacques Leroy's views can be deduced from the fact that after the war he became a Holocaust denier.

There was sufficient anti-Semitic hatred in Belgium for a pogrom to be launched in the spring of 1941. On 14 April around 200 Belgian collaborators, from paramilitary units like the VNV (Volksverwering), set two synagogues on fire in Antwerp and then turned on the home of the Chief Rabbi.[6] The Germans prevented the Belgian fire brigade and police from taking action to extinguish the fire and catch the perpetrators.

Revealingly, those responsible for the attack had just watched *Der Ewige Jude* (The Eternal Jew), an anti-Semitic propaganda film released the previous year. The film is infamous for comparing Jews with rats. It also mounted an attack on Jewish bankers like the Rothschilds, accusing them of opening branches of their bank in different European capitals in an attempt to gain Jewish domination of the banking system. The film thus purported to demonstrate that Jews owed loyalty to each other across international borders, rather than to their country of residence.

Der Ewige Jude was by far the most nauseating piece of anti-Semitic film propaganda produced by the Nazis, and there is evidence that Hitler himself had a hand in its construction. Archival evidence, plus testimony from its director, Fritz Hippler,[7] strongly suggests that Hitler's contribution was to make the film more extreme. Fritz Hippler remembers how, via *Der Ewige Jude*, 'Hitler wanted to bring the "evidence" so to speak with this film that the Jews are a parasitic race . . . who had to be separated from the rest of men.'[8] The comparison of Jews with rats was something that Hitler would have found especially powerful, since he had a special loathing of these particular animals. 'I learnt to hate rats when I was at the front,' he said during the war. 'A wounded man forsaken between the lines knew he'd be eaten alive by these disgusting beasts.'[9]

Goebbels was not a believer in such crude attempts to influence the audience. In July 1941, he outlined how his approach to film propaganda differed from Hitler's: 'A few disagreements over the newsreel. The Führer wants more polemical material in the script. I would rather have the pictures speak for themselves and confine the script to explaining what the audience would not otherwise understand. I consider this to be more effective, because the viewer does not see the art in it.'[10]

In box-office terms, *Der Ewige Jude* was a failure. But although many in the audience disliked it – there were cases of women fainting while watching it – for fanatics, like the Belgian paramilitaries who saw the film in April 1941, it confirmed their view that Jews, like rats, had to be forcibly expelled.

While the synagogues of Antwerp burnt, a very different form of occupation was in force to the north-west, in Denmark. On 9 April 1940, one month before they invaded western Europe, the German Army had moved north, crossing the Danish border. Massively outnumbered and outgunned, the Danes had little choice but to accept the inevitable. Two hours after the first German soldiers arrived the Danish government surrendered. What happened next was surprising, especially in the context of the Nazi governance of neighbouring territory. For the Germans left the Danes largely to themselves. King Christian X carried on as head of state and the Danish police and judiciary functioned almost as before.

The Germans behaved in this comparatively restrained way for several reasons. First, the Nazis regarded the Danes as racial brothers – they had no ideological quarrel with the vast majority of the inhabitants of Denmark. As for the Jews, there were only 7,500 of them living in Denmark – just 0.2 per cent of the population. (This small number was partly because the Danes had refused to help thousands of Jews who were seeking refuge from the Nazis during the 1930s.) Finally, the Nazis wanted to do nothing to jeopardize the export of Danish agricultural produce to Germany. As a consequence, the Nazi occupation of Denmark was less oppressive than that of any other defeated country.

On the eve of the German invasion, Bent Melchior, a Jewish schoolboy living in Denmark, was terrified that his father who had been 'outspoken' in his criticism of the Nazis would be in immediate danger.[11] But after the Germans had arrived, Bent's father suffered no persecution, and life continued for the Danish Jews much as before. Knud Dyby, a Danish policeman during the war, confirms that the Danish Jews remained safe – at work and at home. 'The Jews were absolutely assimilated. They had their businesses and their houses like everyone else.'[12]

The Germans invaded Denmark en route to another Nordic nation, Norway. Hitler wanted to secure Norway for strategic reasons: to gain easy access for the German Navy into the north Atlantic and to protect the shipment of iron ore from neutral Sweden. Despite an attempt by the Allies to prevent the Germans seizing Norway, the country was under Nazi control by the end of the first week of June 1940. Vidkun Quisling, who had established a quasi-Nazi party in Norway in 1933, became the initial ruler immediately after the Germans arrived, but he was replaced within days by a genuine Nazi – Josef Terboven, the former Gauleiter of Essen.

Just as in Denmark, there were only a small number of Jews living in Norway – around 1,700 Jews out of an overall population of 3 million. But, unlike the Danish Jews, they were singled out for persecution. This was partly because of geography. Norway's long Atlantic coastline made it much more vulnerable to Allied attack than Denmark, and the Germans placed naval bases and troops in Norway in significant numbers. The Jews, as we have seen, were always perceived by the Germans as the 'enemy behind the lines' and so were thought to pose a threat to any military installation. But a more hard-line attitude towards the Norwegian Jews was also taken because in Quisling the Nazis possessed a willing anti-Semitic collaborator with a political base.

In the summer of 1940, Quisling managed to convince Hitler to reinstate him as head of the Norwegian government, serving under the authority of Terboven as Reichskommissar. In March 1941 Quisling gave a speech in Frankfurt in which he called for the Jews to be expelled from Norway. He claimed that it was necessary to remove the Jews because they were perverting Norwegian society and 'corrupting' the blood of the Norwegians like 'destructive bacilli'.[13] By the time he spoke those words Norwegian collaborators had already closed a number of Jewish shops and other commercial enterprises.

On 10 May 1940, the Germans invaded another country that had, like Norway, Denmark, Luxembourg and Belgium, attempted to avoid the war by claiming neutrality. Three-quarters of the Jews of this country – the Netherlands – would be killed in the Holocaust: a greater proportion than in any other sizeable nation in western Europe. Just why about 75 per cent of Dutch Jews died in the Holocaust – compared to around 40 per cent of Belgian and Norwegian Jews and 25 per cent of French Jews – is a question that has long troubled historians, and some suggestions as to why there was this eventual disparity are made later in this book.[14]

Unlike the Belgian government-in-exile, the Dutch government-in-exile was not united in its response to the German occupation. While Queen Wilhelmina of the Netherlands was opposed to any collaboration with the Germans, her Prime Minister, Dirk Jan de Geer, took a different view. He believed that the war against the Germans could not be won, and that the Dutch should cooperate with the Nazis in a similar way to the Vichy government in France. True to his beliefs, de Geer secretly left Britain for the Netherlands in September 1940 and subsequently published a pamphlet advocating collaboration with the Germans.[15]

In the absence of strong political leadership, Dutch civil servants played a crucial role. The majority of them decided to assist the Germans in the administration of the country in a professional and diligent way. As the Dutch government-in-exile stated in 1943: 'They [the civil servants] had spent their whole lives accustomed to obey, they were always – and rightly – so proud of the impeccable execution of their tasks and conscientious fulfilment of their duties, that they brought the same conscientiousness and the same fulfilment of duty to the scrupulous organization of the plunder of our country, to the advantage of the enemy.'[16]

Almost all Dutch civil servants agreed to sign forms that confirmed they were of 'Aryan' descent – the so-called 'Aryan attestation' – and in November 1940 they acceded to the German demand that Jews be removed from public service. The civil servants, keen to preserve appearances, considered the Jews 'suspended' from their duties rather than 'dismissed'.[17] It sounded less brutal, but the impact was the same.

Any judgement on the actions of the Dutch civil servants during this period should not, of course, be tainted by our own knowledge of what was to come. Even so, the efficiency with which they facilitated the German desire for all Jews to be individually registered, starting in January 1941, remains startling. This comprehensive system of registration would prove to be of enormous assistance to the Nazis at the time of the deportations of Dutch Jews to the death camps.

By June 1941 a whole range of anti-Semitic measures were in place, directed against the 140,000 Jews living in the Netherlands.[18] Dutch Jews could no longer visit cinemas or public parks or swimming pools; they could not own radio sets or attend mixed schools or work as lawyers or doctors for anyone other than Jewish clients. The Reichskommissar for the Netherlands, Arthur Seyss-Inquart, had demanded all these measures. A committed anti-Semite himself, he was a hard-line Nazi who had grown up in Austria and played a part in the downfall of Chancellor Schuschnigg in 1938. After the invasion of Poland in September 1939 he had served as deputy to Hans Frank, helping to administer and oppress the Poles in the General Government. So by the time he was appointed to his post in the Netherlands he had experienced first hand the bloody reality of the Nazi policy in the east. The fact that the Netherlands was ruled by a brutal racist like Seyss-Inquart, and Belgium by a military governor, General Alexander von Falkenhausen, also partly explains the subsequent disparity between the death rates of Jews in the two countries. Which is not to say that Falkenhausen was any friend of the Jews. He presided over appalling atrocities in Belgium, in part orchestrated by Eggert Reeder, the SS administrator who worked with him, but he still remained an old-school general – one who would eventually be sent to a concentration camp for his complicity in the 20 July plot against Hitler.

Not all institutions in the Netherlands cooperated with the Nazis as efficiently as the civil service. On 26 November 1940, Professor Rudolph Cleveringa of the University of Leiden delivered a devastating riposte to the German order that Jewish professors should be sacked. In the Great Hall of the university he condemned the demand as 'beneath contempt' and drew a stark comparison between 'power based on nothing but force' and the 'noble' example of Eduard Meijers, one of the Jewish professors at the university. Professor Meijers, said Cleveringa, was this 'son of our people, this man, this father to his students, this scholar, whom foreign usurpers have suspended from his duties . . .'.[19] Shortly after he gave this speech, Cleveringa was arrested. He spent the next eight months in prison, and the University of Leiden was closed down.[20]

Hetty Cohen-Koster, a Jewish student of Leiden University, heard Cleveringa speak that day in November. She described his words as 'salve for my doubting soul'. At the time she felt that 'the same thoughts and feelings are being communicated back and forth between us, wordlessly, yet completely and precisely understood by us all. I sit in a community of people sharing the same feelings, the same opinions. I belong here.'[21]

Hetty Cohen-Koster had not experienced any persecution in pre-war Netherlands. At her school in Haarlem there 'was not the slightest sign or trace of anti-Semitism . . . On the contrary, the school had an atmosphere of complete tolerance across all areas: origin, gender, religion and race.' Many Jews in the Netherlands felt the same way. Though in the 1930s there had been isolated anti-Semitic incidents, the idea of persecuting the Jews went against a tradition of Dutch tolerance that dated back to the emancipation of the Jews at the end of the eighteenth century. It was the legacy of this sense of security that led many to feel that the future could not be totally dark. 'At that time,' wrote Hetty Cohen-Koster, 'we believed that the labour camps in Germany were the worst that could happen.'

The Dutch experience thus demonstrates that it is a serious mistake to assume that the amount of pre-existing anti-Semitism in any country is a guide to the level of subsequent Jewish suffering under the Nazis. Other factors, such as the type of Nazi governance, the continuing presence of a functioning system of administration and the degree to which the Nazis desired to undertake anti-Semitic persecution within that specific territory all played an important part.

There were further voices of resistance in the Netherlands. In October many ministers of the Dutch Reformed Church protested against the 'Aryan attestation' by reading a letter of censure to their congregations, and in February 1941 a strike was held – initially in Amsterdam – to protest against the German occupation. All this brave dissent must be remembered, but so must the fact that at a bureaucratic level the Germans were well served by Dutch civil servants who collaborated with the occupying forces in the most 'scrupulous' and helpful way imaginable.

France, the final country that the Germans occupied in their march across western Europe, was treated very differently from the other conquered nations. France had never sought to use the cloak of neutrality as a protection against the Germans. The French and the British had reacted together when the Germans invaded Poland, and both had declared war on 3 September 1939. The French had been supremely confident of victory before the German invasion. General Gamelin, the Commander-in-Chief of the French Army, said that Hitler would 'definitely' be beaten if he tried to attack France in spring 1940.[22] It was an optimism shared by many ordinary French citizens. According to one foreign journalist in Paris on 10 May 1940, the day the Germans launched their assault, the people were 'bubbling with enthusiasm. On the streets and cafés, in the press and on the radio, there was jubilation over the blunder that Germany had just committed.'[23]

Against this background of over-confidence, it is hard to exaggerate the sense of national humiliation felt by the French when the Germans subsequently defeated them in just six weeks. France had been overrun, the French Army disgraced, and more than 1.5 million soldiers captured and taken to camps in Germany. In the wake of this disaster, the French turned to a national hero in an attempt to regain their self-respect – Marshal Philippe Pétain, the victor of the Battle of Verdun during the First World War. Pétain, eighty-four years old at the time of the French defeat in 1940, was the personal embodiment of the dignity of France. Solemn, grave and forbidding, he was tasked with rescuing the French from this physical and emotional catastrophe.

Pétain agreed an armistice with Germany on 22 June, six days after becoming Prime Minister. The terms of the peace treaty with France left the Germans occupying most of France – the north and the south-west – while around 40 per cent of French territory – the south and the south-east – remained technically under the control of the new French government led by Marshal Pétain. Because Paris was within the German-occupied zone, the capital of this new French regime was established at the spa town of Vichy. Once ensconced in Vichy, Pétain – who was now also Chief of State – possessed considerable power over French citizens, and blamed much of the trouble that had engulfed the country on the weaknesses of the Third Republic. He rejected the revolutionary watchwords of 'Liberty, equality, brotherhood' and adopted a new slogan of 'Work, homeland and family'.

A number of politicians and administrators who served Pétain were confirmed anti-Semites. Xavier Vallat, for instance, who became Commissioner-General for Jewish Questions within Pétain's government in spring 1941, subsequently said to Theodor Dannecker, the SS officer who oversaw the deportations of Jews from France, 'I have been an anti-Semite for much longer than you.'[24] There was also Louis Darquier, who replaced Vallat as Commissioner-General: he had founded the French Anti-Jewish Assembly before the war, had served a prison sentence for inciting racial hatred and used to confront Jews in cafés.[25]

Pétain's government acted swiftly to impose anti-Semitic legislation. In October 1940 the Statutes on Jews were passed which deprived Jews of the ability to work in a whole host of professions. They could no longer be civil servants, policemen, journalists or teachers or serve as officers in the army. Only a narrow range of Jews were exempted from these draconian restrictions – such as those who had fought in the First World War. As for foreign Jews, they were treated worst of all and were now liable to be interned in 'special camps' within France.[26]

There is no evidence that the Germans asked the Vichy government to impose these anti-Semitic measures.[27] Indeed, Pétain personally altered a draft of the October statutes in order to make the regulations still harsher.[28] The disturbing truth is that the French authorities persecuted the Jews because they chose to, not because they were told to. For the Jews of France, this evidence that fellow French citizens were prepared to victimize them was devastating. 'I cried last evening,' wrote Raymond-Raoul Lambert in his diary on 19 October 1940, 'as a man might cry who has suddenly been abandoned by the woman who was the sole love of his life, his mentor and the guide of his actions.'[29]

The actions of Vichy seemed all the more outrageous because France was the country of the Enlightenment, of the Rights of Man, the champion of free speech and liberal democracy – indeed, the first European country to emancipate the Jews, as long ago as the end of the eighteenth century. But it was more than that. It was also the country of the Dreyfus affair, in which a Jewish army officer had been falsely accused in the 1890s, and the place where the left-leaning government of Léon Blum in the 1930s had been attacked purely because of Blum's Jewish ancestry. The Jewish Statutes certainly reflected the spirit of that latter legacy of intolerance. The preamble to the statute of 3 October 1940 states: 'In its work of national reconstruction, the government from the very beginning was bound to study the problem of Jews as well as that of certain aliens, who, after abusing our hospitality, contributed to our defeat in no small measure.'[30]

It was no accident that foreign Jews were especially vulnerable under the new legislation. Out of a total of approximately 330,000 Jews in France in December 1940, about 135,000 were not French citizens, but had sought sanctuary in France from other countries. These 'aliens', as the Statutes described them, were particularly hated by French anti-Semites, and would later suffer disproportionately compared to French Jews. While around 10 per cent of French Jews would lose their lives in the Holocaust, more than 40 per cent of foreign Jews in France would die at the hands of the Nazis.[31]

In essence, the Vichy government's policy was to separate and eventually try and expel 'alien' Jews and 'neutralize' – or otherwise assimilate – Jews who were French citizens. Indeed, there was always an element of ambiguity in the Vichy attitude towards French Jews.

Admiral François Darlan, who became French Prime Minister in February 1941, went as far as to say: 'The stateless Jews who have thronged to our country for the last fifteen years do not interest me. But the others, the good old French Jews, have a right to every protection we can give them. I have some, by the way, in my own family.'[32]

Thus, if you were a Jew in occupied Europe during the first year or so of the war, how you were treated could depend not just on the country in which you lived, but whether you were a native of that country or not. Equally, while there was no overarching policy that the Nazis sought to impose on all the Jews under their control, certain core principles were evident across most of occupied Europe. Just as they had in Germany, the Nazis wanted – as a first step – to identify the Jews and isolate them.

As for the longer term, the Nazis had already demonstrated their desire to rob Jews of their wealth and then expel them from all areas under their control. Madagascar, as we have seen, offered one possible destination for the Jews during this period. But since the Madagascar plan depended on the ability of merchant ships carrying the Jews to sail thousands of miles in safety, it was an idea that could only be implemented once the British fleet had been rendered harmless – and the only way to do that was to force Britain out of the war. But that was proving hard to do. Dissatisfied with the Luftwaffe's inability to bomb Britain to the negotiating table, and after it became obvious that the Germans could not mount a successful seaborne invasion of Britain, Hitler increasingly turned his attention to the east. Operation Sealion was postponed – indefinitely as it turned out – after a meeting Hitler held on 17 September 1940 and plans proceeded for an attack on the Soviet Union.

The inability of the Nazis to implement the Madagascar plan did not mean that the idea of deporting Jews out of the Reich had been shelved. That autumn Robert Wagner, the Gauleiter of Baden in the west of Germany, forcibly expelled 6,500 German Jews over the border into Vichy France. Wagner, also the Gauleiter of territory in Alsace-Lorraine, had previously presided over the deportation of French citizens unwanted in this newly 'Germanized' land. This experience appears to have given him the idea of taking the same action against Jews within his domain in Germany. Local police detained German Jews on 22 and 23 October 1940 and forced them to board trains to Vichy. They were each permitted to take with them just 50 kilos of belongings and a maximum of 100 Reichsmarks. Heydrich noted that 'The deportation of the Jews was conducted throughout Baden and Pfalz without incident. The general population was hardly aware of the operation.'[33]

It was an action reminiscent of the deportations that had recently taken place in Poland of Jews from the lands to be Germanized to the General Government. And just as Hans Frank in the General Government had done, the Vichy authorities objected to their territory being used in this way. They had accepted the nine trains of Jews – seven from Baden, two from Saarpfalz – only because they thought they contained French citizens.[34] 'The French government can no longer provide asylum to these foreigners,' the Vichy authorities declared in a protest letter of 18 November 1940. 'It most urgently proposes that the Reich government immediately take the necessary measures so that they are transported back to Germany and the expenditures arising from their stay in France are repaid.'[35] But the Nazis refused to do as their defeated neighbour asked, and the German Jews continued to be held in internment camps in south-west France. A large proportion of them were shipped east in 1942 and eventually died in the Nazi death camps in Poland.

This little-known action in the autumn of 1940 is significant not just because of the importance of remembering the suffering of those German citizens who were suddenly snatched from their homes, but because it offers an insight into the way local initiatives could help shape decision-making. Hitler, as we have seen, did not come up with the idea of deporting the Jews of Baden and Pfalz and then order Wagner to implement the task. Instead, it was Gauleiter Wagner who wanted to send German Jews across the border without telling the French in advance. This initiative was then given the green light by Himmler and, according to one report, by Hitler as well.[36]

All this was possible only because Hitler was a visionary leader who expected his underlings to demonstrate huge amounts of initiative. A month before these deportations took place, he had said to Wagner and Gauleiter Bürckel of the Saar-Palatinate and Lorraine, that 'in ten years' time there was only one report he would want to have from the Gauleiters, namely that their areas were German and by that he meant completely German. He would not ask questions about the methods they had used to make the areas German and could not care less if some time in the future it was established that the methods used to gain the territories had been unpleasant or not absolutely legal.'[37]

In many ways this was a typical Hitler instruction to elite Nazi leaders. This is your goal, accomplish it by whatever means you like. As a consequence, different Gauleiters could pursue wildly different methods of implementation. That is certainly what happened in Poland as rival Gauleiters Albert Forster of Danzig/West Prussia and Arthur Greiser of the Warthegau both sought to impose the 'Germanization' policy desired by Hitler. Arthur Greiser ordered an examination of Poles to see if they could be classed as Germans or not. Those that weren't considered German were subject to deportation. In the next-door *Gau* (administrative region), Albert Forster took a much more laissez-faire approach and categorized some entire groups of Poles as German. Not only did this result in a row between Greiser and Forster, but it also led to the bizarre situation whereby some members of the same family were categorized as German in Foster's *Gau* and others as Poles in Greiser's *Gau*.[38] This mattered a great deal to these Poles – indeed, it could be a matter of life and death, as the ones classed as Germans in Forster's *Gau* were not subject to deportation and received more food than those classed as Poles in Greiser's *Gau*. Yet both Forster and Greiser claimed that they were each implementing Hitler's vision – just in different ways.

The same situation – where two district leaders pursued different policies but each maintained they were following the will of their Führer – occurred in the context of Nazi policy towards the Jews. The Łódź ghetto, established by Arthur Greiser, was in existence at the same time as the Gauleiter of East Upper Silesia, Fritz Bracht, was pursuing a totally different policy. In Bracht's realm, Albrecht Schmelt of the SS compelled Jews to work as forced labour on a variety of industrial and construction projects,[39] with the result that the Jews in the major cities that Bracht controlled, such as Katowice and Będzin, were not imprisoned in ghettos.[40]

This interaction between visionary leadership from above and initiatives from below was characteristic of the way the Holocaust developed. And, as we shall see, in the process of this evolution those involved were influenced not just by their own hate-filled ideology but also by the changing world around them.

• • •

That autumn Hitler was also considering large strategic questions – the most important of which was whether he should finally authorize the invasion of the Soviet Union and launch a war of destruction without parallel in history. It was a dilemma that he resolved after meeting Vyacheslav Molotov, the Soviet Foreign Minister. Molotov arrived for talks with Hitler and Ribbentrop in Berlin on 12 November 1940. He had come armed with a list of detailed questions about the relationship between the two countries – what, for example, were Germany's exact intentions towards the buffer states between them, such as Hungary, Romania and Bulgaria? But Hitler and Ribbentrop didn't want to dwell on such prosaic topics. Instead they talked in grandiose – and vague – terms of a future German world empire. Partly as a result of this mismatch between the practical Molotov and the visionary Hitler, the Soviet official interpreter at the talks described the encounter as 'tiresome and obviously pointless'.[41] A month after this dialogue of the deaf, on 18 December 1940, Hitler signed the plan for the invasion of the Soviet Union – codenamed Operation Barbarossa, after the nickname of Emperor Frederick I, the Holy Roman Emperor who had led the Third Crusade in the twelfth century.

This time German military commanders raised little objection to Hitler's epic plans. In part that was because of the success of the invasion of France, and Nazi ideological teaching which said the Soviets were 'subhuman', but it was also because military intelligence suggested that the Red Army was not much of a threat. Soviet forces had recently performed badly in the war against Finland, and Stalin had purged the Red Army of many of the Soviet Union's finest officers during the 1930s, frightened they were plotting against him. All this led General Alfred Jodl, Chief of the Wehrmacht's Operations Staff, to remark: 'The Russian colossus will prove to be a pig's bladder, prick it and it will burst.'[42]

Hitler's decision to commit to an invasion of the Soviet Union had immediate consequences for Nazi policy towards the Jews. Since the idea of shipping the Jews to 'a colony in Africa' had been shelved, a new policy had to be devised for the Jews imprisoned in Poland in ghettos. The Nazis, as we have seen, had previously imagined that these ghettos were only a temporary measure until the Jews could be expelled from the Reich.

Conditions in the Łódź ghetto were desperate by the summer of 1940. There were food riots in August, with a crowd of starving Jews shouting, 'We want bread, we're dying from hunger!'[43] The Nazi officials in the Warthegau asked Hans Frank to allow the Jews to be deported to the General Government since 'the situation regarding the Jews in the Warthegau worsened day by day' and the ghetto 'had actually only been erected on the condition that the deportation of the Jews would begin by mid-year at the latest'.[44]

True to his past actions, Hans Frank refused to take the inhabitants of the Łódź ghetto into his jurisdiction. So it was left to the authorities in the Warthegau to come up with a solution to their self-created problem. Since the Jews in the ghetto no longer had any money to buy food from the Germans, the Nazis faced a stark choice – let the Jews starve to death or permit them to work in order to earn money to pay for food. The different sides of this dilemma were personified by two people: Hans Biebow, the German chief of the ghetto administration, and Alexander Palfinger, a slightly more junior ghetto official. Estera Frenkiel, a Polish Jew who worked in the office of the Jewish Council within the ghetto, dealt with both of these German bureaucrats in the summer and autumn of 1940. Palfinger, she remembers, was happy to see the Jews in the ghetto 'starve to death'.[45] Her recollection is supported by documentary evidence from the time. 'A rapid dying out of the Jews is for us a matter of total indifference,' wrote Palfinger in a report in late 1940, 'if not to say desirable, as long as the concomitant effects leave the public interest of the German people untouched.'[46] Biebow, on the other hand, took a very different view. As Estera Frenkiel says, 'Biebow had great entrepreneurial spirit. He had great powers of persuasion – something Palfinger lacked. He carried on trying to persuade people until spittle formed at the sides of his mouth.'[47] Biebow proposed that the ghetto become self-sustaining. Factories and workshops could be established for the Jews and the goods they made sold in order to provide money for food.

Biebow's argument won the day. The Nazis gave the Jewish Council within the ghetto a 3 million Reichsmark 'loan' (from money previously stolen from the Jews) in order to set up the necessary infrastructure. This was just what Rumkowski, the Jewish head of the ghetto, had wanted. He had lobbied the Mayor of Łódź for a network of workshops to be established in the ghetto, saying, 'There are in the ghetto about 8–10,000 experts of various branches . . . Shoe and bootmakers (manual and mechan[ized]), saddlers . . . tailors (made to measure and mass production) . . . hat and cap makers, tinsmiths, blacksmiths, cabinet-makers, masons, painters, bookbinders, upholsterers. I could arrange for these [skilled artisans] to work for the authorities . . .'[48]

Biebow's victory was a key moment in this history. For it marked the transition from the ghetto as a temporary measure – a holding area where the Jews were confined, awaiting deportation somewhere else – to an institution that could theoretically become self-sufficient. Rumkowski, in particular, welcomed this development, because he believed the key to the survival of the ghetto was for the Jews to make themselves useful to the Germans. He called this 'Rescue through work'. As a consequence, those who worked in the ghetto received more food than those who were unemployed.[49] Both the Nazis and the imprisoned Jews had an interest in making the new system work. The Jews because they had witnessed how close the Nazis had come to letting them starve to death over the summer, and the Nazis because there was money to be made.

The new system was corrupt on both sides. Arthur Greiser, the ruler of the Warthegau, sought to get personally rich from the ghetto. Biebow regularly transferred money into an account set up in Greiser's name.[50] Estera Frenkiel even witnessed a suitcase full of valuables from the ghetto sent via Biebow to Greiser. On the Jewish side, Rumkowski now possessed even more personal power than he had before, since everything the Germans supplied to the ghetto under this new arrangement was routed through his office. He decided to enrich himself at the expense of others, and in the process created a better standard of living for himself than anyone else in the ghetto. He even, for instance, had a personal carriage and driver.

Meanwhile, just over 70 miles to the east, in Warsaw in the General Government, the largest ghetto of all was about to be sealed off from the outside world. More than 400,000 Jews would be imprisoned in the 1.5 square miles of the Warsaw ghetto – as many Jews in this small area as there were in the whole of France, Denmark and Norway. Around 30 per cent of the population of Warsaw was Jewish, and the enormous scale of this undertaking partly explains why this, the largest of the ghettos, was created relatively late.

The Jews of Warsaw were targeted for persecution from the moment the Germans entered the city just over four weeks after the start of the war. Within days the Nazis had ordered the Jews to create a Jewish Council through which anti-Semitic measures could be communicated to the Jewish population. Over the next few months the Jews of Warsaw were ordered to identify themselves by wearing a blue Star of David on a white armband, Jewish schools were closed and Jewish wealth seized. Jews were captured and made to work as forced labourers, and were frequently tormented by the Germans. 'Here's a game they play at the garages in the Dinance park,' wrote Emmanuel Ringelblum, a Warsaw Jew, in February 1940. 'The workers are ordered to beat one another with their galoshes . . . A rabbi was ordered to shit in his pants. They divide the workers into groups, and have the groups fight each other . . . I have seen people badly injured in these games.'[51] He also recorded that 'Both yesterday and today women were seized for labour. And, it just so happened, women in fur coats. They're ordered to wash the pavement with their panties, then put them on again wet.'[52]

Jews were at risk not just from Germans, but from Poles. Adam Czerniaków, an engineer by training and now the leader of the Warsaw Jewish Council, wrote in his diary in December 1939 that a mad Polish woman 'molests the Jews, striking them and grabbing their hats'.[53] The following month he described how a 'gang of [Polish] teenage hooligans, which for the last several days was beating up the Jews, paraded in front of the [Jewish] Community offices breaking the windows in the houses on the other side of the street'.[54] Other Poles thought that they could now steal from the Jews with impunity. On New Year's Eve 1939, 'two strangers' visited Czerniaków and told him that his apartment was to be 'requisitioned'. It subsequently transpired that the 'requisitioner' of his apartment was 'a driver delivering or distributing soups' – leaving Czerniaków with the problem of whether or not he should ask the SS to punish the Pole who had tried to steal his home.[55]

After the ghetto had been sealed in November 1940, the Nazis pursued the same policy as they had initially in Łódź – they forced the Jews to pay for their own food or starve. Alexander Palfinger, who had lost the argument in Łódź about whether or not to let the Jews die in large numbers, was appointed to run the Transferstelle in Warsaw, the department that assessed how much the goods surrendered by the Jews in the ghetto were worth and how much food they could expect in return. Palfinger's presence was disturbing news for the Warsaw Jews. He had not changed his view – it remained a matter of 'total indifference' to him how many Jews died.

Just as in the Łódź ghetto, those Jews who had valuables to sell or could find some paid work within the ghetto had a chance to stave off starvation. Wealthy Jews bought supplies that had been smuggled into the ghetto – one estimate is that more than 80 per cent of the food in the ghetto was purchased on the black market.[56] If you were unemployed or owned nothing then you were at risk of a swift death. In desperation women even sold themselves. Emmanuel Ringelblum noted in January 1941 that 'streetwalking has become notable' and that 'yesterday, a very respectable looking woman detained me.' The insight he gained into human nature as a result of this experience was bleak. 'Necessity drives people to anything.'[57]

Halina Birenbaum was eleven years old when her family was imprisoned in the ghetto. In the context of the horror of the ghetto, she was fortunate. One of her brothers, Mirek, was a medical student and worked in a Jewish hospital. He 'used to do injections' privately for wealthy Jews within the ghetto, so she did not starve. Watching from her position of relative privilege, she was shocked by the sights she saw. Children lay 'on pavements, in the streets, courtyards of houses . . . so swollen [with hunger] that you could hardly see the eyes in their faces'. She remembers a 'very tall ginger girl' who performed on the street in order to try and gain a few coins to buy food. She recited 'in Yiddish a song she wrote about how they [the Germans] drove her out from her town, how her parents died one after another and her brothers too. And she was saying to God, "How long will it take? Is the glass not yet full of our tears?" I will never forget this girl.'[58]

Just as in Łódź, a crisis point was reached in Warsaw within a few months. The head of the Economic Division of the General Government wrote a report for Hans Frank in which he outlined the fundamental question that had to be answered: was the Warsaw ghetto part of a plan to 'liquidate the Jews'[59] or an attempt to hold the Jews alive for an unspecified period of time? If the latter, then work had to be found for around 60,000 Jews to ensure that enough food could be purchased to feed the rest. Just as he had in Łódź, Palfinger did his best to discredit those who argued that the Jews should be permitted to work in large numbers, and just as he had in Łódź, he lost the argument. Hans Frank sacked Palfinger in April 1941 and replaced him with Max Bischoff, who was charged with making the ghetto productive. At a meeting in May 1941, Adam Czerniaków, now the Jewish leader of the ghetto – the equivalent position to the one Rumkowski held in Łódź – was informed that 'starving the Jews' was not the objective of the Nazis, and that 'there is the possibility that the food rations would be increased and that there will be work or orders for the workers.'[60] During the same meeting Czerniaków was also told that 'the corpses lying in the streets create a very bad impression' and that the 'corpses . . . must be cleared away quickly'.

Although the systematic murder of every Jew by starvation did not now take place, there was still not enough food, despite Nazi promises, to feed everyone in the ghetto. In June 1941, a month after the meeting at which the Nazis had indicated they would increase the food ration, Czerniaków recorded that his work had been interrupted by beggars moaning under his window, 'Bread, bread! I am hungry, hungry!'[61]

At the same time as Jews died from lack of food in the Warsaw ghetto, plans were under discussion elsewhere in the Nazi state to starve millions of people to death in the wake of the invasion of the Soviet Union. On 2 May 1941 the central economic agency of the Wehrmacht stated that since the 'whole' of the invading German Army would have to be 'fed at the expense of Russia' this meant that 'tens of millions of [Soviet] men will undoubtedly starve to death if we take away all we need from the country.'[62] Later that month, on 23 May, the same agency produced another document entitled 'Political-Economic Guidelines for the Economic Organization East' which estimated that 30 million people might die of hunger in the Soviet Union as a consequence of the German Army seizing their food.[63]

Such thinking was not just the product of expediency. German Army planners didn't decide in a vacuum to starve 30 million people to death. Ideological beliefs underpinned their thinking, for they worked in an environment in which German economists calculated how many people in the eastern territories were 'surplus to requirements'.[64] What would be the advantage, the Nazis maintained, in winning new land and yet simultaneously acquiring millions of 'useless eaters'? Himmler certainly understood the genocidal consequences of this logic. Just days

before the invasion of the Soviet Union was launched, he told his senior
SS colleagues that 'the purpose of the Russian campaign' was 'to deci-
mate the Slavic population by 30 millions'.[65]

The Nazis' plan was brutally audacious. During the war against the
Soviet Union, they were planning to starve to death more than the
combined population of Sweden, Norway and Belgium.[66] This objective was in their minds before they had conceived the idea of creating
factories of death in order to exterminate the Jewish people. Understandably, we ask today – what kind of human beings could consider
such an idea? And the answer is – profoundly racist ones. We have
already seen how not just Hitler but the whole Nazi state functioned on
the iron premise of relative racial value. The German soldiers who were
about to invade the Soviet Union were considered more valuable human
beings than the ones they would find there. The Slavs were a 'race' that
Hitler considered 'a mass of born slaves'.[67] Moreover, since some of the
Slavs in the Soviet Union were also both 'Bolsheviks' and Jews, that
meant that there were three separate reasons for the committed Nazi to
loathe one single Soviet citizen, three reasons to despise one human
being who was, at the same time, Slavic, Bolshevik and Jewish.

There was also, according to Hitler, another unchallengeable intellectual justification for taking food from millions of people and starving
them to death. 'The earth continues to go round,' he said, 'whether it's
the man who kills the tiger or the tiger who eats the man. The stronger
asserts his will, it's the law of nature. The world doesn't change; its laws
are eternal.'[68] For Hitler, a sense of common humanity was a sign of
weakness. If you wanted something, you should try and take it. If you
were strong enough to get what you wanted from someone else, then
you deserved it. There was nothing else to say. The great religious leaders, the great humanist thinkers – all of them had been wasting their
time.

On 30 March 1941, Hitler explained to his generals that the forthcoming war with the Soviet Union would be a 'clash of two ideologies',
and reiterated, 'Communism is an enormous danger for our future.' It
followed, he said, that 'We must forget the concept of comradeship
between soldiers. A Communist is no comrade before or after the battle. This is a war of extermination. If we do not grasp this, we shall
still beat the enemy, but thirty years later we shall again have to fight

the Communist foe.' Hitler called for the normal rules of war to be set aside during the fight against the Soviet Union, and demanded the 'Extermination of the Bolshevist commissars and of the Communist intelligentsia'.[69] In his eyes, the war in the east would be an epic struggle for German domination – the epoch-changing conflict that he had dreamt of for years.

Most senior military commanders did not protest at Hitler's characterization of the forthcoming conflict as a war of 'extermination'. A small number, like Field Marshal von Bock, objected to the order to shoot Soviet political officers rather than take them prisoner – the so-called 'Commissar Order' – but Bock's main concern was that these killings might have a negative effect on military discipline. Many more officers would have agreed with the views of Colonel-General Erich Hoepner who said in a directive issued on 2 May 1941, a month before the formal promulgation of the Commissar Order, that the forthcoming war would be 'the old struggle of the Germanic people against Slavdom, the defence of European culture against Moscovite-Asiatic inundation, the repulse of Jewish Bolshevism. This struggle has to have as its aim the smashing of present-day Russia and must consequently be carried out with unprecedented severity. Every military action must in conception and execution be led by the iron will mercilessly and totally to annihilate the enemy. In particular, there is to be no sparing the upholders of the current Russian-Bolshevik system.'[70]

The forthcoming war in the east also offered fresh possibilities for a solution to an existing Nazi problem: just where should the Jews be deported? As early as 21 January 1941, Theodor Dannecker, the SD officer from Eichmann's department based in Paris, had learnt that 'In accordance with the Führer's wishes, after the war a final solution will be found for the Jewish question within the territories ruled and controlled by Germany.'[71] Dannecker added that Reinhard Heydrich had been told to devise a plan to bring this 'huge task' about. One idea was to deport the Jews first to the General Government in Poland, where they would await onward transportation to a destination yet to be decided.[72]

Heydrich's commission to devise a 'final solution' for the 'Jewish question' does not mean that this was the order for the Holocaust. The words 'final solution' do not mean here what they came to mean later. Heydrich was working on a plan not to exterminate the Jews in gas chambers, but to deport them to somewhere under German control once the war was over. Eichmann had already attempted a similar operation at the start of the war with the Nisko plan. Now Heydrich was almost certainly planning to send the Jews even further away – to the extremity of the new Nazi empire in the conquered territory of the Soviet Union.

At the same time as Heydrich was working on this first version of the 'final solution', Himmler was in discussion with Viktor Brack about another method of dealing with the 'Jewish question' – mass sterilization. For Himmler, the benefits of a swift method of sterilizing not just Jews but any other targeted group were considerable. Most obviously, sterilized labourers posed no 'racial' threat to the people around them since they could not reproduce.[73] As a consequence, Brack investigated potential methods of sterilizing people – without those operated on knowing what was happening to them. In a letter dated 28 March 1941, he outlined the challenges: 'If any persons are to be sterilized permanently, this result can only be attained by applying x-rays in a dosage high enough to produce castration with all its consequences, since high x-ray dosages destroy the internal secretion of the ovary, or of the testicles, respectively.'[74] The difficulty with carrying out this procedure in secret was that unless the rest of the body was protected by a lead covering, 'the other tissues of the body will be injured.' Brack suggested that 'one practical way of proceeding' would be to tell the person to be sterilized to 'approach a counter' and fill in some paperwork for 'two or three minutes'. X-rays could then be turned on while most of the victim's body was protected by the counter. 'With a two-valve installation,' wrote Brack, 'about 150–200 persons could be sterilized per day, and therefore, with twenty such installations as many as 3,000–4,000 persons per day . . .'[75] As we have seen, sterilization of the disabled and other groups the Nazis did not wish to see procreate, including children from disturbed backgrounds,[76] had been taking place since 1933, but Brack's proposal called for a radical expansion. Subsequently, Himmler did not progress Brack's idea – though, as we shall see, further sterilization experiments were later conducted at Auschwitz.

Brack's note is more than a bizarre sidelight at this point in the history, because it demonstrates how the Nazis were considering a whole variety of ideas as potential 'solutions' to their 'Jewish question'. It is crucial to recognize that all of them – from the Madagascar plan to ghettoization, to mass sterilization – were ultimately genocidal. Jews would not be destroyed en masse via sterilization, that's true, but over a generation they would all disappear. In Madagascar they would have vanished over time because the territory could not support large numbers of people, and because the Jewish 'reservation' would have been overseen by SS fanatics. In the ghetto they would have perished eventually because the Nazis had created an environment where the death rate was higher than the birth rate and children were treated as 'useless eaters'.

Just suppose for a moment that circumstances had been such that the Nazis had adopted one of these methods, instead of going on as they did to create the death camps. Would the world have been so appalled? Would one of these methods of extermination still have been called a 'Holocaust'? Perhaps not, because the factories of death the Nazis created in the east represented a particular horror – the cold, mechanistic destruction of human life in an instant, a crime that was symbolic of the worst extremes of the industrial age, somehow an even more haunting means of extermination than the mass shootings the Nazi killing squads would carry out elsewhere in the east at the same time. But we should still remember that the death camps were just one means to the same end that all of these other potential 'solutions' offered – the elimination of the Jews.

Hitler's focus on his longed-for war in the east was momentarily diverted in the spring of 1941 by events in the Balkans – and, as a consequence, many more Jews unexpectedly came under German control before the Wehrmacht crossed into the Soviet Union. The problem Hitler faced was Yugoslavia. He had believed in March 1941 that the Yugoslavs had, after considerable persuasion, decided to join the Tripartite Pact, the agreement of cooperation originally made between Germany, Italy and Japan in September 1940 and subsequently signed by other German allies such as Hungary and Romania.

Hitler had wanted to secure the compliance of the Yugoslavs, in order both to prevent any potential problems behind the lines as his armies moved forward into the Soviet Union and to ease a planned German attack on Greece which was to be launched before the start of the war against the Soviets. Following the botched invasion of Greece by the Italians in October 1940, the Germans feared a counter-attack by the Allies through Greece once the Wehrmacht were committed in the Soviet Union. Hence Hitler's pleasure in March 1941 that at least the non-involvement of Yugoslavia in the forthcoming conflict had been achieved.

So it was with enormous anger that he learnt on 27 March, just two days after Yugoslavia had signed the Tripartite Pact, that a group of Serbian officers had mounted a coup and overthrown the regime of Prince Paul. In the face of what Hitler saw as a total betrayal, he ordered the immediate invasion of Yugoslavia. 'This is no joking matter for the Führer,' wrote Goebbels in his diary.[77] But this extra military commitment meant a delay in the scheduled May launch date of the invasion of the Soviet Union.

The Germans attacked both Greece and Yugoslavia on 6 April. The military action was an astonishing success, with Yugoslavia defeated in less than two weeks, and the Greek mainland occupied by the end of April. Suddenly, around 150,000 more Jews were under German control.

In Yugoslavia, the Nazis fuelled the ethnic tensions that had existed for hundreds of years between the various republics that made up the country. Yugoslavia itself was a creation of the peace treaties at the end of the First World War, formed from the amalgamation of territory that had been part of the Kingdom of Serbia with land from the Austro-Hungarian Empire. The Nazis now supported the formation of an Independent State of Croatia under the leadership of Ante Pavelić, a man who had previously conducted terrorist actions against the Yugoslav state in an effort to force the creation of a separate Croatia. Pavelić, and the Ustaše revolutionary movement that he led, were profoundly racist. They asserted that the Croats were not 'Slavic' like the Serbs, but of mainly Germanic descent, and that only those of true Croat 'blood' could take part in the running of Croatia. They possessed an intense hatred of the nearly 2 million Orthodox Christian Serbs who lived within the boundaries of the new Croat state, and the brutal and sadistic way in which the Ustaše treated these Serbs – murdering more than 300,000 (perhaps as many as 500,000) in the course of the war – is a war crime that deserves to be better acknowledged. The 40,000 Jews living in Croatia were also at risk,[78] as the Ustaše maintained that they too were not true Croats. An editorial in a Croatian newspaper in 1939 stated that 'the Jews were not Croats, and they could never become Croatian because by nationality they are Zionists, by race they are Semites, their religion is Israelite . . . I am asking the peoples of the world, how long are we going to kill each other for the interests of the Jews? . . . if we are to kill each other, let us first kill the Jews . . .'[79]

By the Law Concerning Nationality, signed on 30 April 1941, Croat Jews were deprived of their citizenship. Three weeks later, on 23 May, another law was passed that ordered all Jews to be marked with yellow patches on their clothing. Businesses belonging to Croat Jews were seized – often to the benefit of other Croats rather than the government itself – and Jewish lawyers, doctors and other professionals were sacked from their jobs. But still worse was to come in the immediate aftermath of the German invasion of the Soviet Union, when on 26 June Ante Pavelić accused the Jews of profiteering and ordered them to be imprisoned in concentration camps.

However, Pavelić, though undoubtedly responsible for mass murder, was not as ideologically consistent as the Nazis wished. While he believed that 'Communism and Judaism work together against the national liberation of Croatia,'[80] he gave himself the power to decide who was Jewish. He created the term 'Honorary Aryan' in order to allow a number of Jews – including those deemed to have performed meritorious service to the Croat state – to escape persecution. Pavelić's motivation for this act was almost certainly self-serving – his own wife was the daughter of a Jew, and the wives of a number of his colleagues were Jewish.

In neighbouring Serbia the Germans decided to install a military administration aided and abetted by a puppet government. While the overall military command was in the hands of a German air force general, the civilian governance was administered by Harald Turner, an SS officer who would become notorious for his subsequent involvement in the extermination of Serbian Jews.

At the time of the German invasion of Yugoslavia there were about 16,000 Jews in Serbia, the majority living in Belgrade. They were an immediate target for the occupying forces, and the Germans swiftly persecuted them in an all too familiar pattern: passing decrees identifying who was a Jew, banning the Jews from a number of professions, ordering them to wear identifying badges and drafting Jewish men as forced labour.

Most of the rest of what had been pre-war Yugoslavia was swallowed up by a group of greedy neighbours that were already allies of the Nazis. The Italians took southern Slovenia, a section of the Croatian coast and Montenegro; Hungary annexed a chunk of Serbia including the city of Novi Sad and territory to the north; and Bulgaria snatched much of Macedonia.

After the surrender of Greek forces and the flight of British and Greek soldiers to the island of Crete, Greece was split between Bulgaria, Germany and Italy. The Italians took the bulk of the Greek mainland as well as the Ionian and Cycladic islands, the Germans occupied Salonica, and the Bulgarians most of Thrace and another section of Macedonia. The Germans arrested a number of Jews in the wake of the occupation, but although Greek Jewish communities remained at risk, the immediate persecution in Greece was not on the same scale as that in Croatia.

With the conquest of Greece and Yugoslavia, Hitler had secured his southern flank in preparation for the invasion of the Soviet Union. But these were countries that he would have preferred not to have had to conquer by force. Only the coup in Yugoslavia and the inept performance of the Italians in Greece, which drew Allied troops to the region, had compelled him to act.

Now that he had control of this territory he wanted the minimum possible German military commitment consistent with the subjugation of the population. As for the Jews within Greece and Yugoslavia, they were subjected, as we have seen, to varying degrees of persecution in the spring of 1941. But in that context it is important to remember the question of scale. For while the Nazis gained about 150,000 Jews after conquering Yugoslavia and Greece, that was less than half the number that were currently incarcerated within the Warsaw ghetto alone, and a fraction of the number that were about to be encountered in the Soviet Union.

Hitler was focused on the east. And it would be in the midst of his self-proclaimed war of 'extermination' on Soviet territory that the Holocaust would be born.

10. War of Extermination
(1941)

On 22 June 1941 the Germans launched the largest single invasion in the history of the world. Nearly 4 million German troops and their allies crossed into the Soviet Union in three giant thrusts aimed initially at Leningrad, Smolensk and Kiev. For Adolf Hitler it was the moment he had dreamt of for nearly twenty years – the start of the fight to create a vast German empire in the east.

The day before the invasion Hitler had written to Mussolini telling him of his plans. It was a letter full of lies and half-truths: he said, for instance, that invading the Soviet Union was the 'hardest decision' of his life, when it must have been one of the easiest. He also claimed, contrary to the obvious reality, that 'England has lost this war.' But one comment he made in the letter does ring true. He said that having decided to invade he now felt 'spiritually free'.[1] For Hitler that 'spiritual' freedom manifested itself in his desire to wage a war without rules and without compassion for the defeated. 'The Führer says that we must gain the victory no matter whether we do right or wrong,' wrote Goebbels in his diary on 16 June. 'We have so much to answer for anyhow that we must gain the victory because otherwise our whole people . . . will be wiped out.'[2]

Even though the German invasion plan dwarfed anything attempted before, Hitler and his commanders were so massively over-confident that they anticipated reaching the oil of the Caucasus, more than 1,500 miles east of them, in just a few months.[3] Capturing the Soviet oil was just part of the plan, for vast quantities of both food and land were to be seized as well. As for the people who lived in the Soviet Union – the Nazis intended, as we have seen, to starve them to death in their tens of millions.[4]

At the epicentre of the Nazis' hatred lay, as always, the Jews. And in order to confront 'Jewish Bolshevism' directly, Reinhard Heydrich organized four special task units or Einsatzgruppen – a total force of 3,000 – made up of units of the SD and other security forces. These Einsatzgruppen were to follow immediately behind the army groups as they advanced into the Soviet Union. In a document dated 2 July 1941,

Heydrich explicitly ordered these units to shoot 'Jews in the service of the [Communist] Party or the State' as well as other leading Communists. He also insisted that 'No steps will be taken to interfere with any purges that may be initiated by anti-Communist or anti-Jewish elements in the newly occupied territories. On the contrary, these are to be secretly encouraged.'[5] The Einsatzgruppen were not the only units to be involved in so-called 'cleansing' actions behind the front line. By an order of 21 May, Himmler outlined how special detachments of the Order Police and Waffen SS would also enter the Soviet Union in the wake of the invasion – more than 11,000 members of the Order Police alone.[6] These German policemen would commit murder alongside other German security units.

Just how Heydrich's order that the Einsatzgruppen should not 'interfere' with locals who turned against the Jews worked in practice can be seen by the actions of the Germans in Kaunas. German forces reached Kaunas, the second city in Lithuania, on 24 June, just two days after the invasion had begun. Many Lithuanians welcomed the Germans, seeing them as liberators from Stalin's rule. The Soviets had occupied the country in June 1940, having first forced the Lithuanians to accept Red Army soldiers based on their soil the previous year. Once in control, Stalin's forces pursued a ruthless policy of 'Sovietization' in Lithuania: several thousand Lithuanians were imprisoned as 'enemies of the people'; land was nationalized and economic shortages created – in part by the Soviet occupiers buying Lithuanian goods at artificially low prices. Just before the Germans arrived, 17,000 Lithuanians had been deported to Siberia.[7]

It wasn't just the Soviet forces in general who were blamed for all this suffering, it was the Jews in particular. 'Many Lithuanian Jews became the political leaders, joined the police,' says Petras Zelionka, who later collaborated with the German killing squads, 'and everyone was saying that in the security department people were mostly tortured by Jews. They used to put the screws on the head and tighten them, thus torturing the teachers and the professors.'[8] While the idea that under Soviet rule Lithuanian prisoners were 'mostly tortured by Jews' was ludicrous, there was some basis for the belief that Lithuanian Jews were predisposed to be sympathetic to the Soviets. Many Lithuanian Jews had been pleased when the Soviets arrived – they knew, for instance, that in the Soviet Union the Communists had removed a number of the restrictions that the Jews had endured during Tsarist times. But although some Lithuanian Jews did subsequently manage to gain positions in local government and the security forces, thousands of other Jews were deported to Siberia after they had refused to accept Soviet citizenship.[9] So the Jewish experience in Lithuania at the hands of the Soviets was a decidedly mixed one.

It was also the case, of course, that many non-Jewish Lithuanians had collaborated with the Soviet occupiers. As the German troops marched on to Lithuanian soil it became convenient for these collaborators to focus attention on the Jews. By blaming the Jews they hoped to divert attention from their own complicity with the Soviets. They thus sought to 'cleanse themselves with Jewish blood'.[10] Not for the first – or last – time in this history, the Jews were a convenient scapegoat.

On 25 June 1941, the day after the Germans had arrived in Kaunas, locals turned on Lithuanian Jews in a series of bloody murders outside a garage in the centre of the city. A group of civilians, wearing armbands and armed with rifles, forced between forty and fifty Jews on to the forecourt of the garage. Wilhelm Gunzilius, a member of a German air force reconnaissance unit, witnessed what happened next. 'This man pulled someone out of the crowd [of Jews] and used his crowbar, "Whack!" And he went down. The victim received another blow when he was on the tarmac.'[11] Each of the Jews was killed in the same way: 'one man was led up to him at a time and with one or more blows on the nape of the neck he killed each one.'[12] Gunzilius photographed the slaughter, and his pictures show the killings taking place in front of a large group of civilians and members of the German armed forces. 'The conduct of the civilians,' he says, 'among whom there were women and children, was unbelievable. After every blow of the iron bar they applauded . . .'[13]

Viera Silkinaitė, a sixteen-year-old Lithuanian, also witnessed the killings, and remembers how some of the crowd shouted, 'Beat those Jews!' as the murderer smashed their heads open. One man even lifted up his child so that he could see better. 'What kind of person would he [that child] be when he grew up?' asks Viera. 'If, of course, he could understand what he had seen. And what could you expect of the person who was shouting [encouragement]? It was as if he was going to step into that garage and join the beating.' Appalled at what she had seen, Viera ran off into a nearby cemetery. 'I was ashamed,' she says. 'When I went to the cemetery, I sat down and I thought: "God Almighty, I heard before that there were [Jewish] windows broken or something like that done, that was still conceivable, but such an atrocity, to beat a helpless man . . . it was too much." '[14] Back at the garage, once all the Jews had been killed, the man who had smashed their heads open climbed on top of their bodies and played the Lithuanian national anthem on an accordion.[15]

Dr Walter Stahlecker, the commander of Einsatzgruppe A, which operated in the Baltic States, revealed the complicity of the Nazis in actions like these. He wrote in a report that 'local anti-Semitic elements were induced to engage in pogroms against the Jews . . . The impression had to be created that the local population itself had taken the first steps of its own accord as a natural reaction to decades of oppression by the Jews and the more recent terror exerted by the Communists . . . the task of the security police was to set these purges in motion and put them on the right track so as to ensure that the liquidation goals that had been set might be achieved in the shortest possible time.'[16] Heydrich's instruction that 'Jews in the service of the Party or the State' should be killed was thus obviously a statement of the minimum number of murders that was acceptable.

Considerable latitude was given to the local commanders in deciding how best to pursue Heydrich's instructions, and as a result killing rates varied across the different Einsatzgruppen. It is another example of how fixed and unambiguous orders were not always given in connection with the persecution and murder of the Jews. Instead, once again there was a complex relationship between local initiatives and imprecise instructions from on high. There was, however, one guiding principle that an individual Einsatzgruppe commander could use to determine his actions – the most murderous course was almost always the surest. Not killing enough people, or worse still showing mercy, was seen as a sign that you were not doing your job. Hence when Himmler and Heydrich visited Grodno, 90 miles south of Kaunas, they were unhappy with the numbers killed. Despite the fact that Grodno had a large Jewish population, Einsatzkommando 9 had killed 'only' ninety-six Jews.[17] Significantly, there isn't a recorded example of Himmler and Heydrich expressing dissatisfaction that summer because an Einsatzkommando was killing 'too many' Jews.

Four days after the murders in Kaunas, the Romanians demonstrated that they were also prepared to murder Jews. Just as in Lithuania, Jews in Romania were often accused of sympathizing with the Soviets, and the pre-June 1941 government of Romania, under the leadership of Marshal Ion Antonescu, had been virulently anti-Semitic.

The Romanians, allies of the Nazis, enthusiastically took part in the invasion of the Soviet Union. The enormous numbers of Romanian soldiers who entered Soviet territory on 22 June, fighting alongside the Germans, were in part motivated by self-interest. In 1940 the Soviets had occupied Bessarabia and other Romanian territories in the east of the country and now Marshal Antonescu relished the chance to snatch this land back.

Antonescu was an opportunist who believed the Germans would win against the Soviets. When he met Hitler, on 12 June, just before the invasion was launched, Antonescu said to him, 'Whereas Napoleon and even the Germans in 1917 had still had to contend with the huge problems raised by space, the motor in the air and on the ground have eliminated space as Russia's ally.'[18]

One of the first signs that Romanian forces would use the invasion as an opportunity to target Jews was the murderous action that took place in Iaşi in the east of Romania in late June. Antonescu wanted the city purged of Jews, and as soon as the invasion was launched, rumours began to flourish that the 45,000 Jews in Iaşi were somehow helping the Soviets.[19] Starting on the night of 28–29 June a mix of Romanians – including large numbers of police, members of the anti-Semitic Iron Guard and ordinary citizens – rampaged through the city killing Jews. The Germans were also involved, with Major Hermann von Stransky liaising with the locals. Stransky was married to a Romanian and knew the country well.

A prominent member of the Jewish population in Iaşi remembered, 'I saw the crowd flee in total chaos, fired on from rifles and machine guns. I fell on to the pavement after two bullets hit me. I lay there for several hours, seeing people I knew and strangers dying around me . . . I saw an old Jewish man, disabled after the war of 1916–1918 and wearing the Bărbăţie şi Credinţă [Manhood and Faith] decoration on his chest; he also carried with him papers that officially exempted him from anti-Semitic restrictions. However, bullets had shattered his thorax, and he lived his last moments on a garbage can like a dog.' Further along the street lay the son of a leather merchant who 'was dying and sobbing, "Mother, Father, where are you? Give me some water, I'm thirsty" . . . Soldiers . . . stabbed [the dying] with their bayonets to finish them off.'[20] When Vlad Marievici of the city's sanitation department arrived at police headquarters on the morning of 30 June, he found 'a pile of corpses stacked high like logs' that made it difficult for his truck to enter the courtyard. So many Jews had been murdered the previous night that 'the floor was awash with blood that reached the gate; the blood came up to the soles of my shoes.'[21]

At least 4,000 Jews were killed in the city as a result of the pogrom – some estimates put the figure as high as 8,000.[22] Five thousand more Jews were forced on to two trains and deported to the south. Crammed on board sealed freight trucks, the Jews found it hard to breathe, and the Romanian guards refused to let them drink any water. After several days their thirst was all but unbearable. Nathan Goldstein, a Jew from Iaşi, witnessed what happened when his train stopped near a river: 'an eleven-year-old child jumped out the window to get a drink of water, but the [deputy of the train's commander] felled him with a shot aimed at his legs. The child screamed, "Water, water!" Then the adjutant took him by his feet, shouting, "You want water? Well, drink all you want!", lowered him head first into the water of the Bahlui River until the child drowned, and then threw him in.'[23]

The killing of Jews from Iaşi was just the beginning. In the aftermath of the invasion of the Soviet Union, the Romanians went on to murder more than 100,000 Jews in the former Romanian territory of Bessarabia and North Bukovina. Such was the casual brutality employed by the Romanians that even the Germans complained about their behaviour. General von Schobert, for instance, was unhappy with the Romanians for not burying the bodies of those they killed, and the commander of Einsatzkommando 10a criticized the Romanians for 'lacking planning' in their actions against the Jews.[24] Revealingly, it was the Jews who lived in the Romanian territory that had just been 'liberated' from the Soviets who endured the brunt of the violence. Once again, the perceived link between Jews and 'Bolshevism' was a factor in legitimizing the murders as far as the killers were concerned.

In the summer of 1941, the war against the Soviet Union also had an impact on the concentration camps. Heydrich's 2 July directive called for the Einsatzgruppen, operating just behind the front line, to kill 'People's Commissars' – Soviet political officers. However, some of these commissars were not identified immediately after they had been captured, but were only discovered once they had been transferred to POW camps, far away from the Einsatzgruppen area of operation. This created a problem for the Nazis. Once these commissars had been singled out from the hundreds of thousands of other Soviet prisoners, how should they be murdered most efficiently? It was to resolve this issue that systematic mass killing began in concentration camps, in a secret action codenamed 14f14.

In July 1941 several hundred Soviet commissars were sent to Auschwitz. Kazimierz Albin, a Polish inmate of the camp, remembers that 'they wore uniforms, but the uniforms were not [ordinary] soldiers' uniforms but officers' uniforms, very much in tatters. They were unshaven, and extremely emaciated. They impressed me as people who had been in very difficult conditions. And they didn't look like simple soldiers, they looked like intelligent people.'[25] The commissars laboured in a gravel pit near the main gate. Here they were literally worked to death. 'They were beaten all the time,' says Kazimierz Smoleń, another Polish prisoner. 'You could hear those yells all the time. The SS men were yelling, the Kapos were yelling and the people who were being beaten yelled as well.'[26] The commissars were forced to work in the gravel pits for hours on end without respite. If they slackened the pace they were severely beaten or even shot. 'It was just a few days,' says Kazimierz Smoleń, 'and then they ceased to exist. It was the torture and murder of hundreds of people. It was a cruel death they died. It's like in a horror movie, but such a movie will never be shown.'

The Soviet commissars were also sent to other concentration camps to be murdered, and individual SS units often devised their own method of killing. For instance, at Sachsenhausen, outside Berlin, the SS performed an elaborate charade in order to deceive the commissars about their fate. The commissars were taken into a specially converted barracks and told to undress in preparation for a medical examination. Once they were naked they were led one at a time into a room that purported to be a doctor's office. An SS man, dressed in a white coat, looked them over. What the commissars did not know was that the SS man was interested only in whether or not they had any gold teeth or fillings that could be removed after their death. Next they were taken into a third room where they were told that they were to be measured. They stood up against a measuring stick and then, through a small flap connecting this room to an adjacent one, they were shot in the back of the neck. Kapos took the body away and hastily cleaned the execution chamber ready for the next victim. Loud music was played in the waiting room to drown out the sound of the gunfire.

Despite the labour-intensive nature of this killing process, the SS managed to murder a prisoner every few minutes. Over a ten-week period in 1941 they killed several thousand Soviet prisoners of war.[27] But they could not keep the murders secret. One inmate wrote a note, placed it in a jar and managed to conceal it from the SS. Dated 19 September 1941, it reads: 'we've just found out that another 400 Red Guards have been brought to the camp. We're all under the shattering burden of these murders, which have already claimed more than a thousand lives. We aren't in a position to help them at the moment.'[28]

By the time the murder of the Soviet commissars was under way, the adult euthanasia scheme had also spread to the concentration camps. Under action 14f13 concentration camp prisoners who had been selected as unfit to work were transported to euthanasia killing centres. At Auschwitz on the evening of 28 July 1941, around 500 sick prisoners boarded a train to take them to Dresden. The SS had told them that they were leaving the camp so that they could regain their strength elsewhere. 'They had some hope,' says Kazimierz Smoleń, who watched them leave. 'Hope is the last thing that dies.'[29] The sick prisoners were taken to Sonnenstein euthanasia centre and murdered by carbon monoxide poisoning. These were the first Auschwitz prisoners to die by gassing. They were chosen not because they were Jews, but because they were sick, and they died not at Auschwitz but in the heart of Germany.

Just days later, in August 1941, the T4 euthanasia programme came under threat. In one of the most famous statements of resistance in the history of the Third Reich, Clemens von Galen, Bishop of Münster, mounted a powerful attack on the practice of 'euthanasia'. In Münster Cathedral, on the first Sunday in August, he said, 'For several months we have heard reports that people who have been sick for a while and may appear incurable, have been taken away from mental and nursing homes for the mentally ill on orders from Berlin. After a short time, their relatives then receive notification that the patient has died, the body has been burnt, and the ashes can be sent to them. There is widespread suspicion, bordering on certainty, that these numerous cases of the sudden deaths of the mentally ill don't occur naturally, but are being caused intentionally, and that they follow that doctrine that claims that one is justified in destroying so-called "life unworthy of life" – thus to kill innocent human beings, when one thinks that their life is of no value for the people [*Volk*] and the state.'[30] Galen passionately believed that 'This is not about machines, not about horses or cows whose only purpose is to serve mankind, to produce goods for the people! One may annihilate them, butcher them, as soon as they don't fulfil their purpose any more. No, this is about human beings, our fellow human beings, our brothers and sisters! Poor people, sick people, unproductive people if you like! But have they for this reason forfeited their right to live?' He said that if the same principle was applied widely it could also lead to the killing of 'invalids' and, in a warning that had special relevance given the fierce fighting taking place in the east, even of 'brave soldiers' who returned home 'seriously disabled'.

The timing of Galen's intervention was particularly inconvenient for Hitler. Earlier in 1941 the Gauleiter of Bavaria, Adolf Wagner, had ordered all crucifixes to be taken down in schools within his area of control. Hitler did not request that this action take place, and it has never been fully established whether Wagner acted entirely on his own initiative. There was certainly support for attacks against the church at high levels within the Nazi party. Martin Bormann, head of the party Chancellery, had written a note to all Gauleiters in June 1941 – some weeks after Wagner's actions in Bavaria – in which he said that it was important to try and break the power of the church. Both Wagner and Bormann were outspoken critics of Christianity, and it is possible that Bormann in his enthusiasm to act against church authorities misunderstood a passing reference that Hitler might have made as a signal for action.[31]

Whatever the origin of the decision to order the removal of crucifixes from schools in Bavaria, it turned out to be a major tactical mistake for the Nazis. Bavarians, many of them staunchly Catholic, rose up in large numbers to protest in a flurry of petitions, demonstrations and public meetings. They wrote to their sons and husbands on the front line, complaining about what was happening back home. 'Of course we were angry,' says Emil Klein, a committed Nazi from Bavaria who had taken part in the Beer-Hall Putsch in 1923, and was now fighting on the eastern front, 'when we were lying out there in the ditches and we heard that at home they were taking the crucifixes off the walls in Bavaria. We were annoyed about that!'[32]

Hitler could not afford to lose the support of men like Emil Klein, and the crucifix order was rescinded. Once again Hitler's personal reputation was partly protected by the popular notion that he knew nothing about the conduct of some of his underlings. 'You wear brown shirts on top,' read one anonymous protest letter attacking local Nazis, 'but inside you're Bolsheviks and Jews. Otherwise you wouldn't be able to carry on behind the Führer's back.'[33]

Coming on top of the crucifix debacle, Bishop von Galen's sermon condemning the euthanasia killings was especially problematic for Hitler. Though he wanted to see Galen punished, he felt he could not act against him without stirring up discontent among his own supporters who were also Christians. Moreover, the transportation across Germany of disabled patients to be murdered had now become dangerously high profile.

On 24 August 1941, Hitler decided to cancel the T4 action. This didn't mean that all euthanasia killings ceased – individual hospitals continued to starve disabled patients to death and to kill them by fatal injections – but the systematic gassing in the special killing centres no longer took place as before. In turn, this meant that a number of individuals from the T4 programme who possessed expertise in mass murder, like Christian Wirth and Irmfried Eberl, were unemployed. They would shortly be asked to use their particular talents elsewhere.

It is not possible to say that Galen's intervention led directly to the cancellation of the T4 operation, given that Hitler was already anxious about civilian morale in the light of the crucifix controversy and other concerns.[34] Nonetheless, this episode does demonstrate not just the personal courage of Bishop von Galen but also that open resistance was possible in the Third Reich – risky, of course, but possible. It is significant that something similar was not attempted by Bishop von Galen in particular or the German public in general over the treatment of the

Jews. Underlying anti-Semitism amongst much of the population was not the only reason for this lack of action. Protests also did not occur because the Catholic Church in Germany had distanced itself from the persecution of the Jews, fearing the consequences for the church itself of protesting. In addition, most non-Jewish Germans were not personally affected by the way the Jews were treated. By now the Jews were almost completely isolated from the rest of the population. They lived in Jewish houses and their children attended Jewish schools. On the other hand, most German civilians had a relative in the armed forces, and so the adult euthanasia scheme affected them directly. What if their loved ones were murdered by the state after they became severely injured in battle?

Hitler knew that many of his supporters were Christians and that without their support his ambitions would be damaged. Emil Klein was both a committed Catholic and a committed Nazi. It would be fool-hardy to force him to choose between these two faiths. Hitler had no such problem when it came to the Jews. A vanishingly small number of his soldiers on the front line, or their relatives back at home in Germany, cared enough about Jews to risk protesting about how they were treated.

At the same time as the crucifix controversy festered within Ger-many, Hitler's soldiers appeared to be winning the war against the Soviet Union. Minsk, the capital of Belarus, fell to the Germans at the end of June and nearly 300,000 Red Army soldiers were captured. By now, only a week after the launch of the attack, German panzers were almost a third of the way to Moscow. This was not just the largest inva-sion in history – it was the swiftest as well. In conversation with his acolytes, Hitler basked in the glory. He said: 'to those who ask me whether it will be enough to reach the Urals as a frontier, I reply that for the present it is enough for the frontier to be drawn back as far as that. What matters is that Bolshevism must be exterminated.' His plans for Moscow were simple; the city must 'disappear from the earth's sur-face'.[35] Ten days later, on 16 July, Hitler met with leading Nazi figures, including Göring, Bormann and Rosenberg, and announced that he intended to build a 'Garden of Eden' in the eastern territories, using 'all necessary measures' such as 'shooting' and 'resettlements'. Anyone who 'even looks sideways at us', he said, should be killed.[36]

Shortly after the 16 July meeting, Himmler ordered a large increase in the number of security personnel involved in the mass killing of Jews in the Soviet Union; over 16,000 troops, mostly from SS units, were now ordered to help with the murders. Himmler hadn't been present when Hitler said he wanted to build a 'Garden of Eden' on Soviet territory, using 'all necessary measures', but he had nonetheless understood what his boss wanted. That, after all, was how the Reichsführer SS had prospered in the Third Reich. Over the next few weeks he visited the killing squads operating behind the front line – visits that often coincided with an increase not just in the number of people killed, but in the categories of people killed as well. Gradually over the summer and early autumn of 1941, Jewish women and children were murdered alongside men. Now that babies were targeted, there could no longer be any pretence that the Nazis were only killing Jews who posed an immediate threat to their security.

However monstrous these murders seem to us today, the extension of the killing to include Jewish women and children was not a major ideological departure for the Nazis. They were already aware that they were fighting in a war of 'extermination'. The German Army, as we have seen, had been told to let 'millions' starve as soldiers stole the food they needed from the locals. And on 24 June, two days after the invasion began, Himmler ordered Professor Konrad Meyer to work on a 'General Plan for the East' – an epic vision for the Nazi-occupied east that necessitated the deaths of tens of millions of Soviet men, women and children. As Himmler had said just before the war in the east began: 'It is a question of existence, thus it will be a racial struggle of pitiless severity.'[37]

There was also a practical reason, as the Nazis saw it, why these Jewish women and children had to be murdered in the Soviet Union. For once the Jewish men had been shot, many of the women and children had lost their breadwinners and so would likely suffer a slow death by starvation. In the warped world of the Third Reich, one Nazi even argued that it would be more humane to kill the Jews quickly rather than let them starve. Back in Poland, on 16 July – the same day that Hitler held his meeting about establishing a 'Garden of Eden' in the East – SS Sturmbannführer Rolf-Heinz Höppner wrote a memo to Adolf Eichmann about the situation in the Warthegau: 'There is a danger that, in the coming winter, it will become impossible to feed all the Jews. It must seriously be considered whether the most humane solution is to finish off the Jews unfit for labour through some fast-acting means. This would definitely be more pleasant than letting them starve to death.'[38]

However, it was one thing to talk about extending the killing in the abstract, quite another for SS men to stand up close and pull the trigger, a few feet away from naked Jewish women and children. Nonetheless, in the summer and autumn of 1941 thousands of SS men became murderers for the first time as they killed in just such an intimate manner. The 1st SS Infantry Brigade, for example, murdered Jews in Ostrog in the west of Ukraine at the start of August 1941. Ostrog was a predominantly Jewish city, with a population of 10,000 Jews, now swelled by several thousand more who had sought refuge in the city from the surrounding area. On 4 August the SS forced Jews out of Ostrog into the countryside. 'They treated us as cattle,' says Vasyl Valdeman, then a twelve-year-old Jewish boy. 'They [the SS] were armed and had dogs with them. They made the strong [Jews] carry the ill people, and those who had beards were beaten, because they thought they were rabbis, and we saw much blood on their faces. They [the Jews] were crying out, I remember their words, "They are beating us, beating us as dogs."'

When the Jews reached a large sandy field the SS ordered them to sit down. The SS had told the Jews that they were needed to dig fortifications, but it soon became clear that they were to be murdered. 'We were looking at our parents,' says Vasyl, 'and when we saw our grandmother and mother crying we realized that this was something horrible.'[39]

The Jews waited hours in the scorching heat until, one group at a time, they were ordered to undress and all their valuables were stolen. Next they were marched forward to an open pit and shot. But the SS didn't possess the manpower to kill all the Jews in one day, so in the evening the remaining Jews were marched back into Ostrog. The next day the killing began again and continued until the military commander of Ostrog said he needed the remaining Jews to act as forced labour.[40] Almost the whole of Vasyl's family were murdered by the Nazis – including his father, two brothers, two uncles, his grandmother and grandfather. Vasyl and his mother were hidden by non-Jewish neighbours and survived the war. 'They even ran risks so that we could survive,' he says. 'Nobody told the Germans that we were hiding.'

'There were no problems between Ukrainians and Jews in Ostrog,' says Oleksiy Mulevych, a non-Jewish Ukrainian, who was sixteen years old when the Germans arrived. 'What the Germans have done to Jews cannot be forgiven. I felt no difference between the Jews and me. I understood that the next turn would be mine.' Oleksiy thought he and his family might starve because the Nazis 'took all our food away. At the time we had two hectares of land and they took the corn and the cows . . . The Germans were the enemies of all the people. They were like beasts.'[41] Oleksiy knew nothing of the details of the German plan to feed their armed forces at the 'expense' of the local population, but he and his family felt its impact as they struggled to survive on whatever scraps they could find.

Although Vasyl Valdeman and his mother were protected by non-Jewish Ukrainians, not everyone in Ukraine was as supportive of the Jews. There were many cases of non-Jewish Ukrainians profiting from the destruction of their Jewish neighbours. In Horokhiv, for example, 50 miles south of Ostrog, locals stood in queues to buy the murdered Jews' possessions at knock-down prices.[42] In Lwów there were horrific scenes on the streets at the end of June 1941 as Ukrainians participated in the murder of around 4,000 Jews.[43] This orgy of violence was sparked by the discovery that Soviet security forces had killed several thousand prisoners just before the Germans arrived.

Nazi-approved pogroms like the ones in Lwów and Kaunas certainly did take place – one estimate is that there were at least sixty of them in the occupied Soviet Union[44] – but the majority of Jews were murdered that summer and autumn in actions like the one in Ostrog where the Jews were shot at close quarters. Hans Friedrich, an ethnic German from Romania, participated personally in these 'pit' killings as a member of the 1st SS Infantry Brigade. Friedrich says he had 'no feelings' as he shot the Jews. He claims this lack of 'empathy' – indeed his overall 'hatred' of Jews – was because Jews had previously 'harmed' his family by buying animals from their farm too cheaply. The 'motto' of this war, he says, was 'against Communism', and since 'there were connections between Jews and Bolshevism' he thought it understandable that the Jews were considered a target, especially since the Soviet Union was only 'half civilized'.[45]

In the Baltic States in particular, many of those who shot the Jews were locals, murdering alongside German security forces. Petras

Zelionka, for example, was a member of a Lithuanian unit that took part in the killings. He felt justified in murdering innocent Jewish civilians partly because he believed that Jews had tortured Lithuanians during the Soviet occupation of the country – 'we were told what they have done, how they used to kill even the women.'[46] He also reveals that his comrades relished the chance to steal from the Jews. Straightforward avarice could be just as much a reason to commit murder as anything ideological.

A distinguished Lithuanian historian has identified five motivational factors for those who participated in the killings. Revenge (against those who had allegedly helped the Soviets oppress the population), expiation (for those who wanted to show their loyalty to the Nazis after collaborating with the Soviets), anti-Semitism, opportunism (a desire to adapt swiftly to the new situation in Lithuania) and self-enrichment. Having met Petras Zelionka, I believe he matches four of those criteria. Only 'expiation' is doubtful in his case.[47]

An additional motivational factor, not mentioned in this list, was one almost certainly possessed by both Petras Zelionka and Hans Friedrich – sadism. Even long after the war was over – Zelionka was interviewed in 1996 and Friedrich eight years later – neither expressed any remorse for their actions, and they both talked about the killings as if they had gained some base, sadistic kick out of murdering in this intimate way. Friedrich, for example, says that the Jews 'were extremely shocked, utterly frightened and petrified, and you could do what you wanted with them',[48] and Zelionka that he felt a sense of 'curiosity' as he killed children – 'you just pull the trigger, the shot is fired and that is it.'[49]

Zelionka's unit also committed murders at the Seventh Fort in Kaunas, though he claimed he did not take part personally in this particular action. Here there were reports that the killers were sexual sadists. 'Night after night the Lithuanian henchmen would proceed to select their victims: the young, the pretty,' recorded Avraham Tory in his diary. 'First they would rape them, then torture them, and finally murder them. They called it "going to peel potatoes".'[50]

The perverted pleasure that some members of the Einsatzgruppen took in the killing process was obvious to onlookers. 'There were a number of filthy sadists in the extermination Kommando,' said Alfred Metzner, a driver and interpreter. 'For example, pregnant women were shot in the belly for fun and then thrown into the pits . . . Before the execution the Jews had to undergo a body search, during which . . . anuses and sex organs were searched for valuables and jewels.'[51]

In Ukraine, Dina Pronicheva, a Jew who escaped from a killing site, witnessed how some of the German killers were happy to commit what their own ideology considered a 'race crime': 'At the opposite side of the ravine, seven or so Germans brought two young Jewish women. They went down lower to the ravine, chose an even place and began to rape these women by turns. When they became satisfied, they stabbed the women with daggers . . . And they left the bodies like this, naked, with their legs open.'[52]

There were similar sadists not just in the SS but in the ordinary German Army. During the partisan war behind the front line on the eastern front, Adolf Buchner, a member of an SS Pionierbataillon, saw both SS and army soldiers take pleasure in mentally and physically torturing Soviet civilians. 'There were some bastards among them,' he says. 'They undressed them [i.e. the villagers] until they were naked and they killed them once they were naked . . . among our own people there were those who were really hot for it, to be able to let them have it . . . Was there any need, for example, to shoot the children in front of the women and then shoot the women after that? That happened too. That is sadism. There were officers like that, they liked sadistic things, they liked it when the mothers were screaming or children were screaming – they were really hot for that. In my view those people are not human.'[53]

For Walter Fernau, who served on the eastern front with the 14 Panzerjäger-Kompanie, the reason for the atrocities was simple. 'If you give a person a weapon and power over other people,' he says, 'and then allow him to drink alcohol then he becomes a murderer.' There was also, he says, a 'coarsening' and a 'brutalization' that occurred within the German Army during the war in the east, particularly once the 'partisan war' started up: 'then one would meet someone who looked like a partisan . . . [and] he was simply shot.' The final element in this toxic cocktail of emotions was, according to Walter Fernau, straightforward 'fear'. 'You would not believe what sort of feeling it is to be really afraid,' he says. 'When I ever actually spoke to young people . . . about war or anything, I always told them how scared I was.'[54]

As early as 3 July 1941, Stalin had demanded that 'Conditions in the occupied regions must be made unbearable for the enemy and all of his accomplices.'[55] The Germans took this to mean that all civilians in the Soviet territory they controlled were now potential partisans. Since a recurring theme of Nazi ideology was that the Jews were a security threat, it was easy for German forces to conflate 'partisan' and 'Jew'. That was what General von Manstein, commander of the Eleventh Army, did when he issued this order of the day on 20 November 1941: 'Jewry constitutes the mediator between the enemy in the rear and the still fighting remnants of the Red Army and the Red leadership.' Manstein went on to emphasize the racial nature of the war: 'The Jewish–Bolshevik system must be eradicated once and for all. Never again may it interfere in our European living space. The German soldier is therefore not only charged with the task of destroying the power instrument of this system. He marches forth also as a carrier of a racial conception and as an avenger of all the atrocities which have been committed against him and the German people.'[56]

Though a number of German Army commanders issued orders insisting that their soldiers have no part in the SS and Einsatzgruppen killings, the involvement of the Wehrmacht in the pacification actions against the partisans in the east was widespread. For instance, Wolfgang Horn, an NCO with a Panzer artillery unit, personally ordered the burning down of an entire village during the fight against partisans, but he thought little of it because the houses were 'not worth much anyhow . . . we didn't take it so seriously to [set on] fire a Russian house . . . we didn't respect them as as civilized as we are . . . their lifestyle was too primitive for us.'[57]

Many ordinary soldiers, after years of schooling in Nazi ideology, had little doubt that they were fighting inferior human beings. 'Everyone, even the last doubter,' wrote one soldier in July 1941, 'knows today that the battle against these subhumans, who've been whipped into a frenzy by the Jews, was not only necessary but came in the nick of time. Our Führer has saved Europe from certain chaos.'[58]

While there were killers who liked what they were doing, there were also those who had problems participating in the murders. Himmler discovered this for himself on a visit to Minsk in the summer of 1941. On 15 August he watched as around a hundred people – a mix of 'partisans and Jews'[59] according to his work diary – were shot by

Einsatzgruppe B. The victims were forced to lie face downwards in a pit and shot from behind. The next group then had to climb into the pit and lie on the people who had just been shot.

Walter Frentz, an air force cameraman who was stationed at the Führer's headquarters in East Prussia, had asked to accompany Himmler's group to Minsk because he wanted 'to see something else for a change – not always just these four walls at HQ'. Frentz was 'pretty shocked' by what he saw, because he 'didn't know that things like that happened'.[60] Once the killings were finished 'the commander of the auxiliary police approached me, because I was in the air force. "Lieutenant," he said, "I can't take it any more. Can't you get me out of here?" I said, "Well, I don't have any influence over the police. I'm in the air force, what am I supposed to do?" "Well," he said, "I can't take it any more – it's terrible!" '[61]

SS Obergruppenführer (Lieutenant General) von dem Bach-Zelewski claimed that he said to Himmler after the killings in Minsk: 'Reichsführer, those were only a hundred [that had been shot] . . . Look at the eyes of the men in this Kommando, how deeply shaken they are. These men are finished for the rest of their lives. What kind of followers are we training here?'[62]

Himmler gathered the killers around him after the shooting and made a short speech, explaining that 'He alone bore responsibility before God and the Führer for what had to happen.' He said that no doubt his men had noticed that he was not happy that this work had to be fulfilled, but it was a necessary task. Himmler also, according to Bach-Zelewski, told his men that they 'were supposed to look at nature, there was struggle everywhere, not only for humans, but in flora and fauna as well. Those who didn't want to fight simply perished . . . we humans were in the right when we defended ourselves against vermin . . .'[63] Himmler added that although the task they had been set was 'hard' he 'could not see any way round it. They must be hard and stand firm. He could not relieve them of this duty, he could not spare them.'[64] That evening, Frentz heard Himmler say: 'You may be wondering why something like this was done. But if we didn't do this, what would they do to us?' Frentz says he thought these words were 'terrible'.[65] Himmler gave a further glimpse into his murderous mentality the following month, when he said: 'Even the brood in the cradle must be crushed like a puffed-up toad. We are living in an iron time and have to sweep with iron brooms. Everyone has therefore to do his duty without asking his conscience first.'[66]

After witnessing the murders in Minsk in August, Himmler drove on to a mental hospital at Novinki and almost certainly gave the order for the patients to be killed. It is also likely that during or shortly after this visit he discussed with Arthur Nebe, commander of Einsatzgruppe B and a former head of the Criminal Police, other potential methods of mass murder. Himmler had just witnessed, of course, in dramatic personal terms, the potential psychological problems that shooting Jews at close range could cause.[67]

In the weeks following Himmler's visit, Nebe experimented with different killing techniques with the help of Dr Albert Widmann of the Technical Institute of the Criminal Police. Widmann's presence in Minsk was a sign of the growing involvement in the killings in the east of the team that had worked on the T4 euthanasia scheme. Widmann, as we have seen, had helped devise the gas chambers in the euthanasia centres.

It soon became apparent that the killing techniques of T4 could not easily be replicated in the east. The gas chambers in the killing centres in Austria and Germany had used bottled carbon monoxide gas, and it was impractical – partly because of the expense – to transport canisters of carbon monoxide to the various killing locations spread across the occupied Soviet Union. The mobile gas van had been one way round this 'problem', but the physical capacity of the gas van was limited. What the Nazis needed was a cheap and simple method of mass killing that spared the killers the psychological stress caused by facing their victims eye to eye.

In this context, it is a common misconception that gas chambers emerged as the preferred killing method of the Holocaust simply because of the desire of the Nazis to kill Jews in large numbers. That wasn't the case. During the infamous murders at Babi Yar outside Kiev in September 1941, for example, a combination of soldiers from SS police battalions, Einsatzgruppen and local collaborators murdered nearly 34,000 Jews in just two days by shooting them. This was killing on a scale that no death camp ever matched over a similar period. What gas chambers offered was not a way of killing more people in a single day than shooting, but a method of making the killing easier – for the killers.

In the summer of 1941 it wasn't immediately obvious to the Nazis that gas chambers were the most suitable way forward. Widmann and his team also tried – almost unbelievably – imprisoning mental patients in a bunker and blowing them up. The experiment was not a success from the Nazis' point of view. 'The sight was atrocious,' said Wilhelm Jaschke, an officer in Einsatzkommando 8. 'Some wounded came out of the dugout crawling and crying . . . Body parts were scattered on the ground and hanging in the trees.'[68] After the failure of this attempt to murder people, Widmann, Nebe and their colleagues turned their attention once again to carbon monoxide. Was there a way of creating this gas, so effective in killing the disabled in Germany, without using the canisters? The answer turned out to be all around them – in the exhaust gases expelled from cars and trucks. At a mental hospital in Mogilev in Belarus, the Nazis locked patients into a sealed room and piped in exhaust gases from a car engine. When this turned out not to produce enough poisonous gas, they tried a larger engine from a truck until they succeeded in murdering everyone in the room.

Experiments in different methods of killing were not only conducted in the occupied Soviet Union. At Auschwitz, in Upper Silesia, the SS devised another way of murdering prisoners. In the early autumn of 1941, Karl Fritzsch, deputy to the commandant, Rudolf Höss, tried killing sick prisoners and Soviet POWs with a powerful cyanide-based chemical in crystallized form that was used to destroy insects. The crystals, stored in sealed tins, turned into poisonous gas once exposed to the air. The chemical was called Zyklon Blausäure – or Zyklon B for short.

The SS experimented by locking selected prisoners in the basement of Block 11 in Auschwitz. Block 11 was a prison within a prison, the most feared building in the camp, the place where the SS interrogated and tortured prisoners. But just as initial attempts to kill with carbon monoxide exhaust had not been as effective as the Nazis would have liked, so Fritzsch's first attempt to murder with Zyklon B was not – from his point of view – completely successful.

August Kowalczyk, a Polish political prisoner in Auschwitz, witnessed how the SS tried to seal the area in Block 11 where the prisoners were to be gassed by blocking it off with soil and sand. But either the sealing process was ineffective or insufficient Zyklon B was used, because the day after the gassing he saw one SS man running back and forth in an agitated way. It turned out that some prisoners were still alive, so more Zyklon B crystals were poured into the makeshift gas chamber. The terrible agonies faced by these unknown Soviet POWs and sick prisoners as they half suffocated during the night in Block 11 can scarcely be imagined.[69]

The SS, by this murderous trial and error, established the exact amount of Zyklon B crystals required to murder a set number of prisoners. In the process they discovered that the gas was more effective the hotter the room, and the more people that were crammed inside. They also found out that Block 11 was far from the perfect place to conduct mass murder. The difficulty they faced, as August Kowalczyk witnessed, was 'how to evacuate the corpses'. Other prisoners had to enter the basement, disentangle the bodies, carry them back upstairs, place them on handcarts and then push them to the other end of the main camp to be burnt in the crematorium. Not only was this a labour-intensive and time-consuming process, but it was impossible to keep the murders secret from the rest of the camp. After giving the matter some thought, the SS realized that they could short-cut the process by turning one of the corpse-storage rooms in the crematorium into a gas chamber. The prisoners could now be murdered next to the ovens that were used to burn their remains.

These various experiments in the summer and autumn of 1941 were carried out against the background of another campaign of killing that dwarfed the gassings in terms of scale. For during the second half of 1941 the Nazis murdered a staggering number of Soviet prisoners of war. By the end of 1941, out of the 3.35 million Soviet prisoners taken captive by the Germans since the war began on 22 June, more than 2 million were dead. Around 600,000 had been killed as a consequence of the Commissar Order, the rest died of mistreatment of one kind or another, with large numbers starved to death.[70] As one historian of this period remarked, if the war had ended at the start of 1942, 'this programme of mass murder would have stood as the greatest single crime committed by Hitler's regime.'[71]

Georgy Semenyak was one of the minority of Soviet POWs captured at the start of the war who survived. He was imprisoned by the Germans in a camp in the open air along with around 80,000 other POWs and survived on the occasional serving of thin soup, which because the Germans did not issue bowls or cups he had to drink from his forage cap. 'The forage cap is Soviet Army issue,' he says, 'and was intended for summer wear, and the thin soup ran straight through the material.' After a few weeks he was moved to an even larger camp. Here he faced another problem: an infestation of lice. 'This brought about an epidemic of typhus. And people started to die of typhus. Furthermore, there were so many lice that many people's hair was so full of lice that it started to move. Not only were people's hair, clothes and bodies covered with lice, but if you leant over and picked up a handful of sand, the sand moved because of all the lice in it.'[72]

The Soviet prisoners tried to capture rats to eat. 'Sometimes a man would catch a rat by the tail,' says Georgy Semanyak, 'and the rat would bend round and bite his hand. They have two incisor teeth – very strong teeth. So the rat is biting the man's hand, but he won't let go of it. He hits it to kill it, to get a piece of meat to boil or fry.' Soviet prisoners were so desperate that they even ate the dead bodies of their comrades. Semanyak reveals that a number of his comrades cut the buttocks, liver and lungs from corpses and then fried and ate them.

Semanyak also remembers how the Germans played sadistic games on the Soviet POWs, reminiscent of some of the torments they inflicted on Jews: 'A German approaches a crowd of people and asks: "Who wants some food?" What an idiotic question! When you can see that people haven't eaten their fill for months on end, how can you ask: "Who wants food?" Everyone wants food. "OK [says the German], then who can eat a whole bucket of porridge?" Someone raises their hand and says: "I can." "Come forward then." And the German gives him the bucket of porridge. But of course he can't eat the whole bucket. But he stands by the bucket and starts eating. He eats a couple of bowlfuls at the most . . . That's already pretty exceptional. He can't possibly eat any more. And then he says: "That's it!" And the bucket is still three-quarters full. And then they beat him up. So he has to take a beating, but at least he's eaten.'[73]

Hunger dominated the lives of millions who lived under Nazi occupation in the summer and autumn of 1941. True to the intentions they had expressed in secret that spring, the Nazis murdered those they despised not just by the bullet and the gas chamber, but by starvation. This does not mean, however, that the Nazis had the same attitude to killing Soviet POWs as they did to killing Jews. The mental process that allowed them to justify the murders was different. Wolfgang Horn, for example, was a typical soldier in that while he regarded the Soviets 'as uncivilized, nearly savages', he thought the Jews were not 'savages' but intelligent. Horn had been told that the Jews were 'ruling Russia' and were also the reason that the Germans had lost the First World War.[74]

It thus followed logically from Nazi ideology that the Jews were the deadlier enemy – they were not mere subhumans, but a 'race' that was clever enough to plot secretly against Germany. As a consequence it was necessary to remove – in one way or another – every single one of them. As for the Soviet POWs, if they could work as beasts of burden then they might be allowed to serve the Nazi state. When they became 'useless eaters', it was time for them to die. That mentality explains why the mortality rate of Soviet POWs in German hands decreased after Hitler ordered on 31 October 1941 that Soviet prisoners should be employed in large numbers as forced labourers.[75] Significantly, he was not prepared at this stage in the war to countenance the use of Jews as workers within the Reich. In the spring of 1941 Arthur Greiser had been so keen to expel Jews from the Warthegau that he had suggested sending 70,000 Jews to Germany as slave labourers, but Hitler had vetoed the idea.[76] The idea was to expel them from the Reich, not to take them back as workers.

Hitler, of course, was not making every decision about the nature of the killing that took place in the wake of the invasion of the Soviet Union. It is even unclear whether Himmler's instruction to the Einsatzgruppen, to expand the murders in July 1941 in the Soviet Union to include Jewish women and children, was made as a result of a direct order from Hitler. That Hitler knew what the Einsatzgruppen killers were doing, however, is certain. He received direct intelligence detailing how many people they were murdering. On 1 August 1941 the head of the Gestapo, Heinrich Müller, transmitted a message to the commanders of the Einsatzgruppen: 'The Führer is to be sent regular reports from here about the work of the Einsatzgruppen in the east. For this purpose particularly interesting illustrative material is required, like photographs, posters, pamphlets and other documents.'[77] Equally certain is that Hitler approved wholeheartedly of the killings. Later that same month Goebbels wrote in his diary after a meeting with him: 'We talk about the Jewish problem. The Führer is convinced that the prophecy he made in the Reichstag – that if the Jews manage to provoke a new world war, it would result in the extermination of the Jews – is now coming true . . . with almost uncanny certainty. In the east the Jews have had to settle their account; in Germany they have partly paid and will have to pay even more in future.'[78]

Most probably, in extending the killings in the occupied Soviet Union in the summer of 1941, Himmler knew that he was acting within an overall mandate given to him by Hitler about the fate of the Jews during this war of extermination. He was also aware that Hitler would be informed once the operation was under way, and if the Führer was unhappy then the action could be stopped. Tellingly, it was not.

This flexibility in the way the extermination process operated can be detected through the whole chain of command. It is likely, for instance, that when Himmler visited the Einsatzgruppen on location in the east in the summer of 1941 he did not often give written orders, but orally encouraged the Einsatzgruppen to extend the killing where and when possible. And when written orders were issued they could be couched in terms that were imprecise. On 1 August, for example, the 2nd SS Cavalry Regiment, operating in the Pripet Marshes in the occupied Soviet Union, received this message which emanated from Himmler: 'All Jews must be shot. Drive the female Jews into the swamp.' SS Obersturm-bannführer (Lieutenant Colonel) Magill replied: 'Driving women and children into the swamp was not successful because the swamp was not so deep that sinking could occur.'[79]

If there had been an explicit written order from Himmler circulating among the SS and Einsatzgruppen units, this kind of ambiguous communication would not have occurred. In this case, Himmler did not want to be explicit in writing about killing Jewish women and children and hoped his men would read between the lines. But then this particular unit took the order they had received too literally. Magill correctly understood this instruction to be a euphemistic way of saying 'kill the women and children' and so sent his reply explaining that the method of killing he had been told to use – drowning in the swamp – didn't work.

We can learn two important things from this brief exchange. First, that SS functionaries thought it necessary to use camouflage language in writing even between themselves. Second, because orders from the top were sometimes given with an element of ambiguity, some junior officers could be uncertain about what exactly was required of them.

This level of subterfuge even led to other Nazi functionaries trying to stop what they saw as unauthorized killing actions. Hinrich Lohse, for instance, the Reich Commissioner for the Baltic States, wrote on 15 November 1941: 'I have forbidden the indiscriminate executions of Jews in Libau because they were not carried out in a justifiable way.' He asked for clarification whether or not there was an 'instruction to liquidate all Jews in the east' because he was unable 'to find such a directive'.[80] The reply he received from the head of the political department of the Reich Ministry for Eastern Territories was careful not to refer to such a 'directive' in writing, and merely said that Lohse's concern about the 'Jewish question' ought by now to have been 'clarified' via 'oral discussions'.[81]

We cannot know for certain exactly why the Nazis administered their policy of mass killing in this way. But the most persuasive explanation is that they were aware that public knowledge of what they were doing could lead to problems for them. The lesson to take from Bishop von Galen's protests over euthanasia, as far as the Nazis were concerned, would have been to put more effort into keeping killing projects secret. It was not so much that the Nazis would have been concerned about public protests in Germany – although that remained a risk – as the consequences abroad if the rest of the world knew in detail what was happening. Hitler, in particular, would have been concerned about damage to his prestige. He envisaged a life for Germany after the war was won and it would be diplomatically easier for the German head of state if the extermination of the Jews had been kept secret – or at least that he himself had managed to maintain plausible distance from it. Having decided in 1939 to sign a document authorizing the euthanasia scheme, and subsequently seen the way the church attacked the Nazis, Hitler would have been doubly concerned to keep his name out of any other killing actions that might attract negative publicity. While he could stand in front of the Reichstag and predict in principle the extermination of the Jews if there was a world war, that wasn't the same as revealing in detail how Jewish men, women and children were being slaughtered. Much better, from Hitler's perspective, to make sure that no order in his name about this sensitive project ever existed. He was well aware that written orders could come back and haunt the sender. That is one reason he remarked in October 1941, 'it's much better to meet than to write, at least when some matter of capital importance is at issue.'[82]

But no sophisticated state can function if every order is merely spoken, so on occasion it was necessary to refer to the killings in writing. As a result a whole range of euphemisms came to be associated with the destruction of the Jews. 'Special handling', for example, was one way in documents of referring to murder. Equally, the term 'Final Solution' came to mean the plan to exterminate the Jews, even though the words had initially meant only their deportation. It still held this original meaning in a document signed by Göring for Heydrich, dated 31 July 1941. 'To supplement the task that was assigned to you,' the document read, 'on 24 January 1939, which dealt with the solution of the Jewish problem by emigration and evacuation in the most suitable way, I hereby charge you to submit a comprehensive blueprint of the organizational, subject-related and material preparatory measures for the execution of the intended final solution of the Jewish question.'[83] We know that the 'final solution' mentioned in this document was not the mass extermination of the Jews in the death camps, because earlier discussions between Heydrich and Göring about a possible 'blueprint' for the 'final solution' can be traced to March 1941, at a time when the Nazis planned to deport the Jews east after the war. So by far the most convincing explanation of this July 1941 exchange is that Heydrich was still working on a plan to deport the Jews into the furthest reaches of the occupied Soviet Union, with the vast population movements necessary not taking place until the war in the east was over. This interpretation also fits with the thrust of previous Nazi wartime policy against the Jews, which was one of deportation with genocidal consequences in the medium to long term. Just as the Jews sent to Nisko in the General Government at the start of the war had died in large numbers of starvation, disease and other mistreatment, and the Jews would have perished over time had they been sent to Madagascar, so the fate of the Jews sent to the wastelands of the occupied Soviet Union would have been similarly catastrophic.

However, in the late summer and early autumn of 1941 there were discussions about a change in the timetable of the Final Solution. A number of Hitler's most loyal followers wanted the Jews deported east not after the war was over but immediately. When Goebbels met Hitler on 19 August he asked for the Jews of Berlin to be removed from the German capital. Goebbels felt it unconscionable that 70,000 Jews were still able to live in the city while German soldiers were fighting and dying on the eastern front. Hitler did not agree to deport the Berlin Jews at once, but he did accept one of Goebbels' proposals – that German Jews should be marked. Jews in Poland had been forced to wear identification badges for some time, and now it was the turn of German Jews to be subjected to this humiliation.

From 1 September 1941, Jews over the age of six in Germany, Austria and the other incorporated territories had to wear a yellow badge in the shape of the Star of David on their clothing. The effect of this measure was not only to identify Jews and make them more liable to harassment, but to make the persecution of the Jews obvious to every non-Jewish German. Although some Germans abused the now easily identifiable Jews in the streets, there were others who were uneasy at this new development. Uwe Storjohann, for example, remembers that his mother – who, he says, 'probably welcomed' the idea of the deportation of the Jews – nonetheless objected to their 'stigmatization'. Shortly after the Jews of Hamburg had been compelled to wear the yellow badge, Uwe was walking with his mother through a Jewish area of the city when they saw 'an elderly Jew coming along wearing a very torn suit, and carrying a very old suitcase, and he carried it in such a way that his Star of David was covered up. And then he must have been taken by a human need, and he was peering around furtively, thinking whether he could enter a public toilet [which was marked "forbidden to Jews"]. Then he went in there. And my mother stopped, and I thought, why's she stopping? And she said, "Well, have you seen him? That was a Jew, wasn't it? He went in there, and he had his briefcase with the Jewish star hidden underneath it." She waited until he came out. And when he saw my mother, he suddenly had a very anxious expression. I'll never forget this panic, anxiety. He dropped his briefcase, and there you could see the Star of David. And I knew how my mother thought about these things, and I was wondering what would happen next, what she would do. And the Jew too, of course, [was thinking] if she goes to the police now, I'm done for. My mother goes towards him, she points to the Star of David, and says, "We didn't want that." And I said to myself, well, you never expected that. So, at that moment, she must have felt sorry for him. I'm sure she

imagined that you exclude Jews from business life and let them do inferior jobs, or perhaps resettle them into towns where they can then live
nicely among themselves, or something like that, or in their own state,
such as Israel today . . . But this stigmatization, she thought that was
terrible. I became very thoughtful, and thought, well, maybe she isn't
quite as keenly anti-Semitic as I thought she was. But it was also typical
of a large part of the population, who said, "Well, no, that is going too
far, we don't like that." But they wouldn't have done anything. Nothing. They turned their ears and eyes away . . .'[84]

Erna Krantz, a Nazi supporter who lived in Munich, felt similar
emotions after the Jews were forced to wear the Star of David: 'In the
street parallel to us we had a Baroness Brancka, who was married to a
Baron, but was a Jewish shopkeeper's daughter from Hamburg . . . and
she had to wear the Jewish star. I was sorry about that, it was so terrible, because this woman was such a nice woman, that's what you felt.
But really, just like today, when you walk away from people in need,
you can't help everywhere, it was the same then.'[85]

As we have seen, Goebbels had asked for the Jews not just to be marked,
but to be deported as well. And soon other leading Nazis also said they
wanted the Jews to be sent away. On 15 September 1941, the Gauleiter
of Hamburg, Karl Kaufmann, wrote to Hitler asking if the Jews of the
city could be deported. Kaufmann wanted their property to house
non-Jewish Germans who had suffered in the recent air attacks. Hitler
now decided to reverse his previous policy and authorize the deportation of Jews from within the Reich immediately, rather than after the
war was over. Why did he change his mind at this moment, when he
had said to Goebbels just a few weeks before that the Jews could not be
sent east? Nobody knows for certain. One possible explanation is that
Hitler acted out of revenge because of Stalin's decision in August to
deport several hundred thousand ethnic Germans living in the Volga
region to the wastes of Siberia and Kazakhstan. Whether or not this
specific act by Stalin was the trigger for Hitler's action, the overall context of the war against the Soviet Union would surely have played a part
in his decision.

The war still appeared to be going well for the Germans. Though the
soldiers of the Wehrmacht had not – as planned – managed to defeat the

Red Army in a matter of weeks, they were in the process of winning the largest battle of encirclement in history as they fought in the fields around Kiev, capital of Ukraine. On 19 September 1941, the city fell to German forces and 600,000 Soviet soldiers were captured. 'The German soldier has again proved that he is the best soldier in the world,' said Hitler, speaking to his close associates as he basked in triumph. 'The operation now in progress, an encirclement with a radius of more than a thousand kilometres, has been regarded by many as impracticable. I had to throw all my authority into the scales to force it through.' What this success demonstrated, he said, was that 'The Slavs are a mass of born slaves in need of a master.' Moreover, it was 'better not to teach them to read'. Hitler didn't believe that large numbers of German troops would be needed to occupy and administer this new territory, as the 'Slavs' were so clearly inferior. 'The Russian space is our India,' he said. 'Like the English, we shall rule this empire with a handful of men.'[86]

Hitler claimed just a few weeks later, in a speech on 3 October in Berlin, that the Red Army was 'broken' and 'will never rise again'.[87] This belief that the war was all but won might well have played a part in his decision to bring forward the timetable for the deportation of the Jews. Instead of sending the Jews east once the war against the Soviet Union was over, why not deport them now, since Stalin was effectively vanquished? He knew that his ally, Marshal Antonescu of Romania, had been aggressively pursuing a policy of murdering Jews in the east. The centre of the killing was a region beyond the Dniester river, subsequently known as Transnistria. By September, with Transnistria occupied by Romania as an eastern province, Antonescu prepared to expel thousands of Jews from Bukovina and Bessarabia into camps in this new territory. The editor of the Romanian newspaper *Porunca Vremii* wrote in the summer of 1941, 'The die has been cast . . . The liquidation of the Jews in Romania has entered the final, decisive phase . . . To the joy of our emancipation must be added the pride of [pioneering] the solution to the Jewish problem in Europe. Judging by the satisfaction with which the German press is reporting the words and decisions of Marshal Antonescu, we understand . . . that present-day Romania is prefiguring the decisions to be made by the Europe of tomorrow.'[88]

Not surprisingly, Hitler approved of Marshal Antonescu's actions. 'As far as the Jewish problem is concerned,' he said to Goebbels at the end of

August 1941, 'it may be stated with certainty that a man like Antonescu is pursuing much more radical policies in this area than we have so far.'[89] Hitler was still praising Antonescu six weeks later in October, 'Apart from the Duce [Mussolini],' he said, 'amongst our Allies Antonescu is the man who makes the strongest impression. He's a man on a big scale, who never lets anything throw him out of his stride . . .' Moreover, the 'first thing' that Antonescu had to do in order to create a strong Romania, Hitler believed, was to 'get rid of the Jew'.[90]

Hitler now resolved to 'get rid' of the Jews in the Old Reich. But while it was easy to decide to deport them, one vital practical question still remained. Where should they go? Himmler, once again, facilitated a solution. He wrote on 18 September 1941 to Arthur Greiser of the Warthegau, informing him that the Führer had decided to empty the 'Old Reich and the Protectorate' of Jews. As a result, Himmler wanted to send 60,000 Jews to the Łódź ghetto, within Greiser's Warthegau, where they would be accommodated before being sent to an unspecified destination 'further east' the following spring.[91] After protests from Nazi officials in the Warthegau about the inability of the Łódź ghetto to take any more Jews, Himmler reduced the number to 20,000.

In October 1941 the first Jews left Hamburg for Poland. Lucille Eichengreen, one of the Jews sent to Łódź from Hamburg, remembers that as they were marched to the station to begin their journey to Poland a few Germans shouted anti-Semitic comments at them, but most of the non-Jewish population of the city reacted without emotion.[92] Elsewhere, some Jews said that their non-Jewish neighbours expressed sympathy for them, in Frankfurt bringing them 'cookies and other food' and in Vienna crying 'openly' as they were sent away.[93]

The Jews from western Europe were unprepared for what awaited them in Łódź. One Polish Jew, already in the ghetto, wrote of a group of Czech deportees who arrived in October 1941: 'it is said that they asked if it would be possible to get two-room apartments with running water.'[94] But that naivety did not last long, and the western Jews soon discovered the appalling reality of life and death in the ghetto. Most had no friends among the Polish Jews, no connections that would help them get a job or a room in which to live. Many were crammed together in ghetto schools where they had nothing to do, and almost nothing to eat. 'One's belly becomes loose, gradually sinks in,' wrote Oskar

Rosenfeld, who was deported from Prague to Łódź. 'Hesitantly, almost fearfully, one runs one's hand over the restless body, bumps into bones, ribs, runs over one's legs and finds oneself, feels suddenly that one was quite recently fatter, fleshier – and is amazed at how quickly the body deteriorates . . . One word, one concept, one symbol confronts every-body: bread! For bread one would be a hypocrite, a fanatic, a wretch. Give me bread and you are my friend.'[95]

In many cases the shock of the transition proved too much for these Jews from the west to endure. 'They were definitely very depressed,' says Jacob Zylberstein, a Polish Jew already in the ghetto. 'I think because normally they [Jews from the Reich] look down on the Polish Jews – we've been definitely a different category than them. And all of a sudden it hit them that they've come to the same level or maybe lower than us because they cannot live in the conditions we did.'[96] As a conse-quence, the Jews from the Reich and the Protectorate suffered a much higher mortality rate than the Polish Jews already living in the ghetto.[97]

Jews were not just sent to the Łódź ghetto. A number of transports journeyed further east into the killing zones of the Einsatzgruppen in the occupied Soviet Union. Some of these Jews were housed in camps, where many perished in the cold. Others were murdered shortly after they arrived. In late November 1941, for instance, five trains left for Lithuania from Germany and Austria. All of these Jews were murdered by killing squads after they had disembarked in Kaunas. Elsewhere, Wilhelm Kube, Nazi Commissar for Belarus, questioned in December whether Jews from 'our own cultural sphere' should be treated the same way as the 'native brutish hordes'[98] of the east. Just over two weeks before, at the end of November, Himmler had gone so far as to try and prevent the murder – almost certainly temporarily – of one trainload of German Jews sent to Riga while matters were clarified, but his com-munication arrived too late. The Jews had already been killed.[99] All of which demonstrated that there was an element of uncertainty about the intended immediate fate of the Jews from the Old Reich.

At the same time as these Jews from western Europe were being mur-dered in the occupied Soviet Union, preparations were under way for two killing installations in Poland. The first, at Chełmno, 40 miles north-west of Łódź, was primarily created in order to murder Jews from the Łódź ghetto selected as unfit to work. From the perspective of

Arthur Greiser, ruler of the Warthegau, the immediate need for such a murder facility was obvious. He needed a way of easing the intense overcrowding in the Łódź ghetto, a situation that had worsened since the arrival of the Jews from the west. But even as far back as July 1941, as we have seen, Rolf-Heinz Höppner, the SS head of the Emigration Central Office in Posen in the Warthegau, had written that the question of the fate of the Jews in the *Gau* had been the subject of much 'discussion'. He had asked whether – since there was a danger that all of the Jews could not be fed that winter – it might not be more 'humane' to 'finish off' Jews who could not work 'through some fast-acting means'.[100]

Just such a 'fast-acting means' – in the form of a gas van – was already operating in the Warthegau, touring around hospitals and murdering the disabled. Now, in the autumn of 1941, a plan was put in place to use gas vans to kill Jews from Łódź. Herbert Lange, who commanded the unit responsible for killing the disabled, searched for a suitable location to base the vans. His driver, Walter Burmeister, later confirmed that Lange told him that autumn that 'we've got a tough but important job to do.'[101] The village of Chełmno was eventually chosen as the location for the vans, with the Jews subsequently buried in a forest near by.

The second killing installation under construction in Poland during November 1941 was at the village of Bełżec, 75 miles south-east of Lublin in the General Government. Before the invasion of the Soviet Union, the Germans had established a labour camp at Bełżec in order to house Jews who were working on border fortifications between the German and Soviet zones of Poland, but that camp had closed by the end of 1940. This new camp at Bełżec would become the first static, as opposed to mobile, killing facility, purpose-built to murder Jews. Bełżec's location was advantageous to the Nazis in a number of ways. It was relatively remote, away from major centres of population, yet it was next to the main railway line and within easy reach of three cities – Lublin, Kraków and Lwów – each of which contained a large number of Jews.

As well as these two installations under construction in Poland, there is also evidence that discussions were held at the same time about the possibility of building other fixed killing factories in Riga and Mogilev in the occupied Soviet Union.[102] Himmler visited Mogilev in Belarus in October, and the following month a large order was placed with Topf and Söhne to construct a massive cremation installation at Mogilev with thirty-two incinerator chambers.[103] It is possible that this huge crematorium – which was never ultimately built – would have been the centrepiece of a camp which combined the functions of a murder facility with a more conventional concentration camp.[104] Clearly a step change in the way the Nazis were approaching the 'Jewish question' was under way.

But does all this mean that Hitler made a decision in autumn 1941 to exterminate the Jews? Is this when the Holocaust as we know it began? A number of new initiatives certainly came together at this time, including not only the decision to deport Jews from the Old Reich and Protectorate to the east, and the construction of killing installations at Chełmno and Bełżec in Poland, but also Hitler's own comments in private that October about the Jews. Ominously, he quoted from the 'extermination' speech he had given in January 1939. 'From the rostrum of the Reichstag,' he said on 25 October 1941, 'I prophesied to Jewry that, in the event of war's proving inevitable, the Jew would disappear from Europe. That race of criminals has on its conscience the two million dead of the First World War, and now already hundreds of thousands more . . . It's not a bad idea, by the way, that public rumour attributes to us a plan to exterminate the Jews.'[105]

In addition, according to the post-war testimony of Adolf Eichmann, Heydrich told him in the autumn of 1941, 'The Führer has ordered the physical destruction of the Jews.'[106] And Kurt Möbius, one of the SS guards who worked at Chełmno in the early days of the camp, said under interrogation after Germany's defeat, 'We were told by Captain Lange that the order for the extermination of the Jews came from Hitler and Himmler. And as police officers we were drilled to regard any order from the government as lawful and correct . . . At the time I believed the Jews were not innocent but guilty. The propaganda had drummed it into us again and again that all Jews are criminals and sub-humans who were the cause of Germany's decline after the First World War.'[107]

Still more evidence appears to come from an article in the Nazi newspaper *Das Reich* in November 1941, in which Goebbels publicly proclaimed that 'The Jews wanted their war, and now they have it. But they also feel the effect of the prophecy made by the Führer in the German Reichstag on 30 January 1939, that if international financial Jewry should succeed in forcing nations once more into a world war, the result would not be the bolshevization of the earth, but the annihilation of the Jewish race in Europe . . . All Jews belong, due to their birth and race, to an international conspiracy against National Socialist Germany. They wish for our defeat and destruction and do everything in their power in order to help realize this. Every German soldier who is killed in this war is the responsibility of the Jews. They have him on their conscience, and that's why they have to pay for it . . .'[108]

However, despite all these indications, it does not necessarily follow that an absolute decision was taken in the autumn of 1941 to murder all of the Jews currently living in Nazi-occupied territory.[109] A more nuanced interpretation of events in the autumn of 1941 is that Hitler authorized the sending of Jews to the east, but only as and when practicable, with priority always given to the needs of the Wehrmacht. Hitler had wanted the Jews deported from the Reich since the autumn of 1939 – it was just a question of deciding when the time was right. Now, sharing the anger of key lieutenants like Goebbels and Kaufmann at the fact that Jews remained in the Reich, and believing the war in the east was all but over, Hitler resolved to get 'rid' of the Jews once and for all. He was well aware that Soviet Jews were being murdered in the east, and so by sending other Jews into the killing zones he would have known what was likely to happen to them. But whether they were killed on arrival by shooting, or gassed, or starved in ghettos, or worked to death over a longer period – these were all details that could be worked out by others. What was crucial was that once expelled they should never come back. Thus while Hitler authorized the sending of the Jews east to die, he didn't dictate a precise method of killing them or an exact timescale within which their disappearance had to occur.

This was still, therefore, an important moment in the evolution of the Holocaust, but it does not amount to initiating the whole enterprise by one single, overarching decision. A large number of questions remained unresolved in the autumn of 1941. What about the Jews in occupied western Europe, were they also to be sent east to die? If so, when? And what about the rest of the Jews still in the Old Reich? Forty-two thousand Jews were deported from the Old Reich and the Protectorate between October and December 1941, but that still left the majority behind.

What was the timetable for their destruction? Most tellingly of all, what about the nearly 3 million Jews of Poland, was this really the moment their fate was sealed? Why, if there was a decision at this point to kill all the Polish Jews, were the only two killing centres that were actually under construction in Poland on such a small scale? Could not both of them – Bełżec and Chełmno – also be explained as local initiatives created under Himmler's aegis to deal with local 'problems'? In short, doesn't it appear that those on the ground were, to an extent, working out what to do without precise orders from above?

Support for this interpretation can be found in Hitler's own words that autumn. In mid-October 1941 he asked, 'what would happen to me if I didn't have around me men whom I completely trust, to do the work for which I can't find time? Hard men, who act as energetically as I would do myself. For me the best man is the man who removes the most from my shoulders, the man who can take 95 per cent of the decisions in my place.'[110] An example of how this attitude influenced actual events can be found in a note that Greiser wrote to Himmler in spring 1942 about the killing of patients with tuberculosis in the Warthegau. After Greiser's authority to proceed with the killing had been questioned, he said to Himmler, 'I personally don't think we have to consult the Führer again in this matter, all the more since he told me at the last meeting concerning the Jews that I should act according to my best judgment.'[111] All of which suggests that Hitler's position that autumn about the deportation and subsequent treatment of the Jews may well have been similar to the one he took over plans for 'Germanization' where, as we have seen, he told his Gauleiters that he 'would not ask questions about the methods they had used' to make his vision a reality.[112]

Similarly, at Auschwitz in the autumn of 1941, SS personnel were using their 'best judgment' to upgrade the improvised methods of killing they had used so far. As they discussed plans for a new crematorium to be built at the camp they decided on a series of small but significant changes that would allow the building to be turned into a killing factory. Some time between October 1941 and January 1942, the ventilation outlets in the smaller of the two mortuaries in the semi-basement of the building were set back into the concrete of the wall and the fans altered so that they could expel air quickly. The only plausible explanation for these changes in the plans was that this mortuary would now become a gas chamber, with the ducts recessed so that the dying could not wrench them from the wall, and the ventilation system altered so as to allow the poisonous gas to be expelled after the murders had taken place.[113] But it is all but impossible to see how the creation of this one gas chamber at Auschwitz could have been part of a master plan already in existence to murder all the Jews of Europe. Instead, this was surely another example of a local initiative, motivated by the knowledge that gassing with Zyklon B was already taking place in the existing crematorium of the main camp. It would thus make sense, from the perspective of the SS at Auschwitz, to ensure that this new crematorium was also capable of performing the same function.

As the SS at Auschwitz held these discussions, 750 miles away to the east the Germans were fighting arguably the most important series of battles of the whole war. These events on the battlefield – plus a dramatic decision by one of Hitler's allies – were the background against which Nazi policy towards the Jews would harden still further.

11. The Road to Wannsee

(1941–1942)

In October 1941 the Germans still appeared to be winning the war against the Soviet Union. During the giant encirclement action at Vyazma and Bryansk the Germans took 660,000 prisoners and it looked as if the road to Moscow was open. There was panic in the Soviet capital and Stalin's train waited to take him further east to safety. 'How are we going to defend Moscow?' demanded Lavrenti Beria, head of the NKVD, the secret police, in the Kremlin on 19 October. 'We have absolutely nothing at all. We have been overwhelmed . . .'[1]

But the course of the war in the east was about to change drastically. Stalin decided to stay in Moscow and rally his troops – a decision which coincided with the winter rains that turned the landscape around the capital into a morass of mud. Suddenly it seemed unlikely that the Germans could defeat the Soviet Union before the onset of the worst of the Russian winter. This was potentially disastrous for them: German supply lines were stretched almost to the point of collapse and German soldiers possessed little winter clothing, as the war against the Soviet Union had been supposed to last only a few weeks.

At this vital moment in the war Hitler returned from his field headquarters in East Prussia to Munich for celebrations to commemorate the anniversary of the Beer-Hall Putsch, and on 8 November 1941 he gave a speech at the Löwenbräukeller to the party faithful. He was not in the easiest of positions. Just a month before he had told his audience that the Red Army would 'never rise again', and yet it had appeared to do just that. Here he was, facing followers who wanted to bask in more good news, and he had no such news to offer. He could not announce that the war in the east had been won – he could not even say that Moscow had fallen, or was likely to fall in the next few days or weeks. In these difficult circumstances he needed someone to blame for what had happened. And for Hitler, of course, it was always easy to find a scapegoat – the Jews. In his speech he said that although the Jews had influence in France, Belgium, the Netherlands, Norway and

Britain, the 'biggest slave' of the Jews was the Soviet Union where 'only stupid, forcibly proletarianized subhumans remain. Above them, there is a giant organization of Jewish commissars, who in reality are the slave-owners.' He claimed that German forces in the east were fighting in pursuit of a noble goal: 'in this struggle we finally want to free Europe of the danger posed by the east, and . . . at the same time, we [want to] prevent the east with its immense fertility, its immense richness in natural resources and ores, from being mobilized against Europe, and instead place it in Europe's service.' In pursuit of that objective, he said, in words tinged with menace, he would 'make a distinction between the French and their Jews, between the Belgians and their Jews, between the Dutch and their Jews'.[2]

On 15 November, the Germans continued their advance towards Moscow after the mud had frozen, but their energy was almost spent. In a final effort in early December, some forward German units managed to advance to less than 20 miles from Moscow. But this was as far as they would ever get. The whole course of the war in the east – and as a consequence the whole of the war in general – was about to change. Indeed there is a strong case for saying that the events of December 1941 were both the turning point of the Second World War and one of the most decisive periods in the evolution of the Holocaust.

On 5 December the Red Army counter-attacked. Vasily Borisov, a soldier with one of the Siberian divisions now thrown fresh into the battle for Moscow, remembers that 'When they [the Germans] saw Siberians fighting man-to-man they felt frightened. Siberians were very fit guys . . . They [the Germans] had been raised in a gentle way. They were not as strong as the Siberians. So they panicked more in this kind of fighting. Siberians don't feel any panic. The Germans were weaker people. They didn't like the cold much and they were physically weaker too.'[3]

Just as Hitler was absorbing the news of the fight-back of the Red Army, he learnt of the Japanese attack on Pearl Harbor on 7 December. Four days later, on 11 December, Germany declared war on America. At first sight this seems a puzzling decision. Why bring into the war a powerful new enemy several thousand miles away across the Atlantic? But Hitler felt he was merely recognizing the inevitable. Ever since the Atlantic conference in the summer of 1941, when President Franklin

Roosevelt and Winston Churchill had met off the coast of Newfoundland and signed the Atlantic Charter, America's commitment to aiding the British war effort had been obvious. In his November speech, a month before declaring war on America, Hitler was already accusing Roosevelt of taking sides against Germany. He claimed that Roosevelt had been 'responsible' for Poland entering the war and that he had also been behind France's decision to take part in the conflict.[4]

Crucially, Hitler thought that Roosevelt was controlled by the Jews. In his speech to the Reichstag on 11 December 1941, he said that behind Roosevelt's decision to support Britain and oppose Germany was 'the Eternal Jew'. Surrounding Roosevelt, he asserted, were a 'circle of Jews' who were 'driven by Old Testament greediness'. It was the 'satanic perfidy' of the Jews which was responsible for the current state of affairs.[5] As Hitler saw it, the Jews had finally achieved their secret objective – they had created a worldwide conflict from which they hoped to benefit.

On 12 December, the day after his Reichstag speech and Germany's declaration of war on America, Hitler talked to fifty or so leading Nazis in the Reich Chancellery in Berlin. Goebbels recorded what he said in his diary: 'As regards the Jewish question, the Führer is resolved to clear the air. He prophesied to the Jews that if they were to bring about another world war, they would experience their own extermination. This was not a hollow phrase. The world war is here, the destruction of the Jews must be the inevitable consequence. The question must be seen without sentimentality. We are not here to take pity on the Jews, but only to feel sympathy with our own German people. Since the German people has once again sacrificed around 160,000 fallen in the eastern campaign, those who initiated this bloody conflict will have to pay with their lives.'[6] Goebbels could scarcely have been more explicit. Since 'now' there was a 'world war' – with the entry of America into the conflict – 'the destruction of the Jews' was 'inevitable'. This was thus a pivotal moment. There was no ambiguity in Hitler's words.

Hans Frank, ruler of the General Government, was another of the senior Nazis who listened to Hitler's talk in the Reich Chancellery. Four days later, on 16 December, he spoke to key figures in the General Government about the forthcoming fate of the Jews. 'As for the Jews,' he said, 'I will be quite blunt with you, they will have to be finished off one way or the other. The Führer said once: if the united Jewry once again succeeds in unleashing a world war, then the blood sacrifices will not only be made by the peoples who have been hounded into this war. But the Jews in Europe will [also] meet their end . . . As an old National Socialist, I have to say that if the Jewish rabble were to survive the war in Europe, while we had sacrificed our best blood for the preservation of Europe, then this war would only represent a partial success. With respect to the Jews, therefore, I will operate on the assumption that they will disappear.'[7]

As well as outlining the ideological reason why the Jews should 'disappear', Frank also mentioned a practical motive for their destruction. 'The Jews', he said, 'are also tremendously harmful to us through the amount of food they gorge.' Once again, the notion that the Jews were endangering the lives of 'Aryan' Germans simply by drawing breath played a part in explaining why they had to die. If, as a Nazi, you had any difficulty believing that the Jews had via some international conspiracy caused the war – an idea which might stretch the imagination of some, given the real circumstances behind the outbreak of hostilities – then there remained the justification that they were consuming food that otherwise would be eaten by non-Jewish Germans. It was a case, as Hitler always liked to put it, of either/or. If the Jews didn't starve, then the Germans did.

On 7 December 1941 – the day of the Japanese attack on Pearl Harbor and nine days before Frank gave this speech in Kraków – the first fixed-location killing facility built primarily in order to kill Jews began work in Poland. The site was at Chełmno, in the Warthegau, 160 miles to the north-west of Kraków. Greiser, ruler of the Warthegau, had moved ahead more quickly with plans to murder the Jews than his neighbouring Nazi baron Hans Frank. While Frank was just talking about 'finishing off' the Jews en masse, Greiser had actually made a start. A large part of Greiser's motivation in establishing the murder facility at Chełmno was, as he saw it, practical necessity. As we have seen, the Łódź ghetto was enormously overcrowded, in large part because Himmler had decided in September to send tens of thousands of extra Jews from the Old Reich to the ghetto as well as thousands of Sinti and Roma. Chełmno was Greiser's way out of the self-created Nazi 'problem' of ghetto overcrowding.

Greiser realized that he already had at his disposal a murder machine that could swiftly be diverted to kill Jews – the gas van. On 7 December 1939, two years before the same machine was based at Chełmno, the gas van operated by Sonderkommando Lange had begun work murdering mentally disabled Poles at the Dziekanka Psychiatric Hospital in Gniezno in western Poland.[8] Now with the approval of Himmler and Greiser, Lange and his gas van would be set to work killing Polish Jews. In the weeks before the facilities at Chełmno were made ready, Lange's van had already started murdering Jews by taking them from the institutions in which they lived. At the end of October 1941, Lange's van had driven up to a Jewish old people's home near Kalisz, 60 miles west of Łódź, and removed the patients, fifty or so at a time, to be gassed.[9] The following month the van was used to kill several hundred Jews from Bornhagen (Koźminek) labour camp near by.[10]

From the Nazis' perspective, extending the work of the gas van to fulfil the task Greiser now required created several challenges. The first was obvious – a question of capacity. Lange had only one gas van, a large truck with the words 'Kaiser's Kaffee-Geschäft' (Kaiser's Coffee Company) emblazoned on the side. This was the same van that had driven around Poland for nearly two years killing the disabled. So, to increase the number of people Chełmno could murder, Lange was promised several more gas vans.[11] They would finally arrive and be operational at the camp early in 1942. These vehicles, unlike the first van, which used bottled carbon monoxide to gas those trapped inside, murdered by directing the carbon monoxide from the exhaust gases of the engine into the rear compartment. This development in the method of murder used by the gas vans mimicked the evolution of the fixed gas chambers, which had also moved from bottled carbon monoxide to exhaust gas.

But increasing the capacity to kill via the addition of more gas vans did not solve a more fundamental problem the Nazis faced if they wished to use this method of killing to murder the 'unproductive' Jews of Łódź. Lange's original van had travelled around Poland, bringing the gas chamber to where the victims lived, but that was clearly impracticable if the intention now was to kill Jews from the Łódź ghetto. Problems of body disposal and secrecy would arise if the vans were to drive up to the ghetto every day and take Jews away. Hence the selection of Chełmno as a base for the gas vans. The village was in the countryside, far away from any major city and yet with good transport connections to the rest of Poland, and just 40 miles north-west of Łódź. A run-down mansion across from the village church could be converted as a base for the gas-van operation, and the bodies of the murdered Jews could be buried in a nearby forest. The central benefit of the gas vans in the killing process – the mobility of the murder machine – was thus negated. But in exchange the Nazis believed they had gained another, more important advantage – secrecy.

After four to six weeks' preparation, the killing facility at Chełmno was ready for work. The first Jews to be killed were from the surrounding villages, with around 700 Jews transported to Chełmno on 7 December 1941.[12] They were imprisoned in the mansion overnight, having been told that they needed to be disinfected before travelling on to work in Germany.[13] Starting the next day, they were forced in groups into the gas van, killed and their bodies buried in the forest a few miles away.

One of the SS guards at Chełmno, Kurt Möbius, described in detail after the war how the murder factory worked: 'The Jewish people undressed [in the mansion in the village] – they were not separated into sexes – under my supervision. They had already had to give up their valuables; these were collected in baskets by the Polish workers. There was a door in the passage which led to the cellar. On it was a sign: "To the bath" . . . From the door in the passage a staircase led down to the cellar where there was a passage which at first went straight ahead but then, after a few metres, was cut off by another passage at right angles to it. Here the people had to turn right and go up a ramp where the gas vans parked with their doors open. The ramp was tightly enclosed with a wooden fence up to the doors of the gas van. Usually, the Jewish people went quickly and obediently into the gas van trusting the promises which had been made to them [that they were about to be "disinfected"].'[14]

Sometimes, admitted Möbius, the Jews did not go 'quickly and obediently' into the vans. Then Polish workers, forced to work for the Germans, whipped them up the ramp and inside. Zofia Szałek, an eleven-year-old girl living in Chełmno, remembers hearing the Jews as they were shoved into the vans. 'How terribly they were screaming – it was impossible to bear it. Once they brought children and the children shouted. My mother heard it. She said the children were calling, "Mummy, save me!" '[15]

Several of the Poles who were forced to assist the Germans in the kill-ing process at Chełmno appear to have taken advantage of their situation in a shocking way. According to Walter Burmeister, one of the drivers of the gas van, 'It happened sometimes that a woman was selected from the Jews delivered for gassing . . . probably the Poles themselves would choose her. I think that the Poles asked her if she would agree to have sexual intercourse with them. In the basement [of the mansion] there was a room set aside for this purpose where the woman stayed one night or sometimes several days and was at the disposal of these Poles. After-wards, she would be killed in the gas vans with the others.'[16] Another source suggests that there was also at least one instance of members of the SS raping a Jewish woman at Chełmno before murdering her.[17]

Chełmno had been created primarily to kill selected Jews from the Łódź ghetto. But the first transport sent to Chełmno from Łódź, on 2 January 1942, contained not Jews but those the Nazis called 'Gypsies'. These Roma had been sent to Łódź in November 1941 from Austria and had been kept in particularly horrendous conditions. Isolated by barbed wire in a special area within the ghetto, nearly 5,000 Roma had been denied sufficient food and shelter. More than 600 contracted typhus. As a result, the Nazis wanted to destroy this Gypsy camp as a matter of urgency. By 9 January nearly 4,500 Roma from Łódź had been sent to Chełmno, murdered and buried in the forest.[18]

The first Jews from Łódź arrived at Chełmno on 16 January 1942. They had been selected from within the ghetto by the Jewish adminis-tration run by Mordechai Chaim Rumkowski. In a speech he gave on 20 December 1941, Rumkowski announced that 'a special commission comprised of my most trustworthy co-workers determined the list of candidates for dispatch'[19] and that priority had been given to deporting 'undesirable elements' who lived within the ghetto. While at this stage no one could be certain that those sent from the ghetto would be mur-dered, deportation was still a fate that most of the Łódź Jews feared. Better the known horror of the ghetto than the unknown terror that awaited them in German hands outside.

At Chełmno, the gas vans did not offer a quick death. It could take many minutes before those trapped inside were finally asphyxiated, and villagers sometimes heard screams from the vans as they passed by. Once the vans reached the forest and the doors were opened, a team of

Jews – made to work for the Germans or face immediate execution –
had to disentangle the bodies before throwing them into mass graves.
One of the Germans who supervised the Waldkommando (forest commando) was billeted in Zofia Szałek's house, and she remembers how his
shoes stank 'terribly'[20] of decomposing bodies.

Estimates of how many died at Chełmno vary between 150,000 and
300,000 – huge numbers that represent a terrible crime, yet only a fraction of the 3 million Jews in Poland. If the Nazis really intended to kill
not just the Jews of Poland but the Jews of Europe as well, they couldn't
rely solely on local initiatives like Chełmno – they needed a major
coordinated action emanating from the highest reaches of the state. And
on 20 January 1942, four days after the first Jews from the Łódź ghetto
had arrived at Chełmno, a meeting was held at Wannsee on the outskirts of Berlin that many think was convened for just such a purpose.

It is not hard to understand why the Wannsee conference is, in popular
culture, considered the most important single meeting of the Holocaust –
indeed, the moment at which the crime was finally decided upon. The
evolution of the Holocaust is complex and occasionally counter-intuitive.
How much simpler it would be if there was one key moment at which
everything was resolved – if not a decision by Hitler in the autumn of
1941, then a meeting by a lake outside Berlin in January 1942. But it is a
mistake to think that history happened that way. Wannsee was no more
than a staging post along a journey.

Reinhard Heydrich wrote to state secretaries, selected SS officers and
other relevant functionaries and asked them to attend a conference at
56–58 Am Grossen Wannsee outside Berlin. He enclosed with his invitation a copy of Göring's 31 July 1941 letter authorizing him to organize
a Final Solution to the 'Jewish question'. So none of the fifteen people
who attended could have been in any doubt about the purpose of
the gathering or Heydrich's right to convene it. The SS officers who
were invited ranged from the very senior – SS Gruppenführer (Major
General) Heinrich Müller, head of the Gestapo, SS Gruppenführer
(Major General) Otto Hofmann, head of the SS Race and Settlement
Office, and Heydrich, who was an SS Obergruppenführer (Lieutenant
General) as well as head of the Reich Security Main Office – to the relatively junior – SS Obersturmbannführer (Lieutenant Colonel) Adolf

Eichmann, the SD's so-called Jewish 'expert', and SS Sturmbannführer (Major) Dr Rudolf Lange. The latter was asked because of his direct, personal experience of murdering Jews in Latvia with Einsatzgruppe A. Other attendees included Martin Luther, under-secretary at the Foreign Ministry, Dr Roland Freisler of the Reich Ministry of Justice, and Hans Frank's own state secretary from the General Government, Dr Josef Bühler. The original date for the meeting was 9 December 1941, but this was later postponed to 20 January 1942.

The decisions taken at Wannsee had to be acted on by different departments within the government of the Reich, and so it was necessary for them to be recorded. Oral commands alone would never have sufficed. A copy of the minutes, taken by Adolf Eichmann, survived the war, and though they were written in deliberately euphemistic language, they nonetheless offer an insight into the thinking of senior figures involved in the implementation of the Final Solution.

Heydrich announced that with Hitler's 'permission' there was now the possibility of 'evacuating' the Jews 'to the East' rather than forcing their 'emigration'.[21] This would not have been new information to those present in the room. Thousands of Jews from the Old Reich had already been deported. What was new was the scale of the 'evacuation' that Heydrich now outlined. He said that more than 11 million Jews within Europe were potentially subject to the Final Solution including Jews in countries that the Nazis did not even control, like Spain and Britain (which was referred to as 'England'). He outlined how the Nazis now intended to send all of these Jews – or as many as they could get their hands on – to the east to work in 'large labour gangs'. In the course of this work, a 'large number' of the Jews would, said Heydrich, 'drop out' through 'natural wastage'. He singled out for special mention the small number of Jews who would survive this 'natural selection', because they would have proved to be the 'fittest' and could form a 'germ cell' from which the Jewish race could 'regenerate itself'. Consequently, these Jews would have to be 'dealt with accordingly' – by which he could only have meant they should be murdered.

Heydrich was therefore announcing not a fresh strategy, but the extension of an existing one. It was the evolution of a policy that had begun with the desire to see Jews expelled from the Reich to some foreign country, had then morphed into a plan to deport the Jews to the extremity of Nazi-controlled territory once the war was over, and had now become a scheme to work the Jews to death in the Nazi east while the war was still being fought. Heydrich admitted that the 'timing' of each 'large-scale evacuation' would depend on how the war was going. There was no immediate schedule put in place to accomplish this vast task. Indeed, the Nazis would only gradually over the next six months create the killing capacity necessary to murder large numbers of Jews.

Josef Bühler, the representative of Hans Frank, asked if the Final Solution could begin in the General Government. The Jews to be killed were already there, he said, so any 'transport problem' was not serious. After Bühler's request, the meeting discussed 'various' possible 'solutions' to implement the Final Solution – an obvious euphemism for a variety of potential ways to murder the Jews. Much of the rest of the meeting was taken up with an inconclusive discussion about definitions. In particular, just what should be done with those who were considered *Mischlinge* – part-Jews? Heydrich also announced that a small number of Jews – such as those with war decorations – might be transported to a special 'ghetto' at Theresienstadt, north of Prague, rather than directly to the east. This remark confirmed, despite the euphemistic nature of the minutes, that almost all of the Jews were to be sent to a terrible fate.

It is worth noting what was not said at the Wannsee conference. Heydrich did not say that the Jews would be taken to camps in Poland and 'dealt with accordingly' there. He was explicit that Jews would be sent east in order to work in labour gangs. If he had wanted to say that the Jews were to be killed in Nazi-occupied Poland then the minutes could certainly have euphemistically reflected that reality. But they didn't. Heydrich did mention that the Jews were to be 'initially' sent to 'transit ghettos' before they were transported 'further east'.[22] So it is not hard to imagine that, in the months after Wannsee, Poland became out of practical necessity the furthest east the Jews were ever sent, and that consequently they came to be murdered on Polish soil. However, at the moment he chaired the Wannsee conference, Heydrich still appears to have believed that the Jews would eventually be deported into the occupied Soviet Union.

The Wannsee conference was also an opportunity for the SS to assert a pre-eminent role in the Final Solution. Heydrich, for instance, would have been pleased that Josef Bühler, on behalf of Hans Frank, appeared to support the leading role that the SS would play in this vast new operation. Bühler had been a late addition to the list of those invited, after the SS representative in the General Government had warned Himmler that Hans Frank might seek to control Jewish policy in his area.[23] Heydrich and Himmler would not have wanted a repeat of the conflict between Frank and the SS at the time of the deportations of Poles into the General Government. It was also important for Heydrich and Himmler to ensure that the Foreign Office – represented at the meeting by the under-secretary Martin Luther – also accepted the leading position of the SS in the Final Solution. Heydrich and Himmler would have remembered that the Foreign Office had sought at one stage in the summer of 1940 to take a proactive role on the Madagascar plan. Thus gathering all the interested parties together at Wannsee was an obvious attempt by Heydrich to clear a way through the bureaucratic jungle ahead.

According to Eichmann, Heydrich was pleased with the way the meeting had gone: 'After the conference . . . Heydrich, Müller [the head of the Gestapo] and little me sat cosily around a fireplace. I saw for the first time Heydrich smoking a cigar or cigarette, something I never saw; and he drank cognac, which I hadn't seen for ages. Normally he didn't drink alcohol.'[24]

No wonder Heydrich was pleased. No one had raised any objection to the dominance of the SS. It appeared that there would be no infighting within the Nazi leadership over this matter of crucial policy. Nor had anyone protested at the principle of deporting the Jews of Europe to the east to be worked to death. Not that Heydrich would have expected any opposition. After all, he would have reasoned, Soviet Jews had been shot on the eastern front since June, and German and Austrian Jews had been dying in the ghettos of Poland and elsewhere since October. What remained were merely practical questions to do with the expansion of the deportations to western Europe and an intensification of the amount of killing capacity required to eliminate even more Jews than before.

Far from being the single most significant meeting in the history of the Holocaust, the Wannsee conference was a forum for second-level functionaries to discuss ways of implementing their master's wishes. None of the key players attended the meeting. Not Himmler, not Frank, not Goebbels – certainly not Hitler himself. Vital decisions about the fate of the Jews had been taken in the weeks and months before the Wannsee conference. Even then, there had not been one single decision – one day on which Hitler announced 'all the Jews must die, in this way and within this timescale' – but a series of decisions that built, one upon the other, until those around the table at Wannsee would have felt that the extermination of the Jews was inevitable. They still did not know for sure how this end could be achieved, or how long it would take. There remained, for instance, the question of the destruction of the 3 million Polish Jews – a final timetable for their murder, as we shall see, was not to be announced for many months.

There is another aspect of this history that the conference illustrates. The word 'Holocaust' leads us to think that there was one single plan to murder the Jews. But that was not how the Nazis looked at this issue at Wannsee. From their perspective, there were a number of different 'solutions' to their 'Jewish problem'. There was one overall vision, that is true, one that emanated from Hitler – the desire to eliminate the Jews. But how that task was achieved could take many forms. At Wannsee, Heydrich talked first of one 'solution' – the removal of the Jews of Europe to the wastes of the Soviet Union where they would build roads in terrible conditions and perish eventually over a period of time. This idea was not so very far from the Madagascar plan – send the Jews away and let them wither and die over years if necessary. Then there was another sort of 'solution', also discussed at Wannsee, which was the more immediate problem, for the Nazis, of the enormous number of Jews in the General Government. They would potentially be murdered over a shorter timescale and in a different way – though that issue was not finally resolved at the meeting. All this was set against the background of another 'solution', one that already existed – the murder by shooting of the Jews in the Soviet Union. Today, all of these separate Nazi killing actions have been given the collective name 'Holocaust'. But they were not treated as one entity at the time. They were all evolving at different speeds.

And yet – even knowing all this – there is still something about the Wannsee conference that gives it an immense emotional significance. Surely it is this. Those who attended were not mad. They were not deranged. They were all successful men, holding down tough and difficult jobs. Most were highly educated – of the fifteen who sat round the table at Wannsee, eight held academic doctorates. They discussed the extermination of the Jews in elegant and convivial surroundings. The invitation that Heydrich sent out for the meeting had mentioned that lunch would be provided and during the discussions cognac was served. The building they sat in was a stylish villa, with a terrace overlooking the lake – one of the most beautiful and popular recreation spots for Berliners.

It's not just the obvious contrast between the circumstances of these men at Wannsee and the horror experienced by Jews who were simultaneously living and dying in the Łódź ghetto. It's not only that as these men sat in luxurious surroundings and sipped their brandy their victims were choking to death in the back of a gas van at Chełmno. It's that this meeting seems to represent what sophisticated, elegant and knowing human beings are capable of. Not many of them, perhaps, could kill a Jew personally – Eichmann claimed he had a 'sensitive nature' and was 'revolted' at the sight of blood[25] – but they could enthusiastically endorse a policy to remove 11 million people from this world. If human beings can do this, what else can they do?

Finally, it is important to understand the Wannsee conference in the context of the war. As Heydrich and his colleagues met on the outskirts of Berlin, the German Army was struggling to survive west of Moscow. Deprived of warm clothes and equipment capable of working properly in freezing temperatures, and fighting fresh troops from Siberia, the German soldiers only narrowly prevented a breakthrough by the Red Army. The myth of the invincibility of the Wehrmacht had been destroyed.

'The German Army near Moscow was a very miserable sight,' says Fyodor Sverdlov, a company commander fighting the Wehrmacht on the eastern front that winter. 'I remember very well the Germans in July 1941. They were confident, strong, tall guys. They marched ahead with their sleeves rolled up and carrying their machine guns. But later on they became miserable, crooked, snotty guys wrapped in woollen kerchiefs stolen from old women in villages . . . Of course, they were still firing and defending themselves, but they weren't the Germans we knew earlier in 1941.'[26]

Against this background, it might seem surprising that the Nazi leadership spent time planning the deportation of millions of Jews. Would it not have made more sense for them to devote all their time to winning the war? Why tie up any resources in an ambitious plan for the mass deportation of civilians at the same moment that the German Army was fighting to avoid catastrophe?

The answer is that men like Hitler, Goebbels, Himmler and Heydrich did not see this as a contradiction at all. They believed that the Jews behind the front line were just as much an enemy as the Red Army soldiers the Wehrmacht was fighting outside Moscow. Perhaps more so, since the Jews had already demonstrated during the First World War, so Hitler and his colleagues maintained, that they could undermine morale at home and 'stab' the German Army 'in the back'.

As Hermann Göring said: 'This is the great racial war. In the final analysis it is about whether the German and Aryan prevails here, or whether the Jew rules the world . . .'[27] Göring was parroting Hitler's core belief. Hitler had always maintained that this war was not a conflict like any other, but an existential struggle for the future existence of the German nation. 'We are clear in our minds that the war can only end with either the eradication of the Aryan peoples, or with Jewry vanishing from Europe,' said Hitler in a speech in Berlin on 30 January 1942, the anniversary of his appointment as Chancellor. 'I have already spoken out about this on 1 September 1939 in the German Reichstag.' Hitler had not, of course, made this 'prophecy' on 1 September 1939 but seven months before, on 30 January. He found it convenient to redate it to 1 September because that was the day the German Army had invaded Poland and brought about the war. For Hitler the link between the war and the fate of the Jews transcended any desire he might have had for historical accuracy. 'The outcome of this war will be the annihilation of Jewry,' he continued on 30 January 1942. 'This time, the genuine old Jewish law will apply for the first time: "An eye for an eye, a tooth for a tooth!" And the more the fighting expands, the more – world Jewry may mark these words – anti-Semitism will spread. It will find nourishment in every prison camp, in every family whose members are informed about why they have to make their sacrifices at the end of the day. And the moment will come when the most evil enemy of the world of all time will be finished with for at least a millennium.'[28]

Those who had attended the Wannsee conference, held just ten days before Hitler's speech, would thus have been well aware of the importance of their work – they were playing a part in confronting 'the most evil enemy of the world'. Not that the Wannsee conference resulted in a sudden outburst of activity far away from the serenity of the villa at Am Grossen Wannsee. While the gas vans continued to operate at Chełmno, and the first fixed gas chambers built to kill Jews remained under construction at Bełżec, at Auschwitz there was no action taken in January to construct new killing facilities. The crematorium in the main camp, which had been the location for experimental killings in the autumn, carried on functioning as an improvised gas chamber.

By now, in addition to selected Soviet prisoners of war, Jews from the local area who had been identified as unfit to work were also dying in the Auschwitz crematorium. No one knows for sure when the first transport of these Jews arrived, but it was some time between the autumn of 1941 and the start of 1942. Their deaths marked a change in the function of Auschwitz, as these Jews were never formally admitted to the camp as prisoners, but were taken to the gas chamber directly from the surrounding district.

Józef Paczyński, a Polish political prisoner, witnessed how a group of male Jews were killed in the crematorium in the main camp. He worked in the SS administrative building directly across from the crematorium, and managed to climb up to the attic, push aside a roof tile and see what was happening below. 'They [the SS] were very polite with these people,' he says. '"Please take your clothes, pack your things." And these people undressed, and then they made them go in [to the crematorium] and then the doors were locked behind them. Then an SS man crawled up on to the flat roof of the building. He put on a gas mask, he opened a hatch [in the roof] and he dropped the powder in and he shut the hatch. When he did this, in spite of the fact that these walls were thick, you could hear a great scream.'[29] Because of the screaming, the SS started up 'two motorcycles' to try and drown out the noise, but still he heard 'people yelling for fifteen or twenty minutes and becoming weaker and weaker. If someone had seen me I would have been gassed as well.'[30]

Hans Stark, a member of the SS at Auschwitz, told interrogators after the war that in October 1941 he had been present at just such a killing. Indeed, he had been 'ordered' to 'pour Zyklon B into the opening' himself as 'only one medical orderly had shown up.' He said that since the Zyklon B 'was in granular form, it trickled down over the people as it was being poured in. They then started to cry out terribly, for they now knew what was happening to them . . . After some time had passed . . . the gas chamber was opened. The dead lay higgledy-piggledy all over the place. It was a dreadful sight.'[31]

The gas chamber in the main camp at Auschwitz was, as we have seen, improvised within a mortuary in the crematorium. The site always presented problems for the SS of noise, secrecy and capacity. These were issues that Christian Wirth, late of the adult euthanasia scheme and now overseeing the construction of the gas chambers at Bełżec, would have hoped to avoid.

Since Bełżec would become the model for the other specialized death camps – Sobibór and Treblinka – it is worth spending time examining the thinking behind its construction. In conception, Bełżec was very different from the place that would become the most infamous of the camps – Auschwitz Birkenau. Bełżec, unlike Auschwitz, was small. The camp was roughly square, with each side about 300 yards long, and with one side built parallel to the nearby railway line. Within that space the camp was divided into two. The area nearest to the railway contained a roll-call square, barracks where the arriving Jews undressed, accommodation for guards and a small Jewish workforce, and a storage area for the goods stolen from the Jews. The second part of the camp was the place of extermination. This was separated by a fence from the arrival area and connected to it by a narrow passageway known as the 'tube'. Within the extermination section of the camp was space for bodies to be burnt and buried, as well as the three gas chambers themselves. These had been placed in wooden huts disguised as shower blocks and – in an attempt to seal the space hermetically – the double walls had been filled with sand and lined with tin on the inside.

Wirth and his construction team had clearly drawn on their experience in the adult euthanasia scheme in the construction of the camp. Like the patients in the euthanasia centres, the Jews to be murdered at Bełżec were told that they were to take a shower. The only difference was that the gas that came through tubes to kill them was not from bottled carbon monoxide, but from a diesel tank engine placed outside the fake shower blocks.

Unlike Auschwitz, Bełżec was solely a place of murder. The camp had a singularity of purpose that Auschwitz always lacked. That,

19. Hitler and his generals. The officer in the fur coat to the left of Hitler is Heinz Guderian, nicknamed 'Schneller Heinz' (Fast Heinz) because the panzers he led advanced so swiftly. To the left of Guderian, staring at the camera, is Alfred Jodl, Chief of the Wehrmacht's Operations Staff.

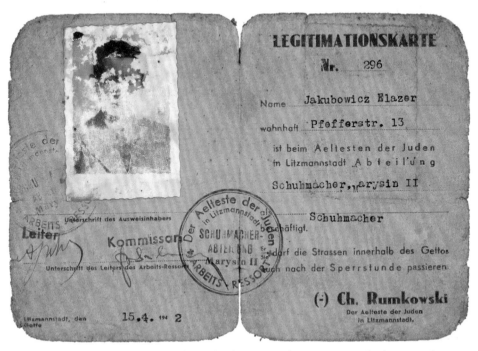

20. A *Legitimationskarte* of a Jew in the Łódź ghetto – or the Litzmannstadt ghetto, as the Germans called it. The document, identifying Elazer Jakubowicz as a shoemaker, also carries the name of the leader of the ghetto, Rumkowski, at the bottom right.

21. Dr Robert Ritter (on the right of the picture) assesses the 'Gypsyness' of this Sinti woman. Starting in the late 1930s Ritter led a team which attempted to decide who should be classed a 'pure Gypsy', who was a 'mixed-blood Gypsy' and who was not a 'Gypsy' at all.

22. One of Ritter's assistants quizzes a Roma family in Austria. Eventually the Nazis would create a vast card index detailing 30,000 Sinti and Roma. Many thousands of people would eventually be murdered on the basis of this bogus classification.

23. Jews take a shower in the Łódź ghetto. It was vital to try and keep free from illness within the ghetto, since those who could not work received less food than those who could.

24. Children in the Łódź ghetto. In September 1942 thousands of the children in the ghetto were deported and murdered.

25. German soldiers march through Paris after their victory in the summer of 1940. In just six weeks the Germans had achieved more success on the western front than they had managed in the entire First World War.

26. Dutch Jews prepare to board trains to take them to the east where the majority will be murdered in a Nazi death camp. The Nazis found it easier to deport Jews from the Netherlands than from any other Western country.

27. Heinrich Himmler (seated in the left front seat of the car) visits the Łódź ghetto in June 1941. He is talking to Mordechai Chaim Rumkowski (with the grey hair and wearing a yellow star), the leader of the ghetto.

28. Mordechai Chaim Rumkowski seated in his private carriage. One of the most controversial Jewish figures of the Holocaust, Rumkowski was accused of exploiting his position as leader of the ghetto for his own benefit – including by sexually assaulting women.

29. Adolf Hitler with Jozef Tiso (on the left of Hitler), the President of Slovakia. Tiso was a Roman Catholic priest and – despite his involvement in the deportation of Slovak Jews – was never excommunicated.

30. Adolf Hitler and Benito Mussolini. Mussolini's rise to power in the early 1920s was an inspiration to the Nazis.

31. Dr Irmfried Eberl, director of the Brandenburg killing centre and subsequently commandant of Treblinka death camp. He presided over the most intense period of killing ever seen at an Operation Reinhard camp.

32. Christian Wirth, one of the most infamous of all Holocaust perpetrators. A veteran of the T4 'euthanasia' programme, he was the first commandant of Bełżec death camp and later inspector of all the Operation Reinhard camps.

33. Pope Pius XII. His refusal to publicly condemn the deportation and extermination of the Jews haunts his reputation to this day.

34. Once the war started to go badly for Adolf Hitler he made fewer and fewer public appearances. But in many of the speeches he did give, he – ludicrously – blamed the Jews for the fact that Germany was losing the war.

of course, explains why Bełżec could be so small. There was no need for space given that virtually all of the people who arrived at the camp would be dead within a matter of hours. Equally, since there was a finite number of people that the Nazis wanted to kill, a specialized death camp like Bełżec would inevitably have a finite period of existence. Unlike Auschwitz, which was planned as a near-permanent feature of Nazi rule, Bełżec was a temporary place. Many of the structures at Auschwitz were built of solid brick, those at Bełżec mostly of wood. All of the specialized death camps would have a transient feel to them – places that were botched together.

In addition, unlike Auschwitz, the Nazis wanted to keep the existence of Bełżec and the other death camps totally secret. Auschwitz, in the tradition of concentration camps like Dachau and Sachsenhausen, was built near a large town. There was no pretence at concealment. Indeed, as a place of terror, it was a positive advantage for the Nazis if the general public knew of its existence. Only when the camp also became involved in mass murder via gas chambers was it necessary to hide part of the function of the place. Bełżec, on the other hand, was a clandestine place from the very beginning. So much so that the 150 Jews who had been forced to build the camp were murdered after they had completed their work. They were the first to die in a test of the new gas chambers.[32]

Just as Chełmno was created to murder the 'unproductive' Jews from the Łódź ghetto, so Bełżec was created to murder the 'unproductive' Jews from the Lublin area, stretching as far as Kraków in the west and Lwów in the south-east. By March 1942 the camp was ready to start killing. Jews were deported from both Lublin and Lwów to Bełżec that month and by the middle of April around 45,000 Jews had been murdered in the gas chambers of the camp and their bodies buried near by.

Bełżec functioned as a killing centre from March 1942 until the end of 1942. No one knows exactly how many people died at Bełżec, but one reliable estimate is that between 450,000 and 550,000 lost their lives there. The vast majority of them were Polish Jews, though a number of Sinti and Roma also perished in the Bełżec gas chambers. Only a handful – some reports say just two – of those sent to Bełżec managed to survive the war. That marks another difference with Auschwitz. For a variety of reasons – not least that the complex of camps we know collectively today as Auschwitz were both work and death camps, and Auschwitz was never focused entirely on the destruction of the Jews – many thousands of people survived incarceration there. But virtually the only chance of emerging from Bełżec alive was to be one of the tiny number selected to work in the camp on arrival and then somehow to effect an escape.

Rudolf Reder, sent to Bełżec from the Lwów ghetto in August 1942, was the only person to write a personal account of the camp. By the time he was travelling in a freight wagon to Bełżec, he believed he knew what awaited him. Despite the desire of the Nazis to keep their activities secret, there were rumours about 'what was going on at Bełżec'.[33] On board the train en route to the camp, 'No one said a word. We were aware that we were headed for death, that nothing could save us; apathetic, not a single moan.' Once they arrived at Bełżec they were ordered to jump down from the trucks – more than 3 feet off the ground – in one huge mass. Some, particularly the elderly and young children, 'broke arms and legs'.

The Jews were gathered together and an SS man gave a speech. 'Everyone wanted to hear,' wrote Rudolf Reder, 'hope dawned suddenly in us – "If they are speaking to us, perhaps we're going to live, perhaps there will be some sort of work, perhaps after all . . ." '[34] The Jews were told by the SS that first they would have to take a bath, and then they would be used as forced labour. 'It was a moment of hope and delusion. For an instant, the people breathed easy. There was total calm.'

Men were separated from women. The men were told to undress before they were forced straight through the 'tube' to the gas chambers. The women were taken to a barracks where their hair was cut. The Germans used the women's hair after their deaths in a variety of industrial processes – for example, in the making of felt. It was as their heads were shaved, says Reder, that the women realized that they were to die, and 'there were laments and shrieks.'

Once their hair had been cut, the women followed the men into the gas chambers. Just like death in the back of a gas van, death in the gas chambers of Bełżec was not quick. Reder remembers hearing the 'moans' and 'screams' of those trapped inside the gas chambers for up to fifteen minutes'.[35]

Reder was spared immediate death only because he was selected to become one of the team of several hundred Jews who were forced to work in the camp, performing tasks like emptying the gas chambers of the dead and burying the bodies. If the SS felt any workers had not performed adequately during the day, they were taken in the evening to the edge of a mass grave and shot. The next day a few more Jews would be selected from an incoming transport to take their place.

The work was the stuff of nightmares. As Reder and the other Jewish workers tried to bury the dead, 'We had to walk across from one edge of a grave to the other, to get to another grave. Our legs sank in the blood of our mothers, we were treading on mounds of corpses – that was the worst, the most horrible thing . . .'[36] The effect of all this was that 'We moved around like people who had no will any more. We were one mass . . . We went mechanically through the motions of that horrible life.'[37]

News about the extermination of the Jews soon reached Goebbels. In his diary, on 27 March 1942, he gave an insight into not just the extent of his own knowledge of the fate of the Jews, but the overall context in which the decision to kill them was taken. Crucially, he points to Hitler's role as the driving force behind the genocide: 'A rather barbaric procedure, that is not to be spelt out, is applied here, and there is not much that remains of the Jews themselves. All in all, we can say that 60% of them have to be liquidated, whereas only 40% can still be used for work . . . A judgement is executed upon the Jews that is indeed barbaric, but which they fully deserve. The prophecy in which the Führer said what they would receive in case of a new world war begins to become reality in the most terrible manner. One must not let sentimentality rule in these matters. If we didn't ward off the Jews, they would destroy us. It is a life-and-death struggle between the Aryan race and the Jewish bacillus. No other government and no other regime would be able to muster the strength to resolve this question in such a wide-ranging manner. Here, too, the Führer is the steadfast champion and spokesman for a radical solution that is necessary under the circumstances and therefore seems inevitable. Thankfully, we have a whole raft of possibilities now during the war that would be blocked in times of peace. The ghettos that become free in the towns of the General Government are now being filled with the Jews deported from the

Reich, and after a certain period of time the procedure is supposed to be repeated here. The Jews' life is no bed of roses, and the fact that their representatives in England and America today organize and propagate a war against Germany has to be paid for very dearly by their representatives in Europe; that is only appropriate.'[38]

After the Wannsee conference, the first Jews from a foreign country to be handed over en masse to the Nazis came from Slovakia. But the history of why Slovak Jews were crammed on to freight trucks on their way to Auschwitz in the spring of 1942 demonstrates once again that the development of the Nazis' Final Solution was anything but straightforward.

We have already seen how Slovakia was formed only in the spring of 1939 as Czechoslovakia disintegrated under Nazi pressure. The Slovak government was, from the beginning, supportive of the Nazis in general and their anti-Semitic views in particular. As early as 20 October 1941, for instance, Himmler had suggested during a meeting with the Slovak President and Prime Minister that it might be possible to deport some of the 90,000 Jews in the country to the General Government.[39]

In a parallel initiative, the Germans were keen for the Slovaks to hand over workers who could be used as forced labour. The Slovak government were not that eager to help – until they thought of an alternative. They asked if perhaps 20,000 of these workers could be Jews. The Slovak government, strongly anti-Semitic, would be glad of the opportunity to deport them. The German Foreign Office replied to this proposal on 16 February 1942, saying that they would be prepared to accept these Jews 'in the course of the measures taken toward a final solution of the European Jewish question'.[40] But it subsequently transpired that the Slovaks wanted to hand over entire Jewish families, and the Germans had no desire to take them. They just sought Jews who could work. In the light of the Wannsee conference, this appears a curious development. Didn't the Nazis want to have all the Jews they could find deported to the east? But it is still part of a pattern. Eichmann and others charged with the practical application of the strategy outlined at Wannsee were well aware that there simply wasn't the current capacity in camps in Poland to accept non-working Jews from Slovakia.

In February 1942, for example, Bełżec was still a month away from opening.

The Slovak authorities held firm. The matter was discussed at a meeting that February between Eichmann's representative in Slovakia, Dieter Wisliceny, and the Prime Minister of Slovakia, Vojtech Tuka, together with Dr Izidor Koso, the chief of his office. The Slovaks maintained that it was 'unChristian' to separate families. Wisliceny understood this to be a hypocritical remark that actually meant that it would be expensive and troublesome for the Slovak authorities to look after those Jews left behind once their breadwinners had been deported.[41] Perhaps, suggested the Slovaks, they might reimburse the Germans for the 'expenses' incurred in taking not just those who were fit to work but whole Jewish families?

The two sides eventually hammered out a deal that was breathtaking in its cynicism. The Slovaks would pay the Germans 500 Reichsmarks for every Jew they took. In return, the Germans promised that they would not assert ownership over the property the Jews left behind, and that the Slovak Jews would never return to Slovakia. This meant that a European country, whose head of state was a Catholic priest – Jozef Tiso – agreed to pay the Nazis to take their Jews away on condition they never came back. Although, at the time they discussed this deal, the Slovak authorities did not have detailed knowledge of precisely what was going to happen to these Jews, they did know that they were being sent into appalling danger. How could the Slovaks pretend otherwise, since just days before their meeting with Wisliceny, Hitler had said in a speech in the Berlin Sportpalast, 'The outcome of this war will be the annihilation of Jewry'?[42]

Heydrich did not finally sign the agreement with the Slovaks until 10 April, and so the initial transports sent to Auschwitz from Slovakia contained only the young and the fit. Linda Breder, an eighteen-year-old Slovakian Jewish woman, was one of the first to be forcibly deported. 'On 24 March 1942,' she says, 'the Hlinka guards [the Slovak People's Party militia] came to every house and collected all the girls from sixteen to twenty-five.' Linda and the other girls were held in a hall in the town of Stropkov in eastern Slovakia. She wasn't 'scared' because 'they told us you are going to Germany to work and you will send money to your parents and then they will join you. So what can I feel? I was happy. Because we would work and then they will have money and then they will come with us.'[43]

The Hlinka Guard now had the Jews in their power – and the opportunity to humiliate them. 'Some of those Slovak soldiers behaved in a really silly way,' remembers Silvia Veselá, another young Jewish woman taken by the Hlinka Guard in March 1942. 'For example, they deliberately crapped on the floor and we had to clean the dirt manually. They called us "Jewish whores" and they kicked us. They behaved really badly. They also told us, "We will teach you Jews how to work." But all of us were poor women that were used to work . . . It's a really humiliating feeling when your personality is being taken away. I don't know whether you can understand it. You suddenly mean nothing. We were treated like animals.'[44]

Michal Kabáč was one of the Hlinka guards who guarded the Jewish women and later forced them on to freight wagons for their journey north to Poland. He was in his early thirties, a staunch Slovak nationalist who believed the anti-Semitic propaganda of his party. 'It was all politics,' he says. 'The state was telling us the Jews were liars and were robbing the Slovaks and never wanted to work, but live an easy life. That is why we were not feeling sorry for them.' Kabáč's own anti-Semitism was more opportunistic than ideological. 'Look,' he says, 'I used to date this Jewish girl. Her father used to have a huge store. He gave me a gift. It was a portrait of a Jew. I knew I'd get imprisoned if they found out I had such a portrait. I had to throw it into the river.'[45]

Kabáč says he had a 'good life' in the Hlinka Guard: 'We had a good salary, accommodation and canteen. We could not complain.' The guards also had the opportunity to steal the possessions of the Jews. Kabáč himself admits he stole a pair of shoes. 'When the Jews came to the camps we used to take their belongings and clothes,' he says. 'All Jews had to show us their belongings and the guards took the more valuable things from them.'[46] Kabáč is relaxed about his role in the Holocaust. 'I was not transporting them to the gas chambers! I was only transporting them to the Polish borders where Germans took over the transport. God knew where they were transported afterwards.'[47]

While in the custody of the Hlinka Guard, Linda Breder clung to the belief that she would be sent to Germany to work. But on 26 March when she was taken to the station to board a train, she saw 'only cattle cars'. 'Where is the regular train?' she asked. 'We already started to feel that something is not right. In the cattle car when you came in there were two buckets there. One with water full, the other one empty to use like a toilet.' Shortly afterwards she realized, 'We are not going to Germany, we are going to Poland.'

Linda Breder was part of the first transport from Slovakia to Auschwitz at the end of March. They were also the first female prisoners to enter the camp. On arrival they were marched under the 'Arbeit macht frei' – 'Work makes you free' – gate at Auschwitz main camp and crammed into one of the prison blocks. There was a struggle, as hundreds of Slovak women were 'screaming and pushing' in an attempt to use the handful of toilets in the block. She and the other women slept on the bare floor, huddled together for warmth since 'it was bitter cold in March in Poland'. The next day she had to undress in front of the SS and a 'gynaecologist' probed her most intimate parts to check if she was 'hiding gold', before she was forced to bath naked in disinfected icy water: 'The SS said to us, "You Jews are dirty, you have lice, you have to be clean." '[48]

All of the Slovak women were admitted directly into the camp. The infamous process of selection on arrival at Auschwitz, by which a proportion of each new transport was sent directly to be killed, had not yet begun. That was not just because the first transports contained only Jews who had been judged fit for work before they left Slovakia, but also because the only gas chamber at Auschwitz in the crematorium of the main camp was an impractical method of killing people on a large scale. One difficulty the Nazis had, as we have seen, was that it was impossible to conduct the killings discreetly in the crematorium because the building was close not just to SS administrative offices, but to the barracks where the prisoners lived.

This 'problem' was about to be solved by the SS at Auschwitz, because a new camp was under construction a mile and a half away from Auschwitz main camp, at a village the Poles called Brzezinka and the Germans Birkenau. In September 1941 Himmler had ordered the creation of a camp at Birkenau capable of holding 100,000 prisoners. Birkenau had originally been intended for Soviet prisoners of war, but at the end of October 1941 Hitler had decided that the Soviet POWs should be used elsewhere in the Reich as forced labour. As a consequence Himmler now said that Birkenau could be a place to send Jews. Subsequently, on 27 February 1942,[49] the commandant of the camp, Rudolf Höss, met with other SS officials and resolved to move the location of the proposed new crematorium from the cramped surroundings of the main camp to the wide spaces of the new Auschwitz Birkenau.

While they waited for the new crematorium to be built at Birkenau, the SS at Auschwitz conceived a stop-gap measure – one designed not just to increase the number of prisoners who could be gassed, but to ensure that the murders could be conducted in greater privacy. In a remote corner of Birkenau, far away from any other habitation, the SS bricked up the windows of a small cottage – known as the 'Little Red House' or 'Bunker I' – and converted two rooms inside so that they could be used as gas chambers. High up in the walls of the cottage they fashioned hatches, through which they could throw Zyklon B crystals. It was a primitive killing machine, but unlike the gas chamber within the crematorium in the main camp, here no one would hear the screams of the Jews as they were asphyxiated. But while the SS had solved one of their problems, they had created another – how to dispose of the dead. Bodies from the Little Red House could not be burnt in the ovens of a crematorium as there was not one near by. The only answer appeared to be to bury them in pits, but that was labour intensive and a potential health hazard for both the inmates and the SS – especially since the ground at Birkenau had notoriously bad drainage.

Notwithstanding the difficulties the SS encountered in disposing of the bodies, the creation of the Little Red House meant that they could murder larger numbers of 'unproductive' Jews than before. Especially when, a few weeks after the killings began in the Little Red House, another cottage about a hundred yards away, known as the 'Little White House', was converted in a similar way into gas chambers.

In early summer 1942, family transports began to arrive from Slovakia for the first time. The SS now began a selection process on the dusty ground next to the railway line, halfway between Auschwitz main camp and Auschwitz Birkenau. In this area, known as the 'ramp', SS medical personnel spent a few seconds assessing each new arrival, and sent those picked to work as forced labour to one side, and those they had chosen to die to another.

In July 1942, Eva Votavová arrived at Auschwitz as a seventeen-year-old with her family. It was the culmination of years of persecution. As a schoolgirl she had heard the Hlinka guards celebrate Slovak independence by shouting 'Slovakia belongs to Slovaks, Palestine belongs to Jews.' 'It was obvious at first sight', she says, 'that they were militants with no moral values.'[50] She felt rejected by the country of her birth and was distraught. 'I could not cope with this,' she says, 'even today, I can't.' In 1942, a commander of the Hlinka Guard lived in her village and wanted her family's house. So he arranged that they would be one of the first Jewish families to be deported. As a result, Eva, together with her father and mother, left Slovakia on 17 July, crammed into 'animal cargo trucks'.

Once on the ramp at Auschwitz her father was selected to join one line and Eva and her mother another. 'From that moment I heard nothing about my father,' she says. 'When I saw him for the last time he looked worried, sad and hopeless.'[51] Her father was taken away and murdered in the gas chamber, while Eva and her mother were assigned to a construction commando. The work was physically demanding and the prisoners received little food or water. As a result, Eva's mother became sick: 'She had a fever and a dark film on her upper teeth – which was an unmistakable sign of deadly typhoid fever. Of course, I did not know this at the time. She told me that evening she needed to go to the hospital [in the camp]. I cried and begged her not to go there at least for one more day. No one ever came back from there.' By now Eva knew that 'people were taken straight to the gas chambers' from the hospital. When Eva came back from work the following day she learnt that her mother had, despite her pleas, been admitted to the hospital. Three days later someone who worked in the hospital told Eva that her mother 'had gone'. Shortly afterwards, Eva was assigned to the 'corpse commando' and collected bodies from all over the camp. Among the pile of human remains, Eva found a pair of glasses. 'I knew they were my mother's – the left glass was broken after my mum had been slapped by a German Kapo.' Holding the glasses, Eva cried, and saw 'all of her [mother's] pain, sickness and misery in front of my eyes'. She kept 'the glasses as the last memory of my mother until stomach typhoid fever infected me. Then they had to burn the pillow I used to hide them in. That is how I lost the last memory of my mother.'[52]

Even if they had been selected for work, many of the new arrivals were now dying at Auschwitz in a matter of weeks – particularly in the newly created women's section of the main camp. Auschwitz had become in a short space of time, and with little or no preparation, one of the biggest women's camps in the Nazi system. Over 6,700 women were held in the main camp in April 1942 and by the time the women's camp was moved to Auschwitz Birkenau in August 1942, an estimated one in three of these women were dead.[53] At Birkenau, conditions were no better. Disease was rife, the Kapos could be brutal, the food was inadequate and the work was often back-breaking – especially for those forced to dig massive ditches to help the drainage.

'We found ourselves in Birkenau,' says Frico Breder, a male Slovak Jew who was sent to Auschwitz in 1942. 'I didn't know anything about that camp at that time. However, as soon as I saw it I thought I was in hell.' One night, shortly after Frico's arrival in Birkenau, his Kapo approached him and said he needed someone 'to do loading' – without mentioning what was to be 'loaded'. He promised Frico that those who completed the task would receive some bread. Frico soon discovered that the task was 'loading dead bodies' on to a cart. As he began moving the corpses, he saw the body of a 'very beautiful woman'. 'She is still in my head,' says Frico. 'She must have come to the camp very recently – she must have committed suicide or something like that . . . It was a clear night and the moon was shining on her . . . It was very beautiful.'[54]

From the moment the camp was established in spring 1940, death had been a constant presence at Auschwitz. But the arrival of the Slovak families and the consequent selections held on the ramp heralded a new era of horror. Those chosen to die were the most temporary visitors imaginable. The old, the sick, the children, all waited by the converted cottages to be gassed. 'They used to sit there,' says Otto Pressburger, a Slovak Jew who worked on the 'corpse commando'. 'They must have been eating their food from home. SS men were around them with dogs. They, of course, didn't know what was going to happen to them. We did not want to tell them. It would have been worse for them. We were thinking that the people who brought them here were not humans but some wild jungle creatures.'[55]

Rudolf Höss, the commandant of Auschwitz, wrote in his memoirs that Jews walked to their death under the 'blossom-laden fruit trees of the cottage orchard'. He recorded that one woman, who clearly realized what was about to happen to her, whispered to him, 'How can you bring yourself to kill such beautiful, darling children? Have you no heart at all?'[56] Höss claimed he found such scenes 'shattering', but these incidents made no difference to his absolute commitment to the killing process.

Jews from Slovakia were not just deported to Auschwitz. At least 24,000 Slovak Jews were transferred to a new murder facility at Sobibór, about 50 miles north-east of Lublin. Sobibór was, after Bełżec, the second camp built as an extermination centre with fixed gas chambers. Like Bełżec the camp was close to a railway line, but the location was even more remote – in forest and marshland a few miles from the River Bug. The countryside around Sobibór was peaceful and picturesque, and the camp was designed to look inviting. 'I imagined Sobibór as a place where they burn people, where they gas people, so it must look like hell,' says Toivi Blatt who was sent to the camp in April 1943, at a time when 'rumours' about the true function of the place had been circulating for months. 'And now what I see is actually nice houses, plus the commandant's villa, painted green with a little fence and flowers.'[57]

In May 1942, when the first large transports of Jews arrived to be gassed, the commandant of Sobibór was a thirty-four-year-old veteran of the T4 euthanasia action called Franz Stangl. Before taking charge at Sobibór he had visited Bełżec and been struck by the 'smell – oh God, the smell. It was everywhere.' He saw pits with 'thousands of corpses' in them, and learnt first hand the practical problems of managing a death camp. He was told that 'one of the pits had overflowed. They had put too many corpses in it and putrefaction had progressed too fast, so that the liquid underneath had pushed the bodies on top, up and over, and the corpses had rolled down the hill.'[58]

At Bełżec, Stangl became reacquainted with Christian Wirth, whom he had known – and disliked – from the euthanasia actions. Wirth was now Stangl's boss, and when he had visited Stangl during the construction of Sobibór he had been dissatisfied with the way the work was progressing. Stangl learnt that Wirth had arrived, 'looked around the gas chambers on which they were still working and said, "Right, we'll try it out right now with those twenty-five work-Jews: get them up here" '. Wirth ordered the Jews pushed into the gas chamber and murdered. According to one of Stangl's colleagues, 'Wirth behaved like a lunatic, hit out at his own staff with his whip to drive them on. And then he was livid because the doors hadn't worked properly.'[59]

Stangl claimed after the war that he had been shocked by the task that had been assigned to him, and that he hadn't wanted to complete it. But eyewitnesses who saw him in the camp at the time tell a different story. 'What was special about him was his arrogance,' said Stanislaw Szmajzner, a Jewish survivor of the camp. 'And his obvious pleasure in his work and his situation. None of the others – although they were, in different ways, so much worse than he – showed this to such an extent. He had this perpetual smile on his face . . . No, I don't think it was a nervous smile; it was just that he was happy.'[60] Erich Bauer, the SS man at Sobibór responsible for the working of the gas chambers, offered another perspective on Stangl, which also contradicts the notion that the commandant did his work unwillingly. 'In the canteen at Sobibor I once overheard a conversation between Frenzel, Stangl and Wagner [all members of the SS at the camp]. They were discussing the number of victims in the extermination camps of Belzec, Treblinka [the last death camp to be built] and Sobibor and expressed their regret that Sobibor "came last" in the competition.'[61]

Despite the experience they had gained in the construction and operation of the death camp at Bełżec, the SS did not create an efficient killing installation at Sobibór. While the remote location was an advantage for them, the railway had only one track. This obviously limited the capacity of the line. An even bigger issue was the nature of the countryside. During August and September 1942 no train could travel to Sobibór because sections of the railway had sunk into the marshland and repairs had to be made.

Even when the camp had been functioning, the SS had created a bottleneck in the killing process. In the early days of the camp's operation, when a train arrived at Sobibór station the SS waited until the Jews who were capable of walking unaided had entered the camp and then gathered up those who were left – the old, the disabled and the injured – and put them on to a horse-drawn cart. The SS told these Jews who were unable to walk that they were to be taken to a hospital. This was said in an attempt to calm them, but it was also a black joke. Because the 'hospital', 200 yards into the forest, consisted of a group of executioners standing by a pit. All of those who had been taken to the 'hospital' on the horse and cart were murdered in sight of each other.

This process did not work as well as the SS wanted. It was time-consuming to get the old and sick on to the horse-drawn cart and for the cart to get to the 'hospital', so the SS made a change to their operating procedure. They constructed a narrow-gauge railway track from Sobibór station up to the killing zone of the 'hospital' so that the weaker Jews could be carried more efficiently to their deaths. The horse and cart were now redundant, replaced by more modern technology.[62]

Only thirty or so SS were needed to staff Sobibór, supported by just over a hundred former Soviet prisoners of war. Many of these men were from Ukraine and had been offered the chance to leave their POW camps, where they stood a high chance of dying of disease or starvation, to work for the Nazis. Trained at Trawniki camp, south-east of Lublin, they were often the most brutal of all the guards. Partly this was because the Germans were keen to give the Ukrainians the bloodiest jobs.[63] At Sobibór, for instance, most of those who shot the Jews at the 'hospital' were Ukrainians.

Just as at Bełżec, the largest category of people working in the camp were the Jewish Sonderkommandos. Every major extermination camp utilized prisoners who were selected from the new arrivals and made to perform a variety of tasks related to the killing process – from the 'Bahnhofskommando' who took the Jews from the station up into the camp, to the most horrific jobs of all which were undertaken by the Sonderkommandos who were forced to empty the gas chambers of the bodies and bury them. Again, as at Bełżec, all of the Sonderkommandos were just a moment away from death themselves. Any of the Sonderkommandos who did not perform as the SS required were murdered and replaced by selected Jews from a new transport.

Toivi Blatt, who at the age of fifteen was selected as a Sonderkommando at Sobibor, was astonished at how the horrific circumstances of the camp could alter the character of those who worked there. 'People change under some conditions,' he says. 'People asked me, "What did you learn?" and I think I'm only sure of one thing – nobody knows themselves . . . All of us could be good people or bad people in these [different] situations. Sometimes, when somebody is really nice to me, I find myself thinking, "How will he be in Sobibor?" '64

As the first anniversary of the invasion of the Soviet Union approached, Hitler and his followers had travelled a long way in a short time – not just in terms of the physical progress the German Army had made inside the Soviet Union, but in the conceptual decisions the SS and others had made about the fate of the Jews and the means by which they sought to kill them.

By June 1942, the first death factories of the Holocaust were in place, and the Nazis had created a method of killing that allowed them to murder in considerable numbers and experience little psychological torment. What they sought now were large numbers of Jews to kill. But since the Nazis could not find every foreign Jew for themselves, they needed willing collaborators. The story of how they acquired them is one of the most troubling parts of this whole history.

12. Search and Kill

(1942)

In their quest to deport the Jews of western Europe to the killing factories in the east, the Nazis faced formidable difficulties. No one country could be dealt with the same way as another. The occupied countries of Belgium, the Netherlands, Norway and Denmark were all administered differently; Italy was an ally; and France was a strange cross between a quasi-ally and a subjugated nation. Not only that, but in the summer of 1942 German forces were focused on the conquest of the Soviet Union – the defining conflict of history, as Hitler saw it. As a consequence, the SS were given minimal resources to accomplish their mission and deport the Jews. They could succeed only with the help of others.

In France in particular, the Nazis were able to exploit many pre-existing prejudices – not just anti-Semitic beliefs, but fear of foreigners and dislike of immigrants. Even before the creation of the Vichy government, the French authorities had opened camps in order to detain unwanted foreigners. In 1939, at Gurs in the Pyrenees, the French set up a camp to imprison people fleeing from the Spanish civil war; not just Spaniards who had fought, and lost, on the republican side, but many other nationalities were held in terrible conditions at Gurs.

However, the worst kind of unwanted foreigner, as far as the French authorities were concerned, was the Jew. 'The Jew is not only an unassimilable foreigner, whose implantation tends to form a state within the state,' said Xavier Vallat, the Commissioner-General for Jewish Questions within the Vichy government. 'He is also, by temperament, a foreigner who wants to dominate and who tends to create, with his kin, a super state within the state.'[1]

The Vichy authorities not only imposed a whole series of restrictive laws targeted at Jews from 1940 onwards, but were also sympathetic in principle to the idea of deporting large numbers of their foreign Jews – many of whom had fled Nazi oppression in Germany and Austria. The Vichy government recognized, however, that solely because of practicalities expelling all these foreign Jews had to be a long-term aim.

'Send them where?' asked Vallat in a speech in 1942. 'By what means, so long as the war is going on? In reality, it will be the victor's business, if he intends to organize a durable peace, to find the means, worldwide if possible, European in any case, to settle the wandering Jew.'[2]

Notwithstanding Vichy's dislike of foreign Jews, the first train filled with Jews that left France for Auschwitz in 1942 was sent not as part of a concerted plan to expel foreign Jews, but in an act of reprisal. The reasons why more than a thousand Jewish men were on that train in March 1942 can be traced back to the summer of 1941. In August 1941, French Communists shot two Germans in Paris, killing one and badly injuring the other. The German invasion of the Soviet Union had released French Communists from the shackles placed on their actions by the pact between Stalin and Hitler. The following month another German was shot dead. In reprisal, the German military authorities killed three Communist hostages. Hitler was incensed. He thought this a trivial response. 'The Führer considers one German soldier to be worth much more than three French Communists,' wrote Field Marshal Wilhelm Keitel in a dispatch from Hitler's headquarters in East Prussia. 'The Führer expects such instances to be responded to with the harshest reprisals . . . At the next assassination at least 100 shootings for each German [killed] are to take place without delay. Without such draconian retribution, matters cannot be controlled.'[3]

However, General Otto von Stülpnagel, the German military commander in France, believed that such 'Polish methods' simply did not work in France.[4] And the evidence on the ground seemed to support that view. There was outrage among many French citizens, for instance, at the German reprisal killing of ninety-eight hostages in Nantes in October 1941. In January 1942 Stülpnagel offered his resignation. He was particularly bitter about having to leave his job because, as he outlined in a letter to Field Marshal Keitel, he thought he had come up with a better way to deter future attacks on Germans: 'I believed that I could accomplish the clearly necessary reprisals for assassinations of personnel by other means, i.e., through limited executions, but primarily through transporting massive numbers of Jews and Communists to the East, which, in my informed opinion, has a far more chilling effect on the French population than these mass shootings, which the French do not understand.'[5]

Stülpnagel's successor, his cousin Carl-Heinrich von Stülpnagel, managed to obtain agreement to try out this policy of reprisal by mass expulsion. Hence the first deportation in March 1942, in response to resistance attacks, of 1,112 Jews from Compiègne to Auschwitz. It didn't matter to the Germans that none of these 1,112 Jews had been found guilty of acts of murderous resistance. Because of the Nazi belief in the iron link between Communism and Judaism, it was sufficient merely that they were Jews.

The train carrying the French Jews reached Auschwitz on 30 March 1942, just a few days after the first transport carrying Slovak Jews had arrived at the camp. The French Jews, like the initial transports of Slovaks, were not selected on arrival and were admitted to the camp, but virtually all of them still perished in Auschwitz. More than 1,000 of them were dead within five months.

It wasn't until the summer of 1942 that the mass deportation of Jews from France as a consequence of the Final Solution began. This action was intended as part of a pattern for western Europe as a whole. On 11 June, SS Obersturmbannführer (Lieutenant Colonel) Adolf Eichmann of the Department of Jewish Affairs convened a meeting in Berlin to discuss the implementation of the Final Solution with his various representatives from France, the Netherlands and Belgium. He told them that Himmler had ordered the deportation of large numbers of Jews from the west, but that 90 per cent of these Jews had to be fit and healthy. Only 10 per cent could be 'not able to work'.[6] Specific targets for the number of Jews to be deported were also fixed at the meeting – 10,000 from Belgium, 15,000 from the Netherlands and 100,000 from France. The French figure was obviously the most ambitious and represented a challenge for Eichmann's representative in Paris, Theodor Dannecker, a twenty-nine-year-old SS Hauptsturmführer (captain).

Dannecker knew that he had to gain the collaboration of the French authorities in order to fulfil his task. There were only around 3,000 German police in the whole of France in 1942, a completely inadequate force to implement the target set by Eichmann – but there were nearly 100,000 French police.[7] At a meeting on 2 July 1942 between German and French officials, René Bousquet, the head of the French National Police, outlined the French position. In the occupied zone of France – the area under the administrative control of the Germans – only foreign

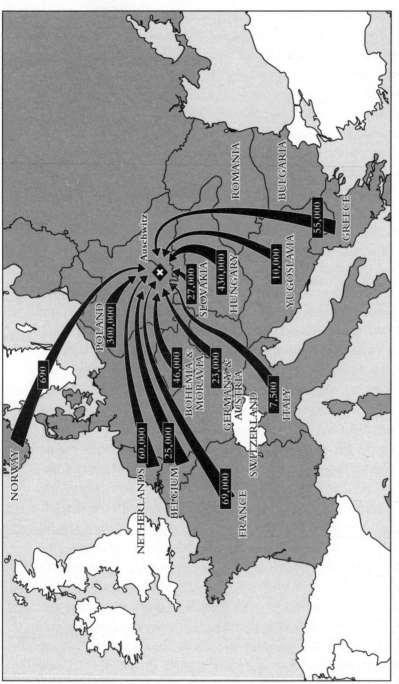

These are the figures of Jews deported to Auschwitz – the great majority of whom died there. Almost all arrived at Auschwitz Birkenau, though the initial transports in 1942 went to Auschwitz main camp. The figures are taken from Franciszek Piper's detailed analytical study, *Auschwitz: How Many Perished*, Oświęcim, Frap Books, 1996, p. 53.

Dr Piper gives an additional figure of 34,000 Jews deported to Auschwitz from concentration camps and 'unknown places'. It is also important to note that his original figure of 438,000 Jews from Hungary was subsequently revised to 430,000, and a Norwegian Royal Commission gives a more exact estimate for the number of Jews from Norway who died in Auschwitz, rather than were deported, at 747 (see p. 290).

Finally, it should of course always be remembered that Jews were deported by the Nazis to many other camps and destinations, and not just Auschwitz.

Jews could be deported. In the unoccupied zone – the area controlled by the Vichy government – the French police would not take part in an attempt to round up any Jews. 'On the French side we have nothing against the arrests themselves,' said Bousquet, but the involvement of the French police 'would be embarrassing'.[8] Bousquet altered his position after the head of the German security police, Helmut Knochen, pointed out that Hitler would object strongly to the French attitude. Bousquet now said that the French police would cooperate in both occupied and unoccupied zones, but they would still target only foreign Jews, not French Jews. He subsequently confirmed that Marshal Pétain had agreed to the deportation of the foreign Jews in all parts of France 'as a first step'.[9] There was no agreement with the Germans that the French Jews would somehow be saved at the expense of the foreign Jews – merely a statement by the French authorities that the foreign Jews would be sent first.

On 4 July, the French Prime Minister, Pierre Laval, met with Dannecker to discuss the forthcoming round-up. Laval said that, as far as the French were concerned, 'during the evacuation of Jewish families from the unoccupied zone, children under sixteen [can] also be taken away.'[10] He went on to express indifference for the fate of the children in the occupied zone. Laval thus voluntarily gave up the Jewish children. The Nazis had not asked for them – at this moment, they appeared not to want them. But the Prime Minister of France, a country with a proud history of protecting the rights of the individual, took the initiative and suggested that the Nazis carry away innocent children. Laval later tried to present his actions as a humanitarian act, but that was always an unsustainable excuse, not least because Laval knew that Hitler had publicly committed himself to 'exterminating' the Jewish race in Europe in the event of a world war. Laval – just as the Slovaks had been – was almost certainly motivated by simple expediency. If Jewish parents were allowed to leave their children behind after they had been deported, their offspring would become a problem for the French authorities. Laval didn't want that problem, so he tried to get rid of them. Laval was not even a fanatical anti-Semite. But he was a cynical and cold-hearted politician.

Over two days, 16 and 17 July 1942, some 9,000 French police took part in one of the most infamous actions in the history of Paris – the round-up known as the *grande rafle*. In the 10th arrondissement, Annette Muller – then just nine years old – remembers the police pushing into her flat and her mother 'begging them to spare her children, to take her [instead] . . . I have the vision of my mother being humiliated by the police officer who pushed her. I remember the scene in front of my eyes.' Annette, her youngest brother Michel and their mother were taken to a hall close by where the French police were temporarily gathering the Jews together. 'I saw people lying on tables who were having fits,' says Annette, 'and others who were vomiting.'[11] Her two elder brothers had managed to escape in the chaos – Annette's mother had encouraged them to run as she was under no illusions as to what might await the family in captivity. Her husband, who was away from the flat that night, was Polish, and had learnt a few months before that many of his close relatives in Poland had been shot by the Germans.

Altogether 12,884 Jews were snatched from their homes by the French police in the course of the *grande rafle* – nearly 10,000 on the first day of the raid, the rest on the second. Several thousand Jews – including Annette, Michel and their mother – were transported to the Vélodrôme d'Hiver, a cycle stadium on the left bank of the Seine where they were confined in atrocious conditions. Michel, just seven years old at the time, still has memories of the terrible stench of diarrhoea that enveloped the Vélodrôme.

From the Vélodrôme d'Hiver, they were sent to Beaune-la-Rolande, a holding camp in the Loiret, south of Paris. Though the whole experience was frightening, Annette and Michel felt comforted because they were with their mother. 'She was there,' says Annette, 'she was warm. We felt protected. We felt that as long as she was there, nothing could happen to us.' Nonetheless, Annette worried about 'what was going to happen to us when we went back to school' because they might 'miss the beginning of classes'.

They were held at Beaune-la-Rolande for three weeks. They didn't know it, but during this time the Nazis were discussing what should be done with the children who had been caught in the round-ups. Dannecker had asked Eichmann for a ruling, and during a telephone call on 20 July Eichmann finally passed on the verdict – the children could be sent east as well, but only once transport complications had been sorted out. The French authorities now decided – instead of waiting until the families could be deported together – to send the parents of the children away first. So much for Laval's claim that he wanted for humane reasons to deport the children along with their parents.[12]

Early in August, parents at Beaune-la-Rolande were separated from their children. 'They brought us together, all of us, in the middle of the camp,' remembers Annette, 'and the police very violently beat the women back. The children were holding on to their clothing . . . there was a lot of screaming, crying, it was really a lot of noise.' Her last memory of her mother is that 'she made a sign with her eyes and we watched her. I had the impression that her eyes smiled at us, as if she wanted to say that she was going to come back.'[13]

The mothers were sent to Drancy in the suburbs of Paris, and a camp that had been established in a half-built housing estate. The majority of the Jews that were deported from France – around 69,000 people – left for the east from Drancy. In 1942 the camp was administered by the French authorities, and conditions were appalling. Not only were sanitation and food wholly inadequate, but this was also a place of emotional despair, especially when the mothers arrived who had been taken from their children. Odette Daltroff-Baticle, an adult who was imprisoned in Drancy that summer, remembers, 'These women naturally were hurt, because they had to leave their children, and some of them threw themselves out of windows. There was one who was saved because she fell on to barbed wire that went around the courtyard [and so her fall was cushioned]. But some of them did die.'[14]

After their mother had been snatched away, life at Beaune-la-Rolande became all but unbearable for Annette and her brother. 'After the departure,' she says, 'for a few days I didn't want to go out of the barracks because I was so sad. I couldn't stop crying. I stayed sleeping on the straw, and I told myself that it was my fault that my mother left, that I wasn't nice with her. All those sorts of things that I could reproach myself with . . . It was a period of constant fear. The Gendarmes had become menacing, threatening, and we needed to stay quiet.'

There was one poignant physical reminder of the mothers who had been separated from the children. 'All the children had gone to go look at the latrine,' says Annette, 'and they had said, "Oh, come look, come look," because at the bottom of the latrine, mixed with the excrement, there was lots of brilliant, shiny things. It was rings. It was wedding rings that the mothers had preferred to throw into the latrines rather than give up, because they had been told to surrender all their jewellery.'[15]

After two weeks or so at Beaune-la-Rolande without their mothers, the children were sent to Drancy. By now their mothers had been deported to Auschwitz. At Drancy, Annette and her brother slept on the concrete floor of a half-finished flat and tried 'not to slip on the stairway because there was so much excrement. We all had diarrhoea.' Though she remembers that she saw some French police 'cry' at the plight of the children, the majority did their work 'with a lot of zeal'.[16]

Odette Daltroff-Baticle tried to look after the children as best she could: 'When they arrived they were in really poor shape. The children were surrounded by insects and they were very, very dirty and had dysentery. We tried to give them showers but we didn't have anything to dry them with. Then we tried to give them food – these children hadn't eaten for several days – and we had a hard time giving them any. Furthermore, we tried to make a full list of their names, but many of them didn't know their family names and so they just said things like, "I'm the little brother of Pierre." So we persisted in trying to find out their names; the older ones, yes, of course, but for the smaller ones it was absolutely impossible. Their mothers had tied little pieces of wood on them with their names, but a lot of them had taken off the pieces of wood and played with them amongst themselves . . . The children always spoke about their parents, of course, they spoke about their mother mostly. They spoke about the moment when they had left their mothers, but we felt in everything they said that they knew that they would never see them again, that's what it seemed to me.'[17]

In one respect, Michel and Annette were fortunate. Unbeknown to them, their father had been trying to get them released for weeks. Through an intermediary he managed to bribe French officials so that they were transferred from Drancy to a holding centre in Montmartre. Here the security was more lax, and he succeeded in taking them away and hiding them in a Catholic orphanage. Most of the other children held in Drancy had no such saviour working to protect them. They were on their own. Had Michel and Annette's father not escaped the initial round-up on 16–17 July, they too would almost certainly have been sent on one of the seven trains that left Drancy for Auschwitz in late August, carrying the newly orphaned children to their deaths.

Odette Daltroff-Baticle remembers that before the children left Drancy they endured one last degradation in the camp: 'they had their heads shaved. It was dreadful. I remember there was a little boy who had relatively long blond hair and he said: "Oh but my mum likes my blond hair so much, we can't cut it." But I saw him later and his head was shaven and [he looked] completely hopeless . . . It was true – he had especially beautiful hair. For the children, particularly the little girls, of ten or twelve years old, when they were shaved it was really a humiliation . . .'[18]

There were protests in France about the deportations, most notably from clerics. Archbishop Jules-Géraud Saliège of Toulouse said on 23 August: 'that children, women and men, fathers and mothers, should be treated like a vile herd of cattle, that members of the same family should be separated from each other and sent to an unknown destination – it was reserved for our time to witness this tragic spectacle.'[19] Other leading churchmen, like the Archbishop of Marseilles, also protested. But there was not one word of public support for these sentiments from Pope Pius XII, and the compassionate remonstrations of the French clerics came to nothing.

A total of 42,500 Jews were deported from France to Poland by the end of 1942. Prime Minister Laval gave every sign that he was pleased to see them go. 'Laval made no mention of any German pressure,' reported a visiting group of Americans who met him in August 1943, 'but stated flatly that "these foreign Jews had always been a problem in France and that the French government was glad that a change in German attitude towards them gave France an opportunity to get rid of them." '[20]

The approach of the French authorities to the persecution and deportation of the Jews was in stark contrast to that of their neighbours to the south – the Italians. It comes as a surprise to many people to learn that the Fascist regime under Benito Mussolini did not deport any Italian Jews. Only the removal of Mussolini as Prime Minister of Italy in the summer of 1943, and the subsequent German occupation, changed that situation. Ironically – since Hitler saw Mussolini's takeover of Italy in 1922 as an inspiration for the Nazi movement – many Italian Jews were also Fascists, with Guido Jung serving as Finance Minister in Mussolini's cabinet from 1932 until 1935. One of Mussolini's most intimate companions was also Jewish – Margherita Sarfatti, who was his mistress for almost twenty-five years. Despite this, however, there is still controversy over Mussolini's own beliefs about Jews during this period, and whether or not he was a committed anti-Semite even at this time.[21] What is certain is that whatever his personal views might have been they didn't stop him working – and sleeping – with Jews.

It wasn't perhaps surprising that Mussolini's Fascists tolerated Jewish Italians. Jews had fought alongside Giuseppe Garibaldi – the great Italian hero and an inspiration to Mussolini – in the battle to unite Italy in the second half of the nineteenth century, and in the wake of Garibaldi's victory official discrimination against Italian Jews had ceased. Italian Jews could now reach the highest positions in the state – for example, in 1902, Giuseppe Ottolenghi became Minister of War and in 1905 Alessandro Fortis became Prime Minister.

It was only after Mussolini had decided to commit to an enduring friendship with Hitler's Germany in the late 1930s that his regime became openly anti-Semitic. In 1938 a whole raft of legislation was introduced, including provisions to outlaw marriage between Jews and non-Jews and prevent Italian Jews from serving in the armed forces. But these measures were primarily motivated by opportunism rather than by deep anti-Semitic conviction. Though there were undoubtedly some Italian Fascists who were Jew-haters, most Italians found it hard to understand why their Jewish neighbours were suddenly the victims of persecution. Even within the Fascist administration there was considerable flexibility in the application of anti-Semitic legislation. In July 1939, for instance, a commission was established which could 'Aryanize' selected Jews – chiefly those who paid large enough bribes.

Italy's entry into the war in 1940 did not herald a massive upsurge in persecution against Italian Jews, though Italian police began to intern foreign Jews living in the country. In the areas outside Italy occupied by the Italian Army, the policy towards Jews was often relatively benign. In Croatia, for example, where the Italians occupied much of the coastline, the Italian Army protected Jews from the Croat Ustaše, the anti-Semitic militia. In 1942 the Croat government agreed with the Nazis that the remaining Jews left alive in the country could be deported. But the Italians would not relinquish the several thousand Jews who had sought sanctuary in the Italian zone. The Germans asked Mussolini to tell his representatives in Croatia to cooperate. Mussolini said he would try, but still the Italian authorities in Croatia procrastinated and kept coming up with reasons why they could not accede to German demands.[22]

In November 1942, in response to the Allied landings in North Africa, the Germans occupied the area of France previously under the control of the Vichy government. At the same time the Germans also agreed that the Italians could send their forces into eight French departments in former Vichy territory, near the Mediterranean coast. This led to a direct confrontation between the Italian and French administrators, and in the process revealed their very different attitudes towards the treatment of the Jews. The Italian General Carlo Avarna di Gualtieri told the Vichy authorities that the Italians would seek to govern their area of France with 'humane legislation'.[23] In pursuit of this aim, the Italians frustrated Vichy's desire to persecute the Jews. For instance, the Italians allowed foreign Jews to carry on living along the coast – Vichy regulations said they should be moved inland – and refused to implement a French demand that the documentation of the Jews should be stamped with an identifying mark. The French authorities did not welcome this more 'humane' approach to the 'Jewish question'. Pierre Laval complained to the Italians about their behaviour and went as far as to ask the German authorities for 'appropriate support'[24] in order to reassert French control.

How can we explain the 'humanity' of the Italians in these occupied areas? Partly it was because the Italians wanted to demonstrate that they were equal partners with their German allies. They were not about to be bullied. Unlike the French, the Italians were not a defeated nation forced into an unwanted relationship with the Germans, but subjects of a proudly independent country that had chosen to be an active belligerent. In addition, Italy, unlike France, had not absorbed large numbers of foreign Jews, nor had Italians been educated to hate Jews as the Germans had. The Italians could now protect Jews in the territory they occupied at little risk to themselves. So why not help them? This is not to say, however, that Italian soldiers were saints – one collection of oral testimony from Italian soldiers on the eastern front reveals that on occasion individual soldiers sexually exploited Jewish women.[25]

At the same time as the Italians were protecting Jews in the areas they controlled, thousands of Dutch Jews were en route to Auschwitz – by the end of 1942 about 40,000 Jews had been sent from the Netherlands to the east. All this was made possible not just because of the continuing cooperation of the Dutch authorities, but as a result of the comprehensive system of registration that the Germans had put in place. In January 1941 all Dutch Jews had been told to register with the authorities and virtually every single one of them had done so – altogether nearly 160,000 registrations.

Unlike in France, the Germans were also able to deal with the Dutch Jews through a single umbrella organization – the Jewish Council. The leaders of the Jewish Council – Dr David Cohen and Abraham Asscher – were later vilified. Many saw their cooperation with the Germans in the deportation process as betrayal. In part this was because the Jewish Council was granted 17,500 exemption certificates by the Germans in 1942 which meant that members of the Council and their families were spared deportation, albeit temporarily. When Cohen and Asscher were themselves eventually deported, they were sent not to the death camps of the east but to concentration camps within the Old Reich and Protectorate, and both survived the war.

At the Berlin meeting on 11 June 1942, Eichmann had originally planned on deporting 15,000 Jews from the Netherlands during the initial series of transports, but by the end of the month he had raised that demand to 40,000. It is possible that Eichmann took that decision because the Nazis found it easier to deport Dutch Jews than they had anticipated. This was in contrast to France, where Dannecker had expressed concern about his ability to meet his quota, as he argued with the Vichy authorities over the deportation of French Jews as opposed to foreign ones.[26]

On 4 July 1942 the first letters were sent out requiring Dutch Jews to present themselves for mass deportation. At the Jewish Lyceum in Amsterdam, Dr Hemelrijk, one of the teachers, remembers the atmosphere: 'The shadow of death hung heavily over the first graduation ceremony (it was also the last) at my school. Girls over the age of fifteen had all received orders to report for transportation to [the] Central Station at one a.m. Destination unknown. All the parents knew was that they had to send their daughters out into the night, defenceless prey, never to be seen again. No one was allowed to accompany these children. The girls went, often after heart-rending domestic scenes, in the hope that by doing so they were sparing their parents. Not that they did.'[27]

No one on the Jewish Council, or within the Jewish community as a whole, knew for certain what was going to happen to these girls or to the thousands of other Jews about to be sent to a 'destination unknown'. But within days of the deportations beginning rumours started to circulate. The underground newspaper *De Waarheid* printed a plea to Dutch policemen on 3 August, saying 'think of your human and professional duty – arrest no Jews and only make a show of carrying out orders directed against them. Let them escape and go into hiding. Remember that every man, every woman and every child you arrest will be killed and that you are their murderer.'[28] On 29 July, Radio Orange, broadcasting from London, had said: 'Just how does it help the German war effort to herd together thousands of defenceless Jewish Poles and do away with them in gas-chambers? How does it help the war effort when thousands of Jewish Dutchmen are dragged out of their country?'[29]

The reference to 'gas-chambers' demonstrates that even this early in the deportation process there was some public knowledge of what was happening to the Jews. In London, on 9 July, at a press conference held by the Polish government-in-exile and attended by Brendan Bracken, the British Minister of Information, journalists had been briefed that the Germans were 'deliberately carrying out their monstrous plan to exterminate Jews' in Poland.[30] But the Allies were still uncertain about the Germans' broader intentions – did they, for instance, just want to kill Polish Jews? Were the Dutch and other European Jews perhaps genuinely to be used as forced labour?

The first firm warning that Hitler had an overall plan of extermination came in August 1942 from Gerhart Riegner of the World Jewish Congress in Geneva. With access to intelligence from German sources in central Europe, Riegner concluded that 'a plan has been discussed, and is under consideration, according to which all Jews in countries occupied or controlled by Germany, numbering three and a half to four millions, should, after deportation and concentration in the East, be at one blow exterminated, in order to resolve once and for all the Jewish question in Europe. Action is reported to be planned for the autumn. Ways of execution are still being discussed including the use of prussic acid. We transmit this information with all necessary reservation, as exactitude cannot be confirmed by us.'[31]

When the leaders of the World Jewish Congress in New York received this news, they did not 'doubt that the information is at least substantially correct' but were concerned that publishing the information might 'have a demoralizing effect on those who are marked as hopeless victims'. As a consequence, they sought 'the best advice possible' about what to do.[32] Riegner's telegram reached the British government by the middle of August and the American government shortly afterwards. To begin with, there was disbelief. It took the best part of four months for the Allies to accept that the news was undoubtedly true, and to make a concerted statement to the world about the Nazis' actions. Only after they had received information from other sources – including an eyewitness account of the Warsaw ghetto – did they commit to condemning the crime in a concerted way.[33]

On 17 December 1942 the British, Americans and Soviets all issued statements expressing outrage at the Nazis' murderous attack on the Jews. In the House of Commons, Anthony Eden, the British Foreign Secretary, drew attention to 'numerous reports from Europe that the German authorities, not content with denying to persons of Jewish race in all the territories over which their barbarous rule has been extended the most elementary human rights, are now carrying into effect Hitler's oft repeated intention to exterminate the Jewish people in Europe. From all the occupied countries Jews are being transported in conditions of appalling horror and brutality, to Eastern Europe . . . None of those taken away are ever heard of again.' Eden said that the Allies 'condemn in the strongest possible terms this bestial policy of cold-blooded extermination' and that they would 'ensure that those responsible for these crimes shall not escape retribution . . .'[34]

Months before Anthony Eden stood up in the House of Commons and revealed what was known about the Nazis' plans, Gerhart Riegner and his colleagues had personally brought intelligence about the destruction of the Jews to the papal nuncio in Switzerland, Monsignor Philippe Bernardini. 'We said, please ask the Vatican to intervene,' says Riegner, 'to preserve, at least in those countries [where it was still possible], what could still be preserved of the Jewish community.'[35] He remembers that the reply from the Vatican was 'wishy-washy' and that 'the attempt to involve the Vatican was a failure.' Pope Pius XII still refused publicly to condemn the extermination of the Jews – though in his Christmas message of 1942 he did speak of those 'who through no fault of their own and sometimes only on grounds of nationality or race, are destined for death or slow deterioration'.[36] But he was not prepared to say the word 'Jews'.

Those who seek to defend the inaction of Pope Pius XII often point to events in the Netherlands in the summer of 1942 as one of the key reasons for his silence. When the Nazis had learnt that Archbishop Johannes de Jong of Utrecht planned to condemn the deportation of the Jews, they warned him that if he did so they would also deport Jews in the Netherlands who had converted to Christianity. Archbishop de Jong stood firm in the face of this blackmail, and on 20 July 1942 his pastoral letter was read from pulpits across the country. The letter referred directly to the 'persecution of the Jews' and included the words of a telegram that had been sent to the 'authorities of the occupying forces' nine days before, which said that 'The undersigned Dutch churches' were 'already deeply shocked by the actions taken against the Jews in the Netherlands that have excluded them from participating in the normal life of society', and had now 'learned with horror of the new measures by which men, women, children, and whole families will be deported to the German territory and its dependencies'. This action was 'contrary to the deepest moral sense of the Dutch people', and so the churches urged the Germans 'not to execute these measures'.[37]

Not surprisingly, the 'occupying authorities' ignored the churches' plea that they should act with common humanity towards the Dutch Jews. Not only that, the Nazis carried out their threat to deport Jews in the Netherlands who had converted to Christianity. No exact figures exist for how many were sent east as a result – it might have been several hundred,[38] though it could have been no higher than ninety-two.[39] Whatever the precise figure, it is argued that a number of people lost their lives as a consequence of Archbishop de Jong's decision to have his letter of protest read in Dutch churches. This was a key reason, it is said, why Pope Pius XII kept quiet. 'The persecution of the Jews in Holland had an enormous effect on the line that Pius XII subsequently took,' says Archbishop Emanuele Clarizio, who worked in the Vatican during the war. 'That's obvious.' Moreover, says Archbishop Gennaro Verolino, who was a papal diplomat at the time, the Pope 'tried every-thing that he could. And if sometimes it seems he didn't go all the way, it's because he was afraid of making the situation worse. That his actions would be misinterpreted and lead to worse reprisals.'[40]

At first sight this appears a powerful justification – it was necessary to keep silent or there might have been more deaths. But it is crucial to remember that Archbishop de Jong was not responsible for the death of the Jewish converts – the Nazis were. They chose to kill them, not him. What Archbishop de Jong must surely have understood was that once you ignored your own feelings about what was right and wrong, your feet rested on quicksand. In any case, who was to say that the Nazis would ever have kept their promise not to deport the Dutch converts even if Archbishop de Jong had kept quiet?[41] More than that, suppose the Nazis had said they would kill an innocent child every day unless Archbishop de Jong publicly renounced his entire faith? Would he then be worthy of condemnation if he had decided to stay true to his beliefs?

Similarly, a common excuse from bureaucrats who collaborated with the Nazis was that they 'sought to change the system from within' and that if they had been replaced the situation would have been 'even worse'. After the war, for instance, Dutch civil servants could point to a number of Nazi measures that were watered down as a result of their involvement. Except that a close examination of the evidence reveals that this excuse lacks validity. That is because the Nazi Reichskommissar's practice was to make deliberately excessive demands, so as to allow the civil servants to think that they had accomplished something when he subsequently reduced his requests to the level he had intended all along. By this simple trick the Nazi leadership helped ensure the administrative cooperation of the civil servants.[42]

As for the Pope, he did not just stay silent about the deportation of the Jews, he did not even publicly express outrage at the atrocities the Nazis were committing against Catholic Poles. 'We all expected something – a word,' says Witold Złotnicki, who fought with the Polish Home Army. 'Some acknowledgement of what we were going through. Some word of sympathy. Some word of hope. But not total silence.'[43]

The Pope, and the Catholic Church as a whole, possessed enormous latent power – particularly in Slovakia. The President of Slovakia, Jozef Tiso, was an ordained Catholic priest and large numbers of the Hlinka Guard were Catholics. At the time of the initial deportations in the spring of 1942, leaders of the Jewish community in Slovakia pleaded with the Catholic Church to protest about the expulsion of the Jews. But they were dismayed by the response. The priority for the church as a whole appeared to be to try and save Jews who had been baptized as Christians.

Some individual churchmen, like Augustín Pozdech, a parish priest in Bratislava, did protest at the inhumanity of the deportation process. His outrage at the actions of the Slovak government and the Nazis was transmitted to the Vatican via the papal nuncio in Budapest. 'I am distressed to the depth of my heart', wrote Pozdech, 'that human beings whose only fault is that they were born Jews should be robbed of all their possessions and should be banished – stripped of the last vestiges of their personal freedom – to a foreign country . . . It is impossible that the world should passively watch small infants, mortally sick old people, young girls torn away from their families and young people deported like animals: transported in cattle wagons towards an unknown place of destination, towards an uncertain future.'[44] But Pozdech was an exception. The bulk of the Catholics in Slovakia made no protest against the deportation of the Jews in 1942.

One of the Pope's closest aides in the Vatican, Monsignor Domenico Tardini, recognized the problem the church faced in not acting against President Tiso. 'Everyone understands that the Holy See cannot stop Hitler,' he wrote in March 1942. 'But who can understand that it does not know how to rein in a priest [i.e. Jozef Tiso, President of Slovakia]?'[45] As for the Pope, he was worried that the Soviet Union might triumph in this war, and was afraid of what the consequences of a Communist-dominated Europe would be for the Catholic Church. In such circumstances, in spring 1942, he might well have doubted the value of publicly breaking Tiso, a Catholic head of state who was confronting the Godless armies of Stalin.

Preaching at a Mass in August 1942, President Tiso said that it had been a Christian act to expel the Jewish 'pests'. He also followed the Nazi line and declared that it was impossible for Jews to be converted into Christians – 'a Jew remains a Jew,' said Tiso, 'even if he is baptized by a hundred bishops.'[46] Yet just two months later Tiso suspended the deportations. It is not clear exactly why he did this. One likely answer is that he thought Slovakia had deported the agreed number of Jews and the deal with Germany had been fulfilled.[47] It is also possible that he was responding both to foreign protests and to the increased knowledge in the world that the majority of Jews had been sent to their deaths. Even at his trial after the war, however, Tiso never claimed that he had stopped the deportations out of any sense of common humanity with the Jews.

By October, when the deportations ceased, around 58,000 Jews had been handed over to the Germans, leaving 24,000 in Slovakia. These remaining Jews were not yet safe, since – as we shall see – in 1944 the situation in Slovakia changed and the deportations started again.

The temptation to stray into counter-factual history is overwhelming at this point. What if the Pope had personally taken action against Tiso once the deportations began in the spring of 1942? As a Catholic priest, Tiso was especially vulnerable. Suppose Pius XII had threatened to excommunicate him – would not that have made Tiso think again? There was a precedent for excommunication during the war. Léon Degrelle, the leader of the Rexists in Belgium, was excommunicated in the summer of 1943 for wearing his SS uniform to Mass. Tiso's crimes were surely greater, and though by the end of the war he had been heavily criticized by the Vatican, he remained a Catholic priest until his dying breath. He was still dressed as a priest while in prison awaiting execution for treason in April 1947.

The Jews languishing in the Warsaw ghetto were also aware that the Pope had the powerful weapon of excommunication at his disposal. We know this as the result of the experiences of an exceptional man called Jan Karski. He was a member of the Polish resistance, who was smuggled into the Warsaw ghetto in 1942 because he wanted to witness first hand the horrific conditions. 'I saw terrible things,' he says, 'I saw horrible things. I saw dead bodies lying on the street. We were walking the streets, [and] my guide said from time to time, "Remember." And I did remember.' Karski met two Jewish leaders inside the ghetto who said they had a request directed at the Pope. They said to him, ' "But we don't know how one does talk to your Pope, we are Jews. But we understand, however, that your Pope has a power to open and close the gates of heaven. Let them close those gates for all of those who persecute us. He [the Pope] doesn't have to say that this concerns [all] the Germans. Only those who persecute and murder the Jews. [That] they may be subjects for automatic excommunication. Perhaps it will help. Perhaps even Hitler will reflect. Who knows? Perhaps some Catholic Germans will reflect and exercise some pressure. In the name of our common roots. We come from the same roots . . . Will you do it?" I said "I will do it, sir." And I did it.'[48] After witnessing the atrocious conditions inside the Warsaw ghetto, Karski managed to escape from Poland and cross occupied Europe. By the end of 1942 he had reached Britain and spoke personally with Anthony Eden. He also tried to influence the Vatican to speak out more strongly against the Nazis. But he feels that 'nothing important happened as a result of my mission. It didn't do any good.'

As the Nazis widened their search for Jews in the summer of 1942, their attention turned to Belgium. At Eichmann's infamous meeting on 11 June, a quota of 10,000 Jews from Belgium had been set, and the first train filled with Jews left the country on 4 August. Queen Elisabeth of Belgium had asked the German authorities to exclude Belgian Jews from the deportations, and at least to begin with this request was met. But agreeing to the wishes of Queen Elisabeth was not difficult for the Nazis as 90 per cent of the 52,000 or so Jews in the country were not Belgian citizens.[49]

The deportation process was not as straightforward for the Nazis in Belgium as it was in the Netherlands. This was partly because of conflict between the military administration and the SS, but also because many of the non-Belgian Jews – having already fled from elsewhere to escape the Nazis – had no reason to trust the Germans when they announced that they wanted the Jews to work as forced labour in the east. Hard as it was to find a place to hide in a foreign country, for a number of the non-Belgian Jews that struggle was preferable to putting their fate back in the hands of their persecutors. The Nazis also faced a tough administrative task in Belgium, because unlike in the Netherlands there was not a fully functioning and cooperative civil service. Despite this, the initial quota of 10,000 Jews was reached by the middle of September 1942, and by the end of the year the Nazis had sent nearly 17,000 to the east.

In the autumn of 1942 the Germans also ordered the deportation of Jews from Norway, and Vidkun Quisling and the Norwegian police collaborated in the practicalities of their arrest.[50] In December 1942, Quisling said in a speech that his administration had 'protected itself against the Jews' by cooperating with the Nazis.[51] Not only that, but the

Norwegian authorities benefited financially from the deportations. At the end of October 1942, Quisling signed a law that allowed the Norwegian state to seize Jewish property and assets.

On 26 November, the merchant ship *Donau* left Oslo for Stettin in the Baltic with 532 Jews on board. Eventually, after further deportations, a total of 747 Norwegian Jews were murdered in Auschwitz. But the majority of the 2,000 Norwegian Jews managed to escape the Nazis, most by fleeing across the border to neutral Sweden.[52]

The Nazis knew that they had to adapt their demands not only according to the individual circumstances of each country, but also according to whether they were dealing with their allies or with conquered nations. While they could decide themselves to deport the Jews of Norway, the Netherlands and Belgium – although to do so they still needed the assistance of the individual administrations – it was more difficult to act as decisively with countries like Italy, Romania, Bulgaria, Hungary and Croatia, which were treated not as conquered nations but as junior partners in an alliance.

One of the most intriguing examples of how the Nazis trod carefully with their allies is the case of Bulgaria. There were around 50,000 Jews living in Bulgaria – less than 1 per cent of the population. While there had been riots directed against the Jews early in the twentieth century and there were still staunch anti-Semites within the Bulgarian government, the country lacked the virulent anti-Semitism that existed, for example, in Slovakia. The regime signed up to the Axis in March 1941 only after Hitler had agreed that they could gain back territory lost to Romania in the First World War. The Bulgarians acquired more territory in April 1941, when they participated with the Germans in the invasion of Greece. Now Thrace and Macedonia became part of a 'Greater Bulgaria'.

The Bulgarians demonstrated their independence by refusing to participate in the war against the Soviet Union, a decision arising from Bulgaria's long historical association with Russia. However, the Bulgarian government was much more accommodating on the question of the Jews. In January 1941 the Bulgarians enacted a Law for the Protection of the Nation, which contained a host of anti-Semitic measures – such as banning marriages between Jewish and non-Jewish Bulgarians and excluding Jews from jobs in the civil service. But it wasn't until March 1943, as we shall see, that the first Jews were deported to their deaths from Bulgarian-occupied territory.

Circumstances were very different in Croatia, another Balkan nation, to the west of Bulgaria. Here, astonishingly, members of the SS were shocked by the level of brutality displayed by the Croat militia, the Ustaše – not towards the Jews, but towards the Serbs. The head of the Security Police and SD in Croatia reported to Himmler in February 1942 that Ustaše units had committed atrocities against 'defenceless old men, women and children, in a beastly manner'.[53] The primitive way the Croats were killing their enemies seems to have had a particular effect on the Germans. Another SS security service report described how the Ustaše had stabbed farmers with 'spear-like sticks'.[54] As far back as July 1941, the German ambassador to Croatia had brought the attention of the Croatian authorities to the numerous 'acts of terror' committed against the Serbs which gave 'rise to serious concerns'.[55] At the Nuremberg war trials in 1946, Alfred Jodl, Chief of the Wehrmacht Operations Staff, said that he had been aware of the 'unimaginable atrocities' committed by one particular Ustaše company in June 1942. The war diary of the Wehrmacht Operations Staff confirmed that the actions of this one Ustaše unit had been thought so appalling that the German Army field police had moved in and disarmed them.[56]

However, the Nazis did not seem to object to the atrocities committed by the Ustaše against the Jews. During 1942 the majority of the 40,000 Jews in Croatia were imprisoned in concentration camps within the country – most in the infamous camp at Jasenovac. The Germans now asked the Croatians to deport the surviving Jews and on 13 August the first transport left for Auschwitz.

Notwithstanding the immense brutality of the Croat Ustaše, the SS could never implement the Final Solution as they wished in Croatia. The fundamental problem for the Nazis, as we have already seen, was the relationship between a number of Croat leaders and individual Jews. As the German police attaché to Croatia, SS Obersturmbannführer (Lieutenant Colonel) Helm, put it in a report April 1944, 'to a great extent the Croatian leadership is related to Jews by marriage.' The ability of the Croatian leadership to declare individual Jews 'Honorary Aryans' meant that it was impossible ever to declare the 'Jewish question' in Croatia entirely 'settled'. As long as Croatia remained an ally, there was little that the Nazis could easily do about this other than, as SS Obersturmbannführer Helm suggested, attempt to 'persuade' the Croatian government to 'eliminate itself those Jews who are still in public positions' and 'apply a more severe standard in granting the rights of Honorary Aryans'.[57]

The Germans also had issues with the Hungarians' attitude to the Jews, even though the authorities had already intensified anti-Semitic persecution. As far back as August 1941 the Hungarians had expelled around 17,000 Jews who did not have Hungarian citizenship, sending them into the maelstrom in the east where almost all of them were murdered by Einsatzgruppen and SS units at Kamenets-Podolsk in western Ukraine. The Hungarians also presided over a brutal occupation of territory in Yugoslavia, and in January 1942 massacred hundreds of Jews at Novi Sad in Serbia. In addition, they forced many Hungarian Jews to serve in Labour Service Battalions where their fate depended on the whim of the commander of their unit. According to one report, a number of Jews in one labour unit were hosed down with cold water in winter so that they resembled 'ice statues'.[58] Another Hungarian officer decided to execute his unit en masse. Ninety-six were killed, thirty murdered by the officer himself. One estimate is that more than 30,000 Hungarian Jews never returned from the eastern front.

However, the Hungarian government were still not willing to deport all of the Jews within the country and the neighbouring territories under Hungary's control – a total of more than 750,000. Admiral Horthy, Hungarian Regent and head of state, was a sophisticated politician, and he balanced the need to be friendly to his German ally with the discontent that had followed from the disappearance of the Jews who had been handed over by the Hungarians to the Germans in 1941 and murdered at Kamenets-Podolsk. In March 1942 Horthy replaced the anti-Semitic and pro-Nazi Prime Minister, László Bárdossy, with the much more pragmatic figure of Miklós Kállay. Horthy had decided to play a long game, waiting to see how the war developed. He understood that it wasn't necessarily in Hungary's interests to hand over large numbers of Jews to the Nazis. After all, he must have thought, suppose the Allies won. What retribution might follow?

Hungary's actions, while disappointing for the Nazis, were not too surprising since Admiral Horthy never hid his pragmatic attitude. What was more unexpected was the behaviour of Romania. The Romanian government had previously demonstrated an enormous commitment to killing Jews. Romanian troops, working alongside Einsatzgruppen, had murdered 160,000 Jews in Ukraine in the wake of the 1941 invasion of the Soviet Union, and the Romanian authorities had deported 135,000 Jews from eastern Romania to Transnistria where around 90,000 died in camps.[59]

In the summer of 1942 it appeared that the Romanians would co-operate with the Germans and expel Jews from the Romanian heartland. On 8 August 1942, the *Bukarester Tagblatt*, a newspaper published in Romania by the German embassy, announced that preparations were being made to clear Romania 'definitively' of Jews.[60] Shortly afterwards the *Völkischer Beobachter* confirmed the news, saying that 'in the course of the next year, Romania will be completely purged of Jews.'[61] But then the discussions about the deportations started to unravel.

Marshal Antonescu prevaricated. He did not say that he was no longer prepared to deport the remaining Jews in Romania, but nor did he commit to an exact date when the deportations would start. He was dithering for a combination of reasons. Information, as we have seen, was reaching the world about the fate of the Jews. This meant that any head of state that handed over Jews to the Germans would now find it hard to plead ignorance at the end of the war. Not that this would matter for the Romanians if the Germans won, but that outcome did not seem certain. Despite the gains that the Wehrmacht were making as they advanced towards the River Volga and the mountains of the Caucasus, the entry of America into the war had caused many of those who had allied themselves to the Germans to reassess what the future might bring. Even some within the German leadership were voicing doubts. In September 1942, for instance, General Friedrich Fromm, who was in charge of the supply of armaments to the German Army, sent a report to Hitler which called for him to negotiate with the Allies and stop the war. Germany, in Fromm's view, simply could not compete with the firepower now at the disposal of the Allies.[62]

There was also an increasing lack of trust between the Romanians and the Germans. The Romanian government were upset by the perceived lack of respect shown to Radu Lecca, the Romanian Commissioner for Jewish Affairs, when he visited Berlin in the summer of 1942. At the same time, Gustav Richter, Eichmann's agent in Bucharest, reported that he thought some Romanian politicians were accepting bribes from Jews.[63] Antonescu was also lobbied by pressure groups within Romania about the fate of the Jews, particularly Archbishop Andrea Cassulo, the papal nuncio in Bucharest. Antonescu, like Admiral Horthy, was making a pragmatic political decision in the summer of 1942. He wasn't suddenly ashamed about the quarter of a million Jews that he had condemned to death the previous year. He was just responding to changing circumstances.

Hitler behaved very differently. He was more intransigent than ever, and gave free rein to his fanaticism in a speech on 30 September 1942. He called the Jews the 'wire-pullers of this insane man in the White House [i.e. Roosevelt]', and said, ominously, 'The Jews once laughed about my prophecies in Germany. I do not know whether they are still laughing today or whether they no longer feel like laughing. Today, too, I can assure you of one thing: they will soon not feel like laughing anymore anywhere.'[64] Many of his followers were just as belligerent. In October 1942, shortly after General Fromm had submitted his memorandum to Hitler saying that Germany was heading for catastrophe, Robert Ley, head of the German Labour Front (the Nazi trade union organization), said at a meeting in Essen in Germany, 'We have burnt all bridges behind us, intentionally we have. We have virtually solved the Jewish question in Germany. That alone is something incredible.'[65] And that same month Göring declared in a speech in Berlin, 'May the German Volk realize one thing: how necessary this fight has become! The terrible situation in which we lived [previously] was unbearable.'[66]

There was now a divergence between those who believed there might be a chance of exiting the war before absolute defeat, and those who understood that they had 'burnt all bridges' and would keep fighting until the end. These fanatics would continue to murder Jews out of conviction – almost regardless of the consequences. Setbacks on the battlefield would never divert them from their course. Indeed, as time went on, many of these same ideologues would feel their resolve to kill the Jews harden as military difficulties increased. For the war against the Jews, they felt, was one fight they could win.

13. Nazi Death Camps in Poland

(1942)

In the Nazi war against the Jews, the main battleground was in Poland – and never more so than during 1942. Not just because all of the major death camps were built on Polish soil, and Poland was the destination for the vast majority of the transports from across Europe, but because more Polish Jews died in the Holocaust than Jews from any other nation – around 3 million.[1] Half of all the Jews murdered in the course of the entire Final Solution.

On 19 July 1942, on a visit to Poland, Himmler ordered that the 'resettlement of the entire Jewish population of the General Government' should be 'carried out and completed by 31 December 1942'.[2] According to Himmler, a 'comprehensive clearing out' was necessary. This was a euphemistic way of saying that he wanted virtually all of these Jews to be murdered by the end of the year.

Enormous numbers of Polish Jews would now be sent direct to death camps where the vast majority would be murdered within hours of arrival. Only a handful would either temporarily be spared deportation because their work was deemed essential or be selected for the Jewish Sonderkommando units when they arrived at the death camp, and be forced to help the SS with the extermination process.

Himmler's order is a key moment in the history of the Holocaust – a vital part of an evolutionary process. At the start of 1942 the Nazis did not know for sure how many Jews they were going to kill in the short term. For Heydrich at Wannsee the confrontation with the Jews was still potentially a long-term process of attrition with large numbers of Jews worked to death over a period of time. What Himmler did in July 1942 was to say in effect, 'We will kill vast numbers of Jews, right now.' While that was a leap forward, it was one that was possible only because the Nazis had previously embarked on a gradual process of killing selected Jews. Only because of that past history, and the experience that they had gained along the way, could Himmler now be confident of committing mass murder on such a scale.

This was undoubtedly a decision taken in the weeks and months after the Wannsee conference, rather than the implementation of a decision taken at Wannsee or before. We know this partly because of the physical changes that were needed at the two existing specialized death camps with fixed gas chambers. Neither Bełżec nor Sobibór had the capacity to murder the numbers of Jews that Himmler now imagined. Only at this point were both expanded. At Bełżec all transports were temporarily suspended in June while larger gas chambers were built which would allow just over a thousand people to be murdered simultaneously. In the second week of July, transports began again, just in time to fulfil Himmler's programme of expansion. Similarly, at Sobibór there was a halt in the extermination programme – this time at the end of July. This was partly to allow repairs to be made to the railway line that transported Jews to the camp, but also to enlarge the existing gas chambers. Killing capacity now increased from 600 people at a time within the gas chambers to 1,200. Most significantly of all, an entirely new extermination camp at Treblinka – close to the main railway line to Warsaw, 60 miles away to the south-west – opened on 23 July just four days after Himmler's announcement. More Jews would eventually be murdered at Treblinka than at any other camp with the exception of Auschwitz.

A number of other factors came together at this point – all of which had occurred since the Wannsee conference. The first was an administrative change of considerable consequence. During the early months of 1942 Hans Frank, ruler of the General Government, had been called to account over allegations of corruption. As Frank's power weakened, Himmler assumed control over Jewish policy within the General Government subject only to Hitler's wishes. This was especially important because more Jews lived in the General Government than anywhere else – around 1.7 million. Himmler already had a subordinate in place in Lublin in the General Government – the Higher SS and Police Chief, Odilo Globocnik – who could be relied upon to organize the practical side of any expansion in the extermination plan.

There was also the question of the availability of food. A cut in rations to the German people in April 1942 had proved understandably unpopular, and the Nazi leadership remained determined that before any German went short of food others should starve first. Göring expressed this view at a meeting on 6 August 1942 when he imposed new demands on the occupied territories. 'This everlasting concern about foreign peoples must cease now, once and for all,' he told a group of senior officials. 'I have here before me reports on what you are expected to deliver. It is nothing at all when I consider your territories. It makes no difference to me in this connection if you say that your people will starve. Let them do so, as long as no German collapses from hunger.'[3] A few days before the meeting, Himmler had ordered that food deliveries to Warsaw in August should be restricted, and any farmers who didn't hand over the produce the Germans expected should be executed.[4] Another way, of course, of reducing the demand for food in the occupied territories was to kill many of the people who were currently eating it. In this case the Jews of the General Government.

An additional external event that would have intensified the murderous determination of both Hitler and Himmler was the assassination of Reinhard Heydrich. In an operation planned by the British SOE (Special Operations Executive), two Czech operatives attacked Heydrich's open-top Mercedes as he drove through Prague on the morning of 27 May 1942. Heydrich died of his wounds eight days later. At his funeral on 9 June, Himmler said, 'We have the sacred duty to atone for his death, to carry forward his work, and now, even more than before, mercilessly to annihilate the enemies of our people without showing any weakness.'[5] That evening, at a gathering of senior SS figures, Himmler declared that 'within a year . . . no one [i.e. Jews] will be migrating any more. For now things have finally got to be sorted out.'[6] The action to murder the Jews of the General Government would be named Operation Reinhard in honour of Heydrich.

Himmler met Hitler on many occasions during this period, and one persuasive analysis is that crucial discussions between them about the expansion of the killing were held on 23 April and 3 May. Himmler even met Hitler in July the day before he announced the 'comprehensive clearing out' of the Jews in the General Government, and it is inconceivable that the two of them did not once again discuss the forthcoming killings.[7] When Hitler crowed that the Jews would 'soon not feel like laughing anymore' two months later, it is very possible that he was referring obliquely to the massive increase in the extermination programme in Poland that had occurred since July.

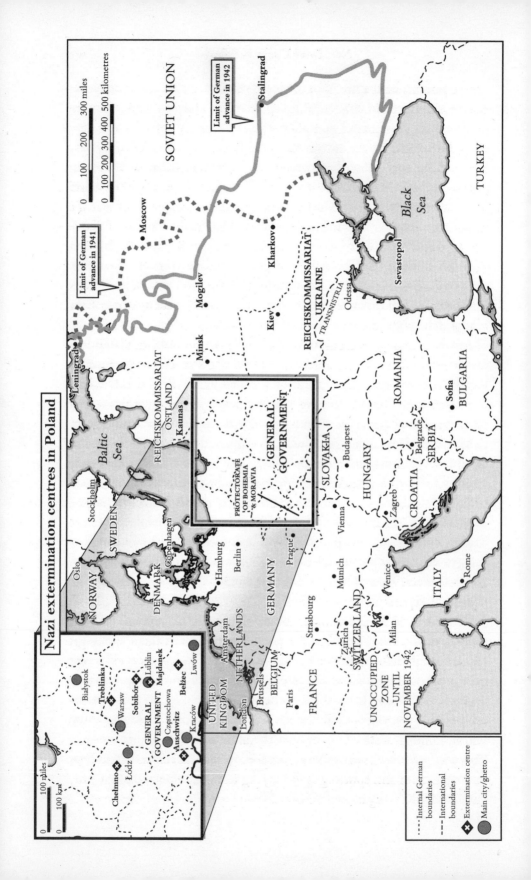

Nazi extermination centres in Poland

Around this same time, Himmler and Hitler were also contemplating the mass murder of millions of non-Jews. On 16 July, three days before he gave the order that almost all the Jews of the General Government should be killed by the end of the year, Himmler remarked privately that he had experienced the 'happiest day of his life', because he had just discussed with Hitler 'the greatest piece of colonization which the world will ever have seen'[8] and his own key role in creating it. This was the infamous General Plan for the East by which tens of millions of Slavic people would be condemned to slavery and death. Indeed, an indication of how ruthless Himmler would now be in pursuit of racial 'cleansing' occurred in the months following this 'happiest day'. In a massive 'Germanization' action that has not received the public attention post-war that it deserves, Himmler ordered the expulsion of large numbers of Poles from the region around Zamość in south-east Poland. Himmler's senior commander in Lublin, Odilo Globocnik, oversaw the forcible deportation of more than 50,000 Poles. The idea was that this whole area, rich in fertile soil, would be colonized by ethnic Germans. But once again the Nazis had overestimated their ability to accomplish the task, and their racial arrogance worked against them. Many Poles fled to the forests, formed resistance units and fought back. It was obviously impractical at this moment for the Nazis to pursue this plan in addition to the deportation of the Jews, and Himmler's colonization of the region was left unrealized.[9]

In the General Government more Jews were imprisoned in the Warsaw ghetto than anywhere else. More than twice as many Jews lived in this one small area of the Polish capital than Eichmann had said he wanted to deport that summer from France, Belgium and the Netherlands put together. Not surprisingly, therefore, in the summer of 1942 the more than 300,000 Jews in the Warsaw ghetto were an immediate target for the SS. Adam Czerniaków, chairman of the Jewish Council in the ghetto, wrote in his diary on 18 July that there were 'rumours' about deportation. The next day he recorded that he had done his best to reassure those Jews who were anxious. 'I try to hearten the delegations which come to see me,' he wrote. 'What it costs me they do not see. Today I took 2 headache powders, another pain reliever, and a sedative, but my head is still splitting. I am trying not to let the smile leave my face.' The following day an SS officer said to Czerniaków that he could tell the ghetto population that all talk of deportations was 'utter non-sense'. But it was a lie. Two days later, on 22 July, Czerniaków wrote: 'We were told that all the Jews irrespective of sex and age, with certain exceptions, will be deported to the East. By 4 p.m. today a contingent of 6,000 people must be provided. And this (at the minimum) will be the daily quota.'[10] Czerniaków's despair was focused, in particular, on what he called the 'tragic dilemma' of the children in orphanages. Did he have to hand them over as well? The answer, of course, was bound to be yes. The SS saw the children as a particular target – to them they were the most 'useless' of 'useless eaters'.

Unbeknown to Adam Czerniaków, one of Odilo Globocnik's officers had arrived several days before to plan the deportations with the help of the SS who oversaw the ghetto. They now sought the coopera-tion of the Jewish Council in organizing the transports via a combination of incentive and threat. The incentive was simple: the SS offered to exclude the members of the Jewish Council and their families from deportation. The threat was even more straightforward – if the Jewish Council didn't cooperate, their loved ones would be killed. Czerniaków was told on 22 July that 'if the deportation was impeded in any way' his wife would 'be the first one to be shot as a hostage'.[11]

All this was too much for Adam Czerniaków. On 23 July he commit-ted suicide by swallowing a capsule of cyanide. This made no difference to the SS or to the deportations. They appointed another head of the Jewish Council, Marek Lichtenbaum, and carried on as before. More than 2,000 members of the Jewish Order Police within the ghetto now helped organize the deportations. Like the members of the Jewish Council, by doing so they saved – temporarily at least – their own lives and the lives of their wives and children.

No one living inside the ghetto knew for certain what would happen to the Jews who were deported. But some information about what was happening to Jews had filtered back to Warsaw. Emmanuel Ringelblum was particularly well informed and had even heard about one of the death camps by name. He wrote in his diary in June 1942, just before the deportations began, that the Germans were 'following this plan: The "non-productive elements", children up to the age of ten and old people over sixty, are locked in sealed railroad cars, which are guarded by a German detail and transported to an unknown destination . . . where every trace of the "resettled" Jews disappears. The fact that no one has so far succeeded in escaping from the death camp in Belzec, that up till now not a single Jewish or Polish witness of the extermination operation in Belzec has survived, is the clearest indication of how careful they are that the news not be published among their own people.'[12]

Ringelblum was particularly critical of the role of the Jewish police during the deportations, who 'said not a single word of protest against this revolting assignment to lead their own brothers to the slaughter'. In his judgement, and based on his own observations, 'For the most part, the Jewish police showed an incomprehensible brutality . . . Merciless and violent, they beat those who tried to resist.'[13]

The action against the Jews of the Warsaw ghetto, starting on 23 July, was one of the most atrocious of all the horrors of the Holocaust. 'The turmoil and terror is appalling,' wrote Abraham Lewin in his diary on 1 August. 'Mothers lose their children. A weak old woman is carried onto the bus. The tragedies cannot be captured in words. The Rabbi from 17 Dzielna Street has been seized and apparently shot. Children walking in the street are seized.'[14]

Halina Birenbaum, then twelve years old, remembers, 'Every day there were less and less people, every day more and more empty apartments.' The Jews took to hiding within the fabric of their apartments 'behind the wardrobe or behind the bed', but soon 'the Germans and their Ukrainian helpers, together with the Jewish police', started to 'go from floor to floor in each apartment breaking the doors with iron bars . . . I heard when they were getting the Jews out, and the screaming, and the shots. Every day is like that – from the morning until evening.'[15]

Sixty-five thousand Jews were deported to Treblinka in the first ten days of the action. To begin with the SS didn't deport those who had been granted exemption, but soon, if they had trouble filling a train, they would take anyone they could find. The Jewish police were told that if they did not serve up five people each – every single day – then their own loved ones would be sent in their place. By such methods the great majority of the Jews were expelled from the ghetto by the end of September.

Almost all of the Jews from the Warsaw ghetto were sent to the death camp at Treblinka. This, the last specialized death camp to be constructed, was the largest and most deadly.[16] Around 850,000 people – some estimates say over 900,000 – were murdered here between summer 1942 and autumn 1943. And within that timeframe, the most murderous period was from the end of July until the end of August 1942 when an estimated 312,500 people were killed – around a quarter of a million of them from the Warsaw ghetto.[17] The SS achieved this appalling killing record in part because Treblinka had been built with a railway spur leading directly into the camp. This was of great assistance to the SS, who were able to speed up the unloading of the Jews and their transportation to the gas chambers. As for the internal layout of the camp, it was similar to Bełżec and Sobibór. There was an arrival area and an extermination area containing the gas chambers, with the two connected via a narrow pathway or 'tube', plus separate sections for the guards' and Sonderkommandos' accommodation.

Another reason for the astonishing scale of the murders at Treblinka in the summer of 1942 was not technical, but personal – the ambition of thirty-one-year-old Dr Irmfried Eberl, the commandant of Treblinka and the only medical doctor ever to run an extermination camp. Dr Eberl has already featured in this history, when he was the director of the euthanasia killing centre at Brandenburg. He thus had plenty of experience in mass murder before starting work at Treblinka. And just as he showed every sign of liking his work at Brandenburg, so he appeared to relish the opportunity to murder Jews. In June 1942, while preparing the extermination camp for the arrival of the first transport from Warsaw, he wrote to his wife, Ruth, that his life was 'very busy' and that he 'enjoyed it'.[18] In another letter to her at the end of July, shortly after the Jews had started arriving, he said: 'I know that I haven't written much lately, but I couldn't help that, as the last "Warsaw weeks" have gone by in an unimaginable rush.' He said that even if the day had 'a hundred hours' it would not be 'quite enough' for him to complete his work, and that in the pursuit of his duties he had managed to gain 'nerves of steel'. He was also, he claimed, able to get his staff to 'go along' with him and he was 'glad and proud of this achievement'.[19]

The key to operating an efficient death camp, the SS had learnt from experience, was subterfuge. So Treblinka was disguised as a transit camp, with the new arrivals hurried through the killing process as swiftly as possible towards the 'showers' in the 'disinfecting' block. An obvious precondition for this deception was that the presence of large numbers of dead bodies was hidden from the arriving Jews. This was accomplished not just by seeking to bury the corpses as quickly as possible but also by weaving dead branches into the wire fences that divided different areas within the camp in order to hide what was happening.

To begin with, the killing appeared to progress efficiently for the SS, with about 5,000 to 7,000 Jews murdered each day. But around the middle of August the systems at the killing factory at Treblinka started to fall apart. Part of the reason was an increase in the number of Jews sent to the camp – arrivals almost doubled to over 10,000 a day. This meant that the SS and their helpers could not adequately clean up the camp between transports in order to preserve the fiction that this was merely a transit camp. Once this task was not accomplished on schedule, the consequences for the rest of the murder process were immediate. The SS had to order arriving trains to wait at Treblinka station before the carriages were shunted up the railway spur into the camp. This only exacerbated the collapse of the deception, because it meant that large numbers of Jews died within the freight wagons. Cleaning the wagons of corpses took much longer than escorting the Jews to the gas chambers, adding yet more delays to the working of the camp.

There was also the problem, for the Nazis, of the smell. The air around the camp was filled with noxious odours. Eugenia Samuel, then a schoolgirl who lived close by, remembers that 'the smell of the disintegrating corpses was just terrible. You couldn't open a window or go out because of the stench. You cannot imagine such a stench.'[20]

Oskar Berger was one of the Jews who arrived at Treblinka just as the fabric of the camp was collapsing. When he disembarked from the train, on 22 August 1942, he saw 'hundreds of bodies lying all around'.[21] The SS and their Ukrainian helpers attempted to control the new arrivals by shooting at them from the roofs of buildings. This only made the panic worse, as the 'air was filled with screaming and weeping'.

Another new arrival, Abraham Krzepicki, was 'confronted' in the camp 'by a staggering sight: a huge number of corpses, lying one next to the other. I estimate there were 20,000 corpses there . . . most of whom had suffocated in the freight cars. Their mouths remained open, as if they were gasping for another breath of air.' He was selected by the SS to help clear up this nightmare scene. But, notwithstanding the terrible situation at the camp, the relentless train schedule did not stop: 'At night another transport arrived at the camp. We ran toward the cars. I was shocked. All the cars were filled only with the dead – asphyxiated. They were lying on top of one another in layers, to the ceiling of the freight car. The sight was so awful, it is difficult to describe.'[22]

Irmfried Eberl's immense over-confidence, as well as the increase in the numbers of transports in August, was behind this horror. 'Dr Eberl's ambition', said August Hingst, a member of the SS at Treblinka, 'was to reach the highest possible numbers and exceed all the other camps. So many transports arrived that the disembarkation and gassing of the people could no longer be handled.'[23] There were also rumours that discipline had broken down at Treblinka and that some valuables stolen from the Jews had not been sent back to the Reich but taken by the guards at the camp – even that Dr Eberl, when he was drunk, ordered a female Jew to dance naked for him.[24]

When reports of the disintegration of Treblinka reached Dr Eberl's superiors they decided to pay him a visit. Towards the end of August, Odilo Globocnik travelled to the camp together with a group of senior officers, including Christian Wirth, the first commandant of Bełżec and the newly appointed inspector of the Operation Reinhard death camps. 'In Treblinka, everything was in chaos,' said SS man Josef Oberhauser, who worked for Wirth and saw what happened when the delegation arrived at the camp. 'Dr Eberl would be dismissed immediately . . . Globocnik said in the course of this conversation that if Dr Eberl were not his fellow countryman, he would arrest him and bring him before an SS and police court.'[25]

Wirth chose Franz Stangl, currently commandant of Sobibór, to replace Dr Eberl. Because Sobibór was temporarily closed while the railway line that ran next to the camp was repaired and the gas chambers enlarged, Stangl was free to take over almost at once. Even so, Wirth decided to stay on at the camp for a few weeks to oversee the cleaning-up process, together with Stangl. This was a major undertaking, as witnessed on his arrival by one of the cruellest of all the SS figures working in the death camps, SS Oberscharführer (Company Sergeant Major) Kurt Franz, an SS officer nicknamed 'Doll' because of his supposed baby-faced looks: 'In the camp there were bodies lying everywhere . . . These bodies were dragged through the camp to the upper section by Jews. The working Jews were forced to keep moving by the [Ukrainian] guards, also by the Germans . . . There was tremendous confusion and a horrible din . . . During my walk I established that some of the guard squads were with girls and had put down their rifles.'[26] Kurt Franz's specialty at Bełżec had been dealing with the auxiliaries – guards who had been selected from Soviet POWs to work at the death camps – collectively known, as we have seen, as 'Ukrainians'. So he now tried to establish order among them.

Transports to Treblinka had to be suspended between 28 August and 3 September while the camp was cleared of thousands of corpses. The dead bodies were burnt in ditches and the smoke that filled the sky was noticeable for miles around. Throughout this process, Christian Wirth was the dominant force. 'Wirth conducted talks with the German staff, mainly at 11 o'clock in the evening,' said SS Scharführer (Sergeant Major) Franz Suchomel. 'These talks took place in the presence of Stangl . . . His [Wirth's] instructions were detailed.'[27]

Just as there had been at Sobibór, there were tensions between Stangl and Wirth. According to Suchomel, after Stangl had examined the extermination operation at Treblinka, he recommended that buckets should be placed in the tube – the path that led from the arrival area of the camp to the gas chambers – because the women 'all defecated you know, while they ran, or stood there, waiting'. Stangl said he had previously put buckets in the tube and it had proved helpful. Wirth answered, 'I don't care a damn what you did with the shit in Sobibor. Let them beshit themselves. It can be cleaned up afterwards.'[28]

Christian Wirth, like Dr Eberl, gave every indication that he revelled in his work. His adjutant, Josef Oberhauser, remarked that 'His most outstanding features were iron relentlessness, unconditional obedience, belief in the Führer, absolute insensitivity and ruthlessness. These traits already characterized him in the euthanasia [action], where I got to know him; but he really was in his element when it came to the extermination of the Jews.'[29] With Wirth 'in his element', the extermination process at Treblinka began again with the resumption of transports from the Warsaw ghetto on 3 September.

Kalman Taigman was one of the Jews from the Warsaw ghetto crammed into a freight wagon that September en route to Treblinka. While some Jews on the train believed that they were being sent to their deaths, he still thought that the Nazis might have spoken the truth about what lay ahead. 'We were told when we were still in the ghetto', he says, 'that we were going to the east to work in all kinds of factories. So I thought that I was a young and healthy man and that I was probably being taken to work.'[30] But on arrival at Treblinka these illusions were swiftly shattered. 'It was unbelievable,' he says. 'They opened the freight cars and started yelling, "Get out!" in German, of course, yelling, and many of the people who were still standing and breathing came out, but there were some who were already corpses inside the freight cars and they didn't come out.' From the healthy Jews who arrived, the SS made a selection and Kalman Taigman was one of those they picked. A relatively large number of Jews were chosen to work in the camp from these early transports to Treblinka in September, in order to ensure that the camp was kept clean and the chaos of Eberl's regime was not repeated. Out of those chosen from Kalman's transport, one group started emptying the freight wagons of bodies and another began sorting out the belongings of the Jews who had been taken to the gas chambers.

Kalman was later part of a commando that cleaned out the barracks where the women had their heads shaved before entering the gas chambers. 'When we cleaned these barracks of the clothing,' he remembers, 'there were cases where we found babies underneath these piles. I guess the mothers left them there, maybe so they might be rescued.' When he and his comrades found these babies they carried them to a fenced-off area of the camp where the sick were taken, known as the *Lazarett* (German for military hospital). But when Jews arrived at the *Lazarett* they discovered that, just as at Sobibór, it wasn't a hospital at all but an execution area where the sick were shot and then thrown into a pit. 'There was a white fence around it,' says Kalman, 'and on this fence there was a sign of the Red Cross, so people who came there didn't know where they were going at all . . . such things are hard to describe.' He remembers that the babies found in the barracks were either shot and thrown into the pit or – if bodies were already being burnt – thrown directly on to the fire. 'How did I feel?' says Kalman. 'I didn't feel anything . . . I became an automaton. No thoughts. I only worried about not getting beaten and sometimes I worried about having a full stomach and that's it. I didn't think and I didn't feel. I saw hell if such a thing exists.'[31]

The new SS regime at Treblinka ensured that the camp was kept as spotless as possible. 'The path that led to the gas chambers had to be clean and tidy,' says Kalman. 'Each time we had to bring new clean yellow sand and scatter it.' During his time at the camp, he says, 'the death machinery worked there very efficiently.'

By the end of the third week of September most of the Warsaw Jews had perished in the gas chambers of Treblinka. The German authorities now decided temporarily to halt the deportations from Warsaw after a final mass selection that allowed 35,000 Jews to remain for the moment in the ghetto – around 10 per cent of the pre-deportation ghetto population. There were also more than 25,000 other Jews left in the ghetto – those who had managed to hide themselves, often in cellars, in attics and behind walls.

The pause in the deportations from Warsaw allowed the Nazis to send Jews from other ghettos in Poland to die in Treblinka. The biggest ghetto clearance during this new phase occurred in Częstochowa, west of Lublin, where about 35,000 Jews were forced on to trains and sent to Treblinka. Jews were also sent to the death camp from many other ghettos, large and small. Samuel Willenberg, for instance, then nineteen years old, was caught in Opatów in south-east Poland and transported to Treblinka during this new phase. By now – the autumn of 1942 – rumours about the fate of the Jews were widespread, and as his train passed through a station he heard Polish children shout out, 'Jews! You'll be turned into soap!'[32] But, like many other Jews transported to the death camps during the Holocaust, those crammed into Samuel Willenberg's freight car found it difficult to accept that the Nazis wanted to kill them all. Many still hoped that such a place could not really exist. 'It was hard to believe,' says Samuel. 'I was here [Treblinka] and still I could not believe it at first.'

Almost everyone on Samuel Willenberg's transport died within a few hours of arriving at the camp. He survived only because of a chance encounter. One of the Jewish Sonderkommandos, already working in the camp, asked him where he was from. Samuel, who thought the man looked familiar, answered that he was from Opatów, but had also spent time in Warsaw and Częstochowa, where he had been born. 'Częstochowa,' echoed the prisoner, who was obviously from the same place. The prisoner asked Samuel for his name, and added cryptically, 'Say you are a bricklayer.'

As a result of this short conversation, Samuel Willenberg escaped the gas chambers. The SS lined up the Jews who had just entered the camp and asked if there were any bricklayers among the new arrivals. Samuel immediately volunteered. He thought, correctly as it turned out, that he could acquire enough of the trade quickly enough to fool the SS. So he became a member of the Sonderkommando.

Samuel observed first hand how efficiently the SS dealt with new arrivals. He saw that when the women had their heads shaved they 'gained hope, for if they are going to have their hair cut, it means there is going to be some life after . . . for hygiene is necessary in a camp'. Making the incoming Jews take off their clothes also worked to the advantage of the SS. 'A man who takes his shoes off and then is ordered "Strip!" and is naked – that man is no longer a human being,' says Samuel, 'no longer a master of himself. He covers certain parts of his body, he is embarrassed. Suddenly, he has a thousand problems of which he has not been aware in his normal life, which he did not have as he was never forced to walk about naked – except perhaps as a child – among people, among friends. Suddenly everyone is naked! And the Germans, you see, took advantage of that. And on top of that, the lashing, "Quick! Schnell!" At that point one wanted to run somewhere as fast as one could, run somewhere, no matter where.'

At Treblinka, Samuel spent much of his time sorting out the belongings of the murdered Jews. 'It looked like a Persian bazaar,' he says, 'open suitcases, spread-out sheets, and on each sheet lay different things. Trousers separately from shirts, from woollen things, it all had to be sorted. The gold lay separate in the bags . . . Each of us had a sheet spread out next to him where we put photos, documents, diplomas.' Samuel and the rest of his commando were often supervised by Kurt Franz. He remembers Franz as 'The worst of them [of the SS] . . . He was a handsome man, posing as Napoleon and demanding constant admiration. Those were his happiest days! He had a great time here. He was a bandit, a real bandit.'[33]

Franz took pleasure in setting his dog, a massive St Bernard called Barry, on the prisoners. He also enjoyed personally administering pain. 'He was an expert at whipping, twenty-five or fifty lashes,' wrote Oskar

Strawczynski, another Sonderkommando. 'He did it with pleasure, without hurrying. He had his own technique for raising the whip and striking it down.'[34]

Franz was a committed Nazi and had worked at Buchenwald concentration camp before the war. Like a number of other guards in the death camps, he had also spent time in the T4 euthanasia programme. He had thus been working for many years in an environment, and for an organization, that preached absolute hatred of Jews and asserted that it was legitimate to kill those the state thought 'unworthy of life'. As a result, he almost certainly thought the people he was dominating, torturing and killing were not really 'human' at all. But that can't be the whole explanation for his sadistic actions, since some other SS in the same situation did not appear to take the same pleasure in inflicting the pain that Franz did. It is a reminder that members of the SS who decided to carry on working in a death camp still had a choice about how to behave – one between becoming a sadistic murderer, or merely a cold-hearted one. Kalman Taigman's view, having observed the SS and their Ukrainian helpers closely at Treblinka, is that 'each person has the instincts of an animal, but since we live in a normal way we don't show it – it doesn't come out. But there are times when a person turns into something else and what comes out of him is what was hidden [all along].'

Only a fraction of all those sent to the death camps of Sobibór, Bełżec and Treblinka survived the war – perhaps not more than 150 people. And each of these individuals owed their survival to a large extent to good fortune. Samuel Willenberg, for instance, says, 'It could have turned out differently in a thousand different ways. It did not matter what I said or did – I could have been burnt just as well. I would have ended up in the ash. It was all a question of luck . . . and maybe a bit of hot-headedness.'[35] Luck was part of the reason why he survived, but it was not the whole reason. Both Samuel Willenberg and Kalman Taigman also possessed particular attributes that helped them endure their experience at Treblinka. Both were young at the time – in their late teens when they arrived at the camp – and both were strong and determined. Both were also men – far fewer women were selected for Sonderkommando work. Taigman coped in part, as we have seen, by turning himself into an 'automaton', while Willenberg had an extraordinary ability to look on the positive side – even in a death camp. After the war, he remarked that 'others suffered more. It wasn't like I was actually one of those forced to work in the gas chambers. They worked in terrible conditions. They had to drag the corpses out of the gas chambers as fast as they could.'[36] So, surprising as it may seem, he drew some comfort from the fact that other Jewish workers at Treblinka were suffering even more than he was. Both he and Taigman were eventually to escape from the camp during the revolt in August 1943.

In addition to Treblinka, Sobibór and Bełżec, a fourth murder camp under the aegis of Odilo Globocnik was in operation during 1942. This place, called Majdanek, was situated just 3 miles away from Globocnik's office in Lublin. Majdanek was an unusual camp within the system: neither a prisoner-of-war camp nor a concentration camp, nor a specialized death camp, nor a massive combination of concentration and death camp like Auschwitz, but a mixture, on a smaller scale, of all of them. Even the Nazis seemed unsure how to label the camp. Until early 1943 the place was officially the 'Prisoner of War Camp of the Waffen SS in Lublin', while other German documents at the same time called it a 'concentration camp'.[37]

Majdanek's evolution mirrored in many ways the development of the Nazis' Final Solution. Like Auschwitz Birkenau, it was originally conceived as a camp for Soviet prisoners of war. Construction began in the autumn of 1941, and barracks for around 20,000 prisoners were completed by the end of the year. From the start Majdanek was a place where death was commonplace. Starving prisoners slept on the bare ground in unheated barracks through the freezing Polish winter of 1941–2. They were at risk from a range of infections, including typhoid. But by the time new arrivals came to the camp in the spring of 1942, Majdanek's function had changed. No longer a prisoner-of-war camp, it had now become a sorting centre for the Final Solution. Several thousand Slovak Jews were sent to the camp between the end of March and the middle of June 1942. Occasionally trains transporting Jews to Sobibór would stop near by and a selection would be made, with some Jews diverted to Majdanek as forced labourers.

Gas chambers were constructed behind the shower blocks at Majdanek. No other camp had the gas chambers so close to the genuine showers used by arriving Jews who had passed the initial selection. The position of the gas chambers meant that, just as with the gassings at the crematorium in the main camp at Auschwitz, the SS had difficulty in keeping the killings secret, and – as at Auschwitz – the SS had to rev motor engines at Majdanek next to the gas chambers in order to drown out the screams of those trapped inside.[38]

While there were rumours about the true function of Treblinka and some of the other death camps, Majdanek remained relatively unknown. When, for example, Halina Birenbaum was sent to the camp with her mother from the Warsaw ghetto, in the second wave of deportations in the spring of 1943, she remembers that there was 'hugging and kissing' among the Jews when they discovered that they were not en route to Treblinka. 'If it's not Treblinka,' she says, 'and we hadn't heard of Majdanek, then it's a sign that we are going to a labour camp and not to our deaths. So, big celebration!'[39] Halina was further reassured by her first sight of Majdanek. 'There is a camp, and there are barracks, and we will work. Now they'll take us to a shower and give us different clothes, and they'll take us to these barracks and whoever is willing and can work, nothing will happen to you. The barracks you see over there, there's probably beds and food and water and everything will be good.'

The SS directed Halina along with a group of other Jews to one of the shower blocks at the camp. As she entered the building she suddenly became anxious: 'My mum is not coming in, and everything is turning upside down in my stomach. What? Is she not going to come? She'll never be here again, my mother?' Halina looked frantically around to try and find her but without success. Suddenly she realized that her mother must have been taken away, and that Majdanek, like Treblinka, was a place of murder: 'I have no words at all. I didn't cry. It was beyond tears. It's all over. There is nothing any more. There is no sky. No more earth. As if they took and broke my legs and hands. So I started to go round the shower. "Mother is gone. Mother is gone. Mother is gone."'[40]

Halina was admitted to Majdanek, and after a short time she consoled herself with the knowledge that at least her mother had been spared the experience of life in the camp. When she saw how the prisoners were beaten she couldn't bear the thought that her 'distinguished, modest, clean' mother would have been hurt in such a way. 'What could be worse than Majdanek?' she says.[41]

Stefania Perzanowska, a Polish doctor imprisoned in Majdanek, confirmed the brutality of the regime in the camp. 'Above all there was beating,' she said. 'Beating for any reason and for no reason. Beating over the head with a bullwhip at roll call, with a fist to face, over a special stool with a piece of rubber or cane . . . They all beat us.' She remembers one SS guard 'who was capable of coming into the hospital even at two in the morning to beat us across the face because he was drunk and had to take it out on someone, right down through all the camp ranks'. But it was a female guard called Else Ehrich who 'probably broke all the records. She beat women with a passion with frigid cruelty in her eyes. No SS woman could match her for strength or inflicting pain. She always beat us until she drew blood.'[42]

Another Majdanek survivor confirms how violent Else Ehrich could be towards inmates. 'It seemed to us that she hit us with complete intentionality, short and hard,' said Hanna Narkiewicz-Jodko, 'and employed particularly humiliating and denigrating language. She usually kicked and hit us with her riding crop, which I saw over and over again.'[43]

Such testimony reminds us that it was not just men who abused prisoners in the camps, women participated in the mistreatment as well. Known as *Aufseherinnen*, 'female overseers', a number of women were used as guards in camps such as Majdanek and Auschwitz – their appearance coinciding with the arrival of female prisoners. Himmler never gave the *Aufseherinnen* full SS status, although they nonetheless held the power of life and death over the inmates. But women only ever made up a small percentage of the overall garrison of these particular camps – there were just twenty-eight during the period of operation of Majdanek, for instance, and fewer than 10 per cent of concentration camp guards were women across the whole Nazi system during the war.[44]

Though the regime was particularly brutal, Majdanek always remained small in comparison to Auschwitz. Just under 25,000 prisoners were incarcerated in Majdanek at peak capacity in the spring of 1943. And uniquely among the camps that contained gas chambers, Majdanek's killers could murder with either bottled carbon monoxide – like the extermination chambers of the adult euthanasia scheme – or Zyklon B – like the gas chambers of Auschwitz. Why Majdanek, of all the camps, had the capacity to kill with both methods has never been determined.

For many years after the war it was only possible to calculate the death toll approximately at the camps of Majdanek, Treblinka, Bełżec and Sobibór. But in 2000 a decrypted German telegram was found in files held at the Public Record Office in London that revealed the Nazis' own estimate. This telegram, dated 11 January 1943 and written by SS Sturmbannführer (Major) Hermann Höfle, one of the organizers of Operation Reinhard, recorded in detail the number killed at each of the camps up to the end of 1942: the figures were 24,733 at Majdanek, 101,370 at Sobibór, 434,508 at Bełżec and 713,555[45] at Treblinka – a total of 1,274,166 human beings murdered.[46]

The Nazis managed to commit mass murder on this incredible scale with only a small number of SS supervising the process. Treblinka, the camp where more than half of this vast total died, required only two dozen or so SS to oversee the whole extermination operation. The contrast with the thousands and thousands of SS, Einsatzgruppen and other security forces needed to shoot Jews en masse in the Soviet Union is stark. Significantly, Majdanek, the place on Höfle's list that killed fewest people, needed a larger SS garrison than the others, because more prisoners were kept alive for longer.

The insight the Höfle telegram offers is thus straightforward. Just a handful of SS could kill large numbers of their fellow human beings in a small area, as long as mechanized means were employed and the new arrivals were killed within hours of disembarking.

At the start of 1942 the Nazis had not known if it was possible to kill so many people so quickly. By the end of the year they had discovered the answer – it was.

14. Killing, and Persuading Others to Help
(1942–1943)

All these murders took place against the background of the bloodiest war in history. And the course of that war would, in turn, influence the extent to which the Nazis' allies were willing to cooperate with the Holocaust. But it was not always easy, during 1942, for observers to work out exactly what the result of the war was likely to be.

While it was certainly true that the Red Army had prevented the Germans taking Moscow in December 1941, that Soviet victory had been followed by defeat. In May 1942 the Soviets had attacked the Germans around Kharkov in Ukraine, at a point where the Red Army had a large advantage, outnumbering the Germans two to one. But, in an action that demonstrated that numerical superiority does not guarantee success if tactics are deficient, the Soviet soldiers soon ran into trouble. The Germans retreated and allowed the Red Army to move forward, only to move in subsequently from the flanks and encircle large numbers of them. Soviet soldiers panicked. Many tried to run, but they were already caught in the German trap. More than a quarter of a million Red Army soldiers were killed, wounded or captured.

Boris Vitman, an officer in the Soviet 6th Army, was one of those who were taken prisoner. Once captured, he remembers how the Germans immediately demonstrated that they were fighting a brutal, ideological war. The Germans first looked for Jews and commissars among the Red Army prisoners, and when they found them, they split them into two groups. They took the commissars away and Boris Vitman never saw them again, but he did witness what happened to the ten or so Jews they had identified: 'The Jews were given spades and told to dig a trench. It began to rain. After a while I could only see the tops of their heads. An SS man was hitting them to make them dig faster. When the trench was deep enough, he picked up a Russian machine gun and fired, shooting several salvos into the trench. We could hear them moaning. Then some more SS men turned up and finished them off. They were killed only because they were Jews. This had a shocking effect on me because then I saw what Nazism was. We were told [by the Germans] that the Jews and commissars cannot have control over us any more, that the Germans had come to liberate us and soon we're going home. But I only knew I had to fight the Germans to the very end.'[1]

Having humiliated the Red Army at Kharkov, Hitler now launched his own offensive, codenamed Operation Blue. The idea was for the Wehrmacht to advance towards the River Volga in the south-east of the Soviet Union and then down into the mountains of the Caucasus and the Soviet oil fields that lay beyond. It was a wildly ambitious plan. And to start with, it seemed to be working. But the problem the Germans faced was that the further they advanced to the east, the more their supply lines were stretched, a difficulty that was exacerbated by Hitler's decision to separate his forces and send one thrust south to the Caucasus and the other east to the Volga. As far as General Halder, Chief of Staff of the German Army, was concerned, Hitler was in danger of letting his over-confidence damage his judgement. 'This chronic tendency to underrate enemy capabilities is gradually assuming grotesque proportions and develops into a positive danger,' Halder wrote in his diary on 23 July 1942. 'The situation is getting more and more intolerable.'[2] Halder's words were prophetic. A few months later the German Army was engaged in an intractable, war-defining fight in the streets of a city on the western bank of the Volga called Stalingrad.

The Germans didn't have the resources or expertise to remove the Red Army soldiers from the rubble in Stalingrad. 'The Russians had the advantage in trench warfare and hand-to-hand combat – there's no doubt,' says Joachim Stempel, a German officer who fought in Stalingrad. 'As a tank unit, we were used to driving tanks and trying to bring the enemy down with tanks and then stopping, clearing the area and moving forward. But that was all forgotten in the past, a long time ago.'[3] Now it was the turn of the Red Army to show that they could mount encirclement operations on a large scale. On 19 November 1942, the Soviets launched Operation Uranus, an attempt to trap the German Sixth Army in Stalingrad. The plan worked and the Sixth Army finally surrendered on 2 February 1943.

Hitler had told the German people in a speech on 30 September 1942: 'you can rest assured, no man will take us away from this place [Stalingrad].'[4] Now his promise was revealed as worthless. To make matters worse for the Germans, the defeat at Stalingrad was part of a pattern that seemed to show by the start of 1943 that they were losing the war. In the autumn of 1942 Field Marshal Erwin Rommel's forces had been defeated at El Alamein – less because of the talents of the British commander Bernard Montgomery than because Rommel's soldiers, who were outnumbered by the Allies, didn't have enough fuel to manoeuvre their tanks effectively. At sea, the German fleet was hampered by a combination of lack of fuel and inadequate air cover. Finally, on 8 November 1942, the Allies had landed in North Africa and begun the long fight that would eventually take them in the summer and autumn of 1943 first into Sicily and then on to the Italian mainland.

In January 1943, the Allies had publicly proclaimed at the Casablanca conference that they would accept nothing less from the Germans than 'unconditional surrender' and that they intended to 'impose punishment and retribution in full' on the 'guilty, barbaric leaders'[5] of the countries currently opposing them. But behind the scenes matters were not quite as clear cut. Take the case of Admiral François Darlan, the former Prime Minister of Vichy France and collaborator with the Nazis. He was captured during the Allied invasion of North Africa but he wasn't imprisoned, or tried for any offence. Instead, in an extreme example of pragmatic politics, he was confirmed by the Allies as head of the civil government in French North Africa. The Allies needed to ensure the cooperation of the former Vichy forces in France as swiftly as possible, and this was one way to do it. Admiral Darlan remained deeply unpopular with the British and Americans, and was killed on Christmas Eve 1942 by an anti-Vichy assassin.

Shortly after Darlan's death, President Roosevelt revealed the same deeply pragmatic side of his nature during discussions about the Jews with General Charles Noguès, the former Vichy commander in Morocco. At the time of the Casablanca conference, General Noguès remarked that it would be 'sad' if after the war the Jews could dominate the economy of North Africa. Roosevelt sought to dispel his anxiety by saying that if the Jews were restricted to a certain proportion of professions, this would 'eliminate the specific and understandable complaints which the Germans have towards the Jews in Germany, namely, that while they represented a small part of the population, over fifty percent of the lawyers, doctors, school teachers, college professors, etc, in Germany were

Jews'.[6] Leaving aside the obvious factual inaccuracies in Roosevelt's statement – Jewish representation in these professions in Germany had certainly not been 50 per cent – his words demonstrated how even the leader of the largest Western democracy was prepared to give voice to slurs against the Jews.

This kind of confidential conversation was not made public during the war. So the message that went out from Casablanca remained one of unshakeable resolve to punish the 'guilty' and 'barbaric' leaders of the countries that opposed the Allies. For the Nazi leadership, of course, such threats were meaningless as they already knew there was no way back. In March 1943, Goebbels recorded in his diary a conversation with Hermann Göring that revealed their thinking: 'Göring is fully aware of what we would be faced with if we weakened in this war. He has no illusions about this. Particularly when it comes to the Jewish question, we are so involved that there is no escape for us any more. And that is a good thing. Experience shows that a movement and a people that have burnt all bridges, fight with even more determination than those who still have an opportunity of retreat.'[7]

For those who collaborated with the Germans, the situation was not so clear cut. Many of them did not appear to think they had necessarily 'burnt all bridges'. In France, for example, the French police were less cooperative with the Germans than they had been the previous year. The police particularly disliked arresting and sending French nationals to Germany as forced labour – a measure the Germans had introduced in February 1943.[8]

In Romania, events over the winter of 1942–3 had strengthened the resolve of Marshal Antonescu, and he now refused outright to hand over the remaining Romanian Jews to the Nazis. He met Hitler in April 1943 and resisted pressure to cooperate further on the Jewish question. The meeting was a clash between one political leader – Hitler – who believed that any setbacks on the battlefield should act as an incentive to treat the Jews still more harshly, and another – Antonescu – who was looking for a way out of the mess in which he and his country were now wallowing. Some members of Antonescu's government were even trying to contact the Allies in order to extricate their country from the war – a development that Hitler knew about.[9]

Hitler was even more forthright in the discussions he held shortly afterwards with another ally, Admiral Horthy. In Hitler's view, Horthy's Hungary had been extremely dilatory in its treatment of the Jews. And like Antonescu, Horthy's colleagues were attempting to sound out the Allies about a way of exiting the war. This wasn't a surprising development, since Horthy knew better than most the scale of the Stalingrad defeat. The Hungarian Second Army, fighting alongside the Germans on the eastern front near Stalingrad, had been virtually annihilated. Half of the army of 200,000 soldiers were killed outright, and most of the rest were wounded or taken prisoner. A unit of Jewish forced labourers from Hungary, attached to the Second Army, also suffered appalling casualties. It was one of the worst battlefield defeats in Hungary's history.

Hitler deployed all his powers of persuasion in an attempt to convince Horthy to keep fighting. He told him that 'Germany and its allies were in a boat on a stormy sea. It was clear that anyone who wanted to get off in this situation would drown immediately.' Hitler also attacked Horthy's policy over the Jews, saying that 'the pro-Jewish attitude in Hungary was completely incomprehensible to him . . . Why should the Jews be handled with kid gloves? After all, they had incited the world war.' When the meeting resumed the next day Horthy demanded to know what more he was expected to do, since he had already stopped the Jews earning a living and 'he could not kill them.' Joachim von Ribbentrop, the Nazi Foreign Minister, replied that the Jews should be imprisoned in camps or 'annihilated'. Hitler pointed out approvingly that the Jewish situation in Poland had been 'thoroughly cleaned up' and explained to Horthy that the Jews 'were to be treated like tuberculosis bacilli that could infect a healthy body. This was not cruel if you considered that even innocent creatures of nature like rabbits and deer would have to be killed in [such a situation] in order that no harm would be caused. Why should the beasts that wanted to bring Bolshevism to us be spared?'[10]

The talks with Horthy were not a success from Hitler's perspective. And Goebbels thought he knew the reason why. As he wrote in his diary on 7 May 1943, the 'Hungarians are clear in their mind that a war cannot be won with words alone. They obviously know our weak position and are slowly adjusting to it.'[11] Moreover, a report of 30 April by Edmund Veesenmayer, an SS officer sent to Hungary to assess the situation, revealed that the Hungarian authorities 'see the Jews as a guarantee for the protection of 'Hungarian interests', and they believe that through the Jews they can provide proof that they waged this war alongside the Axis Powers only out of necessity, but that in practice they have indirectly made a contribution to the enemies of the Axis Powers through hidden sabotage [by not handing over the Jews].'[12]

Hitler responded to the vacillations of the Hungarians and Romanians in a typical way. He concluded – as he told his Gauleiters in May 1943 – that 'small states' should be 'liquidated as fast as possible'. After all, he said, 'today we live in a world of destroying and being destroyed.'[13] It was an early sign that Hitler might contemplate a German occupation of Hungary if Horthy didn't do what he was told.

Hitler had similar problems with another ally in the spring of 1943 – Bulgaria. The official communiqué after the meeting between Hitler and King Boris of Bulgaria on 3 April stated that they had 'a long and cordial talk', which was characterized by 'the spirit of traditional friendship' that existed between Germany and Bulgaria.[14] But the reality was that the Bulgarians, like the Romanians and Hungarians, were wavering in their support – especially over the question of the Jews. In February 1943, Alexander Belev, the Bulgarian government's Commissar for the Jewish Question, had agreed with Eichmann's representative, Theodor Dannecker, that the Bulgarians would hand over 20,000 Jews to the Germans. Just like the French, the Bulgarian authorities found it much more acceptable to offer up Jews who were not Bulgarian citizens. The Bulgarians knew – or at least must have strongly suspected – that they were sending these Jews to their deaths, especially in the wake of the public statements of the Allies the previous December about the Nazis' extermination programme. Notwithstanding this knowledge, towards the end of March 1943 the Bulgarians cooperated in the deportation of around 11,000 Jews from the Bulgarian-occupied territory of Thrace and Macedonia. Virtually every single one of these Jews perished in the gas chambers of Treblinka.

However, when the authorities moved to deport Jews from inside the old borders of Bulgaria, there were public protests. Anti-Semitism had never been much of a tradition in Bulgaria, and the government's introduction of legislation that persecuted the Jews in late 1941 had been motivated less by ideological conviction and more by an attempt to please their German ally.[15] Now, faced with the deportation of Jews who lived among them, many Bulgarian citizens and members of the government were unhappy – knowledge that the Germans had just lost at Stalingrad would almost certainly have played a part in their unhappiness, of course. Instead of sending the Jews to their deaths, the Bulgarian authorities now passed legislation that expelled Jews from their homes in the capital Sofia and distributed them around various provincial towns. This made it almost impossible for them to be deported, but also caused the Jews considerable hardship. After the war a number of Bulgarians sought to portray their country's history as a noble one in which 'their' Jews had been saved. It was anything but an honourable history, especially given what happened to the Jews from Thrace and Macedonia.

During April and May 1943, Hitler was aware not only of the attitude of his allies towards the Jews, but also of the resistance that the Jews themselves were demonstrating in Warsaw. On 19 April German forces entered the ghetto to begin the deportation of the remaining Jews. They were met with small-arms fire, grenades and home-made bombs. Marek Edelman, then twenty-four years old, was one of the Jews who fought back against the Germans, and he reveals that he and his colleagues in the Jewish Combat Organization were motivated by the knowledge that the Germans wanted to transport them to their deaths – knowledge they had gained from a witness to events at Treblinka who had managed to return to Warsaw and told them what awaited at the camp. 'It was difficult to believe that you were killed for nothing,' says Marek Edelman. 'But that's the way it was.'[16] After the initial shock of hearing the news about Treblinka, Marek and his comrades resolved to fight back. 'It's obvious', he says, 'that the death camps were the factor that caused the resistance.' The decision of the Germans to split up families and send old people and children to Treblinka, leaving just healthy, fit Jews within the ghetto also played a part. The resistance fighters could now fight free of any family responsibilities.

Members of the resistance within the ghetto had armed themselves with guns obtained from the Polish Home Army and stolen from the Germans. They also, says Marek Edelman, 'made grenades out of metal pipes and gunpowder'. Initially, the German forces entering the ghetto were surprised at the level of resistance and made little progress towards their objectives. As Marek Edelman puts it, 'The first few days were our victory.' Many of the resistance fighters, like Aharon Karmi, another young Jewish man, were exhilarated by the opportunity to confront the enemy: 'I shot with my pistol into the mass [of Germans] that was passing by. The Germans yelled, "Help!" and took shelter behind a wall. It was the first time we saw Germans running away. We were used to being the ones who ran away from the Germans. They had no expectation of Jews fighting like that. There was blood and I couldn't take my eyes off it. I said, "German blood." '[17]

Neither Marek Edelman nor Aharon Karmi, nor most of the other Jews who attacked the Germans in the ghetto, had previously been trained as soldiers. But this did not hold them back. 'It's very easy to learn how to shoot,' says Marek Edelman. 'You don't need to be trained. It's not the front where the general plans a battle. This is guerrilla warfare. The German goes walking down the street and when there's an opportunity you shoot at him. And if he doesn't see the person who's shooting all the better. You just have to have the will to fight and the weapons, that's all.'[18] Against the superior firepower of the Germans, the resistance fighters knew they had no chance of eventual victory. 'Yes,' says Marek, 'we knew we wouldn't win but we had to show the Germans that we're human beings like everybody [else]. During the war you're a human being when you kill the enemy.'

Under the command of SS Brigadeführer (Brigadier) Jürgen Stroop, German forces entered the ghetto and began setting fire to buildings, block by block. Marek Edelman remembers flames engulfing the ghetto as the Germans tried to burn them out, and that he and his comrades had to move from house to house as the fire pursued them. 'Until we left the ghetto there was no peace, [but] the Germans couldn't say they had won before we left.' Both Marek Edelman and Aharon Karmi eventually managed to escape from the ghetto, just two of the handful of Jews who were able to cross to the non-Jewish side of Warsaw – most of them smuggled out via sewers or tunnels.

The ghetto uprising was suppressed by the middle of May, and in his report Stroop claimed that he and his soldiers had captured 56,065 Jews – a figure that appears to be an overestimate[19] – at a cost of only a hundred or so German casualties. In purely military terms the Warsaw Jews had achieved little, other than to postpone for a short time the inevitable destruction of the ghetto and the murder of the majority of the Jews. But symbolically the importance of their resistance was enormous. The Jews had fought back in large numbers and demonstrated tremendous courage. 'When they started liquidating the ghetto we had to resist,' says Marek Edelman. 'It was not an uprising, it was a defence of the ghetto. When the Germans wanted to liquidate us then they met with resistance, that was the point . . . What would you like me to say [to them]? Please kill me immediately?'

Just days before the Germans entered the Warsaw ghetto in an attempt to clear the area of Jews, an event of enormous importance occurred in the development of Auschwitz. In March 1943, the first of a series of new killing facilities opened at Auschwitz Birkenau. Originally, as we have seen, the SS intended to place this crematorium/gas chamber in the main camp, but they subsequently changed its location to Birkenau. During the design stage various changes were made so that the building could function not just as a crematorium but also as a gas chamber. In August 1942 three more crematoria had been ordered – one virtually the same as the existing commission, and two of a different design. These two new crematoria, eventually to be known as Crematoria IV and V, marked a radical change.

The revolution encapsulated in the design of Crematoria IV and V was simple. They were the first buildings at Auschwitz that from the initial design stage were intended to function solely as places of murder. They had undressing rooms, gas chambers and crematoria ovens all on one level – a kind of conveyor belt of death. The other two new crematoria still betrayed in their design their origins as places to burn human remains, rather than to kill them as well. Crematoria II and III had the undressing room and gas chamber in the semi-basement, because the function of these rooms had originally been to store dead bodies. Now that they had been converted, it meant that once people had been murdered their bodies had to be transported in a corpse lift up to the level of the crematorium to be burnt.

These four buildings at Auschwitz Birkenau – numbered Crematoria II to V, since Crematorium I still existed in Auschwitz main camp – represented a new stage in the evolution of the Holocaust. In part this was because they were solid and looked from the outside like factories. By contrast, the Reinhard death camps of Bełżec, Sobibór and Treblinka were all temporary places, and once their murderous work was completed, they would be destroyed. The new red-brick crematoria/gas-chamber buildings at Auschwitz, however, were an integral part of a growing SS presence in Upper Silesia. They were at the centre of a vast network of nearly thirty Auschwitz sub-camps which provided forced labour for a range of industrial operations, including cement works, armaments factories and – biggest of all – the IG Farben chemical plant at Monowitz in the suburbs of Auschwitz town. The crematoria/gas chambers of Birkenau were – in essence – the physical manifestation of the idea of extermination through labour. Once Jewish workers at Monowitz, for example, could no longer function as required, they were transported the short distance to Birkenau for annihilation. These buildings were something more than a means of killing the men, women and children the Nazis hated and feared; they symbolized a system in which only the productive deserved to live. They were inhumanity memorialized in brick.

All four of the new crematoria/gas-chamber complexes at Birkenau were working by the summer of 1943. Karl Bischoff, the SS officer in charge of their construction, wrote that in total the ovens could dispose of 4,416 corpses in twenty-four hours – that is to say that Auschwitz Birkenau now had the capacity to turn 1.6 million people into ashes in one year.[20] This, it should be said, was a low estimate. According to eyewitness testimony, the number burnt could be as high as 8,000 bodies a day, by the simple expedient of putting more than one corpse into an oven at a time.[21]

The process of killing was broadly similar to that employed in the Operation Reinhard camps. New arrivals were ushered into the undressing room and told that they had to take their clothes off before having a shower. They were then directed into the gas chamber, which they were told was the shower room. Once the hermetically sealed door was closed, and everyone was trapped inside, crystals of Zyklon B were inserted through hatches in the roof (in the case of Crematoria II and III) or high in the wall (in the case of Crematoria IV and V). After everybody had been murdered, the residual gas was cleared, and Sonderkommandos entered. Only the means of gassing, Zyklon B as opposed to carbon monoxide, and the fact that the women's hair was shaved after death rather than before, marked a significant difference from the way in which the operation was conducted in the Reinhard camps.

Just like the Reinhard camps, the murder factories in Birkenau needed only a handful of SS men to oversee the whole process. The manual labour – including the horrendous task of untangling the dead from the gas chambers – was performed by Sonderkommandos. But, revealingly, it was always SS personnel who dropped the Zyklon B into the gas chambers.

Henryk Mandelbaum, a Polish Jew, worked as one of the Sonderkommandos in the new Auschwitz crematoria/gas chambers in 1944. 'You can't really think about it,' he says. 'I thought I was in hell. I remember that sometimes when, if I did something wrong at home, my parents would tell me don't do it because you'll go to hell. But when I saw many human corpses, people who were murdered through gassing and they were being burnt . . . It was beyond anything I could imagine and I didn't really know what to do. If I refuse [to work there] then I'll be gone right? I knew they would kill me. I was young. I lost my family. They were gassed – my father, my mother and my sister and brother. So I was aware of it and I wanted to live and I fought. I struggled to live all the time.'

Henryk Mandelbaum remembers that, despite the efforts of the SS to keep an atmosphere of calm as the Jews were ushered into the gas chamber, sometimes people 'started to sense something was wrong. There were too many people and some wanted to withdraw, but the SS men would hit them on the head with sticks and blood was flowing. So there was no chance of withdrawing or getting out, but by force they would be pushed into the gas chambers. When it was full they would lock the door – the doors were hermetic like in refrigerators.' He recalls that behind every transport 'there was an ambulance with a red cross [on it]' and, in a cynical act, 'in that red cross ambulance they [the SS] had Zyklon B gas [crystals].' Once the crystals had been thrown into the gas chamber, 'the gassing lasted about twenty minutes to half an hour. After the gassing, after the twenty or thirty minutes, we opened the doors. You could see how these people died – standing. Their heads were to the left or to the right, to the front, to the back. Some vomited or had hemorrhaged, and they would shit with loose bowels. Before the burning we had to cut their hair and pull out the gold teeth. And also had to look whether people kept anything in their nostrils, or valuables in the mouth – women in their vaginas.'[22]

Eventually, in the spring of 1944, a railway spur would be constructed, right into the heart of Birkenau, which allowed trains to deliver transports to within easy reach of the gas chambers in Crematoria II and III. Before that transports still arrived at the ramp – the unloading area halfway between Auschwitz main camp and Auschwitz Birkenau. For many of those arriving at Auschwitz, this was the first stage in their journey to the gas chambers. Günther Ruschin, a young German Jew, remembers that when he arrived at the ramp and saw women with children separated out, 'I was thinking, a fool that I was, that they were going into a family camp.' Selections at the ramp were always conducted by an SS doctor. This preserved the fiction that Auschwitz was an institution governed by scientific principles – that those to be murdered were chosen not out of arbitrary vindictiveness but by medical criteria. It was a lie, of course, even in Nazi terms, as there was never any proper medical examination, merely a glance at each individual. The SS would also trick new arrivals by asking if anyone wanted a lift in a vehicle to Birkenau, rather than walk to the camp. Sometimes fit young men and women would accept the ride. But everyone who chose not to walk to the camp was sent straight to the gas chambers.[23] They had, the SS thought, betrayed their weakness and so did not deserve to live.

Günther Ruschin was taken with others who had been selected for forced labour to the camp at Monowitz, next to the IG Farben works. Several days later his father, who had also been selected for work, was injured in an accident. Günther was told that his father would be sent to 'hospital' for 'an X ray'. But shortly afterwards a Polish Jew told him that his father would not receive medical treatment, but would be 'gassed' instead. Günther's immediate reaction was that he wanted to be selected for Birkenau so as to be near his father since maybe by some miracle he still lived. 'This is the feeling', he says, 'of a boy who was very close to his father.' But the Polish Jew convinced Günther that his father was dead and that he should remain working at Monowitz. So Günther decided to stay where he was and vowed to try and survive. 'We went to work in lines of five men in groups,' he says. 'I always tried to be in the middle, so as not to be hit by the SS, and that helped. And

I tried always not to be seen by the troops. I am not a man who says I must do something, some sabotage or something, no. I wanted to stay alive, to try to help others.'

En route to Auschwitz, when Günther's train had stopped at a station in eastern Germany, the Jews in the freight wagons had shouted out, 'Please give us some water.' But 'the people who were there [said], "Damned Jews! Didn't they kill you yet?"' Günther was 'depressed and upset' by what happened at the station, but he still didn't believe that his fellow Germans could possibly want to murder him. 'We knew that we weren't going first class,' he says. 'But we didn't know that the majority of us would go into the gas chambers. We didn't know of the existence of the gas chambers.'[24]

The SS did what they could to keep the new crematoria/gas-chamber buildings at Birkenau separate from the rest of the camp. The buildings were fenced off and the Sonderkommandos lived on site. Paradoxically, the Sonderkommandos – who had the worst jobs in the whole of Auschwitz – lived in better conditions than most of the other prisoners. 'We had nice quarters, with beds,' confirms Dario Gabbai, one of the Sonderkommandos who worked at Birkenau in 1944. 'We ate well. We didn't need the soup from the camps.'[25] The SS usually allowed the Sonderkommandos to keep the food left behind in the undressing room by the Jews taken to the gas chambers. This led to an atmosphere of plenty in the Sonderkommandos' quarters in the crematorium. Dr Miklós Nyiszli, a Romanian Jew imprisoned at Auschwitz, described a memorable dinner with them. 'The table awaiting us', he wrote, 'was covered with a heavy silk tablecloth . . . The table was piled high with choice and varied dishes, everything a deported people could carry with them into the uncertain future: all sorts of preserves, bacon, jellies, several kinds of salami, cakes and chocolate.'[26]

Some Sonderkommandos took the valuables of the Jews who were killed – in particular jewellery that had been secreted either in their clothes or within the orifices of their bodies. They then tried to exchange these valuables for other goods they wanted. They could do this because, despite the isolation of the crematoria, contact between the Sonderkommandos and other prisoners in the camp was still possible. Otto Pressburger, sent to Auschwitz in 1942 from Slovakia, remembers how he had an opportunity to visit the Sonderkommandos because he drove a horse and cart transporting various goods around Birkenau. And he was always keen to do 'business' with them. 'They [the Sonderkommandos] wanted alcohol and cigarettes, and they had plenty of gold [to pay for them]. The "business" in the crematorium was the best. I always wanted to be delivering cargoes to the crematorium. You could always buy things there . . . Once I came to the crematorium asking if they had something to sell. I got offered a jewelled spider. Very rich Jews who used to have jewellery stores came to the camp at that time. I asked what they [the Sonderkommandos] wanted for the spider. They said a hundred cigarettes. I said if the spider is worth it then I will bring the cigarettes. We used to trust each other. The spider was beautiful. There was a big stone in the middle and the legs were covered in brilliant [jewels]. I took the spider to our Polish civilians [construction workers who lived outside the camp but worked inside during the day] and offered it to them . . . Each of us made a profit.'

This trade was strictly prohibited and Otto Pressburger risked his life to pursue it. 'There was always an SS man at the gates to the crematorium,' he says. 'I used to make up fake reasons for my arrival. Most of the time I said I was told to deliver sand to the crematorium. But of course I was coming to do "business". So they let me in. Sand was never a reason and I always dumped it. The problem was to hide the goods. They [other prisoners involved in the trading] made me a little wooden storage box [on the cart] under my feet . . . Once I was delivering a thousand cigarettes to the crematorium. As I was taking them out of my storage box someone hit me on my back and over my head. It was an old SS man. He always used to ride a bicycle around and watch for prisoners doing "business" . . . He asked where I got the cigarettes from and accused me of doing "business". But I lied. I said I was only hungry and had stolen a bag believing I would find a sandwich inside. Instead I found the cigarettes. He said that was a lie . . . He was only a corporal but I called him officer, which apparently helped a lot. He punched me in my face and I pretended it hurt much more than it really did. At the end he took my cigarettes and let me go. If he had reported the incident I would have been killed the same day.' As Otto Pressburger saw it, he had 'no choice' but to get involved in 'doing "business"' within the camp because he 'wanted to live'.[27]

The Sonderkommandos formed relationships not just with prisoners in the rest of the camp, but also with the SS who supervised their work in the crematoria/gas chambers. The SS had already discovered at death camps like Sobibór that it was counter-productive for them to kill all the Sonderkommandos after a brief period and then select a new group. Similarly, at Auschwitz it became common for the Sonderkommandos to be kept alive for many months. As a result, and because of the proximity in which they worked with the SS, a kind of intimacy developed, with the SS overseers often treating the Sonderkommandos much better than other prisoners at Auschwitz. Dr Miklós Nyiszli even witnessed them playing football together – a team of Sonderkommandos versus a team of SS.[28] Dario Gabbai remembers one Dutch member of the SS almost with fondness, describing him as 'a very nice guy'.[29] Morris Venezia, another Sonderkommando, confirms that this Dutchman was 'The best guard we had in the crematoria. He treated us sometimes to a cigarette. Sometimes we treated him to a cigarette. A very, very good man, very friendly with us.' But even this 'nice guy', says Morris, 'was always willing to go and kill people. And he was one of the best of our guards. I couldn't understand that – why?'[30]

Other SS working at the crematoria/gas chambers took the opportunity to indulge their sadistic desires. In testimony written at the time by a member of the Sonderkommando and discovered only after the war, a chronicler describes how one particular SS man liked to feel the sexual parts of naked young women as they walked by him on the way to the gas chamber.[31]

Chief among these sadists was Otto Moll, the SS man who supervised the operation of the crematoria. Dario Gabbai remembers how he liked to kill naked girls by shooting them 'on their breasts'. In 1944, when the arrival of enormous numbers of Hungarian Jews meant that bodies had to be burnt in the open air in giant pits – since the crematoria could not cope with the volume – Moll on occasion threw children directly into the flames so that they were burnt alive.[32] Alter Feinsilber, one of the Sonderkommando, witnessed another of Moll's sadistic acts. Moll ordered a naked woman to jump about and sing on a pile of corpses near the flaming pit while he shot prisoners and threw their bodies into the fire. When he had finished shooting them, he turned his gun on the woman and killed her.[33] Such was Moll's all-pervasive sadism that long after the war was over Dario Gabbai's heart still 'bumps at maybe two hundred a minute' whenever he hears a motorcycle engine – because Moll used to arrive at the crematoria on a motorbike. 'When you see this guy [Moll],' says Dario, 'it's just problems – nothing else. You don't want to be around him. In 1951 I was going to the city college in Los Angeles to learn English, and the first thing that teacher told me was to write something about the camps you were in. The first thing I wrote – I still have it from 1951 – I wrote two pages about Moll.'[34]

Many of the Sonderkommando were profoundly troubled by their work. Not just the appalling nature of it, but the knowledge that they were assisting the SS in the destruction of fellow Jews. 'We became animals,' says Morris Venezia. 'We feel that we should kill ourselves and not work for the Germans. But even to kill yourself is not so easy.' Dario Gabbai found that 'After a while you don't know nothing. Nothing bothers you. That's why your conscience gets inside of you and stays there until today. What happened? Why did we do such a thing?' The only explanation Dario can give is that 'You always find the strength to live for the next day,' because the desire to live is so 'powerful'.[35]

One account, written by a member of the Sonderkommando during the war, described how children from Lithuania, just before they died, admonished the Jews who were helping the Germans. One young girl shouted at a Sonderkommando who tried to undress her younger brother, calling him a 'Jewish murderer'. She said that she was her brother's 'good mummy' and that her brother 'will die in my arms, together with me'. Another child asked a Sonderkommando why fellow Jews were taking the children to be killed – was it, the child suggested, 'only in order to live' themselves? Was their life among the 'murderers' really worth 'the lives of so many' other Jews?[36]

'We got liberated,' says Morris Venezia. 'For what? To remember all those barbarous things? We didn't want our lives actually. This is the way we feel – we're still feeling. Until now I'm just saying, why [did] God let me live, for what? To remember all those things? Always, even now, when I'm going to bed, everything comes in my mind before I close my eyes. Everything, everything, every night, every night.'[37]

The purpose-built crematoria/gas chambers of Birkenau began their murderous work after the majority of Jews had died in the Holocaust. Around 1.1 million were killed in 1941 and 2.7 million in 1942.[38] Most of these Jews died either in the Einsatzgruppen actions in the east, or in the Reinhard death camps within Poland. Auschwitz accounted for 200,000 deaths in 1942, a fraction of the total catalogue of murder. In 1943 the number of dead fell to 500,000 – with around half that number murdered in Auschwitz. The newly created murder machinery in Auschwitz Birkenau was thus functioning well below capacity. In part this reduced figure for 1943 reflected the difficulties that the Nazis encountered in finding and transporting Jews to the death camps once it became clear that the Germans were losing the war.

During 1943, the Nazis didn't just transport Jews to Auschwitz. They also sent other categories of people they considered a threat, including Sinti and Roma – those the Nazis called 'Gypsies'. A Gypsy camp was created within Birkenau, and the first transport of several hundred Sinti and Roma arrived at Auschwitz in February 1943. At its height the Gypsy camp at Birkenau contained 15,000 people. Unusually, the Sinti and Roma were not selected on arrival but were permitted to stay in family groups. This was most probably because a final decision about their collective fate had not yet been taken, but the fact that they could remain together did not mean that the Sinti and Roma received preferential treatment in any physical sense – they were still brutally mistreated. Hermann Höllenreiner, who came from a Sinti background and was sent to Birkenau as a child, remembers that he and the other children were so hungry that 'We would pull out the grass like rabbits so that we could just eat it. And if an SS caught us we would get beaten. That was also bad. But then everything that happened in Birkenau was bad . . . We lived in constant fear. Every moment we thought now they will beat my father or my mother to death, or that we will be gassed; we knew that every moment could be the one we are gassed.'[39]

Franz Rosenbach, also from a Sinti family, was fifteen when he was sent with his mother to Auschwitz Birkenau. He remembers that when he arrived at the camp he was shocked that he and his mother had to get completely undressed in front of each other. 'I don't know if you know that we have our own customs,' he says. 'A mother would never get undressed in front of her children, nor would the father. There is some kind of sense of shame and respect. But in this instance, we were forced to do it. We were undressed and I called out, "Mum, where are you?" She was standing behind me, she was hiding behind me. And when her hair was cut off – her braid – I wanted to go and grab it. So I was hit a few more times on the back with a rubber truncheon or something like that, some kind of hosepipe. You know, it was a sight that you cannot imagine. The SS came in with a cane and hit the men's penises, making a point of [saying] . . . please excuse the expression, I can't say it, something like "Gypsy dick" or whatever you call it . . . that kind of thing, derogatory terms, discriminatory terms.'[40]

Imprisoned with his mother in the Gypsy camp, Franz Rosenbach was 'totally shocked' at the conditions in which the Sinti and Roma existed. 'The atmosphere was terrible, because many of the small children and [other] people in the blocks were ill, everyone was mixed up together. The children were screaming, "Mum, I'm hungry, Mum, [give me] something to eat, do we have anything to drink?" They weren't allowed to drink the water because of the risk of [catching] typhoid fever and that kind of thing. "Mum, [give me] . . ." this and that. And the women had nothing to give them, they didn't have anything. We were beaten, kicked, degraded, but you didn't know why, you had no idea why . . . You know, these young SS men, the older ones too, had been trained, [to think] that we, the Sinti and Roma, were not human beings. We weren't people. We were to be destroyed. Anyone could do whatever he liked to us. The Sinti were fair game to them, do you understand?'

Women imprisoned in the Gypsy camp were particularly vulnerable to sexual abuse. Hermann Höllenreiner recalls how Kapos would come into the camp at night, select individual women – the 'beautiful Gypsies'[41] – and then take them outside to be raped. Franz Rosenbach, also imprisoned in the Gypsy camp, recalls members of the SS committing the same crime. 'I witnessed this twice,' he says. 'At night, young SS men would come in with a torch and approach the women. Most of the time the women didn't know what was going on, they had to take off their headscarves so that they could get a look at them. Sometimes they picked out young women and [took them] behind the block . . . you didn't hear a shot ring out, you didn't hear a thing. Next morning they'd be lying there dead. They'd been murdered.'[42] According to Sonderkommando Alter Feinsilber, there were also instances of women in the Gypsy camp selling themselves out of desperation. He said that prisoners from outside the Gypsy camp, 'who could afford a bribe', would give cigarettes to the *Blockführer* of the Gypsy camp and then enter the camp 'with the SS man's leave. There they had sexual relations with Gypsy women, who were starving and were ready for sexual intercourse to get some cigarettes or some other trifle. The husbands or fathers of the Gypsy women put up with this state of things as they were starving, too . . .'[43]

Though around 23,000 Sinti and Roma were sent to Auschwitz, Nazi policy about the Gypsies remained confused. The Nazis, for instance, never put the same kind of pressure on their allies to send Sinti and Roma to the camps as they did Jews. Not that Sinti and Roma escaped persecution. While, for example, the considerable Sinti and Roma population in Romania was not subjected to systematic extermination, thousands were still deported to Transnistria. In Croatia, during the same period, the Ustaše targeted 'Gypsies', passing discriminatory legislation, imprisoning them in camps and eventually murdering around 26,000 Sinti and Roma.[44] Undoubtedly, enormous numbers of Sinti and Roma died during the war – the precise figure is unknown, but it was certainly more than 200,000.

Part of the reason for the lack of clarity in Nazi policy towards Sinti and Roma was that Himmler himself did not offer precise guidelines to those under his command. On the one hand the Einsatzgruppen in the east regularly killed Sinti and Roma along with Jews, and thousands of Sinti and Roma were deported to ghettos in Poland from the Old Reich, but on the other hand Himmler issued a decree on 13 October 1942 stating that 'racially pure' Sinti might be allowed to wander over designated areas under 'Gypsy headmen'.[45] This order arose from the work conducted by Dr Robert Ritter, Himmler's 'expert' on Gypsies. Ritter had concluded that 'racially pure Gypsies' living in the Reich were not a threat, but that the much larger number of Sinti and Roma who had 'mingled' their blood with other races were potentially dangerous. This was not just bad science, but produced a discriminatory policy almost impossible to implement in practice.

Even so, when Himmler issued a further decree on 29 January 1943 which resulted in the deportation of the Sinti and Roma to Auschwitz, specific exceptions were made – for example, for those considered 'racially pure', for Gypsies married to Germans who could be vouched for by the police and so on. They were still liable to sterilization, but they had – in theory at least – a chance to escape Auschwitz and the other camps. In practice, however, all these various distinctions were largely ignored during the deportation process.[46]

At the same time as the Sinti and Roma suffered in Auschwitz, Hitler was digesting what for him was dispiriting – almost disastrous – news on the military front. The surrender of the Sixth Army at Stalingrad had been bad enough for the Germans at the start of 1943, but the series of defeats that followed made matters even worse. By mid-May that year the Wehrmacht had lost their campaign in North Africa, and Hitler – according to Goebbels – feared that the defeat of the Germans at Tunis might 'be on the scale of Stalingrad'.[47] That same month Grand Admiral Dönitz ordered U-boat action in the north Atlantic to stop – Allied counter-measures had made it almost impossible for the U-boats to wage war successfully.

None of these setbacks, serious as they were, altered Hitler's desire to murder the Jews. He told Goebbels on 13 May 1943 that because they were 'parasites' there was 'nothing else open for modern people to do other than to eradicate the Jews'. He added, 'World Jewry believes it is on the brink of a world victory. This world victory will not come . . . The peoples who were the first to have recognized and fought the Jew will instead gain world domination.'[48]

Hitler's obsession with Jews had not abated. If anything it seemed to have intensified – as events in the summer and autumn of 1943 would confirm in the most disturbing ways imaginable.

15. Oppression and Revolt
(1943)

One of the many tragic aspects of this history is that so many Jews lost their lives even though they lived in countries that had, by now, decided they wanted to exit the war. But there was no easy way out of this conflict, and Hitler's vengeance on those of his Axis partners who sought to break with him could be devastating.

The Italians, for instance, certainly recognized by the summer of 1943 how disastrous it had been to link themselves with Nazi Germany. On 10 July 1943 the Allies landed in Sicily and on 19 July Rome was bombed. 'Everybody understood that the war was lost,' says Mario Mondello, an Italian diplomat and member of the Fascist Party. 'And, of course, everybody was thinking that Italy had to get out [of the war] and not to stay with Mussolini . . . We're more realistic sometimes than the Germans are. Of course being more realistic we are not faithful to the present chief, and so on. I don't say it is a noble thing, but it is our character.'[1]

On 24 July 1943, at a meeting of the Fascist Grand Council, Mussolini was criticized by his colleagues and his policies attacked. The next day, at an audience with the King, the Duce was told his services were no longer required as Prime Minister. He was arrested as he left the room.

Marshal Badoglio replaced Mussolini as Prime Minister and tried to negotiate a way out of the war. On 3 September 1943, the same day the first Allied troops crossed from Sicily to the Italian mainland, the new Italian government agreed an armistice, and on 8 September General Eisenhower, broadcast the news that the Italians had surrendered unconditionally.

The exit of Italy from the Axis alliance proved calamitous for the Jews living in the country. The time lag between Mussolini's removal and the final surrender of the Italians allowed the Germans to prepare their response, and as soon as the Italians quit the war German forces seized Italian bases and installations. By 10 September the Germans were in control of Rome and most Italian troops had been disarmed. The same day the Germans occupied the Italian capital, Hitler recorded a speech, broadcast that evening. In it he denounced the duplicity of the new

Italian government and said that Germany would never surrender in such a way. 'We all know', he said, 'that in this merciless struggle the loser will be annihilated, in accordance with the wishes of our enemies, while only the victor will retain the means for living.'[2]

It would not have gone unnoticed – especially to Germany's other allies – that one way of interpreting events was that the Italians had managed to avoid fighting to the end because they were not party to the crime of mass extermination. Even though Mussolini's regime had persecuted the Jews inside Italy, they had not sent Jews en masse to be murdered in the Nazi death camps. Not just that, but up until the moment of their surrender, the Italians had been protecting Jews from deportation on territory outside Italy. In spring 1943, for instance, at the same time as the Bulgarians were deporting Jews from Thrace and Macedonia, the Italian consul in German-occupied Salonica organized the transfer of a number of Greek Jews to relative safety in Athens, then in the Italian zone of Greece.[3] There were even cases of Italian soldiers visiting the camps in which the Germans held Jews in Salonica and claiming that selected women were their 'wives' and so could not be deported.[4]

The surrender of the Italians meant that this protection was removed in an instant. The lives of Jews both in the former occupied zones and within Italy itself changed suddenly for the worse. For example, as soon as the Germans entered Nice in the south of France – a city that had been under Italian control – they began searching for Jews in an action that became infamous for its brutality. Thousands of Jews had taken refuge in Nice, protected for the last ten months since the fall of Vichy by the Italians. But now the Germans took their revenge. On entering Italian territory itself, the Germans were similarly heartless. Around Lake Maggiore in the north of Italy the SS began searching for Jews, and at Meina at the southern end of the lake they came across a number of Jews in a hotel. They murdered sixteen of them, and threw their bodies into the lake.[5]

Less than a month later, on 16 October 1943, German forces moved against the Jews of Rome. This, one might think, ought to have been a risky operation for them, since they were snatching Jews close to the Vatican. For while it was true that Pope Pius XII had not yet publicly condemned the extermination of the Jews, surely he would not ignore this outrage? Ernst von Weizsäcker, German ambassador to the

Holy See, certainly thought he wouldn't. He believed that deporting the
Jews of Rome would result in such censure from the Pope that it would
damage Germany.[6] But Weizsäcker was wrong. Not only did the Pope
not threaten to condemn any attempt to deport the Jews from Rome, he
never even spoke out against the action after it had happened.

Early in the morning of 16 October, Settimia Spizzichino, a twenty-
two-year-old Roman Jew, suspected that something was wrong: 'That
night was a slightly different night from the others. One could feel that
there was something in the air. A kind of cottonwool silence. I can't
describe it. And towards four in the morning we started hearing footsteps, heavy footsteps. Soldiers' footsteps, marching. So we went to the
windows to see what was going on and we saw the Germans breaking
into the houses and taking the Jews. We took fright because we saw them
coming into our building.'[7] Settimia was taken with her family to a
prison close to the Vatican, where she describes conditions as 'horrendous', and from there to Auschwitz. She was one of 1,800 Jews deported
from Rome during the German occupation. 'I came back from Auschwitz on my own [at the end of the war],' she says. 'I lost my family
there. My mother. Two sisters, my little niece and then one brother. Had
the Pope spoken out a number of Jews would have fled. They would
have reacted. Instead he kept quiet. He played into the Germans' hands.
The Pope was very near. We were right under his nose. But he didn't lift
a finger. He was an anti-Semitic Pope. He didn't take a single risk.'

While it is understandable, given what happened to her, that Settimia
Spizzichino believes that the Pope was anti-Semitic, the charge is hard
to sustain. Not least because the Pope certainly did not prevent priests
and nuns from hiding Jews in Italy. 'The Pope issued the order that the
convents could open up,' says Sister Luisa Girelli of the Sisters of Sion.
'It lifted the rule of enclosure – opening the door to any escapee.'[8] En-
richetta Di Veroli was just one of the Jews hidden by the Sisters of Sion,
and will never forget how they saved her life. 'We were accepted here
with no problems,' she says, 'the nuns were very nice. These nice nuns
represented nine months of my life. They were important. I feel much
more than gratitude.'[9] Over 4,000 Jews were protected by the Catholic
Church and hidden in convents, monasteries and other church buildings. Several hundred even found refuge inside the Vatican.[10]

But what the Pope would not do, even having been told that the Nazis were almost certainly exterminating the Jews, was to speak out about the crime. Most likely, he was frightened for a number of reasons. He feared, first of all – as we have noted before – the victory of the Godless 'Bolsheviks' and the subsequent threat to the Catholic Church. Second, he worried that if he condemned the Nazis' attack on the Jews, the Germans might enter church property and in doing so capture the Jews who were hidden there. Finally, he was anxious lest the Germans bomb the Vatican itself.[11] So he kept his mouth shut. By this course of action he undoubtedly also served, as he saw it, the interests of the Catholic Church as an institution. But, as we have already seen in the case of the Dutch Jews, we can't know for sure what would have happened if he had taken a stronger line. Maybe the Germans would have moved against the church, or maybe – given the reluctance Hitler had already shown to attack the church in Germany – they would have done nothing. What we do know is that if the Pope had spoken out he would have offered moral guidance to the world.

It was not just the Germans who conducted the Jewish deportations in Italy. Italians were also involved, in particular members of Fascist groups like the Brigate Nere (the Black Brigades) and other military units attached to the so-called Italian Social Republic – the area of northern Italy still ruled by Benito Mussolini, who had been rescued from imprisonment by German paratroopers.

Altogether around 7,000 Jews were deported from Italy and murdered.[12] More than 80 per cent of Jews in Italy thus survived the war – most by hiding or escaping across the border into neutral Switzerland. Initially, even after the Germans had occupied Italy, the Swiss maintained that Italian Jews had no right to asylum in Switzerland unless they 'qualified' in some way – for example, if they were children, pensioners or married to a Swiss citizen. These instructions were relaxed in December 1943, and replaced entirely by more liberal measures only in July 1944. Throughout the war, as far as Italian Jews seeking refuge in Switzerland were concerned, a great deal depended on the compassion – or lack of it – of individual Swiss border guards.[13]

The fact that just under 20 per cent of Jews in Italy were murdered remains a disturbing one, even given that in a country like the Netherlands 75 per cent of Jews died. That's because, unlike in the Netherlands, the full-scale persecution of the Jews in Italy came relatively late in the war, and the threat was eliminated in large parts of the country by the Allied advance. Rome, for example, fell to the Allies less than nine months after the Italian surrender, on 4 June 1944. The opportunity for the Germans to identify, capture and deport the Jews was thus necessarily limited.

The history of the Holocaust in Italy is especially bleak when compared to events in another country occupied by the Germans, 700 miles to the north. Denmark was home to about 7,500 Jews, and the Nazis planned on moving against them for the first time in the autumn of 1943, around the same time as they were deporting Italian Jews. The relatively light-touch Nazi occupation of Denmark had come to an end during the summer in the wake of strikes and other protests. When the Danish government resigned in August, a state of emergency was imposed by the Germans and the Nazi plenipotentiary, Werner Best, pressed for action against the Jews. The idea was to detain the Danish Jews on the night of 1–2 October 1943, and then deport them. But just a few days before the planned action, Werner Best did something extraordinary. Through an intermediary, Georg Duckwitz, the German naval attaché, Best told the Danish Jews what was about to happen to them. Best briefed Duckwitz on the planned deportations, knowing that Duckwitz, a man sympathetic to the plight of the Danes, would pass the information on to members of the Danish elite, and that they in turn would warn the Jews.

'We heard that [the news about the impending deportations] at the police station,' says Knud Dyby, a Danish policeman. 'Of course we heard it at the same time as the journalists and the politicians heard it. It was a great surprise to all of us. We never thought – after more than two years – that the Germans would arrest the Danish Jews.'[14] Knud Dyby, who like his colleagues 'did not believe in discrimination', felt compelled to help the Jews, in part because he knew about the likely fate of the Jews from the 'underground press'.

Up to the moment the Germans decided on the deportation, 'The situation of the Jews in Denmark was quite a happy one,' says Bent Melchior, who was fourteen years old in 1943. 'We were not very many Jews at any point and we were well integrated into the Danish society. Over the centuries there has been a lot of intermarriage and people who were not Jews might have a Jewish great-grandfather or mother. So I would say there was a pro-Semitic atmosphere, and we were no threat – not to the church, not to the country. On the contrary, many Jews played a very important role in public life in Denmark, in the arts, in the science, even in politics.'[15]

Bent Melchior remembers that, if you felt in any danger, you could 'ask any policeman in the street to help you, without fearing that this would have given anything away to the Germans'. The atmosphere in Denmark was very much one of the Danes – regardless of religion – together as one nation against the Germans.

After learning about the proposed German action, Jewish leaders gave warnings in synagogues and throughout the Jewish community. As a result, many of the Jews living in Copenhagen left the city to hide in houses in the countryside or moved in with their non-Jewish neighbours.

Non-Jewish Danes also made a major effort to warn the Jews. 'I went from house to house in the streets of the neighborhood,' said Robert Pedersen, then seventeen years old. 'Whenever I saw a name plate that indicated a Jewish family, I rang the doorbell and asked to talk to them. Sometimes they did not believe me. But I succeeded in persuading them to pack and come with me to Bispebjerg Hospital which had been turned into a gathering place for Jewish refugees . . . After that the doctors and nurses took care of them. And then I went back to my neighborhood and collected more Jews.'[16]

The most common escape route was across the narrow channel to neutral Sweden. Volunteer guides, such as Knud Dyby, escorted small groups of Jews through the streets of Copenhagen to the fishing port. 'It was always done at night,' he says. 'We preferred the worst weather because we didn't want any light evenings where everybody could see us.' Once at the harbour, 'we would hide ourselves in the small sheds that the Germans normally used for nets and tools' until called on to the boat by a fisherman. 'I was scared all the time,' he says. 'I had to move many places to rest my aching body and I had no trouble finding Danes that would give me room and board, without payment at all, just to help me out as an underground person.'[17]

The church in Denmark also tried to protect the Jews. 'Wherever Jews are persecuted for racial or religious reasons,' said the Bishop of Copenhagen, in an unequivocal statement of support on 3 October, 'it is the duty of the Christian Church to protest against such persecution . . . Irrespective of diverging religious opinions, we shall fight for the right of our Jewish brothers and sisters to keep the freedom that we ourselves value more highly than life.'[18]

As a result of this resistance, the German action on 1–2 October largely failed – most Jews were not at home when the Germans called. Out of the 7,500 or so Danish Jews, fewer than 500 were ever deported. Those that were captured by the Germans were sent not to the death camps of the east but to Theresienstadt concentration camp in Czech territory, and the majority survived the war.

The Danish experience of the Holocaust is singular. This was the only country under Nazi domination where large numbers of Jews – around 95 per cent – were saved by their fellow countrymen. There is no simple explanation for why this happened in Denmark and nowhere else – a combination of factors all came together at this moment. In the first place, there was a historical culture of Danes sticking together against their powerful neighbour, Germany. There was also a profound sense of the importance of individual human rights. 'It is a question of what I call Danish fairness and justice,' says Rudy Bier, a Jewish teenager who was saved by his fellow Danes in the autumn of 1943. 'I think we want to protect each other and we do not easily give in or up on things.'[19] The proximity of a neutral country also played a part. Sweden was near by and offered an immediate place of refuge – especially after the Swedes had broadcast on radio on 2 October 1943 that they would welcome any Danish Jews who could make the crossing.

Another factor – notwithstanding the fact that around a thousand of the Jews in Denmark at the time were foreign – was the perception, as Knud Dyby puts it, that the Jews were 'all Danish'. The suspicion thus remains that the Danes were not so much rescuing Jews, as rescuing fellow Danes who happened to be Jewish. Had Denmark not placed such strong restrictions on foreign Jews entering the country in the 1930s, and instead allowed many more Jews to take refuge, the situation might possibly have been different in the autumn of 1943. We cannot, of course, know for sure.

Finally, there is the most crucial reason why so many Jews in Denmark were saved – the attitude of the Germans. The rescue was possible only because Werner Best, the leading German representative in the country, sent out a warning that he knew would reach the Jewish community. Furthermore, the German Navy made little effort to police the water between Denmark and Sweden, thus allowing the Jews to escape. 'I always maintain', says Rudy Bier, 'that if the Germans had wanted to stop that operation, they could have done it extremely easily because the whole of the water between Denmark and Sweden is not that wide, nor that long, and with four or five motor torpedo boats the whole operation would have gone flat.'[20] That is not to say that the Germans ignored the flight of the Jews entirely. On the Danish mainland some German security personnel did try to capture Jews – the amount of effort depending, it seems, on the enthusiasm of the individual German units.

However, at the top of the German hierarchy in Denmark, the position was clear. Werner Best wanted to allow the Jews to escape. Yet before this action, Best had previously been no friend of the Jews. He was a committed Nazi who had worked closely with Reinhard Heydrich, helping to devise and implement Nazi racial policy in France. There is no evidence that he had suddenly developed a sense of compassion for the plight of the Jews. He was acting out of self-interest, not humanity. A clue to his real thinking is contained in a document he wrote for the authorities in Berlin, dated 5 October 1943: 'As the objective goal of the *Judenaktion* in Denmark was the de-judaization of the country, and not a successful headhunt, it must be concluded that the *Judenaktion* has reached its goal.'[21] In essence, Best was arguing that since his job was to clear the Jews out of Denmark, he had succeeded. It was just that he had achieved success not by deporting the Jews to their deaths, but by letting them escape to Sweden. He could also have added that the political situation in Denmark had always been different from that in other Nazi-occupied countries. The Nazis had largely permitted the Danes to enforce their own occupation, in order to ensure that Danish food supplies kept arriving in the Reich, and the bad feeling caused by the forced deportation of the Jews would have been considerable. Much better, Best must have thought, to achieve the desired 'goal' by more subtle means than used elsewhere.

There was almost certainly another reason for Best's actions – one that he would never have told his fellow Nazis. Best was a sophisticated man. A trained lawyer, he was appointed a judge when he was still in his twenties. So it is not unreasonable to suppose that by the autumn of

1943 he had worked out that the Nazis would lose, and that he needed to start improving his CV as far as the Allies were concerned. It was a strategy that worked, because despite his close association with Heydrich and his past record of crimes, he was only imprisoned briefly after the end of the war. He subsequently became an executive with a large German industrial conglomerate.

It is thus a mistake to believe that the Danish example shows that heroic resistance was the most significant factor in determining how many Jews survived in any particular country. Even more important was another element – how much in each instance the Nazis wanted to find and deport the Jews concerned. That conclusion is supported by studying the experience of the Greek Jews. In Greece, despite a number of instances of resistance, around 80 per cent of the 70,000 Jews in the country died during the war.[22] In large part that was because, unlike in Denmark, the Germans were determined to expel the Jews of Greece.

The Germans moved into the Italian zone of Greece in September 1943 and at once started planning mass deportations. There were immediate protests from non-Jewish Greeks. Archbishop Damaskinos, the Greek Orthodox Bishop of Athens, not only made representations to the Germans, but also called on his fellow clergy to hide Jews. Academics at the University of Athens also protested. The Germans responded by closing the university and arresting hundreds of clergy.

Though anti-Semitism was not unknown in Greece and some Jewish communities had few non-Jewish friends to count on, the broad picture in Greece was one of sympathy and support for the Jews. As one scholar of the history of the Holocaust in Greece concludes, 'the mass of Greeks offered hospitality to Jews who asked for assistance.'[23]

The most famous act of resistance was on the island of Zakynthos. When asked by the Germans to produce a list of every Jew on the island, the local mayor and bishop handed over a piece of paper that contained just two names – their own. Meanwhile the Jews were hidden in the houses of non-Jewish islanders. All 275 Jews survived. We don't know exactly why the Germans chose not to pursue the Jews on Zakynthos. Most probably they simply decided there were too few Jews on the island to justify the resources needed to find them. But it was, once again, the decision of the Germans not to try and take the Jews that was crucial. The incident on Zakynthos is famous because the Jews survived. But there were many more cases in Greece where despite similar heroics the Jews were captured and deported.

Salonica, the area in Greece with the highest percentage of loss, had been under German control from spring 1941. About 95 per cent of the Jews of Salonica died in the war – up to 48,500 men, women and children. Both the fact that so many Jews were concentrated in this one place, and the fact that the Germans had been in control for two years before the deportations, help explain why such a high percentage of Greek Jews from this area died. In addition, unlike in many other parts of Greece, the Jews of Salonica were not largely assimilated into the local population. Before the war there had been a small but vociferous group criticizing the Jews – many of whom were economically successful – and the Germans were able to build on these tensions.[24]

Enormous numbers of Jews were sent from Greece to Auschwitz – altogether around 55,000. The majority of them were murdered immediately, and the survival rate of the rest within the camp was notoriously low. The Greek Jews found the harshness of the Polish climate hard to take and few of them spoke German, the language in which all commands in the camp were spoken.

What the history of the Greek and Danish Jews demonstrates once again is how the Germans could implement their Final Solution in radically different ways in different countries. And in deciding how much they wanted to find and deport Jews in each individual place – something that, as we have seen, was a crucial element in determining how many Jews subsequently died – the Germans would, of course, have been influenced by a whole range of other factors. Such as how easy it was to deport the Jews in practical terms, the political consequences of deporting them, how 'racially' dangerous they considered the particular Jews to be, whether the Jews lived near the front line or not, and so on.

Unlike the Jews of Greece, the Jews of Denmark survived in such large numbers in large part because the Germans chose – for a variety of reasons – not to pursue them all ruthlessly. None of that, it has to be said, takes anything away from the bravery of those who helped the Danish Jews. The heroism of the Danish resisters remains undimmed. But we should also remember the courage of the Greeks who helped the Jews in their country – notwithstanding the fact that so many Greek Jews were subsequently murdered by the Nazis.

Shortly before Danish Jews crossed the sea to safety in Sweden, Jews in the largest Reinhard death camp in Poland were planning their own escape. In the summer of 1943, at Treblinka, the SS were about to face armed resistance from the inmates for the first time. Superficially, in the months leading up to the attempted breakout, all seemed to be running smoothly for the SS. The chaotic rule of Irmfried Eberl had been replaced by a new regime of order and deception – all designed to calm the arriving Jews. 'They turned the platform, where the people arrived, into a kind of village train station,' says Kalman Taigman, a member of the Treblinka Sonderkommando. Signs were erected reading 'first class, second class, third class' and 'waiting room'. There was a door with a sign over it saying 'station manager'.[25] Oskar Strawczynski, another Jewish prisoner at Treblinka, also witnessed the transformation of the camp. 'In a prominent spot,' he wrote, 'a fake clock, with a 70-centimeter diameter, is hung. All this decoration understandably served to disorient the new arrivals, to give them the momentary impression that they have simply come to a transit station.'[26] Samuel Willenberg, also an inmate of the camp, was appalled at the trickery employed by the SS. As he saw it, the Jews now 'alighted on to the platform in the usual manner, as if they had arrived in a health resort. And here, on this small plot of land, was taking place the greatest murder that ever took place in Europe, in the entire world.'[27] In addition to the transformation of the arrival area, other facilities at the camp were expanded. 'There were also workshops,' says Kalman Taigman, 'there were tailors who would sew new clothing for the SS. There was a metal works and a carpenter shop and an electricians' shop.'[28]

But despite this air of seeming permanence, the Jews working inside the death camp knew that the intention of the Germans was – in the words of Oskar Strawczynski – that 'we will never leave Treblinka alive.'[29] Fearing for their future, a group of Sonderkommandos started to plot a way out of the camp. In this enterprise they were helped by the arrogance of the SS and the complacency of their Ukrainian helpers, who were used to seeing Jews terrified and cowed. Moreover, as we have seen, the SS had decided that it was impractical to kill all the Jewish workers in the camp at regular intervals and replace them – not least because training new workers and educating them about the mechanics of the camp was time consuming. Keeping the Sonderkommandos alive for a longer period made the lives of the SS easier, but the risk of an uprising was consequently greater – especially as over time the security tended to become more lax.

Notwithstanding the arrogance of their SS overseers, the difficulties faced by the conspirators within the Sonderkommandos were immense. If the SS had the slightest sense that any resistance was planned, they would torture those they suspected in order to find out the details of the plot. That was the reason that one of the organizers of the planned revolt, Dr Julian Chorążycki, took poison in April 1943 when he was discovered with a large amount of money with which he had hoped to bribe one of the guards. He chose to kill himself rather than risk betraying his comrades.

By the summer of 1943 the Sonderkommandos at Treblinka were becoming increasingly alarmed. They were concerned that soon the camp would be closed and, as part of that process, they would inevitably be killed. Finally, on 2 August, they decided to act. 'We were sick of our miserable existence,' wrote Yankel Wiernik, an inmate at Treblinka, 'and all that mattered was to take revenge on our tormentors and to escape . . . The long processions, those ghastly caravans of death, were still before our eyes, crying out for vengeance. We knew what lay hidden beneath the surface of this soil. We were the only ones left alive to tell the story. Silently, we took our leave of the ashes of our fellow Jews and vowed that, out of their blood, an avenger would arise.'[30]

The conspirators managed to steal weapons from the armoury in the camp, and on the afternoon of 2 August they attacked the SS and the other guards. At the same time other prisoners doused wooden buildings with petrol and set them on fire. Several hundred prisoners now rushed for the barbed wire. 'Some of us were mowed down by the machine guns,' says Samuel Willenberg, who escaped from Treblinka that day. 'And I ran over those corpses.' The perimeter fence at Treblinka was not electrified, and using blankets to cover the wire, Samuel and the rest of the prisoners rushed towards the nearby forest, all the time under fire from the guards. Samuel remembers that as he ran he 'screamed like a madman: "The hell has been burnt!"'[31]

Around 300 prisoners managed to escape, but – as we shall see – getting past the wire fence was just the first of many dangerous challenges that prisoners who broke out from a death camp had to face.

• • •

Surprisingly, the SS did not learn lessons from the uprising at Treblinka, and a similar breakout occurred at Sobibór less than three months later. Just as at Treblinka, the Sonderkommandos at the death camp of Sobibór understood that once their usefulness to the Germans ceased, they would be killed. Their own existence depended on the murder factory continuing to function. This tragic dichotomy – their lives were prolonged by the deaths of others – was not lost on them. 'For some time again there had been a lull in transports,' wrote Toivi Blatt, a member of the Sobibór Sonderkommando. 'Food was scarce, and we were hungry, because we previously supplemented our diet with the food we found in the luggage of new arrivals. Suddenly the Nazis ordered us to prepare for a transport that would arrive the next day. Somewhere on the distant rails of Poland, a doomed train was rolling toward Sobibor. Karolek [another Sonderkommando] turned toward me and said, "Tomorrow there will be plenty of food." I thought: Are we still humans?'[32]

Between March and July 1943, the deportation of nearly 35,000 Dutch Jews to Sobibór brought considerable wealth to the camp. These Jews, direct from the Netherlands, carried food and jewels with them. It was unusual for large transports from western Europe to arrive at a Reinhard death camp. The decision to deport Dutch Jews to Sobibór was probably taken because thousands of Jews had just been sent to Auschwitz from Greece, and Sobibór had spare killing capacity. But whatever the precise motive for it, this decision was one of the reasons why the overall death toll of Jews from the Netherlands was so high. Unlike at Auschwitz, where a proportion of new arrivals were selected on the ramp to work as forced labour, at Sobibór more than 99 per cent of the people on each transport were dead within a few hours of arrival. Out of the 35,000 Dutch Jews who were sent to Sobibór, fewer than two dozen survived. So while it is understandable that historians focus on the domestic factors within the Netherlands that might have contributed to the large proportion of Dutch Jews who lost their lives in the Holocaust – such as the cooperative attitude of the Dutch civil service – it is important to remember that this German decision to send the Dutch Jews to Sobibór also had some, albeit limited, impact.[33]

When the Dutch Jews entered the camp, many believed the Nazi lie that they had arrived at a hygiene stop. 'This trap was so perfect,' says

Toivi Blatt, one of the Sonderkommando who dealt with the Dutch transports, 'that I'm sure that when they were in the gas chambers and gas came out instead of water, probably they were thinking that this was some kind of malfunction . . . When the job was finished, when they were already taken out of the gas chambers to be burnt, I remember thinking to myself that it was a beautiful night [with] the stars really quiet . . . Three thousand people died [in that one transport]. Nothing happened. The stars are in the same place.'[34]

At Sobibór, it took the arrival of a group of Soviet prisoners of war in September 1943 – all of them sent to the camp because they were also Jews – to act as the catalyst for a mass escape. About eighty of the POWs were selected to work as builders within the camp and they soon realized the special nature of Sobibór. As one of them, Arkadiy Vajspapir, says, 'we knew that the Germans would not leave anyone alive, especially in that camp.'[35] Under the leadership of a Red Army officer called Alexander Pechersky, they conceived a daring plan. The idea was to ask individual members of the SS to come to the cobblers' workshop and the tailors' shop in the camp for fittings. The prisoners believed – and it turned out they were correct – that the Germans, all asked to come at set intervals, would arrive exactly on time. Once they sat down, waiting for the fitting, they would be killed by a prisoner who had hidden in the back of the hut.

On 14 October 1943 they put their plan into action. At half past three in the afternoon, Arkadiy Vajspapir, together with a comrade called Yehuda Lerner, hid behind a curtain at the back of the cobblers' hut. 'The German came in for a shoe fitting,' says Arkadiy. 'He sat down just in front of me. So I stepped out and hit him. I didn't know that you should do it with the flat side of the axe. I hit him with the blade. We took him away and put a cloth over him. And then another German came in. So he came up to the corpse and kicked him with his leg and said, "What is this? What does this disorder mean?" And then when he understood [what was happening] I also hit him with the axe. So then we took the pistols and ran away. Afterwards I was shivering. I couldn't calm down for a long time. I was sick. I was splashed with blood.'[36]

While Arkadiy Vajspapir and Yehuda Lerner killed two Germans in the cobblers' workshop, their colleagues attacked three more members of the SS in the tailors' shop. By late afternoon the majority of the SS men in the camp had been killed, but the SS commander, Karl Frenzel, was still alive. 'I found Sasha [Alexander Pechersky, the leader of the uprising] and told him we had killed two Germans,' says Arkadiy. 'And he said that we should kill Frenzel. We should go to his room . . . and I said that I couldn't. My hands were shaking. I was shivering all over my body, I said I couldn't do it . . . he understood, and he didn't . . . push me. So I didn't kill anyone else.'[37]

Just before six o'clock in the evening the prisoners moved towards the main gate. They now came under fire not just from the guard towers, but from Frenzel who turned a machine gun on them. Many of the prisoners ran straight for the wire, but when Toivi Blatt reached the fence it collapsed on him: 'My first thought was, "This is the end!" People were stepping over me, and the barbed wire points went into my coat. But finally I had a stroke of genius. I left the leather coat in the barbed wire and just slid out. I started to run. I fell down about two or three times; each time I thought I was hit, but I got up, nothing happened to me, and finally [I reached] the forest.'[38]

Just as at Treblinka, the majority of prisoners who escaped from Sobibór did not survive the war. Out of the 300 who crossed the wire of the camp, perhaps sixty made it through to the end of the conflict. They had to survive less than two years in the country in which many of them had been born – they spoke the language, they knew the landscape. Yet so many perished. The reasons why this happened are complex, but the experience of Toivi Blatt encapsulated many of the difficulties the escapees faced. He was well aware, for instance, that he had not reached 'safety' when he got to the forest, for 'it wasn't safe at all.'[39] Not only did he run the risk of the pursuing Germans catching up with him, and local farmers capturing him for a reward, but he was worried that he might encounter groups of armed 'bandits' – Poles who had sought refuge in the forest and now lived by robbing others.

Toivi desperately wanted to stay with Sasha, the Red Army officer who had led the revolt, as he felt much safer under his protection. But the day after the breakout Sasha announced that he and eight other members of his unit were going off on their own. 'Sasha said, "Now we must find out where we are, so a group of us will go to check the area and maybe buy food,"' remembers Toivi, 'and he ordered us to give him some money . . . he just promised that he will be back, and he left and he never came back.'[40] Toivi was devastated. After the war he confronted Sasha about what had happened. Toivi told him that while he would always be a hero 'not only in my eyes, but the eyes of other survivors' he had 'done something which I think you shouldn't have', because 'you took nine people with nine guns and left us with practically nothing. So he told me – "Listen, I was a soldier, my first obligation was to go back to the army." He explained this with some kind of a little bit of shame. But nevertheless he said, "I was a soldier and a soldier is supposed to go back." '

Sasha led his armed group east and they managed to make contact with Soviet partisans. 'Only those who flocked together could survive,' says Arkadiy Vajspapir, one of Sasha's unit. 'The only thing that helped us to survive – that we kept together all nine of us. We had many brave and courageous people, but they were not respected as much as Sasha.'[41]

But in saving his comrades Sasha had left the rest of this group of forty or so escapees in disarray. Small factions formed and argued with others. Without leadership some of the stronger wanted to discard the weaker. Eventually, Toivi and two others detached themselves from the main group and made for his hometown of Izbica. With winter approaching, they were desperate to find shelter. When they eventually reached Izbica, Toivi approached one villager, who he knew had venerated his father, and begged her to hide them. She refused, fearing German retribution. She said that her husband had been taken to Auschwitz and she wanted to save her son. 'By the terror etched in her face,' wrote Toivi, 'I could clearly see we represented a deadly plague, the Black Death of the twentieth century.'[42]

They moved on and met a farmer who was prepared, in return for the gold and jewels the escapees had carried with them from the camp, to hide them in a pit at the back of his barn. But the farmer was interested only in what he could take from them, and after several months – once he had 'borrowed' many of their clothes – he attempted to kill them with the help of some friends. Toivi escaped only because after they had fired a shot that grazed his jaw he pretended he was dead. Having fled from the farm, Toivi hid in a ruined brickworks in Izbica and relied on acquaintances to bring him food. But he was almost as much at risk here as he had been in the hands of the murderous farmer. Armed groups from the forest sometimes came and searched the area – some of them were partisans and some were simply bandits. Toivi was afraid of both.

Many of the partisans were anti-Semitic – one group, even though it included one of Toivi's childhood acquaintances, refused to let him join simply because he was a Jew.

Starving, Toivi approached his former teacher and begged her for help. She replied that she was frightened, because the Germans had recently captured a Jew and then tortured him to make him reveal the names of the people who had assisted him. Toivi turned away, but the woman was overcome by pity and gave him a loaf of bread. Eventually, outside Izbica, Toivi met a farmer who had known him since childhood. The farmer agreed that Toivi could stay with him – as long as he pretended to be a non-Jewish Pole and looked after the cows.

Toivi was protected by the farmer until the Red Army liberated Poland. 'I should have jumped for joy,' wrote Toivi of his reaction to surviving the war. 'So why did I feel such sadness, such tremendous sorrow, such emptiness in my soul? What my survival instincts had suppressed now hit me with full force. My loved ones were gone, my world was gone. I felt empty, sad and alone.'[43]

Looking back, Toivi believes that there are 'three basic ingredients' of anti-Semitism, and that they were all present in Poland during the war: 'Religious prejudice which was very strong in Poland; economic and social difficulties – the country had some problems – and of course it was very easy to point at [that is, blame] the Jew. And the third one is simple jealousy, mostly Jews made a living for themselves.'[44] But Toivi also accepts, despite the widespread anti-Semitism, that it was only because of the kindness of a number of Catholic Poles that he was able to survive at all.

Toivi Blatt's story illustrates many of the difficulties that Polish Jews faced even if they managed to escape from German hands. The destruction of Jewish communities meant that they had no safe place to hide – no fellow Jews on whom they could rely. Moreover, a German decree of 15 October 1941 stated that not only would the Germans execute Jews who were found outside a camp or ghetto without permission, but that any Poles who had assisted them would also be killed. So giving a Jew a crust of bread meant death if you were caught. Jews were also at risk of blackmail from non-Jewish Poles, and Jews would often have to pay large amounts of money for a place of refuge. As a result, Jews without financial resources were intensely vulnerable. Female Jews who sought somewhere to hide were particularly at risk of sexual exploitation. There were also strong incentives for Poles to denounce Jews. In some areas of the General Government, for example, any Pole that betrayed a Jew could expect to receive as much as a third of that Jew's property as a reward.[45]

Israel Cymlich escaped in April 1943 from a labour camp close to Treblinka and – just like Toivi Blatt – he found it hard to survive in Nazi-occupied Poland. He managed to reach Warsaw, but soon came to the conclusion that, even if Jews could make it beyond the wire of the ghetto, 'In many cases, having failed to find a shelter, overcome by hunger, and realizing the hopelessness of his situation, such a person voluntarily surrendered to the police.'[46]

But this is only part of the history, for Israel Cymlich – just like Toivi Blatt – owed his life to the compassion of non-Jewish Poles. A Polish couple, Mr and Mrs Kobos, sheltered him in the attic of their house in Warsaw, letting him stay even after his money had run out. They risked their lives, motivated by a sense that they were doing what was right. Israel Cymlich wrote that he was 'puzzled' by 'the fact that those people did so much for me and had been keeping me for so long. For people as poor as they were, this was a serious burden.'[47]

Large numbers of non-Jewish Poles helped the Jews, and the methods they used were often ingenious. Dr Eugene Lazowski, for instance, managed to convince the Germans that there was an outbreak of typhoid in the area around Rozwadów. He did this by injecting the population – including many Jews – with a safe substance that mimicked typhoid so that when the Germans conducted blood tests they believed the whole district was infected. As a result the Germans stayed well clear of the area and thousands of Jews and Poles were not deported.[48]

In Warsaw, around 28,000 Jews lived in defiance of German restrictions outside the ghetto. Most were hidden by non-Jewish Poles. Of these 28,000 Jews, about 11,500 survived the war. One credible estimate is that between 7 and 9 per cent of the non-Jewish population of Warsaw gave assistance to the Jews – that is 70,000–90,000 people.[49] It is a statistic that gives the lie to the lazy stereotype that the Poles did little to help the Jews. In fact, as one scholar concludes, the survival rate of Jewish fugitives in Warsaw 'was not much less than that observed in a Western European country such as the Netherlands'.[50]

A similar, nuanced judgement needs to be made about the actions of the resistance forces fighting within Poland, most notably the Polish Home Army. That's because while there were undoubtedly many units in the Home Army that were anti-Semitic, there were also units that accepted Jews into their ranks. Samuel Willenberg, for instance, who had escaped from Treblinka, joined the Home Army and participated in the Warsaw uprising in the summer of 1944. He remembers that he took a risk in revealing to the non-Jewish Poles that he was a Jew, but he wanted to 'die under my own name'. While, he says, 'there were characters in the Home Army who gave me trouble,' in the particular section he belonged to they were 'nice people' and even though they 'knew I was a Jew' it was not a problem.[51]

The Home Army also occasionally helped Jewish resistance fighters. They provided some weapons to Jews for use during the Warsaw ghetto uprising, for instance, though some Jews felt they should have given much more assistance than they did. The truth, as one scholar says, is that 'because the Home Army was an umbrella organization of disparate Polish organizations numbering more than 300,000, from all regions ranging from socialists to nationalists, its attitude and behavior towards the Jews varied widely.'[52] The history – as Samuel Willenberg experienced personally – was thus a multifaceted one.

During 1943 the Nazi leadership watched as the morale of the German population fell still further. The fire bombing of Hamburg by the RAF in late July had a devastating effect; 40,000 Germans died – more than British losses in the whole of the Blitz. 'The losses in Hamburg were great,' said Albert Speer, Nazi Armaments Minister, after the war, 'the greatest we had suffered in any raid, particularly from the burning houses. And the depression among the population was extraordinary.'[53] In such circumstances, it was vital for Hitler that the Nazi leadership stand firm. As he said in his speech on 10 September, 'the party must set an example in everything.'[54] An obvious concern lay behind his words – some Nazis might try and follow the example of the Italians, and exit the war.

Himmler knew one way of countering such defeatism – broaden the knowledge of the extermination of the Jews. This crime, which up to now had been conducted in such secrecy, would now be talked about in meetings attended by more than a hundred Nazi leaders. It was a remarkable turnaround of policy, but the thinking behind it was clear. Once many more Nazis understood the extent of the atrocities that had been committed in their name, what choice would they have but to 'burn their boats' and never give up? The Italian elite – the King and senior Fascists – had been able to walk away from the war untainted by the crime of mass murder, but that was not going to be an option for the broader Nazi leadership.

In October 1943 Heinrich Himmler gave two speeches at Posen in Poland – one to around ninety senior SS leaders and another to senior party figures including Reichsleiters and Gauleiters. In these speeches Himmler was open about the extermination of the Jews and thus made everyone who listened into a co-conspirator. For example, he told the Reichsleiters and Gauleiters on 6 October, 'I didn't believe myself to be justified in eradicating the [Jewish] men – that is killing them or having them killed – and then letting their children grow up to take revenge on our sons and grandsons. The tough decision to make this people disappear from the face of the earth had to be taken. For the organization which had to carry out the task, it was the hardest we have ever had to undertake.'[55] Himmler could scarcely have been more explicit.

In parallel with telling Nazi leaders the true extent of their collective guilt, Himmler wanted to wind up the extermination operation of the Reinhard camps. The revolts at Treblinka and Sobibór, together with the Jewish resistance in a number of ghettos – not only in Warsaw in April, but more recently in Białystok in August – had reinforced his desire to centralize much of the killing process on the more secure facility at Auschwitz.[56] He was also influenced by bureaucratic considerations. He wanted to eliminate the possibility that the Jews in the area could be used as forced labour by any German agency other than the SS.[57] As a result, in October 1943, he told Friedrich-Wilhelm Krüger, the SS and police chief in the General Government, to liquidate the large camps still operating in the Lublin district.[58]

Himmler's order to murder the remaining Jews at Majdanek in the suburbs of Lublin was carried out in November 1943 in a series of massacres known as the Harvest Festival killings. Henryk Nieścior, a Polish political prisoner in Majdanek at the time, witnessed the preparations for the crime. 'Near the crematorium in Field V [different areas within Majdanek were known as "fields"] in late October 1943 the Germans

assigned Jews to dig ditches, which were dug in zigzag form.'[59] He
remembered that the Germans tried to reassure the Jews that the ditches
were nothing sinister – merely defence works, necessary because the
front line was getting ever closer. On 3 November, the Germans ordered
all the Jews in the camp to 'step forward' and they were taken up towards
the area where the ditches had been dug. Shortly afterwards the SS
started shooting the Jews with machine guns while music played
through loudspeakers.

Jews from surrounding camps were also murdered in Majdanek.
They were ordered in small groups to lie down in ditches and then shot.
Members of the next group to be killed were told to lie on top of the
corpses of those who had just died and then the guns were turned on
them. Not everyone died at once and it was to drown out their screams –
and the screams of the Jews who were about to die – that two 'radio cars'
blared out popular music.[60] On 3 November around 18,000 people were
killed at Majdanek – the largest number ever killed in a death camp on
a single day. It is another reminder that gas chambers were not needed
in order to murder en masse.

The overall Harvest Festival operation also included killings in two
other nearby camps, Trawniki and Poniatowa. At Poniatowa a number
of Jews resisted as the Germans attempted to kill them. They managed
to snatch some weapons and opened fire on their captors, but the Germans set fire to the barracks in which they sought refuge and burnt
them alive. Their brave resistance would only have confirmed to
Himmler that his judgement that the Jews in these camps should be
liquidated was correct. In total around 43,000 Jews died as a result of the
Harvest Festival action.

Treblinka and Sobibór ceased to operate as death camps around the
same time. Both were now dismantled and an attempt was made to
eliminate all traces of the crime. These camps – along with Bełżec, the
first Operation Reinhard fixed-killing installation – had always been
seen by the Nazis as transitory places, and since by now there were
hardly any Jews left alive in the General Government, and Auschwitz
had more than adequate killing capacity for Jews from western Europe,
there was no need for them to exist. Bełżec had ceased to kill people in
large numbers by December 1942 and was fully dismantled by the summer
of 1943. As for Treblinka, the last transport arrived in August 1943, two

weeks after the revolt, and the camp was subsequently destroyed during the autumn. Sobibór was the final Reinhard death camp to be dismantled. And since the prisoners who had not managed to escape had been killed the day after the revolt, another Sonderkommando unit was sent to take the camp apart. After they had completed their task, they too were murdered.

By December 1943 all these camps had vanished. In their place were farms and fields. 'For reasons of surveillance,' wrote Globocnik to Himmler, 'a small farm was created in each camp which is occupied by a guard. A pension must be paid regularly to him in order that he can maintain the farm.'[61] But a problem remained for the Nazis: a large number of the local population knew what had been going on. Many of them believed that jewellery, gold and other valuables left by the murdered Jews lay concealed among the soil and the ashes of the site. So one function of the 'farmer' was to stop the locals scavenging for plunder.

Operation Reinhard was officially over. On 30 November 1943, Himmler wrote to Globocnik thanking him for the 'great and unique services that you carried out for the German people by implementing Operation Reinhard'.[62] In total, around 1.7 million people had been murdered in this action between March 1942 and November 1943. Most of them had died in one of three camps – Bełżec, Sobibór or Treblinka.

When images are used to symbolize the Holocaust, it is mostly Auschwitz that is featured. The centrality of Auschwitz in the memorialization of the crime is almost ubiquitous. In Britain, the very date of Holocaust Memorial Day is the anniversary of the liberation of Auschwitz. Of course, Auschwitz did, as we shall see, go on to become the most murderous death camp of them all. But there is a danger that these three Reinhard camps – Bełżec, Sobibór and Treblinka – become, if not forgotten, then somehow overlooked. The Nazis would have approved of this. They wanted no one to remember these places. But in many respects it is these camps that symbolize the singularity of the crime. It needed only a handful of Germans to direct the murder of 1.7 million people. Every one of these individuals died not because of anything they had ever done, but simply because of who their grandparents had happened to be. Once their lives had been erased, the places in which they had been murdered were erased as well. One does not see images of Bełżec, Treblinka or Sobibór in Holocaust memorialization because there are no images of the camps to show. In a way, that, as much as anything else, demonstrates the bleakness of the crime. Those who were murdered were turned to nothing, and the places where they died were turned to nothing along with them.

As for the leading perpetrators, they swiftly left the scene of the crime. In September 1943, Globocnik departed for northern Italy, where he had been appointed Higher SS and Police Leader. He took many of his co-conspirators with him, including Christian Wirth and Franz Stangl. They soon found use for their particular talents in Trieste, in a region now annexed to the Reich. At Risiera di San Sabba, a factory in the south of the city, they helped to create one of the most notorious concentration camps and prisons in the Mediterranean. The majority of those killed here were not Jews, but partisans. At least 3,000 people were murdered at Risiera di San Sabba – most beaten to death or executed by firing squad in the courtyard of the building. Just as at Majdanek, music was played loudly in an attempt to drown out the noise of the killing. From April 1944, the bodies of those who had been murdered were burnt in a purpose-built crematorium on the site – created by Erwin Lambert, who had previously constructed gas chambers not just for the T4 programme but also at Sobibór and Treblinka. Once the bodies had been burnt, the ashes were thrown into the nearby harbour.[63]

Franz Stangl, former commandant of Treblinka, believed that he knew the reason why he and the other Operation Reinhard staff had been sent to this hazardous area – one designated a *Bandenkampfgebiet*, a 'bandit-fighting district'. 'I realized quite well', he said after the war, 'that we were an embarrassment to the brass: they wanted to find ways and means to "incinerate" us. So we were assigned the most dangerous jobs – anything to do with anti-partisan combat in that part of the world was very perilous.'[64] But while it is true that Christian Wirth was killed in May 1944 by partisans, both Stangl and Globocnik survived the war – Globocnik only by a matter of days, since he committed suicide after the British captured him on 31 May 1945. As for Franz Stangl, he escaped to South America where he was eventually arrested in 1967. He was subsequently sentenced in West Germany to life in prison.

The era of the Reinhard camps was over. But the most infamous period in the life of Auschwitz – one that would make this place the site of the largest mass murder in history – was just about to begin.

16. Auschwitz

(1943–1944)

Only now did Auschwitz become central to the Holocaust. But it is important to remember that even after the new gas-chamber complexes had opened at Birkenau, vastly increasing the camp's capacity to kill, Auschwitz continued to perform a variety of functions in the Nazi state – not just extermination.

One of the most surprising, given the reality of what took place there, was to provide a possible propaganda alibi for the Nazis. In early September 1943, 5,000 Jews were sent to Auschwitz Birkenau from Theresienstadt, north-west of Prague.[1] Uniquely among the Jewish prisoners, they were permitted to live in a 'family camp' within Birkenau. Though men lived in separate barracks from women, children were not sent directly to the gas chambers, but were allowed to live with one of their parents. The Jews were told to write postcards to their relatives still in the camp at Theresienstadt. The idea was that the Red Cross staff who inspected Theresienstadt would, via this ruse, believe that Birkenau was merely a labour camp. Several months later, once the Nazis had used them in this way, almost all of the Jews in the family camp were murdered in the gas chambers.

Another function of Auschwitz, which distinguished the place from the Reinhard camps, was the increasing instance of medical experimentation. The most infamous medical practitioner at Auschwitz arrived in spring 1943 – Dr Josef Mengele. His 'research' into twins and dwarfs would shock the world when it was revealed in all its cruelty. In his work he was assisted by a number of prisoners. One of them was Wilhelm Brasse, who had been sent to Auschwitz as a Polish political prisoner in 1940 at the age of twenty-two, and so by 1943 was one of the longest-serving inmates in the camp. He had trained as a photographer, and it was this skill that the German doctors at Auschwitz sought to exploit. 'I spoke to Dr Mengele,' he says. 'He explained to me that he would send women to me, Jewish women, twins and triplets and all kinds of cases, and he wanted photos to show the whole person from the

front, from the side, profile and from the back. Also naked [photos] . . .
These women were very much ashamed and intimidated. The children
were terribly intimidated. They were afraid even to speak to one
another. As far as what they looked like those were young women,
young girls just developing – they were not worn out. He [Mengele]
would take them from the transports . . . I felt ashamed and it was painful, unpleasant . . .' Wilhelm Brasse took pictures of some appalling
sights. 'He [Mengele] explained to me he would send from the Gypsy
camp a case of water cancer. I've forgotten the other name of this illness,
the professional name [a disease known as noma, which was prevalent in
the Gypsy camp] . . . They sent a young Gypsy who had the cancer,
water cancer on his face, you could see the whole jaw, you could see the
bone visible, and he [Mengele] explained to me it must be photographed
from profile so the bone would be visible . . . These things are constantly
before my eyes. After the war I had recurring dreams, either of someone
brought from Dr Mengele or they're looking for me, taking me to be
shot.'[2]

Dr Mengele and his activities have dominated the public memory
about the corruption of medical ideals at Auschwitz. And it is not hard
to see why. Mengele was thirty-two years old when he arrived at
Auschwitz, a handsome, decorated veteran of the war. He was undoubtedly
brave – he had won the Iron Cross for rescuing two soldiers from a
burning tank – and he was always perfectly turned out. Survivors often
remark, for instance, on his immaculate uniform and his beautifully
polished boots. He was the opposite of the caricature image of the
sweating, red-faced SS killer.

Mengele was a staunch Nazi. He had joined the party in 1937 and had
demonstrated a commitment to the nationalist cause even before Hitler
came to power. He was also a dedicated racist and believed he was a
member of a master race. But nothing in his previous background before
Auschwitz suggested that he had a capacity for sadism on a gigantic
scale – yet that is what he demonstrated in the camp. He seemed to
relish the power he had during selections, not just on the ramp but in
the hospital barracks when he chose who was to die from among the
existing inmates.

For Mengele, Auschwitz was an enormous medical playground. He
could devise whatever medical experiments he liked in pursuit of his

'racial' research, limited only by his imagination. His special interest was always genetics, and how genes were passed on within families – he was thus particularly keen to experiment on twins. Vera Alexander, a Kapo who looked after twins selected by Mengele, recalls how they often returned to the block screaming with pain after his attentions. Having observed him at close quarters, she says that she simply cannot 'understand his cruelty'.[3] The overwhelming advantage for Dr Mengele of studying twins was that once an experiment had been completed on one twin, both could be murdered and their bodies dissected to compare the two. As Dr Miklós Nyiszli, a prisoner who assisted Dr Mengele, said, 'Where, under normal circumstances, can one find twin brothers who die at the same place and at the same time?' But at Auschwitz 'there were several hundred sets of twins, and therefore as many possibilities of dissection.'[4]

Mengele was not the only Nazi doctor who conducted medical experiments at Auschwitz. In a specially equipped medical block, for instance, Professor Carl Clauberg and Dr Horst Schumann both conducted research into sterilization. Wilhelm Brasse, who took photos for Mengele, also took photographs of women under anaesthetic who had been subjected to these sterilization experiments. The women were placed in a special gynaecological chair and the doctors 'would stretch the vagina and take the uterus out with forceps, and I would take photos of it. Not the whole person but just the sexual parts and the uterus. In several cases I used colour film. We didn't develop it in our lab as we didn't have a colour film lab, we sent it to Berlin . . . For me it was the worst – seeing this terrible sight. I had information that in many cases such operated women were [subsequently] given a shot [an injection] and killed.'[5]

Carl Clauberg had previously held the post of professor of gynaecology at the University of Königsberg, and was, like Mengele, a committed National Socialist. Himmler had taken an interest in his work and had personally approved his use of Auschwitz as a human research laboratory. As we have seen earlier in this history, sterilization was a subject of considerable interest for the Reichsführer SS. In pursuit of his experiments, Clauberg injected various substances into women in order to prevent fertilization. 'Those women were in horrible pain, and had high temperature,' says Silvia Veselá, a Slovak Jew who assisted Clauberg. 'I measured their temperature, did X-rays, and so on.'[6]

While Clauberg experimented with the use of injections, his colleague Dr Schumann gave his subjects massive doses of radiation.
Silvia Veselá recalls that 'the impact of X-ray intensity on [the] small
intestine was tested on them. It was more than awful. Those women
were throwing up all the time. It was really terrible.'[7] During her time
in Auschwitz, Silvia confesses that she became emotionally numbed to
suffering: 'If you are beaten too hard, after a while you feel nothing. Do
you know that feeling? No, you don't, because you haven't experienced
such a treatment. But as I said before: if you are beaten too hard, after a
while you feel nothing, because you are apathetic. That was the only
rescue . . . To become apathetic.'[8] She herself was forced to take part in
one of Clauberg's medical trials. 'I was ill and they carried out some
experiments on me . . . Unfortunately, after the war when I got married, in spite of those experiments I got pregnant. I had to undertake a
very loathsome abortion. Doctors told me, "That's enough! Don't dare
to be pregnant any more." '[9]

Medical experiments on inmates were not confined to Auschwitz.
Doctors in other concentration camps also participated. Soon after the
war began, doctors at Sachsenhausen exposed prisoners to mustard gas
in order to measure the effect of the poison. But it was at Dachau that
some of the most infamous experiments took place, supervised by Dr
Sigmund Rascher. In 1942 prisoners were locked in airtight chambers
and tested to see how much pressure their bodies could endure. Other
prisoners were thrust into icy water to assess how long downed aircrew
could survive in a freezing sea.

The potential value to the Luftwaffe of these experiments was obvious. But not everyone in the German Air Force was content that human
beings had died in the course of the trials. When, in October 1942, Dr
Rascher presented his findings to senior figures in the Air Ministry, he
detected an element of disquiet among his audience. Just before the
meeting Himmler had stated his own position on the subject in a letter
to Dr Rascher: 'I believe that people objecting to these human experiments still today, who would rather German soldiers died of the
consequences of this hypothermia, are high traitors, and I shall not
refrain from mentioning the names of these gentlemen to the authorities
in question.'[10] There is even evidence that Himmler sought Hitler's
approval for this research, and that Hitler took the view that 'in

principle as far as the welfare of the state is concerned, human experimentation has to be tolerated.'[11]

In one of the most bleakly bizarre episodes of Nazi human experimentation, Dr Rascher attempted to revive a prisoner who was unconscious as a result of exposure to freezing conditions, by placing him between two naked female prisoners. Himmler had been the one who had suggested the idea, because he thought that 'a fisherwoman could well take her half-frozen husband into her bed and revive him in that manner.'[12]

In Dachau and Sachsenhausen many of the prisoners selected to be tortured for medical experimentation were non-Jews, but that wasn't so surprising given that by the start of 1943 there were fewer than 400 Jews in the concentration camps in the Reich that had been built before the war.[13] Even in Auschwitz, as we have seen, Dr Mengele could choose Sinti and Roma to die just as easily as he could choose Jews. For someone like Mengele, Nazi ideology justified a raft of murderous schemes: from the extermination of the Jews to deadly medical experiments. It was all part of a world in which medical professionals were the arbiters of life and death within the racial state.

Auschwitz had by now become a vast enterprise that encompassed many different functions and goals – and the lines between them all were sometimes blurred. That was certainly the case with the treatment of Polish political prisoners. The personal history of Tadeusz Smreczyński, for instance, demonstrates how the suffering of non-Jewish Poles became linked in the gas chambers of Birkenau with that of the Jews. Tadeusz was fifteen years old when the Germans invaded Poland in September 1939. He lived with his family in Zator, only a few miles from Auschwitz. The Germans prevented Poles like him from receiving any further education and he was forced to leave school. In September 1940, at the age of sixteen, he was sent to Germany to work as a forced labourer, but in November he escaped, and fled to Kraków where he lived with an aunt. Five months later he returned home to Zator in the hope that the Germans had forgotten about him. He now started, on his own initiative, to work against the Germans. He helped people cross the nearby border between Upper Silesia, which had been incorporated into the Reich, and the General Government. He also produced leaflets criticizing the Germans. In December 1943 he developed a plan to help

Poles imprisoned in the nearby camps and, as a first step, passed on several bread-ration cards to a friend. 'He was planning to get some bread,' says Tadeusz, 'and give it away to the prisoners when SS men were not around. I arranged these coupons for him. Unfortunately he had a tendency to drink alcohol and he got involved in a brawl at the railway station in Auschwitz. He was subsequently arrested and those coupons were found on him. He told me later that he was beaten and had no choice but to disclose that I had fled Germany and that I had distributed the leaflets and assisted the fugitives.'[14]

Tadeusz was found, arrested and taken to Mysłowice prison – a place where inmates were 'beaten and forced to confess'. Here, he signed the confession the Germans put in front of him since 'there was no point in denying anything.' At Mysłowice assessments were made in order to decide where the prisoners should be sent next. The place Tadeusz most feared was Auschwitz, because he knew that a 'police court' with a terrifying reputation was held inside Block 11 in the main camp. In the spring of 1944, he learnt his fate. He, and fifty or so other prisoners, were loaded on to a truck and driven out of the prison, escorted by police on motorbikes. 'After the convoy turned left,' he says, 'we knew we were going to Auschwitz. We were all sitting quietly, thinking about our fate and our families because we knew that this was the last day of our lives.'

They arrived at Auschwitz main camp and marched under the entrance gate, inscribed 'Arbeit macht frei'. They turned right, past the red-brick buildings where the inmates lived, until they reached the walled courtyard between Blocks 10 and 11. Here they were joined by more than a hundred prisoners who had been taken up from the cells in Block 11. Shortly afterwards, says Tadeusz, 'The Gestapo commander, a Doctor of Law from Katowice, with two officers in tow arrived and the administration of justice began. Each one of us was called to report individually. We had to climb a few stairs leading from the courtyard to the block and then wait in a corridor. When my turn came I went into the room and was asked to provide my personal details. All the charges against me were read out.' He was then told to join one of three groups of prisoners. There was no 'trial', no chance for him to defend himself; the 'court' merely announced which group each individual prisoner should join. 'They [the members of the court] were taking lunch breaks and dinner breaks and so it all lasted till evening.' Once the selection of all the prisoners was over, the first of the three groups was sent immediately to Birkenau and gassed. Among this group was a schoolteacher who had shared his cell at Mysłowice prison. 'Before they left he said to me,' says Tadeusz, ' "If you survive, tell Poland how we died." '[15] The second group of prisoners was sent to the gas chambers of Birkenau two days later. Only the small number of prisoners in Tadeusz's third group were admitted to the camp.

By this point in the evolution of Auschwitz the gassing of Polish political prisoners was not unusual. On 29 February 1944, for instance, 163 Poles who had been sent to Block 11 from Mysłowice prison were transported to Crematorium IV in Birkenau, along with forty-one other prisoners from Auschwitz. Among the condemned was a young Polish woman who, once she reached the crematorium, told the SS that everyone knew they were about to die in the gas chambers so the secrecy that had once surrounded this crime was no more. The Germans, she said, would one day be called to account for what they had done. As they entered the gas chamber, the Poles sang 'Poland Is Not Yet Lost' and 'To the Barricades'.[16] It is a reminder, both of the bravery of these individuals when faced with certain death, and that not only Jews perished in the gas chambers of Birkenau.

As for Tadeusz Smreczyński, he was 'surprised' that he had not been killed immediately after his 'trial' in Block 11. Once admitted to the main camp he benefited from a piece of luck. He encountered two prominent prisoners who felt a personal connection to him. The first was a Kapo: 'That man apparently recognized me from Mysłowice where I used to carry pots of food around to various blocks. The man told me he was going to take care of my safety which was something extraordinary and which made me stronger psychologically.'

On the following day Tadeusz met the second man who would offer him support: 'He introduced himself and said that he had known my father who he had worked with when my father was a mayor. He gave me his daily bread ration which was an extremely valuable gesture . . . and he said to me, "Do not let them kill you. Remember never to stand on the sides or at the front or at the back of the columns when marching or during assemblies. This is where they hit most often. So stick to the middle of the column," and he repeated "Do not let them kill you" before he departed. He did not survive the camp. The beginning was in a psychological sense very favourable to me because I became aware that I was not alone.' Tadeusz also soon learnt that it was vital to try and work 'inside' the camp. The work commandos that marched outside to dig ditches or build roads had to suffer in the freezing cold or the pouring rain and few survived for long. Tadeusz was assigned to a building commando that stayed within the confines of the main camp and so managed to avoid this fate.

Tadeusz Smreczyński was well aware that one of the functions of Auschwitz was to murder Jews. Indeed, once in the middle of the night he witnessed the emotional aftermath of a mass killing when he heard 'some commotion' outside his block: 'I peeped through the window very discreetly so as not to be seen and shot. There were men – only young and middle-aged – all naked. Their families had been gassed and they were brought to the main camp. They were ordered to stand in compact groups of five but they were in panic and each wanted to be close to his nearest relative: brother, father or a friend. SS men with dogs and Kapos were beating them. It was a teeming mass of human bodies reflected in the light of the lamps. It was a horrible sight.' He imagined how he would have felt if 'my parents had just been gassed and I stayed alive. It must have been a terrible experience – that sense of helplessness in the face of fate. One could do absolutely nothing to save one's loved ones.'

He tried to understand how the SS could be responsible for the appalling cruelty in front of him and yet still consider themselves civilized. In Birkenau he heard 'the camp's orchestra playing masterpieces by German, Austrian and Italian composers. SS men were sitting by the crematorium where children, mothers, women and men were burning, but they were just sitting there. Now I think that they were pleased to have properly completed their work and were due for a cultural entertainment. They had no dilemmas. The wind from Birkenau blew the smoke from the death camp in but they were just sitting and listening to Mozart and others. This is what a human being is capable of . . .' Experiences like this confirmed the view of the world that he had formed as a child. 'As a thirteen-year-old boy I used to read a lot and I listened to the radio, and I had the conviction that Earth is embraced by crime and there is so much evil among people. I came to a conclusion that life has no sense.'[17]

But for Oskar Groening, a member of the Auschwitz SS garrison, what was happening in the camp made at least a kind of sense. In 1943 he was twenty-two years old, and worked in the economic department of the camp, counting the money stolen from the arriving Jews. A committed nationalist, he had absorbed the key principles of Nazism: 'We were convinced by our world-view that there was a great conspiracy of Jewishness against us, and that thought was expressed in Auschwitz – that it must be avoided, what happened in the First World War must be avoided, namely that the Jews put us into misery. The enemies who are within Germany are being killed – exterminated if necessary. And between these two fights, openly at the front line and then on the home front, there's absolutely no difference – so we exterminated nothing but enemies.'[18]

It was one thing, however, to believe this in theory, quite another to watch mass murder in practice. Normally Oskar Groening could avoid the horror as most of his working hours were spent in an office, but when he saw the bloody evidence of the killings he was shocked. Once he came across bodies being burnt in the open at Birkenau: 'The fire was flickering up and the Kapo there told me afterwards details of the burning. And it was terribly disgusting – horrendous. He made fun of the fact that when the bodies started burning they obviously developed gases from the lungs or elsewhere and these bodies seemed to jump up, and the sex parts of the men suddenly became erect in a kind of way that he found laughable.'[19] But for the most part life in the camp was comfortable for Groening – almost luxurious compared to the other postings that he might have received. He, like many of the 3,000 SS serving in the Auschwitz complex, never had to bloody his own hands since only a tiny number of SS worked in the murder factories of the crematoria. For him, this 'distance' from the killing was 'the decisive thing' that enabled him to carry on working in a relatively contented way.[20] So much so that in his leisure time he liked to participate in sports. For instance, he represented the Auschwitz SS athletics team at the high jump.

In many respects Auschwitz was thus an attractive posting for a member of the SS. Not only was there little danger of getting killed, but the food and drink were excellent – much of it stolen from the arriving Jews. There was also the opportunity to get rich. An SS officer tasked with investigating corruption in the camp in 1943 later said that

'The conduct of the SS staff was beyond any of the standards that you'd expect from soldiers. They made the impression of demoralized and brutal parasites. An examination of the lockers yielded a fortune of gold, pearls, rings, and money in all kinds of currencies.'[21]

But it wasn't just the chance to get rich that motivated the SS to work at Auschwitz. As Oskar Groening says, they were told that their work was important for the security of the Reich, that the Jews were behind Bolshevism, and that it was necessary to keep fighting in this war to prevent the Red Army destroying Germany. As a result, Groening and his comrades remained committed to participating in the mass murder of civilians – from the very old to the very young.

Oskar Groening would have likely understood the reasoning behind the sentiments Adolf Hitler expressed in a speech on 30 January 1944 – the eleventh anniversary of his appointment as Chancellor. Hitler chose to deliver his speech at his headquarters in East Prussia and to have his words broadcast on the radio. Gone were the days of the fawning crowds at the Berlin Sportpalast. There was little good news to celebrate, and so Hitler preferred to hide himself from the masses. In his speech he still seemed bemused that 'England' – as he persistently called Great Britain – had chosen to side with the Soviet Union rather than Germany. 'The victory of Germany means the preservation of Europe,' he declared, 'and the victory of the Soviet Union means its annihilation.' The problem was, according to Hitler, that 'the guilty war criminals in London' now found they had no way of 'liberating themselves from their own entanglement' because their 'way back' had been cut off by 'their Jewish wire-pullers'. They had made a mistake in dealing with the Jews, said Hitler, as 'every state, once it has devoted itself to Jewry like England, will die from this plague, unless it pulls itself together at the last minute and forcibly removes these bacteria from its body. The view that it is possible to live peacefully together or even reconcile one's own interests and those of this ferment of the decomposition of peoples, is nothing else than hoping that the human body is able to assimilate plague bacilli.'[22]

Hitler's worldview, as he demonstrated in his 30 January 1944 speech, remained as consistent as it was warped and murderous. The Jews were to blame for Germany's misfortune. Just as they had sabotaged the war effort in 1914–18, they were sabotaging the war effort now. All that was clear to Hitler. The only thing that was incomprehensible was why the 'English' didn't come to their senses and realize that they were being duped by the Jews.

It is impossible to quantify how many Germans actually believed this fantasy when they heard Hitler speak these words in January 1944. What is certain is that approval for Hitler and his regime was in decline after the defeat in Stalingrad at the start of 1943. A whole host of indicators demonstrated that truth – not least the Nazi party's own reports of the public's mood. A typical one stated that members of the public were now 'daring to express open criticism of the person of the Führer and to attack him in hateful and mean fashion'.[23] One of the many jokes now told was that Hitler was currently writing a follow-up to *Mein Kampf* – My Struggle – to be called *Mein Fehler* – My Error.[24] Of course, if such views had reached the Gestapo then the retribution inflicted on the individual concerned would have been draconian.

But the threat from the 'Bolsheviks' in the east remained real whether one believed Hitler's rhetoric or not – arguably, even whether Germany surrendered or not. The Italians could change sides in this war and face a comparatively benign occupation by the Western Allies. The Germans knew that their soldiers were fighting a 'war of extermination' on the eastern front and that the Red Army was approaching. That reality meant that Hitler's warning that a defeated Germany faced 'annihilation' sounded less like a rhetorical exaggeration and more like an accurate forecast of the future. In such circumstances there seemed little practical option to many people but to fight on. As Fritz Darges, Hitler's SS adjutant, puts it, one cannot 'get off a moving train'.[25]

Hitler, when he spoke in private to his generals on 26 May 1944, emphasized the importance of the battle against the Jews in the context of the rest of the war. 'By removing the Jew,' he said, 'I have eliminated the possibilities of the formation of any revolutionary nucleus. Of course, you can say to me: "Well, couldn't you have solved this more simply – or not more simply, because everything else would have been more complicated, but more humanely?" Gentlemen, officers, we are in a life-or-death struggle.'[26]

Consequently, the war against the Jews continued, indeed it intensified. The capitulation of Italy, combined with the German occupation of the whole of France and the resulting changes in French security personnel, meant that the Germans were in a stronger position to enforce the deportation of Jews in a number of territories than they had been before. In France, the appointment of Joseph Darnand in December 1943 as General Secretary of the Police symbolized the desire of the Germans to move swiftly against French Jews.[27] Darnand, leader of the Milice, the French paramilitary collaborators, had previously accepted the SS rank of Sturmbannführer (Major). This meant that by the end of 1943 a French SS man ran the French police force. There was now a sudden increase in the number of Jews deported from France – between 20 January and 17 August 1944 nearly 15,000 Jews were sent to Auschwitz.[28] All pretence that the French security forces were somehow protecting French Jews was cast aside.

Early in 1944, Ida Grinspan, a teenage Jew hiding in the village of Le Jeune Lié in the south-west of the country, was shocked when French police came for her. 'I didn't understand,' she says. 'I thought they would be German policemen. I didn't know that the French police were making arrests. So when the policemen arrived I said, "How can French policemen arrest someone like me, a French girl who was born here?" I felt a sort of contempt. And that's why I held in my tears, and that I did not want to cry, I stayed firm.'[29]

Once she arrived in Auschwitz that same strength of will enabled her to cope: 'You had to adapt to that way of life. Do you see what I'm saying? You had to adapt to sleeping in conditions like that, you had to adapt to working hard, you had to adapt to spending hours and hours being ordered about, poorly dressed. Yes, when the mentality is there the body adapts. If you're not there mentally, the body won't follow suit . . . That is why young people managed much better than those who were thirty-five or forty years old. Forty was the maximum. The will to survive was stronger in us younger ones.'

Soon after she arrived she was told by other inmates that 'there are gas chambers here,' but it just didn't seem possible that such places could exist. 'Nobody believed them,' says Ida. 'Not one of us believed them. It was beyond belief. We said either they're joking or they've lost their minds.' Only after she smelt the noxious odours coming from the Birkenau crematoria did she 'finally' accept that 'perhaps they were right about the smell, that they were actually burning people.'

Ida says she never felt 'why me?' as she tried to survive in Auschwitz. She always knew who was really guilty for her arrest and her subsequent suffering. And to this day, as a proud Frenchwoman, she has never forgotten the role her fellow countrymen played in facilitating the Nazis' murderous assault on the Jews.[30]

Even though Jews from all over occupied Europe were now dying in the gas chambers of Birkenau, and the whole mechanism of what we now call the Holocaust had long been established, the overall picture was still not a straightforward one. For example, while the majority of ghettos in Poland had been liquidated, there remained one major exception – the Łódź ghetto, a place where large numbers of Jews still survived. The continued existence of the Łódź ghetto into 1944 demonstrates once again how the way the Holocaust was implemented could alter from place to place. At the start of 1944 there were still more than 75,000 Jews in the Łódź ghetto, permitted to live because Arthur Greiser, the ruler of the Warthegau, had convinced Himmler that the work produced by the Jews justified their continued existence.

Mordechai Chaim Rumkowski, the leader of the ghetto, had done whatever he thought necessary in order to please the Germans. Notoriously, in September 1942, he had collaborated with the Germans in the deportation of thousands of the most vulnerable Jews. On 4 September 1942, he gave a speech in the ghetto in which he said: 'I never imagined that I would be forced to deliver this sacrifice to the altar with my own hands. In my old age I must stretch out my hands and beg: Brothers and sisters, hand them over to me! Fathers and mothers, give me your children!'[31] Rumkowski spoke those words because the Nazis had told him that they wanted to reduce the number of 'useless eaters' in the ghetto – and, since small children could not work, in the eyes of the Nazis they were 'useless'. The reaction of the audience was one of 'terrifying wailing' at the news that children would be taken from their parents and sent out of the ghetto. But Rumkowski didn't only say the children would be deported. The sick would also have to leave. 'There are, in the ghetto,' he said, 'many patients who can expect to live only a few days more, maybe a few weeks. I don't know if the idea is diabolical or not, but I must say it: "Give me the sick. In their place, we can save the healthy."'[32] Rumkowski pleaded with the inhabitants of the ghetto to 'think logically' and to put themselves in his place. Then, he claimed, 'you'll reach the conclusion that I cannot proceed any other way.'[33]

Many who listened to him felt very differently about the plan. 'I was seventeen when I heard that speech,' says Lucille Eichengreen. 'I could not comprehend how somebody could ask parents for their children. I still cannot comprehend that. People were crying out, "How can you ask this? How can we do this?"'[34] Jacob Zylberstein was another Jew in the ghetto who heard the speech, and he too was outraged by it. 'Rumkowski was such a coward,' he says. 'He should have killed himself before giving the children away.'[35]

When the Jewish police came for the children and the sick, the scenes were – predictably – emotionally devastating. 'And it's no use that the child is clinging with both little arms to the mother's neck,' wrote Josef Zelkowicz in his diary. 'It's no use that the father throws himself down before the threshold and howls like a dying ox: "Only over my dead body will you take my child." It's no use that the old man clings with his bony arms to the cold walls and bed: "Let me die here quietly" . . . It's no [use] that the old woman falls at their feet, kisses their boots, and pleads: "I have grown grandchildren just [as old as you]." It's no use that the sick man buries his feverish head in the damp, sweat-covered pillow and there sobs out perhaps his last tears. It's no use. The police must deliver their consignment.'[36]

The German security forces, who worked alongside the Jewish police in organizing the deportations, were extremely brutal during the action. When one mother refused to give up her four-year-old daughter she was given three minutes to reconsider her decision. When she still refused, both she and her daughter were shot.[37]

Estera Frenkiel, a young woman who worked in the ghetto administration, remembers that as the children were snatched from their parents 'their screams reached the sky.' But she herself, in the context of the ghetto, was relatively fortunate. Though she had no children herself, she had been given ten release forms that would save the lives of ten children or sick people – and she could choose who to give them to. Just like the Jewish police who participated in the action, members of the ghetto administration staff could save their own loved ones. 'I also had close family,' she says. 'I had an uncle who had to be saved. I had a cousin. To me, one's own family is always closer. I had to take care of them all. Out of these certificates I had first to consider my own relatives . . . in these cases tears are shed, but when there are so many tears, then one thinks only of one's own situation.'[38]

The fact that a small proportion of Jews could save their own families – and that those who benefited were often the very ones charged with taking the children of others – caused considerable resentment. The Łódź ghetto chronicle, a record of life in the ghetto compiled by Jews at the time, mentioned that those who were saved from deportation in this way 'were not people who were making any contribution to society, not even people able to perform any especially valuable work in the ghetto but were, we repeat, people with connections'.[39]

During the action, Jacob Zylberstein discovered that his mother was about to be deported from a hospital within the ghetto. Panic-stricken he ran to the hospital and discovered two Jewish policemen standing outside the entrance. Luckily, one of them was a friend called Romek. He and Romek went into the hospital and Jacob started shouting, 'Mamma, Mamma, Mamma!' The hospital was packed, and it was hard to find her. But eventually he heard his mother calling back, 'Here! Here!' from behind a locked door. Jacob opened the door, and let loose an avalanche of people. 'I grabbed my mother,' says Jacob, 'and went to the second floor, because the Jewish police started to run to put everybody back into the room.' Using Romek as an intermediary, he attempted, with the offer of a watch, to bribe a German policeman who now guarded the entrance to the hospital. But that failed. 'The only way out' was via the window. So, with his mother hanging on to him, Jacob climbed down a cast-iron drainpipe to the ground and took her back home. Then, says Jacob, they had 'the biggest celebration ever'.[40]

Although no one in the ghetto could be certain that the children and the sick were being sent to their deaths, they knew that a horrible fate of some kind awaited them. After all, they reasoned, why would the Nazis want to care for children or the sick? So those left in the ghetto – the parents in particular – were tormented by the idea of the suffering that their loved ones would now be forced to endure on their own.

Over time, knowledge of the existence of the death camps seeped through the ghetto. By the start of 1944, for instance, Jacob Zylberstein knew all about Auschwitz. He had met a Polish carpenter on a building site who had said to him, 'I was in Auschwitz.' Jacob 'took no notice, because I never heard of the city of Auschwitz. And I passed by. On the way back, he stopped me and said, "Do you know what Auschwitz is?" And I said, "Where is Auschwitz?" And he said, "Not far from Kraków. But you know what they do there? They are gassing and killing Jews." And I said, "How do you know that?" He said, "I was there, I was working as a carpenter there." Of course, for me it was the biggest shock ever.' Jacob hurried to seek an audience with Rumkowski, to tell him what he had heard. Having listened to him, Rumkowski slapped Jacob in the face and 'started to scream at me, "I'll send you out from the ghetto [he said], if you say one word to anybody I'll send you out from the ghetto" '.[41]

After the deportations of September 1942, the ghetto entered a period of comparative calm. But within the Nazi leadership a power struggle developed over the future of the place. Arthur Greiser wanted to keep the ghetto within his aegis. Almost certainly he was motivated in large part by personal greed, since he siphoned off money from the ghetto for himself. Even those in the ghetto administration, like Estera Frenkiel, knew that the Nazi in direct charge of the ghetto, Hans Biebow, was sending Greiser backhanded payments. 'Biebow took it for granted', says Estera, 'that if he turned up with presents for high-ranking people then he would be allowed to keep the ghetto going and he would still be master of life and death.'[42]

In 1943 Himmler tried to gain control of the ghetto by turning it into a concentration camp. But he faced opposition not just from Greiser but from the Wehrmacht, who saw the ghetto as a useful source of forced labour. The dispute rumbled on, with Greiser's staff at one point demanding a huge payment for handing over the ghetto – a request which was refused.[43] By May 1944 Himmler had finally lost patience with the negotiations and ordered that the ghetto should cease to exist. External events shortly made such a course of action inevitable, since the following month the Red Army began a major advance that threatened to break through towards Łódź. As a consequence, on 23 June the first of ten transports, taking in total around 7,000 people, left for the 40-mile journey to the gas vans at Chełmno – the murder facility that had been reopened for the task of murdering the Łódź Jews.

In 1942 the static facilities at Chełmno had been destroyed, after the initial transports of Jews selected from Łódź and elsewhere in Poland had ceased and the Reinhard death camps had been established. This attempt to erase the evidence of the crime had included blowing up the building known as the 'mansion' that had served as the base for the gas vans in Chełmno village. Now that the killing squad had returned, under the command of SS officer Hans Bothmann, they had to rethink the mechanism of the murder process. They decided, instead of basing the gas vans in the village, to transfer the killing operation to the nearby forest where the bodies had previously been buried. They built barracks, which they pretended were part of a larger camp, and a crematorium near by. When the first transport arrived from Łódź in June 1944, the Jews were taken to spend the night in the church in the village. The next day they were transferred to the barracks in the forest in groups – the number in each group determined by the capacity of the gas vans that were now based in the forest. Once assembled outside the barracks, the Jews were told that they were to be sent to Germany to work. A specific city was always named as their destination. This was a more sophisticated attempt to reassure the Jews than usual, as the name of the city was identical to the one the Jews had been told was their ulti-mate destination on leaving the Łódź ghetto. The SS then said that the Jews would have to be medically examined and disinfected in a delous-ing station, so it was necessary for them to take their clothes off. Once inside the barracks, after a mock examination by an SS man dressed in a white coat masquerading as a doctor, the Jews were led forward into a space they thought was the disinfecting chamber. In fact, it was the back of the gas van. 'The doors were closed, locked and bolted,' said Szymon Srebrnik, a member of the Chełmno Sonderkommando. 'The motor was started. The exhaust gas was directed into the van by a special exhaust pipe and it poisoned the people inside . . . Screams and knock-ing on the walls of the van continued . . . When the screams ceased, the van moved and took the bodies to the crematorium.'[44]

A few of the Jews were spared immediate death and told to write postcards back to the ghetto, pretending that they were already in Ger-many. Once they had done this, they too were killed. The sinister trick seemed to work. 'Thirty-one postcards have arrived,' reads an entry in the Łódź ghetto chronicle for 25 July 1944, 'all of them postmarked July 19, 1944. Fortunately, it is apparent from these cards that people are faring well and, what is more, that families have stayed together . . . The ghetto is elated and hopes that similar reports will soon be arriving from all the other resettled workers.'[45]

While the gas vans, from the Nazi perspective, had many advantages as a method of murder, chiefly that they could be deployed swiftly, they also had many weaknesses – most obviously that they could not murder in large numbers. That had been the case in the spring of 1942 when the gas vans had been unable to compete with the fixed gas chambers at places like Bełżec and Sobibór, and it remained the case now when compared with the potential murder capacity of Auschwitz Birkenau. The SS realized that it would take a considerable time for Chełmno to kill all the remaining Łódź Jews, and so the plan was changed. Deportations to Chełmno stopped on 15 July, and when they began again in August the destination for the Łódź Jews was not Chełmno but Auschwitz Birkenau.[46]

Just over 70,000 Jews from Łódź ghetto arrived in Auschwitz that summer. Among them were Max Epstein and his mother.[47] 'The ghetto was no picnic,' says Max, 'and I'm not trying to defend the style there, but it was still home. It was still families . . . as pitiful as it was, it was something.'[48] It took Max a mere 'twenty minutes' to realize that Auschwitz was an altogether different place. 'The smell,' he says, 'it was like burning film or hair, you know, organic. So it was crystal clear [that the SS were killing people].' Because Max's transport contained skilled workers who had specialized in the repair of communications equipment, they were not selected on arrival but admitted straight into the camp.

Shortly after they arrived Max remembers: 'I was sitting with my mother and they brought us water. Now in the ghetto we had a lot of typhoid fever, so we never drank unboiled water. So I turned to my mother and I said, "I presume it's not boiled." So she got into hysterical laughter, I mean, she has got on her hands an idiot of a kid, who thinks that now he's going to worry about boiled water. The people around, who are sitting there, thought that she'd become hysterical because she heard about the crematorium.'[49] Max's mother was sent to the women's quarantine camp at Birkenau. While he was 'upset' to see his mother leave, he didn't 'start screaming'. He realized that he had to contain his emotions or 'I wouldn't be living two minutes afterwards.' Subsequently he shouted through the wire to his mother, 'Why are you crying, why are you crying? We are going to be dead anyway, so what's the point?'

Max and his mother were unusual, because they survived the war. Most of the Jews from the Łódź ghetto sent to Auschwitz died there – including Mordechai Chaim Rumkowski. In the end all his collaboration, all his machinations, did not save him from the gas chamber. But, ultimately, what other realistic options did he have, other than to bow to German demands? His counterpart in Warsaw, Adam Czerniaków, killed himself when the deportations from the ghetto began, but that was of little help to his fellow Jews.

Whether or not Rumkowski should be criticized because of his eager collaboration with the Germans is debatable. What is certain is that he should be utterly condemned because of his personal conduct towards his fellow Jews – especially the way that he used his immense power within the ghetto to sexually assault young women. There had been rumours about his sexual behaviour before the war when he ran an orphanage, and once he had power in the ghetto he assaulted women with impunity.[50] Lucille Eichengreen, for example, remembers vividly how Rumkowski 'molested' her when she was a teenager in the ghetto. She felt that, if she did not let him do what he wanted, 'her life was at stake' since he had the power to have her deported. He chose to exploit her intense vulnerability for his own sexual pleasure.[51] Other Jews confirm that Rumkowski was a sexual predator.[52] His abuse of the Jews he led was a terrible crime for which, had he lived, he should have been called to account.

By the time the Jews from Łódź arrived at Auschwitz Birkenau in the summer of 1944 the camp contained inmates from many different countries, including Italy, Belgium, Poland, Germany, the Netherlands, France, Slovakia and Greece. Jews had even been sent to Auschwitz from the Channel Islands. But it was the deportations from one particular place that came to dominate the camp during 1944 – Hungary. And, for a whole variety of reasons, the history of the extermination of hundreds of thousands of Hungarian Jews at Birkenau sheds light on the unparalleled nightmare of the Holocaust.

17. Hungarian Catastrophe
(1944)

At the end of February 1944, Adolf Hitler left the claustrophobic surroundings of his military headquarters in a forest in East Prussia and travelled to the Berghof, his home in the mountains of southern Bavaria. The reason for his change of location illustrated Germany's fortunes at this point in the war – his headquarters in East Prussia were no longer safe from air attack and had to be fortified. So while that work took place, he returned home to the landscape that had inspired him since the 1920s.

When Hitler stood on the terrace of the Berghof he could stare across at the Untersberg, the mountain in which according to legend the mighty warrior Frederick Barbarossa lay sleeping. But by now his own dream of becoming an all-conquering hero stood little chance of turning into reality. German forces were in retreat. The Wehrmacht had abandoned the vital Ukrainian iron-ore mines, and Germany's supply of oil from Romania was threatened. In late February 1944 the Americans had launched a series of massive bombing raids against Germany's industrial base. These attacks, later known as 'Big Week', didn't just destroy key factories, but demonstrated that Germany's air defences were wholly inadequate to deal with the Allied threat.

Yet Hitler was nothing if not self-confident. Despite all these setbacks, when Goebbels visited him at the Berghof in early March he found his Führer 'fresh and relaxed' – almost upbeat. The new front line in the east was shorter, said Hitler, and that was to Germany's advantage. Moreover he was 'absolutely certain' that the expected Allied landings in France would be repelled. German soldiers could then be moved from the west for a new offensive in the east. 'I hope these prognoses made by the Führer are correct,' wrote Goebbels in his diary. 'Lately, we've been disappointed so often that you feel some scepticism rising inside you.'[1]

Hitler's anger was directed, as always, against the Jews. The week before his meeting with Goebbels, he had spoken to Nazi leaders in the banquet hall of the Hofbräuhaus in Munich on the twenty-fourth anniversary of the foundation of the party. In his speech he had promised that the Jews of Britain and America would be 'smashed down' just as the Jews of Germany had been. His words had been greeted with 'thundering applause'.[2] Now, back at the Berghof, he brought up with Goebbels once again the question of troublesome partners – to begin with, Germany's difficulties with Finland. The Finns, whom Hitler had always thought unreliable friends, looked to be trying to exit the war, just as the Italians had done. He didn't need to mention – since both he and Goebbels knew it – that the Finns, even more than the Italians, had refused to cooperate in the deportation of their Jews. Not that the Germans had particularly pressed them, since they knew in advance that the Finnish government would be loath to agree to German demands for a comprehensive 'solution' to the 'Jewish question' in Finland. While the Finns had handed over to the Germans several thousand Soviet prisoners of war, a number of whom were almost certainly Jewish, and eight non-Finnish Jewish refugees, the remainder of the Jews in Finland – fewer than 2,000 – had been kept safe. Moreover, the Finns had not put in place any anti-Semitic legislation, and Finnish Jews were even serving in the Finnish Army fighting against the Soviets. This led to the ideologically strange situation, from the perspective of the Nazis, of Jews fighting on the same side as the Germans against Bolshevism, an ideology that the Nazis believed was backed by Jews.[3]

Just as he realized he could do little to make the Finns cooperate over the deportation of the Jews, Hitler accepted that he could not do much to prevent them leaving the war.[4] It certainly wasn't, from his point of view, worth the effort to try and force them by military means to do what he wanted. But, as he told Goebbels, that was not the case with every one of the Germans' recalcitrant partners. In particular, said Hitler, the situation in Hungary was very different. While the Hungarians – like the Finns – were trying to extricate themselves from the war, Hungary – unlike Finland – possessed not just enormous numbers of Jews but also valuable raw materials, food stocks and other supplies of use to the Germans. So Hitler had decided that he wanted to confront the Hungarian leader, Admiral Horthy, occupy the country, seize whatever the Germans wanted and deal with the Hungarian Jews once and for all.

Hitler met Admiral Horthy at Klessheim Castle near Salzburg on 18 March 1944. Horthy had hoped Hitler would be prepared to discuss bringing home Hungarian soldiers from the eastern front. He was wrong. Hitler wanted to talk about something else entirely. As soon as they met, Hitler launched into a tirade. He said he knew about the continuing Hungarian attempts to renege on their alliance with the Germans, and claimed that the best way forward was for Hungary to contribute more to the war, not less. The problem, as Hitler had said many times before, was that the Hungarian government refused to deal with the Jews who lived in Hungary. Germany would not tolerate this security threat existing so close to the approaching enemy. As a result, Hitler said, he was about to order the German occupation of Hungary and he demanded Horthy agree to this course of action. Horthy refused and started arguing with Hitler. When Horthy said he would resign sooner than sign, Hitler threatened that if that happened he could not guarantee the safety of Horthy's family. Horthy, outraged, left the room.

Eventually, after the Germans had employed various tricks to prevent Horthy leaving – such as pretending the phone lines were down and faking an air raid on the castle – Horthy was persuaded to agree to the Wehrmacht entering Hungary and to the deportation of 100,000 Jews. The next day, 19 March, German troops occupied Hungary and two days after that Adolf Eichmann was installed in Budapest, ready to implement the destruction of the Jews.

The occupation of Hungary was not, as the Nazis saw it, an act motivated only by a desire for vengeance against the Jews, even though Hitler certainly believed that the Jews had sabotaged the Hungarian will to fight. The Nazis had a good deal to gain in practical terms from Hungary. Not just raw materials and strategic military advantage – given that the Red Army were advancing ever closer to Hungary's borders – but also the wealth of the Hungarian Jews. Not only could the Jews be robbed, but those who were deemed fit enough could also be used as forced labour. Given the enormous numbers of Jews in Hungary, that prospect appeared an attractive one to the Nazis.

For many of the Jews of Hungary, the sudden arrival of the Germans, although frightening, did not seem necessarily to mean their obliteration. 'I could see the fear on my parents' faces,' recalls Israel Abelesz, a teenager living in the south of Hungary, 'and I could see the whole atmosphere had changed. [Maybe] it's the beginning of something horrible. Though we were hoping this was just a military manoeuvre and the Jewish population will not be affected.' He read in the newspapers that 'the Germans had to occupy Hungary in order that they could carry on the war better. We thought it won't affect the Jewish population. That was the hope. That was the hopeful side. I mean, in a situation like that there's always hope and despair – it keeps on alternating in one's mind.'[5]

Despite the German occupation, Eichmann and his team knew that it would be impossible to deport the Jews without the support of the Hungarian authorities. Eichmann had studied what had happened in Denmark and knew that lack of local assistance had caused immense difficulties, so it was vital for the Nazis to have Hungarian administrative and police help. And that is just what they received. The new Prime Minister, Döme Sztójay – the former Hungarian ambassador in Berlin – was appointed only after the Germans had given their approval, and the two state secretaries with responsibility for the Jewish 'question' were both proven anti-Semites. One of them, László Endre, was particularly eager to assist the Nazis. Endre enthusiastically collaborated with the Germans and implemented a whole series of restrictive measures against the Jews – such as banning them from owning vehicles and phones and compelling them to list all their valuables. Also keen to help was a commander of the Hungarian gendarmerie, another anti-Semite called László Ferenczy,[6] and Eichmann soon struck up a warm relationship with him.

The recent background to anti-Semitism in Hungary would have been familiar to Eichmann. Hungarian anti-Semites – like German and Austrian anti-Semites – had pointed to the influence that Jews were alleged to possess in the media and in key professions, and also to the supposed links between Judaism and the hated creed of Communism. At the end of the First World War there had even been a Communist government of Hungary for a brief period, dominated by the revolutionary Béla Kun who was of Jewish origin.

Despite this history, and a group of Hungarian anti-Semites willing to assist him, Eichmann knew he was embarking on a vast enterprise that was fraught with difficulties. The potential, from the Nazis' perspective, for the whole project to fall apart was large. Suppose the Jews learnt that they were all to be shipped to Auschwitz, where the majority of them – particularly the most vulnerable – would be murdered? Wouldn't they then do all they could to hide and even resist? Eichmann was aware of the precedent of the Warsaw ghetto uprising – what if something similar happened in Budapest?

Eichmann, given the chance for the first time to be the man on the spot rather than directing operations from a desk in Berlin, was determined to avoid the issues that had dogged Nazi plans in both Denmark and Warsaw. To this end, he not only ensured that compliant anti-Semites were in key positions within the new Hungarian administration, but he also moved to calm the anxious Jews about their fate. As a first step, Jewish leaders were told to form a Jewish Council. On 31 March, Eichmann met with four members of the newly formed council at his office in the Hotel Majestic in Budapest and told them that while measures were to be introduced against the Jews – such as the wearing of the yellow star – they should not be concerned about what was going to happen to them, as long as they behaved themselves. He said that 'the Jews had to understand that nothing was being demanded of them except discipline and order. If there was discipline and order, then not only would Jewry have nothing to fear, but he would defend Jewry and it would live under the same good conditions as regards payment and treatment as all the other workers.'[7]

The members of the Jewish Council seemed to have been reassured by Eichmann. In one way, the restrictive measures against the Jews implied that the Germans were not going to kill them, but might be seeking a longer-term accommodation. In short, why make Jews wear the yellow star if you just want to shoot them? That was certainly the interpretation that Israel Abelesz and his family favoured. 'After a few days they came out with restrictions,' he says. 'We thought, all right, this is something which we can live with. Because we were aware that the war was not going well for the Germans. It's just a question of time. They will be defeated. Look – we had been brought up strongly in Jewish history and we realized that all through the generations in different places, Jews have suffered for being Jews. I mean, the original anti-Semitism of course originates from the Jews not accepting that Jesus is a saviour, and that kind of hostility to the Jews has persisted through the centuries. And so we're not surprised at all that we are being discriminated [against]. It's just a question of to what degree.'[8]

Again learning from mistakes that had been made by Nazis elsewhere, Eichmann planned on conducting the deportations not in one massive operation but piecemeal. He would start with the Jews in the east of Hungary, far from Budapest. This had the double benefit, from the Nazis' point of view, of first tackling the Jews who were closest to the advancing front line under the pretext of military security, while simultaneously not yet attempting the difficult task of deporting the large number of Jews in Budapest, who had more opportunities to hide than Jews in the countryside.

Jews in the east of Hungary – including many who lived on land that had been annexed by the Hungarians – were forced into ghettos as soon as early April. In an operation of great speed, which would have been impossible without the cooperation of the Hungarian gendarmerie, nearly 200,000 Jews were imprisoned in ghettos or in hastily constructed temporary camps in less than two weeks.

The initial agreement with the Hungarian authorities had been that the Germans would deport 100,000 Jews, but once the ghettoization process began the Hungarians themselves lobbied for all the Jews to leave. A crucial element in their thinking was the question of what they would do with the Jews who had not been selected for forced labour. Just as in Slovakia two years before, the Hungarian authorities believed they were better off asking the Germans to take all their Jews, including old people and children.

As the Hungarian Jews waited in the ghettos, most were still uncertain about what lay ahead. Though sometimes they heard clues. Alice Lok Cahana, a fifteen-year-old schoolgirl who lived with her family in western Hungary, remembers one non-Jewish Hungarian saying to her, 'You know, we make soap out of you.' 'I said "Really? So remember if you wash yourself with the good-smelling soap it's me."' Later she 'cried' and felt 'so humiliated that he dared to say something like that, so vile, so horrible to me'.[9] But such offensive remarks still did not amount to proof that they were to be killed. Many Jews, like Israel Abelesz and his family, still thought they might be sent to work as 'compulsory' labour. 'That was the best hope,' he says, 'the families will stay together and we'll just have to survive for another few months, because the war is coming to an end. I mean, we were taken away in the last stage of the war.'[10]

At first sight this lack of certainty among Hungarian Jews about the fate they faced at the hands of the Germans seems strange. Several thousand Hungarian Jews, for instance, had returned home in 1943 from work in labour battalions in the heart of the killing zone in Ukraine, and they would surely have learnt what was happening. Indeed, one Hungarian writer confirmed that by 1943 'we had already heard much about the massacres from Hungarian soldiers and Jewish conscripts back from the Eastern front.'[11]

However, not only would there almost certainly have been a different level of knowledge between sophisticated Jews in Budapest and Jews in remote agricultural areas, but a potent mix of uncertainty and hope still remained in many people's minds. There were always ways of rationalizing what was going on. For example, even if the Germans had been killing Jews in the east, perhaps that policy of murder applied only to Soviet Jews? It simply made no sense, so one argument went, for the Germans to be killing Jews now that the war was going badly for them. Surely they now needed workers more than ever before? It was these kinds of thoughts that Eichmann encouraged with his promise of safety for Jews who kept their 'discipline and order'.

What the Jews did know for certain was that the Hungarian gendarmerie, as well as many other Hungarians, were getting rich at their expense. Israel Abelesz watched as members of the gendarmerie searched the Jews and stole 'money and jewellery', while Alice Lok Cahana's family lost not just their house but their whole business – sold for a pittance to a non-Jewish man called Mr Krüger. 'I was so embarrassed,' she says, as she and her family were forced out of their town. 'The scene of going out of Egypt came to my mind. And here was Mr Krüger watching us go by, not with compassion but with glee – the owner of our factory, the owner of our house.'[12] Elsewhere in Hungary there were even reports that the gendarmerie tortured Jews to make them reveal where they had hidden their money.[13]

Central to Eichmann's plan for the deportation of the Jews in Hungary was the role of Auschwitz. This place was not the crude 'solution' to the Nazis' 'Jewish problem' that had been offered by the Reinhard camps. No, the complex of camps at Auschwitz offered a multifaceted answer to the perennial Nazi question of how to deal with the Jews. Part of that, as we have seen, was the sense of permanence of the place, and the development of a more efficient killing process during 1943 with the opening of four new crematoria/gas-chamber complexes at Birkenau. But there were also more recent 'improvements'. It was only now, for example, that a railway spur was completed that allowed new arrivals to enter under an arch in the red-brick guardhouse of Birkenau directly into the camp. Previously the arrival ramp had been close to the main railway line, roughly halfway between Auschwitz main camp and Birkenau. But with the new railway track inside Birkenau the journey to the crematoria and gas chambers for those selected to die was just a few minutes' walk. It had taken four years for Auschwitz to evolve to this point, but the images of Auschwitz Birkenau from this short period of a few months have become emblematic not just of Auschwitz but of the entire Holocaust – to a large extent because photographs taken by the SS of the arrival of a transport of Hungarian Jews at Birkenau survived the war.

However, more important than any enhancements in the murder procedure was what Auschwitz had become in conceptual terms. For Auschwitz was not just the biggest murder factory ever built – where people became ashes just a few hours after arrival – it was also, by now, an efficient sorting machine for human beings. The idea was that Hungarian Jews would first be selected on arrival inside the camp at Auschwitz Birkenau, with the old, children and others who looked unfit sent straight to the gas chambers. The remaining Jews would usually be held in a 'quarantine' camp within Birkenau for several weeks, and then either allocated to work camps in the Auschwitz area or sent further away, often to camps near industrial concerns within the Reich. Those working in the camps near to Auschwitz would be returned to Birkenau to be murdered once they were deemed no longer useful.

Himmler, working to the wishes of his Führer, had finally devised a physical institution that appeared to solve the question that had dogged Nazi policy on the Jews since the beginning of the extermination process – how does one reconcile the usefulness of the Jews as workers with the ideological desire to eliminate them? Heydrich at the Wannsee conference in January 1942 had talked about working the Jews to death by making them build roads in the east, but the practical details of how this could be put into effect had never been thought through. Instead there had been a series of disputes between those who wanted to preserve the Jews to exploit their labour and those who wanted to kill them. Not only did Auschwitz bridge those two apparently irreconcilable objectives – as long as there remained a steady supply of replacement workers – but it did so within a secure environment. There was little risk of revolt at Auschwitz – the secure area around Auschwitz, known as the 'zone of interest', extended far beyond the wires of Birkenau and the main camp, and within Birkenau the various sections of the camp were fenced off from each other. A mass escape along the lines of the uprisings at Treblinka or Sobibór was all but inconceivable. Auschwitz and its network of sub-camps serving various industrial concerns was a self-contained universe. Once inmates entered it, they could live, work and die there – at every stage under the controlling eyes of the SS. It is this – the fact that Auschwitz by this point had become the practical manifestation of the Nazis' ideological imperative – that helps make Auschwitz the most potent symbol of the Holocaust.

In July 1944, Israel Abelesz experienced first hand how Auschwitz impacted on the Hungarian Jews. He and his family arrived at Auschwitz Birkenau in a freight train after several days' journey from western Hungary. His train travelled down the new railway spur, under the archway in the guardhouse, directly into the camp. The doors were opened and everyone was ordered out of the wagons. 'We were told just the people should get out,' he says, 'and they should leave their luggage behind – the luggage will be distributed later.' He remembers that while 'everything went so fast', the arrival process still seemed well organized. 'The prisoners who came out to receive us,' he says, 'they brought water. So everybody who was thirsty could drink water.' He believes this was so that the new arrivals would not get 'panicky'. 'We just asked them,' he says, "what is it here?" They said, "It's a labour camp."'[14]

The Sonderkommandos on the ramp helped organize the separation of the Jews into two groups: 'They said, children with their mother, they should go in one row' and men into another. 'That's when I saw my little brother who was eleven years old, he went with my mother, being a child, and that's the last time I saw them. And I was standing in front of a smart-looking German officer with my father and my older brother, who was sixteen at that time. And the German officer looks at me and he says to me in German, how old are you? So I said to him, "I am fourteen."' Israel added that his birthday had been just a few days before. The SS man 'smiled back, "Oh, Geburtstag, sehr gut [birthday, very good]. You go with your brother." And my father also was sort of following us, and he says [to him], "No, no, you go this way." In a nice [way], just pointing with a little baton.'

35. German soldiers steal pigs during the war against the Soviet Union. Just before the invasion, the central economic agency of the Wehrmacht stated that 'tens of millions' would die 'if we take away all we need from the country'.

36. German units advance against a village on the eastern front. Hitler had said, during the planning stages of the invasion, that this would be a war of 'extermination'.

37. Jewish women wait to be murdered by Nazi security forces in the occupied Soviet Union. Increasingly, from July 1941, the Nazi killing squads targeted women and children as well as adult male Jews.

38. Nazi security forces in action in the occupied Soviet Union. On the eastern front the Nazis' belief that any civilian might also be a partisan meant the Germans could shoot, as Hitler said, 'anyone who even looks askance at us'.

39. A fraction of the 5.7 million Soviet soldiers captured by the Germans during the course of the war against the Soviet Union. The majority – around 3.3 million – would die in German captivity.

40. Jewish civilians captured by the Germans in the aftermath of the Warsaw ghetto uprising in spring 1943. Though militarily the uprising achieved little, as a statement of the Jewish desire to fight back against the Germans the action was of immense importance.

41. Hungarian Jews arrive at Auschwitz Birkenau in 1944. The majority of the people in this photograph – including all the small children – would be dead within a matter of hours.

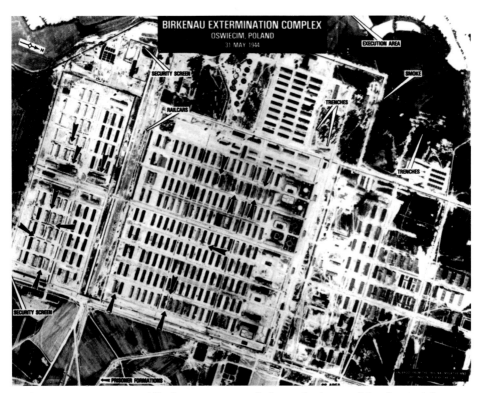

42. Starting in spring 1944, Allied reconnaissance flights took photos of Auschwitz. This photograph is of Auschwitz Birkenau during the Hungarian deportation action.

43. This photograph captures the moment of selection – of life or death – at Auschwitz Birkenau during the Hungarian action. Most new arrivals would be told to join a group destined immediately for the gas chamber.

44. Staff at Auschwitz relax. Oskar Groening, a former member of the SS at Auschwitz, later remarked that working at the camp 'led to friendships which I'm still saying today I like to think back on with joy'.

45. Crematorium III at Auschwitz. This killing factory, which opened in 1943, had the gas chambers and undressing rooms in the semi-basement of the building.

46. Crematorium IV at Auschwitz. Unlike Crematoria II and III, which were altered at the design stage to incorporate gas chambers, this building (together with Crematorium V) was conceived from the beginning as a place of mass murder. The gas chambers and undressing room were on the same level as the ovens where the bodies were burnt.

47. The Nazi doctor Fritz Klein stands on top of a pile of the dead from Bergen Belsen concentration camp. Klein was forced to help bury the dead by British forces after the liberation of the camp.

48. Oskar Groening, a member of the SS garrison at Auschwitz. He worked in the economic administration, counting the money stolen from those the Nazis killed.

49. Petras Zelionka, a Lithuanian who participated with the German Einsatzgruppen in murdering Jewish civilians in the occupied Soviet Union. After the war he served twenty years in a Soviet prison.

Israel Abelesz remembers the SS wanted 'everybody' to 'be reassured' so they didn't make 'any scenes'. 'Their purpose', he says, was 'really speed, like in a factory. It was like on a conveyor belt, and there shouldn't be any hitch in the conveyor-belt system.' When he witnessed what was happening, he 'thought everything's going to be all right. We are going to work here – like everybody else. I saw those Jewish prisoners, [and thought] we are going to be prisoners like them and we are going to be sent out to work somewhere near by.' As for his mother, father and younger brother who had been selected to join a different group, he 'thought they would also be all right. They would be in a different camp.' After all, that's what the arriving Jews were told by the prisoners who met them on the ramp. 'They said, "They're going to a different camp."'

After Israel had been at Birkenau for about three weeks, one dramatic event convinced him that his mother, father and younger brother had been murdered. On the night of 2 August, he heard 'screaming and crying . . . and dogs barking'. The noise came from the direction of the Gypsy camp, near his own prison barracks. And 'in the morning there were no Gypsies in the camp.' Overnight, following orders from Himmler, the entire Gypsy camp had been liquidated – around 2,800 Roma and Sinti had been murdered. 'Then I realized', says Israel, 'that if they do that to the Gypsies, they would do that to us – or they have done it to us. And gradually it came to our mind that, yes, those people who were not able to work, they went to the gas chambers.'

For the whole summer of 1944 Israel lived in a section of Birkenau that he describes as a 'labour pool'. There were regular selections from within the group, and the chosen prisoners were taken away to work as forced labour, either within the Auschwitz zone of interest or elsewhere in the Nazi empire. Now that he realized that Birkenau contained gas chambers, Israel was desperate to 'get away from Auschwitz'. As a consequence he 'always volunteered' whenever the SS announced they were selecting workers. But they didn't pick him. He was small – even for a fourteen-year-old – and bigger and stronger prisoners were taken ahead of him.

Israel became increasingly anxious. Not only was he never picked, but he was growing weaker. 'Every day there was rationing of food – it was just not enough, a starvation diet. And the overwhelming feeling besides the fear of death is the feeling of hunger. The feeling of hunger is such an overpowering feeling that it covers up any other feeling, any other human feelings . . . [you become] just like a dog who is looking for food.'[15]

After three months at Birkenau he saw a new and terrifying sight. Just outside his hut the Germans assembled a measuring bar. Those who reached the required height would be sent to one group, those who were under that height to another. Israel just 'couldn't reach it' so he was put with the group who had failed the test. They were predominantly children between the ages of twelve and sixteen who had survived the initial selection at the ramp because, as Israel had witnessed, 'there was always a few borderline cases. I mean, both through the upper age and the lower age.'

Israel and the others 'were told that they are going to the children's camp. Where they are going to have much better treatment. I didn't believe it.' A number of others in the group didn't believe the promise either, but 'I suppose they were in such despair by then that they just said it's no good. No good to fight, we're giving up, sort of. I mean there were people who went to the electric wires and just killed themselves. They just didn't want to live like that . . . they gave up. There's no purpose in life. I mean it was a terrible situation. People who were part of a family, they lived in a family, suddenly they were thrown into the worst part of hell . . . your people are getting sent to the gas. It was not a gradual transformation, just suddenly. And it was such a shock for people, they couldn't take it . . . In my experience there was no hysterics. The people accepted fatalistically what's going to happen to them. There was no screaming. Maybe – I heard in the night when they were taking them in the gas chamber there was a bit of screaming. Otherwise, what is to scream? To whom do you scream? You accept your fate. Well, a condemned man in his cell is screaming all night? I don't think so.'

Determined to survive, he used the confusion of the selection process to his advantage and simply 'ran over to correct side' where he hid with the group who had passed the test. But it was only a short reprieve. Shortly afterwards he failed another selection. This time he was saved because he started 'crying' and pleading with the SS man, saying, 'But I'm fit to work, I can work.' A Kapo slapped him and told him to shut up, but the German SS man said to the Kapo, 'Oh, leave him, leave him alone.' As a result 'he took somebody else instead of me. I just don't know why I was spared . . . But that's what happened with me. So I had the feeling that I've been fated by God to survive. I had this strong feeling by then that somehow I will manage to survive. After I managed to get through the selections, I always had a strong feeling . . . I mean it's a series of fortunes that I'm here.'

However, Israel didn't rely entirely on the belief that he was 'fated by God to survive'. He also looked out for himself. 'I had with me my brother,' he says, 'who was two years older than me and he had more feeling [for others] . . . I never had this feeling. I was a bit more selfish. For instance, I remember one of the children was crying one morning that his ration of bread was stolen in the night and he's so hungry. I remember my brother gave a piece of his bread to this boy . . . I said to him, but why have you given it away, you don't need [to do] this. "His need is bigger than mine" [said his brother]. This is something I always admired in him.'

By a combination of luck and sharp wits, Israel Abelesz managed to survive until the camps were liberated. But though he was no longer in the hands of the Nazis, he was still tormented by what he had experienced. 'I don't know how to deal with it . . . hardly a day passes when I'm lying in bed and I cannot sleep for one reason or another, [I] always look at those faces of the children [selected to die] and my imagination goes: what's happened in their last minute? When they were in the gas chambers and the Zyklon B started and they couldn't breathe any more? And they realized that we are going to get suffocated from the gas. What was in their mind?'

The lethal reality of life in Auschwitz forced many to reconsider their faith. 'I became an atheist immediately after deportation,' said Ruth Matias, another Hungarian Jew sent to Auschwitz in 1944. 'My father never wronged a soul, and not only was he wronged, but also so many small innocent children. I saw it with my own eyes, they caught them by their feet, banged them against the wall and their brains split open . . . Now I am fatalist.' In Auschwitz she also saw how traditional family bonds of care were tested to breaking point. 'I saw a girl hitting her mother. The mother would not eat anything but gave her entire ration to her daughter, and still, if the mother took as much as one spoon of food for herself, the daughter hit her . . . The mother would defend her daughter; be angry at our interference, "Don't mix in, I'm not hungry." '[16]

As the Hungarian Jews discovered, the Nazis were selecting Jews to work not just in the factories around Auschwitz, but also within the territory of the pre-war Reich. Yet for years a basic tenet of Nazi ideology had been that the Jews should be expelled from these lands. So once again the Nazis demonstrated that there was no absolute ideological clarity in the way they implemented their Final Solution, given that this change in policy was purely pragmatic and was designed to address a labour shortage. It also meant, of course, that unlike the Jews who worked in the network of factories and mines in the immediate area of Auschwitz, the Jews working in the Reich were out of the reach of the gas chambers of Birkenau. Many of them would still die of starvation, disease and beatings, but they did so out of the orbit of Auschwitz.

At the same time as the Hungarian Jews suffered in Auschwitz Birkenau, a mile and a half away Tadeusz Smreczyński tried to survive in Auschwitz main camp. Most of the Poles he had arrived at Auschwitz with a few weeks before had already been sent to the gas chambers, and in early July 1944 he thought it was his turn to die. In the middle of the night, the SS ordered him to join a group of several hundred prisoners and march to Birkenau. 'Nobody told us what was going to happen,' he says. 'During our march we were surrounded by SS men, and one of my friends proposed that we attack them if they are taking us to the gas chambers, because a fast death from a bullet is better than being suffocated for a dozen minutes.'[17]

But Tadeusz and the rest of his group were not on their way to the gas chambers. They were loaded on to freight wagons at the ramp in Birkenau and taken far away, across the border into Austria to a destination that was almost as infamous as Auschwitz. For Tadeusz Smreczyński had been transferred to one of the most notorious concentration camps in the entire Reich – Mauthausen, near Linz in Austria. Mauthausen opened in the summer of 1938, and had been conceived from the beginning as a very different kind of camp from the traditional Dachau model. To begin with, unlike Dachau, the location of Mauthausen camp had been selected primarily for economic reasons. The camp was next to a vast granite quarry, and prisoners were forced to work here under the most appalling conditions, lugging blocks up the 'stairs of death' from the quarry floor.

Before the war, few Jews were sent to Mauthausen. The inmates were primarily those the Nazis claimed were 'incorrigible' criminals or 'anti-socials'. But that policy changed in 1941 when hundreds of Dutch Jews were deported to the camp in reprisal for acts of resistance in the Netherlands. Most of these Dutch Jews were dead in a matter of weeks. So dreadful was the experience for the Dutch Jews at Mauthausen that the Nazis in the Netherlands subsequently used the place as a threat – if the Jews did not agree to be deported to the east, then more Jews would be sent to Mauthausen. The reality of this Austrian concentration camp was therefore presented as a more terrifying prospect than the unknown fate that awaited the Dutch Jews if they boarded the deportation trains. The Nazis themselves even recognized the special brutality of Mauthausen. When Reinhard Heydrich had split concentration camps into categories, Mauthausen had been placed in the most severe group of all. Thus while many inmates in Birkenau longed to be selected for a transport out of Auschwitz, simply leaving the Auschwitz zone of interest was no guarantee that their prospects of survival would improve.

Mauthausen was at the heart of an enormous series of business concerns – some owned by the SS, others by private enterprise. The granite quarry was under the aegis of DEST – Deutsche Erd- und Steinwerke GmbH, the German Earth and Stone Company – a commercial venture run by the SS. But Mauthausen also supplied workers for outside companies involved in a variety of manufacturing businesses – from armaments to pharmaceuticals. As a consequence, scores of sub-camps were established to service these factories, and the complex rivalled Auschwitz in terms of scale and variety. Mauthausen was also similar to Auschwitz in another respect – a gas chamber was built at the camp. It was used for the first time in spring 1942 around the time that gassings began in the Little Red House at Birkenau. Like the gas chambers at Auschwitz, the one at Mauthausen, though smaller, used Zyklon B. But despite the presence of the gas chamber, Mauthausen was never a camp primarily concerned with the Final Solution, even at the height of the extermination process elsewhere. About 200,000 prisoners were sent to Mauthausen in the course of its existence. Poles made up the largest ethnic group, with approximately 40,000 Polish prisoners deported to the camp. Altogether around half of all those sent to Mauthausen died there, including an estimated 14,000 Jews.[18]

'They brought us to Mauthausen,' remembers Tadeusz Smreczyński.

'SS men from Mauthausen surrounded our train. Meanwhile the armed SS escort from Auschwitz were standing on the platform doing their best to kick or hit everybody leaving the train with their rifle butts, as if saying goodbye. I saw what was happening. I waited at the back of the train, gathered speed and jumped out of the wagon a few metres away from the escorting guards. I did it to avoid being hit and I was not. New SS guards escorted us to Mauthausen camp. Dawn was breaking. The windows [of the houses] were shut but you could see the curtains open slightly as the Austrians discreetly watched what was happening. We reached the camp. It was situated on a hill with beautiful scenery around and the Alps visible – an area of exceptional beauty where people were meeting their tragic fate.'[19]

Once in the camp, Tadeusz and the others were told to strip naked and their heads were shaved. 'The SS men returned from their breakfast,' he says, 'and inspected the prisoners standing in lines. We were naked. They walked up and down along our lines and slapped us in our faces, hitting us in the abdomen and stamping on our feet. I waited for my turn. Out of the corner of my eye I noticed a young, blue-eyed and blond SS man, maybe in his early twenties. He took a step in my direction. I kept looking straight into his eyes, as he was looking straight into mine for a few seconds, and he did not hit me. He moved towards the next prisoner and hit him. Later my friends were asking how was it possible that he did not hit me. I do not know. I do not know what was on that boy's mind.'[20]

Tadeusz found conditions in the barracks at Mauthausen even worse than those he had endured in the main camp at Auschwitz. Not only were there no spare beds to sleep on, but 'space was very limited and about sixty of us had to stand during the night. They could lie down [only] if someone left his place to go to the toilet, and on his return he would join the standing.' Next morning they were ordered to assemble in the roll-call square. 'It was a very hot day and prisoners were reluctant to stand in lines for hours because those who fell down as a result of the heat were finished off. I was standing in the first line. Those too slow to form the lines were beaten with a truncheon. The beating gained such impetus that they started hitting those who did form the lines and I was suddenly hit on the back of my head. I fell down. Luckily the strike was not too strong and nothing happened to me, but at that very moment I remembered the Polish prisoner [in Auschwitz] who advised me not to stand in the most exposed sides of the prisoners' lines and not to let them kill me.'[21]

Tadeusz was one of a group selected to travel a dozen miles west of Mauthausen to the city of Linz. Here they were told to build a new camp – part of a network of labour camps in the area. Though one or two wooden barracks and a barbed-wire fence were already in place, the prisoners had to construct everything else themselves. The work was so physically debilitating that Tadeusz realized that he stood little chance of surviving for long. But then he heard that a few prisoners were to be selected for easier work in the kitchen. 'We ran to the kitchen gate where the chef, and an SS man – a *Rapportführer* – were standing and choosing ten out of a group of sixty candidates. By the time we reached them they had already selected nine, so I only had one chance. I was asked in German about my age and whether I was healthy and strong and what my occupation was. I responded in German and told them I was a baker because I had worked in a bakery before I got arrested. After some deliberation in low voices they took me on as the tenth one. For me it was the happiest moment of the war.'

As a result of working in the kitchen, he was able to escape the worst vicissitudes of life in the camp – in particular, the hunger. 'The conditions [in the rest of the camp] were horrible,' he says. 'The hunger grew and prisoners fainted from hunger and were dying. Once I saw prisoners carrying a bowl of soup which looked like water from a puddle . . . As they were walking the soup spilled on the ground covered with trodden snow . . . and people were licking it out of the snow. Horrible sight.'

The prisoners were at risk not just as a result of their treatment at the hands of the Nazis, but from Allied bombing as well. Shortly after Tadeusz arrived at the camp in Linz, American bombers targeted military factories close by. Suddenly bombs exploded within the camp. 'I was seized by an enormous panic,' he says. 'Those who were running in front of me simply vanished – they were torn apart and [their bodies] scattered. I noticed a hole in the fence and six prisoners the other side of the wires and I followed them unconcerned that any voluntary departure from the camp meant a death sentence for the prisoners.' Tadeusz and the other prisoners ran about a mile away from the camp and then rested on grass near an embankment. 'After fifteen or twenty minutes we suddenly heard "Hände hoch!" We stood up with our hands up. Wehrmacht soldiers stood behind the trees with their machine guns aimed in our direction. They were part of the anti-aircraft artillery and having shot down a few bombers they took us for American paratroopers. They were shouting "American parachutists!" At that moment I had a sort of revelation and I shouted back that we are not Americans but the prisoners of the Mauthausen Camp, Linz 3, which had been bombed by the Americans . . . and that we were waiting there for our SS men to come and take us back. It later turned out that it saved our lives'. Other prisoners who had fled from the camp were executed, but Tadeusz's prompt explanation of his conduct meant that he and the other prisoners with him were spared. He remembers that the day after the bombing, 'two young Russians who had escaped with me' came 'to thank me for saving their lives'.

The bombing of the camp had another lasting impact on Tadeusz Smreczyński. As he watched the doctors, who were also prisoners, tending the wounded he had a sudden insight: 'I felt that life could only regain sense if you try and do good to other people. I decided that if I survived, I would become a doctor. I was inspired by prisoners who were doctors who were helping others in the camp.'[22] After the war, Tadeusz did indeed become a doctor in his native country. But because he refused to join the Polish Communist Party, his career was blighted and he was denied the opportunity to pursue medical research. 'I totally rejected Communism in the form it existed,' he says. 'It was not at all about the poor, the working classes and the peasants; it was for the benefit of the so-called leaders.' He stayed true to the life philosophy he had developed as a prisoner of the Nazis. 'Life has sense only when one does good. Am I right? I did not feel the urge to live a public life. I did not care about financial incentives that would let me compare my car with someone else's car. I did not need to impress anyone.'[23]

At Auschwitz, the arrival of the Hungarian Jews in the spring and summer of 1944 led to the most intense period of killing in the history of the camp. Around 430,000 Jews from Hungary were transported to Auschwitz between May and July 1944.[24] The majority of them were killed on arrival, with the proportion selected for immediate death varying between 70 and 90 per cent of each transport. To accommodate the vast numbers to be killed, large cremation pits were dug near crematoria/gas chambers IV and V, not far from the original improvised Birkenau extermination centres in the Little Red House and Little White House.

Amid the vast numbers arriving at Birkenau, individual members of the SS felt free to indulge their sadistic imagination. Morris Venezia, one of the Jewish Sonderkommandos working in the crematoria, remembers that two young Jewish sisters and their friend asked one of the SS men if they could be killed together. He was 'very happy' to do as they asked, and in the process thought that he would try and see if he could kill all three of them with one bullet. He placed them in a line and pulled the trigger. All three girls collapsed and appeared to be dead. 'Right away,' says Morris, 'we took them and threw them in the flames [of the open pit]. And then we heard some kind of screaming [from the pit].' It transpired that one of the girls had only fallen down and had not been killed, so now she was burnt alive. 'And that German officer was so happy because he killed two of them at least with one shot. These animals . . . No human brain can believe that or understand it. It's impossible to believe it. But we saw it.'[25]

Not all Jews in Hungary were sent to Auschwitz. Back in Budapest, Eichmann and other members of the SS were pursuing a parallel strategy in an attempt to extort the Jews' wealth. Kurt Becher, as head of the economic department of the SS in Hungary, spent his time wresting large quantities of money, jewels and other valuables from Jews in exchange for a promise that their lives would be spared. He allowed members of the Weiss family, for example, one of the richest and most prominent Jewish families in Hungary, to escape to a neutral country once they had transferred ownership of the enormous Weiss Steel and Metal Works to the Nazis.

Eichmann was also directly involved in attempts to extort goods from Hungarian Jews, and in the process he made one of the most extraordinary proposals of the Final Solution. On 25 April 1944 he met a leading Budapest Jew called Joel Brand and told him that the Nazis were prepared to let 'one million' Jews go free as long as a suitable ransom was paid. 'We are interested in goods, not in money,' said Eichmann. 'Travel abroad and liaise directly with your international authorities and with the Allies. And then come back with a concrete offer.'[26] It is likely that Eichmann knew that such an offer was doomed from the beginning. Why would the Allies bargain for Jewish lives by supporting the Nazis with equipment that could be used to prolong the war? Especially when the Nazis said that any material the Allies handed to the Nazis in exchange for Jews would not be used on the western front – an obvious attempt to split the Alliance. But even if the negotiations stood little chance of success, Eichmann must have thought he would still benefit by them. That is because by suggesting this offer he would demonstrate to Himmler that he too could be as flexible as Becher, his SS colleague, at a time when the German war machine needed all the raw materials it could get.

On 17 May 1944, Brand – together with a shady figure called Bandi Grosz – left Hungary for Istanbul to make contact with the Allies and propose a deal whereby 1 million Jews would be 'saved' if the Allies provided the Germans with 10,000 trucks. Once in Istanbul Brand met with the Turkish representatives of the Jewish leadership from Palestine. Subsequently, on 26 May, the British High Commissioner for Palestine, Sir Harold MacMichael, was told of the proposed exchange. The Americans also soon learnt of the Nazi plan, and a divergence in the British and American response to the proposal began to appear. Although both sides rejected the idea in principle, they had different opinions about whether or not to use it to open up negotiations. In America the War Refugee Board, established by Roosevelt in January 1944 to assist those persecuted by the Nazis, took an interest in the idea. The perception of the British, expressed at a meeting of a war cabinet committee on refugees on 30 May, was that Henry Morgenthau, the driving force behind the War Refugee Board, had promised that America would 'rescue' Jews, and that this might lead to an 'offer' from the Germans 'to unload an even greater number of Jews on to our hands'.[27] Morgenthau, as the British knew, was Jewish, and that thought, plus other factors such as the difficulties the British authorities already had in Palestine, and the challenge of transporting large numbers of Jews during wartime, would have made the British wary of the idea.

The British and Americans had already discussed the problem of rescuing Jews at the Bermuda conference the year before, in April 1943. This gathering of second-tier politicians and advisers rivalled the Evian conference of 1938 for the reluctance shown to offer safe haven to large numbers of Jews. Just as at Evian, the conference was not even officially about the Jews, but about 'refugees'. And just as at Evian, the British would not commit to accepting substantial numbers of Jews into Palestine. Only a handful of journalists were permitted into Bermuda to cover the conference and the 'proposals' reached were kept 'confidential' – ostensibly because they needed to be discussed by the respective governments but also, one suspects, because they amounted to virtually nothing. It was in the wake of this ineffectual response to the extermination of the Jews that Roosevelt created the War Refugee Board.

By the start of July 1944 the divergent views of the British and Americans over the Brand mission had hardened. The Americans believed that shelter should be offered to 'Jews and similar persons in imminent danger of death', while the British countered with a suggestion that such an offer should be made only for certain categories of Jews – like children and religious leaders.[28] This discussion turned out to be of little practical importance because on 7 July the Americans decided to notify the Soviets about the Brand mission.

It is not hard to imagine why the Americans felt it important to tell the Soviets about Eichmann's proposal. This was a particularly sensitive moment in the relationship between the Western Allies and the Soviet Union. Not only had D Day just been launched in the west, but in the east the Red Army had started Operation Bagration, a massive attack on German Army Group Centre that dwarfed D Day in scale. There were also unresolved political issues connected with the Soviet advance, relating to the future of the eastern European nations that the Red Army was about to liberate. Now was not the time, the Americans felt, to keep the Soviets in the dark about a proposal from the Nazis that would destabilize the alliance. The Soviets, not surprisingly, rejected the Brand deal outright.

But there was another – sensational – element to the Brand mission that the British discovered in Cairo only once they started to interrogate Bandi Grosz, the minor intelligence agent who had accompanied Brand on his trip. Grosz said that he had been told by leading figures in the SS in Budapest to use the mission to 'arrange a meeting in any neutral country between two or three senior German security officers and two or three American officers of equal rank, or as a last resort British officers, in order to negotiate for a separate peace between the Sicherheitsdienst [SD] and the Western Allies'.[29] This idea that the real purpose of the mission was to open negotiations with the West about a way out of the war was certainly what Joel Brand came to believe. 'My impression was', said Brand in 1961 at Eichmann's trial, 'that Himmler used the Jews as a bribe, as it were, in order to have a visiting card with which to enter into bigger things. [Eichmann] made it clear to me that the deal originated with Himmler.'[30]

That Himmler knew about the 'Jews for trucks' deal is confirmed by Kurt Becher's post-war testimony and by contemporary documents.[31] Indeed, it is scarcely possible that the mission could have gone ahead without his knowledge and approval. Himmler would have felt he already had permission to pursue such an approach because in December 1942 Hitler had authorized him to ransom Jews for hard currency – as long as such an action brought in substantial amounts of foreign money.[32] But it is unlikely that Himmler also received authorization from Hitler to start discussions about a separate peace with the Western Allies, even if only in an attempt to cause discord between the Western Allies and Stalin. Although Hitler was open to the spreading of false intelligence – he authorized the leaking in Spain, for example, of a fictitious attempt by the Soviets to seek a separate peace[33] – it is hard to see how he would ever have entered substantive peace negotiations, not least because if news of the talks became public the consequences for German morale would be disastrous.

As for Himmler, it is likely that he did attempt to open discussions about a way out of the war at this point. In that context there is an intriguing mystery around a record of a British decrypt made of a telegram from 'Himmler' on 31 August 1944. The message was sent direct to Churchill, who clearly didn't want the document to exist. 'Himmler telegram. Kept and destroyed by me,'[34] he wrote on a note in the file. This is the only record of a decrypted message from Himmler, and apparently the only one out of thousands of other German documents that was destroyed by Churchill. What was in the message – an offer of peace negotiations? It appears we will never know.

A few months later, in December 1944, Theodor Ondrej, an SS intelligence officer, was shocked to learn from his boss, the Nazi foreign intelligence chief Walter Schellenberg, that Himmler wanted to find a way out of the war. 'One day, by mid- or end of December 1944, Schellenberg told me that Himmler was trying to secure a separate peace,' says Ondrej. 'Schellenberg trusted me, so he also told me that Himmler had taken him into his confidence only because Schellenberg, as Germany's highest intelligence officer, would learn about peace feelers from his foreign agents anyway. This is why he took him into his confidence. My first thought was that Himmler was the least suitable man for a separate peace settlement. SS General Schellenberg smiled and said, "It's amazing, isn't it? I support this, even though I know that he is the least suitable man for this." So Schellenberg was absolutely clear about it, but at the time we were clutching at straws.'[35]

As we will see later, by the spring of 1945 Himmler was pursuing a number of different options in an attempt to deal with the West, ultimately, as Hitler saw it, 'betraying' Germany. So it is not too far fetched to imagine that he was behind the Bandi Grosz suggestion in the summer of 1944. Maybe at that time he just wanted to create a split between the Allies with the suggestion of a separate peace, or perhaps he was seriously looking for a way out of the war and wanted to progress talks. Or, equally possible, he hadn't decided between those two options and was waiting to see what developed. What is extraordinary, as both Schellenberg and Ondrej remarked, is that the man who in a speech in Posen in October 1943 had boasted that he had helped make the Jews 'disappear' could imagine that little more than a year later the Allies would negotiate with him. But Himmler's ability to delude himself was immense.

In Budapest, in late May and June 1944, Eichmann awaited news of the Brand mission. While he waited, Brand's wife, Hansi, and an enterprising Hungarian Jew called Rudolf Kasztner held a series of meetings with him. They tried to persuade Eichmann to offer a gesture to the Allies to show that the Nazis were serious about releasing Jews. These discussions crystallized around a proposal to send a trainload of Jews to Switzerland. From Eichmann's perspective this was not an unwelcome idea. It would demonstrate good faith to the Allies, and also be a means of extorting more money from the Hungarian Jews, as the Nazis could demand payment for every place on the train. Given Eichmann's interest, Rudolf Kasztner took on the practical task of trying to make it happen. In the process 'Kasztner's train' would become the focus of criticism from the Jewish community – and the repercussions would lead to Kasztner's assassination in Israel after the war.

In part, Kasztner was attacked because the train contained many of his own relations – including his mother and brother – as well as a disproportionate number of Jews from his hometown of Cluj. Out of a total of 1,684 passengers, 388 came from this one small city in Transylvania. Éva Speter, then twenty-nine years old, was selected for the Kasztner train, along with her husband and son. Their places had been assured because her father was one of those, along with Kasztner, who chose who travelled. 'Everybody tried for himself to stay alive,' she says. 'If you have to save your life you'll try it in every way, even in a criminal way if it comes to that, but you have to save yourself. Your life is the first, you are nearest to yourself, whatever people try to say.'[36]

Éva Speter and her family were well aware of what had happened to the Hungarian Jews who were deported. She believed that the Germans wanted 'to kill all the 11 million Jews who are living in Europe, including the Jews of Russia'. She had even learnt that the Germans gassed Jews after pretending that they were about to take a shower. And just before she left Budapest she discovered that many more people also knew that the Germans were deporting Jews to their deaths: 'There came a working woman, and she had seen my son, we were all with the yellow star, [and she] said: "Give me your son, I'll take care of him. He will grow up, and don't take him to be murdered with you." Of course I didn't give her my son, but I thought – this working woman, whom I never knew, wanted this beautiful little child to grow up: a Jewish child. For that I can't be really angry with the Hungarians.'[37]

When Éva Speter left Budapest on 30 June aboard the Kasztner train she didn't trust the Germans to keep their word, and when the train stopped at Linz in Austria she grew increasingly concerned about what was going to happen to them. Here the Jews were told to disembark because they were to be medically examined and had to take a 'shower'. She remembers that 'I was standing naked before the doctor, and still looking very proud, into his eyes, and I thought he should see how a proud Jewish woman is going to die.' Once in the showers, from the taps came 'fine warm water . . . a very relieving experience after we were ready to die there.'[38] The Nazis, it turned out, had told the truth about the showers for once.

But in at least one respect Eichmann had lied, because the train's immediate destination was not Switzerland but the concentration camp of Bergen-Belsen in the north of Germany. A section of the camp had been set aside for so-called 'exchange Jews' – those the Nazis might try and ransom – and these Jews received better treatment than Jews elsewhere. For example, Shmuel Huppert, who was sent to the exchange camp with his mother in 1943, remembers that not only did he receive enough food to survive in Bergen-Belsen, but he also learnt to play chess in the camp.[39] The Jews from the Kasztner train received similar preferential treatment, and after months of protracted negotiations the vast majority eventually reached safety in Switzerland.

After the war Kasztner was criticized not only for giving places on the train to his friends and relations, but for causing the deaths of large numbers of other Hungarian Jews by not warning them that the Nazis planned on deporting them to Auschwitz. On the first charge he is guilty, but on the second the evidence is less clear cut. While it is true that on a visit to his hometown of Cluj he didn't alert people to the Nazis' true intentions, it is doubtful if an intervention by him would have made any difference. Jewish youth movements within Hungary, like Hashomer Hatzair, Maccabi Hatzair and Bnei Akiva, had made a concerted effort to warn Jews in the provinces of the dangers they faced, but in every case their warnings were ignored.[40] In part that was because of the lack of options the Jews faced – there were few mountains or thick forests in which to hide, and many of the non-Jewish locals were anti-Semitic – and partly it was a desire to block out the idea that the terrible rumours might be true. 'People didn't listen to whatever they heard,' says Éva Speter, 'because people don't want to believe – never want to believe – the worst. They always try to believe something that's better . . . Hope is one of the best qualities that men get from when they are born.'[41]

Kasztner knew about the mass killings at Auschwitz because he had read a report written by two former inmates, Rudolf Vrba and Alfred Wetzler. They had managed to escape from the camp in April 1944 and had made their way back to their homeland of Slovakia. There they recorded what was happening at Auschwitz Birkenau. Prior to this, few people in the world knew about the true function of Birkenau. Because Birkenau was partially a work camp, at the centre of a whole network of other work camps, many observers outside the Reich had misunderstood its primary purpose. Richard Lichtheim, for instance, of the

Jewish Agency in Geneva, had thought – prior to reading the Vrba–Wetzler report – that the Germans were deporting Jews to Auschwitz in order 'to exploit more Jewish labour in the industrial centres of Upper Silesia'.[42] But the Vrba–Wetzler report left no room for doubt about the real purpose of Auschwitz. It accurately described the opening of the new crematoria/gas-chamber complexes at Birkenau in 1943 and the way in which the murders were conducted. It wasn't surprising that the report was so authentic, because one of the Sonderkommandos working in the crematoria, Filip Müller, had told the two Slovaks exactly what went on there. 'I had handed to Alfred [Wetzler] a plan of the crematoria and gas chambers as well as a list of names of the SS men who were on duty there,' wrote Müller after the war. 'In addition I had given to both of them notes I had been making for some time of almost all transports gassed in crematoria 4 and 5. I had described to them in full detail the process of extermination so that they would be able to report to the outside world . . .'[43]

The Vrba–Wetzler report circulated in Budapest during May 1944. By late June the news had reached London and by early July the authorities in Washington had been informed. Armed with such authentic intelligence, a whole variety of people – from Roosevelt to the King of Sweden – protested to Admiral Horthy about the deportation of the Hungarian Jews. Even the Pope wrote to Horthy in a letter of 25 June, calling on him to reconsider his actions.[44] Archbishop Gennaro Verolino, a papal diplomat in Budapest, remembers that even before the Vrba–Wetzler report had surfaced, 'Gradually we came to the conclusion that "compulsory work abroad" meant deportation. And deportation meant extermination, annihilation. We then protested very vigorously, at first the nuncio himself, and then with the other diplomats.'[45] The papal nuncio in Hungary gave up to 15,000 letters of safe conduct to Jews in Budapest. 'It saved my life once,' says Ferenc Wiener, a Hungarian Jew. 'It saved my life when I showed it to a German officer. And they were executing all the others. I was next to be killed. I then showed my letter and the officer told me I could move on.'[46] In the light of incidents like this, Gerhart Riegner, the wartime representative of the World Jewish Congress in Switzerland, maintains that the Vatican's intervention in Hungary was 'the only example in the history of the Holocaust where the Vatican systematically took the right decision.'[47]

Admiral Horthy now had to decide what to do. Should he try and stop the transports to Auschwitz and so incur the wrath of the Germans, or let them continue despite the protests? Leading Nazis like Joseph Goebbels had previously felt secure in their hold over him – not just because they had successfully bullied Horthy into 'inviting' German troops into Hungary in March and cooperating in the deportation of the Jews, but because they believed that he now welcomed the chance to expel the Jews from his country. 'At any rate,' wrote Goebbels in his diary on 27 April, 'he now no longer obstructs the cleansers of public life in Hungary; on the contrary, he is now murderously angry with the Jews and has no objections to us using them as hostages. He even suggested the same thing himself . . . At any rate the Hungarians will not escape the rhythm of the Jewish question. Whoever says A must say B, and the Hungarians, having started with *Judenpolitik*, can for that reason not halt it. From a certain point onwards *Judenpolitik* propels itself.'[48] This is a particularly revealing diary entry, for Goebbels states unequivocally how he believed the Nazis could handle their allies over the question of the Jews. If the Nazis managed to get blood on the hands of their allies, they would have no choice but to stick with the Third Reich come what may.

But Horthy didn't react as predicted. Even though he was already massively compromised, he reversed his position and on 6 July told the Germans that he wanted the deportations to end. The transports to Auschwitz officially stopped three days later. The pressure on Horthy had been just too much. While he had felt able to sanction the deportations when there were only rumours – however strong and compelling – that the Jews were being killed, now that there was clear evidence that the Jews were being sent to a murder factory he wasn't prepared to permit them to continue. Especially when not only was he receiving protests from the international community, but Budapest was under direct attack from the Allies with the Americans bombing the Hungarian capital on 2 July. Now that the Western Allies were fighting in France and the Red Army was advancing into eastern Europe, there was no hiding from reality – the Germans were losing the war, and one day the victorious powers would call their collaborators to account. By stopping the deportations now Horthy must have thought he stood a chance of constructing an alibi for himself. His judgement was right. Notwithstanding Hungarian participation in previous atrocities against the Jews, Horthy escaped without punishment at the end of the war. He retired to a seaside town near Lisbon where he died in 1957 aged eighty-eight.

The Germans, having already deported 430,000 Jews from Hungary to Auschwitz, were prepared to pause before deporting the rest. After all, this was just one setback the Nazis faced that summer among many. They had to deal not just with the desperate situation on the front line, but with a crisis at the top of the Nazi state when, on 20 July, disaffected Wehrmacht officers tried to kill Hitler by exploding a bomb at his headquarters in East Prussia. Hitler was not seriously hurt, but the search for the perpetrators now became an immediate priority for the German security services.

In the aftermath of the attack on his life Hitler – always at heart an angry man – became even angrier. According to General Heinz Guderian, newly appointed Chief of Staff of the German Army, 'the deep distrust he [Hitler] already felt for mankind in general, and for General Staff officers and generals in particular, now became profound hatred . . . It had already been difficult enough dealing with him; it now became a torture that grew steadily worse from month to month. He frequently lost all self-control and his language grew increasingly violent.'[49]

A month later another disaster loomed for the Germans – this time on the diplomatic front. The Romanians wanted to quit the war. On 5 August, Hitler met the Romanian leader, Marshal Antonescu, and used all his rhetorical skills to try and convince him to keep fighting, but mere words could not alter the dire reality for the Romanian soldiers on the front line. On 20 August large sections of the Romanian Army simply fell apart as the Red Army attacked in the Jassy–Kishinev offensive. On 23 August, Antonescu was removed from office. The Romanians now changed sides and announced that they were at war with Germany.

But Hitler, true to character, would not alter course. And his determination to prolong the war until Red Army soldiers were in the streets of Berlin led inevitably to one final period of appalling destruction.

18. Murder to the End
(1944–1945)

In the wake of Hitler's resolution to fight to the end, the Allies had their own politically controversial issues to confront – not least what to do with the detailed knowledge they now possessed about the murders the Nazis were committing at Auschwitz.

One point on which they all agreed was the magnitude of the horror. 'There is no doubt that this is probably the greatest and most horrible crime ever committed in the whole history of the world,' wrote Churchill on 11 July 1944, 'and it has been done by scientific machinery by nominally civilized men in the name of a great State and one of the leading races of Europe . . . Declarations should be made in public, so that everyone connected with it will be hunted down and put to death.'[1] But words of outrage and threat on their own, of course, didn't directly help the Jews who were dying in Auschwitz.

Various Jewish groups suggested one practical response to the crime – drop bombs on the camp. The World Jewish Congress in Geneva called in June for the Americans to destroy the gas chambers, and Churchill, when he heard about the idea, wrote on 7 July to Anthony Eden: 'Get anything out of the Air Force you can and invoke me if necessary.'[2] But calls to bomb Auschwitz were ultimately rejected. In Britain the Air Ministry was unenthusiastic about the idea for practical reasons. One problem was the difficulty of bombing the gas chambers while avoiding killing many of the prisoners at Birkenau. The British suggested that the request be considered by the Americans, who specialized in daytime bombing. On behalf of the Americans, John McCloy, the Assistant Secretary of War, was dismissive. He expressed doubts about the feasibility of the plan, and said that in any case it would divert bombers from other, more important operations.[3]

However, even if the immense practical difficulties could have been overcome and the gas chambers of Auschwitz bombed, it is hard to see how this would have stopped the killings. The Harvest Festival massacre at Majdanek the year before had demonstrated that the Germans did not need gas chambers to murder large numbers of Jews – machine guns could kill just as many.

Nonetheless, the dismissive way in which many of those involved in the decision-making process treated the question of the bombing of Auschwitz – one of McCloy's staff even wrote an inter-office memo admitting that McCloy wanted to 'kill' the idea[4] – reflects a broader issue of significance. It is encapsulated by a question to the Allies posed by David Ben Gurion, chairman of the Jewish Agency executive and later one of the founders of modern Israel, in a speech on 10 July 1944: 'If instead of Jews, thousands of English, American or Russian women, children and aged had been tortured every day, burnt to death, asphyxiated in gas chambers – would you have acted in the same way?'[5]

The answer to Ben Gurion's question is, almost certainly, no. The Allies would surely not 'have acted in the same way' if, for example, British prisoners of war were being gassed at Auschwitz. That is a judgement that is supported by the evidence. As we have seen, the Allies didn't want to commit themselves at the Bermuda conference in 1943 to admitting large number of Jews into their countries – even though at the end of 1942 they had condemned the Nazis' extermination of the Jews. In Washington in March 1943, a month before the Bermuda conference, Anthony Eden, the British Foreign Secretary, had said in a meeting that it was imperative 'to move very cautiously about offering to take all Jews out of a country' because 'if we do that, then the Jews of the world will be wanting us to make similar efforts in Poland and Germany. Hitler might well take us up on any such offer, and there simply are not enough ships and means of transportation in the world to handle them.'[6] To paraphrase Ben Gurion's question in the light of Eden's words, does anyone think such an excuse for inaction would have been thought acceptable if the Germans were murdering British or American prisoners of war? Would the British and Americans seriously have let their soldiers be massacred just because ships couldn't be diverted to take them across the English Channel to safety, especially when ships were found during the war to transport several hundred thousand captured enemy prisoners across the Atlantic to North America? No, Eden's excuse is simply not credible.

Linda Breder, a Jewish inmate of Auschwitz, felt that 'God forgot us and [the] people of the war forgot us, didn't care about what's going on and they knew what's going on [at Auschwitz].' She says, 'We wanted them to put the bombs on the camp, at least we could run and hundreds and hundreds of planes were coming [to bomb other targets in Poland] and we are looking up and no bombs. So this we could not understand.'[7]

The Allied position regarding the Jews remained simple – the only sure way to stop their extermination was to defeat the Nazis. In the summer of 1944 that strategy seemed to enjoy some success when the Red Army captured Majdanek camp in late July. Majdanek was a revelation to the world. Much of the extermination machinery had not been destroyed by the retreating Germans, and the remaining gas chambers and crematorium were incontrovertible proof of the Nazis' murderous activities. 'What I am now about to relate is too enormous and too gruesome to be fully conceived,' wrote Konstantin Simonov, a Soviet war correspondent, after examining the camp. Simonov described how the gas chambers functioned, with 'specially trained operators wearing gas masks' who 'poured the "cyclone [sic]" out of the cylindrical tins into the chamber'. He was also appalled by the immense number of shoes he saw, taken from those who had been murdered. 'They spill over out of the hut through the windows and the doors. In one spot the weight of them pushed out part of the wall, which fell outwards together with piles of shoes . . . it is hard to imagine anything more gruesome than this sight.'[8]

At Auschwitz, after the Hungarian transports had stopped in early July, and the majority of the Łódź ghetto Jews had been murdered a few weeks later, the peak period of killing was over. As a result, the SS decided to reduce the number of Sonderkommandos in the camp from the high point of 900 reached at the time of the Hungarian transports to a much lower figure. They planned to do this by murdering surplus Sonderkommandos. 'We knew that our days were always numbered and we didn't know when the end would be,' says Dario Gabbai, one of the Sonderkommando at Birkenau. The Nazis, especially in the light of the publicity about Majdanek, did not want any Sonderkommandos to survive the war. They knew too much about the intimate details of the killing process. So at the end of September, SS Scharführer (Sergeant Major) Busch asked for 200 'volunteers' from the Sonderkommandos at Crematorium IV to come forward. He claimed that they would be transported to a new camp. But the Sonderkommandos were aware that the number of transports to the camp had been tailing off, and had no doubt what that meant for their own fate. 'Was Busch really so naïve, I thought,' wrote Filip Müller, one of the Auschwitz Sonderkommando, 'to believe any one of us would volunteer for his own slaughter?'[9] Not surprisingly, no one came forward. So Scharführer Busch was forced to pick the 200 Sonderkommandos himself. Of course, there was no 'new camp' and the selected prisoners were taken away and killed. That night – in an unprecedented event – the SS themselves burnt the bodies of the Sonderkommandos in crematoria ovens away from the eyes of the other prisoners. Their excuse was that they were burning the bodies of people killed in an Allied bombing raid. The remaining Sonderkommandos were not deceived, and their suspicions about the fate of their comrades were confirmed when several of the bodies were found in the ovens the next morning, burnt but still recognizable. As a consequence, when the SS told the Kapos at the crematoria to come up with a list of 300 more Sonderkommandos who were allegedly to be transferred to 'rubber factories', the Sonderkommandos decided to launch an uprising.[10]

As we have already seen, the security levels at Auschwitz were of a higher level than other death camps like Sobibór and Treblinka. The crematoria/gas-chamber buildings were in their own fenced-off sub-camps within the giant complex of Auschwitz Birkenau, which itself sat within the security area of the Auschwitz zone of interest. There had been attempts at a mass breakout before – most notably a revolt of Poles within the penal company at Birkenau on 10 June 1942. But of the fifty or so prisoners who attempted that escape, only one is known for certain to have survived.

However, even knowing that the chances of a successful uprising were slim to non-existent, on 7 October 1944 the Sonderkommandos at Crematoria IV turned on their SS guards. They fought with axes and hammers against SS armed with guns, and managed to set the crematorium on fire. Hearing the noise coming from Crematorium IV, the Sonderkommandos at Crematorium II also attacked their SS overseers, killing two of them – even throwing one into a burning furnace. SS reinforcements arrived and started to hunt down any prisoners who had managed to escape the perimeter of the camp. When they found some Sonderkommandos hiding inside a barn they set it on fire. Not one of the Sonderkommandos who rose up against the SS that day survived the attempted escape. Around 250 Sonderkommandos had taken part in the revolt and the SS made sure every single one of them died. But the revenge of the SS did not stop there. In an attempt to terrorize the remaining Sonderkommandos they selected a further 200 and killed them as well.[11] Henryk Mandelbaum, one of the Auschwitz Sonderkommando, remembers that they 'told us to lie face down on the ground holding our hands behind our backs and every third person was shot. Some of my friends in the Sonderkommando lost their lives and the rest had to go back to work. There was never much hope for us. I'm telling it like it is.'[12] Despite enduring this ordeal himself, and witnessing the death of so many of his comrades, Henryk Mandelbaum still feels that those who fought back 'did a good thing' because 'we were the living dead, you have to remember. Now we're speaking freely, peacefully and we can have assumptions, we can pose questions, we can add, we can subtract, but then it was very different. Human beings were condemned . . .'[13]

After the war, Auschwitz survivors sometimes had to endure taunts that they had lacked the courage to resist. Halina Birenbaum remembers that when she reached Israel in 1947 she was distraught when other members of the kibbutz said to her, 'You just followed like sheep. You didn't defend yourselves. Why didn't you defend yourselves? What happened to you? You're to blame. You didn't do anything. That kind of thing wouldn't happen to us. Don't tell us about it. It's a disgrace. Don't tell the young people, you'll crush their fighting spirit.'[14]

The history of the Sonderkommando revolt at Auschwitz in October 1944 demonstrates the injustice of such accusations. The Sonderkommandos did not go like 'sheep' to the slaughter. They fought back and died as a consequence. They lost their lives because effective resistance in Auschwitz was almost impossible. Auschwitz lasted as an institution for four and a half years and in that time out of the more than 1 million people sent there, about 800 attempted to escape. But fewer than 150 of them managed to get away from the area and an unknown number of these successful escapees were subsequently killed in the war.[15] It was thus not so much lack of courage that prevented the mass of inmates from escaping as lack of opportunity.

By the time of the Sonderkommando revolt in October 1944, the Germans had lost yet more allies. On 8 September, the Red Army entered

Bulgaria and hours later the Bulgarians followed the example of the Italians and Romanians – they changed sides and declared war on Germany. Less than two weeks later Finland exited the war as well.[16] Hitler's erstwhile friends had recognized the inevitable – the Germans had lost the war. Even members of the Nazi elite wanted to explore ways of escape. Not just Himmler, but Joseph Goebbels as well. When Goebbels heard via Japanese sources a rumour that Stalin might possibly consider a separate peace, he composed a letter to Hitler supporting the idea. 'What we would attain', he wrote on 20 September 1944, 'would not be the victory that we dreamed of in 1941, but it would still be the greatest victory in German history. The sacrifices that the German people had made in this war would thereby be fully justified.'[17] But Hitler didn't even bother to engage with Goebbels' suggestion and never discussed it with him. For Hitler, either Germany triumphed or Germany would be destroyed. What had been his greatest strength in the eyes of supporters like Goebbels – his refusal to compromise – was now revealed as his greatest weakness.

One obvious consequence of Hitler's intransigence was that the suffering of the Jews continued. In Slovakia, for instance, German security forces deported more than 12,000 Jews between September and December 1944, after the Germans suppressed an uprising by the Slovak resistance. In Hungary, Hitler's determination to stop Admiral Horthy from taking the country out of the war led to another crisis for the Hungarian Jews. After ending the deportations to Auschwitz in early July, Horthy had once again been plotting to make peace with the Allies. In early October, a Hungarian delegation even signed a deal with the Soviets in Moscow. On 15 October, the Germans responded. Otto Skorzeny, the SS officer who had led the team that rescued Mussolini from prison the year before, captured Horthy's son Miklós in Budapest, rolled him up in a carpet and took him to Mauthausen camp in Austria. The Germans now blackmailed Horthy into transferring power to Ferenc Szálasi, leader of the Hungarian fascist party, the Arrow Cross. Horthy, wanting to save his son, collaborated with the Germans once again, and then spent the rest of the war as Hitler's 'guest' in a castle in Bavaria.

With Horthy out of the way and Hungary in the hands of fascists, the Jews were vulnerable once again. On 18 October Eichmann began discussions with Szálasi about deporting Jews – not this time to Auschwitz, but direct to the Reich as forced labourers. Eichmann's problem was that there was no means of transporting tens of thousands of Jews to the west. But he came up with a solution. If the Jews could not be carried by railway or truck, then they could walk – for more than a hundred miles. By the end of November, 27,000 Jews were walking to the Reich and 40,000 more were supposed to follow them. Conditions on the march were, predictably, appalling. Indeed, they were so bad that when a group of SS officers passed the marching Jews they were so concerned about what they saw that they complained to Otto Winkelmann, Higher SS and Police Chief for Hungary. Incredibly, one of those who voiced their objections was Rudolf Höss, one-time commandant of Auschwitz and now in an administrative role in the SS. It wasn't that Höss had suddenly developed a sense of humanity, but that he didn't see the value in sending Jews to the Reich who, when they arrived, couldn't work.[18] Another SS officer, Kurt Becher, who had been involved in the negotiations about the Hungarian Jews earlier in the year, complained to Himmler about Eichmann's actions. This led to an extraordinary meeting in Himmler's private train in the Black Forest in November 1944. Himmler told Eichmann to stop deporting the Budapest Jews, adding, 'If until now you have exterminated Jews, from now on, if I order you, you must be a fosterer of Jews.'[19]

Himmler's apparently bizarre remark was, like Höss's, motivated not by a change of ideological heart, but by purely practical concerns – not just the desire to use the Jews as both potential labour and hostages in any future discussions with the Allies, but also an understanding of the military reality. As Himmler talked to Eichmann, the Red Army were advancing further into Hungary. Thus discussions about any potential deportation of Hungarian Jews were shortly to become of only theoretical interest.

By late December the Red Army had encircled Budapest. Hitler declared the city a 'fortified place' and called on the defenders to fight to the death. The ensuing battle lasted until 13 February 1945 and around 40,000 civilians died. In the aftermath of the Soviet victory, soldiers of the Red Army attacked the women of Budapest and thousands were raped – one estimate is as many as 50,000. Barna Andrásofszky, a medical student, witnessed the aftermath of one such attack in a village outside Budapest. He was called to help a young woman who said she had been gang-raped by 'maybe ten or fifteen men'. Barna could not stop the woman's massive internal bleeding and she was taken to hospital. 'It was very difficult to come to terms that this was happening in the twentieth century,' he says. 'It was very difficult to see as a reality what the Nazi propaganda was spreading. But here we could see that in reality. And also we heard about many other terrible situations like this.'[20]

Such testimony is relevant in a history of the Holocaust because it reminds us once again that the extermination of the Jews took place in the context of a war of the most horrendous brutality, though that must not, of course, be considered any form of excuse for the Nazis' crime. Significantly, the appalling scenes in Budapest were not replicated in Bucharest in Romania or in Sofia in Bulgaria after the Red Army arrived. Hitler had, to a large extent, brought this suffering upon the Hungarians. For a necessary precondition of the Red Army's atrocities in Hungary had been Hitler's decision that the Hungarians were to be prevented, unlike the Romanians and Bulgarians, from changing sides as the Soviets neared. Hitler's stubbornness was ultimately futile anyway. At the end of December, with Budapest surrounded, the new Hungarian government, sponsored by the Soviets, declared war on Germany.

Hitler continued, in the face of the Allied advance, to voice his hatred of the Jews. In a decree of 25 September 1944 he referred to 'the total annihilatory will of our Jewish-international enemies',[21] and in a proclamation in Munich on 12 November he talked about the Jews' 'satanic will to persecute and destroy'.[22] In a sign of Hitler's own reluctance to face an audience when events were going against him, the Munich address was actually delivered by Himmler, but the sentiments were undeniably Hitler's. Yet again the German leader marvelled at the 'incomprehensible absurdity' of the Western democracies in forming an alliance with the forces of 'Bolshevism', and claimed that this apparently nonsensical position could be explained 'at the moment you realize that the Jew is always behind the stupidity and weakness of man, his lack of character on the one hand, and his deficiencies on the other'. The reality, he said, was that 'the Jew is the wire-puller in the democracies, as well as the creator and driving force of the Bolshevik international beast of the world.' Hitler thus remained a consistent fantasist. For this was the same argument he had made in the beer halls of Munich in the early 1920s when he alleged that the Jews were simultaneously behind both 'Bolshevism' and the excesses of capitalism.

In a piece of the most twisted logic imaginable, Hitler even argued in his 1945 New Year proclamation to German soldiers that the fact that Germany was now engaged in 'a merciless struggle for existence or non-existence' was because 'the goal of the Jewish-international world conspiracy opposing us is the extermination of our *Volk*.' The correct explanation, of course, was that Germans were now in danger because Hitler had pursued a racist war of expansionism that had backfired, not that 'the Jewish-eastern Bolshevism reflects in its exterminationist tendencies the goals of Jewish-western capitalism.'[23]

As Hitler offered this New Year message to German soldiers, their 'Bolshevik' enemies were not far from Auschwitz, where around 67,000 inmates still remained. In a new offensive, beginning on 12 January, Soviet soldiers from the First and Fourth Ukrainian Fronts closed in on Kraków, little more than 30 miles east of the camp. At Auschwitz, the Germans now followed orders not to allow their prisoners to fall into enemy hands. The SS marched most of the remaining Auschwitz prisoners – around 58,000 of them – out into the icy wind and snow of the Polish winter. The prisoners left behind, just under 9,000, were judged too sick to embark on the march. They were supposed to be shot by SS Sturmbannführer (Major) Franz Xaver Kraus and his men before the Red Army liberated Auschwitz. SS units did go on to murder about 300 prisoners at Birkenau, together with several hundred more in four sub-camps, but most of the sick at Auschwitz survived. Once again, this wasn't because the SS had suddenly become ashamed of their murderous work, but because the discipline of the SS had started to crack as the Red Army approached. Rather than spend time killing the inmates, the SS preferred to increase their chances of saving themselves by escaping the area. Prisoners recalled that during the 'evacuation' there was 'chaos' and 'panic' among 'the drunken SS'.[24]

Amid this confusion, even some of the Sonderkommando managed to survive. Morris Kesselman, an eighteen-year-old member of the Sonderkommando, remembers that as thousands of prisoners were milling about, waiting to join the march out of the camp, the 'guy in charge' of his block – 'a French Jew' – came and said that the SS appeared to have left the immediate area because the camp was being 'liquidated'. 'So we all went out,' says Morris, 'we mixed in [with the other prisoners] and marched out.'

During his time in the Auschwitz Sonderkommando, Morris Kesselman had tried to 'strengthen himself' with 'whatever [food] was available'. He had also learnt to give himself an edge during selections in Birkenau by standing next to someone who looked weak. 'If it wouldn't be him it would be me,' he says. 'Did I feel sorry? Sure I felt sorry, but I couldn't help him. But at that point I only watched out for myself. I was not in a position to help anybody.'[25] Once assigned to the Sonderkommando, though horrified by the work he had to do, he believes his chances of survival were increased by the fact that he was young and 'didn't know much about anything'. He remembers that it was predominantly the 'elderly people, the intelligent people' who committed suicide by flinging themselves on the electric fences. He believes the young and less well educated found it easier to cope. As a member of the Sonderkommando he had access to the clothes of the murdered Jews and so in January 1945, 'when I marched out of the camp . . . I was very well dressed. I had a Russian hat, a fur hat, with a heavy coat, and good shoes. And the only thing is, I don't know what made me do it, but I had my pockets full of lumps of sugar. Why I did it, I don't know – other people took meat. The sugar and the snow [mixed together], I survived because of that.'[26]

Conditions on the march out of Auschwitz were life-threatening. Dario Gabbai, another Sonderkommando who had managed to join the exodus, remembers that 'The German Army was killing anyone who couldn't walk.'[27] Silvia Veselá, a Slovakian Jew who had spent more than two years in Auschwitz, confirms that 'Those who couldn't go further were shot dead. We were all mixed up, men and women. The road was covered in dead . . .'[28]

The guards shot prisoners not only because they could not keep up with the pace of the march, but for stopping to urinate or to bend down and tie their laces. At night, there wasn't space in the barns or other shelters for all the prisoners, so many slept in the open.[29] After several days on the road, Ibi Mann, a Czech Jew, remembers, 'it seemed to me to be the end of the world already, it was very hard . . . There were less and less and less people marching . . . we weren't hungry but we were thirsty. We were terribly thirsty and people simply dropped. They dropped or they were shot.'[30]

The majority of prisoners were marched to one of two destinations – either Gliwice, 30 miles to the north-west, or Wodzisław, a similar distance due west. There they were shoved on to open railway trucks for the next stage of their ordeal. Morris Venezia, a Greek Jew, remembers that it was 'terrible' in the trucks because 'the snow was coming down on top of us' and 'the wagon was packed.' As a result 'many people died' on the journey to camps further away from the front line.[31]

Just days after the march out of Auschwitz, at Stutthof concentration camp in West Prussia, thousands of other prisoners were also forced out into the snow. Around 11,000 inmates, mostly Jews, were marched out of Stutthof and nearby satellite camps. Some headed towards Königsberg in East Prussia while others headed due west.[32] On the journey the accompanying guards shot around 2,000 of the prisoners. 'On both sides of the road,' recalled Schoschana Rabinovici, one of those forced to march through the freezing cold, 'we saw corpses of the prisoners from the columns marching in front of us. You could tell that some of the dead had collapsed and died of hunger, others had been shot, and the blood flowing from their wounds turned the snow red.'[33] On 31 January several thousand prisoners were machine-gunned on the seashore at Palmnicken on the Sambian peninsula in the far east of Prussia, after an attempt to trap them in an amber mine and blow them up had been thwarted.[34] Only 200 are thought to have survived the massacre.

Six months earlier the commandant of Stutthof had been ordered by the SS economic and administrative department to ensure that no Jewish prisoner at the camp was left alive by the end of 1944. As a consequence gas chambers had been improvised in the camp. Starting in the early autumn of 1944, the gassing took place in a converted delousing room, but after a short time a new gassing installation was created in a railway wagon in a siding near the crematorium. The idea was that the prisoners to be gassed were first tricked into believing that they were boarding a train, rather than entering a gas chamber. To assist in that deception an SS man put on a railway uniform 'complete with signal whistle' and told the prisoners to hurry up and get on board as the train was about to leave for Danzig.[35] But the capacity of these makeshift gas chambers was limited, and there were still many thousands of Jews left alive at Stutthof by the end of the year.

What the Stutthof massacre confirmed was that for all Himmler's talk of 'fostering' the Jews, a desire to murder them still existed within the Nazi state, even as the Red Army moved ever closer. Although the situation was certainly confused – almost chaotic – on the ground, the ideological imperative to destroy the Jews still remained. While Himmler understood that for tactical reasons it might be worth bargaining with the Allies over the lives of some Jewish 'hostages', the central objective had not altered.

The level of suffering on what became known as the 'death marches' was immense. One estimate – almost certainly on the low side – is that out of 113,000 concentration camp prisoners who were forced on to the winter roads in January and February 1945, more than one in three died.[36] In Poland there were examples of locals trying to offer help to the desperate prisoners as they trudged by,[37] but within Germany, while there may well have been individual displays of kindness, the general attitude was less forgiving – summed up by the comment of one German bystander at the sight of prisoners on a death march: 'What crimes they must have committed to be treated so cruelly.'[38]

Once the surviving prisoners reached their destinations their torment continued. Most were sent to camps within the Reich, including Buchenwald, Dora-Mittelbau and Mauthausen. About 20,000 former Auschwitz prisoners ended up at Bergen-Belsen, north-west of Hanover. The camp had been the holding destination for the so-called 'exchange Jews' in 1943, but conditions had deteriorated badly by the time the prisoners from the death marches arrived. In part that was the result of gross overcrowding. The camp expanded from 15,000 inmates at the end of 1944 to 60,000 in April 1945. 'Bergen-Belsen cannot be described in human language,' says Alice Lok Cahana, who was sent there from Auschwitz. Prisoners cried out 'for "Mother! Water! Water! Mother!" You heard chanting, day and night.' The Kapo in charge of Alice's group of prisoners 'went berserk' and started whipping them 'because she wanted to silence the dying'. During the night the Kapo kicked out at the prisoners. Once she stamped on Alice's head, and Alice knew that 'if I move she [the Kapo] will beat me to death.'[39]

A Polish Catholic woman imprisoned in Bergen-Belsen remembered the arrival of Hungarian Jews. 'During December 1944 and January and February 1945 multitudes of women stood for hours in this freezing weather,' she said, in testimony she gave immediately after the end of the war. 'This horrible picture was not enough to describe the conditions of those miserable Hungarian Jewish women, particularly the elderly ones who dropped like flies from starvation and cold. [A] special detail of Ukrainian prisoners picked up the corpses lying by the blocks and carted them off to be cremated. Each night women died in [their] blocks and each day they died during the roll calls. They came from transports that lasted for days, sometimes even weeks, were totally exhausted, became crowded into blocks one thousand or twelve hundred in each, having to use one bed by four people.'[40] Another prisoner recalled that there was no water and that 'intestinal illnesses were rampant; diarrhea and typhoid fever decimated people.'[41]

As the Third Reich neared collapse, conditions at other camps were equally horrific. Mauthausen and the network of sub-camps close by became vast zones of death – 11,000 died in April 1945 alone. At Ravensbrück, north of Berlin, conditions had been worsening during 1944, and early in 1945 a gas chamber was improvised to murder several thousand prisoners.[42] Estera Frenkiel, who had previously been in the Łódź ghetto, was sent to Ravensbrück in the summer of 1944. She remembers the camp as 'pure hell'. 'The ghetto was a story in its own right,' she says. 'That was a tale of hunger. That was a battle for food, avoiding deportation. But there [in Ravensbrück] it was hell: neither day, nor night.'[43]

Yet, at the same time as the death marches left the camps, Himmler personally negotiated the ransom of Jews. In January 1945 he met in the Black Forest with Jean-Marie Musy, a Swiss politician, and discussed releasing a number of Jews for money. In early February a transport containing around 1,200 Jews left Theresienstadt camp, north-east of Prague, for Switzerland. Rita Reh, one of the Jews on board, remembers, 'When we were on the train the SS came and told us to put on some make-up, comb our hair and dress up, so we'd look all right when we arrived. They wanted us to make a good impression on the Swiss. They didn't want us to look like camp inmates, overworked. They wanted us to look good.'[44] When Himmler's 'humanitarian' gesture was publicized in the Swiss papers, Hitler was furious.[45] Even though he had agreed in December 1942 that Himmler could pursue the ransoming of Jews, this was too much. Almost certainly, he was concerned about the sense of despair that might emanate from sending Jews to safety at a time when the German people were suffering as the bombing attacks intensified. Hitler ordered Himmler to stop ransoming Jews at once. It was clear once again that Hitler would fight to the very end. Bernd Freiherr Freytag von Loringhoven, an adjutant to the army Chief of Staff, who observed Hitler during this period, maintains that 'Officially there was no political solution. Foreign policy did not exist any more. For Hitler there was only a military solution. A political solution was beyond discussion, and if it had been mentioned, Hitler would have labelled it as defeatism.'[46]

Himmler's relationship with Hitler was now under great strain. Hitler was already furious with Himmler for his perceived failure as a military leader. Dissatisfied with the performance of his traditionally trained military experts, Hitler had recently appointed him to a series of leadership posts, including Commander of Army Group Vistula. But having an amateur commander – albeit one with the necessary ideological fervour – had not benefited the soldiers concerned, and Himmler had been no more successful at holding back the Red Army than his predecessors had been. On 15 March 1945, according to Goebbels, Hitler remarked that Himmler bore 'the historic guilt' for the fact that 'Pomerania and a large part of its population had fallen into the hands of the Soviets'.[47] The following day Hitler told Goebbels that he had given Himmler 'an exceptionally vigorous telling off'.[48] Goebbels' consequent judgement on Himmler was cutting: 'Unfortunately, he was tempted to pursue military laurels, but he has failed completely. He'll do nothing but ruin his good political reputation by this.'[49]

However, by this point Himmler seems to have been less concerned with his 'political reputation' among the Nazi elite, and a great deal more interested in how he might be perceived by the victorious powers. He ignored Hitler's instructions and instead decided to intensify his contacts with the West. During February and March 1945 he met with Count Folke Bernadotte of the Swedish Red Cross and discussed sending Scandinavian prisoners held in concentration camps to Sweden. Himmler's personal masseur and physical therapist, Felix Kersten, played a part in lobbying Himmler to release not just the Scandinavian prisoners – both Jews and non-Jews – but also large numbers of Jews of other nationalities. It was in this context that Himmler wrote a bizarre letter to Kersten in the middle of March, in which he revealed how he would try and explain his previous actions to any representative of the Jews. He said that he had always wanted to allow Jews to move safely to the West 'until the war and the irrationality unleashed by it' made this policy impossible. He now wanted 'all differences' to be put to one side so that 'wisdom and rationality' and 'the desire to help' would appear in their place.[50]

We see Himmler's words today, understandably, as wholly mendacious. But it is possible that he genuinely believed what he was writing. The words reflect the warped, paranoid world in which the Nazi leadership existed. Himmler almost certainly thought that, had the war not intervened, the policy Eichmann had operated in Vienna in 1938 – of robbing the Jews and deporting them – might have removed all the Jews from the Reich. This policy had been thwarted, the Nazis argued at the time, only by the unwillingness of the rest of the world to take the Jews. From the Nazi perspective, the problem had been not that the German government wanted to expel the Jews, but that none of the nations of the world gathered at the Evian conference in 1938 had wanted to receive them. In this context, Himmler would have argued that the Nazis were the true victims. Not just that, but – according to the Nazis – the war was not their fault either. It had happened because Germany had been denied the return of territory stolen after the end of the First World War. As for the extermination camps, they had been constructed only because the British had irrationally acted against their best interests and refused to make peace in the summer of 1940. Likewise, Germany had been forced to fight a preventative war against the Bolsheviks who, had Germany not intervened, would have invaded and conquered Europe. The fact that the Bolsheviks were even now fighting their way towards the Atlantic was proof that this analysis had been correct all along.

It was all a fantasy, of course – not least because Hitler had for years intended to launch a war of territorial conquest in the east. But within the confines of the Nazi universe Himmler's arguments made sense. Outrageous and full of falsehoods as his letter of explanation to Kersten was, it remains valuable as an insight into how he seriously thought he could argue that the Holocaust was not his fault.

Given that Himmler had no problem deluding himself about the fate of the Jews, what about the mass of ordinary Germans? What did they know about the Final Solution and how many of them were prepared to help the Jews? That there was some German opposition to the Nazis' treatment of the Jews is undeniable. Most famously the White Rose group in Munich, including brother and sister Hans and Sophie Scholl, distributed a series of leaflets in 1942 and 1943 protesting about many aspects of Hitler's rule. But while the White Rose group condemned the Nazi treatment of the Jews, the wording of their protest leaflet is enlightening. They focused on the murder of 'three hundred thousand Jews' in Poland 'in the most bestial manner imaginable', which they saw as 'a terrible crime against the dignity of mankind, a crime that cannot be compared with any other in the history of mankind'. However, they immediately felt the need to add these words: 'Jews are human beings too – it makes no difference what your opinion is regarding the Jewish question – and these crimes are being committed against human beings. Perhaps someone will say, the Jews deserve this fate. Saying this is in itself a colossal effrontery.'[51] That the White Rose protesters felt the need to argue against those who thought the Jews 'deserve their fate' is significant. They obviously believed that, because the victims were Jews, they could not count on all their fellow non-Jewish Germans to condemn the crime automatically.

It must not be forgotten, however, that there were a number of brave Germans who protected Jews during the war. In Berlin, for example, Otto Jogmin, a caretaker living in a house in Charlottenburg, concealed Jews in the basement of his building and managed to supply them with food and medicine. He was one of around 550 Germans who were honoured in Israel after the war as 'Righteous among the Nations'.[52]

Altogether around 1,700 Jews managed to survive the war in hiding in Berlin, and an estimated 20,000 to 30,000 non-Jewish Germans assisted them in one way or another.[53] That is a much smaller number of Jews than were helped in Warsaw during the same period. As we have seen, around 28,000 Jews were hidden in Warsaw, of whom about 11,500 survived the war. Up to 90,000 non-Jewish Poles risked their lives to help them.

The stark fact is that nearly seven times as many Jews survived the war in Warsaw, helped by non-Jews, as in Berlin. Yet Berlin was more than three times the size of the Polish capital, albeit with fewer Jewish inhabitants at the start of the war (about 80,000) than Warsaw (350,000). While there are a number of possible explanations for this disparity, the most persuasive is that there was simply less desire among the broad German population to take risks for the Jews. As one leading scholar concludes: 'Many, probably the great majority of the population, were convinced by 1939 if not before that the Jews had been a harmful influence in German society, and that it would be better if those still remaining left (or were forced to leave) as soon as possible.'[54] That is not to say, of course, that large numbers of Germans were content that the Jews should be killed.

As for the ordinary German's knowledge of the fate of the deported Jews, that varied considerably. But while detailed information about the murder factories was not commonplace, the idea that something bad was happening to the Jews in the east was widespread. After all, as we have seen, in a number of speeches during the war Hitler referred openly to the fulfilment of his 'prophecy' about the extermination of the Jews in the event of a 'world war'. In that context, the concern of many non-Jewish Germans seems to have been less for the Jews and more for their own fate if the war did not go to plan. One SD report for Franconia in southern Germany from December 1942 reads: 'One of the strongest causes of unease among those attached to the church and in the rural population is at the present time formed by news from Russia in which shooting and extermination of the Jews is spoken about. The news frequently leaves great anxiety, care and worry in those sections of the population. According to widely held opinion in the rural population, it is not at all certain that we will win the war, and if the Jews come again to Germany, they will exact dreadful revenge upon us.'[55]

Charles Bleeker Kohlsaat, an ethnic German living in the Warthegau in Poland, heard this fear expressed first hand. His uncle had learnt what was happening in Auschwitz and warned: 'Should the world ever find out what is going on there, we have had it.' Bleeker Kohlsaat asked his mother: 'Mummy, what does Uncle Willy mean?' And she replied: 'Well, it is very difficult to explain, and there is no need for you to know.' He remembers that 'We [had] assumed it [Auschwitz] to be a severe prison or something of the kind, where people received extremely meagre food and might even be treated badly, meaning that they were shouted at – not beaten – but received meagre food and had to work very hard. That's what we believed. We thought they were being punished in a severe prison, that's what we imagined. Our imagination did not stretch far enough to guess what was concealed behind the scenes.'[56]

When Manfred von Schröder, a German officer, discovered the reality of Auschwitz before the end of the war, he was 'terrified' and thought, 'Oh goodness, what will happen to the Germans when we lose that war?' Previously, fighting against the Red Army, he had felt that 'Human life is cheap in a war. If you hear that somewhere near by some Russian prisoners or partisans or even Jews have been shot, then the feeling was – when the same day five of your comrades were shot – you think, And, so what? There were thousands dying every day . . . so you thought, "How do you try to be alive yourself?" And everything else doesn't interest you very much, you know.'[57]

Himmler was certainly concerned about his own fate once Germany lost the war. As part of his strategy to show himself in the best possible light, he allowed Bergen-Belsen to be captured intact on 15 April 1945. But the plan – from his perspective – was a disaster. When the British entered the camp they saw the surviving prisoners living in the most horrendous conditions. 'I think they [the British soldiers] were the bravest people I ever saw in my life,' says Jacob Zylberstein, previously of the Łódź ghetto but who was now in Bergen-Belsen, 'because there was typhus, dysentery, cholera, everything there.'[58] Shortly afterwards 'the English bulldozers started to dig graves' for the thousands of dead.

Himmler's reaction was to protest, on 21 April, to Norbert Masur, a Swedish official of the World Jewish Congress – and a Jew – that he had not received the thanks he deserved for handing over the camps to the Allies.[59] During the discussion he also repeated many of the self-serving lies and excuses he had made in his letter to Kersten in mid-March: the Jews were a foreign element in Germany and had needed to be removed; the Jews were dangerous because they were linked to Bolshevism; he had wanted peaceful emigration for the Jews, but other countries had not cooperated; Jews from the east carried typhus and the Germans had built crematoria to dispose of the sick who had died; the German people had suffered along with the Jews in this war; concentration camps were really re-education camps, and so on.

After the Masur meeting, Himmler still persevered in a doomed attempt to refashion his reputation. Two days later, on 23 April, he told the Swedish diplomat Count Bernadotte he could approach the Allies and tell them that Germany would surrender unconditionally to Britain and America on the western front – but not to the Soviet Union. At the time, Himmler thought that Hitler might already have committed suicide. But Hitler was still very much alive in his fortified bunker beneath the garden of the Reich Chancellery, and he was outraged when he learnt of Himmler's offer of surrender, broadcast on radio on 27 April. 'The news hit the bunker like a bombshell,' remembers Bernd Freiherr Freytag von Loringhoven. 'It had the greatest impact on Hitler.'[60] Himmler's attempt to surrender to the Western powers was, said Hitler, 'the most shameful betrayal in human history'.[61] He now prepared to commit suicide, believing that his 'loyal Heinrich' had turned against him at the last.

In the middle of the afternoon on 30 April 1945, Hitler killed himself. He left behind his 'political testament' in which he stated that he had never wanted war in 1939, but that the conflict had been caused by 'those international statesmen who are either of Jewish origin or work for Jewish interests'. He also hinted that he was responsible for – indeed proud of – the extermination of the Jews. He said that he had 'never left any doubt' that the 'actual guilty party' for starting the war would be 'held responsible'. This was, according to him, 'the Jews'. 'Further,' he said, 'I have not left anybody in the dark about the fact that this time, millions of adult men would not die, and hundreds of thousands of women and children would not be burnt or bombed to death in the cities, without the actual culprit, albeit by more humane means, having to pay for his guilt.' The very last words he dictated in the second and final part of his political testament, read: 'Above all, I oblige the leadership of the nation and its followers to keep the racial laws scrupulously and to resist mercilessly the world poisoner of all peoples, international Jewry.'[62]

Hitler was not sorry for the destruction he had brought into the world. Far from it. But he was angry that the West – the British in particular – had not understood the dangers of 'Jewish Bolshevism' and joined together with the Nazis in the fight. His hatred of the Jews, as captured in his political testament, remained at the core of his being. He was pleased, even as Germany came crashing down about him, that he had brought about the death of 6 million Jews.

• • •

This moment in the history is also an appropriate time to review the role of the Nazi leader in creating and orchestrating the Holocaust. As we have seen, Hitler did not simply devise a blueprint for the scheme and then order his underlings to complete the task. His involvement in the crime was much more complex than that, and reflects the nature of his leadership of the Nazi state. Though he was undoubtedly a charismatic leader, he did not 'hypnotize' Germans to do his bidding. Instead, he tried to convince them that he was right. 'My whole life', he said, 'can be summed up as this ceaseless effort of mine to persuade other people.'[63]

In the context of the Holocaust, Hitler's primary role was to set a vision. That vision was relatively consistent from the moment he entered politics at the end of the First World War. He hated the Jews with a passion that was almost overwhelming. They were to blame for Germany's misfortune. They needed – somehow or other – to be neutralized and rendered harmless. As we have seen, how that goal should be accomplished varied from time to time, determined largely by what Hitler thought was politically acceptable at any given moment. There were thus many different milestones on the journey to the Holocaust. Some of the most crucial along the way were: the invasion of the Soviet Union; Hitler's decision to send the Jews from the Old Reich and Protectorate to the east in the autumn of 1941; his response to the entry of the United States into the war a few months later; and the order to kill the Jews of the General Government in the summer of 1942. The most appalling atrocity in history was thus caused not by one single, monumental moment of decision, but by a series of moments of escalation, which cumulatively built into the catastrophe we call the Holocaust.

The structure of the Nazi state also played a part in the way the Holocaust developed. The fact that different death camps used different means of gassing Jews – Zyklon B at Auschwitz, carbon monoxide from engines at Treblinka and gas vans at Chełmno – demonstrates the extent to which the Nazi system encouraged subordinates to devise their own way of best fulfilling the overall vision.

All this needs to be set against another fact that is often overlooked, which is that during the war most of Hitler's time was spent trying to think of ways to defeat his enemies on the battlefield. While the racist and anti-Semitic views held by him and many others in Nazi Germany made a confrontation with the Jews an inevitable consequence of this war, Hitler's day-to-day attention was predominantly on military matters. That partly explains why the implementation of the Holocaust was often under-resourced and haphazard.

This is not to say that Hitler was not the individual most responsible for the crime. Unquestionably he was. As the world's leading expert on Adolf Hitler says: 'No Hitler, no Holocaust'.[64] Without Hitler this crime could not have happened in the way it did. At key moments he demonstrably intervened to make the process still more extreme.[65] No one who studies this history can conclude anything other than that Hitler was primarily responsible for the Holocaust. But – partly because of the way the Nazi regime functioned – many, many others have to take part of the blame as well.

The Third Reich did not last long after the removal of its architect, and in the early hours of 7 May, at Reims in France, Alfred Jodl, Chief of the Wehrmacht Operations Staff, signed the unconditional surrender of German armed forces in the presence of the British and Americans. The next day, in Berlin, Field Marshal Keitel surrendered on behalf of Germany to the Soviets. As for Himmler, he had ordered that no prisoners at Dachau and Flossenbürg concentration camps should be taken alive when the Allies arrived. As a result, even in the last hours of the Third Reich, new death marches were formed and thousands more lost their lives. One estimate is that out of 714,000 inmates alive in concentration camps at the start of 1945, between 240,000 and 360,000 died before Germany capitulated.[66] As for Himmler, he survived the end of Nazism by only a matter of days. On 23 May he committed suicide by biting into a poison capsule, after his British captors had discovered that he was not Sergeant Heinrich Hitzinger as he pretended to be, but Heinrich Himmler, former Reichsführer of the SS and one of the world's most notorious war criminals.

For those Jews in the labour camps that were now liberated, the mood was not one of simple joy. Giselle Cycowicz remembers how she, and the other Jewish women imprisoned with her, learnt that the war was over: 'We hear whistling – you know they have whistles like these police whistles to mean roll call. We run out. It's a beautiful sunny day. It's a big field; the girls are on one side of the field, lining up, feverishly because we cannot dilly-dally. And suddenly we hear through a loud-speaker, somebody [one of the SS] says, "Today the war was declared over. And you are free, you can go wherever you want to and you can do whatever you want to. But we were asked to stay here with you and watch you until the Russian army arrives . . ." Let me tell you why this is traumatic . . . Because the minute he said we are free – especially, he used these magic words of "you can go wherever you want" – [I thought] where would I want to go? What place is there for me to go to? Should I go back to where they sent me away from . . . the Jewish houses that we left . . . Everything my parents possessed was left open [i.e. unpro-tected] in the house . . . people were already taking out the possessions of the Jews. So I want to go back there? Who wants to live in a place where everybody stood by when the Jews were meted out terrible evil, who wants to go there? And where is there another place in the world [for me]?

'You know I keep reading about the world's rejection of any approach to let them [the Jews] come in before the killing took place. Nobody wanted the Jews to come in, nobody. There was no Israel open for us. There was no England, no America, no Canada with its open spaces, Australia with its open spaces – nobody wanted the Jews. So should I be happy that I'm liberated? I'm eighteen years old, what am I? I am nothing . . . It was very traumatic. And why was it so traumatic? Because a minute before I realized that I am free and can do whatever I want, there was nothing else in the world that interested me but how do I get something to put into my mouth. Seventy years, I cannot get over it. I cannot get over the evil.'[67]

Postscript

I want to conclude with a few words about why I thought it appropriate to subtitle this work 'a new history', together with some reflections on the challenges of writing about the Holocaust. As anyone who has just read this book will appreciate, this is not a straightforward history to explain. Surprisingly perhaps, it is not made easier by the word 'Holocaust' – a word which originally meant 'burnt offering' or 'sacrifice' and only came to be associated in the popular consciousness with the extermination of the Jews relatively recently.

In the first place there is no universal agreement about what precisely the word now signifies. Is it confined to the murder of the Jews, or can it refer to any genocide? Was Genghis Khan's treatment of the Persians a Holocaust, for example? But there's an even bigger issue, which is that if the Holocaust is restricted just to the extermination of the Jews we risk not understanding the breadth of the murderous thinking of the Nazis. That is because the murder of the Jews should not be taken out of the context of the Nazis' desire to persecute and kill large numbers of other people – for example, the disabled via the euthanasia actions, or millions of Slavs via a deliberate policy of forced starvation, and so on. Not just that, but the Holocaust as we know it was implemented around the same time as another wide-ranging murderous scheme was under discussion – the General Plan for the East. This plan, which the Nazis were only prevented from pursuing because they were defeated, would have resulted in the death of tens of millions of additional people.

None of this is to say, however, that any of these other initiatives was analogous with the desire of the Nazis to exterminate the Jews – for hatred of the Jews was always at the core of Nazi thinking. So, against this background, I have taken the word 'Holocaust' to mean the Nazi persecution of the Jews, culminating in the implementation of a desire to exterminate them, but I have also accepted that this crime cannot be understood unless set into a broader picture.

You might ask, legitimately enough: if I have issues with the word why have I titled this book 'The Holocaust'? In part it is simply to acknowledge that this is what the crime is now called and trying to call it something else would not be helpful for the reader. But, more significantly, I think the word is appropriate here because it reflects the fact that the extermination of the Jews was a crime of singular horror in the history of the human race.

I know that last sentence will provoke debate. Indeed, I have taken part myself in many lively discussions about whether or not it is possible to point to some kind of 'singularity' about the Holocaust or whether it has to be considered as just one ghastly atrocity among many in history. Ultimately, though, I agree with the late Professor David Cesarani who, in conversation with me a few years ago, put the claim for the special nature of the Holocaust eloquently: 'Never before in history, I think, had a leader decided that within a conceivable time frame an ethnic religious group would be physically destroyed, and that equipment would be devised and created to achieve that. That was unprecedented.'[1]

Another important issue to consider, when writing about the Holocaust, is the role of eyewitness testimony. I have benefited from meeting hundreds of people who experienced this history personally and – not surprisingly, you might think – I believe that their testimony is of enormous value. Indeed, there is an almost existential point to be made about the advantage of meeting people and questioning them about their experiences. It is that while you talk to these people the history still lives.

It is the presence of this testimony in the book – most of which has never been published before – that was one of the key reasons that I thought I should subtitle the work a 'new' history. In particular, not one word from any of the interviews conducted for my most recent project, *Touched by Auschwitz* – with Halina Birenbaum, Giselle Cycowicz, Max Epstein, Ida Grinspan, Hermann Höllenreiner, Tadeusz Smreczyński and Freda Wineman – has previously appeared in book form.

I was privileged to be one of the last generation that could access the history of this period in this way. In fact, I was fortunate in two ways. The first was that when I – together with my TV production team – started to meet former Nazis twenty-five years ago, they had mostly just retired from their careers so they no longer felt constrained by their employers from speaking freely, yet they were still young enough not to be beset by the vicissitudes of old age. The second was that the fall of the Berlin Wall meant that we could travel to the countries of eastern Europe and the former republics of the Soviet Union, and interview eyewitnesses who had never previously been able to speak freely about their wartime experiences. As a result, we were among the first to access this important primary material.

I have always believed, however, that it is vital to look at every source with a certain amount of scepticism. As a consequence, I believe that the safeguards we all took in researching and filming this eyewitness material were second to none. I have written elsewhere, in detail, of how we approached this difficult task[2] and of the way in which, for instance, we checked wherever possible that each interviewee's story was consistent with documents of the period. It was a long and laborious process, and if at the end of it we had any misgivings about the authenticity of a potential interviewee's testimony then we never recorded the interview.

In the course of our researches we also discovered that even after a considerable number of years people could often still recall crucial events in their lives extremely powerfully. I think we can all recognize the truth of this. The example I point to from my own life is the death of my mother nearly forty years ago. Although I could not tell you what I had for lunch on a specific day just a couple of months ago, I can still recall in intense detail the manner in which my mother died. One event was insignificant, the other life changing.[3]

There were, of course, special factors that we had to consider when interviewing survivors of the Holocaust. One of the most crucial was always to remember that the survivors of camps like Auschwitz, Sobibór and Treblinka did not represent the normal experience of those who were sent there. The normal experience was to be murdered. So we cannot, of course, speak to anyone who suffered the fate of the majority.

I also thought it important to write about the Holocaust only after I had been informed by the geography of the crime – and this is another area in which I hope this book offers something different. I believe I benefited hugely from the insights to be gained by visiting the places where these events took place. I will never forget, for example, the experience many years ago when my friend Mirek Obstarczyk, one of the talented historians working at the Auschwitz museum, took me round every one of the locations across Auschwitz main camp and Birkenau where the Nazis committed mass murder using Zyklon B. I visited these sites with Mirek in the chronological order in which the

Nazis used them as killing locations: from the basement of Block 11 in the main camp to the crematorium by the SS administration offices; from the site of the Little Red House and Little White House in a remote area of Auschwitz Birkenau to the remains of the massive crematoria/gas-chamber complexes that emerged at Birkenau only in 1943. Experiencing first hand this geographical progression helped me to understand the conceptual journey the Nazis took at the camp – something I hope I have conveyed in this book.

I found it just as valuable to visit hundreds of other locations associated with this history: from the site of the death camp at Sobibór, where the branches of the trees blow in the wind and the sense of isolation is total, to the vast expanse of the semi-circular roll-call area at Sachsenhausen concentration camp outside Berlin; from the ruins of Hitler's military headquarters at what was Rastenburg in East Prussia to the killing fields of Belarus and Ukraine.

It is also possible, of course, to combine the insights to be gained from physical geography with those you receive from meeting eyewitnesses. Some of the most memorable moments of my working life have been when the two have coalesced. I remember, for example, filming a man in Belarus who had been forced to walk with other villagers down a road the Nazis believed was riddled with mines. German soldiers followed a safe distance behind them, waiting for these human mine detectors to be blown up and render the road safe. Luckily for him, he made it to the next village alive. We filmed him at the very place where this happened, and his interaction with the landscape was extraordinarily moving as he showed us how he had tried to deal with one of the most terrible dilemmas imaginable. Should he step on what he believed was a mine and be killed, or walk around it and risk one of the Germans who were following standing on it instead? If one German soldier had been killed by a mine, the surviving Germans would have murdered all the villagers at once. Die by a mine or die by a bullet – that was the choice he thought he would have to make on that remote road in Belarus. Fortunately for him, he did not see any mines in front of him on that terrifying journey.

Equally, I must add, I would not want this work to rely solely on oral testimony, which is why the book also draws on many speeches, diaries and documents of the time. My aim was to weave all this material into an examination of the decision-making process of the Holocaust, informed by the immense amount of outstanding scholarship conducted in this area since the war.

Over the last twenty-five years I have read many astonishing Holocaust memoirs and a number of insightful academic histories of the crime, but I have not come across a general work that sought to combine both the emotional power of first-hand interview testimony with an analysis of the machinations of the Nazi state in quite the way that I intended here. Hence my hope that, in this respect too, the book is something of a 'new' history.

During the last quarter of a century, in conversations with many of the world's leading academic historians, I have seen the intellectual landscape shift. When I started out, opinion was largely divided between intentionalists – who pointed to Hitler's key role in the decision-making process and who argued that he might well have intended to kill the Jews for years before the Holocaust – and functionalists – who believed that the best way of understanding what happened was to look at the complex interaction between Hitler and a multitude of outside forces. Over time, fewer and fewer serious historians took the intentionalist position and the debate shifted among the functionalists to an attempt to identify the precise moment when we can say the Holocaust was decided. I have heard many different dates suggested. Some believe that the key decision was taken in July 1941, others in October 1941, still more in December 1941 and a few even assert that it was as late as the summer of 1942. More recently the debate has moved away from the attempt to find a single point of decision and instead to identify a number of different moments when Nazi anti-Jewish policy intensified.

I was never convinced by the intentionalist argument, nor was I fully persuaded by the attempt to point to one moment of decision. From quite early in my interaction with this history I had seen how some people had decided that, because the crime of the extermination of the Jews was so horrendous, it must have been orchestrated and planned at one monumental moment. But it seemed to me that this was a mistaken leap. As I hope this book demonstrates, the journey to the Holocaust was a gradual one, full of twists and turns, until it found final expression in the Nazi killing factories.

Finally, although the contents of the book you have just read are distressing, I believe it is still important to understand how and why this crime happened. For this history tells us, perhaps more than any other, just what our species can do.

Acknowledgements

Since this book draws on twenty-five years' work, you won't be surprised to learn that there are a considerable number of people who helped me along the way and who deserve my gratitude. In particular I want to give enormous thanks to the talented members of the many different production teams that worked with me. To begin with, I mention my German colleagues, Tilman Remme and Detlef Siebert, whose commitment to historical research over the years was breathtaking. Others who were of special help at various times included Tanya Batchelor, Saulius Berzinis, Martina Carr, Sallyann Kleibel, Wanda Koscia, Michaela Lichtenstein, Elodie Maillot, Nava Mizrahi, Dominic Sutherland, Anna Taborska and Elena Yakovleva. I am profoundly grateful to them all. I also need to remember here Dr Frank Stucke. He was a brilliant researcher and penetrating intellectual who worked on many of my TV series. If it had not been for his pioneering journalism a number of our most important interviews with former Nazis would never have happened. I was proud to call him my friend. He died, tragically young, in February 2016, and is missed by us all.

This book has also benefited from the indefatigable research talents of the German historian Julia Pietsch. She also read through the book in manuscript and made many helpful comments. In addition, I thank all the various copyright holders for permission to quote from their material, including the Hoover Institution for permission to publish extracts from the diaries of Heinrich Himmler and, of course, the BBC.

My thinking on this subject has been influenced by a large number of academic historians – in particular by the opportunity to discuss this history over many years with my dear friend Professor Sir Ian Kershaw. Anyone who has even a passing interest in this subject is aware of his immense gifts as a historian. He has been a constant source of encouragement and help to me with this project, from the moment of its conception through to reading the final book in manuscript. I am also grateful to two other distinguished historians, Antony Beevor and

Andrew Roberts, for reading this book before publication and giving me a wealth of wise advice.

I also benefited from the chance to discuss this period of history a few years ago with many of the world's other leading thinkers on Nazism and the Holocaust for my educational website W W2History.com. They include Professor Omer Bartov, Professor Christopher Browning, Professor Sir Richard Evans, Professor Norbert Frei, Professor Richard Overy and Professor Adam Tooze. I also make special mention of Professor David Cesarani, who worked with me on my Auschwitz project. David and I shared many lively discussions about the Holocaust in particular and the world in general. His death in October 2015 robbed the world of a great scholar.

At Viking, my publishers, I give thanks to my editor Daniel Crewe, who has shown great faith in this project, as well as to my copy editor Peter James. I must also mention the considerable debt I owe to my former editor at Ebury Press, Albert DePetrillo. And, as ever, I thank my literary agent, the legendary Andrew Nurnberg.

In addition, I want to express my gratitude to the staff of the Holocaust Educational Trust for their help and support over many years. In particular, the Chairman Paul Phillips, the Chief Executive Karen Pollock and the Head of Education Alex Maws.

My wife Helena has helped me every step of the way with this book. Her comments were always incisive and to the point. This book would be much poorer without her. My children, Oliver, Camilla and Benedict, offered cheerful encouragement, particularly during the difficult moments on this project.

This book is dedicated to my daughter Camilla, an Oxford history graduate herself. Not just because she is the most wonderful daughter that a father ever had, but because she carefully read the whole of this book in draft and made many useful suggestions.

My final thanks go to the interviewees whose testimony we recorded over the last twenty-five years. Since there were several hundred of them, I cannot list them all individually here. But my gratitude is no less sincere and heartfelt.

Laurence Rees
London, September 2016

Notes

Abbreviations of Archives Cited

BArch	Bundesarchiv
BayHStA	Bayerisches Hauptstaatsarchiv
FAH	Familien-Archiv Hügel (Historisches Archiv Krupp, Essen)
HHStAW	Hessisches Hauptstaatsarchiv Wiesbaden
Nds. HStAH	Niedersächsisches Hauptstaatsarchiv Hannover
PRO	Public Record Office, Kew
StAN	Staatsarchiv Nürnberg
ZStL	Zentrale Stelle der Landesjustizverwaltungen zur Aufklärung nationalsozialistischer Verbrechen in Ludwigsburg

Prologue

1 Previously unpublished testimony. For ease of recognition, testimony which has been gathered for the documentary series which I wrote and produced over the last twenty-five years is shown in this book in the present tense – that is, he (or she) says, rather than said.

Chapter 1: Origins of Hate

1 BayHStA, Abt. IV, R W GrKdo, Bd 50/08. In English in J. Noakes and G. Pridham (eds.), *Nazism 1919–1945*, vol. 1: *The Rise to Power 1919–1934*, University of Exeter Press, 1991, pp. 12–14.

2 See Brigitte Hamann, *Hitlers Wien. Lehrjahre eines Diktators*, Piper, 1996.

3 See Thomas Weber, *Hitler's First War*, Oxford University Press, 2010, p. 177.

4 John 7:1.

5 Ibid. 8:59.

6   Ibid. 8:44.

7   Michael R. Marrus and Robert O. Paxton, *Vichy France and the Jews*, Stanford University Press, 1995, p. 27. The authors point out also that 'From 1959 to 1963, Pope John XXIII removed from the liturgy this and other passages offensive to Jews.'

8   Martin Luther, *On the Jews and Their Lies*, 1543, in *Luther's Works*, vol. 47, Fortress Press, 1971, pp. 268–93.

9   Christian Wilhelm von Dohm, *Über die bürgerliche Verbesserung der Juden*, 1781, in English in Paul Mendes-Flohr and Jehuda Reinharz (eds.), *The Jews in the Modern World: A Documentary History*, Oxford University Press, 2011, p. 30.

10   George L. Mosse, *The Crisis of German Ideology: Intellectual Origins of the Third Reich*, Howard Fertig, 1998, p. 149.

11   Wilhelm Heinrich Riehl, *Land und Leute*, 1854, vol. 1 of *A Natural History of the German People as a Basis for a German Social Politics*, in English in Michelle Facos, *An Introduction to Nineteenth-Century Art*, Routledge, 2011, p. 271.

12   Quoted in Susanne Karstedt, 'Strangers, Mobilisation and the Production of Weak Ties: Railway Traffic and Violence in Nineteenth-Century South-West Germany', in Barry S. Godfrey, Clive Emsley and Graeme Dunstall (eds.), *Comparative Histories of Crime*, Willan Publishing, 2003, pp. 89–109, here p. 93.

13   David Welch, *Propaganda and the German Cinema: 1933–1945*, Oxford University Press, 1985, p. 105.

14   Ibid., p. 107.

15   Laurence Rees, *The Dark Charisma of Adolf Hitler*, Ebury Press, 2012, p. 44.

16   Previously unpublished testimony.

17   Alyssa A. Lonner, *Mediating the Past: Gustav Freytag, Progress, and German Historical Identity, 1848–1871*, Peter Lang, 2005, says that *Soll und Haben* was 'one of [the] – if not *the* – most widely read books of the [nineteenth] century', p. 37.

18   Quoted in Alex Bein, *The Jewish Question: Biography of a World Problem*, Associated University Presses, 1990, p. 617.

19   Heinrich Class writing as Daniel Frymann, *Wenn ich der Kaiser wär': Politische Wahrheiten und Notwendigkeiten* (If I Were Kaiser: Political Truths and Necessities), 4th edn, Dieterich, 1913. In Harry Pross (ed.), *Die Zerstörung der deutschen Politik: Dokumente 1871–1933*, trans. Richard S. Levy, Fischer, 1959.

20 Arthur de Gobineau, *Essai sur l'inégalité des races humaines*, 1855, in English in *The Inequality of the Human Races*, William Heinemann, 1915.

21 Algernon Freeman-Mitford, 1st Baron Redesdale, Introduction, in Houston Stewart Chamberlain, *Foundations of the Nineteenth Century*, vol. 1, Elibron Classics, 2005, first published by F. Bruckman, Munich, 1911, pp. v–vi.

22 Ibid., p. 350.

23 Ian Kershaw, *Hitler: 1889–1936, Hubris*, Penguin, 2001, p. 660 n. 116.

24 Mosse, *German Ideology*, p. 104.

25 BArch NS 33/89, p. 41, The Reichsführer SS (SS-HA/ZK./Az. B 17a), Berlin, 11 April 1938, regarding selection of candidates as SS leaders, mailing list V. Also see Tom Segev, *Soldiers of Evil: The Commandants of the Nazi Concentration Camps*, Diamond Books, 2000, p. 97.

26 Francis Galton, *Hereditary Genius*, Macmillan, 1869, Introduction, p. 1.

27 Alfred Ploetz, *Die Tüchtigkeit unsrer Rasse und der Schutz der Schwachen* (The Efficiency of Our Race and the Protection of the Weak), quoted in Peter Watson, *The German Genius*, Simon & Schuster, 2011, p. 434.

28 Calculation by Professor Richard Levy of the University of Chicago, in his 15 May 1996 review of Daniel Goldhagen's *Hitler's Willing Executioners*, http://www.vho.org/aaargh/engl/crazygoldie/reviews96.html.

29 Robert Weinberg, 'The Pogrom of 1905 in Odessa: A Case Study', in John D. Klier and Shlomo Lambroza (eds.), *Pogroms: Anti-Jewish Violence in Modern Russian History*, Cambridge University Press, 2004, pp. 248–89.

30 Joshua Sobol, *Weiningers Nacht*, Europa-Verlag, 1988, pp. 145–6.

31 BArch R 8034 III/295, Reichslandbund Pressearchiv, Lup-Lz, p. 11a, R. Tag Z. Nr. 121, 13 March 1910, Lueger speech, 11 January 1894, state parliament of Lower Austria.

32 See Hamann, *Hitlers Wien*.

33 Kershaw, *Hitler: Hubris*, p. 67.

34 Ibid., p. 96.

35 Quoted in Jay Winter, *Remembering War: The Great War between Memory and History in the Twentieth Century*, Yale University Press, 2006, p. 84.

36 Ibid., p. 87.

37 Rathenau letter, 4 August 1916, quoted in Antony Loewenstein, *My Israel Question*, Melbourne University Press, 2007, p. 130.

38 Quoted in Nigel Jones, *The Birth of the Nazis: How the Freikorps Blazed a Trail for Hitler*, Constable & Robinson, 2004, pp. 194–5.

39 See Rees, *Charisma*, p. 22. The passage quoted here also includes previously unpublished testimony from Fridolin von Spaun.

40 Previously unpublished testimony.

Chapter 2: Birth of the Nazis

1 Robert Waite, *Vanguard of Nazism*, W. W. Norton, 1969, p. 206.

2 Rudolf von Sebottendorff, *Bevor Hitler kam. Urkundliches aus der Frühzeit der nationalsozialistischen Bewegung*, Deukula-Verlag Grassinger, 1933, pp. 41–3.

3 Ibid., pp. 57–60.

4 Joseph Howard Tyson, *Hitler's Mentor: Dietrich Eckart, his Life, Times, & Milieu*, iUniverse, 2008, p. 50.

5 Ibid., p. 15.

6 *Auf gut deutsch. Wochenschrift für Ordnung u. Recht*, ed. Dietrich Eckart, vol. 1, 1919, no. 2, p. 18.

7 Ibid., vol. 2, 1920, no. 30/34, p. 392.

8 Balthasar Brandmayer, *Meldegänger Hitler 1914–1918*, Walter, 1933, pp. 71–2. In English in Laurence Rees, *The Dark Charisma of Adolf Hitler*, Ebury Press, 2012, p. 13.

9 Joachim C. Fest, *Hitler*, Harcourt Brace Jovanovich, 1974, p. 133.

10 Quoted by Margarate Plewnia, *Auf dem Weg zu Hitler*, Schünemann Universitätsverlag, 1970, p. 67. She in turn quotes Albert Zoller, *Hitler privat – Erlebnisbericht seiner Geheimsekretärin*, Droste, 1949, p. 118. In English in Rees, *Charisma*, p. 47.

11 *Hitler's Table Talk, 1941–1944*, Phoenix Press, 2000, p. 217, night of 16–17 January 1942.

12 Ibid.

13 Tyson, *Hitler's Mentor*. See also Eberhard Jäckel and Axel Kuhn (eds.), *Hitler. Sämtliche Aufzeichnungen 1905–1924*, Deutsche Verlags-Anstalt, 1980, p. 117. Otto Dietrich, *12 Jahre mit Hitler*, Isar Verlag, 1955, p. 178. BArch NS 26/514, Letter of Gottfried Grandel to the main archive of the NSDAP, Freiburg i. B., 22 October 1941.

14 Ernst Deuerlein (ed.), *Der Aufstieg der NSDAP 1919–1933 in Augenzeugenberichten*, Rauch, 1968, p. 60. In English in J. Noakes and G. Pridham

(eds.), *Nazism 1919–1945*, vol. 1: *The Rise to Power 1919–1934*, University of Exeter Press, 1983, p. 14.

15 Eberhard Jäckel and Axel Kuhn (eds.), *Sämtliche Aufzeichnungen 1905–1924*, Deutsche Verlags-Anstalt, 1980, p. 366, speech by Hitler at a NSDAP meeting in Rosenheim, 21 April 1921.

16 N. H. Baynes (ed.), *Speeches of Adolf Hitler: Early Speeches, 1922–1924, and Other Selections*, Howard Fertig, 2006, p. 17, speech of 12 April 1921.

17 Ibid., p. 42, speech of 18 September 1922.

18 Ibid., p. 13, speech of 12 April 1922.

19 Ibid., p. 30, speech of 28 July 1922.

20 Ibid., p.17, speech of 12 April 1922.

21 Ibid., p. 21, speech of 28 July 1922.

22 A. Hitler, 'Rathenau und Sancho Pansa', *Völkischer Beobachter*, 13 March 1921, p. 2.

23 Previously unpublished testimony.

24 Rees, *Charisma*, pp. 30–31.

25 Previously unpublished testimony.

26 Previously unpublished testimony.

27 Sönke Neitzel, *Tapping Hitler's Generals: Transcripts of Secret Conversations 1942–45*, Frontline Books, 2013, p. 67, words of General Ludwig Crüwell.

28 Baynes (ed.), *Speeches of Adolf Hitler*, pp. 15–16, speech of 12 April 1922.

29 Ibid., p. 42, speech of 18 September 1922.

30 Peter Longerich, *Holocaust: The Nazi Persecution and Murder of the Jews*, Oxford University Press, 2012, p. 13.

31 'An die Brüder der USP., MSP., KPD.', *Deutscher Sozialist*, Folge 1, 4 June 1920, in Julius Streicher, *Ruf zur Tat. Aufsätze aus den Kampfjahren 1920–1922*, Verlag Der Stürmer, 1937, pp. 11–13. Also see Randall L. Bytwerk, *Julius Streicher*, Cooper Square Press, 2001, p. 10.

32 Bytwerk, *Streicher*, p. 2.

33 StAN, Polizeipräsidium Nürnberg-Fürth 541, doc. 187, Copy of a judgment against Streicher, court of lay assessor at the district court Schweinfurt, for an offence against religion, 5 September 1922.

34 Ibid., doc. 103, Report from 22 December 1922 on the meeting of the National Socialists on 21 December 1922 in the Kulturverein in Nuremberg.

35 Ibid., City Council of Kitzingen to the state police department Nuremberg-Fürth, 16 May 1922, 'Remarks from the meeting of the Deutsche Werkgemeinschaft in the Kolosseumssaal in Kitzingen on 7 May 1922. From a speech by the elementary teacher J. Streicher from Nuremberg'.

36 *Hitler's Table Talk*, p. 154, night of 28–29 December 1941.

37 Nuremberg Trial Proceedings, vol. 12, p. 308, 115th day, Friday 26 April 1946. Also Bytwerk, *Streicher*, p. 15.

38 Ibid., Nuremberg, and also Rees, *Charisma*, p. 49.

39 Deuerlein (ed.), *Aufstieg*, p. 146. In English in Noakes and Pridham (eds.), *Nazism*, vol. 1, pp. 25–6.

40 Peter Viereck, 'Stefan George's Cosmic Circle', *Decision*, October 1941, p. 49.

41 Rees, *Charisma*, p. 76.

42 Werner Jochmann (ed.), *Nationalsozialismus und Revolution. Dokumente*, Europäische Verlags-Anstalt, 1963, pp. 88–9, Hitler Memorandum of 7 January 1922. In English in Noakes and Pridham (eds.), *Nazism*, vol. 1, p. 23.

43 Baynes (ed.), *Speeches of Adolf Hitler*, p. 40, Hitler speech of 28 July 1922.

44 BArch N 1126/8, Leseliste No. 107.

45 BArch N 1126 141 K, Himmler's diary entry for 12 January 1922. Originals in Hoover Institution, Stanford University, Stanford, California.

46 Ibid., entry for 24 June 1922.

47 Ibid., entry for 22 November 1921.

48 Ibid., entry for 27 May 1922.

49 Ibid., entry for 7 June 1922.

50 For example, at the December 1924 general election, the biggest party was the Social Democrats with 26 per cent of the vote. They were opposed to the anti-Semitic policies of the Nazis, as were parties like the German People's Party with 10.1 per cent, the Communist Party with 9 per cent and the German Democratic Party with 6.3 per cent.

51 Rees, *Charisma*, p. 37.

52 Albrecht Tyrell (ed.), *Führer befiehl . . . Selbstzeugnisse aus der 'Kampfzeit' der NSDAP. Dokumentation und Analyse*, Droste, 1969, pp. 281–3. In English in Noakes and Pridham (eds.), *Nazism*, vol. 1, pp. 34–5.

Chapter 3: From Revolution to Ballot Box

1 Words of Ernst Hanfstaengl, quoted in article in *Der Spiegel* by Jan Friedmann, 23 June 2010: http://www.spiegel.de/international/germany/adolf-hitler-s-time-in-jail-flowers-for-the-fuehrer-in-landsberg-prison-a-702159.html.

2 Adolf Hitler, *Mein Kampf*, Houghton Mifflin, 1971, pp. 118–19.

3 Ibid., pp. 180–81.

4 Ibid., p. 57.

5 Ibid.

6 Ibid., p. 63.

7 Ibid., p. 59.

8 Ibid., p. 65.

9 Ibid., pp. 62–3.

10 Ibid., p. 206.

11 Ibid., p. 305.

12 Aldous Huxley, 'Notes on Propaganda', *Harper's Monthly Magazine*, December 1936.

13 Hitler, *Mein Kampf*, p. 679.

14 *Hitler's Table Talk, 1941–1944*, Phoenix Press, 2000, 25 October 1941, p. 87.

15 Hitler, *Mein Kampf*, p. 65.

16 First published in *Völkischer Beobachter*, 22 April 1922. Also see Laurence Rees, *The Dark Charisma of Adolf Hitler*, Ebury Press, 2012, p. 29.

17 A remark in conversation with General Ludendorff. See Wilhelm Breucker (Ludendorff's adjutant), *Die Tragik Ludendorffs*, Rauschenbusch, 1953, p. 107; also in English in J. R. C. Wright, *'Above Parties': The Political Attitudes of the German Protestant Church Leadership 1918–1933*, Oxford University Press, 1974, p. 78; also see Rees, *Charisma*, p. 135.

18 Albert Speer, *Inside the Third Reich*, Phoenix Press, 1995, p. 150. Also see Rees, *Charisma*, pp. 135–6.

19 Elke Fröhlich (ed.), *Die Tagebücher von Joseph Goebbels*, Teil I: *Aufzeichnungen 1923–1941*, vol. 9, K. G. Saur, 1998, pp. 233–5, entry for 8 April 1941. Also see Rees, *Charisma*, p. 138.

20 Max Domarus, *Hitler: Speeches and Proclamations 1932–1945*, vol. 2, *1935–1938*, Bolchazy-Carducci, Hitler speech of 23 November 1937, p. 980.

21 Hitler, *Mein Kampf*, p. 232.

22 Ibid., p. 316.

23 Ibid., p. 255.

24 Ibid., p. 654.

25 Konrad Heiden, Introduction, ibid., p. xv.

26 Roger Moorhouse, *His Struggle: Hitler in Landsberg Prison, 1924*, Endeavor Press, 2015. Kindle edition, location 556–600.

27 Otto Leybold, Governor of Landsberg Prison, 'Report on Adolf Hitler', September 1924, at http://alphahistory.com/nazigermany/hitlers-prison-report-1924/.

28 Moorhouse, *His Struggle*, Kindle edition, location 625–31.

29 Kurt Lüdecke, *I Knew Hitler*, Jarrolds, 1938, pp. 217–18. Also see Rees, *Charisma*, p. 66.

30 Report, *Der Nationalsozialist (T Leipzig)*, vol. 1, no. 29 from 17 August 1924, quoted in Eberhard Jäckel and Axel Kuhn (eds.), *Hitler. Sämtliche Aufzeichnungen 1905–1924*, Deutsche Verlags-Anstalt, 1980, p. 242.

31 Dennis Mack Smith, *Mussolini: A Biography*, Vintage, 1983, p. 172. Also see Rees, *Charisma*, p. 64.

32 Previously unpublished testimony.

33 Previously unpublished testimony.

34 Fröhlich (ed.), *Die Tagebücher von Joseph Goebbels*, Teil I, vol. 1/1, K. G. Saur, 2004, pp. 116–17, entry for 31 March 1924.

35 Ibid., p. 312, entry for 8 June 1925.

36 Ibid., p. 50, entry for 14 November 1923.

37 Ibid., p. 121, entry for 10 April 1924.

38 Ibid., p. 147, entry for 10 June 1924.

39 Laurence Rees, *The Nazis: A Warning from History*, BBC Books, 1997, p. 33.

40 Fröhlich (ed.), *Die Tagebücher von Joseph Goebbels*, Teil I, vol. 1/1, p. 108, entry for 17 March 1924.

41 Ibid., pp. 108–9, entry for 20 March 1924.

42 Ibid., p. 201, entry for 19 August 1924.

43 Ibid., p. 253, entry for 23 December 1924.

44 Ibid., pp. 326–7, entry for 14 July 1925.

45 Ibid., Teil II: *Diktate 1941–1945*, vol. 2, K. G. Saur, 1996, pp. 498–9, entry for 13 December 1941.

46 Ibid., Teil I, vol. 1/1, p. 108, entry for 17 March 1924; pp. 326–7, entry for 14 July 1925.

47 Peter Longerich, *Goebbels*, Vintage, 2015, pp. 62–3.

48 Fröhlich (ed.), *Die Tagebücher von Joseph Goebbels*, Teil I, vol. 1/2, K. G. Saur, 2004, pp. 55–6, entry for 15 February 1926.

49 Ibid., p. 73, entry for 13 April 1926.

50 Gerhard L. Weinberg (ed.), *Hitler's Second Book: The Unpublished Sequel to Mein Kampf*, Enigma Books, 2006, p. 234, Kindle edition, location 3978.

51 Ibid., p. 234, location 3986.

52 Ibid., p. 129, location 2367.

53 *Völkischer Beobachter*, no. 35, 12 February 1927, quoted in Detlef Mühlberger, *Hitler's Voice*, vol. 1: *Organisation and Development of the Nazi Party*, Peter Lang, 2004, p. 240.

54 *Verhandlungen des Deutschen Reichstags*, vol. 395, docs 13717–18, 24 March 1928. Also in Peter Longerich, *Holocaust: The Nazi Persecution and Murder of the Jews*, Oxford University Press, 2010, p. 15.

55 Previously unpublished testimony.

56 Albrecht Tyrell (ed.), *Führer befiehl . . . Selbstzeugnisse aus der 'Kampfzeit' der NSDAP*, Gondrom, 1991, pp. 235–6. In English in J. Noakes and G. Pridham (eds.), *Nazism 1919–1945*, vol. 1: *The Rise to Power 1919–1934*, University of Exeter Press, 1983, p. 55.

57 Uriel Tal, *'Political Faith' of Nazism Prior to the Holocaust*, Tel Aviv University, 1978, p. 28. Rees, *Charisma*, pp. 81–2.

58 Max Domarus, *Hitler: Speeches and Proclamations 1932–1945*, vol. 1: *1932–1934*, Bolchazy-Carducci, 1990, p. 112, Hitler speech, 27 January 1932.

59 Previously unpublished testimony.

60 Previously unpublished testimony.

61 Rees, *Nazis*, p. 74.

62 Previously unpublished testimony.

63 Rees, *Nazis*, p. 46.

64 David Redles, 'Nazi End Times: The Third Reich as Millennial Reich', in Karolyn Kinane and Michael A. Ryan (eds.), *End of Days: Essays on the Apocalypse from Antiquity to Modernity*, McFarland, 2009, pp. 173–96, here p. 182.

65 *Der Angriff*, 9 September 1929, quoted in Longerich, *Goebbels*, pp. 91–2.

66 Nds. HStAH, Hann. Des. 310 I A, Nr. 35. In English in Noakes and Pridham (eds.), *Nazism*, vol. 1, p. 76.

67 Status report of the district president of Hanover to the Interior Minister of the Reich for the months of December 1934/January 1935, 4 February 1935, in Klaus Mlynek (ed.), *Gestapo Hannover meldet . . . Polizei- und Regierungsberichte für das mittlere und südliche Niedersachsen zwischen 1933 und 1937*, Verlag August Lax, 1986, p. 315. Original source of Mlynek: Nds. HStAH, Hann. 180 Hannover Nr. 799, ff. 191–203.

68 Laurence Rees, *Selling Politics*, BBC Books, 1992, p. 24.

69 Previously unpublished testimony.

70 Lion Feuchtwanger, 'Wie kämpfen wir gegen ein Drittes Reich?' (How Do We Struggle against a Third Reich?), *Welt am Abend*, 21 January 1931. In English in Anton Kaes, Martin Jay and Edward Dimendberg (eds.), *The Weimar Republic Sourcebook*, University of California Press, 1994, p. 167.

71 Heinrich Mann, 'Die deutsche Entscheidung' (The German Decision), *Das Tagebuch*, vol. 12, no. 51, 19 December 1931. In English in Kaes, Jay and Dimendberg, *Weimar Republic Sourcebook*, pp. 164–6.

72 Previously unpublished testimony and Rees, *Nazis*, 1997, p. 171.

73 Strasser speech, Berlin Sportpalast, 23 October 1931, *CV-Zeitung. Blätter für Deutschtum und Judentum*. Organ des Central-Vereins deutscher Staatsbürger jüdischen Glaubens e. V., Berlin, 11 December 1931, vol. X, no. 50, p. 572.

74 Otto Meissner, *Aufzeichnung über die Besprechung des Herrn Reichspräsidenten mit Adolf Hitler am 13. August 1932 nachmittags 4.15*, quoted in Walther Hubatsch, *Hindenburg und der Staat. Aus den Papieren des Generalfeldmarschalls und Reichspräsidenten von 1878 bis 1934*, Musterschmidt, 1966, p. 338. In English in Noakes and Pridham (eds.), *Nazism*, vol. 1, p. 104.

75 Max Domarus, *Hitler. Reden und Proklamationen 1932–1945. Kommentiert von einem deutschen Zeitgenossen*, vol. 1: *Triumph*, R. Löwit, 1973, p. 158, Meissner to Hitler, 24 November 1932.

76 Konrad Heiden, *Adolf Hitler. Das Zeitalter der Verantwortungslosigkeit. Eine Biographie*, Europa-Verlag, 1936, p. 278.

77 Jewish Telegraphic Agency report, 3 August 1934.

78 *Evening Standard* interview, 16 May 1933. Also see Jewish Telegraphic Agency report of the same date.

79 *Völkischer Beobachter*, Norddeutsche Ausgabe, vol. 46, no. 6, 6 January 1933, p. 1. Also Domarus, *Hitler. Reden und Proklamationen*, vol. 1, p. 175.

Chapter 4: Consolidating Power

1 Elke Fröhlich (ed.), *Die Tagebücher von Joseph Goebbels*, Teil I: Aufzeichnungen 1923–1941, vol. 2/3, K. G. Saur, 2006, p. 119, entry for 30 January 1933.

2 Laurence Rees, *Their Darkest Hour*, Ebury Press, 2007, pp. 206–7, but also includes some previously unpublished testimony.

3 Previously unpublished testimony.

4 Previously unpublished testimony.

5 Excerpts from the diaries of Mrs Luise Solmitz, 4 January 1932 to 5 March 1933, in Werner Jochmann, *Nationalsozialismus und Revolution. Ursprung und Geschichte der NSDAP in Hamburg 1922–1933. Dokumente*, Europäische Verlagsanstalt, 1963, pp. 400–32, here pp. 422–3.

6 Previously unpublished testimony.

7 Previously unpublished testimony.

8 Rees, *Darkest Hour*, p. 136. But also includes some previously unpublished testimony.

9 Previously unpublished testimony.

10 Max Domarus, *Hitler: Speeches and Proclamations 1932–1945*, vol. 1: *1932–1934*, Bolchazy-Carducci, 1990, pp. 246–7, Hitler speech, 10 February 1933.

11 Ibid., p. 253, Hitler speech, 15 February 1933.

12 Fröhlich (ed.), *Die Tagebücher von Joseph Goebbels*, Teil I, vol. 2/3, p. 137, entry for 28 February 1933.

13 Previously unpublished testimony.

14 Domarus, *Hitler* (English edn), vol. 1, pp. 298–302.

15 *Völkischer Beobachter*, no. 89, 30 March 1933, quoted in Max Domarus, *Hitler. Reden und Proklamationen 1932–1945. Kommentiert von einem deutschen Zeitgenossen*, vol. 1: *Triumph*, R. Löwit, 1973, pp. 251–2.

16 Laurence Rees, *The Nazis: A Warning from History*, BBC Books, 1997, p. 105.

17 Leni Yahil, *The Holocaust: The Fate of European Jewry, 1932–1945*, Oxford University Press, 1991, pp. 95–7.

18 Jürgen Matthäus and Mark Roseman (eds.), *Jewish Responses to Persecution*, vol. 1: *1933–1938*, AltaMira Press/US Holocaust Memorial Museum, 2010, CV press release dated 24 March 1933, in *CV-Zeitung*, 30 March 1933, document 1-5, p. 15.

19 Rees, *Nazis*, pp. 71–2, together with previously unpublished testimony.

20 Ibid., pp. 72–3, together with previously unpublished testimony.

21 Previously unpublished testimony.

22 Previously unpublished testimony.

23 US Holocaust Museum figures, http://www.ushmm.org/.

24 Yahil, *Holocaust*, p. 92.

25 Previously unpublished testimony.

26 Previously unpublished testimony.

27 Reich Statistical Office Figures for 1933, quoted in J. Noakes and G. Pridham (eds.), *Nazism 1919–1945*, vol. 2: *State, Economy and Society 1933–1939*, Exeter University Press, 1991, p. 522.

28 StAN, LG Ansbach, Strafprozessakten, Große Strafkammer 50/34, Bär, vol. II, p. 185, Testimony of Kurt Adolf Bär, 14 April 1934.

29 Ibid., p. 63, Testimony of Marie Breinl, 4 April 1934.

30 BayHStA, StK 6410, pp. 100–101, 103–4, 105, 113, 127, 128, 146, 147, Verdict in the action against Kurt Bär and accomplices on violation of the public peace on 14 July 1934.

31 BayHStA, MInn 73708, p. 48, Report on the events in Gunzenhausen on 25 March 1934, by the senior prosecutor at the district court in Ansbach.

32 Ibid., pp. 15–16, Letter from the deputy of the Supreme SA leader of the government of Central Franconia, 27 March 1934.

33 BayHStA, StK 6410, p. 160, The Minister of the Interior of the Reich in Berlin to the state chancellery of the Free State of Bavaria in Munich, 25 July 1934.

34 Ibid., p. 73, Indictment, 11 August 1934, against Kurt Bär and two others for murder and attempted murder.

35 BayHStA, MJu 23436 Office of U.S. Chief of Counsel, APO 124 A, U.S. Army, Memo to: Commanding Officer, Company B, Third Military Government Regiment, APO 170, U.S. Army, subject: Murder of German Jewish Subject. From the interrogation of Dr Benno Franz Theodor Martin taken at Nürnberg on 19 October 1945.

36 Barbara Distel and Ruth Jakusch (eds.), *Concentration Camp, Dachau 1933–1945*, Comité International de Dachau, 16th edn, 1978, p. 40.

37 E. F. M. Durbin and John Bowlby, *Personal Aggressiveness and War*, Routledge, 2007, p. 134.

38 Matthäus and Roseman (eds.), *Jewish Responses to Persecution*, vol. 1, Kurt Rosenberg, diary entry for 20 and 31 August 1933, document 2-2 LBINY AR 25279, pp. 37–8.

39 Nikolaus Wachsmann, *KL: A History of the Nazi Concentration Camps*, Little, Brown, 2015, p. 30.

40 *Münchner Neueste Nachrichten*, 13 March 1933, quoted in Peter Longerich, *Himmler*, Oxford University Press, 2012, p. 150.

41 See pp. 58–9.

42 Distel and Jakusch (eds.), *Dachau*, p. 48, document on the release of Johann Deller, 12 October 1934.

43 Göring testimony, 18 March 1946, 84th day Nuremberg trials, http://law2.umkc.edu/faculty/projects/ftrials/nuremberg/Goering1.html.

44 Rudolf Hoess, *Commandant of Auschwitz*, Phoenix Press, 2001, p. 71.

45 Tom Segev, *Soldiers of Evil: The Commandants of the Nazi Concentration Camps*, Diamond Books, 2000, p. 28.

46 Christopher Dillon, *Dachau and the SS: A Schooling in Violence*, Oxford University Press, 2015, p. 37.

47 Previously unpublished testimony and Rees, *Nazis*, p. 51.

48 *Münchner Neueste Nachrichten*, 13 March 1933, quoted in Longerich, *Himmler*, p. 150.

49 Max Abraham, *Juda verrecke. Ein Rabbiner im Konzentrationslager* (Death to Juda: A Rabbi in a Concentration Camp), reprinted in Irene A. Diekmann and Klaus Wettig (eds.), *Konzentrationslager Oranienburg. Augenzeugenberichte aus dem Jahre 1933*, Verlag für Berlin-Brandenburg, 2003, pp. 117–67, here p. 128.

50 Max Abraham, *Juda verrecke. Ein Rabbiner im Konzentrationslager*, Druck- und Verlagsanstalt Teplitz-Schönau, 1934, p. 154.

51 Landesamt für Bürger- und Ordnungsangelegenheiten Berlin, Reg. No. 50909, Entschädigungsakte Max Abraham.

52 *Manchester Guardian*, 1 January 1934, http://www.theguardian.com/world/2015/jan/01/dachau-nazi-germany-second-world-war.

53 Hans Beimler, *Im Möderlager Dachau*, available online (in German) at www.hs-augsburg.de/~harsch/germanica/Chronologie/20Jh/Beimler/bei_da00.html.

54 *Amper-Bote*, 7 September 1933, in Dillon, *Dachau*, p. 228.

55 Previously unpublished testimony.

56 Previously unpublished testimony.

57 Previously unpublished testimony.

58 Previously unpublished testimony. He expands on this belief in Rees, *Nazis* (1997 edn), p. 53.

59 Previously unpublished testimony.

60 Dillon, *Dachau*, p. 44.

61 Franciszek Piper, *Auschwitz 1940–1945: Central Issues in the History of the Camp*, vol. 3: *Mass Murder*, Auschwitz-Birkenau State Museum, 2000, p. 71.

62 Ibid.

63 Dillon, *Dachau*, p. 52.

64 Ibid.

65 Laurence Rees, *Auschwitz: The Nazis and the 'Final Solution'*, BBC Books, 2005, p. 25. Also see Danuta Czech, 'The Auschwitz Prisoner Administration', in Yisreal Gutman and Michael Berenbaum (eds.), *The Anatomy of the Auschwitz Death Camp*, Indiana University Press, 1998, p. 364.

66　Hoess, *Commandant of Auschwitz*, p. 78.

67　Ibid., pp. 65–6.

68　*Als sozialdemokratischer Arbeiter im Konzentrationslager Papenburg*, Verlags-genossenschaft ausländischer Arbeiter in der UdSSR, 1935, p. 20. (See note 70 below.)

69　Wolfgang Langhoff, *Die Moorsoldaten. 13 Monate Konzentrationslager*, Aufbau-Verlag, 1947, pp. 251–2.

70　*Als sozialdemokratischer Arbeiter im Konzentrationslager Papenburg* was written by a former prisoner of Börgermoor and was credited only as 'anony-mous' in order to protect his family. The preface of the book, vouching for its accuracy, was written by Willi Bredel, another concentration camp inmate.

71　*Als sozialdemokratischer Arbeiter*, p. 35.

72　Rudolf Diels, *Lucifer ante Portas . . . es spricht der erste Chef der Gestapo . . .*, Deutsche Verlags-Anstalt, 1950, pp. 260–62.

73　Langhoff, *Moorsoldaten*, pp. 251–2.

74　*Als sozialdemokratischer Arbeiter*, p. 51.

75　Langhoff, *Moorsoldaten*, pp. 251–2.

76　Report by Max Hempel, quoted in Hans-Peter Klausch, *Tätergeschichten. Die SS-Kommandanten der frühen Konzentrationslager im Emsland*, Edition Temmen, 2005, p. 231.

77　In English in J. Noakes and G. Pridham (eds.), *Nazism 1919–1945*, vol. 1: *The Rise to Power 1919–1934*, University of Exeter Press, 1991, p. 175.

78　Dillon, *Dachau*, p. 88.

79　Wachsmann, *KL*, p. 83.

Chapter 5: The Nuremberg Laws

1　Previously unpublished testimony.

2　Nikolaus Wachsmann, *KL: A History of the Nazi Concentration Camps*, Little, Brown, 2015, p. 90.

3　Yehuda Bauer, *Jews for Sale? Nazi–Jewish Negotiations, 1933–1945*, Yale University Press, 1994, p. 9.

4　Aaron Berman, *Nazism, the Jews, and American Zionism, 1933–1948*, Wayne State University Press, 1990, p. 39.

5   Adolf Hitler, *Mein Kampf*, Houghton Mifflin, 1971, p. 325; also see Jeffrey Herf, *The Jewish Enemy: Nazi Propaganda during World War Two and the Holocaust*, Belknap Press, 2006, p. 75.

6   See p. 65.

7   Previously unpublished testimony.

8   Laurence Rees, *The Nazis: A Warning from History*, BBC Books, 1997, p. 75, together with previously unpublished testimony.

9   Herbert Michaelis et al. (eds.), *Ursachen und Folgen. Vom Deutschen Zusammenbruch 1918 und 1945 bis zur staatlichen Neuordnung Deutschlands in der Gegenwart*, vol. IX, Wendler, 1964, p. 397. In English in J. Noakes and G. Pridham (eds.), *Nazism 1919–1945*, vol. 2: *State, Economy and Society 1933–1939*, Exeter University Press, 1991, p. 530.

10 Noakes and Pridham (eds.), *Nazism*, vol. 2, pp. 531–2.

11 Max Domarus, *Hitler: Speeches and Proclamations 1932–1945*, vol. 2: *1935–1938*, Bolchazy-Carducci, 1992, p. 706, Hitler speech, 15 September 1935.

12 *Jewish Post*, Indiana, 13 September 1935, https://newspapers.library.in.gov/cgi-bin/indiana?a=d&d=JPOST19350913-01.1.1.

13 Domarus, *Hitler* (English edn), vol. 2, p. 707, Göring speech, 15 September 1935.

14 Hans Mommsen, 'The Realization of the Unthinkable: "The Final Solution of the Jewish Question" in the Third Reich', in Michael R. Marrus (ed.), *The Nazi Holocaust*, vol. 3: *The 'Final Solution': The Implementation of Mass Murder*, Meckler, 1989, pp. 224–53, here p. 223.

15 This interpretation is suggested not by Mommsen but by the present author.

16 Reinhard-M. Strecker, *Dr. Hans Globke. Aktenauszüge, Dokumente*, Rütten & Loening, 1961, p. 115, quoted in Noakes and Pridham (eds.), *Nazism*, vol. 2, p. 541.

17 Supplementary Decree of the Reich Citizenship Law, 14 November 1935. Noakes and Pridham (eds.), *Nazism*, vol. 2, pp. 538–9.

18 Quoted in Max Domarus, *Hitler. Reden und Proklamationen 1932–1945. Kommentiert von einem deutschen Zeitgenossen*, vol. 1: *Triumph*, R. Löwit, 1973, p. 538, Hitler speech, Reichstag, 15 September 1935. Also in Domarus, *Hitler* (English edn), vol. 2, p. 707.

19 *Völkischer Beobachter*, 16 September 1935.

20 Previously unpublished testimony.

21 In the words of the parents of Lucille Eichengreen.

22 Laurence Rees, *Their Darkest Hour*, Ebury Press, 2007, pp. 191–2, together with previously unpublished testimony.

23 Adam Tooze, *Wages of Destruction: The Making and Breaking of the Nazi Economy*, Penguin, 2007, p. 65.

24 Ian Kershaw, *Hitler: 1889–1936, Hubris*, Penguin, 2001, p. 558.

Chapter 6: Education and Empire-Building

1 There are many different English translations of *völkische* in this context – 'people's', 'racist', 'ethnic', 'folkish' are just some of the attempts at conveying what the word meant at this time. 'Ethnic' is probably the nearest to the original meaning.

2 Adolf Hitler, *Mein Kampf*, Houghton Mifflin, 1971, p. 404.

3 *Deutschland-Berichte der Sozialdemokratischen Partei Deutschlands (Sopade) 1934–1940. Zweiter Jahrgang, 1935*, Verlag Petra Nettelbeck/Zweitausendeins, 1980, p. 1043.

4 Martin Broszat et al. (eds.), *Bayern in der NS-Zeit*, Oldenbourg, 1977, vol. 1, pp. 466–7. Also see J. Noakes and G. Pridham (eds.), *Nazism 1919–1945*, vol. 2: *State, Economy and Society 1933–1939*, Exeter University Press, 1983, p. 546.

5 Max Domarus, *Hitler: Speeches and Proclamations 1932–1945*, vol. 2: *1935–1938*, Bolchazy-Carducci, 1992, pp. 700–701, Hitler speech, 14 September 1935.

6 Previously unpublished testimony.

7 Previously unpublished testimony.

8 Laurence Rees, *Their Darkest Hour*, Ebury Press, 2007, p. 193, together with previously unpublished testimony.

9 Previously unpublished testimony.

10 Gregory Wegner, *Anti-Semitism and Schooling under the Third Reich*, Routledge, 2002, Kindle edition, location 4325–31.

11 Ernst Hiemer, *Der Giftpilz*, Stürmerverlag, 1938.

12 Fritz Fink, *The Jewish Question in Education*, 1937, at http://research.calvin.edu/german-propaganda-archive/fink.htm. Also see Wegner, *Anti-Semitism*, location 1618–43.

13 Previously unpublished testimony. Boehm-Tettelbach's assertion that lawyers in Berlin were 'mostly' Jews is false – German Jewish lawyers were never a majority.

14 David Welch, *Propaganda and the German Cinema*, Oxford University Press, 1983, p. 122. Also see Helga Grebing, *Der Nationalsozialismus: Ursprung und Wesen*, Isar Verlag, 1959, p. 65.

15 *Völkischer Beobachter*, Bayernausgabe, 7 August 1929, p. 1.

16 Previously unpublished testimony.

17 Welch, *Propaganda*, p. 123.

18 Michael Burleigh, *The Third Reich: A New History*, Pan, 2001, p. 381.

19 Henry Friedlander, *The Origins of Nazi Genocide: From Euthanasia to the Final Solution*, University of North Carolina Press, 1995, p. 62.

20 Figures from the United States Holocaust Memorial Museum, http://www.ushmm.org/learn/students/learning-materials-and-resources/mentally-and-physically-handicapped-victims-of-the-nazi-era/forced-sterilization.

21 Robert Jay Lifton, *The Nazi Doctors: Medical Killing and the Psychology of Genocide*, Basic Books, 2000, p. 29.

22 Claudia Koonz, *The Nazi Conscience*, Harvard University Press, 2003, p. 105. Also see Boaz Neumann, 'The Phenomenology of the German People's Body (*Volkskörper*) and the Extermination of the Jewish Body', *New German Critique*, vol. 36, no. 1, 2009, pp. 149–81.

23 Ian Kershaw, *The 'Hitler Myth': Image and Reality in the Third Reich*, Oxford University Press, 2001, p. 78.

24 Rees, *Darkest Hour*, p. 192.

25 Laurence Rees, *The Nazis: A Warning from History*, BBC Books, 1997, p. 74.

26 Previously unpublished testimony.

27 *Daily Express*, 17 September 1936.

28 In his article, Lloyd George asserted that 'the German temperament takes no more delight in persecution than the British', and expressed the hope that in future 'Goebbels' ranting speeches will not provoke another anti-Jewish manifestation'.

29 Tom Segev, *One Palestine, Complete: Jews and Arabs under the British Mandate*, Little, Brown, 2014, p. 33.

30 Previously unpublished testimony.

31 Previously unpublished testimony.

32 *Sunday Express*, 19 June 1938, quoted in article by Edie Friedman, 'Britain as Refuge: The Real Story', 23 October 2008, http://www.thejc.com/comment/essays/britain-refuge-real-story.

33 Segev, *One Palestine*, pp. 37-9.

34 Domarus, *Hitler* (English edn), vol. 2, p. 938, Hitler speech, 13 September 1937.

35 Hildegard von Kotze and Helmut Krausnick (eds.), *Es spricht der Führer. 7 exemplarische Hitler-Reden*, Mohn, 1966, pp. 123–77, Rede Hitlers vor Kreisleitern auf der Ordensburg Vogelsang am 29. April 1937.

36 Elke Fröhlich (ed.), *Die Tagebücher von Joseph Goebbels*, Teil I: *Aufzeichnungen 1923–1941*, vol. 4, K. G. Saur, 2000, pp. 429–30, entry for 30 November 1937.

37 *Documents on German Foreign Policy*, Series C, vol. V, no. 490.

38 Nuremberg Trial Document 46-EC.

39 Fröhlich (ed.), *Die Tagebücher von Joseph Goebbels*, Teil I, vol. 3/2, K. G. Saur, 2001, pp. 251–2, entry for 15 November 1936.

40 J. Noakes and G. Pridham (eds.), *Nazism 1919–1945*, vol. 3: *Foreign Policy, War and Racial Extermination*, Exeter University Press, 2006, pp. 72–9.

41 Joachim Fest, *Hitler*, Harcourt Brace Jovanovich, 1974, p. 42.

42 Richard S. Geehr, *Karl Lueger: Mayor of Fin de Siècle Vienna*, Wayne State University Press, 1990, p. 181.

43 Ibid., p. 200.

44 Kurt von Schuschnigg, *Austrian Requiem*, Victor Gollancz, 1947, pp. 21, 23.

45 Previously unpublished testimony and Rees, *Nazis*, p. 107.

46 Max Domarus, *Hitler. Reden und Proklamationen 1932–1945. Kommentiert von einem deutschen Zeitgenossen*, vol. 1: *Triumph*, R. Löwit, 1973, p. 803, Hitler speech, Reichstag, 20 February 1938.

47 *Völkischer Beobachter*, Norddeutsche Ausgabe, 26 February 1938, p. 2.

48 Previously unpublished testimony.

49 Previously unpublished testimony.

50 Previously unpublished testimony.

51 Previously unpublished testimony.

52 Rees, *Nazis*, p. 114.

53 Ibid., p. 112.

54 Ibid., p. 114.

55 William L. Shirer, *Berlin Diary: The Journal of a Foreign Correspondent, 1934–1941*, Johns Hopkins University Press, 2002, pp. 110–11.

56 Nikolaus Wachsmann, *KL: A History of the Nazi Concentration Camps*, Little, Brown, 2015, p. 140.

57 Ibid., p. 177.

58 Ibid.

59 Jürgen Matthäus and Mark Roseman (eds.), *Jewish Responses to Persecution,* vol. 1: *1933–1938,* AltaMira Press/US Holocaust Memorial Museum, 2010, Report to the Jewish Telegraph Agency in Paris on persecution in Austria in June 1938, document 10-7, pp. 283–4.

60 Shirer, *Berlin Diary,* p. 109, entry for 19 March 1938.

61 Fröhlich (ed.), *Die Tagebücher von Joseph Goebbels,* Teil I, vol. 5, K. G. Saur, 2000, p. 225, entry for 23 March 1938.

62 David Cesarani, *Eichmann: His Life and Crimes,* Vintage, 2005, p. 61.

63 Ibid., p. 65.

64 Ibid., p. 67.

65 Peter Longerich, *Holocaust: The Nazi Persecution and Murder of the Jews,* Oxford University Press, 2012, p. 106.

Chapter 7: Radicalization

1 Max Domarus, *Hitler. Reden und Proklamationen 1932–1945. Kommentiert von einem deutschen Zeitgenossen,* vol. 1: *Triumph,* R. Löwit, 1973, pp. 845–6, Hitler speech, 6 April 1938.

2 Ibid., p. 845, Hitler speech, Klagenfurt Festival Hall, 4 April 1938.

3 Ibid., p. 844, Hitler speech, Graz, 3 April 1938.

4 See pp. 33–4.

5 *Hitler's Table Talk, 1941–1944,* Phoenix Press, 2002, pp. 142–5, here p. 144, 13 December 1941.

6 Ibid., p. 145.

7 Domarus, *Hitler. Reden und Proklamationen,* vol. 1, p. 606, Hitler speech, 14 March 1936.

8 Ibid., p. 848, Hitler speech, 9 April 1938.

9 Peter Longerich, *Holocaust: The Nazi Persecution and Murder of the Jews,* Oxford University Press, 2010, p. 92.

10 Nikolaus Wachsmann, *KL: A History of the Nazi Concentration Camps,* Little, Brown, 2015, p. 177.

11 Y. Arad, Y. Gutman and A. Margaliot (eds.), *Documents on the Holocaust: Selected Sources on the Destruction of the Jews of Germany and Austria, Poland and the Soviet Union,* Bison Books, 1999, pp. 98–9.

12 Beate Meyer, Hermann Simon and Chana Schütz (eds.), *Jews in Nazi Berlin: From Kristallnacht to Liberation,* University of Chicago Press, 2009, p. 25.

13 To be faithful to both the history and the different sensitivities of today, in this book the word 'Gypsy' will be used when discussing Nazi policy and 'Sinti and Roma' when referring more generally to the individuals concerned.

14 Guenter Lewy, *The Nazi Persecution of the Gypsies*, Oxford University Press, 2000, pp. 2–3.

15 Aristotle Kallis, *Genocide and Fascism: The Eliminationist Drive in Fascist Europe*, Routledge, 2009, p. 55, words of Albert Krantzius, at the start of the sixteenth century.

16 Ibid.

17 Cesare Lombroso, *Die Ursachen und Bekämpfung des Verbrechens*, Bermühler, 1902.

18 Lewy, *Nazi Persecution*, p. 7.

19 Previously unpublished testimony.

20 Previously unpublished testimony.

21 Lewy, *Nazi Persecution*, p. 42.

22 Michael Burleigh and Wolfgang Wippermann, *The Racial State: Germany 1933–1945*, Cambridge University Press, 1991, pp. 120–21. Also see Lewy, *Nazi Persecution*, pp. 135–8.

23 Permanent exhibition at Sachsenhausen concentration camp memorial.

24 Christian Goeschel and Nikolaus Wachsmann (eds.), *The Nazi Concentration Camps, 1933–1939: A Documentary History*, University of Nebraska Press, 2012, pp. 204–5.

25 Report from the police post of St Johann, Austria, 12 January 1939, quoted in Lewy, *Nazi Persecution*, pp. 61–2.

26 M. James Penton, *Jehovah's Witnesses and the Third Reich*, University of Toronto Press, 2004, pp. 275–84.

27 Laurence Rees, *Auschwitz: The Nazis and the 'Final Solution'*, BBC Books, 2005, p. 210, together with previously unpublished testimony.

28 Michel Reynaud and Sylvie Graffard, *The Jehovah's Witnesses and the Nazis: Persecution, Deportation, and Murder, 1933–1945*, Cooper Square Press, 2001, p. 21.

29 Wachsmann, *KL*, p. 126.

30 Reynaud and Graffard, *Jehovah's Witnesses*, pp. 89–90.

31 Rudolf Hoess, *Commandant of Auschwitz*, Phoenix Press, 2001, pp. 88–9.

32 Ibid., p. 89.

33 Ibid., p. 91.

34 Reynaud and Graffard, *Jehovah's Witnesses*, p. 31.

35 Previously unpublished testimony.

36 Bradley F. Smith and Agnes F. Peterson (eds.), *Heinrich Himmler. Geheimreden 1933 bis 1945 und andere Ansprachen*, Propyläen Verlag, 1974, pp. 93–4, 96–7, speech to SS group leaders on 18 February 1937.

37 *Völkischer Beobachter*, Bayernausgabe, 2 August 1930 (182. Ausgabe, 43. Jg.), p. 1.

38 Testimony of Wolfgang Teubert and Emil Klein, quoted in Laurence Rees, *The Dark Charisma of Adolf Hitler*, Ebury Press, 2012, pp. 127–8.

39 *Völkischer Beobachter*, 1 July 1934, and Rees, *Charisma*, p. 127.

40 Wachsmann, *KL*, pp. 127–8.

41 See http://www.ushmm.org/learn/students/learning-materials-and-resources/homosexuals-victims-of-the-nazi-era/persecution-of-homosexuals. The museum estimates that 5,000–15,000 homosexuals were sent to concentration camps.

42 Wachsmann, *KL*, p. 134.

43 Domarus, *Hitler. Reden und Proklamationen*, vol. 1, p. 870, Hitler order, 30 May 1938.

44 Adam Tooze, *Wages of Destruction: The Making and Breaking of the Nazi Economy*, Penguin, 2007, p. 255.

45 PRO FO 371/22530, 13 March 1938, quoted in Fiona Horne, 'Explaining British Refugee Policy, March 1938–July 1940', thesis, University of Canterbury, New Zealand, 2008, p. 5.

46 Major Sir George Davies, Conservative MP for Yeovil, speaking in the House of Commons on 22 March 1938, PRO FO 372/3282.

47 Martin Gilbert, *Exile and Return*, Lippincott, 1978, p. 203. Spoken in a Cabinet Committee on Refugees, 20 July 1938.

48 David Clay Large, *And the World Closed its Doors*, Basic Books, 2004, p. 72.

49 G. S. Messersmith, Berlin, to William Phillips, Undersecretary of State, Washington, 26 June 1933, George S. Messersmith Papers in the University of Delaware Library, http://udspace.udel.edu/handle/19716/6176.

50 Joseph S. Nye Jr, *Presidential Leadership and the Creation of the American Era*, Princeton University Press, 2013, p. 38.

51 Clay Large, *And the World Closed its Doors*, p. 70.

52 *Diaries of William Lyon Mackenzie King*, entry for 29 March 1938, http://www.bac-lac.gc.ca/eng/discover/politics-government/prime-ministers/william-lyon-mackenzie-king/Pages/item.aspx?IdNumber=18924&.

53 Ibid., entry for 29 June 1937. After the Anschluss, King did remark in his diary that he could not 'abide' the Nazis' 'oppression of Jews' but nonetheless felt that the world would still come to see Hitler as 'a very

great man-mystic': see Mackenzie King diary, entry for 27 March 1938. After Kristallnacht, he wrote that he had 'sympathy' for the Jews 'in their plight': see Mackenzie King diary, entry for 23 November 1938.

54 Ibid., entry for 30 June 1937.

55 Jürgen Matthäus and Mark Roseman (eds.), *Jewish Responses to Persecution*, vol. 1: *1933–1938*, AltaMira Press/US Holocaust Memorial Museum, 2010, WJC Memorandum, July 1938, USHMMA RG 11.001 M.36, reel 106 (SAM 1190-1-257), document 11-3, pp. 314–18.

56 Deborah Dwork and Robert Jan van Pelt, *Flight from the Reich: Refugee Jews 1933–1946*, W. W. Norton, 2009, p. 99, Roger Makins, Memorandum 25 March 1938, PRO FO 371/2231.

57 Emanuel Melzer, *No Way Out: The Politics of Polish Jewry, 1935–1939*, Hebrew Union College Press, 1965, p. 90.

58 David Cymet, *History vs. Apologetics: The Holocaust, the Third Reich, and the Catholic Church*, Lexington Books, 2010, p. 125.

59 Golda Meir, *My Life*, Weidenfeld & Nicolson, 1975, p. 127.

60 Francis R. Nicosia, *The Third Reich and the Palestine Question*, Transaction, 2013, p. 125.

61 Winston Churchill speaking in a House of Commons debate, 23 May 1939, Hansard, vol. 347, col. 2178. See Daniel Todman, *Britain's War: Into Battle 1937–1941*, Allen Lane, 2016, pp. 162–6.

62 Cabinet Committee Minutes, PRO CAB 24/285, 20 April 1939; also see correspondence to Winston Churchill reporting that the British Minister in Bucharest was 'strongly anti-Semite', despite the 'persecution' of Jews there. Quoted in Gilbert, *Exile and Return*, p. 226.

63 Irving Abella and Harold Troper, *None Is Too Many: Canada and the Jews of Europe, 1933–1938*, L. & O. Dennys, 1982, p. 35.

64 Ibid., p. 9, Blair letter dated 13 September 1938.

65 William L. Shirer, *Berlin Diary: The Journal of a Foreign Correspondent, 1934–1941*, Johns Hopkins University Press, 2002, p. 120, entry for 7 July 1938.

66 *Völkischer Beobachter*, 13 July 1938, and Rees, *Charisma*, p.189.

67 Max Domarus, *Hitler: Speeches and Proclamations 1932–1945*, vol. 2: *1935–1938*, Bolchazy-Carducci, 1992, p. 1153, Hitler speech, 12 September 1938.

68 Joshua D. Zimmerman, *The Polish Underground and the Jews, 1939–1945*, Cambridge University Press, 2015, p. 20.

69 Leonidas E. Hill (ed.), *Die Weizsäcker Papiere 1933–1950*, Propyläen Verlag, 1974, p. 142.

70 Longerich, *Holocaust*, pp. 106–7.

71 Domarus, *Hitler*, vol. 2 (English edn), p. 1223, Hitler speech, 9 October 1938.

72 Matthäus and Roseman (eds.), *Jewish Responses to Persecution*, vol. 1, letter from Josef Broniatowski, Częstochowa (Poland), no date (most likely early November 1938), document 12-2, pp. 345–7.

73 Hannah Arendt, *Eichmann in Jerusalem*, Penguin, 1997, p. 228.

74 Elke Fröhlich (ed.), *Die Tagebücher von Joseph Goebbels*, Teil I: *Aufzeichnungen 1923–1941*, vol. 6, K. G. Saur, 1998, p. 180, entry for 10 November 1938.

75 This testimony is previously unpublished, but also see Laurence Rees, *The Nazis: A Warning from History*, BBC Books, 1997, pp. 75–6, and Rees, *Charisma*, pp. 191–2.

76 Previously unpublished testimony.

77 Ruth Levitt (ed.), *Pogrom: November 1938. Testimonies from 'Kristallnacht'*, Souvenir Press/The Wiener Library for the Study of the Holocaust and Genocide, 2015, p. 33, report B12.

78 Gendarmerie-Station Muggendorf Monthly Report, 26 November 1938, in Walter H. Pehle (ed.), *November 1938: From Reichskristallnacht to Genocide*, St Martin's Press, 1991, p. 39. Quoted in 'Reactions to Kristallnacht' at www.jewishvirtuallibrary.org.

79 Levitt (ed.), *Pogrom*, pp. 86–7, report B66.

80 Previously unpublished testimony.

81 Levitt (ed.), *Pogrom*, pp. 28–9, report B8.

82 'Juden, was nun?', *Das Schwarze Korps. Zeitung der Schutzstaffeln der NSDAP, Organ der Reichsführung SS*, Berlin, 24 November 1938, issue no. 47, vol. 4, front page.

83 'Dieses Pack ist schlimmer!', *Das Schwarze Korps. Zeitung der Schutzstaffeln der NSDAP, Organ der Reichsführung SS*, Berlin, 17 November 1938, issue no. 46, vol. 4, front page.

84 'Damit wir uns recht verstehen . . .', *Das Schwarze Korps. Zeitung der Schutzstaffeln der NSDAP, Organ der Reichsführung SS*, Berlin, 1 December 1938, issue no. 48, vol. 4, p. 2.

85 'Das genügt fürs erste!', *Das Schwarze Korps. Zeitung der Schutzstaffeln der NSDAP, Organ der Reichsführung SS*, Berlin, 24 November 1938, issue no. 47, vol. 4, p. 14.

86 'Juden, was nun?', *Das Schwarze Korps*, 24 November 1938.

87 David Cesarani, *Final Solution: The Fate of the Jews 1933–49*, Macmillan, 2016, p. 214.

88 Previously unpublished testimony.

89 PRO CAB 27/624 32, 14 November 1938, quoted in Rees, *Charisma*, p. 221.

90 Previously unpublished testimony.

91 Source of English translation: Stenographic Report of the Meeting on 'the Jewish Question' under the Chairmanship of Field Marshal Goering in the Reichs Air Force Ministry, 12 November 1938, in United States Chief Counsel for the Prosecution of Axis Criminality, *Nazi Conspiracy and Aggression*, vol. IV, United States Government Printing Office, 1946, Document 1816-PS, pp. 425–57.

92 Longerich, *Holocaust*, p. 115.

93 Max Domarus, *Hitler: Speeches and Proclamations 1932–1945*, vol. 3: *1939–1940*, Bolchazy-Carducci, 1997, pp. 1447–9, Hitler speech, 30 January 1939.

94 Conversation between Hitler and the Hungarian Foreign Minister Count Csáky on 16 January 1939, 5–6 p.m., *Akten zur deutschen auswärtigen Politik 1918–1945*, Serie D, vol. V: *Polen, Südosteuropa, Lateinamerika, Klein- und Mittelstaaten, Juni 1937–März 1939*, Imprimerie Nationale, 1953, p. 305.

95 Minutes of the meeting of the Czechoslovakian Foreign Minister Chvalkovský with Hitler on 21 January 1939, 5–6 p.m., *Akten zur deutschen auswärtigen Politik 1918–1945*, Serie D, vol. IV: *Die Nachwirkungen von München, Oktober 1938–März 1939*, Imprimerie Nationale, 1951, pp. 170–71.

96 James Mace Ward, *Priest, Politician, Collaborator: Jozef Tiso and the Making of Fascist Slovakia*, Cornell University Press, 2013, p. 177.

97 Ibid., p. 185.

98 Previously unpublished testimony.

99 Previously unpublished testimony.

100 David Dilks (ed.), *The Diaries of Sir Alexander Cadogan, OM, 1938–1945*, Cassell, 1971, p. 161, entry for 20 March 1939.

101 American Presidency Project: 15 April 1939, press conference, www.presidency.ucsb.edu.

102 Domarus, *Hitler*, vol. 3 (English edn), pp. 1585–92.

103 *Documents on German Foreign Policy*, Series D, vol. VII, pp. 200–204, meeting of 22 August 1939. Also see J. Noakes and G. Pridham (eds.), *Nazism 1919–1945*, vol. 3: *Foreign Policy, War and Racial Extermination*, Exeter University Press, 1991, pp. 739–43.

Chapter 8: The Start of Racial War

1 Laurence Rees, *World War II: Behind Closed Doors*, BBC Books, 2008, p. 32.

2 Jürgen Matthäus, Jochen Böhler and Klaus-Michael Mallmann (eds.), *War, Pacification, and Mass Murder, 1939: The Einsatzgruppen in Poland*, Documenting Life and Destruction: Holocaust Sources in Context, Rowman & Littlefield, 2014, p. 44, document 5: Diary notes by SS Hauptsturmführer Erich Ehlers, Einsatzgruppe II, for 1 to 5 September 1939.

3 Ibid., p. 54, document 12: Report by Helmuth Bischoff, leader of Einsatzkommando 1/IV, on his deployment in Bydgoszcz, 7 and 8 September 1939, undated (late 1939), IPN W, NTN 196/180.

4 Laurence Rees, *The Nazis: A Warning from History*, BBC Books, 1997, pp. 127–8.

5 Ibid., p. 130.

6 Previously unpublished testimony.

7 Tomasz Szarota, 'Poland under German Occupation 1939–1945', in Bernd Wegner (ed.), *From Peace to War: Germany, Soviet Russia, and the World, 1939–1941*, Berghahn Books, 1997, pp. 47–61, here p. 54.

8 Laurence Rees, *The Dark Charisma of Adolf Hitler*, Ebury Press, 2012, p. 251.

9 Matthäus, Böhler and Mallmann (eds.), *War, Pacification, and Mass Murder*, p. 29.

10 Alexander B. Rossino, *Hitler Strikes Poland: Blitzkrieg, Ideology, and Atrocity*, University Press of Kansas, 2003, p. 16.

11 Ibid., pp. 66–7 and 129.

12 Christopher Browning, *The Origins of the Final Solution*, Heinemann, 2004, pp. 36–7. David Cesarani, *Final Solution: The Fate of the Jews 1933–49*, Macmillan, 2016, p. 257.

13 Previously unpublished testimony.

14 Peter Longerich, *Holocaust: The Nazi Persecution and Murder of the Jews*, Oxford University Press, 2010, pp. 151–2.

15 Christopher Browning, *Nazi Policy, Jewish Workers, German Killers*, Cambridge University Press, 2000, p. 8, Hans Frank speech, 25 November 1939.

16 Ibid., p. 6.

17 Previously unpublished testimony.

18 Rees, *Nazis*, p. 139.

19 Browning, *Origins*, p. 57.

20 Rees, *Charisma*, p. 294, Goebbels diary entry for 24 January 1940.

21 Testimony of Fritz Arlt, published here for the first time. But see also Arlt's testimony in Rees, *Nazis*, pp. 151–2, and Laurence Rees, *Auschwitz: The Nazis and the 'Final Solution'*, BBC Books, 2005, p. 34.

22 Rees, *Nazis*, p. 136.

23 Previously unpublished testimony.

24 Browning, *Origins*, p. 93.

25 Himmler memo, 15 May 1940, 'Some Thoughts on the Treatment of the Alien Population in the East', J. Noakes and G. Pridham (eds.), *Nazism 1919–1945*, vol. 3: *Foreign Policy, War and Racial Extermination*, Exeter University Press, 1991, p. 934.

26 See p. 145.

27 Tatiana Berenstein et al. (eds.), *Faschismus – Getto – Massenmord. Dokumentation über Ausrottung und Widerstand der Juden in Polen während des zweiten Weltkrieges*, Röderberg-Verlag, 1960, pp. 78–81, here p. 81. Circular of the district president of Kalisz, Uebelhoer, 10 December 1939. Also printed in *Dokumenty i materialy z czasów Okupacji Niemieckiej w Polsce*, vol. 3: *Getto Lódzkie*, Towarzystwo Przyjaciół Centralnej Żydowskiej Komisji Historycznej, 1946, pp. 26–31.

28 Alan Adelson and Robert Lapides (eds.), *Łódź Ghetto: Inside a Community under Siege*, Viking, 1989, p. 11, Diary of Dawid Sierakowiak.

29 Previously unpublished testimony.

30 Rees, *Nazis*, p. 153.

31 Isaiah Trunk, *Łódź Ghetto: A History*, Indiana University Press, 2008, p. xxxiv.

32 Ibid., p. 21.

33 Yehuda Leib Gerst, *From the Straits* (Hebrew), Jerusalem: Safra Fund, 1949, p. 26, quoted in Michal Unger, *Reassessment of the Image of Mordechai Chaim Rumkowski*, Yad Vashem, 2004, p. 8.

34 Raul Hilberg, Stanislaw Staron and Josef Kermisz (eds.), *The Warsaw Diary of Adam Czerniakow*, Elephant, 1999, pp. 236–7, entry for 17 May 1941.

35 Rees, *Nazis*, p. 154. Testimony of Egon Zielke.

36 Previously unpublished testimony.

37 Longerich, *Holocaust*, p. 136.

38 See p. 99.

39 Previously unpublished testimony, but also see Rees, *Nazis*, p. 83.

40 Browning, *Origins*, p. 186.

41 Robert Jay Lifton, *The Nazi Doctors: Medical Killing and the Psychology of Genocide*, Basic Books, 1986, p. 280. Brack was a failed medical student.

42 Henry Friedlander, *The Origins of Nazi Genocide: From Euthanasia to the Final Solution*, University of North Carolina Press, 1995, p. 75.

43 Ibid., p. 81.

44 C. F. Rüter et al. (eds.), *Justiz und NS-Verbrechen. Sammlung deutscher Strafurteile wegen nationalsozialistischer Tötungsverbrechen 1945–1966*, vol. XXVI, Amsterdam University Press/K. G. Saur, 2001, pp. 555–83, here pp. 558–9. Also quoted in Ernst Klee, *Euthanasie im NS-Staat. Die 'Vernichtung lebensunwerten Lebens'*, S. Fischer Verlag, 1983, pp. 84–5.

45 Klee, *Euthanasie*, p. 118.

46 Karsten Linne (ed.), *Der Nürnberger Ärzteprozeß 1946/47. Wortprotokolle, Anklage- und Verteidigungsmaterial, Quellen zum Umfeld*, Mikrofiche-Edition/K. G. Saur, 1999, ff. 2687–8, transcript of Hans Heinrich Lammers' testimony, Nuremberg Medical Case, 7 February 1947. Also note that preliminary experiments with carbon monoxide as a killing agent were made in the Warthegau in November 1939. Browning, *Origins*, p. 188.

47 Lifton, *Nazi Doctors*, p. 72.

48 See, for example, Józef Paczyński's testimony, p. 255.

49 Lifton, *Nazi Doctors*, p. 72.

50 Figures from the Sonnenstein Museum.

51 Michael Grabher, *Irmfried Eberl. 'Euthanasie' Arzt und Kommandant von Treblinka*, Peter Lang, 2006, p. 35. Original in Hearing of Aquilin Ullrich in Frankfurt, 10 October 1962, HHStAW 631a, no. 1726.

52 Ute Hofmann and Dietmar Schulze, '. . . *wird heute in eine andere Anstalt verlegt*'. *Nationalsozialistische Zwangssterilisation und 'Euthanasie' in der Landes-Heil- und Pflegeanstalt Bernburg – eine Dokumentation*, Regierungspräsidium Dessau, 1997, p. 111.

53 Grabher, *Eberl*, p. 105. Original in Hearing of Heinrich Bunke in Frankfurt, 17 April 1962, HHStAW 631a, no. 1666.

54 Hans-Walter Schmuhl, 'Brain Research and the Murder of the Sick: The Kaiser Wilhelm Institute for Brain Research, 1937–1945', in Susanne Heim, Carola Sachse and Mark Walker (eds.), *The Kaiser Wilhelm Society under National Socialism*, Cambridge University Press, 2009, pp. 99–119, here p. 113.

55 Quoted in http://chgs.umn.edu/histories/documentary/hadamar/ignorance.html, University of Minnesota, Center for Holocaust Studies.

56 Ernst Klee (ed.), *Dokumente zur 'Euthanasie'*, S. Fischer Verlag, 1985, p. 125.

57 Gitta Sereny, *Into That Darkness: From Mercy Killing to Mass Murder*, Pimlico, 1995, p. 54.

58 Longerich, *Holocaust*, p. 138.

59 Browning, *Origins*, pp. 188–9.

60 Ibid., pp. 191–2; but note that one Jewish hospital at Bendorf-Sayn was exempt from this – these patients were later killed as part of the Final Solution.

61 Nikolaus Wachsmann, *KL: A History of the Nazi Concentration Camps*, Little, Brown, 2015, pp. 231–2.

62 http://www.buchenwald.de/en/457/.

63 Wachsmann, *KL*, pp. 221–5.

64 Previously unpublished testimony.

65 Previously unpublished testimony.

66 Previously unpublished testimony.

67 Previously unpublished testimony.

68 Previously unpublished testimony.

69 Noakes and Pridham (eds.), *Nazism*, vol. 3, pp. 932–4.

70 Yitzhak Arad, Yisrael Gutman and Abraham Margaliot (eds.), *Documents on the Holocaust*, University of Nebraska Press, 1999, pp. 216–18, Rademacher memo, 3 July 1940.

71 Ibid., p. 218, Frank speech, 12 July 1940.

72 Kurt Pätzold, *Verfolgung, Vertreibung, Vernichtung. Dokumente des faschistischen Antisemitismus*, Reclam, 1991, pp. 269–70.

73 Arad et al. (eds.), *Documents*, pp. 216–18, Rademacher memo, 3 July 1940.

74 Longerich, *Holocaust*, pp. 162–4.

75 Charles Burdick and Hans-Adolf Jacobsen (eds.), *The Halder War Diary, 1939–1942*, Greenhill Books, 1988, p. 76, entry for 3 November 1939.

76 Georg Mayer (ed.), *Generalfeldmarschall Wilhelm Ritter von Leeb. Tagebuchaufzeichnungen und Lagebeurteilungen aus zwei Weltkriegen*, Deutsche Verlags-Anstalt, 1976, pp. 187–8, entry for 9 October 1939.

77 David Jablonsky, *Churchill and Hitler: Essays on the Political–Military Direction of Total War*, Frank Cass, 1994, p. 155; also see Alexander Pollak, *Die Wehrmachtslegende in Österreich. Das Bild der Wehrmacht im Spiegel der österreichischen Presse nach 1945*, Böhlau, 2002, p. 62.

78 *Documents on German Foreign Policy*, Series D, vol. VII, pp. 200–204, Hitler speaking to his military commanders at Berchtesgaden, 22 August 1939. Also see Noakes and Pridham (eds.), *Nazism*, vol. 3, pp. 739–43.

79 Max Domarus, *Hitler. Reden und Proklamationen 1932–1945. Kommentiert von einem deutschen Zeitgenossen*, vol. 2: *Untergang*, R. Löwit, 1973, pp. 1422, 1425–6, Hitler speech, 23 November 1939.

80 Ibid., pp. 1553, 1558, Hitler speech, 19 July 1940.

81 Burdick and Jacobsen (eds.), *Halder War Diary*, pp. 241–6, entry for 31 July 1940.

Chapter 9: Persecution in the West

1 The figure 4,500 is the total suggested by the United States Holocaust Memorial Museum (www.ushmm.org) – 3,500 citizens of the country and 1,000 refugees. Yad Vashem suggest a lower total of 3,500 (www.yad-vashem.org). Yehuda Bauer, *American Jewry and the Holocaust: The American Jewish Joint Distribution Committee 1939–1945*, Wayne State University Press, 1981, p. 53, suggests 3,500 in 1939 and 2,000 in 1940.

2 Gustav Simon was head of the civil administration of Luxembourg and Gauleiter of neighbouring Moselland.

3 Bauer, *American Jewry* pp. 53–5.

4 Emmanuel Debruyne, 'The Belgian Government-in-Exile Facing the Persecution and Extermination of the Jews', in Jan Láníček and James Jordan (eds.), *Governments in Exile and the Jews during the Second World War*, Vallentine Mitchell, 2013, pp. 197–212, here p. 201.

5 Laurence Rees, *Their Darkest Hour*, Ebury Press, 2007, p. 165.

6 Lieven Saerens, 'Antwerp's Attitude toward the Jews from 1918 to 1940', in Dan Michman (ed.), *Belgium and the Holocaust*, Yad Vashem, 1998, pp. 159–94, here pp. 192–3.

7 Laurence Rees, *Selling Politics*, BBC Books, 1992, pp. 18–25.

8 Ibid., p. 24.

9 *Hitler's Table Talk, 1941–1944*, Phoenix Press, 2002, p. 99, entry for 30 October 1941.

10 Rees, *Selling Politics*, p. 24, Goebbels diary entry for 5 July 1941.

11 Previously unpublished testimony.

12 Laurence Rees, *Auschwitz: The Nazis and the 'Final Solution'*, BBC Books, 2005, p. 217. Though note that around twenty Jewish refugees were

handed over to the Nazis. The Danish Prime Minister apologized for this in 2005 on behalf of Denmark.

13 Hans Fredrik Dahl, *Quisling: A Study in Treachery*, Cambridge University Press, 1999, p. 222.

14 See p. 346.

15 Jeroen Dewulf, *Spirit of Resistance: Dutch Clandestine Literature during the Nazi Occupation*, Camden House, 2010, p. 48.

16 Bob Moore, *Victims and Survivors: The Nazi Persecution of the Jews in the Netherlands 1940–1945*, Arnold, 1997, p. 195, Broadcast on Radio Oranje, 2 October 1943.

17 Jacob Presser, *Ashes in the Wind: The Destruction of Dutch Jewry*, Souvenir Press, 2010, p. 25.

18 140,000 is the estimated number of Jews liable for deportation under the Nazi administration. See www.rijksmuseum.nl/en/rijksstudio/timeline-dutch-history/holocaust.

19 Presser, *Ashes in the Wind*, pp. 27–8.

20 Willem Ridder, *Countdown to Freedom*, Author House, 2007, p. 252.

21 Testimony of Hetty Cohen-Koster, then a law student at Leiden University, http://www.news.leiden.edu/news-2015/hetty-cohen-koster-was-present-at-cleveringas-speech.html.

22 Ernest R. May, *Strange Victory: Hitler's Conquest of France*, I. B. Tauris, 2000, p. 283, Gamelin talking to General Edouard Réquin.

23 Ibid., p. 386.

24 Quoted in David Carroll, 'What It Meant to Be "a Jew" in Vichy France: Xavier Vallat, State Anti-Semitism, and the Question of Assimilation', *SubStance*, vol. 27, no. 3, 1998, pp. 36–54. Also see Olivier Wieviorka, *Orphans of the Republic: The Nation's Legislators in Vichy France*, Harvard University Press, 2009, p. 195.

25 Ralph W. Schoolcraft III, 'Darquier de Pellepoix', in Richard S. Levy (ed.), *Antisemitism: A Historical Encyclopedia of Prejudice and Persecution*, vol. 1, ABC Clio, 2005, pp. 161–2, here p. 162.

26 Yves Beigbeder, *Judging War Crimes and Torture: French Justice and International Criminal Tribunals and Commissions, 1940–2005*, Martinus Nijhoff, 2006, pp. 143–7.

27 Michael R. Marrus and Robert O. Paxton, *Vichy France and the Jews*, Stanford University Press, 1995, p. 5.

28 See the *Guardian*, 3 October 2010, http://www.theguardian.com/world/2010/oct/03/marshal-petain-nazi-zealous-anti-semitism.

29 Renée Poznanski, 'The Jews of France and the Statutes on Jews, 1940–1941' at www.yadvashem.org/yv/en/education/courses/life_ghettos/pdfs/reading5.pdf.

30 Vicki Caron, 'The Path to Vichy: Antisemitism in France in the 1930s', United States Holocaust Memorial Museum, Center for Advanced Holocaust Studies, J. B. and Maurice C. Shapiro Annual Lecture, 20 April 2005, pp. 1–2.

31 Susan Zuccotti, *The Holocaust, the French and the Jews*, Bison Books, 1999, p. 3.

32 Jérôme Carcopino, *Souvenirs de sept ans*, Flammarion, 1953, p. 359; Also Marrus and Paxton, *Vichy*, p. 85.

33 Bella Gutterman and Naomi Morgenstern, *The Gurs Haggadah: Passover in Perdition*, Devora Publishing and Yad Vashem, 2003, p. 17.

34 Christopher Browning, *The Origins of the Final Solution*, Heinemann, 2004, pp. 89–93.

35 Ibid., p. 92.

36 Ibid., p. 90.

37 J. Noakes and G. Pridham (eds.), *Nazism 1919–1945*, vol. 3: *Foreign Policy, War and Racial Extermination*, Exeter University Press, 2006 edn, p. 471.

38 Laurence Rees, *The Nazis: A Warning from History*, BBC Books, 1997, pp. 141–2.

39 Sybille Steinbacher, 'In the Shadow of Auschwitz: The Murder of the Jews of East Upper Silesia', in Ulrich Herbert (ed.), *National Socialist Extermination Policies: Contemporary German Perspectives and Controversies*, Berghahn Books, 2000, pp. 276–305, here p. 284.

40 David Cesarani, *Final Solution: The Fate of the Jews 1933–49*, Macmillan, 2016, p. 274.

41 Laurence Rees, *World War II: Behind Closed Doors*, BBC Books, 2008, p. 80.

42 David Stahel, *Operation Barbarossa and Germany's Defeat in the East*, Cambridge University Press, 2012, p. 73.

43 Isaiah Trunk, *Łódź Ghetto: A History*, Indiana University Press, 2008, p. 109.

44 Christopher Browning, *Path to Genocide: Essays on Launching the Final Solution*, Cambridge University Press, 1993, p. 33.

45 Previously unpublished testimony.

46 Browning, *Genocide*, p. 36, Palfinger's report of 7 November 1940.

47 Previously unpublished testimony.

48 Trunk, *Łódź Ghetto*, p. 83, document no. 55 YI-1212, 5 April 1940, Rumkowski to the Łódź Mayor.

49 Ibid., p. 111.

50 Michal Unger, *Reassessment of the Image of Mordechai Chaim Rumkowski*, Yad Vashem, 2004, p. 37 n. 82.

51 Jacob Sloan (ed.), *Notes from the Warsaw Ghetto, from the Journal of Emmanuel Ringelblum*, iBooks, 2006, p. 19, entry for 12 February 1940.

52 Ibid., p. 17, entry for 7 February 1940.

53 Raul Hilberg, Stanislaw Staron and Josef Kermisz (eds.), *The Warsaw Diary of Adam Czerniakow*, Elephant, 1999, p. 100, entry for 16 and 17 December 1939.

54 Ibid., p. 112, entry for 28 January 1940.

55 Ibid., p. 104, entry for 31 December 1939 and 2 January 1940.

56 Cesarani, *Final Solution*, p. 339.

57 Sloan (ed.), *Journal of Emmanuel Ringelblum*, p. 120, entry for January 1941.

58 Previously unpublished testimony.

59 Browning, *Genocide*, p. 38.

60 Hilberg et al. (eds.), *Warsaw Diary of Adam Czerniakow*, p. 239, entry for 21 May 1941.

61 Ibid., p. 247, entry for 9 June 1941.

62 Nuremberg Trial Files, vol. 31, Minutes of meeting on 2 May 1941, document 2718-PS, p. 84. Rees, *Auschwitz*, p. 53.

63 Nuremberg Trial Files, vol. 36, *Political-Economic Guidelines*, pp. 135–7.

64 Goetz Aly and Susanne Heim, *Architects of Annihilation*, Weidenfeld & Nicolson, 2002, pp. 63–4.

65 Ibid., p. 237. Rees, *Auschwitz*, p. 54.

66 At population levels of 2016.

67 *Hitler's Table Talk*, p. 33, 17 September 1941.

68 Ibid., p. 38, 23 September 1941.

69 Charles Burdick and Hans-Adolf Jacobsen (eds.), *The Halder War Diary, 1939–1942*, Greenhill Books, 1988, p. 346, 30 March 1941.

70 Ian Kershaw, *Hitler: 1936–1945, Nemesis*, Allen Lane, 2000, p. 359.

71 Noakes and Pridham (eds.), *Nazism*, vol. 3 (2006 edn), pp. 478–9.

72 Ibid., p. 479.

73 Vivien Spitz, *Doctors from Hell: The Horrific Account of Nazi Experiments on Humans*, First Sentient Publications, 2005, pp. 190–94.

74 Ibid., p. 195.

75 Robert Jay Lifton, *The Nazi Doctors: Medical Killing and the Psychology of Genocide*, Basic Books, 1986, p. 279.

76 See Paul Eggert, pp. 98–9.

77 Elke Fröhlich (ed.), *Die Tagebücher von Joseph Goebbels*, Teil I: *Aufzeichnungen 1923–1941*, vol. 9, K. G. Saur, 1998, p. 210, entry for 29 March 1941.

78 This 'new' Croatia with 25,500 Jews also included Bosnia-Herzegovina with 14,000 Jews. In total there were around 80,000 Jews in the former Yugoslavia and 72,000 in Greece.

79 Esther Gitman, *When Courage Prevailed: The Rescue and Survival of Jews in the Independent State of Croatia, 1941–1945*, Paragon House, 2011, pp. 12–13.

80 Ibid., p. 17.

Chapter 10: *War of Extermination*

1 Laurence Rees, *The Nazis: A Warning from History*, BBC Books, 1997, p. 175. Full text of letter at United States, Department of State, Publication No. 3023, *Nazi–Soviet Relations 1939–1941: Documents from the Archives of the German Foreign Office*, Government Printing Office, 1948, pp. 349–53.

2 Elke Fröhlich, 'Joseph Goebbels und sein Tagebuch', *Vierteljahrshefte für Zeitgeschichte*, vol. 35, no. 4 (1987), Goebbels diary entry for 16 June 1941.

3 Adam Tooze, *The Wages of Destruction: The Making and Breaking of the Nazi Economy*, Penguin, 2007, pp. 452–60.

4 See pp. 197–8.

5 Laurence Rees, *Auschwitz: The Nazis and the 'Final Solution'*, BBC Books, 2005, p. 56, Heydrich's directive of 2 July 1941.

6 Peter Longerich, *Holocaust: The Nazi Persecution and Murder of the Jews*, Oxford University Press, 2012, p. 186.

7 Robert van Voren, *Undigested Past: The Holocaust in Lithuania*, Rodopi, 2011, p. 27. Around 13.5 per cent of those deported to the Soviet Union were Jews – a disproportionately high number compared to the proportion of Jews in the overall population.

8 Laurence Rees, *Their Darkest Hour*, Ebury Press, 2007, pp. 11–12.

9 David Cesarani, *Final Solution: The Fate of the Jews 1933–49*, Macmillan, 2016, p. 362.

10 Michael MacQueen, 'Lithuanian Collaboration in the "Final Solution": Motivations and Case Studies', in *Lithuania and the Jews: The Holocaust*

Chapter, Symposium Presentations, Center for Advanced Holocaust Studies, United States Holocaust Memorial Museum, 2004.

11 Testimony from *The Nazis: A Warning from History*, Episode 5: *Road to Treblinka*, written and produced by Laurence Rees, first transmission October 1997, BBC2.

12 Aleks Faitelson, *The Truth and Nothing But the Truth: Jewish Resistance in Lithuania*, Gefen Books, 2006, p. 26.

13 Testimony from *The Nazis: A Warning from History*, Episode 5: *Road to Treblinka*, written and produced by Laurence Rees, first transmission October 1997, BBC2.

14 Rees, *Nazis*, pp. 179–82.

15 Ernst Klee, Willi Dressen and Volker Riess, *'The Good Old Days'*, Konecky & Konecky, 1991, p. 31.

16 Ibid., pp. 24–7.

17 Peter Longerich, *The Unwritten Order*, Tempus, 2005, p. 113.

18 Jean Ancel, *The History of the Holocaust in Romania*, Yad Vashem, 2011, p. 215. Protocol of the talk between Hitler and Antonescu in Munich, in *Documents on German Foreign Policy*, vol. 12, doc. 614, p. 1006.

19 Ancel, *Romania*, pp. 445–6.

20 Radu Ioanid, *The Holocaust in Romania: The Destruction of Jews and Gypsies under the Antonescu Regime, 1940–1944*, Ivan R. Dee, 2008, p. 74; Kindle edition, location 1738–45.

21 Ancel, *Romania*, p. 453.

22 Ancel, ibid., p. 455, says 8,000, the US Holocaust Memorial Museum says 'at least 4,000'. Figure from US Holocaust Memorial Museum, http://www.ushmm.org/information/museum-programs-and-calendar/ first-person-program/first-person-podcast/haim-solomon-hiding-during-the-pogrom-in-iasi.

23 Ioanid, *Holocaust in Romania*, p. 81; Kindle edition, location 1884–90.

24 Ancel, *Romania*, pp. 230–32.

25 Previously unpublished testimony.

26 Previously unpublished testimony.

27 Testimony of Emilio Büge, Sachsenhausen Museum, and Nikolaus Wachsmann, *KL: A History of the Nazi Concentration Camps*, Little, Brown, 2015, pp. 262–5.

28 Testimony of unknown inmate, discovered in 1954, Sachsenhausen Museum.

29 Previously unpublished testimony.

30 Peter Löffler (ed.), *Bischof Clemens August Graf von Galen. Akten, Briefe und Predigten 1933–1946*, vol. 2: *1939–1946*, Matthias-Grünewald-Verlag, 1988, pp. 876–8. Original in Bistumsarchiv Münster, Fremde Provenienzen, A 8, Niederschrift der Predigt des Bischofs von Münster, Sonntag, den 3. August 1941, in der St. Lambertikirche in Münster.

31 Ian Kershaw, *Hitler: 1936–1945, Nemesis*, Allen Lane, 2000, pp. 424–5.

32 Previously unpublished testimony.

33 Kershaw, *Hitler: Nemesis*, p. 426.

34 Cesarani, *Final Solution*, p. 284. Richard Evans, *The Third Reich at War*, Allen Lane, 2008, pp. 93–101.

35 *Hitler's Table Talk, 1941–1944*, Phoenix Press, 2000, p. 5, night of 5–6 July 1941.

36 Christopher Browning, *The Origins of the Final Solution*, Heinemann, 2004, pp. 309–10.

37 Ibid., p. 240.

38 Götz Aly, *'Final Solution': Nazi Population Policy and the Murder of the European Jews*, Arnold, 1999, p. 214.

39 Previously unpublished testimony, but see also Laurence Rees, *Auschwitz: The Nazis and the 'Final Solution'*, BBC Books, 2005, pp. 64–5.

40 Yitzhak Arad, *The Holocaust in the Soviet Union*, University of Nebraska Press, 2009, p. 165.

41 Previously unpublished testimony.

42 Laurence Rees, *War of the Century*, BBC Books, 1999, pp. 93–4.

43 The city of Lwów had many different names in the twentieth century. For example, it was called Lemberg by the Germans, Lviv by Ukrainians and Lvov by the Russians. The spelling used here is the Polish version, because at the start of the war this was the name of the city. The figure of 4,000 for the pogrom in 1941 is the estimate by the United States Holocaust Memorial Museum.

44 Peter Longerich, *Heinrich Himmler*, Oxford University Press, 2012, p. 526.

45 Previously unpublished testimony and Rees, *Auschwitz*, pp. 63–6.

46 Rees, *Darkest Hour*, p. 13.

47 Alfonsas Eidintas, *Žydai, Lietuviai ir Holokaustas*, quoted in MacQueen, 'Lithuanian Collaboration in the "Final Solution": Motivations and Case Studies'.

48 Rees, *Auschwitz*, p. 63.

49 Rees, *Nazis*, p. 190.

50 Avraham Tory, *Surviving the Holocaust: The Kovno Ghetto Diary*, Harvard University Press, 1991, p. 24, entry for 4 August 1941.

51 Ernst Klee, Willi Dressen and Volker Riess, '*The Good Old Days*', Konecky & Konecky, 1991, p. 179.

52 Anatoly Podolsky, 'The Tragic Fate of Ukrainian Jewish Women under Nazi Occupation, 1941–1944', in Sonja M. Hedgepeth and Rochelle G. Saidel (eds.), *Sexual Violence against Jewish Women during the Holocaust*, Brandeis University Press and University Press of New England, 2010, pp. 94–107, here p. 99.

53 Rees, *Nazis*, p. 213, together with previously unpublished testimony.

54 Previously unpublished testimony.

55 Leonid D. Grenkevich, *The Soviet Partisan Movement, 1941–1944: A Critical Historiographical Analysis*, Frank Cass, 1999, p. 75.

56 Manus I. Midlarsky, *The Killing Trap: Genocide in the Twentieth Century*, Cambridge University Press, 2005, p. 147.

57 Rees, *Darkest Hour*, p. 68, together with previously unpublished testimony.

58 Kershaw, *Hitler: Nemesis*, p. 467.

59 Peter Witte et al. (eds.), *Der Dienstkalender Heinrich Himmlers 1941/42*, Hans Christians Verlag, 1999, p. 195.

60 Previously unpublished testimony.

61 Rees, *Auschwitz*, p. 68, together with previously unpublished testimony.

62 Ibid.

63 'Leben eines SS-Generals. Aus den Nürnberger Geständnissen des Generals der Waffen-SS Erich von dem Bach-Zelewski', *Aufbau*, vol. XII, no. 34, 23 August 1946, p. 2.

64 Recollection of former SS General Karl Wolff, *The World at War*, Thames Television, 27 March 1974, quoted in Martin Gilbert, *The Holocaust: The Jewish Tragedy*, Collins, 1986, p. 191.

65 Previously unpublished testimony.

66 Michael Burleigh, *The Third Reich: A New History*, Pan, 2001, p. 614.

67 Browning, *Origins*, p. 283. Also Longerich, *Himmler*, p. 534. A total of 120 inmates of the hospital were gassed five weeks later.

68 Testimony of Wilhelm Jaschke, Vilsbiburg, 5 April 1960, BArch 202, AR-Z 152/159. And Rees, *Auschwitz*, p. 69.

69 Previously unpublished testimony, and Rees, *Auschwitz*, p. 71.

70 Tooze, *Wages of Destruction*, pp. 482–3.

71 Ibid., p. 483.

72 Previously unpublished testimony.

73 Previously unpublished testimony.

74 Previously unpublished testimony.

75 Longerich, *Holocaust*, p. 315.

76 J. Noakes and G. Pridham (eds.), *Nazism 1919–1945*, vol. 3: *Foreign Policy, War and Racial Extermination*, Exeter University Press, 2006, p. 481.

77 Peter Klein (ed.), *Die Einsatzgruppen in der besetzten Sowjetunion 1941/42. Die Tätigkeits- und Lageberichte der Sicherheitspolizei und des SD*, Hentrich, 1997, p. 342.

78 Elke Fröhlich (ed.), *Die Tagebücher von Joseph Goebbels*, Teil II: *Diktate 1941–1945*, vol. 1, K. G. Saur, 1996, p. 269, entry for 19 August 1941.

79 Browning, *Origins*, pp. 281–2.

80 *Der Prozess gegen die Hauptkriegsverbrecher vor dem Internationalen Militärgerichtshof, Nürnberg, 14. November 1945–1. Oktober 1946*, vol. XXXII, Nuremberg, 1948, document 3663-PS, p. 436.

81 Ibid., document 3666-PS, p. 437.

82 *Hitler's Table Talk*, pp. 56–7, evening of 13–14 October 1941.

83 Rees, *Auschwitz*, p. 67.

84 Previously unpublished testimony.

85 Rees, *Nazis*, p. 222.

86 *Hitler's Table Talk*, pp. 31–5, night of 17–18 September 1941.

87 Max Domarus, *Hitler: Speeches and Proclamations*, vol. 4: *1941–1945*, Bolchazy-Carducci, 2004, p. 2491, Hitler speech, Berlin Sportpalast, 3 October 1941.

88 Ioanid, *Holocaust in Romania*, p. 120; Kindle edition, location 2726–34.

89 Ansel, *Romania*, p. 243.

90 *Hitler's Table Talk*, p. 67, 17 October 1941.

91 Noakes and Pridham (eds.), *Nazism*, vol. 3, pp. 519–20.

92 Rees, *Auschwitz*, p. 76.

93 Alan Adelson and Robert Lapides (eds.), *Łódź Ghetto: Inside a Community under Siege*, Viking, 1989, p. 175, Diary of Shlomo Frank, entries for 19 and 23 October 1941.

94 Ibid., p. 171, Diary of David Sierakowiak, entry for 17 October 1941.

95 Ibid., pp. 178–81, Notebook of Oskar Rosenfeld.

96 Rees, *Auschwitz*, p. 85.

97 Isaiah Trunk, *Łódź Ghetto: A History*, Indiana University Press, 2008, p. 217.

98 Helmut Heiber, 'Aus den Akten des Gauleiters Kube', *Vierteljahrshefte für Zeitgeschichte*, vol. 4, no. 1 (1956), p. 75.

99 Kershaw, *Hitler: Nemesis*, p. 486.

100 Aly, *'Final Solution'*, p. 214.

101 Statement by Walter Burmeister, 24/01/1961, p. 3, BArch ZStL 203 AR-Z 69/59, vol. 4. (ZStL is the central legal administration office dealing with National Socialist crimes in Ludwigsburg.)

102 Browning, *Origins*, p. 367.

103 Longerich, *Holocaust*, p. 282.

104 Although note that two smaller camps – at Maly Trostenets and Bronna Gorá – were established in Belarus where Jews were murdered. Maly Trostenets started operation in May 1942 – its chief function to murder the Jews of Minsk. Bronna Gorá in western Belarus began killing Jews from the surrounding area shortly afterwards. Though the exact number killed in these camps is unknown, neither approached the scale of the Operation Reinhard camps.

105 *Hitler's Table Talk*, p. 87, 25 October 1941.

106 Browning, *Origins*, p. 362.

107 Testimony from 8 November 1961, BArch ZStL 203 AR-Z 69/59, vol. 3, pp. 5–6. And Rees, *Auschwitz*, p. 92.

108 Dr Goebbels, 'Die Juden sind schuld!', *Das Reich*, no. 46, 16 November 1941, pp. 1–2.

109 For Professor Christopher Browning's own detailed analysis, see his *Origins*, pp. 358–73.

110 *Hitler's Table Talk*, pp. 57–8, night of 13–14 October 1941.

111 Patrick Montague, *Chełmno and the Holocaust*, I. B. Tauris, 2012, p. 34.

112 See pp. 190–91.

113 Michael Thad Allen, 'The Devil in the Details: The Gas Chambers of Birkenau, October 1941', *Holocaust and Genocide Studies*, vol. 16, no. 2, Autumn 2002, pp. 189–216. Rees, *Auschwitz*, pp. 82–3.

Chapter 11: The Road to Wannsee

1 Account by V. S. Pronin, President of the Moscow Soviet, *Voenno-istoricheskii Zhurnal*, vol. 10 (1991), pp. 335–41.

2 Max Domarus, *Hitler. Reden und Proklamationen 1932–1945. Kommentiert von einem deutschen Zeitgenossen*, vol. 2: *Untergang*, R. Löwit, 1973, pp. 1773, 1779, Hitler speech, 8 November 1941.

3 Laurence Rees, *World War II: Behind Closed Doors*, BBC Books, 2008, p. 114.

4   Domarus, *Hitler. Reden und Proklamationen*, vol. 2, pp. 1773–4.

5   Ibid., pp. 1804, 1808, Hitler speech to the Reichstag, 11 December 1941.

6   Elke Fröhlich (ed.), *Die Tagebücher von Joseph Goebbels*, Teil II: *Diktate 1941–1945*, vol. 2, K. G. Saur, 1996, pp. 498–9, entry for 13 December 1941.

7   Werner Präg and Wolfgang Jacobmeyer (eds.), *Das Diensttagebuch des deutschen Generalgouverneurs in Polen 1939–1945*, Deutsche Verlags-Anstalt, 1975, pp. 452–9, here p. 457.

8   Patrick Montague, *Chełmno and the Holocaust*, I. B. Tauris, 2012, p. 22.

9   Ibid., p. 43.

10 Christopher Browning, *The Origins of the Final Solution*, Heinemann, 2004, p. 417.

11 Ibid., p. 372.

12 Montague, *Chełmno*, p. 64.

13 Browning, *Origins*, p. 418.

14 Eugen Kogon et al., *Nationalsozialistische Massentötungen durch Giftgas*, S. Fischer Verlag, 1983, pp. 122–3. Also J. Noakes and G. Pridham (eds.), *Nazism 1919–1945*, vol. 3: *Foreign Policy, War and Racial Extermination*, Exeter University Press, 1991 edn, p. 1140.

15 Laurence Rees, *Auschwitz: The Nazis and the 'Final Solution'*, BBC Books, 2005, p. 91.

16 Montague, *Chełmno*, p. 59.

17 Ibid.

18 Ibid., pp. 65–6.

19 Isaiah Trunk, *Łódź Ghetto: A History*, Indiana University Press, 2008, p. 370, Rumkowski's speech of 20 December 1941, document no. 122: YI-1221.

20 Rees, *Auschwitz*, p. 91.

21 Noakes and Pridham, *Nazism*, vol. 3, pp. 1127–34.

22 David Cesarani, *Eichmann: His Life and Crimes*, Vintage, 2005, p. 114.

23 Browning, *Origins*, p. 406.

24 Cesarani, *Eichmann*, p. 114.

25 Sister Margherita Marchione, *Consensus and Controversy: Defending Pope Pius XII*, Paulist Press, 2002, p. 71.

26 Laurence Rees, *War of the Century*, BBC Books, 1999, pp. 78–80.

27 Michael Burleigh, *The Third Reich: A New History*, Pan, 2001, p. 571, cited in Jost Dülffer, *Deutsche Geschichte 1933–1945*, Kohlhammer, 1992, p. 125.

28 Domarus, *Hitler. Reden und Proklamationen*, vol. 2, pp. 1828–9, Hitler speech, Berlin Sportpalast, 30 January 1942.

29 Rees, *Auschwitz*, p. 97.

30 Previously unpublished testimony.

31 Quoted in Ernst Klee, Willi Dressen and Volker Riess, *'The Good Old Days'*, Konecky & Konecky, 1991, p. 255.

32 Browning, *Origins*, p. 420.

33 Rudolf Reder, *Belzec*, Auschwitz Museum, 1999, p. 115.

34 Ibid., pp. 118–20.

35 Ibid., pp. 124–5.

36 Ibid., p. 130.

37 Ibid., pp. 132–3.

38 Fröhlich (ed.), *Die Tagebücher von Joseph Goebbels*, Teil II, vol. 3, K. G. Saur, 1994, pp. 557–63, entry for 27 March 1942.

39 Peter Longerich, *Holocaust: The Nazi Persecution and Murder of the Jews*, Oxford University Press, 2012, p. 295.

40 Yehuda Bauer, *Jews for Sale? Nazi–Jewish Negotiations, 1933–1945*, Yale University Press, 1994, p. 66.

41 See Wisliceny's post-war testimony in *Slovakia*, 6–7 May 1946 (Statny oblastny archive v Bratislave, Fond Ludovy sud, 10/48) and 12 August 1946 (Statny oblastny archive v Bratislave, Fond Ludovy sud, 13/48), plus Koso's testimony of 11 April 1947 (Statny oblastny archive v Bratislave, Fond Ludovy sud, 13/48).

42 Domarus, *Hitler. Reden und Proklamationen*, vol. 2, pp. 1828–9, Hitler speech, Berlin Sportpalast, 30 January 1942.

43 Previously unpublished testimony.

44 Rees, *Auschwitz*, p. 108.

45 Previously unpublished testimony.

46 Previously unpublished testimony. Also see Rees, *Auschwitz*, p. 108.

47 Previously unpublished testimony.

48 Previously unpublished testimony.

49 Rees, *Auschwitz*, p. 110.

50 Previously unpublished testimony.

51 Rees, *Auschwitz*, p. 114.

52 Previously unpublished testimony.

53 Nikolaus Wachsmann, *KL: A History of the Nazi Concentration Camps*, Little, Brown, 2015, p. 299.

54 Previously unpublished testimony.

55 Rees, *Auschwitz*, p. 114.

56 Hoess, *Commandant*, pp. 149–50.

57 Rees, *Auschwitz*, p. 207.

58 Gitta Sereny, *Into That Darkness: From Mercy Killing to Mass Murder*, Pimlico, 1995, pp. 111–12.

59 Ibid., pp. 113–14.

60 Ibid., p. 131.

61 Klee et al., *'The Good Old Days'*, p. 232.

62 Jules Schelvis, *Sobibor: A History of a Nazi Death Camp*, Berg, 2007; see Chapters 3, 4 and 5, but in particular pp. 63–6.

63 Even though a number of the Soviet POWs were not from Ukraine, they were collectively known in the camp as 'Ukrainians' and so that usage is adopted here.

64 Rees, *Auschwitz*, pp. 210–11.

Chapter 12: Search and Kill

1 Michael R. Marrus and Robert O. Paxton, *Vichy France and the Jews*, Stanford University Press, 1995, p. 88. Vallat made this statement at his trial after the war, though it was 'almost identical' to a speech he had given in sping 1942.

2 Ibid., p. 90.

3 Ulrich Herbert, 'The German Military Command in Paris and the Deportation of the French Jews', in Ulrich Herbert (ed.), *National Socialist Extermination Policies: Contemporary German Perspectives and Controversies*, Berghahn Books, 2000, pp. 128–62, here p. 139.

4 Ibid., p. 140.

5 Ibid., p. 143.

6 David Cesarani, *Eichmann: His Life and Crimes*, Vintage, 2005, pp. 139–40.

7 Marrus and Paxton, *Vichy*, p. 243.

8 Serge Klarsfeld, *French Children of the Holocaust*, New York University Press, 1996, p. 34.

9 Marrus and Paxton, *Vichy*, pp. 233–4.

10 Susan Zuccotti, *The Holocaust, the French and the Jews*, Bison Books, 1993, p. 99. Dannecker is the source for the Laval quotation; Laval's words to the Council of Ministers six days later also tally with this previous statement reported by Dannecker.

11 Previously unpublished testimony. Also see Laurence Rees, *Auschwitz: The Nazis and the 'Final Solution'*, BBC Books, 2005, pp. 126–31.

12 Klarsfeld, *French Children*, p. 45. Marrus and Paxton, *Vichy*, p. 263.

13 Rees, *Auschwitz*, p. 130.

14 Previously unpublished testimony.

15 Previously unpublished testimony.

16 Previously unpublished testimony.

17 Rees, *Auschwitz*, p. 132, together with previously unpublished testimony.

18 Previously unpublished testimony.

19 Michael Phayer, *The Catholic Church and the Holocaust, 1930–65*, Indiana University Press, 2000, pp. 92–3.

20 Marrus and Paxton, *Vichy*, p. 261.

21 Margherita Grassini Sarfatti, *My Fault: Mussolini as I Knew Him*, ed. Brian R. Sullivan, Enigma Books, 2014, p. 84.

22 Susan Zuccotti, *The Italians and the Holocaust: Persecution, Rescue and Survival*, University of Nebraska Press, 1996, p. 77. Michele Sarfatti, *The Jews in Mussolini's Italy: From Equality to Persecution*, University of Wisconsin Press, 2006, pp. 159–60.

23 Marrus and Paxton, *Vichy*, p. 317.

24 Ibid.

25 Nuto Revelli (ed.), *Mussolini's Death March: Eyewitness Accounts of Italian Soldiers on the Eastern Front*, Kansas University Press, 2013. See in particular the testimony of Bartolomeo Fruttero in Warsaw, pp. 219–20.

26 Bob Moore, *Victims and Survivors: The Nazi Persecution of the Jews in the Netherlands 1940–1945*, Arnold, 1997, p. 91.

27 Jacob Presser, *Ashes in the Wind: The Destruction of Dutch Jewry*, Souvenir Press, 2010, p. 142. And Moore, *Victims and Survivors*, p. 93.

28 Presser, *Ashes*, p. 147.

29 Ibid.

30 Martin Gilbert, *Auschwitz and the Allies*, Pimlico, 2001, pp. 46–7.

31 Michael Fleming, *Auschwitz, the Allies and Censorship of the Holocaust*, Cambridge University Press, 2014, p. 106.

32 Ibid., p. 107, note from Maurice Perlzweig of the WJC, in late September 1942.

33 See Jan Karski's testimony, pp. 288–9.

34 Fleming, *Auschwitz*, p. 116, Anthony Eden, House of Commons, 17 December 1942.

35 Testimony from Gerhart Riegner in *Reputations: Pope Pius XII: The Pope, the Jews and the Nazis*, produced by Jonathan Lewis, executive producer Laurence Rees, transmitted on BBC2 in 1995.

36 This translation taken from *Reputations: Pope Pius XII*. See also http://catholictradition.org/Encyclicals/1942.htm.

37 Translation of letter at http://rorate-caeli.blogspot.com/2012/07/70th-anniversary-of-pastoral-letter-of.html.

38 http://www.patheos.com/blogs/labmind/2011/01/archbishop-de-jong-the-cost-of-speaking-up.html?repeat=w3tc.

39 Research for *Reputations: Pope Pius XII*.

40 Testimony from *Reputations: Pope Pius XII*, transmitted on BBC2 in 1995.

41 See Phayer, *Catholic Church*, p. 94. Phayer contends that the argument that de Jong's protest caused the deportation of baptized Jews 'rings hollow' and that 'The archbishop's protest was simply an excuse the Nazis used to seize these Jewish converts prematurely.'

42 Moore, *Victims and Survivors*, p. 79, quoting the work of Dr Jacob Presser.

43 Testimony from Witold Złotnicki in *Reputations: Pope Pius XII*, transmitted on BBC2 in 1995.

44 Livia Rothkirchen, 'The Churches and the Deportation and Persecution of Jews in Slovakia', in Carol Rittner, Stephen D. Smith and Irena Steinfeldt (eds.), *The Holocaust and the Christian World*, Yad Vashem, 2000, pp. 104–7.

45 James Mace Ward, *Priest, Politician, Collaborator: Jozef Tiso and the Making of Fascist Slovakia*, Cornell University Press, 2013, p. 232.

46 Rothkirchen, 'Persecution of Jews in Slovakia'.

47 Mace Ward, *Jozef Tiso*, pp. 234–6.

48 Testimony from Jan Karski in *Reputations: Pope Pius XII*, transmitted on BBC2 in 1995.

49 Peter Longerich in *Holocaust: The Nazi Persecution and Murder of the Jews*, Oxford University Press, 2012, p. 362, gives a figure of 52,000 Jews in Belgium at the end of 1940.

50 Ibid., p. 372.

51 Hans Fredrik Dahl, *Quisling: A Study in Treachery*, Cambridge University Press, 2008, p. 287.

52 Figures from the Norwegian Royal Commission (NOU 1977: 22) quoted in ibid.

53 Ladislaus Hory and Martin Broszat, *Der kroatische Ustascha-Staat 1941–1945*, Deutsche Verlags-Anstalt, 1964, pp. 120–21.

54 Ibid., pp. 101–2. Original: Nuremberg document NOKW-1071.

55 Ibid., p. 99.

56 *Der Prozess gegen die Hauptkriegsverbrecher vor dem Internationalen Militär-gerichtshof, Nürnberg, 14. November 1945–1. Oktober 1946*, vol. XV, p. 327.

57 *Akten zur deutschen auswärtigen Politik 1918–1945*, Serie E: 1941–1945, vol. VII, 1. Oktober 1943 bis 30. April 1944, doc. no. 352, pp. 658–60.

58 Randolph L. Braham, *The Hungarian Labor Service System 1939–1945*, East European Quarterly, 1977, p. 28. Also see Robert Rozett, *Conscripted Slaves: Hungarian Jewish Forced Labourers on the Eastern Front during the Second World War*, Yad Vashem, 2013, pp. 158–63.

59 Cesarani, *Eichmann*, p. 151.

60 I. C. Butnaru, *The Silent Holocaust: Romania and its Jews*, Greenwood Press, 1992, p. 138.

61 Ibid., p. 139.

62 Bernhard R. Kroener, Rolf-Dieter Müller and Hans Umbreit, *Organization and Mobilization in the German Sphere of Power: Wartime Administration, Economy, and Manpower Resources 1942–1944/5*, vol. 5, issue 2 of *Germany and the Second World War*, Oxford University Press, 2003, p. 855. Also Adam Tooze, *The Wages of Destruction: The Making and Breaking of the Nazi Economy*, Penguin, 2007, p. 587.

63 Cesarani, *Eichmann*, p. 152.

64 Max Domarus, *Hitler: Speeches and Proclamations*, vol. 4: *1941–1945*, Bolchazy-Carducci, 2004, pp. 2679–80, Hitler speech, 30 September 1942.

65 Lothar Gall (ed.), *Krupp im 20. Jahrhundert. Die Geschichte des Unternehmens vom Ersten Weltkrieg bis zur Gründung der Stiftung*, Siedler, 2002. Werner Abelshauser, *Rüstungsschmiede der Nation? Der Kruppkonzern im Dritten Reich und in der Nachkriegszeit 1933 bis 1951*, pp. 267–472, here p. 412. Original in FAH, 5 C 48.

66 Domarus, *Hitler* (English edn), vol. 4, p. 2687, Göring speech, 4 October 1942, in Berlin.

Chapter 13: Nazi Death Camps in Poland

1 There were also camps in Belarus, for example, at Maly Trostenets and Bronna Górá where Jews were murdered, but neither had fixed gas chambers.

2 Tatiana Berenstein et al. (eds.), *Faschismus – Getto – Massenmord. Dokumen-tation über Ausrottung und Widerstand der Juden in Polen während des zweiten Weltkrieges*, Röderberg-Verlag, 1960, p. 303. In English in J. Noakes and G. Pridham (eds.), *Nazism 1919–1945*, vol. 3: *Foreign Policy, War and Racial Extermination*, Exeter University Press, 1991, pp. 1159–60.

3 Léon Poliakov and Joseph Wulf, *Das Dritte Reich und seine Diener*, Ull-stein, 1983, pp. 471ff. Also in document 170-USSR, in *Der Prozessgegen die Hauptkriegsverbrecher vor dem Internationalen Militärgerichtshof, Nürnberg, 14. November 1945–1. Oktober 1946*, vol. XXIX, 1949, pp. 385ff. Stenographic report of the meeting of Reich Marshal Göring with the Reich Commis-sioners for the occupied territories and Military Commanders on the food situation, 6 August 1942.

4 Adam Tooze, *The Wages of Destruction: The Making and Breaking of the Nazi Economy*, Penguin, 2007, p. 545.

5 Peter Longerich, *Heinrich Himmler*, Oxford University Press, 2012, p. 570. Also see pp. 561–8 for his analysis of the reasons behind Himmler's 19 July statement.

6 Ibid.

7 Ibid., pp. 564 and 572.

8 Felix Kersten, *The Kersten Memoirs, 1940–1945*, Hutchinson, 1956, pp. 132–4, entry for 16 July 1942. These memoirs have to be treated with considerable care and are not always reliable. This section, how-ever – also quoted in part by Adam Tooze in *Wages of Destruction*, p. 526 – is credible.

9 Joseph Poprzeczny, *Odilo Globocnik: Hitler's Man in the East*, McFarland, 2004, pp. 320–21. Also Longerich, *Himmler*, pp. 583–4.

10 Raul Hilberg, Stanislaw Staron and Josef Kermisz (eds.), *The Warsaw Diary of Adam Czerniaków*, Elephant, 1999, pp. 381–5.

11 Ibid., p. 385.

12 Jacob Sloan (ed.), *Notes from the Warsaw Ghetto, from the Journal of Emmanuel Ringelblum*, iBooks, 2006, p. 292, entry dated 'June 1942'.

13 Ibid., pp. 330–31 (no precise date given).

14 Abraham Lewin, *A Cup of Tears: A Diary of the Warsaw Ghetto*, Fontana, 1990, p. 145, entry for 1 August 1942.

15 Previously unpublished testimony.

16 Auschwitz was the only place where more Jews were murdered, but unlike Treblinka Auschwitz was never solely a death camp.

17 Laurence Rees, *Auschwitz: The Nazis and the 'Final Solution'*, BBC Books, 2005, p. 162.

18 Michael Grabher, *Irmfried Eberl. 'Euthanasie' Arzt und Kommandant von Treblinka*, Peter Lang, 2006, pp. 70–71, letter from Irmfried Eberl to Ruth, 20 June 1942, HHStAW 631a, no. 1631.

19 Ibid., p. 73, letter from Irmfried Eberl to Ruth, 30 July 1942, HHStAW 631a, no. 1631. Also quoted in Ute Hofmann and Dietmar Schulze, '. . . *wird heute in eine andere Anstalt verlegt'. Nationalsozialistische Zwangssterilisation und 'Euthanasie' in der Landes-Heil- und Pflegeanstalt Bernburg – eine Dokumentation*, Regierungspräsidium Dessau, 1997, pp. 67–8.

20 Rees, *Auschwitz*, p. 162.

21 Yitzhak Arad, *Belzec, Sobibor, Treblinka: The Operation Reinhard Death Camps*, Indiana University Press, 1999, p. 84.

22 Ibid., p. 85.

23 Ibid., p. 87.

24 Gitta Sereny, *Into That Darkness: From Mercy Killing to Mass Murder*, Pimlico, 1995, pp. 160–61.

25 Rees, *Auschwitz*, p. 163.

26 Ernst Klee, Willi Dressen and Volker Riess, *'The Good Old Days'*, Konecky & Konecky, 1991, p. 244.

27 Arad, *Belzec, Sobibor, Treblinka*, p. 96.

28 Sereny, *Darkness*, p. 161.

29 Volker Rieß, 'Christian Wirth – der Inspekteur der Vernichtungslager', in Klaus-Michael Mallmann and Gerhard Paul (eds.), *Karrieren der Gewalt. Nationalsozialistische Täterbiographien*, Wissenschaftliche Buchgesellschaft, 2004, pp. 239–51, here p. 247. Original in BArch 208 AR-Z 252/59, vol. 9, pp. 1689ff., hearing of Josef Oberhauser, 13 December 1962.

30 Previously unpublished testimony.

31 Previously unpublished testimony.

32 Laurence Rees, *The Nazis: A Warning from History*, BBC Books, 1997, p. 165.

33 Previously unpublished testimony.

34 Arad, *Belzec, Sobibor, Treblinka*, p. 190.

35 Laurence Rees, *Their Darkest Hour*, Ebury Press, 2007, p. 94.

36 In conversation with author; see ibid., p. 94.

37 Tomasz Kranz, *Extermination of Jews at Majdanek Concentration Camp*, State Museum, Majdanek, 2010, p. 13.

38 Ibid., p. 59.

39 Previously unpublished testimony.

40 Testimony from *Touched by Auschwitz*, written and produced by Laurence Rees, transmitted on BBC2, 20 January 2015.

41 Previously unpublished testimony.

42 Testimony displayed at the State Museum, Majdanek.

43 Elissa Mailänder, *Female SS Guards and Workaday Violence: The Majdanek Concentration Camp, 1942–1944*, Michigan State University Press, 2015, p. 242.

44 Ibid., pp. xi–xiii.

45 The total for Treblinka is given in the decoded telegram as 71,355, but this is an obvious misprint, as in order to get the total contained in the telegram of 1,274,166 the number killed at Treblinka has to be 713,555 – a number that is also confirmed as credible by other documentary evidence.

46 PRO HW 16/10.

Chapter 14: Killing, and Persuading Others to Help

1 Laurence Rees, *War of the Century*, BBC Books, 1999, p. 128.

2 Charles Burdick and Hans-Adolf Jacobsen (eds.), *The Halder War Diary, 1939–1942*, Greenhill Books, 1988, p. 646, entry for 23 July 1942.

3 Rees, *War of the Century*, p. 159.

4 Max Domarus, *Hitler. Reden und Proklamationen 1932–1945. Kommentiert von einem deutschen Zeitgenossen*, vol. 2: *Untergang*, R. Löwit, 1973, p. 1916, Hitler speech, Berlin Sportpalast, 30 September 1942.

5 FDR address 12 February 1943, http://avalon.law.yale.edu/wwii/casablan.asp.

6 Theodore S. Hamerow, *Why We Watched: Europe, America, and the Holocaust*, W. W. Norton, 2008, p. 349. The Roosevelt–Noguès and the Roosevelt–Giraud Conversations at the President's Villa, noon and 4:20 p.m., 17 January 1943, Roosevelt Papers, McCrea Notes, in *Foreign Relations of the United States: The Conferences at Washington 1941–1942 and Casablanca 1943*, US Department of State, 1968, pp. 608–11.

7 Elke Fröhlich (ed.), *Die Tagebücher von Joseph Goebbels*, Teil II: *Diktate 1941–1945*, vol. 7, K. G. Saur, 1993, p. 454, entry for 2 March 1943.

8 Michael R. Marrus and Robert O. Paxton, *Vichy France and the Jews*, Stanford University Press, 1995, pp. 321–6.

9 Ian Kershaw, *Hitler: 1936–1945, Nemesis*, Allen Lane, 2000, p. 582.

10 Andreas Hillgruber (ed.), *Staatsmänner und Diplomaten bei Hitler. Zweiter Teil. Vertrauliche Aufzeichnungen über Unterredungen mit Vertretern des Auslandes 1942–1944*, Bernard & Graefe, 1970, pp. 234–63, here pp. 238, 240, 245, 256–7, meeting on 16 April and 17 April 1943.

11 Fröhlich (ed.), *Die Tagebücher von Joseph Goebbels*, Teil II, vol. 8, K. G. Saur, 1993, p. 225, entry for 7 May 1943.

12 Record by SS-Oberführer Veesenmayer, in *Akten zur deutschen auswärtigen Politik 1918–1945*, Serie E: 1941–1945, vol. VI, 1. Mai bis 30. September 1943, pp. 78–80, here p. 79.

13 Fröhlich (ed.), *Die Tagebücher von Joseph Goebbels*, Teil II, vol. 8, pp. 236, 238, entry for 8 May 1943.

14 Domarus, *Hitler. Reden und Proklamationen*, vol. 2, p. 2003, communiqué concerning the meeting of Hitler and King Boris, 3 April 1943.

15 Christopher Browning, *The Origins of the Final Solution*, Heinemann, 2004, p. 212. Also Peter Longerich, *Heinrich Himmler*, Oxford University Press, 2012, pp. 663–4.

16 Previously unpublished testimony.

17 Laurence Rees, *Auschwitz: The Nazis and the 'Final Solution'*, BBC Books, 2005, p. 176.

18 Previously unpublished testimony.

19 This is a suspiciously exact figure, to be treated with caution. (The fact that it is the same forwards as backwards only adds to that suspicion.)

20 Nikolaus Wachsmann, *KL: A History of the Nazi Concentration Camps*, Little, Brown, 2015, p. 316.

21 Jadwiga Bezwińska and Danuta Czech (eds.), *Amidst a Nightmare of Crime*, Howard Fertig, 1992, p. 47, deposition of Alter Feinsilber (also known as Stanislaw Jankowski).

22 Previously unpublished testimony.

23 Bezwińska and Czech (eds.), *Amidst a Nightmare*, p. 52.

24 Previously unpublished testimony.

25 Previously unpublished testimony.

26 Dr Miklós Nyiszli, *Auschwitz: A Doctor's Eyewitness Account*, Penguin, 2012, p. 24.

27 Previously unpublished testimony.

28 Nyiszli, *Auschwitz*, p. 42.

29 Previously unpublished testimony.

30 Previously unpublished testimony.

31 Bezwińska and Czech (eds.), *Amidst a Nightmare*, p. 119.

32 Ibid., p. 56, deposition of Alter Feinsilber.

33 Ibid.

34 Previously unpublished testimony.

35 Rees, *Auschwitz*, pp. 236–7.

36 Bezwińska and Czech (eds.), *Amidst a Nightmare*, p. 119.

37 Previously unpublished testimony.

38 Robert Jan van Pelt, *The Case for Auschwitz: Evidence from the Irving Trial*, Indiana University Press, 2002, p. 80.

39 Testimony from *Touched by Auschwitz*, transmitted on BBC2, 20 January 2015, and previously unpublished testimony.

40 Previously unpublished testimony.

41 Previously unpublished testimony.

42 Previously unpublished testimony.

43 Bezwińska and Czech (eds.), *Amidst a Nightmare*, p. 59.

44 Kurt Jonassohn, with Karin Solveig Björnson, *Genocide and Gross Human Rights Violations in Comparative Perspective*, Transaction, 1999, p. 283.

45 Wim Willems, *In Search of the True Gypsy: From Enlightenment to Final Solution*, Routledge, 2013, p. 251.

46 Donald Kenrick and Grattan Puxon, *Gypsies under the Swastika*, University of Hertfordshire Press, 2009, pp. 38–9.

47 Kershaw, *Hitler: Nemesis*, p. 584.

48 Fröhlich (ed.), *Die Tagebücher von Joseph Goebbels*, Teil II, vol. 8, p. 288, entry for 13 May 1943.

Chapter 15: Oppression and Revolt

1 Testimony from *The Nazis: A Warning from History*, Episode 6: *Fighting to the End*, written and produced by Laurence Rees, first transmission October 1997, BBC2.

2 Max Domarus, *Hitler: Speeches and Proclamations*, vol. 4: *1941–1945*, Bolchazy-Carducci, 2004, p. 2818, Hitler speech, 10 September 1943.

3 Martin Gilbert, *The Righteous: The Unsung Heroes of the Holocaust*, Black Swan, 2003, p. 439.

4 Susan Zuccotti, *The Italians and the Holocaust: Persecution, Rescue and Survival*, University of Nebraska Press, 1996, p. 81.

5   Renzo De Felice, 'Hunting Down the Jews', in Stanislao G. Pugliese (ed.), *Fascism, Anti-Fascism, and the Resistance in Italy: 1919 to the Present*, Rowan & Littlefield, 2004, pp. 200–206, here p. 202.

6   José M. Sánchez, *Pius XII and the Holocaust: Understanding the Controversy*, Catholic University of America Press, 2002, p. 143.

7   Testimony from *Reputations: Pope Pius XII: The Pope, the Jews and the Nazis*, produced by Jonathan Lewis, executive producer Laurence Rees, transmitted on BBC2 in 1995.

8   Ibid.

9   Ibid.

10 Zuccotti, *Italians and the Holocaust*, p. 133.

11 Michael Phayer, *The Catholic Church and the Holocaust, 1930–1965*, Indiana University Press, 2000, pp. 240–45.

12 Figures from Zuccotti, *Italians and the Holocaust*, p. xxv. Note this is the figure for those who died. The estimate on p. 274 is for the number deported to Auschwitz.

13 Zuccotti, *Italians and the Holocaust*, pp. 235–6.

14 Previously unpublished testimony.

15 Previously unpublished testimony.

16 Emmy E. Werner, *A Conspiracy of Decency: The Rescue of the Danish Jews during World War II*, Westview Press, 2002, p. 49.

17 Previously unpublished testimony.

18 Michael Mogensen, 'October 1943 – The Rescue of the Danish Jews', in Mette Bastholm Jensen and Steven L. B. Jensen (eds.), *Denmark and the Holocaust*, Department for Holocaust and Genocide Studies, 2003, pp. 33–61, here p. 45.

19 Previously unpublished testimony.

20 Laurence Rees, *Auschwitz: The Nazis and the 'Final Solution'*, BBC Books, 2005, pp. 221–2.

21 Mogensen, 'Rescue', p. 33. See also Leni Yahil, *The Rescue of Danish Jewry: Test of a Democracy*, The Jewish Publication Society of America, 1969.

22 The United States Holocaust Memorial Museum gives a figure of 72,000 Jews in Greece at the time of the occupation and 'nearly 60,000' who died in the Holocaust: https://www.ushmm.org/wlc/en/article.php?ModuleId=10005778. Steven B. Bowman, *The Agony of Greek Jews, 1940–1945*, Stanford University Press, 2009, p. 77, states that nearly 90 per cent of Greek Jewry perished.

23 Bowman, *Agony of Greek Jews*, p. 177.

24 David Cesarani, *Final Solution: The Fate of the Jews 1933–49*, Macmillan, 2016, p. 600. Also see Mark Mazower, *Inside Hitler's Greece*, Yale University Press, 2001, for a description of the deportation of the Jews from Salonica, pp. 238–46.

25 Previously unpublished testimony.

26 Israel Cymlich and Oskar Strawczynski, *Escaping Hell in Treblinka*, Yad Vashem, 2007, p. 167.

27 Laurence Rees, *The Nazis: A Warning from History*, BBC Books, 1997, p. 170.

28 Previously unpublished testimony.

29 Cymlich and Strawczynski, *Escaping Hell in Treblinka*, p. 178.

30 Yankel Wiernik, *A Year in Treblinka*, General Jewish Workers' Union of Poland, 1945, Chapter 13. www.zchor.org/treblink/wiernik.htm.

31 Previously unpublished testimony.

32 Thomas Toivi Blatt, *From the Ashes of Sobibor*, Northwestern University Press, 1997, p. 129.

33 Cesarani, *Final Solution*, pp. 676–7. Although this impact should not be exaggerated. Very few Dutch Jews survived Auschwitz.

34 Rees, *Auschwitz*, p. 210.

35 Previously unpublished testimony.

36 Rees, *Auschwitz*, p. 214.

37 Previously unpublished testimony.

38 Rees, *Auschwitz*, pp. 214–15.

39 Previously unpublished testimony.

40 Previously unpublished testimony.

41 Previously unpublished testimony.

42 Blatt, *Ashes of Sobibor*, p. 167.

43 Ibid., p. 222.

44 Previously unpublished testimony.

45 Tatiana Berenstein et al. (eds.), *Faschismus – Getto – Massenmord. Dokumentation über Ausrottung und Widerstand der Juden in Polen während des zweiten Weltkriegs*, Röderberg-Verlag, 1960, p. 352, Circular by SS and Police Chief of Warsaw district, 13 March 1943.

46 Cymlich and Strawczynski, *Escaping Hell in Treblinka*, p. 58.

47 Ibid., p. 61.

48 Naomi Baumslag, *Murderous Medicine: Nazi Doctors, Human Experimentation, and Typhus*, Praeger, 2005, p. 117.

49 Statistics taken from Gunnar S. Paulsson, *Secret City: The Hidden Jews of Warsaw, 1940–1945*, Yale University Press, 2002, pp. 2–9 and 231.

50 Ibid., p. 231.

51 Previously unpublished testimony.

52 Joshua D. Zimmerman, *The Polish Underground and the Jews, 1939–1945*, Cambridge University Press, 2015, pp. 9–10.

53 Gian P. Gentile, *How Effective Is Strategic Bombing? Lessons Learned from World War II to Kosovo*, New York University Press, 2001, pp. 59–60.

54 Domarus, *Hitler* (English edn), vol. 4, p. 2819, Hitler speech, 10 September 1943.

55 BArch NS 19/4010. Also reproduced in Bradley F. Smith and Agnes F. Peterson (eds.), *Heinrich Himmler. Geheimreden 1933 bis 1945 und andere Ansprachen*, Propyläen Verlag, 1974, pp. 162–83, here pp. 169–70.

56 Rees, *Auschwitz*, pp. 215–16. Also see Yitzhak Arad, *Belzec, Sobibor, Treblinka: The Operation Reinhard Death Camps*, Indiana University Press, 1999, p. 366.

57 Tomasz Kranz, *The Extermination of Jews at Majdanek Concentration Camp*, Majdanek, 2010, p. 64.

58 Peter Longerich, *Holocaust: The Nazi Persecution and Murder of the Jews*, Oxford University Press, 2012, p. 382.

59 Testimony of Henryk Nieścior, State Museum, Majdanek, permanent exhibit.

60 Kranz, *Majdanek*, p. 66.

61 *Der Prozess gegen die Hauptkriegsverbrecher vor dem Internationalen Militärgerichtshof, Nürnberg, 14. November 1945–1. Oktober 1946*, vol. XXXIV, 1949, doc. 4024-PS, pp. 58–92, here p. 72.

62 Ibid., pp. 69–70, Himmler letter, 30 November 1943.

63 Zuccotti, *Italians and the Holocaust*, pp. 185–6.

64 Gitta Sereny, *Into That Darkness: From Mercy Killing to Mass Murder*, Pimlico, 1995 edn, p. 261.

Chapter 16: Auschwitz

1 More Jews were sent to the 'family camp' in two subsequent transports in December 1943 and March 1944 – giving a final total of 17,500 inmates.

2 Previously unpublished testimony.

3 Previously unpublished testimony.

4 Dr Miklós Nyiszli, *Auschwitz: A Doctor's Eyewitness Account*, Penguin, 2012, p. 35.

5 Previously unpublished testimony.

6 Previously unpublished testimony.

7 Laurence Rees, *Auschwitz: The Nazis and the 'Final Solution'*, BBC Books, 2005, p. 187.

8 Previously unpublished testimony.

9 Rees, *Auschwitz*, p. 187.

10 Wolfgang U. Eckart and Hana Vondra, 'Disregard for Human Life: Hypothermia Experiments in the Dachau Concentration Camp', in Wolfgang U. Eckart (ed.), *Man, Medicine, and the State: The Human Body as an Object of Government Sponsored Medical Research in the 20th Century*, Franz Steiner Verlag, 2006, pp. 157–66, here p. 163.

11 Ibid.

12 Maura Phillips Mackowski, *Testing the Limits: Aviation Medicine and the Origins of Manned Space Flight*, Texas A&M University Press, 2006, p. 94.

13 Nikolaus Wachsmann, *KL: A History of the Nazi Concentration Camps*, Little, Brown, 2015, p. 334.

14 Previously unpublished testimony.

15 Previously unpublished testimony.

16 Danuta Czech, *Auschwitz Chronicle 1939–1945: From the Archives of the Auschwitz Memorial and the German Federal Archives*, I. B. Tauris, 1990, p. 591.

17 Previously unpublished testimony.

18 Rees, *Auschwitz*, p. 143.

19 Ibid., p. 167.

20 Previously unpublished testimony.

21 Hermann Langbein, *Der Auschwitz-Prozess. Eine Dokumentation*, Neue Kritik, 1995. See the testimony of Konrad Morgen in Frankfurt am Main on 8 March 1962, at the Auschwitz trial, ibid., pp. 143–5.

22 Max Domarus, *Hitler. Reden und Proklamationen 1932–1945*, vol. 2: *Untergang*, R. Löwit, 1973, p. 2083, Hitler speech, 30 January 1944.

23 Ian Kershaw, *The 'Hitler Myth': Image and Reality in the Third Reich*, Oxford University Press, 2001, p. 193.

24 Ibid., pp. 210–11.

25 Laurence Rees, *The Dark Charisma of Adolf Hitler*, Ebury Press, 2012, p. 381.

26 Hans-Heinrich Wilhelm, 'Hitlers Ansprache vor Generalen und Offizieren am 26. Mai 1944', *Militärgeschichtliche Mitteilungen*, vol. 20, no. 2 (1976), pp. 141–61, here p. 156, Hitler's address to generals and officers, 26 May 1944. In English in Peter Longerich, *The Unwritten Order*, Tempus, 2005, p. 212.

27 Clive Emsley, Eric Johnson and Pieter Spierenburg (eds.), *Social Control in Europe*, vol. 2, Ohio State University Press, 2004, p. 312.

28   David Cesarani, *Final Solution: The Fate of the Jews 1933–49*, Macmillan, 2016, p. 727.

29   Previously unpublished testimony.

30   Previously unpublished testimony.

31   Alan Adelson and Robert Lapides (eds.), *Łódź Ghetto: Inside a Community under Siege*, Penguin, 1991, p. 328.

32   Ibid., p. 329.

33   Ibid., p. 331.

34   Rees, *Auschwitz*, p. 102.

35   Previously unpublished testimony.

36   Isaiah Trunk, *Łódź Ghetto: A History*, Indiana University Press, 2008, p. 281, Josef Zelkowicz's description of the September Action, 'In Those Nightmarish Days', no. 102: YI-54.

37   Trunk, *Łódź Ghetto*, p. 246.

38   Laurence Rees, *Their Darkest Hour*, Ebury Press, 2007, pp. 109–10.

39   Lucjan Dobroszycki (ed.), *The Chronicle of the Łódź Ghetto 1941–1944*, Yale University Press, 1984, p. 252, entry for 14 September 1942.

40   Previously unpublished testimony.

41   Previously unpublished testimony.

42   Testimony from *The Nazis: A Warning from History*, Episode 4: *The Wild East*, written and produced by Laurence Rees, first transmission October 1997, BBC2.

43   Trunk, *Łódź Ghetto*, p. 250.

44   Patrick Montague, *Chełmno and the Holocaust*, I. B. Tauris, 2012, p. 162.

45   Dobroszycki (ed.), *Chronicle of Łódź Ghetto*, p. 534, entry for 25 July 1944.

46   Note also the timing of the change from sending the Łódź Jews to Chełmno to sending them to Birkenau. That's because by the start of August the mass killing of Hungarian Jews at Auschwitz was over and the gas chambers of Birkenau now had the spare capacity to kill the Łódź Jews.

47   Max's father had died in the ghetto; see pp. 159–60.

48   Previously unpublished testimony.

49   Previously unpublished testimony.

50   Michal Unger, *Reassessment of the Image of Mordechai Chaim Rumkowski*, Yad Vashem, 2004, p. 13.

51   Rees, *Auschwitz*, pp. 104–5.

52   Ibid.

Chapter 17: Hungarian Catastrophe

1   Elke Fröhlich (ed.), *Die Tagebücher von Joseph Goebbels*, Teil II: *Diktate 1941–1945*, vol. 11, K. G. Saur, 1994, pp. 396, 399–400, entry for 4 March 1944.

2   Ibid., p. 348, entry for 25 February 1944.

3   Simo Muir and Hana Worthen (eds.), *Finland's Holocaust: Silences of History*, Palgrave Macmillan, 2013. Also Elina Suominen's work, *Kuoleman laiva s/s Hohenhörn* (Death Ship S/S Hohenhörn), WSOY, 1979, and *Luovutetut: Suomen ihmisluovutukset Gestapolle* (The Extradited: Finland's Extraditions to the Gestapo), WSOY, 2003, the latter title written under her married name Elina Sana.

4   The Finns signed an armistice with the Soviet Union and the United Kingdom on 19 September 1944.

5   Previously unpublished testimony.

6   Randolph L. Braham, *The Politics of Genocide: The Holocaust in Hungary*, Wayne State University Press, 1994, p. 110.

7   David Cesarani, *Eichmann: His Life and Crimes*, Vintage, 2005, p. 167.

8   Previously unpublished testimony.

9   Previously unpublished testimony.

10   Previously unpublished testimony.

11   Yehuda Bauer, *Jews for Sale? Nazi–Jewish Negotiations, 1933–1945*, Yale University Press, 1994, pp. 150–51.

12   Laurence Rees, *Auschwitz: The Nazis and the 'Final Solution'*, BBC Books, 2005, p. 230.

13   Gerald Jacobs, *Sacred Games*, Hamish Hamilton, 1995, pp. 63–7.

14   Previously unpublished testimony.

15   Previously unpublished testimony.

16   Ilana Rosen, *Sisters in Sorrow: Life Histories of Female Holocaust Survivors from Hungary*, Wayne State University Press, 2008, pp. 192–3.

17   Previously unpublished testimony.

18   US Holocaust Memorial Museum figures, https://www.ushmm.org/wlc/en/article.php?ModuleId=10007728.

19   Previously unpublished testimony.

20   Previously unpublished testimony.

21   Previously unpublished testimony.

22 Testimony from *Touched by Auschwitz*, written and produced by Laurence Rees, transmitted on BBC2, 20 January 2015.

23 Previously unpublished testimony.

24 Franciszek Piper, *Auschwitz: How Many Perished?*, Frap Books, 1996, p. 53, writes of 438,000 Hungarian Jews taken to Auschwitz (from within Hungarian wartime borders), but Mirek Obstarczyk of Auschwitz museum informs me that the figure is now revised to 430,000.

25 Rees, *Auschwitz*, p. 235.

26 SIME report no. 1 on the interrogation of Joel Brand, 16–30 June 1944, file no. SIME/P 7769, PRO FO 371/42811. Also Rees, *Auschwitz*, p. 227.

27 Bauer, *Jews for Sale?* p. 178.

28 Ibid., p. 186.

29 Ibid., p. 166.

30 Ibid.

31 Ibid., p. 167.

32 *Himmler, Hitler and the End of the Reich*, produced by Detlef Siebert, executive producer, Laurence Rees, transmitted on BBC2, 2001.

33 Peter Longerich, *Heinrich Himmler*, Oxford University Press, 2012, p. 720.

34 Document discovered by the research team of *Himmler, Hitler and the End of the Reich*, PRO HW 1/3196.

35 Testimony from *Himmler, Hitler and the End of the Reich*, transmitted on BBC2, 2001.

36 Previously unpublished testimony.

37 Previously unpublished testimony.

38 Rees, *Auschwitz*, pp. 243–4.

39 Testimony from *Himmler, Hitler and the End of the Reich*, transmitted on BBC2, 2001.

40 Bauer, *Jews for Sale?*, pp. 158–9.

41 Previously unpublished testimony.

42 Robert Jan van Pelt, *The Case for Auschwitz: Evidence from the Irving Trial*, Indiana University Press, 2002, pp. 145–6.

43 Filip Müller, *Eyewitness Auschwitz: Three Years in the Gas Chambers*, Ivan R. Dee, 1999, p. 121. Also quoted in part in van Pelt, *Case for Auschwitz*, p. 149.

44 We can't know for certain if the Pope had read the Vrba–Wetzler report before sending his note to Horthy, but it is very likely he knew about it, since Vrba met a papal representative in Bratislava on 20 June 1944.

45   Testimony from *Reputations: Pope Pius XII: The Pope, the Jews and the Nazis*, produced by Jonathan Lewis, executive producer Laurence Rees, transmitted on BBC2 in 1995.

46   Ibid.

47   Ibid.

48   Peter Longerich, *Holocaust: The Nazi Persecution and Murder of the Jews*, Oxford University Press, 2012, pp. 407–8, Goebbels diary entry for 27 April 1944.

49   Heinz Guderian, *Panzer Leader*, Penguin, 2009, p. 342.

Chapter 18: Murder to the End

1   PRO FO 371/42809, online at http://www.nationalarchives.gov.uk/education/worldwar2/theatres-of-war/eastern-europe/investigation/camps/sources/docs/5/transcript.htm.

2   Michael J. Neufeld and Michael Berenbaum (eds.), *The Bombing of Auschwitz*, St Martin's Press, 2000, Martin Gilbert, *The Contemporary Case for the Feasibility of Bombing Auschwitz*, p. 70. And see Martin Gilbert's lecture to the US Holocaust Memorial Museum, 8 November 1993, http://www.winstonchurchill.org.

3   Laurence Rees, *Auschwitz: The Nazis and the 'Final Solution'*, BBC Books, 2005, pp. 248–52.

4   Neufeld and Berenbaum (eds.), *The Bombing of Auschwitz*, p. 68. Rees, *Auschwitz*, p. 248.

5   Yehuda Bauer, *Jews for Sale? Nazi–Jewish Negotiations, 1933–1945*, Yale University Press, 1994, p. 195.

6   Martin Gilbert, *Auschwitz and the Allies*, Pimlico, 2001, p. 127.

7   Testimony from *Auschwitz: The Nazis and the 'Final Solution'*, Episode 5, written and produced by Laurence Rees, transmitted on BBC2, February 2005.

8   Robert Jan van Pelt, *The Case for Auschwitz: Evidence from the Irving Trial*, Indiana University Press, 2002, pp. 155–6. Simonov's first report on Majdanek was released by the Soviet embassy in Washington on 29 August 1944.

9   Filip Müller, *Eyewitness Auschwitz: Three Years in the Gas Chambers*, Ivan R. Dee, 1999, p. 153.

10   Henryk Świebocki, *Auschwitz, 1940–1945: Central Issues in the History of the Camp*, vol. 4: *The Resistance Movement*, Auschwitz Birkenau State

Museum, 2000, pp. 244–9, and Franciszek Piper, *Auschwitz, 1940–1945: Central Issues in the History of the Camp*, vol. 3: *Mass Murder*, Auschwitz Birkenau State Museum, 2000, pp. 186–7.

11 Ibid.

12 Testimony from *Auschwitz: The Nazis and the 'Final Solution'*, Episode 5, transmitted on BBC2, February 2005.

13 Previously unpublished testimony.

14 Testimony from *Touched by Auschwitz*, transmitted on BBC2, 20 January 2015.

15 Świebocki, *Auschwitz*, vol. 4, pp. 232–3.

16 While Italy, Bulgaria and Romania were allies of Nazi Germany, the Finns considered the arrangement with the Nazis to be one in which they were 'co-belligerents', not formal allies.

17 Ian Kershaw, *Hitler: 1936–1945, Nemesis*, Allen Lane, 2000, pp. 728–31.

18 David Cesarani, *Eichmann: His Life and Crimes*, Vintage, 2005, pp. 189–92.

19 See the testimony of Kurt Becher, 10 July 1947, cited in *Eichmann Interrogations: Trial of Adolf Eichmann*, Jerusalem, vol. VIII, pp. 2895–6. Online at http://www.nizkor.org/hweb/people/e/eichmann-adolf/transcripts/Testimony-Abroad/Kurt_Becher-04.html note 42.

20 Laurence Rees, *World War II: Behind Closed Doors*, BBC Books, 2008, p. 326.

21 Max Domarus, *Hitler. Reden und Proklamationen 1932–1945*, vol. 2: *Untergang*, R. Löwit, 1973, p. 2152, Hitler proclamation, 25 September 1944.

22 Max Domarus, *Hitler: Speeches and Proclamations*, vol. 4: *1941–1945*, Bolchazy-Carducci, 2004, pp. 2965–6, Hitler speech, delivered by Himmler, 12 November 1944.

23 Ibid., p. 2993, Hitler's New Year 1945 proclamation to the Wehrmacht.

24 Danuta Czech, *Auschwitz Chronicle 1939–1945: From the Archives of the Auschwitz Memorial and the German Federal Archives*, I. B. Tauris, 1990, p. 783, report of Józef Cyrankiewicz and Stanisław Klodiński, 17 January 1945.

25 Previously unpublished testimony.

26 Previously unpublished testimony.

27 Previously unpublished testimony.

28 Previously unpublished testimony.

29 Andrzej Strzelecki, *Auschwitz, 1940–1945: Central Issues in the History of the Camp*, vol. 5: *Epilogue*, Auschwitz Birkenau State Museum, 2000, pp. 29–36.

30 Previously unpublished testimony.

31 Previously unpublished testimony.

32 Shmuel Krakowski, 'Massacre of Jewish Prisoners on the Samland Peninsula – Documents', *Yad Vashem Studies*, vol. 24 (1994), pp. 349–87, here p. 367. See also Janina Grabowska, *K. L. Stutthof*, Temmen, 1993, p. 60.

33 Schoschana Rabinovici, *Dank meiner Mutter*, Fischer Taschenbuch Verlag, 2009, pp. 220–47.

34 Daniel Blatmann, *Die Todesmärsche 1944/45. Das letzte Kapitel des national-sozialistischen Massenmords*, Rowolth Verlag, 2010, p. 203.

35 Irene Sagel-Grande, H. H. Fuchs and C. F. Rüter, *Justiz und NS-Verbrechen. Sammlung deutscher Strafurteile wegen nationalsozialistischer Tötungsverbrechen 1945–1966*, vol. XIV, University Press Amsterdam, 1976. *Massenvernicht-ungsverbrechen in Lagern, KZ Stutthof*, Herbst 1944 (Lfd. Nr. 446: LG Bochum vom 16.12.1955, 17 Ks 1/55), pp. 147–234, here pp. 156–60.

36 Ian Kershaw, *The End: Germany 1944–45*, Allen Lane, 2011, p. 234.

37 Strzelecki, *Auschwitz*, vol. 5, pp. 35–6.

38 Kershaw, *The End*, p. 334.

39 Previously unpublished testimony, and from Rees, *Auschwitz*, p. 270.

40 Testimonies held at Lund University, Sweden, Testimony no. 22 at www.ub.lu.se/en/voices-from-ravensbruck-3.

41 Ibid., http://www3.ub.lu.se/ravensbruck/interview18.pdf.

42 Nikolaus Wachsmann, *KL: A History of the Nazi Concentration Camps*, Little, Brown, 2015, p. 568.

43 Laurence Rees, *Their Darkest Hour*, Ebury Press, 2007, p. 112.

44 Rees, *Auschwitz*, p. 272.

45 Testimony from *Himmler, Hitler and the End of the Reich*, transmitted on BBC2, 2001.

46 Ibid.

47 Elke Fröhlich (ed.), *Die Tagebücher von Joseph Goebbels*, Teil II: *Diktate 1941–1945*, vol. 15, K. G. Saur, 1995, p. 514, entry for 15 March 1945.

48 Ibid., p. 521, entry for 16 March 1945.

49 Ibid., p. 564, entry for 22 March 1945.

50 Reproduced in Felix Kersten, *Totenkopf und Treue. Heinrich Himmler ohne Uniform. Aus den Tagebuchblättern des finnischen Medizinalrats Felix Kersten*, Mölich, 1952, pp. 358–9, Himmler to Kersten, 21 March 1945.

51 Leaflet 2 of the White Rose protest, http://www.white-rose-studies.org/Leaflet_2.html. Hans and Sophie were both caught and executed in February 1943.

52   http://db.yadvashem.org/righteous/family.html?language=en&itemId=92 21536.

53   Estimate of Johannes Tuchel, head of the German Resistance Memorial Center, http://www.raoulwallenberg.net/press/2007/museum-created-germans-hid/.

54   Ian Kershaw, *The 'Hitler Myth': Image and Reality in the Third Reich*, Oxford University Press, 2001, pp. 229–30.

55   Ian Kershaw, 'The Persecution of the Jews and German Popular Opinion in the Third Reich', *Yearbook of Leo Baeck Institute*, vol. 26 (1981), pp. 261–89, here p. 284. Also Laurence Rees, *The Nazis: A Warning from History*, BBC Books, 1997, p. 223.

56   Previously unpublished testimony.

57   Previously unpublished testimony and from Rees, *Darkest Hour*, p. 210.

58   Previously unpublished testimony.

59   Felix Kersten, *The Kersten Memoirs*, Hutchinson, 1956, pp. 286–90.

60   Testimony from *Himmler, Hitler and the End of the Reich*, transmitted on BBC2, 2001.

61   Kershaw, *Hitler: Nemesis*, p. 819.

62   Domarus, *Hitler. Reden und Proklamationen*, vol. 2, pp. 2236–7, 2239, Hitler's Political Testament, 29 April 1945.

63   *Hitler's Table Talk, 1941–1944*, Phoenix Books, 2002, p. 221, 18 January 1942.

64   Interview with Professor Sir Ian Kershaw conducted by Laurence Rees in 2009 for the educational website WW2History.com, http://ww2history.com/experts/Sir_Ian_Kershaw/Hitler_and_the_Holocaust.

65   See, for instance, pp. 259–60 for Fröhlich (ed.), *Die Tagebücher von Joseph Goebbels*, Teil II, vol. 3, K. G. Saur, 1994, pp. 557–63, entry for 27 March 1942.

66   Peter Longerich, *Heinrich Himmler*, Oxford University Press, 2012, p. 731.

67   Previously unpublished testimony.

Postscript

1   http://ww2history.com/experts/David_Cesarani/Hitler_s_ruthlessness_vs_Stalin_s.

2   Laurence Rees, *Their Darkest Hour*, Ebury Press, 2007, pp. viii–ix.

3   Ibid., especially p. ix.

Index